Mirages of Transition

The three northern altiplano provinces (Azángaro, Carabaya, and Lampa), which belonged to the bishopric of Cuzco in the late eighteenth century. The map was probably drawn in 1786. Archivo General de Indias.

ROBB.ᴬ

LOS PARTIDOS DEL COLLAO.

Estan situados (esenta los Valles de Carabaya) en unos dilatados llanos que hacen las faldas de la Cordillera, su temperamento es mui Frio, y seco, pero aunno su terreno abunda en muchos pastos con el quese mantiene crecido numero de ganado maior, y menor, carneros de la tierra, bicochas, guanacos, bicuñas, sierbas vs ai mucha caza maior, y menor; su comercio que es considerable, consiste en los ganados referidos, que estan apacentados en unas Haciendas q.ᵉ llaman estancias, en chalonas, sevos, quesos, lanas, baietas en engerga, costales togas, pellones à imitacion de los de Chile, ponchos, alfombras, jauon, lora, y lo q.ᵉ es mas claro, y plata que se trabaja con conocida utilidad. En Lampa está el antiguo mineral de Vilavila en la Doctrina de Pucara q.ᵉ Fue opulento, oy se estan beneficiando en Pamari, y unpoco metales de mui buena ley. En Arangaro estan los minerales de oro, y plata de Poto y Ananea, con bastante decaden- cia aun antigua grandeza. En Carabaia el unico mineral de Vcuntaia, cuia emi- nencia es de plata de 58 marcos, y sus faldas y demas Cerros de este partido de metales, y lauaderos de oro, oy se halla mui descaecidas por falta de Fomento

PARTE DE PAUCAR COLLA

PARTE DE MOQUEGUA

CURATOS		
LAMPA	Lampa, Capital de su Partido con un añj	
	Caraqato con 2 anejos.	
	Juliaka	
	Asuncolla	
	Cabana	
	Cauanilla	
	Vilq.ᵉ con Mañaro	
	Pucara, con Vilavila,	
	Aiauiri	
	Vmachiri con Ocubiri	
	Macari con Llalli, y Cupi.	
	Nuñoa con S.ᵗᵃ Rosa	
	Orurillo	
ARANGA RO	Arangaro, con Muñani Poto y Ananea.	
	Asillo	
	Putina con Chupa	
	Arapa con la Villa de Vexansos	
	Saman	
	Taraco	
	Puri	
	Cuiminaca, con Achaia, y Nicasio en Lamp.ᵃ	
	Pupuja	
CARA BAIA	Sandia con 8 anejos.	
	San Juan del oro, con Quiaca, y Sina	
	Coaza con 5.	
	Para con 4.	
	Aporoma	
	Atapata con 5.	

Mirages of Transition

THE PERUVIAN ALTIPLANO, 1780–1930

NILS JACOBSEN

University of California Press

BERKELEY   LOS ANGELES   LONDON

This book is a print-on-demand volume. It is manufactured using toner in place
of ink. Type and images may be less sharp than the same material seen in traditionally
printed University of California Press editions.

The publisher gratefully acknowledges the grant provided by the Oliver M.
Dickerson Fund of the Department of History, University of Illinois at
Urbana-Champaign.

University of California Press
Berkeley and Los Angeles, California

University of California Press, Ltd.
London, England

Library of Congress Cataloging-in-Publication Data

Jacobsen, Nils, 1948–
    Mirages of transition : the Peruvian altiplano, 1780–1930 / Nils
Jacobsen.
        p.   cm.
    Includes bibliographical references and index.
    ISBN 0-520-07938-8 (alk. paper). — ISBN 0-520-08291-5 (pbk. :
alk. paper)
        1. Azángaro (Peru : Province)—Economic conditions.   2. Azángaro
(Peru : Province)—Social conditions.   I. Title.
HC228.A93J3   1993
338.985'36—dc20   92-33342
                                                                CIP

Printed in the United States of America

Meinem Vater, Hans Jacobsen,
und dem Gedenken an meine Mutter,
Alice Jacobsen, gewidmet

Contents

Maps, Tables, and Figures

Figures

ERRATUM

In the title of table 5.6 (page 173) the units of measurement should read "metric tons," not "1,000 metric tons."

Preface

A quixotic struggle against the law of diminishing returns has led me to publish this book years after it should have come out. As a result, it may be more balanced, but it is also overly complex because of the years of mulling over old problems and old and new data. My long rethinking also meant that the manuscript was becoming longer and longer and required extensive cutting to avoid trying the patience and goodwill of the reader. Much empirical data has been eliminated. Some of this information can be found in my dissertation, and other material can be obtained directly from me. (I refer to some of the eliminated tables on which conclusions are based in the notes.)

The help I have received in working on this project since 1975 is enormous. The notaries Don Francisco Santa Cruz Zegarra and Don Manuel Aparicio Gómez (both of Azángaro) and the late Don Guillermo Garnica Ormachea (of Puno) generously allowed my wife and me to work in their offices with their invaluable holdings of notarial registers. Dr. Mauro Paredes, a lawyer in Azángaro, gave me unlimited access to his archive and library and shared his rich knowledge of local history in discussions and correspondence. Dr. Humberto Rodríguez Pastor, then director of the Archivo del Fuero Agrario in Lima, was very helpful and kind during my work at that unique repository of documentation. In Sucre, Dr. Gunnar Mendoza expertly steered me to valuable sources on the northern altiplano in the Archivo Nacional de Bolivia, which he has directed with great dedication and scholarly understanding. I am also grateful to the staff of the former Subdirección de Reforma Agraria of the Ministerio de Agricultura, the Municipal Library, and the Registro de la Propiedad Inmueble, all in Puno, the Archivo Departamental in Arequipa, and the Archivo General de la Nación and the Biblioteca Nacional in Lima for granting me access to their collections. My wife and I deeply appreciated the hospitality shown to us in Peru, especially by Graciela Ormachea Frisancho and Ignacio Cruz Mamani and their families in Puno; Fathers Ronald Llerena, René Pinto, and their *equipo pastoral* in Azángaro; Mariel Romero de Farfán in Lima; and María Mayer, Martin Scurrah, and their family in Lima.

My understanding of the issues raised in this book owes much to discussions with friends and colleagues in Peru, Europe, and the United States, especially the following: Gordon Appleby, Heraclio Bonilla, Manuel Burga, John Coatsworth, the late Alberto Flores Galindo, Luis Miguel Glave, Jürgen Golte, Michael Gonzales, Erwin Grieshaber, Marcel Haitin, Thomas Krüggeler, Reinhard Liehr, Enrique Mayer, Rory Miller, Magnus Mörner, Scarlett O'Phelan Godoy, Benjamin Orlove, Franklin Pease G. Y., Vincent Peloso, Hans-Jürgen Puhle, Susan Ramirez, Augusto Ramos Zambrano, Karen Spalding, and Charles Walker. Some of them have generously provided me with documentation.

David Cahill, Frederic Jaher, Erick Langer, Rory Miller, and members of the Social History Group at the University of Illinois have read and commented on chapters of the manuscript. Tulio Halperín, Joseph Love, Fiona Wilson, and three anonymous readers for the University of California Press have read and commented on drafts of the entire manuscript. Their suggestions were important for making the book better, and I greatly appreciate their efforts. Of course, the remaining errors and misconceptions are entirely mine. Dan Gunter, Eileen McWilliam, and Mark Pentecost from the University of California Press have made the process of getting the manuscript into press as painless as it could be and made the book as good as the raw material I provided them allowed. I thank them for this crucial help. Hans-Jürgen Puhle and Joseph Love, my senior Latin Americanist colleagues at the University of Bielefeld and at the University of Illinois, provided guidance and council on scholarly and professional issues and assured me that this was a worthwhile project to complete. So has Tulio Halperín, my teacher at the University of California at Berkeley, who supervised the dissertation on which this book continues to be based. Their support has been invaluable and I am deeply grateful to them. It was a singular stroke of luck to have had the opportunity to study with Tulio Halperín and to be able to continue counting him as a friend. His rich, penetratingly analytical, dialectic, subtly ironic, yet humanistic approach to history remains my model of how historians should approach the past. Whatever may be of value in this book owes a great deal to him.

I gratefully acknowledge funding for this project from the following sources: the Doherty Foundation, the University of California Regents' Fellowship, the University of California (Berkeley) Center for Latin American Studies, the Tinker Foundation, the Mabelle McLeod Lewis Foundation, Foreign Language Area Fellowships, the Research Commission of the University of Bielefeld, and the Research Board and the History Department at the University of Illinois. Barbara Harned expertly typed an earlier version of the manuscript for word processing. I have received able research assistance from Monica Garrido, Klaus Hartung, and Paulina Mendoza. The map in chapter 1 was professionally drawn by P. Blank. A big "Thank you!" to them all for their help.

I thank Johanna Jacobsen for showing understanding for my preoccupation with this project, even when that meant sacrificing plans for undertaking something together. Teresa Jacobsen has helped in every phase of the project, from gathering information to making final revisions of the manuscript. Without her emotional support I could not have completed it. It is more than gratitude that I feel for her. To all I am thankful for not having lost confidence that I could complete this project.

List of Abbreviations

A.	Asiento (in Puno's Registro de la Propiedad Inmueble)
AFA	Archivo del Fuero Agrario, Lima
AFA-P	Archivo del Fuero Agrario, Picotani Files
AFA-R	Archivo del Fuero Agrario, Ricketts Files
AFA-S	Archivo del Fuero Agrario, Sollocota Files
AGN	Archivo General de la Nación, Lima
AJA	Archivo del Juzgado de Primera Instancia, Azángaro
ANB	Archivo Nacional de Bolivia, Sucre; Materiales Sobre Tierras e Indios
BLAR	Bulletin of Latin American Research
BMP	Biblioteca Municipal, Puno
BNP	Biblioteca Nacional del Perú, Lima; Sala de Investigaciones
CIF	"Cost, insurance, freight"; price of a commodity delivered to the importer's warehouse in the port of destination
Dir.	Dirección
F.	folio
fn.	footnote
FOB	"Free on board"; price of a commodity placed on board ship in the port of exportation
HAHR	Hispanic American Historical Review
JLAS	Journal of Latin American Studies
Lb.	Letterbook (in the Ricketts correspondence, AFA-R)
Min.	Ministerio
MPA	Private archive of Mauro Paredes, Azángaro
OMR	Ovejas madres en reducción; conventional livestock tallying unit in the altiplano
p.	Partida (of Puno's property registry)

prot.	Protocollization (of an informal contract in the notarial registries)
RA	Revista Andina
REPA	Registro de Escrituras Públicas, Azángaro
REPAr	Registro de Escrituras Públicas, Arequipa
REPC	Registro de Escrituras Públicas, Cuzco
REPP	Registro de Escrituras Públicas, Puno
RPIP	Registro de la Propiedad Inmueble, Puno
T.	Tomo (volume)

1 Introduction

Why, Where, and How Many?

On the evening of June 23, 1965, in the middle of Lima's damp, gloomy winter season, a group of prominent social scientists and literary critics gathered around a table in the auditorium of a spacious villa owned by the Institute of Peruvian Studies. They had come to meet the writer and anthropologist José María Arguedas for a public discussion of his latest novel, *Todas las sangres*. One of Peru's foremost indigenista authors, Arguedas had sought to portray, through the prism of provincial society in the southern highlands, the multiple conflicts dividing the country: conflicts between landowners, who wanted to build efficient agricultural enterprises and who despised their Indian work force, and the *gamonales* (strongmen), who, while brutally exploiting their *colonos* (labor tenants), shared with them notions about the religious and personalistic nature of their world; conflicts between owners of large estates and adjacent Indian communities whose lands and labor they coveted; conflicts within communities between the old hierarchy of authorities, who still clung to the annual cycle of celebrations and the multifarious rituals enacting solidarity in the fields, around the houses, and in the chapels, and newfangled leaders, educated in schools, in the army, or in stints as wage laborers in the cities, who were pointing toward revolution when they talked about solidarity and diagnosed class exploitation of the peasantry rather than the brutality or beneficence of this or that gamonal.

Arguedas had expressed his hope that, despite the advance of modern, capitalist economic and social structures, the brotherly and magical worldview held by many of the Andean peasants might somehow emerge victorious. Several of the panelists gathered on that June evening took Arguedas to task for the image of Peruvian society portrayed in the novel and the directions of change suggested. A young French anthropologist, Henri

Favre, denied that caste society still existed in the Andes: "I have lived for
two years . . . in Huancavelica . . . and did not find Indians, but only
exploited peasants." In the intellectual and political debate about the future
course of Peruvian society, Favre exclaimed, the antiquated vision espoused
in Arguedas's novel could have only "a rather negative impact."[1] The
young Peruvian sociologist Anibal Quijano, soon to become a major pro-
ponent of dependency theory, faulted Arguedas for not having captured the
transition from a caste to a class society. As Quijano saw it, Arguedas had
failed to integrate his notions of an Indian solution to the current agrarian
problem of Peru with the evident rapid change from "traditional" to
"modern" values, norms, and structures.[2]

Arguedas felt crushed by this massive critique from some of Peru's
avant-garde intellectuals of the day. That same night he penned a note
renouncing his will to live. "I think today my life has entirely lost its reason
of existence. . . . Two erudite sociologists and one economist [have] basically proven that my book *Todas las sangres* is negative for the country;
I have nothing left to do in this world. My strength and willpower have
declined, I believe for good. . . . I shall go to where I was born and there
I will proceed to die immediately."[3] Somehow Arguedas gathered enough
strength to go on living and writing for another four years, but in late 1969
he killed himself.

This intensely creative and sensitive man perceived a rift between the
Andean world of his birth, with its legacy of communitarian values and
naturalistic spirituality, and the rationalistic, urban, and Western world in
which he worked and communicated, and try as he might, he could not
bridge this rift in his own mind. He had begun his intellectual career late
in the first wave of pro-Indian writing during the 1920s and 1930s, when
many of Peru's intellectuals had steadfastly offered a vague Indian solution
to the problems of Peru's national identity and development; now he could
not reconcile himself to the brash, progressive visions of the socialists and
developmentalists of the 1960s, who foresaw the rise of integrated mestizo
culture and society through revolution or social and economic reform.

Today, after more than a decade of a huge foreign debt burden, capital
flight, an uncontrollable cocaine trade, runaway inflation, unemployment
or starvation wages for growing numbers of workers, and a brutal civil war,
most Peruvians have abandoned the optimism of the 1960s and early 1970s.
Having lost any certainty and vision about where Peru might be heading,
Peruvian intellectuals are now embracing the sobering realization that
racism and violence are deeply ingrained in Peruvian society and that
extreme differentials of power continually reproduce high levels of social
inequality and a polarized vision of the polity. In this atmosphere Argue-

das's account of the unresolved conflict between the Andean peasant world and that of capitalist urban Peru seems to some observers as much prophetic as anachronistic in its details. Although society has continued to undergo rapid change both in the highlands and on the coast, the legacies of colonialism appear stronger and more enduring than many Peruvians had hoped twenty-five years ago.

This book explores the cycles and long-term transformations of a provincial agrarian economy and society in the Andean highlands of Peru during the century and a half from the crisis of the colonial order to the crisis of the export economy. Although focusing on issues concerning trade, land, labor, and livestock raising and the shifting configuration of the social groups involved, throughout I seek to establish how specific constellations of power have influenced the scope and direction of socioeconomic change. The broadest conclusion is that the persistent legacy of colonialism was the crucial factor in blocking the transition to capitalism in the Peruvian altiplano. By "legacy of colonialism" I do not mean primarily the impact of Hispanic cultural, juridical, and political norms and structures on postindependence Peru. Although such legacies are undeniable, broad cultural distinctions—such as the one that contrasts thrifty, goal-oriented, Protestant Anglo-Americans with Catholic, rent-seeking Latin Americans—do not have much validity in explaining why one society achieved the transition to a highly productive, capitalist industrial economy while the other did not or achieved only a warped and inefficient version of such an economy.[4]

Nor does "legacy of colonialism" signify the notion that Peru tumbled helplessly from Spain's formal colonialism into an informal neocolonialism controlled first by England and later, since about 1900, by the United States. It is now becoming increasingly clear that the rapid "internationalization" of Peru's trade between the 1820s and 1850s did not signify the instant achievement of foreign domination. Indeed, foreign influence was probably weaker during the early independence period than during the late colonial period and the late nineteenth and early twentieth centuries, and anti-free-trade coalitions held considerable sway in debates over economic policy.[5]

Clearly the influence of foreign merchants, financiers, mining and industrial entrepreneurs, and owners of railroads and other infrastructure became very strong during the age of the "mature export economy" between the 1890s and the Great Depression of 1929–32. But it has proved difficult to explain the failure to achieve sustained increases of productivity, deepening of markets, and capital accumulation as a more or less automatic consequence of an economy specializing in raw materials exports and depending on foreign capital.[6] Moreover, Peru's dependent relationship with European and North American entrepreneurs, corporations, and technical elites was molded according to the interests of various regional and national domestic groups, who used their foreign interlocutors as best they could to foster their own projects. Dependency, in the case of the Peruvian altiplano, served as a catalyst for changes in its economy and society, but the nature of those changes cannot be seen as linear, inevitable, or predetermined by foreign, capitalist penetration.

What, then, is meant by "legacy of colonialism"? It means the tendency of most social groups in the altiplano—Indian community peasants, hispanized large landholders, traders, priests, government officials, police, and military—to use polarized visions of society, such as those of colonizers/colonized, Spaniards/Indians, civilized notables/barbaric peasants, to construct, define, and fortify their own power and social identity. As the pattern of trade, the relations of production, the composition of the social groups, and the nature of the state underwent important changes between the 1780s and 1930, most social actors in the altiplano repeatedly appealed to and relied on such polarized visions, distilled from the memory of the colonial past, to increase or defend their access to economic resources.

Between the late eighteenth century and 1900 the political and administrative structure of the colonial regime, its pattern of taxation, its legal notions of corporate landholding, and its social categorization scheme were gradually dismantled. By 1900, moreover, estate owners, traders and governmental authorities were a rather different group from the dominant elites of the mid-eighteenth century, many having risen from humble backgrounds as muleteers, petty traders, and modest landholders since independence. The Indian communities of 1900 had undergone great changes in the preceding century, and in some ways the very identity of "the Indian" was distinct from the colonial antecedent. Although altiplano society and economy thoroughly changed in response to growing demand for its raw materials on the world market and new currents of political and social ideas, the colonial cleavages and modes of constructing power did not disappear: they took on a new garb.

Up-and-coming owners of estates justified the incorporation of more and more labor tenants on their haciendas by claiming smallholding Indian peasants to be unproductive and culturally degenerate. Indian peasants insisted on reconstituted notions of communal solidarity because they could not fully trust the public order to protect their individual activities as livestock producers, agriculturalists, or traders. Commercial agents, itinerant traders, and shopkeepers sought to strengthen their business and stabilize their profits by creating quasi-monopolistic ties to their suppliers and customers through credit, symbolic kinship (*compadrazgo*), or brute force. The implantation of bourgeois legal norms protecting property largely failed in the countryside, compromised by the contradictory and self-serving use and disregard of its precepts by large landholders and peasants alike. Throughout the altiplano, neocolonial hierarchical power relations were resurrected during the late nineteenth and early twentieth centuries, just as commercial networks became denser and competition for land more keen.

In the last fifteen years many authors have posited the transition to capitalism as the most meaningful paradigm for analyzing the multifaceted changes of Latin American agrarian societies and economies, especially for the century after independence from colonial rule. Some authors, mostly associated with the dependency and world capitalist systems approaches, have located this transition in the century after the Spanish conquest, highlighting the rise of agricultural production for markets.[7] However, most empirically well-supported studies have located the transition between the 1860s and 1930 or even during the mid-twentieth century, depending on the specific circumstances of the region analyzed. These scholars stress rapidly changing class structures and relations of production in Latin America's agrarian complexes as a consequence of a closer integration into the burgeoning international markets dominated by capitalist industrial economies in Western Europe and North America.[8]

As an ideal type, capitalism means the existence or, more accurately, the gradual rise to dominance of three crucial conditions of organizing economic activity and social relations. (1) An internal, tendentially "price-setting" or self-regulating market contributes to a deepening of the division of labor concurrently with the process of capital accumulation.[9] (2) Growing numbers of producers are separated from the means of production, and wage labor becomes dominant in the manufacturing and service sectors. In agriculture, capitalism may take the form of large enterprises relying on rural workers, often former peasant smallholders, or of family farms, not necessarily employing wage labor, which through reinvestment of earnings constitute increasingly capital-intensive entities. Common to both paths is the massive displacement of the least efficient rural producers, especially small peasants or farmers, as capital intensity and productivity of agricultural production increases. (3) Private property is legally recognized, effectively protected, and conventionally accepted. Without a commonly accepted notion of private property, effectively sanctioned by the state, the dynamic of capitalism cannot fully unfold. Complex, disputed, and overlapping understandings of the rights to use and dispose of land, often accompanied on the ground by vague boundaries, discourage landholders from seeking to optimize their capital investment by reinvesting profits in improved, more productive operations.

The Peruvian altiplano saw at best a truncated version of these processes in the century and a half between the late colonial period and the onset of the Great Depression. A whole range of processes critical in the development of a capitalist agrarian economy was initiated or intensified. Rural producers were increasingly pushed into monetarized markets; a revolution in transport and communication allowed the establishment of a fairly dense network of traders and commercial agents. In a series of initiatives the late colonial Bourbon regime and several of Peru's nineteenth-century national administrations gradually adjusted the legal framework of property to the liberal ideal. Indeed, corporate landholding by peasant communities and the Catholic church had shrunk to insignificance by the early twentieth century. Something that at first sight looked like an active land market had sprung up in the altiplano. At that time a number of progressive estate owners also sought to undo the system of privileges and obligations of their labor tenants and convert them into more productive and specialized rural wage workers.

However, all of these processes either remained stuck in midstream—often for half a century or longer—or produced outcomes unexpected in the framework of a transition to capitalism. The deepening web of monetarized commerce took the form of intensifying exchange based on social relations of hierarchy, clientalism, and entrapment. Even during sustained periods of price rises for their principal products, most owners of livestock estates saw little reason to do away with the cumbersome system of labor tenancy, although it limited the productivity of their haciendas. The few hacendados who attempted to switch over to a system of specialized wage laborers encountered enormous resistance, delaying change for thirty to forty years. Also in reaction to incentives from the market and the penetration of liberal property notions, the buying, selling, and mortgaging of land increased considerably. But many of these transfers, instead of solidifying a convention of secure, unambiguous, and complete title rights to property, relied on clientalism, deception, or force and failed to allay the pandemic strife over use rights and disputed borders of property.

In short, the process of change in the Peruvian altiplano was driven by the same forces that propelled the transition to capitalism elsewhere—impulses from the market, the labor process, and the legal norms on property. Yet these forces provoked a reawakening and readjustment of an older set of social forces that constituted serious obstacles to the emergence of capitalism: monopoly, clientalism, and communal solidarity. Pressure from the market and the redefinition of the labor process and of legal norms were not strong enough to defeat those older social forces—understood as ingrained modes of behavior tending toward institutionalization. They remained catalysts for a direction of change sui generis. The transition to agrarian capitalism thus remained a mirage: something that one hoped or feared as imminent, something whose outline was always visible, but that never materialized.

In recent years historians have become critical of the notion that the rise of industrial capitalism in Western Europe, especially in England and France, provides the classical case of development against which all other cases should be measured. The critique is two-pronged. On the one hand, it does not make sense to set up the experience of any single country as the classical model that all others ought to follow if they wish to achieve proper progress. The timing, direction, and modalities of change in every society depend to a very large extent on a host of variables specific to that society—from landscape and climate to cultural norms, education, infrastructure, class relations, and the distribution of power. On the other hand, it is increasingly evident that even the countries of the classical model underwent a much less neat transition to capitalism than previously thought: aristocracies remained powerful during the century after the presumed bourgeois revolutions, markets were far more constrained by externalities than previously thought, and agriculture in certain regions was very slow to adopt scientific farming.[10]

In this study I seek to portray the complex pattern of continuity and change in the Peruvian altiplano as a unique, open-ended process with phases of rapid change, stalemates between the major social forces, patterns of cyclical change, and, only one among various possible patterns, linear transformations. I wish to go beyond the above-mentioned critique and reject the teleological view that changes in a given Latin American society and economy ineluctably prepare the triumph of capitalism. In the Peruvian altiplano the transition to capitalism began in the decades after the Spanish conquest, with the introduction of money, the payment of wages to mine workers, and limited trade in land. This transition continues today, with a growing number of agrarian enterprises operating on the basis of capitalist relations of production.

With the demise of the conflict between capitalism and socialism as the central issue of the world political-economic arena, it is necessary for social scientists to develop the capacity to imagine the end of the capitalist era in world history other than through a proletarian revolution, unless they are willing to accept the notion of a final victory of capitalism over socialism and "the end of history." As new paradigms begin to define the central conflicts in an increasingly interconnected world, between nation-states, ethnic and religious communities, transnational corporations, international agencies, and citizens' movements, not all the regions and societies in the world will be leaving the "age of capitalism" fully transformed according to the internal logic of that historical way of organizing economy and society. The Peruvian altiplano is such a region. It has been powerfully affected by capitalism, but it has not been totally remade in its image, as recurring stalemates between its social forces that were the consequence of colonialism led to the revitalization of older norms and modes of economic behavior, a type of defensive change.

Those who wish to assert that capitalism has increasingly subsumed, directly or indirectly, all areas of economic activity in Latin America emphasize its logic of unequal development.[11] This is undoubtedly one of capitalism's hallmarks, but it does not follow that all unequal developments in the modern world find their explanation in capitalist penetration. The centralization of political power, initiated by the Spanish Hapsburgs through bureaucratic patrimonialism and mercantilism and heightened by the Bourbons through more efficient and penetrating administrative and fiscal controls, was never really abandoned by the independent Peruvian state.[12] The establishment of Lima's ever-more-glaring urban primacy, as well as that of most departmental and provincial capitals in their respective territories, has as much to do with the unequal distribution of resources by the administrative fiat of those in positions of power—extraction from the countryside and the interior provinces and accumulation among those associated with the state in the capitals, especially Lima—as it does with different rates of profit and capital accumulation. In short, there are dynamics of inequality, some surviving from the colonial era, others newly arising in the last century, that have roots independent of the capitalist economy. These dynamics ought to be considered before assigning any particular instance of regionally or socially unequal development to the workings of capitalism. This is especially true for regions in which capitalist relations of production have not come to dominate directly even today.

The process of change analyzed in this book is one full of ambiguities, and it may help to briefly mention the three principal ones at the outset. The altiplano's society before 1930 can be cast in two contradictory images. Dimensions such as income distribution and ownership of land lie on a finely gradated scale, with "middle sectors," including middling and affluent peasants and hispanized owners of small haciendas, much more prominent than commonly assumed. At the same time altiplano society was also highly polarized, mainly in the understanding of the people themselves about honor and status and in social interactions based on this understanding. Both images of altiplano society need to be taken into account to grasp its dynamics of change.

Second, the multifarious process of historical change simultaneously brings losses and gains to specific social groups. The rise of liberalism, for example, not only brought an attempt to liquidate the communitarian traditions of the Indian peasantry but also prepared for new forms of association and political participation. Few broad historical processes (in contrast to discrete events and actions) do not show ambivalent effects on the interests of one and the same social group.[13]

As mentioned before, the economic and social development in the altiplano are here viewed as characterized by both cycles and transformations. "Cycles"—aside from the annual pattern of production and social life in the countryside and the roughly seven-year pattern of rising and falling water levels in Lake Titicaca, correlated with periods of drought and flooding—can be observed in secular movements of global economic activity: periods of about seventy years of growth followed by intervals of roughly the same length of stagnation and crisis. Shorter upward and downward rhythms occur within these secular waves. The relation of forces between the altiplano's hispanized elite and the peasantry was linked to these broad economic cycles, with eras of overall stagnation favoring the autonomy of the Indian communities and eras of growth seeing offensives by hispanized landholders and traders. Of course, each phase of the cycles also saw countervailing outcomes. Individual hispanized landholders expanded estates even during an era of stagnation; and although the autonomy of peasant communities was seriously challenged during phases of large landholder offensives and economic growth, it is far less certain that most peasants simultaneously experienced declining income levels. "Cycles," in the most abstract sense, also refers to the reconstruction of colonial cleavages in the postcolonial altiplano. Eras of hierarchy and monopoly in southern Peru's economy and structures of power have alternated with eras of more open, competitive, horizontal socioeconomic structures.[14]

But this cyclical pattern of development never returns the altiplano's economy and society to the starting point. Cycles are not closed circles. Institutions may regain strength after a period of decay, and old norms and privileges are cited by peasant communities and provincial elites in defense of their rights. At the same time, new patterns of markets and transportation, new currents of ideas, new channels of articulating political power, new arenas of social conflict—all will alter these norms and institutions, although they remain continuous in the minds of the interested groups. This is what is meant here by transformations. In the altiplano, cyclical patterns of development and transformative patterns are conjoined in such a way that we may speak of conservative modernization.[15]

In this book I tackle several important issues in the transformation of Latin American societies and economies between the late colonial period and the Great Depression:

1. The changing nature of markets: I explore the shifting range of commodities traded, the spatial patterning of commercial circuits, the decay and reconstruction of social hierarchies of traders, and the fate of parallel networks of exchange based on different notions of utility. This exploration leads to a reevaluation of the effects of dependency on regional economic development, which turns out to be less powerful than is often assumed. It is not the strength but the weakness of the foreign merchants, even during the era of export-led growth, that demands explanation.[16] Although they benefited more than anybody else from the altiplano's wool export economy, in the end they failed to achieve the kind of transformation of the production region for which they had been pushing.

2. The distribution of land and the issue of latifundism: I question the notion of a long-standing predominance of haciendas since colonial times; in the context of a major transfer of land from the peasant communities to the estate sector during the era of export expansion, widely recognized in the literature, the growing importance of rather small estates needs to be emphasized. I also question whether the increasingly frequent transfers of land in the late nineteenth and early twentieth centuries can aptly be described as a land market, an issue closely associated with the conventional meaning of land among the various social groups in the altiplano.

3. Continuity and change in the peasant communities: The continued and, indeed, revitalized solidarity of communities occurred simultaneously with a process of increasing demographic, land-related, and commercial pressures and a changing relationship to the state. The community is seen as a conflictive construct, shaped by and expressing not only shifting external challenges but also the internal constellations of power between different groups and families with changing aspirations.

4. Paternalism, subordination, and autonomy in the haciendas: The dominance of large landholders over their resident labor force was perhaps more fragile than often assumed, even if it was all encompassing. Indeed, my work supports the notion of parallel constructions of power between hacienda and community, recently suggested for the central Peruvian sierra by Gavin Smith, which is helpful in comprehending the dynamic of subordination and autonomy experienced by Andean colonos.[17]

5. The rationality of the hacendado's economic strategies: Although it is possible to speak of the efficiency of seigneurial estates, I dispute the

notion, introduced by the revisionist modelers of the Andean estate during the 1970s, that it is useful to portray the hacendado as a profit optimizer in neoclassical terms. As Alan Knight has recently suggested for Porfirian Mexico, we need to take contemporary critics of the hacienda more seriously, though without returning to their evolutionist schemes.[18]

These issues are explored through the study of one altiplano province, Azángaro, over a period of some one hundred and fifty years, from the 1770s to 1930. Tracing the complex and contradictory process of change of a rural economy and society over a century and a half makes it possible to detect the longer cycles identified above. It offers some protection against exaggerating the staying power of short-range, dramatic changes and opens the view to long-term characteristics of a regional society, the impact of its culture, its environment, and its historically evolved relations of power and status.

The altiplano offers a fascinating setting to explore the issues mentioned above. Its peoples look back on a long, proud history. One of the focal points of Andean civilization, the region first entered the limelight with the rise of Tiwanaku, a state centered just south of Lake Titicaca and holding a kind of cultural hegemony over great parts of the southern Andes for much of the first millennium of our era. The ethnic kingdoms of the Lupakas and Kollas, which dominated the northern altiplano between the decline of Tiwanaku and the region's forced incorporation into the Inca empire in the mid-fifteenth century, have become models for modern ethnographers' understanding of prehispanic Andean polities, with their emphasis on "nested kinship units" tied by reciprocal exchanges of material and ritual resources and sustained through the maximum use of different ecological levels, from the oasis settlements on the Pacific coast to colonies just above the tropical rain forests east of the Andes.

During the centuries of Spanish colonial rule the altiplano was in the center of the trading circuits linking the rich silver-mining districts of Upper Peru (modern-day Bolivia) with the viceroyalty's administrative and mercantile hub, Lima. In the nineteenth century the northern altiplano was one of the first interior regions of Peru to be integrated into world markets, while its population continued to be overwhelmingly monolingual, Quechua- or Aymara-speaking Indian community peasants. With the decline of the export economy and the consolidation of the Lima-centered Peruvian national state during the mid-twentieth century, the altiplano has become increasingly marginalized, a poor, "backward" region in the country's *mancha India*, or Indian belt. In the long run of two thousand years the region's history may be read as one of decline, from the power and splendor of Tiwanaku, through the subordination, on relatively favorable terms, to

Incaic imperialism, Spanish colonialism, and European capitalist expansion, to a poor backwater in the Peruvian nation.

But its history may also be read as contradictory and ambiguous. For centuries the altiplano has been an open transit space for conquering armies, trade, and ideas. The region's inhabitants have actively adapted to changing institutions, relations of production, and state structures introduced by powerful outside forces, perhaps responding more willingly than peoples in other parts of the Andes have done. Yet the altiplano was also a redoubt of Andean resistance to European colonization: the Spanish population remained scarce, and before the twentieth century no major urban center developed for a stretch of some five hundred kilometers between Cuzco and La Paz. Even today, educated and well-to-do citizens of Lima think that only the half-mad would choose to live in the altiplano, which they consider a cold, desolate place lacking minimal urban amenities. During the century and a half with which this book is concerned, the altiplano was at the forefront of most rebellions and civil wars convulsing Peru. Again we have an image of a regional society that embraces change but has a strong sense of distinct identity, through which it seeks to mold and temper externally introduced changes.

In this study I concentrate on one province, Azángaro, located just north of Lake Titicaca in the department of Puno. The province, in its borders between 1854 and 1989, was more than twice as large as the Grand Duchy of Luxembourg and a bit larger than the state of Delaware. A province such as Azángaro, which has been in existence in some form at least since the mid-sixteenth century, constitutes a legitimate unit of study, as authority structures, social networks, and channels of commercialization have given meaning to this administrative unit. Since the nineteenth century its inhabitants have identified themselves as Azangarinos, although that identity has frayed in outlying districts. In 1989 the town of Putina succeeded in a decades-old campaign to become capital of a new province, taking with it territories of old Azángaro province that figure prominently in this study.

The study is divided into two parts and nine chapters. The remainder of this introduction outlines basic characteristics of the altiplano environment and of Azángaro's demographic history, fundamental for understanding the region's development. The following three chapters form part 1, which deals with the age of crisis between about 1780 and the mid-1850s. Chapter 2 concerns the crisis of the colonial commercial circuits into which the altiplano was bound and the gradual reconstruction of new circuits since the 1820s. In chapter 3 I examine how the region's agrarian structure and the colonial mechanisms of surplus extraction from the Indian peasantry were affected by the onset of the crisis between the 1780s and 1820. In chapter 4 I explore how owners of estates and community peasants dealt with the challenges and opportunities of Peru's political independence under the conditions of a continued commercial slump.

The four chapters in part 2 cover the age of expansion between the late 1850s and 1920. Chapter 5 begins with a reappraisal of the marketing system and circuits. This is followed, in chapter 6, by an analysis of land transactions, hacienda expansion, and the various modes of acquiring and retaining land. In chapter 7 I take a closer look at peasant communities in the context of commercial pressures, changing constellations of local power, and the state. In chapter 8 I turn to the labor regime and the economy of altiplano livestock estates and valiant attempts at changing them. Chapter 9 demonstrates how the northern altiplano again entered a period of crisis and stalemate by the early 1920s and draws together the major points of the book.

Geography and Ecology of Azángaro

The traveler arriving in the altiplano either from the narrow inter-Andean valley system of Cuzco to the northwest, with its verdant valley bottom agriculture and the steeply sloping, reddish gray rock formations, or from the desolate wastelands of the western cordillera, which one must traverse coming from Arequipa, cannot help but marvel at the sight offered as one descends into the huge inter-Andean basin of which Peru's department of Puno forms only the northernmost part. The view here is opened to a plain stretching to the horizon and glowing in the golden colors that the intense sun of the altiplano grants to the endless grasslands during the long dry season from April to November.

The Titicaca basin forms the northern third of the altiplano, which extends for some twelve hundred kilometers from the dividing line of the modern departments of Puno and Cuzco southward to the border between Argentina and Bolivia. It is surrounded by the eastern and western cordillera of the Andes, which bifurcate at the northeastern extreme of the basin, the Nudo de Vilcanota, at fourteen and one-half degrees south latitude. On the Bolivian side, some four hundred kilometers to the southeast, the Titicaca basin is divided from further hydrographic basins only by some hills in the vicinity of La Paz.[19]

At an altitude of 3,812 meters above sea level, Lake Titicaca, nearly two hundred kilometers long and up to seventy kilometers wide, provides the special environment that has allowed the altiplano to become one of the most densely settled areas anywhere on our planet at comparable altitudes.

It has moderated the harsh climate and favored agricultural production in a narrow belt around its shore. Lacustrine plants and fishery resources provide construction materials and a natural food reserve for the dense lakeside population in times of scarcity. Ever since pre-Columbian times, but especially since the introduction of steam navigation, the lake has facilitated communication and transport.

The province of Azángaro, covering an area of 6,643 square kilometers in its boundaries of 1854–1989, is located at the northern rim of the altiplano (map 1.1). Extending at its widest and longest points for about one hundred and forty kilometers from north to south and one hundred kilometers from east to west, the province nearly touches Lake Titicaca at the mouth of Río Ramis on its southern border. Toward the north and northeast it slopes upward to the crest of the Cordillera de Carabaya at altitudes above five thousand meters. To the west the border with the province of Lampa follows fairly closely the course of Río Pucará. From Tirapata in the northwest Azángaro's border with Melgar province follows an ill-defined line in a northerly direction until reaching the crest of the eastern cordillera beyond Potoni. The southeastern border facing Huancané province runs from a point between the mouth of Río Ramis and Huancané town in a northeasterly direction up to the crest of the cordillera in the vicinity of Ananea.

Azángaro covers a good part of the drainage basin for the three major tributaries of Río Ramis, the largest of the feeder rivers of Lake Titicaca. Two of these tributaries, Río Crucero (called Río Azángaro south of Asillo) and Río Putina, trisect the province in a north-south direction. The westernmost districts of Azángaro descend to plains facing the third river, Río Pucará. In the central part of the province, the rivers meander through wide pampas separated by chains of hills.

In the northern and northeastern parts of the province river valleys become narrow. Here the cordillera slopes climb to heights above five thousand meters, as at Cerro Surupana in San José district, which retains its snowcap year round. Toward the south and southwest of the province the pampas widen. In the districts of Saman, Achaya, Caminaca, and the southern part of Arapa the landscape becomes flat. No more hills divide the runs of Ríos Pucará and Azángaro during the last ten or fifteen kilometers before they join to form Río Ramis. In the area of Saman and Taraco, the latter district part of Huancané province since 1854, the river reaches a width of one hundred meters and a depth of eight to ten meters. By the end of the rainy season, it frequently floods surrounding fields and pastures, causing considerable damage.[20]

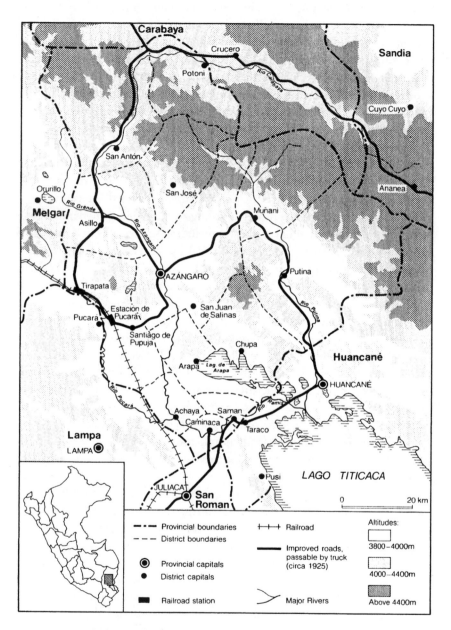

Carabaya

Crucero

Sandia

Potoni

Rio Carabaya

Cuyo Cuyo

San Antón

Ananea

Orurillo

Rio Grande

San José

Muñani

Melgar

Asillo

Rio Azángaro

Putina

AZÁNGARO

Rio Putina

Tirapata

San Juan
de Salinas

Estación de
Pucará

Pucara

Santiago de
Pupuja

Chupa

Huancané

Arapa   *Lag de
Arapa*

HUANCANÉ

Rio Pucara

Achaya   Saman

Rio Ramis

Caminaca

Taraco

Lampa

LAMPA

LAGO TITICACA

Pusi

0   20 km

JULIACA
San
Roman

Provincial boundaries   Railroad

District boundaries

Altitudes:

Provincial capitals   Improved roads,
passable by truck
(circa 1925)

District capitals

3800–4000m

Railroad station   Major Rivers

4000–4400m

Above 4400m

MAP 1.1.   Azángaro Province, circa 1920

In addition to numerous rivers and creeks, smaller lakes and ponds aid Azángaro's inhabitants in dealing with periodic scarcity of water. The southern end of the largest of the lakes, Lago de Arapa, with a circumference of about fifty kilometers, is only two kilometers from Lake Titicaca. The much smaller Laguna de San Juan de Salinas, some ten kilometers north of Arapa, holds considerable importance for the province as a steady source of high-quality salt. A mineral spring on an island constantly replenishes its brackish waters. As the shoreline recedes during the dry season, Indian peasants harvest the crystallized salt from the dry lake floor. Marketed until the nineteenth century throughout the northern altiplano and adjacent areas in the Cuzco valley system, the salt from San Juan de Salinas has been an important resource at least since Incaic times.[21]

The soils of the province, in many places exhausted for centuries,[22] generally differ from each other according to the relief of the land. In the immediate shore belt of Lake Titicaca, including some plains in Azángaro's southernmost districts, the soil is formed by alluvial and lacustrine deposits.[23] Ranging from moderately acidic to neutral, deficient both in nitrogen and phosphates, these soils contain a relatively high percentage of organic contents and do not need to rest for more than a year in order to replenish themselves naturally.[24] The pampas and softly sloping hills further away from the lake have superficial, stony soils less than thirty centimeters deep, as well as well-drained dark brown to brown-gray clay soils of greater depth. In depressions badly drained soils form little swamps. All of these soils are also deficient in nitrates and phosphates. Where there is no adequate drainage, salt and minerals accumulate, leaving the soil completely infertile;[25] such infertile, saline spots, called *collpares* in Azángaro, are prized features of a landholding, as they serve to combat livestock diseases. The soils on the steep slopes of the cordillera above four thousand meters are shallow and rocky.

Two factors influence Azángaro's climate more than any others: potential frosts for about seven months during the year and sharply marked seasonal rainfall for three to four months with great year-to-year fluctuations. Mean temperatures fluctuate greatly within each twenty-four hour-period. During the day the tropical sun lets the thermometer rise to the mid-twenties (Celsius); immediately after sunset a chill sets in, with temperatures often sinking below zero. Month-to-month fluctuations of temperatures are slight, ranging from an average of 10.2 degrees Celsius in January to 6.5 degrees Celsius in July on Puno's lakeshore. But they do make the difference between above-zero temperatures and night frosts.[26] Between April and October farmers have to contend with night frosts, leaving only a short growing season. In the cordillera, at altitudes above four thousand meters, frosts occur throughout the year.

Precipitation in the northern altiplano strongly fluctuates both from year to year and within each year. Annual rainfall may dip below 500 millimeters and climb as high as 1,000 millimeters, with a thirty-year mean of 580–600 millimeters.[27] Rainfall patterns divide the year into a rainy and warm summer season and a dry, cold winter season. The period from May to August is virtually free of rain, and 90 percent of the precipitation falls between mid-November and early April, with the peak in January and early February. Precipitation between September and mid-November, small in absolute terms, is of strategic importance for agriculture. Because soils dry out and harden during the winter months, the September rains are crucial for sowing the crops, providing an adequate growing period for plants to reach maturity before the April frosts. Delayed early rains can have consequences as devastating as those of veritable droughts.[28] In either form, droughts are frequent and cause severe subsistence crises and starvation among the altiplano's peasantry.[29] The other extreme, superabundant rainfall, also occurs, periodically flooding the areas of most intensive agriculture around the lakeshore and river valleys and destroying crops.

Frost and hail occur frequently. In years when severe frosts come, say, by early April, the greater part of the harvest may be destroyed. With such severe weather, optimal conditions for agriculture and livestock raising are rare. In 1831 José Domingo Choquehuanca, keenly interested in progress for his native province, observed that Azángaro had not been blessed with "good pastures" in four of the past five years because of excessive rains, drought, or severe frosts.[30] Microclimates play an important role in efforts to thwart the effects of harsh weather on crops. Plants might be killed by frost in one spot, while only thirty yards away they remain unaffected. For planting, farmers carefully choose spots sheltered from the wind, on hillsides or in small depressions or canyons, avoiding the windswept and frost-prone pampas. Fear of frost and hail has given rise to numerous invocations and rites among the Indian peasantry.[31]

At altitudes of above thirty-eight-hundred meters only the altiplano's proximity to the equator and the intense sun have made possible a vegetation sufficient to sustain large animal and human populations. This vegetation gets sparser the further south, reaching desert conditions in the salt flats at the southwestern edge of the altiplano in Bolivia. Even Puno's vegetation is relatively poor. Few trees thrive in this environment. The indigenous *kkolli (Polylepis racemosa)* and *kuenua (Budleya coriacea)* survive mostly in bushy patches on hill slopes, with tree-sized specimens only rarely gracing an altiplano town's *plaza de armas* or the roadway leading to a hacienda's building complex. For centuries these trees have been overexploited as construction material and firewood.[32] The eucalyptus tree, introduced from Australia, has adapted well in the lakeshore zone, but few grow in the altiplano proper.

By and large the altiplano is a treeless grassland, reminiscent of the steppes of inner Asia. The most common flora are grasses—*chillihua (Festuca dissitiflora), chillihua crespillo (Festuca rigescens), grama (Poa meyeni), chije (Sporobulus)*, and *cebadilla (Bromus unioloides)*—which cover plains and hillsides in varying density according to altitude, micro-climates, degree of moisture, and soils.[33] Differences of quantity and quality of pastures have played an important role in the locations of the area's livestock operations and have influenced land values. Some altiplano grasses can make livestock sick, especially the *ichu* or *paja brava (Stipa pungens)*, a tough grass with thorny tips that grows in tufts up to two feet tall on the slopes of both cordilleras.[34] In badly drained parts of the pampas and in shallow water close to the shorelines of lakes there thrives a variety of semiaquatic plants, including the prized *llacho (Miriophilium titicacensis)*, which provide fodder during the dry season.[35]

Only an estimated 22,400 hectares were dedicated to crops in the province in 1959, about 3.5 percent of the total provincial surface, while over 90 percent of land consisted of natural pastures—a distribution not likely to have changed greatly over the past two hundred years. Yet agriculture was and continues to be of strategic importance for the livelihood of the rural population. The degree to which the region's crops provide the necessary food for peasant families determines their freedom of disposition over their livestock herds. With insufficient crops greater numbers of animals have to be sold or bartered to acquire necessary foodstuffs. Thus, the harvests directly influence the size of stock populations, the key aspect of the region's economic well-being.[36]

Many temperate-climate food plants do not mature in the altiplano, and harvests are highly insecure because of the frequent climatic calamities. Since prehispanic times potatoes, native to the Andes, have constituted by far the most important food crop in the northern altiplano.[37] With an upper limit of cultivation around thirty-nine-hundred meters, the potato is grown in all districts of Azángaro province.[38] Although part of the crop is eaten fresh during the months after harvest, a greater part has historically been consumed in freeze-dried form, known as *chuño*.[39] Other native tubers, such as the *oca (Oxalis tuberosa)* and the *papa lisa* or *olluco (Ullucus tuberosus)*, are produced in smaller quantities.[40]

Compared with the persistent and overwhelming importance of tubers, the fortunes of other crops have undergone considerable changes. Such changes have marked in particular the Andean grains *quinua (Chenopo-*

dium quinoa) and *canihua (Chenopodium canihua),* whose production was concentrated in the lakeshore areas. Until the early colonial period these grains were cultivated considerably more widely than they were during the nineteenth century. Partly because production per hectare is lower than with potatoes and partly because urban consumers have not favored them, the production of Andean grains continued to decline until the 1970s, when the military government promoted them because of their high nutritional value.[41] Barley has taken acreage away from quinua and canihua since the seventeenth century.[42] Because barley reaches its upper limit of cultivation at about four thousand meters, it usually does not reach maturity in the altiplano, and stalks and foliage are used as forage.[43] During the late 1950s production still lay slightly below that of the indigenous Andean grains.[44] Planted throughout Azángaro, barley is found principally in the districts of Arapa and Saman, where the crop has been used as forage by cattle-fattening enterprises at least since the late nineteenth century.

Since the colonial period peasants and estate owners have attempted to plant a variety of vegetables, among them onions, carrots, cabbages, and—most important—lima beans. Although some of these plants reach maturity in well-protected hillside niches in Arapa and Chupa districts, only small quantities can be grown. This also holds true for maize and wheat, which rarely reach maturity in the altiplano. The supply of these cereals, important food items since prehispanic and colonial times respectively, had to be obtained through a lively trade with the valleys around Cuzco and with areas on the Andes' eastern and western slopes.[45]

The largest animals existing in the altiplano in historic times are the cameloids. The two domesticated species of this family, the llama and the alpaca, are the most common of the region's big mammals. Until the first quarter of this century the two nondomesticated species of cameloids, the huanaco and the vicuña, still roamed the isolated hillsides and cordillera slopes of Azángaro province in appreciable numbers. Vicuñas, living in highly stratified herds of about fifty animals, have been hunted for their extraordinarily fine fur since colonial times. An Andean variety of deer *(Cervus anticiencis),* pumas *(Felix concolor),* and foxes have also been hunted regularly. Pumas and foxes prey on flocks of smaller domesticated animals, causing frequent losses.[46] Several smaller animals are hunted as well, including the *viscacha (Lapidum peruvianum),* a rodent, and wild ducks, which are abundant in sheltered bays of the lakes.[47] Although hunting may have commercial motives—as in the case of vicuñas—or serve to eliminate livestock predators—as with the hunt for pumas and foxes—it has also served a more elemental function: in years of meager harvests and insufficient food supplies, the region's rural population will turn to hunting, along with the gathering of wild roots and berries, for survival.[48]

Although the fauna of the lakes and rivers consists of only a limited number of species, some types of fish have become an important additional source of food and income, particularly for the population living on the shores of Lakes Titicaca and Arapa. The preferred edible lake fish are *bogas* (*Orestia pentlandi*) and *humantus*, esteemed also by urban dwellers. *Carachis* (*Orestia albus*), rather small and skinny fish, are a cheap source of protein and have been traded throughout the region in dried form. Azángaro's rivers contain the largest edible indigenous fish of the altiplano, the *suche* (*Trychomicterus dispar*), which grows up to thirty-five centimeters. During the nineteenth and early twentieth centuries some varieties of altiplano fish found markets as far away as Cuzco and Arequipa.[49]

Two conclusions may be drawn from this overview of the northern altiplano's environment: (1) Because the environment approaches the limit for sustaining large human populations, it has been less malleable by humans than that of other, more favored climatic zones. The people of the altiplano cannot easily shift from a predominantly pastoral orientation to become surplus producers of food crops. Under technological conditions prevailing during both the colonial and republican periods, a drastic extension of acreage planted to crops would bring diminishing returns because of the harsh climate. Evidence suggests that the prehispanic societies put a considerably larger acreage into crop production through the use of hillside terraces and ridged fields in the pampas, solving the problems of drainage, irrigation, and protection against frosty winds.[50] Still, even before the coming of the Spaniards the region's principal wealth consisted in its abundant stock herds.[51] (2) Nevertheless, it should be emphasized that the environment allows a number of other primary economic activities. In spite of its limited scale, agriculture, with its notable local differentiation, has been of strategic importance. Hunting and fishing help to sustain populations in years of crop failure and high livestock mortality, besides offering a small number of people a regular income. It would be wrong to consider the altiplano, at any point in its history, as a monocultural livestock economy.

The Long-term Development of Azángaro's Population

Peruvian demographic history has only recently begun to provide fairly reliable population estimates for the prestatistical era. Most figures up to the 1940 census still have to be considered with caution because of a plethora of errors in data gathering as well as imprecisions and shifts in the administrative units covered. What is offered here on Azángaro's population should be viewed as rough approximations of major trends and turning points.

In contrast to New Spain, population decline in Andean Peru, and in Azángaro province in particular, continued for at least one hundred and fifty years after the Spanish conquest. Here the nadir was reached with the epidemics that swept much of Lower and Upper Peru in 1687 and again from 1718 to 1720. During the seventeenth century the onerous *mita de Potosí*, a mining labor draft imposed on Azángaro's indigenous population along with that of sixteen other provinces, also contributed to population losses and fueled massive migration aimed at escaping this and other Spanish impositions. By 1700 a large share of inhabitants in Azángaro's communities were *forasteros*, people whose ancestors were not born in the community where they now resided. The priest of the parish of Chupa reported to the Bishop of Cuzco in 1690 that all of his Indian parishioners were forasteros.[52] This growing segment of the population was apparently not regularly included in tribute recounts of the communities where they resided until the mid-1720s. Indian population growth between 1690 and 1725—unlikely in the face of reported losses during the 1718–20 epidemic of more than 50 percent—thus merely reflects new methods of counting.[53]

Available figures (tables 1.1 and 1.2) suggest a rapid increase of population during the following sixty-five years until the mid-1780s, in spite of the heavy loss of life suffered during the Túpac Amaru Rebellion at the beginning of that decade. The tribute recounts carried out during the 1750s were too low, and administrative reforms undertaken during *visitas* (inspections) of Areche and Escobedo allowed officials to capture a greater part of actual Indian population in the recount of 1786 and the episcopal census of 1798.[54] Whatever the precise rate, there can be little doubt that Azángaro's Indian population grew rapidly during the second and third quarters of the eighteenth century.[55] It was also during this period of economic growth that the non-Indian segment of the population, beyond the few dozen families of Spanish miners, landholders, and officials evident since the sixteenth century, became more visible.

For the remainder of the colonial period, until the mid-1820s, Azángaro's Indian population increased at a modest rate of about 1.0 percent annually. During the first two decades of the nineteenth century the altiplano suffered severe epidemics and droughts as well as the dislocating effects of the Wars of Independence, with repeated recruitments of the peasantry.[56] But such calamities had not been absent during the fifty years preceding the 1786 recount. Beyond the general congruence with

TABLE 1.1. Population of Azángaro Province, 1573–1972, According to Censuses and Tribute Counts

	Indians	Total
1573/78	25,482	n.a.
1615[a]	22,443	n.a.
1690	6,855	7,192
1725[a]	9,129	n.a.
1754[a]	10,228	n.a.
1758/59	12,604	n.a.
1786	26,573	n.a.
1798[a]	28,844	32,103
1826	36,052	n.a.
1825/29	37,579	43,291
1845[a]	n.a.	38,471
1850[a]	46,133	48,144
1862	n.a.	46,954
1876	n.a.	45,252
1940	92,845	97,038
1961	n.a.	111,468
1972	n.a.	122,210

Note: The figures here exclude Taraco, Pusi, and Poto.

[a]I subtracted 11.39 percent from the provincial totals, the average for the *doctrinas* of Pusi and Taraco, and the *anexo* or *vice-parroquia* of Poto in the counts for 1786, 1826, and 1825/29.

Sources: Cook, "Population Data for Indian Peru," 113; Vollmer, *Bevölkerungspolitik,* 281–84; Villanueva Urteaga, *Cuzco 1689,* 111–26; Wightman, *Indigenous Migration and Social Change,* 66; Macera, *Tierra y población,* 161–62 (multiplication of the number of tributarios for 1758/59 and 1786 by 4.5 as an estimate of total Indian population; subtraction of 1.6 percent for the population of Poto, not listed separately); Mörner, *Perfíl,* between pp. 132 and 133; Kubler, *Indian Caste,* 11, 28, 34; Choquehuanca, *Ensayo,* 15–53 (for 1825/29 I multiplied the number of tributarios by 4.5 as an estimate of total Indian population); *Correo Peruano,* July 30, 1845, as quoted by Castelnau, *Expedition* 4:129; 1862 census, BMP; national censuses of 1876, 1940, 1961, and 1972.

TABLE 1.2. Demographic Growth Rates for Azángaro Province, Derived from Population Counts

Years	Absolute Growth (percent)	Span (years)	Annual Rate (percent)
	Indians		
1573/78–1725	−64.2	ca. 150	−.43
1615–1725	−59.3	110	−.54
1725–1786	291.1	61	3.13
1725–1798	316.0	73	2.96
1725–1825/29	411.6	ca. 102	3.05
1786–1825/29	41.4	ca. 41	1.01
1798–1825/29	30.3	ca. 29	1.04
	Total Population		
1825/29–1876	4.5	ca. 49	.09
1825/29–1850	11.2	ca. 23	.49
1825/29–1862	8.5	ca. 35	.24
1850–1862	−2.5	12	−.21
1850–1876	−6.0	26	−.23
1876–1940	114.4	64	1.79
1940–1972	25.9	32	.80

Sources: See table 1.1.

semisecular economic rhythms in the region, it is still difficult to account for this demographic slowdown.

Uncertainties do not diminish for the century after independence. The counts of the late 1820s, 1850, and 1862 were not based on modern statistical methods and have generally been considered unreliable.[57] Even the 1876 census, carried out after painstaking preparations, contained numerous errors and confused categories.[58] And for the altiplano there is a most unfortunate gap without any useful population counts for the long interval between the 1876 and 1940 censuses.

If we are to believe the census data, Azángaro's global population grew at an annual rate of 0.49 percent between the immediate postindependence years, 1825–29, and 1850, only to decline during the following twenty-six years, until 1876, to a level just 4.5 percent above that of fifty years earlier. Only during the subsequent sixty-four years until 1940 did the long-term population growth that had begun during the second quarter of the eighteenth century set in again with an increase of 114 percent. With its population fluctuating between about 43,000 and 54,000 from the 1820s to 1870s, Azángaro's average population density was about seven or eight inhabitants per square kilometer. Some areas, particularly in the districts close to Lake Titicaca and certain sectors of Asillo and Azángaro districts, had a much higher population density, while the hilly ranges interlacing the broad valley plains and the slopes of the Cordillera de Carabaya were sparsely settled by a few livestock herding families. With the increase to over 97,000 inhabitants by 1940, Azángaro's average population density reached a level of about fifteen persons per square kilometer.

The 1850 census may have deliberately overstated Azángaro's population since it was prepared by the Ministry of War to "buttress a presidential decree ordering the recruitment of fresh troops" for impending hostilities with Bolivia.[59] Regardless of its veracity, we need to explain either the decline of population between 1850 and 1876 or its near stagnation between 1825–29 and 1876. Unfortunately, we cannot measure the impact of migration and military recruitment, although both factors clearly played some role.[60] Various sources refer to at least seasonal migration by male peasants to the eastern piedmont of the Andes (the *ceja de la selva*) in Apolobamba and Pelechuco (Bolivia) and, less frequently, to Carabaya, Sandia, and the Cuzco valley system.[61] During the civil wars following independence, young men were at times rounded up in altiplano peasant communities to build the regiments of warring caudillos. Some of these peasant recruits never returned home.[62]

We can say a bit more about epidemics. A severe disease, probably typhus or typhoid fever, struck the Peruvian and Bolivian highlands from Jauja in the north to Potosí in the south between 1856 and 1858, coinciding with the interval when Azángaro's population growth of the previous thirty years was reversed. According to the Swiss traveler Johann Jakob von Tschudi, the epidemic killed about three hundred thousand Indians, totally depopulating some villages.[63] Although losses were greatest in the department of Cuzco, the British Consul in Islay expressly reported its horrible sweep through the department of Puno.[64]

We can thus explain the decline of Azángaro's population between the censuses of 1850 and 1862 as largely caused by the 1856–58 epidemic. But there is no evidence to account for the continued—although minimal—decline until 1876. To be sure, in this period Azángaro and Huancané provinces were shaken by the "Bustamante Rebellion" of 1866–68. In the subsequent repression authorities planned to resettle complete Indian communities implicated in the uprisings in the ceja de la selva of Carabaya.[65] But after strong public protest the reprisals were never carried out to the extent planned, and population decline between the census figures of 1862 and 1876 is lower for some of the centers of the rebellion (Saman, Putina, and Muñani) than for districts not implicated. Although other short-term developments during this interval cannot be excluded with certainty, mere census errors, too high a figure for 1862 or too low a figure for 1876 or both, appear just as likely. A notable undercount in the 1876 census appears most plausible.

The province's strong demographic growth over the following sixty-four years, averaging 1.8 percent annually according to the census data, would have been produced although on the surface none of the major factors influencing population had much changed. Recruitment drives by the army and Guardia Nacional continued even after the termination of the War of the Pacific and the ensuing civil war in 1895.[66] In addition, migration to the ceja de la selva may have intensified. Between 1900 and 1930 peasants from the altiplano districts closest to the eastern cordillera such as Muñani, Putina, Rosaspata, and Conima were drawn through *enganche* contracts (credit advances) to work as rubber collectors in the Tambopata valley of Sandia province. Coffee and coca production in this southernmost piedmont province of Peru also attracted growing numbers of peasants from the altiplano, while others continued to migrate to the Bolivian ceja de la selva around Apolobamba and Pelechuco.[67] Only the depression of the early 1930s and the outbreak of the Chaco War between Bolivia and Paraguay in 1932, which created fears among Peruvian workers in the Bolivian piedmont that they might be recruited into that republic's army, brought a brief respite to the gradual increase of outward migration from the altiplano.

By 1940 as many as 35,688 persons, 6.2 percent of those born in the department, had migrated from Puno department to other parts of Peru, nearly half of those to the department of Arequipa. Only a third as many persons migrated into the department, the largest contingent (36.7 percent) coming from Bolivia. By 1940 Puno's net migration loss amounted to more than 23,000 persons, 4.2 percent of the department's population. Though small compared to the massive migration losses common since the 1950s, this loss further diminished population growth rates. Many migrants from Azángaro went to Arequipa or Cuzco. In 1907, for example, we find Gertrudis Quispe Amanqui, a peasant woman from *parcialidad* (community) Ccacsani in Arapa district, living permanently in Arequipa and selling cheeses in the market.[68]

Epidemics continued to exact a toll on Azángaro's population during the intercensus period between 1876 and 1940. The only medical doctor in the province, Manuel E. Paredes, a descendant of an important hacendado family, reported that in 1919 "influenza appeared and wreaked havoc upon the Indians with a most terrifying percentage of fatal cases." Typhus and smallpox also became epidemic during certain seasons, and measles had caused "considerable mortality" among children in years past. However, gastrointestinal infections and tuberculosis were rare because of healthy drinking water and low population density.[69]

During the early decades of the twentieth century the death toll from infectious diseases remained high in Azángaro. There are references to an epidemic (possibly bubonic plague) in 1903 and the outbreak of exantemic typhus in 1908, both causing many deaths. The 1903 epidemic killed forty-five shepherds in Haciendas Checayani and Caravilque alone.[70] With evidence for continued army recruiting, gradually increasing emigration, and a number of serious epidemics, it is difficult to account for the mean 1.8 percent annual population increase between 1876 and 1940 suggested by the censuses of those years.

A look at birth and death rates for the years 1924–25 makes lower growth rates for the period 1876 to 1940 highly plausible.[71] Records on births are likely to be fairly accurate, since nearly everybody considered baptism of newborn children essential; deaths, by contrast, often went unreported since peasants sought to avoid the expense of a church funeral.[72] The rate of birth of 2.6 percent in 1924–25 for six districts in Azángaro province is nearly identical with the rate of between 2.1 and 2.6 percent for the years 1941 to 1945 reported by Peru's statistical office for the whole of Puno. However, the reported mortality rate of 0.35 percent for the six districts in 1924–25 compares with mortality rates of between 1.1 and 1.4 percent for the whole of Puno department from 1941 to 1945. This difference strongly suggests that most deaths went unreported in 1924–25. Whereas relying on this unbelievably low mortality rate would render a rate of natural population increase of 2.2 percent for 1924–25, an application of the more dependable mortality figures from 1941–45 (a mean rate of 1.26 percent) would result in a rate of natural population increase of 1.34 percent for the mid-1920s. This is nearly one-third lower than the mean rate required to achieve the population increase suggested by the censuses for the period from 1876 to 1940.

If we assume both the 1940 figure for Azángaro's total population and the 1924–25 figures of births to be fairly reliable, the 1876 census must have undercounted the provincial population by about 15 percent. Choquehuanca's data for 1825–29 underestimated Azángaro's population as well. Although a mortality rate of 2.8 percent seems plausible for those years, a birth rate of 4.6 percent is highly improbable. On the assumption of fairly accurate birth statistics, this error could have been the result only of low overall population figures and mortality rates.

In conclusion, I would like to present a model of Azángaro's probable long-term demographic development. The province's population declined between the conquest period and the late seventeenth century, but not to such low levels as suggested by the 1690 count. Only the devastating epidemic of 1718–20 marked the nadir of Azángaro's Indian population. The seven decades after the epidemic saw rapid population recovery, perhaps on the order of 2 percent annually, a rebound of fertility well known from aftermaths of major European epidemics. This recovery was spread more evenly throughout the period than suggested by the tribute recounts of the 1750s. It coincided with an era of economic growth and saw the entrenchment of a significant sector of non-Indian population in Azángaro, although the province would remain about 90 percent Indian well into the twentieth century. Azángaro's population growth slowed down between the 1790s and mid-1820s; this slowdown coincided with the onset of a long period of economic crisis, discussed in the next chapter.

Among the early censuses of the republican era those of the late 1820s and of 1876 are likely to have undercounted Azángaro's population, whereas those of 1850 and 1862 were closer to the mark or too high. During the first quarter century after independence the province's population continued to grow at the modest rate of the late colonial era. The epidemic of 1856–58 caused major population losses still not overcome five years later, at the time of the 1862 census. Contrary to the indications from the 1876 census, we may safely assume a growing population during the following decade, but the 1850s epidemic had a major impact on Azángaro's demographic development for the whole intercensus period from the late 1820s to 1876. In contrast to recent regional and national studies, I estimate that the population of altiplano provinces such as Azángaro underwent only minimal growth during this half century.[73] This near stasis occurred largely during the remainder of the long-term economic crisis that began during the 1780s and came to a close during the mid-1850s. During the following long intercensus period, 1876–1940, regional population growth became sufficiently robust to overcome the effects of epidemics, emigration, and military recruitment. Yet because of the undercount of 1876 it was considerably lower than suggested by the raw census data, perhaps around 1.3 percent annually, commensurate with preindustrial population growth in eighteenth-century Europe.

Between the conquest and 1720 and again from the 1930s onward, Azángaro's population development cannot easily be correlated to long-term economic cycles. In the earlier phase the Indians' lack of immunity to European diseases and, since about the 1930s, the dramatic impact of antibiotics and public health campaigns have been the predominant factors influencing population trends, regardless of economic cycles. But during the roughly two hundred intervening years, from 1720 to the 1930s, we may note a certain correlation between population and economy: an era of growth during the middle decades of the eighteenth century followed by a period of crisis between the 1780s and mid-1850s and another period of growth since the 1860s. This is not a neat and tidy correlation, to be sure, and it is especially messy at the first seam, the transition from growth to stagnation during the late eighteenth and early nineteenth centuries, where the economic downturn appears faster and more drastic than the demographic crisis. Nor is there sufficient information to say with certainty whether population drove the economic cycles (as suggested by Esther Boserup and so convincingly applied to the region of Guadalajara, Mexico, during the eighteenth century by Eric Van Young)[74] or whether, as in the Malthusian model, the economy determined demographic patterns. Over the long run of the two hundred years an interdependent relation between the altiplano's economic and demographic trends offers the most realistic model, although during shorter periods one or the other factor may have been overwhelmingly influential. As we try to understand the socioeconomic evolution of the Peruvian altiplano in the ensuing chapters, it is of critical importance to keep in mind both the region's long-term population development and its harsh yet surprisingly varied ecology.

I CRISIS AND REALIGNMENT, 1780–1855

2   From the "Andean Space" to the Export Funnel

"The province of Azángaro is extremely abundant in livestock, which constitutes the principal base for its commerce, as well as wool, tallow, and hogs."[1] This description of the province's economy, written by the geographer Cosme Bueno around 1770, hardly differs from those given by travelers a hundred years later. Azángaro's wealth has rested primarily on the products of its livestock herds since pre-Incaic times. But the way in which these livestock resources were exploited changed in important ways between the mid-eighteenth and the second half of the nineteenth centuries. Azángaro's economy had to adapt to changing commercial circuits, which redefined the relations of peasants, estate owners, and traders with the outside world and simultaneously brought shifts in the distribution of income and modes of exploitation between the various social groups in the region.

On the highest level of integration this change was marked by the gradual demise of the colonial mining supply economy and the subsequent integration of southern Peru's livestock-growing areas into an expanding world market for wools, a transition that spanned the decades between the 1770s and the 1850s. The three developments that contributed most to this transition were the crisis of silver mining in the southern Andes; the political and social upheavals between the 1780s and 1840s that led to the creation of the independent states of Peru and Bolivia and to the fracturing of the "commercial space" that had its core in the altiplano; and European industrialization, which fostered a new quality of commodity, capital, and labor flows on a world scale.

Yet as strong as the impact of these macroregional and even global forces of change were on the northern altiplano, much in the agrarian economy and society of the altiplano remained untouched by them. Despite the

31

disruption of the colonial market since the last decades of the eighteenth century, the northern altiplano maintained an active commercial interchange with neighboring, ecologically distinct regions of southern Peru. The low-level local trade in foodstuffs and household goods, characteristic of entrenched peasant societies, continued unabated.

In this chapter I trace the variegated development of markets for the northern altiplano livestock economy from the mature colonial period through the era of crisis. I pursue the following kinds of questions: How did upswings or downturns in demand for livestock products affect the various social groups in Azángaro? To what degree did peasants participate in the market? What was the nature of this market, and can it be viewed in isolation from the distribution of power and the sociocultural structure of altiplano society?

Azángaro's Integration into the Commercial Circuits of Colonial Peru

During most of the colonial period Azángaro's primary economic function lay in the supply of the viceroyalty's mining centers.[2] In their role as "indispensable but secondary annex" to the mining economy Azángaro and the neighboring altiplano *partidos* (provinces) of Lampa and Paucarcolla contributed sheep and alpaca wool, furs and leather, dried mutton, alpaca and llama meat, tallow, and chuño to the mining camps and towns between Cuzco and Potosí.[3]

Although the most important mining centers—Potosí, Porco, and Oruru—were located at the southern end of the central Andean altiplano, some five hundred to eight hundred kilometers from Azángaro, the present-day departments of Puno and Arequipa were mining centers of some significance in their own right, in need of supplies from the livestock-producing regions in the northern altiplano. For a brief period in the mid-seventeenth century the Laikakota mines outside of Puno town produced one and a half million pesos per year in royal taxes alone. The silver mines of San Antonio de Esquilache were located in the western cordillera some thirty or forty kilometers west of Puno. And according to Emilio Romero, the Carabaya gold-mining district, which stretched from the high plateau of the eastern cordillera around Ananea and Poto to the ceja de la selva valleys of the Tambopata and Inambari rivers, produced 139 million pesos of gold during the whole colonial period, more than one-third of the viceroyalty's total production.[4]

Around 1770 lead mines were being worked in the vicinity of Asillo within the province of Azángaro. At that time a variety of mines, although of low-grade ores, continued to be operated in the province of Lampa.[5] On the western slopes of the Andes, in the bishopric of Arequipa, the mines of the partido of Cailloma during the mid-eighteenth century were increasing their production.[6] By contrast, by the late eighteenth century most of Puno's mining districts had been abandoned altogether or had declined to shadows of their former selves. Nevertheless, the area of the department of Puno still produced 1,765,632 marks of silver at seven to nine pesos the mark between 1775 and 1824.[7]

Azángaro's trade during the colonial period was not limited to the supply of mining centers. Because of the peculiar ecology of the central Andean range, neighboring regions of differing elevations complemented each other by producing agricultural and livestock goods ranging from those of a tropical climate to those of cold-weather zones. Since pre-Incaic times the altiplano had maintained a lively interchange of goods with the coastal areas to the west, the inter-Andean valleys to the north, and the ceja de la selva to the east. Up to the time of the Spanish conquest this interchange had taken place within the framework of the altiplano ethnic kingdoms, among them the Lupakas and the Kollas (whose domain included the modern area of Azángaro), which had founded colonies on both the western and eastern slopes of the Andes to have access to a maximum of ecological levels and their agricultural products.[8] This vertical interchange of goods continued throughout the colonial period and, indeed, continues today. However, the penetration of indigenous Andean societies by Spanish colonial structures altered the organization and rationale of this interchange. The Spanish colonial policy of stabilizing the Indian population in one location began to cut off access of kinship groups to land on other ecological levels. In the prehispanic era this access had permitted the self-sufficiency of extended kinship groups, but during the colonial period vertical interchange became monetary trade or barter between individuals living in spatially separated indigenous communities or Spanish towns that had no kinship ties.

This is the framework for Azángaro's late colonial trade with Arequipa and its surrounding agricultural valleys, with Cuzco and the towns of the Vilcanota and Urubamba valleys, and with the ceja de la selva regions of Carabaya and Larecaja. In 1791 the Viceroyalty of Buenos Aires, to which the northern altiplano belonged between 1776 and 1796, exported 214,000 pesos worth of dried meats and livestock on the hoof to the Intendency of Arequipa in the Viceroyalty of Peru.[9] Most of these goods came from the partidos of Azángaro, Lampa, Paucarcolla, and possibly Chucuito.[10] The city of Arequipa alone annually purchased 54,800 sheep on the hoof, 1,500 cows on the hoof, and 100,000 *chalonas* (dried and salted mutton carcasses) from the altiplano, valued at 99,000 pesos. Arequipa further imported from Azángaro and its neighboring provinces 11,000 pesos worth of tallow, 1,000 pesos worth of raw wool, and considerable quantities of chuño, butter, and cheese. In exchange, Azángaro received alcohol, constituting nearly 75 percent of Arequipa's exports to High Peru, as well as wine, corn, oil, cotton, wheat flour, chili peppers, and sugar.[11]

Although smaller in quantity, the range of goods exported from Azángaro and the neighboring altiplano provinces to Cuzco in 1791 was much the same as the goods exported to Arequipa. Besides 30,000 pesos worth of wool and 25,000 pesos worth of cheap woolen fabrics, the region sold 120,000 head of sheep on the hoof for 60,000 pesos to the Intendency of Cuzco.[12] Furthermore, Cuzco received from the northern altiplano 18,000 pesos of tallow, 500 pesos of cheese, and 8,750 pesos of dried mutton. In return, the northern altiplano bought from the valleys of Cuzco sugar and other sweets, chili peppers, a small amount of coca leaves, flour, and, most important of all, corn. A small part of Cuzco's voluminous cloth exports to the Viceroyalty of Buenos Aires may also have been sold in Azángaro and the neighboring provinces. Azángaro supplied the ceja de la selva valleys of Carabaya and Larecaja provinces with much the same products that it sent to Cuzco and Arequipa. In return, the valleys supplied Azángaro with coca in great amounts, some corn, and a variety of tropical fruits in small quantities.

This trade of the northern altiplano with the neighboring, ecologically distinct regions cannot be explained primarily as a function of Peru's mining economy. Azángaro and the adjacent provinces balanced ecologically imposed nutritional deficits with imports of cereals, sugar, chili peppers, and a variety of fruits, herbs, and other foods from Cuzco, Carabaya, and Arequipa. In return, their exports furnished these regions with scarce livestock products for food, clothing, lighting, and other industrial uses. Many items of this complementary exchange responded to rather inelastic demands, and the long-term trend in the volume of the trade depended primarily on the rise of the population and the degree of competition from alternative sources of supply (e.g., imports). Because much of this trade could take the form of barter, it was only indirectly dependent on the conjuncture of the mining sector and its supply of specie to the monetary economy. But for some commodities this mining nexus was important, as was the case with *aguardiente* (a raw liquor distilled from wine) from Arequipa. Matheo Cossio, Arequipa's deputy of trade, explained slumping alcohol sales in 1804: "Because of the lack in the workings of the mines in the provinces of the sierra . . . , there was no monetary circulation in them, and consequently they have had no consumption of aguardiente."[13]

Some of the altiplano products were not sent to centers of consumption in their raw form but were processed by artisans or in manufactories either in the province itself or in neighboring regions. In particular, wool was made into blankets, rough cloth, saddle bags, and other textiles before being transported to Potosí, Oruro, and other mining centers. During the seventeenth and eighteenth centuries this processing took place in part in the notorious *obrajes*, technologically backward textile manufactories owned by Spaniards, creoles, wealthy mestizos and caciques, and even religious communities. Until 1781 one such obraje was located in Muñani in the province of Azángaro, and there were a few others in neighboring altiplano partidos.[14] During the eighteenth century the most important concentration of obrajes was in some of the southern partidos of the bishopric of Cuzco, most prominently Canas, Canchis, Quispicanchis, and Chumbivilcas.[15] Much of Azángaro's wool was transported to these obrajes, where it was processed into rough woolen cloths for the markets in High Peru. Even in 1791, a period of crisis for southern Peru's textile manufactories, the Viceroyalty of La Plata was still exporting to Cuzco thirty thousand arrobas (750,000 pounds) of wool, most of which came from Azángaro and the neighboring provinces of Lampa and Paucarcolla.[16] Wool shipments from the northeastern altiplano to Cuzco had been larger before 1776.

Curiously, in 1791 the Viceroyalty of Buenos Aires was also exporting 200,000 yards of woolen cloth to the Viceroyalty of Lima via the Cuzco route.[17] This cloth (*jerga*) was cheaper than that exported from Cuzco to High Peru and was probably produced by rural, indigenous weavers in the northern altiplano provinces in home production. That it could be marketed at all in an area in which a great deal of wool was processed into cloth sheds some light on the structure of the market in the southern Andes at that time. Instead of one integrated marketing system in which all social classes were consuming goods produced through essentially similar processing techniques, several fairly segregated markets existed for the same type of goods (such as woolen textiles) separated by the socioeconomic condition and local custom of consumers and divergent production processes. Although affluent sectors of colonial society in the larger cities were accustomed to buying cloth manufactured in European factories, the poorer classes in the cities and the large mining populations, who had no immediate access to the cloth woven by rural peasant artisans, had to rely on products turned out by obrajes.[18] The cloth produced on the looms in peasant households still found a market among peasants who did not produce sufficient wool to cover their own clothing needs and also among the poor in towns, who could afford only the very cheapest material.

The great majority of Indian peasant households in Azángaro spun and wove sheep and alpaca wools. Numerous other rural crafts were practiced by smaller groups of peasants. An industrial census of the partido of Lampa from 1808 enumerates twenty different artisanal goods, besides the great variety of textiles, that were elaborated in the partido, such as hats, shoes, spoons, ceramics, reed mats, soap, and even a few wheels for the mineral mills.[19] Several Indian communities of Azángaro's parish of Santiago de Pupuja produced—and still do so today—ceramic cooking utensils "of good quality and very special glaze, . . . which if brought to Lima would be esteemed, because they are better than those produced there."[20] Although most artisanal goods were produced in small quantities, they nevertheless sufficed to constitute a marketable surplus.

Rural crafts were an integral part of Azángaro peasants' household economy, complementing income from scanty crops and livestock. In contrast to European protoindustrial complexes during the eighteenth and early nineteenth centuries, for most altiplano peasant households income from craft production was subsidiary to their income from agriculture. In the province of Lampa, for example, during the early years of the nineteenth century the value of all textiles and crafts goods amounted to less than half the value of crops, livestock products, and the corresponding herds. If all craft goods had been sold, each peasant household would have taken in an average of six to eight pesos annually. The three peasant communities in the parish of Santiago de Pupuja sold some two thousand pesos of pottery annually in the first years of the nineteenth century, on average just over five pesos per household.[21]

European protoindustrial complexes such as the Flemish and Westphalian linen regions produced for vast export markets. In a complex interaction between population pressure, socioeconomic differentiation within peasant societies, and merchant adaptation to changing market structures, spinning and weaving for external markets allowed a burgeoning subpeasant strata to remain on the land despite insufficient land resources. This rural industry thus sustained population growth and led to a notable widening of the internal market for locally produced foodstuffs, as a growing number of cottagers needed to buy cereals and industrial raw materials from the more affluent peasant strata.[22]

In the eighteenth-century altiplano the production of woolen textiles and other craft goods in peasant households did not have its origins in similar demographic and socioeconomic processes, nor did they lead to an appreciable intensification of the region's internal market. The impressive population increase in the northern altiplano during the last century of the colonial regime, caused by the diminishing effect of epidemic diseases on the Indian population, was sustained by rising agricultural and livestock production, which could grow at par with population because of underutilization of land in an era of low population densities. In contrast to the experience of Western European protoindustrial regions, rural craft production in the altiplano was thus not the decisive element or necessary precondition for population growth.[23] An expression of what O. Hufton has called the peasants' "economy of survival," characterized by an aggregation of labor in households rather than any tendency toward further division of labor, rural crafts supplied needed goods for home consumption as well as for defraying the costs of modest purchases in local and regional markets and for the payment of civil and religious fees and taxes.[24] On the local markets, these goods could be exchanged for staple foods in years when the producers' own crops fell short or, for those with too little land, on a more permanent basis. These goods—like livestock products—were also exchanged in the interregional markets of Arequipa and Cuzco for supplementary foodstuffs and intoxicants such as maize, coca leaves, and alcohol. Although these exchanges were important for the peasants' livelihood, they necessarily remained on a low level of intensity and could not form the basis for a dynamic internal market.

This condition was exacerbated by the asymmetrical nature of many commercial exchanges involving peasants. Blankets, baize cloth, saddle bags, other textiles, and livestock products were extracted from the peasant economy by a small number of provincial power holders through a variety of coercive mechanisms at the very heart of the colonial regime. Especially the *corregidores*, the highest royal officers in the provinces, their lieutenants, and some of the powerful *kurakas* and priests combined their positions of authority with commercial activities in which the peasants of their jurisdiction constituted both a captive market and the inevitable source for some of the commodities of their trading circuit.

In Azángaro some communities in the eighteenth century were still forced to pay tributes in cloth, a kuraka kept for himself the annual increase of livestock belonging to a communal fund, and a corregidor in the 1690s had live sheep—probably acquired from peasants—marketed as far as Lima and Potosí. As official inquests, petitions by communities to the Protector de Indios in La Plata, court cases before the audiencia of that city, and brief but violent local revolts attest, corregidores, kurakas, and priests in Azángaro used a great variety of ruses to get at the most marketable products of the Indian peasants.[25] In this pattern of asymmetrical trade, prices were set not by the market but by the power holders. While these profited doubly from selling dearly to, and buying cheaply from, the peasants, the purchasing power of the latter was severely reduced. In brief, the local markets of the northern altiplano remained feeble during the eighteenth century both because of the intrinsic nature of exchanges between undifferentiated peasant households and because of asymmetrical surplus extraction schemes facilitated by the colonial regime. To speak of a strong internal market for this region during the last century of colonial rule is unwarranted.

The northern altiplano occupied a central location in the circuits of long-distance trade that had tied together the vast "Andean space" since the late sixteenth century.[26] Much of the goods transported between Lower and Upper Peru had to pass through the transit corridor along the shores of Lake Titicaca. The great road that connected Lima, administrative and commercial hub of the viceroyalty, with the crucial mining center of Potosí straddled the western border of Azángaro province for some twenty or thirty kilometers. The spinal cord of the Peruvian viceroyalty at least until the 1770s, the road functioned southbound as a funnel for all supplies needed in Potosí and the other mining centers of High Peru, while northbound it carried precious metals to Lima and the large mule herds from Tucuman and Salta to be sold in all parts of Lower Peru.[27] Another road that fed into the major transverse road at Lampa connected the altiplano with Arequipa and its coastal valleys. Although not as important for the long-distance trade as the Lima–Cuzco–La Paz–Potosí route, it was of great importance for the vertical interchange between the northern altiplano and the agricultural production zones around Arequipa.[28]

This strategic location brought an uncommonly high level of trade and transport business through the northern altiplano. However, merchants and muleteers from the Spanish towns of Cuzco, Arequipa, La Paz, Potosí, and La Plata and their surrounding valleys controlled most of this trade and reaped most benefits from it. In a way, the northern altiplano had become an internal space since the late sixteenth century, dominated by the primary Spanish centers of the colonial economy. For the mercantile interests in these cities, the importance of Azángaro and its neighboring provinces lay as much in their strategic location as in the livestock products contributed by the region itself. Nevertheless, by the eighteenth century kurakas, corregidores, and small-scale, independent muleteers had increased their activities as traders and transport entrepreneurs throughout the southern Peruvian Andes. Some mules driven northward from Tucuman and Salta were retained in the northern altiplano both for the muleteers' own use and in order to resell them after some weeks or months of putting them out to pasture.[29]

The strategic location of the northern Titicaca basin for the colonial trading circuits created both additional burdens and opportunities for the peasantry. As *mitayos* working for the corregidor, as *yanaconas* of estate owners, or merely as more or less forced "free" laborers in the employ of anyone with power or influence in the province, peasants regularly had to leave their communities and accompany mule or llama strings to Potosí, Arequipa, or even Lima. Viceregal regulations regarding work conditions for the Indians employed on such journeys were routinely disregarded. Corregidores and kurakas routinely required the peasants to use their own pack animals and refused to compensate them for loss of the animals. Pay was insufficient, and the peasants were responsible for loss or damage of goods entrusted to them. The *trajín*, as these treks with transport animals were called, thus became a serious form of exploitation of the northern altiplano's peasants.

At the same time, this geo-economic centrality made it easier for quite a few Indian peasants from Azángaro, Lampa, Paucarcolla, and Chucuito provinces to enter the trade and transport business on a small scale. They could supplement their subsistence economy not just by selling their own livestock products and artisanal goods but also by hiring out their services as muleteers with their own llamas or mules or even by purchasing goods for later resale. This type of Indian trader was a frequent figure on the roads of the eighteenth-century altiplano.[30]

By the mid-eighteenth century, then, Azángaro and the neighboring provinces occupied a relatively favorable position in the complex colonial economy of the southern Andes. True, the region's own mining production had declined since the late seventeenth century, yet the population of neighboring urban centers had increased, and mining in Upper Peru had recovered. As prices for textiles declined since the early eighteenth century because of growing European imports, the competing obraje complex of Quito ceded market shares in Upper Peru to the Cuzco obrajes, which profited from lower transport costs. Textile production briefly flourished there during the first three quarters of the eighteenth century, and demand for altiplano wools grew as a consequence.[31] These, then, were the factors that fostered demand for altiplano's livestock goods in long-distance trade until the 1770s.

Beyond the trade circuits articulated through the mining economy, there existed other, less cyclical bases for marketing livestock products and artisanal goods from the northern altiplano. Both the interchange of commodities with neighboring ecologically distinct regions, especially the Cuzco valley system and Arequipa and its agricultural hinterland, and the local market, which was based on recurring scarcities in relatively undifferentiated peasant households, would be affected only indirectly by the ups and downs of the silver-mining circuits.

Most of the trade in the altiplano relied on the products, labor, and resources of the Indian peasantry. Only the extraction of surplus from the peasants' economy, in the spheres of both production and circulation, allowed merchants and muleteers to trade throughout the Andean space with its extremely difficult transport conditions and still take in a good profit. But the scant pay that Indian peasants received for their labor, wool, or hides and the requisitioning of their pack animals free of charge reinforced their "economy of scarcity," the attempt to provide most of a family's subsistence needs through household production. The potential of the internal market was thus limited by the essential features of Peru's colonial economy. By the mid-eighteenth century prosperous trade for the northern altiplano's elite depended not only on the fortunes of the mining economy and the competitiveness of southern Peru's obrajes but also on political stability in the broadest sense.

The Late Colonial Crises of Southern Peru's Commercial Circuits

Between the last quarter of the eighteenth century and the turbulent three decades following Peru's independence in 1821 a seemingly unending series of events rent asunder the commercial circuits that had brought Azángaro modest prosperity during the mid-eighteenth century, events that inflicted heavy blows on the productive base of the province's livestock economy itself. These events ranged from political acts and administrative decrees, to destruction and dislocation by war and rebellion, to more gradual changes in commercial and economic structures. All contributed to the slow paralysis of the mining economy in the south of the old Peruvian viceroyalty.

The first visible step in this process was the separation of a new Viceroyalty of Buenos Aires from the Viceroyalty of Peru in 1776. It included the Audiencia of Charcas and with it the northern altiplano. For the economic and fiscal interests of Lima, the loss of control over Potosí and the other mining centers of High Peru was a heavy blow. Although the new viceroyalty ostensibly was intended to strengthen Spanish defenses against Portuguese and English military and commercial expansion in the Banda Oriental (modern Uruguay) and on the Patagonian coast, it also corresponded to a shift in the center of gravity of the Spanish Empire in South America from the Pacific to the Atlantic coast.[32] Since early in the eighteenth century a lively contraband trade had diverted part of High Peru's silver production from the monopolistic export route via Callao and Portobelo to Buenos Aires, and the latter port imported goods for the interior. This trend strengthened after the 1740s with the authorization of the *registro suelto* (single, licensed ships sailing outside the fleet system) and the route around Cape Horn, which increased contraband between Buenos Aires and High Peru. Miners and merchants in the southern altiplano favored the imperial reorganization of the 1770s because they could receive European goods more cheaply via the Río de la Plata.[33]

The economic consequences of this reorganization for the truncated Viceroyalty of Peru and, indirectly, for the immediately bordering area of the northern altiplano became obvious only too soon. In 1777 Viceroy Cevallos of Buenos Aires decreed that the silver and gold production of High Peru could henceforth be minted only in Potosí, not in Lima, and that no unminted silver and gold could be exported to Lower Peru. He thus sought to channel all of High Peru's production of precious metals through Buenos Aires instead of Lima. The decree forced much of Lower Peru's trade with the mining center of High Peru into illegality. Up to 1777 the textiles, cereals, sugar, alcohol, and other supplies that were brought in great quantities from Cuzco, Arequipa, and other parts of Lower Peru to Potosí and Oruro had been paid for largely in unminted silver (*plata piña*). Because High Peru's range of exportable products other than precious metals was insufficient to pay for such imports, prohibiting the export of unminted silver and gold contributed to the growing difficulties that now hindered trade between both viceroyalties.[34]

Azángaro and the whole of the northern altiplano saw its important trade with the regions of Arequipa and Cuzco, now separated from the Titicaca basin by the border between two viceroyalties, seriously affected. Traders and producers on both ends of the commercial circuit between the altiplano and the coastal and inter-Andean valleys of Arequipa and Cuzco were increasingly short of coined money. Although altiplano residents had access to unminted silver from Potosí and mines closer by, they could not use it for purchasing goods from Arequipa or Cuzco, insofar as their trade was controlled by royal authorities. We may assume that during this period of cash shortages, barter again became more important.

On October 12, 1778, King Charles III issued the Ordinance of Free Trade that topped off the trade reforms in the Spanish Empire undertaken at an accelerating pace since the calamitous capture of the ports of Havana and Manila in 1762 by the British. The ordinance allowed direct trade between thirteen peninsular ports and most major Spanish colonial areas, including four ports on the west coast of South America. The ambitious goals of the ordinance were, in the words of John Fisher, "to provide the combination of freedom and protection which would promote the settlement of empty territory, eliminate contraband trade, generate increased customs revenues, . . . and, above all, develop the empire as a market for Spanish products and a source of raw materials for Spanish industry."[35] The full effect of the measure was felt only after 1783, when the Peace of Paris terminated hostilities between England and Spain. In the following years European goods flooded Spanish American markets and exerted strong downward pressures on retail prices for manufactured goods. In 1785 imports from Spain into Spanish America had increased more than sixfold over 1778 levels. Against the older notion of a general economic crisis in late colonial Peru, Fisher has conclusively demonstrated that the truncated viceroyalty fully participated in this enormous upswing of transatlantic trade.[36]

Peru's capacity to import European goods remained tied to its production of precious metals throughout the waning decades of the colonial regime and through the first quarter century after independence. It is not surprising, then, that the vast upsurge of transatlantic trade was accompanied by an impressive growth in silver output. Based on the exploitation of newly discovered lodes at Cerro de Pasco in the central Peruvian sierra and at Hualgayoc in the northern intendency of Trujillo, the silver output of the truncated viceroyalty more than doubled between the mid-1770s and the end of the century, continued on a high level until 1810, and then began a precipitous decline over the next fifteen years. In Upper Peru silver production, after its long depression between the 1630s and 1740s, also recovered until 1802, albeit much less vigorously, and gradually declined to depression levels during the following three decades (fig. 2.1).

Although Lower Peru had accounted for less than a quarter of total silver output in the old viceroyalty during the first two centuries of colonial rule, by the early nineteenth century it had surpassed Upper Peru's production (fig. 2.1). But this second Andean mining boom, comparable in quantity to the first bonanza of the late sixteenth and early seventeenth centuries, did not have the same integrative and vitalizing effect on the whole of the "Andean space." Rather, it served as motor for the growth and entrenchment of distinct and separate commercial spaces in central and northern Peru on the one hand and in the southern Andes on the other. In Lower Peru more than two-thirds of the silver was produced in the central and northern sierra. Livestock producers from Puno and textile manufacturers from Cuzco could not compete with ranchers and obrajeros in the intendencies of Tarma, Lima, and Trujillo for supplying the newly expanded mining camps and the buoyant market of the growing city of Lima. In Upper Peru, particularly in Potosí, the recovery of silver output was

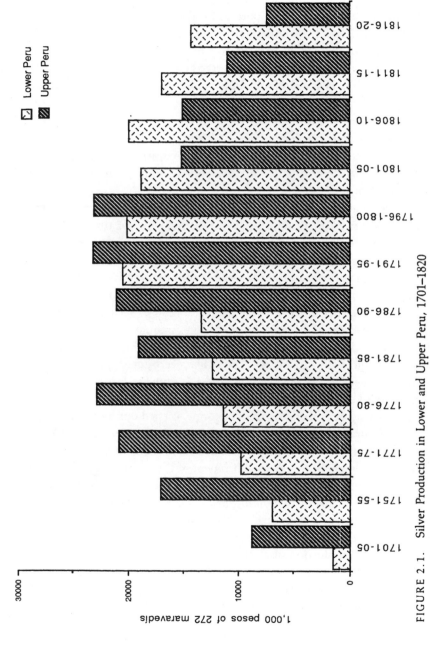

FIGURE 2.1. Silver Production in Lower and Upper Peru, 1701–1820

Source: TePaske, "Silver Production."

achieved through more intensive exploitation of mitayo labor while Potosí's population continued its long-term decline.[37]

Thus, demand for supplies did not grow proportionately with silver output in Upper Peru. More important for the economies of the northern altiplano and Cuzco, the southern altiplano increasingly oriented its trade patterns toward the Río de la Plata, to where the bulk of the silver now flowed and from where the region received European imports, especially textiles, as well as a wide range of locally produced supplies. Although trade with Upper Peru continued to be important for the merchants and producers in Puno, Cuzco, and Arequipa through the last decades of the colonial period and even during the first century after independence, by the mid-1780s the fabric of the erstwhile "Andean space" was wearing thin, and trade flows decreasingly reflected positive mining conjunctures in Potosí or Oruro.

As a consequence of the Free Trade Ordinance, European goods were now sold at lower prices than before 1778, and some of them seriously competed with Peruvian goods. European woolen and cotton textiles turned out by steam-powered factories began to undersell similar Peruvian obraje products. They not only entered Peru through Callao but increasingly were imported into Lower Peru through Buenos Aires. Transport costs lay at the root of the problem. According to Cespedes del Castillo, after 1778 a *tercio* of Bretaña linen sold in Arequipa cost 337 pesos if shipped from Cádiz via Buenos Aires but 361 pesos if shipped via Callao.[38] Merchants and textile producers of Lower Peru were not only losing market shares in Upper Peru but increasingly ceding ground to European imports in home markets such as Arequipa and Cuzco.

The fiscal aspects of the Bourbon reforms, carried out by Charles III's enlightened or protoliberal corps of bureaucrats, hit the southern Andes in full force during the late 1770s and exacerbated the disruptions of trade circuits brought about by the establishment of the Viceroyalty of the Río de la Plata. Concerned with increasing colonial revenue for the benefit of the metropolis, Madrid raised the *alcabala*, a sales tax on most commodities traded by Spaniards and mestizos, from 2 to 4 percent in 1772 and to 6 percent in 1776. In 1778 Viceroy Manuel de Guirior imposed a tax of 12.5 percent on the production of alcohol, Arequipa's major item of trade.

These new revenue measures were seriously implemented only in 1777, after Visitor General Antonio de Areche arrived in Lima, but then the scheme was undertaken with a vengeance. Circulars to the corregidores charged them with collecting the alcabala and enforcing measures against contraband of unregistered silver and gold. The alcabala now had to be paid by persons previously exempted, especially Indians, and was levied on a broader range of goods, including coca. First in Upper Peru (Cochabamba in 1774, La Paz in 1776) and then in the southern cities of Lower Peru (Arequipa and Cuzco in 1780), customs houses were established to ensure compliance with taxes and fees on trade. Thus, not only were levies on regional trade increased enormously, but enforcement became much tougher in the southern Andes, making it difficult for merchants to elude payment.[39]

These stringent fiscal measures contributed much to forging the fragile but broad coalition of interests that in 1780 erupted in the complex cycle of social movements commonly referred to as the Túpac Amaru Rebellion, the most serious challenge to Spanish authority anywhere in its American possessions since the conquest. Different social groups in the southern Andes had various causes for dissatisfaction with the political economy of the Bourbon regime, but the drastic increase of the alcabala and the novel, rigorous scheme to collect it through internal customs hurt Indians, mestizos, and creoles alike.[40]

Originating in the corregimiento of Tinta, close to the southeastern rim of the Cuzco valley system in the very center of obraje textile production, the rebellion soon spilled over into the Lake Titicaca basin, where the struggle reached its greatest intensity, brutality, and duration. José Gabriel Condorcanqui, cacique of Tungasuca, who adopted the name Túpac Amaru II and claimed descent from the last Inca, initiated the rebellion as a means of forcing the viceregal administration to root out abuses against creoles, mestizos, and Indians. Soon after his initial military successes in the Vilcanota valley, Túpac Amaru crossed over into the altiplano with a rebel army measuring in the thousands. Meeting ineffective resistance from the corregidores of Azángaro, Carabaya, and Lampa, he took control of the whole altiplano north of the city of Puno. On December 13, 1780, Túpac Amaru entered Azángaro town, installing his own administrators and taking particular care to destroy the extensive urban and rural properties of the family of Kuraka Diego Choquehuanca, who had staunchly supported the royalist cause throughout.[41]

José Gabriel Túpac Amaru was captured in April 1781, a scarce five months after the beginning of the rebellion. After a trial he and many relatives were executed in Cuzco with exemplary cruelty on May 18, 1781. But this was not the end of the rebellion. Its focus now shifted to the altiplano, both north and south of Lake Titicaca, where major towns were besieged and several of them, Puno and Oruro, taken by the rebels. The northern altiplano was effectively under rebel control between December 1780 and early 1782, and in some isolated parts peasant warlords continued fighting until the following year.

Diego Cristóbal Túpac Amaru, supreme commander of the northern movement after his cousin José Gabriel's capture, established his headquarters at Azángaro. From there troops were sent and instructions dispatched throughout the altiplano. After April 1781 the movement became more radical, and Indians assumed a growing leadership role as creoles and mestizos withdrew their support, apprehensive about losing social privileges and the possibility of a "race war" unleashed by the mobilized Indian peasantry. Diego Cristóbal never achieved in the northern altiplano the disciplined, hierarchical command structure that his cousin had in his family's base in the Vilcanota valley. In Azángaro and adjacent provinces more or less independent leaders, often minor or disgruntled kurakas with a strong base in peasant communities, increasingly pursued their own local agendas. The Indian peasants ceased to pay tribute, did not perform their mita obligations in Potosí, and abducted livestock from the estates of the church, creoles, and kurakas. With the flight of the corregidores, the forced *repartos* (distributions of goods to peasants) obviously collapsed.

The clashes between royalist and rebel armies as well as the random killing, destruction, and theft by both armies devastated Azángaro's population, its livestock capital, and productive infrastructure. A Peruvian priest, describing the rebellion two years after its suppression, estimated deaths at around 100,000 Indians and 10,000 peninsular and American Spaniards.[42] Azángaro was one of the areas where the death toll had been so terrible that "one could not count the dead Indians." The number of peasants just from this province killed either in battle or in punitive actions committed by royalists and rebels alike may well have numbered in the thousands.[43]

Although small compared to Indian losses, the deaths and permanent emigration among the white and mestizo population were of great consequence for the economy of the northern altiplano. Spanish or mestizo traders, landholders, and crown officials fled with their families, leaving all their belongings behind. From the parish of Arapa alone twenty-three "Españoles," creoles from a largely mestizo ethnic background, emigrated during the rebellion to La Paz, Buenos Aires, and even Spain.[44]

Destruction of property accompanied the depopulation of the altiplano. The longest-lasting damage to Azángaro's economic base was done by the decimation of the livestock herds. Sheep, cows, and transport animals were requisitioned by both armies from any estate that lay close to their path, with Túpac Amaru's troops purportedly consuming up to four thousand sheep daily.[45] Many animals were taken by soldiers or peasants from abandoned or inadequately protected estates to enrich themselves. Peasants stocked their own estancias with the stolen animals, while the royalist troops sent from Arequipa and Moquegua to retake the altiplano sold stolen sheep at a discount in those cities.[46] When the rebellion was defeated after two long years of bloodshed and destruction, the damage to Azángaro's livestock economy could not be repaired in a few months or even a year or two. In a dramatic plea to Viceroy Jauregui, the corregidores of Azángaro and Carabaya, Lorenzo Sata y Zubiría and Miguel de Urviola, predicted that the impoverished northern altiplano would "exhaust the royal treasury for its sustenance" for a long time to come.[47] In 1784, more than a year after tranquility had been reestablished, the parish priest in Juliaca, only a few kilometers from Azángaro, described the consequences of the rebellion as follows: "The estates of the churches, convents, monasteries, and private persons are seen today in the utmost decadence; many years will still pass by to rebuild them. Many houses in the towns and other places are burned, through actions of both Indian rebels and Spanish troops, who destroyed the towns. In some places one is caused to cry upon seeing their ruins."[48]

By the mid-1780s both conjuncture and structure of the commercial circuits that tied the northern altiplano to the wider colonial economy had undergone a major sea change, the outcome of three separate developments: the implementation of reformist Bourbon policies, the penetration of Andean markets by European textiles, and the destruction and power realignments resulting from the Túpac Amaru Rebellion. Contemporaries observed a "notable decadence" of woolen exports from the Cuzco obrajes to High Peru because of the "increased imports of European woolens via the Río de la Plata."[49] This shrinking control of Cuzco's obrajes over the markets of Upper Peru and even to a degree over markets in the south of Lower Peru was certainly one of the main factors of the Cuzco region's economic decline during the late eighteenth century.[50] It had a similarly depressing effect on stock raising in the northern altiplano, whose wool production found its outlet largely through the Cuzco obrajes. After 1782 the scarcity of circulating currency, the flooding of markets with cheap European imports, and the obstacles to trade between the viceroyalties of Peru and Buenos Aires prevented a strong recovery of Cuzco's obraje production and the northern altiplano's livestock economy from the ravages of the rebellion.

The authorities in Lima and Madrid showed increasing concern about the economic decline of what is today the southern Peruvian sierra and in particular the Intendency and City of Cuzco, a decline dramatized by the destruction wrought by the Túpac Amaru Rebellion. In 1788 an audiencia was established in Cuzco to attempt to halt this decline and to revitalize the city and surrounding rural areas by focusing more government attention on the region and by making long and costly appeals of litigation to the distant Audiencia of Lima unnecessary. Azángaro, Lampa, and Carabaya provinces became judicially dependent on the Audiencia of Cuzco, whereas the remaining provinces of the Intendency of Puno stayed under the jurisdiction of the Audiencia of Charcas. The three northern altiplano provinces were thus judicially and ecclesiastically dependent on Cuzco in the Viceroyalty of Peru while administratively still belonging to the Viceroyalty of Buenos Aires. The awkwardness of this arrangement, realized as early as the mid-1780s by Visitador Escobedo, persuaded the crown to reintegrate the Intendency of Puno with the Viceroyalty of Peru on February 1, 1796.[51] But this change merely shifted the dividing line between the two viceroyalties from the altiplano's northern rim to the southern shore of Lake Titicaca. The administrative barrier splitting the northern altiplano's commercial space did not disappear.

In 1801 a plan drawn up by Francisco Carrascón y Sola, prebendary of the Cathedral in Cuzco, suggested a quite different administrative arrangement for the altiplano. The cleric proposed the creation of a new viceroyalty centered in Puno to cover the whole territory of the Audiencia of Charcas and the intendencies of Puno and Cuzco.[52] Carrascón saw the major advantage of such a far-reaching administrative change as improved political and military control over the densely populated area of the northern altiplano, whose unruly indigenous population had produced the fiercest rebels during the uprising of Túpac Amaru. But more important, the plan demonstrates that the whole of the altiplano, with an extension into the adjacent parts of modern southern Peru, was still conceived as one culturally, socially, and economically unified region. Any border that split this region into two, whether it ran across the altiplano at the Río Desaguadero, close to the southern end of Lake Titicaca, or at the northwestern rim of the altiplano basin, failed to correspond to long-standing trade and settlement patterns.

While expressing shifts in the political and economic power structure on the axis between Lima and Buenos Aires, any such administrative division tended to marginalize the altiplano areas lying on both sides of the border. The project for a new viceroyalty centered at Puno was soon forgotten, and the administrative division of the altiplano was not reversed and took on a much more serious character with the establishment of the independent republics of Peru and Bolivia in the 1820s.

During the remaining three decades before Peru's independence in 1824 the northern altiplano's trade continued to be affected by great instability. International war, rebellions, and military campaigns fought nearly continuously in one area or another of the southern Andes between Cuzco and Potosí since 1809, as well as a series of devastating droughts, led to short-term fluctuations of prices and access to markets. Trade based on peasant production seems to have withstood this instability better than did that based on commercial goods from Spanish and creole enterprises.

In 1803 the Consulado of Lima reported that the woolen cloth production of the obrajes around Cuzco had declined to about 700,000 varas per year from a level of 3,000,000 varas only thirty or forty years earlier. This decline necessarily depressed the wool production of Azángaro and the neighboring provinces. In addition to the continued presence of European woolens in the markets of Lower and Upper Peru, beginning in the 1790s Cuzco's textile production encountered growing competition from obrajes in La Paz, La Plata, and Córdoba.[53]

There are indications that textiles produced by Indian peasants on the looms in their own homes did not decline as drastically as did those of the obrajes in the waning decades of the colonial era.[54] The cheap woolens produced by home industry were not yet affected by competition from European imports. Another factor may have been that these dispersed production sites suffered less destruction during the Túpac Amaru uprising than the large obraje plants had. Whatever the reasons, in the early years of the nineteenth century the Intendency of Puno maintained a lively trade in "flannels, quilts, ticking, coarse baizes, blankets, friezes, homespun cotton cloth, and carpets" produced by Indian peasants with various places on the coast, "particularly the city of Arequipa, where these textiles are bought up for the use by poor folk, and these goods even make their way to Lima."[55] The economic situation of the peasants was not as severely affected by the dislocation and disruptions that plagued the livestock operations, textile industry, and commercial networks controlled by the upper strata of northern altiplano society from the last quarter of the eighteenth century well into the republican era.

Only about thirty years after the Túpac Amaru Rebellion had been quelled, Azángaro saw itself embroiled in another uprising that represented the beginning of the struggle for political independence in the southern Peruvian sierra. During the Pumacahua Rebellion, initiated in 1814 by the creole citizenry of Cuzco against peninsular officials in that city, the rebel leaders again directed their military campaign southward and occupied most of the Intendency of Puno. Their forces were strengthened by Indians from Azángaro and Carabaya provinces, "some of whom had served in the Túpac Amaru rebellion and wanted to carry out revenge against the Spanish."[56] Although rapidly suppressed by royal forces under Marshal Ramirez, the Pumacahua Rebellion had much the same devastating effects on Azángaro's rural economy as had the movement headed by Túpac Amaru. The province found itself again in one of the centers of the uprising

and subsequent royalist military operations, which continued in Azángaro
months after the rebels' rout at Umachiri in March 1815.[57]

After mid-1815 the intelligent administration of Viceroy Abascal—
seizing on the turn of the tide in Europe after Waterloo favorable for
legitimist forces—was able to recapture lost ground for the royalist cause
in Peru and some adjacent colonial territories. But the structural depression
facing southern Peru's commerce, textile production, and livestock-raising
operations could not be overcome until the end of the colonial era. When
Abascal wrote his report to his successor, Joaquín de Pezuela, in 1816, he
was keenly aware of the persistence of these problems.

> The rough cotton and woolen textiles provided the towns of the
> whole country with cheap clothing and the surplus was exported
> in considerable quantity to the Kingdom of Chile. After the
> [royal decree of free trade of October 1778] the [production of]
> woolen textiles decayed because of the better quality and lower
> prices of the common cloth of Spain and lately also [the
> production of] cotton textiles has decayed because of contraband.
> As a consequence, having lost their markets, estancias which
> produced the primary goods and the obrajes which elaborated the
> textiles have simultaneously entered a state of ruin.[58]

The military campaigns that led to Peru's independence from Spain
between 1820 and 1825 affected southern Peru's commerce in varying ways.
After the occupation of much of the coast between Arica and Payta by the
insurgents in late 1820, the Spanish army under Viceroy La Serna withdrew
to the southern sierra, making the intendencies of Cuzco and Puno the
staging ground for repeated forays into regions controlled by the insurgents. The royalist army relied on provisions from the region's haciendas
and textile sweatshops, and most of its soldiers were recruited here, a pattern
established since the first campaigns against the rebellions in Upper Peru
and the invasions by the Río de la Plata insurgents in 1809–10.[59]

At the same time, the northern altiplano briefly regained unlimited
access to its precrisis markets. After several attempts by patriot armies from
Buenos Aires to occupy Upper Peru had failed, the southern altiplano once
more became part of the Viceroyalty of Peru between 1818 and the royalists' defeat in late 1824. Woolen cloths, hides, and dried meats could again
pass without restrictions from Cuzco and the northern altiplano to Potosí
and other urban and mining centers of Upper Peru. The competition that
Cuzco and Puno had suffered prior to 1810 from textile producers in the
interior provinces of Argentina and imports from Europe via Buenos Aires
was reduced to the level of clandestine trade.[60] The Spanish merchant De

la Cotera, resident in Arequipa and privileged in the trade with Upper Peru "due to his influence with Viceroy La Serna," annually sold close to 500,000 pesos worth of woolen textiles from Cuzco's obrajes in Potosí between 1820 and 1824, a level of sales considerably higher than that in 1791.[61] José Domingo Choquehuanca must have been referring to these years when he wrote in 1831 that Azángaro's "sales of black and colored baizes, blankets, bags, and ponchos to High Peru before the revolutions for Independence were very lucrative."[62]

The Rise of the Wool Export Commercial Circuit after Independence

The final defeat of the royalists at Ayacucho in December 1824, Azángaro's integration into an independent Peru, and the establishment of Bolivia as a separate republic brought an end to this favorable conjuncture and reinforced the structural crisis for the region's livestock economy that had become evident four decades earlier. Two secular trends now forced hacendados and traders to readjust the commercialization of their products: the accelerating decline in the marketability of regionally produced woolen textiles and the growing demand for raw wool in industrializing Europe. Both trends began to influence southern Peru's regional economy when, after the battle of Ayacucho, the markets and products of the intendencies of Cuzco, Puno, and Arequipa became directly accessible to European and North American merchants in the coastal ports.

Until the 1840s Great Britain and the other industrializing nations viewed Peru and all of Latin America primarily as an important market for their growing output of manufactured goods.[63] In the years following the defeat of the royalists Peru was flooded with goods much beyond its capacity to consume them. Samuel Haigh, a British commercial agent who stayed in Arequipa between June 1825 and February 1827, lamented the flooding of the city with British manufactured goods, "the prices having lowered in proportion as the free trade was thrown open." He blamed the system of sales by commission for this unsatisfactory state of affairs. British manufacturers, without knowledge of market conditions, were remitting a "large and constant supply" of goods to Peru, maintaining a "glut of heavy goods in the market without either assortment or selection, as to quantity and quality." Shippers were generally experiencing "great losses," and "the commission merchant derives little advantage in proportion to his trouble." He concluded that "the South American markets have been much overrated."[64]

The single most important group of European imports were cotton and woolen textiles. During the 1830s and 1840s they represented an astounding 81 percent of all British imports to Peru.[65] What was potentially most damaging about such imports was the fact that their prices fell rapidly after 1820. The price of cottons at British ports fell by 72 percent and that of woolens by 63 percent from 1817 to 1850. According to some estimates, Peruvian import prices plunged by about 50 percent just in the early 1820s.[66]

The impact of these European goods on multifarious groups of artisans and manufacturers in Peru and, indeed, throughout Latin America has been highly controversial in the literature, in part because the issue lies at the core of the debate about dependency but also because contemporary evidence is as contradictory as it is vague. Petitions and public denouncements by politicians and merchants from southern Peru in the postindependence decades seem to lend much support to those authors who espouse the extreme dependency position that Peru passed smoothly from the Spanish mercantilist sphere into a British-dominated commercial system in which the country produced only raw materials for the world market, importing all its manufacturing goods, with a concomitant rapid destruction of domestic textile production.

Already in mid-1826 the Prefect of Puno, Aparicio, was claiming that the manufacture of flannels, coarse baizes, rough camlets, and other woolen textiles, which hitherto had employed between fifteen and twenty thousand families in the department, had ceased completely because the locally produced textiles had been undersold by European imports due to their "extreme cheapness." Significantly, Aparicio went on to explain that another reason for the ruin of Puno's wool manufacture lay in the fact that the foreigners were buying up wool "in all the towns of the Collao."[67] British and French merchants operating from Arequipa could pay higher prices for raw wool than the owners of obrajes could. Thus, not only the massive imports of woolen textiles from Europe but the very beginnings of wool exports contributed to the heightened pressure on southern Peru's wool-processing industries.

Aparicio's alarmist report reflected the position of owners of obrajes and livestock estates as well as merchants in Cuzco and Puno, who perceived the new wave of textile imports as the death knell of their once flourishing businesses. Until the late 1840s they were advocates of protection for wool and cotton cloth against competing European goods.[68] Although there still exists no thorough study on the textile trades in Cuzco and Puno during the early independence period, it is becoming increasingly clear that the crisis had a complex array of causes: declining sales on the Bolivian markets, rising transport costs, disruption of trade during the civil wars, and lack of capital to modernize the inefficient manufactories, which in turn arose from the depressed agrarian economy of the southern Andes. The rapid decline in the price of many textiles following the wave of imports during the early and mid-1820s merely exacerbated these problems and accelerated the withdrawal of obraje products from Andean markets between Arequipa and Potosí.

Nevertheless, the colonial circuits for obraje textiles from Cuzco and Puno, dominated by merchants from the imperial city, died a slow death. The glut of imported cloth after the mid-1820s led to the bankruptcy of a number of European import merchants and the withdrawal of others from trade with the interior, hounded by a host of protectionist legislation and the hostility of creole mercantile elites in Arequipa, Cuzco, Ayacucho, and other cities. The level of textile imports declined during much of the 1830s, and the brief Peruvian-Bolivian Confederation under Andrés Santa Cruz (1836–39) brought some respite to the surviving obrajes by giving their products free access to Bolivian markets.[69]

Most of the remaining obrajes closed their doors between 1841 and 1846. During these years military strife (arising both from internal Peruvian conflicts and renewed war with Bolivia) was particularly severe, protectionist sentiment was growing in Bolivia, and maritime freight rates dropped sharply as steamboats began to ply the Pacific coast between Valparaiso and Central America, bringing a new surge of European imports at lower prices.[70] The 1840s thus saw the final demise of a venerable colonial industry and trade that had been crucial for the prosperity of estate owners, muleteers, and merchants in Puno and Cuzco. Although some of the old textile merchants may have survived by expanding the coca trade, increasing sales of imports, or participating in the wool export trade, for many merchants in Cuzco the demise of obraje production brought impoverishment as the city ceased to be a major commercial entrepôt in the southern Andes.

But the disappearance of commercial wool manufactories in Cuzco and Puno in no way implied the end of household textile production by peasants in the altiplano and numerous areas in the Peruvian Andes. In part this was subsistence production for the peasants' own households and was quite impervious to any price changes in the market for cloth comparable to the various qualities of homespun textiles. Yet altiplano peasants also continued to sell or barter their textiles throughout the southern Andes in spite of the dramatic fall of prices. In contrast to obraje owners and textile merchants, they could withstand declining prices because they relied on family labor and used their own llamas or mules to transport their product to market. Moreover, as monopolistic control over peasant commercialization gradually disintegrated beginning with the prohibition of the corregidores' reparto trade in 1783, the share of the final market price retained by the peasant producer rose. Thus, rapidly declining market prices for textiles translated into a smaller decline in the price retained by the peasant producers.[71]

Seven years after Prefect Aparicio claimed the virtual destruction of the altiplano's textile production, José Domingo Choquehuanca, the learned scion of Azángaro's most powerful kuraka family, published a statistical treatise that covered everything from births and deaths to fisheries and gold production in the province during the years 1825–29.[72] Here a totally different picture emerges of the impact of European imports and wool exports on the production of woolens in one of Peru's major stock-raising provinces, far removed from coastal ports (see table 2.1).

According to Choquehuanca's estimates, Azángaro still received more than one-third of its total "export earnings" from the sale of serges, colored baizes, blankets, and coca bags, while only 7,300 arrobas (about eighty-four metric tons) of wool—at most a third of total production—was shipped out of the province annually in raw form, both to the obrajes in Cuzco and for export through Islay, the port on Arequipa's Pacific coast. In fact, with overseas wool exports still very low, the province probably sold considerably less raw wool during the late 1820s than it had prior to the decline of obraje textile production in Cuzco and Huamanga in the 1780s. Choquehuanca's careful estimates suggest that close to six thousand looms were still operated in the province immediately after independence, most of them in peasant households. They produced nearly twice as much for subsistence use as was marketed outside the province.

The avalanche of European imports reaching Peruvian ports during the mid-1820s appeared as a mere trickle in remote interior provinces such as Azángaro, where they amounted to just over 8 percent of the province's outside purchases. Consumption of European textiles clearly was limited to the few dozen priests, hacendados, bureaucrats, and professionals and their families, delighted that reduced import prices allowed them to dress in "delicate materials" whereas their fathers before independence could afford only "rough materials" produced by obrajes. European textiles served more as emblems of the emerging tiny elite in rural southern Peru, a mark of their "civilization," than as items of consumption for the great majority of Indian peasants.[73]

Among rural elites and urban middle classes European imports had cut deeply into the market for obraje textiles because their rapidly declining prices offered machine-produced textiles, which were relatively high in quality and culturally desirable, at prices that the Cuzco manufacturers

TABLE 2.1. Annual Exports and Imports of Azángaro Province, 1825–29

Exports	Value (pesos)	Imports	Value (pesos)
Lead, 400 quintales	1,600	Flour, 2720 fanegas	19,040
Baizes, 2970 pieces	35,640	Maize, 3190 cargas	9,570
Baizes in color, 20,000 varas	5,000	Sugar, 325 arrobas	2,275
Blankets, 6000	3,000	Sugar in loaves	2,575
Coca bags, 5000	1,250	Coca leaves, 5790 bags	40,530
Pottery	1,500	Alcohol, 1240 quintales	24,800
Candles	500	Butter, 67 arrobas	808
Cheese	17,000	Wine, 124 arrobas	744
Lard	150	Vinagre, 25 arrobas	150
Tallow, 1179 quintales	14,148	Oil, 9 arrobas	81
Chalonas, 39,500 pieces	19,750	Dried peppers, 1420 arrobas	4,260
Vicuña skins, 160	80	Dried figs, 385 arrobas	750
Wool, 7,300 arrobas	3,650	Tobacco, 555 bundles	337
Cows, 1,190 head	7,140	Chocolate, 174 arrobas	1,740
Young bulls, 1,910 head	7,640	Cotton, 154 arrobas	385
Sheep, 16,200 head	8,100	Indigo, 642 pounds	2,568
Fish	1,100	Brazilwood, 705 pounds	352
		European goods	9,960
Total	127,248	Total	120,925

Note: These figures exclude Pusi, Taraco, and Poto.
Source: Choquehuanca, *Ensayo.*

could not match. But it was another matter to wean the Indian peasantry and the poorest urban strata, domestic servants, poor artisans, carriers, and transport workers from the use of homespun materials, a process spanning at least a century after independence. Before independence, authorities in Azángaro punished Indians for wearing Castilian clothes, considered insolent. After independence, although sumptuary laws fell into disuse, Indians continued to wear homemade serges even if they could afford imported materials, because "to the person who dresses with decency the parish administrators say, 'you are dressed with costly materials, thus you have money, thus you have to pay more [parish fees].'"[74]

To be sure, when the import of textiles again expanded rapidly at ever lower prices during the 1840s and 1850s, certain imported materials, mostly light cotton "drills," "domestics," and "shirting" but also some woolen serges, seem to have become items of mass consumption in southern Peru. For some items of clothing, such as shirts and underclothes, the peasantry increasingly recurred to cheap English imports after midcentury. But ponchos, *licllas* (kerchiefs), skirts, and women's vests continued to be woven in peasant households. So did blankets, saddlebags for llamas, woolen belts, and coca bags. Locally produced woolen felt hats continued to be fashionable even among urban mestizos, and the knitting of skullcaps, socks, and gloves may have increased during the second half of the nineteenth century.[75] In fact, when traveling through the altiplano province of Lampa in 1860, Paul Marcoy encountered many women from peasant and even impoverished creole households selling spun sheep and alpaca wool in town, evidence for the survival of a rudimentary division of labor in Puno's textile trades.[76]

A conservative estimate suggests that more than 50 percent of southern Peru's annual sheep wool production between 1837 and 1840, years of rising exports, was retained for domestic consumption.[77] In years of peak exports, such as 1840 and 1841, exports might have accounted for up to 60 percent of total production; however, until the late 1850s exports were generally lower than in those peak years, and thus rates of domestic retention would have been above 50 percent. Although early data for alpaca populations are less accurate, it appears that after 1840 a considerably higher percentage of alpaca wool was exported. With the withdrawal of creole and mestizo manufacturers and merchants from textile production, an increasing share of the raw wool retained in southern Peru stayed in control of peasants for processing, subsistence consumption, and barter and trade.

This "peasantization" of the textile trades in Azángaro had set in before independence. Even by the 1780s much cloth throughout the southern Andes was produced, transported, and sold by peasants. The Wars of Independence, while diminishing the trade, further reduced the role of mestizo and creole merchants. Professional traders from Upper Peru ceased to come to Azángaro to buy cloth. By 1830 the province's textiles were sold in reduced circuits, mostly by peasant traders and possibly their kurakas on their periodic journeys to the valleys of Cuzco and Arequipa and nearby Bolivian montaña regions such as Apolobamba; these journeys also served for buying supplies of maize, chile peppers, coca leaves, and alcohol.[78] Just as in many parts of postindependence Mexico, the collapse of the commercial economy controlled by creoles and mestizos in the northern altiplano was accompanied by the survival and greater autonomy of peasant trading activities.[79]

One of the main problems affecting the Peruvian altiplano's livestock and agricultural economy lay in the vicissitudes of access to the Bolivian markets. After 1825 the commercial flow crossing what had become an international border at the Río Desaguadero never again attained the volume still prevailing in 1791, after the onset of the late colonial crisis of the region. Southern Peru's textile exports to Bolivia were hit hardest and as early as 1826 had sunk to the low value of about 50,000 pesos. For the commercial and landholding interests of La Paz it was of great importance, as the Hungarian historian Tibor Wittmann has noted, "to cut the communication with the provinces of Arequipa and Cuzco so that La Paz itself could dominate the agricultural supplies of the mining regions."[80]

Yet even beyond midcentury Bolivia depended on imports from southern Peru for the provision of some key agricultural goods. Bolivia's yearly imports from Peru amounted to 414,000 pesos in 1826 and 592,000 pesos in 1851. Roughly 80 percent of these imports were agricultural products from the valleys around Arequipa and Cuzco: alcohol, wine, sugar, chile peppers, and—of declining significance—raw cotton. The altiplano contributed only the remaining 20 percent of these exports: cattle on the hoof, dried meats, butter and cheese, and potatoes and chuño. These imports were particularly odious to Bolivian protectionists as the Bolivian altiplano was producing the same goods.[81] Bolivia's balance of trade with Peru was highly negative during the first three decades of independence. For the year 1826 the British consul Pentland reported a value of exports to Peru of 153,000 pesos, including "a great quantity of flour and corn" from Cochabamba for the department of Puno. By 1851 this amount had dwindled to a mere 52,000 pesos, largely coca leaves from the Yungas for sale in Puno.[82]

This trade deficit was extremely irksome to the commercial interests of La Paz and contributed to repeated clashes between Peru and Bolivia between the 1830s and 1850s. It led to the flooding of Peru with debased Bolivian silver coins, which by 1847 had become just about the only currency used in the internal circulation of the country. Furthermore, it led to increasing protectionist Bolivian tariffs on Peruvian goods, mutual trade recriminations, the repeated threat of war, and temporary interruptions of trade between both countries, which reached their peak during the Bolivian administrations of Manuel Isidoro Belzú and José María Linares between 1850 and 1860.[83]

The long slump of Bolivian silver mining between the early 1800s and the 1850s, as well as the stagnation of the altiplano's urban population, diminished the demand for livestock products such as meat, tallow, and cheese and lowered prices. Although only partially successful, protectionism against southern Peru's competing livestock goods was deemed essential to stop the price decay. In this unstable trade environment, it was primarily the peasant traders from bordering Peruvian altiplano provinces who continued small-scale trade or barter in livestock goods with La Paz. As Erick Langer has noted, the collapse of High Peru's state-supported silver-mining industry brought about the "fall [of trade] from abnormally high levels to more 'normal' levels consistent with the largely peasant population of the region."[84]

Hacendados from the Peruvian altiplano found it difficult to accept the decline of their trade with the regions South of Lake Titicaca that were now incorporated into a separate sovereign republic. It was not only their commercial interests that caused members of the northern altiplano's administrative, landholding and commercial elite to persist in seeking a "reunification" of the altiplano. Just as important were a variety of other links, such as frequent family ties, a common culture of the Indian peasantry on both sides of the Río Desaguadero, and generally a parallel social and economic adaptation to a shared geographic and climatic environment. Already in 1829, Colonel Rufino Macedo, owner of several haciendas in Azángaro province, headed a short-lived conspiracy in Puno aimed at uniting Puno, Arequipa, and Cuzco with Bolivia and relied on the active support of Bolivian President Andrés Santa Cruz.[85] When Santa Cruz finally succeeded in establishing the confederation between Peru and Bolivia under his leadership in 1836, he found much support among the notables in the department of Puno.[86] Even those refusing to support Santa Cruz, because they considered him an "invader of [the] fatherland," favored the reunification of the two neighboring Andean republics, albeit in a centralist Peruvian fashion: that is, the reannexation pure and simple of Bolivia, a plan pursued by Santa Cruz's major adversary, the Cuzqueño caudillo Agustín Gamarra.[87]

The failure of political reunification between Peru and Bolivia only underscored the irreversible disruption of the colonial commercial circuits that had linked large parts of Peru with the altiplano mining centers. The declining exports of livestock products from Puno to Bolivia and the collapse of their textile trades forced ranchers and merchants in the Peruvian altiplano to adapt to a totally distinct commercial pattern: exports of raw materials, this time as a "secondary but indispensable annex" to Europe's industrial economies. Small amounts of vicuña, sheep and alpaca wool from the altiplano, and chinchona bark (from which quinine is extracted), gathered in the tropical rain forests of Carabaya province adjacent to Azángaro, had found their way to Cadiz since the mid-eighteenth century.[88] But only after 1825 did the quantities of such exports attain a level at which they could begin to reshape the commercial system of the region's agrarian economy.

Statistics on Peruvian wool exports during the nineteenth century are problematic. The government did not begin to publish export statistics regularly until 1891. Earlier export statistics from Peruvian published sources exist only for scattered years. This lack of data has led several scholars, notably Shane Hunt and Heraclio Bonilla, to construct export statistics based on import figures of Peru's major overseas trading partners—Great Britain, France, the United States, and some others.[89] For the years up to the 1850s the scattered Peruvian data and the studies by Bonilla and Hunt offer widely differing figures for both volume and value of wool exports. Because of obvious inaccuracies and errors in the available sources, Peruvian wool exports before mid-century can only be estimated.[90]

The two major types of wool exported from Peru were sheep and alpaca wools. For both, the southern highlands—the altiplano and mountain slopes of the department of Puno as well as adjacent provinces in the departments of Arequipa and Cuzco—have constituted the most important production zone. The central Peruvian highlands in Junin and surrounding departments have been the other major production area of sheep wool, but in the centuries after conquest they lost most of their cameloid herds. Between 60 and 80 percent of sheep wools were exported through Islay and, after 1873, its successor port of Mollendo, both on the rocky and barren coast of Arequipa department, with the remaining bales channeled mostly through Callao and Arica. For alpaca wools Islay's share was even greater. Although most wool from Puno and the neighboring provinces was shipped through Islay and Mollendo, some was exported through Arica, which also served as port for wool shipments from the Bolivian altiplano.

During the first decade after independence Peru's sheep wool exports remained at a low level, never exceeding a value of 75,000 pesos and in some years during the early 1830s dwindling to almost nothing. Until the 1830s the European and especially the English woolen industry received most of its raw materials from nearby sources—the British Isles, Spain, Germany, and Russia. It is thus no surprise that the commercial agent Samuel Haigh, frantically looking for "returns" from southern Peru in the mid-1820s, did not even consider wools a relevant commodity.[91]

Sheep wool exports surged between the mid-1830s and 1841, leading the Swedish traveler Carl August Gosselman, collecting information on South American trade for his government, to remark that "in time sheep wool will probably become the principal export article of Peru."[92] Between 1835 and 1841 Peru's sheep wool export nearly doubled from 763 to 1,446 metric tons. As a consequence both of intensifying civil wars in Peru, which disrupted supplies, and an industrial crisis in England, sheep wool exports plummeted by 50 percent in 1842 and stayed depressed at least until 1846, possibly even until 1851.[93] As this long slump during the 1840s coincided with the final crisis of obraje textile production, hacendados were particularly hard hit, much as they were in the years immediately after independence. Seeing their hopes for renewed wealth based on wool exports temporarily dashed, they turned, as mentioned above, one last time toward a campaign for protecting the domestic markets and urgently sought favorable trade agreements with Bolivia.[94]

The decades between the 1840s and 1870 saw the rapid growth and technological transformation of the woolen and worsted industries of the United Kingdom, Peru's most important wool purchaser. After having lagged behind the cotton industry in the adoption of power equipment, woolen mills went through a stormy period of innovation and growth during the third quarter of the century as the total quantity of wools consumed in the United Kingdom more than doubled between 1845–49 and 1870–74 and the number of power looms installed in the wool and shoddy section of the industry—lagging behind worsteds—jumped from 9,439 in 1850 to 48,218 in 1870. This expansion occurred while British sheep herds stagnated after the 1830s and ranchers in continental Europe were faced with increasing domestic demand, leaving a declining share of wool production for export to Great Britain. Although wool from overseas represented barely 1 percent of British wool imports in 1815, it accounted for two-thirds of imports as early as 1849, and its share continued to rise over the next two decades even as total consumption was climbing rapidly.[95] By the mid-1850s Peruvian sheep wool exports had begun to benefit from this surge in demand for overseas wool. Exports steadily climbed no later than 1854, with volume topping 1,000 metric tons in 1857 for the first time since 1841. Even more important, prices (FOB) at 26 pesos per quintal (washed) in 1856 had more than doubled over the level prevailing in the first expansionary phase of the late 1830s.[96]

The export of alpaca wool to Europe began later than that of sheep wool. Only some twelve years after independence were the first samples of the fiber sent to England by British export houses, notably that of Mohens and Company. Since the alpaca fiber is much finer than sheep wool and can reach up to one foot in length, its processing required special machinery. Once this machinery was developed by the British manufacturer Titus Salt, the volume of Peruvian exports soared. From a humble beginning of fifty-seven quintales in 1834, within the short period of seven years total alpaca wool exports from Peruvian ports reached 16,500 quintales by 1840.[97]

In contrast to the development of sheep wool exports, the 1840s apparently did not witness a sharp decline of alpaca wool exports. Only in two years, 1844 and 1845, did exports drop below 14,000 quintales, and they reached new highs in the second half of the decade. By that time, only ten years after its commercial introduction, alpaca wool had found great esteem in European markets as one of the finest light wools, even replacing silk in such uses as the lining of gentlemen's coats.[98] This esteem was reflected in prices. A few years after its introduction it fetched more than twice the price of Peruvian sheep wool. Alpaca wool prices continued to climb in the 1850s. In 1857, at 74 pesos, 4 reales per quintal (FOB), the fiber brought nearly three times the price of Peruvian sheep wool.[99]

During the early years of the trade, at least until 1840, sheep wool dominated wool exports from Islay. In the following decade the volume of alpaca wool exports reached a parity with sheep wool, a balance that continued until the early 1870s. The story is different with regard to the value of exports. Sheep wool contributed the major share to the combined value of wool exports from Islay only until 1838. By 1839 the value of alpaca wool exports had overtaken that of sheep wool, and during the early 1850s it reached a level of twice and in some years even three times that of sheep wool exports from all Peruvian ports. Thus, already by the 1850s alpaca wool overshadowed sheep wool as the most important export from southern Peru's livestock economy.

Before the 1850s wools were far from the only important product exported from southern Peru. Until the late 1830s the fibers contributed less to the region's export earnings than did precious metals, currency, or chinchona bark.[100] Yet the key colonial commodity, precious metals, failed to insert renewed vigor into the regional economy through direct exportation. Only a secondary center of silver production during the late eighteenth century, the mines in the western and eastern cordilleras of the department of Puno had decayed notably between the early 1800s and the termination of the Wars of Independence, as mercury became scarce, transport was disrupted, and mining labor was recruited into the royalist and patriot armies. By 1825 the majority of mines were abandoned, and many had been flooded. Others were worked in haphazard fashion. Azángaro's colonial mines were largely abandoned, and in 1826 only the placer gold–mining district of Poto was being exploited [101]

But during the following fifteen years, Puneños and especially foreigners—among them merchants, men who had participated in the Wars of Independence, and adventurers—made numerous attempts to reopen abandoned mines and invested some capital in imported mining equipment. These efforts brought success for a brief period. Puno's share of Peru's total silver output grew from 8.4 percent between 1800 and 1820 to 10 percent between 1825 and 1834. The high point of this feeble recovery was reached between the late 1830s and early 1840s. Yet in 1845 Puno produced only about 40,000 marks of silver at seven to nine pesos per mark, compared to some 52,000 marks in 1805, the apex of the late colonial recovery.[102]

Typical of the short-lived attempts to resuscitate the northern altiplano's silver mining sector was the Manto mine on the outskirts of Puno town. In 1826 it was granted to General O'Brien, an Irish participant in the Wars of Independence. After failing to reopen the mine, he passed it on to the English merchant John Begg, who in 1830 completed a drainage tunnel begun in the early eighteenth century under the auspices of the Marqués de Villa Rica. Although Begg imported expensive mining machinery from England and employed a British engineer, he gave up his attempts to make a profit out of the Manto mine in 1839 and died a year later in Chile a poor man. Peruvian entrepreneurs continued to operate the mine on a modest scale, but it was abandoned soon after 1851. Although the mines around Puno town still employed 932 workers during the years immediately preceding independence, by 1845 this number had declined to 30.[103]

In contrast to silver, Puno was a major gold-producing region in Peru. The metal was found in placer mines in the eastern cordillera around Poto, part of Azángaro until 1854, and in river washings further east in the montaña of Carabaya province. Gold was of minor importance for Peru's economy as a whole both during the colonial period and in the century after independence, but José Deustua has plausibly suggested that it was considerably more important in the south, where upwards of two-thirds of total national output was produced during the early independence period.[104] The geographical isolation of the gold region, however, inhibited commercial exploitation on a grand scale. Transport to the tropical valleys of Carabaya on steep, narrow mule paths was difficult, and the price of all supplies in the production region, including much of the food hauled from the altiplano, was more than twice that in Puno or Cuzco. Labor had to be brought in to the sparsely populated valleys from adjacent districts in Azángaro, Huancané, and Lampa provinces, but highland peasants were reluctant to commit themselves to labor in the hot and humid river valleys for extended periods. Political authorities, landholders, and entrepreneurs from the altiplano who wanted to exploit the gold fields complained about the difficulties of finding laborers despite relatively high wages—four reales per day plus provisions, compared to two reales for public works in the altiplano.[105]

Commercial gold production in Carabaya thus remained small-scale during the early republic. In the dry season and after harvests had been completed in the altiplano, hacendados led a few hundred estate colonos and community peasants down to the Inambari, Tambopata, and Challuma rivers to pan the river sediments for gold dust. A large part of the gold was produced by altiplano peasants operating on their own, combining a few weeks of gold panning with trips to sell livestock products in the valleys and to supply themselves with coca leaves and other tropical and subtropical goods. As long as transport to the montaña remained prohibitively expensive, the region allowed no more than fleeting temporary incursions of commercial enterprises controlled by creole and mestizo entrepreneurs. A hell for altiplano peasants under conditions of forced labor, Carabaya remained a refuge for them when it was part of their autonomous economic undertakings aimed at supplementing household subsistence. Peasants sold the gold dust they had collected to traders at annual trade fairs at Crucero and Rosaspata on the slopes of the Cordillera de Carabaya descending to the altiplano. From there much of the gold found its way to the Cuzco mint. In contrast to silver, a substantial share of gold was not exported but kept circulating within the domestic economy.[106]

In 1849 a minor gold rush developed in Carabaya when two brothers named Poblete, Arequipeños involved in the chinchona bark trade, discovered great amounts of gold dust in the sands of the Challuma, one of the tributaries of the Madre de Dios. Prospectors from all over the world arrived in Carabaya, and many hacendados from the altiplano also tried their luck in the gold washings. Among them was the Puneño Manuel Costas, a large landholder, founder of a long-lived wool trading company, and briefly Peruvian president in 1878. Despite investments in processing machinery and housing for management and a few workers, his enterprises failed. Most other prospectors were also unsuccessful. By 1852 the Carabaya gold-mining region was again reverting to its usual state of casual gold washings by Indian peasants and a few local adventurers in the season when not much work was required for agriculture and livestock raising in the altiplano.[107]

In sum, mining in southern Peru and in the department of Puno in particular remained important for the regional economy during the first quarter century after independence as foreign and Peruvian entrepreneurs invested capital in the revival of the ailing industry. But the years between 1840 and 1852 saw the failure of these efforts, and as foreigners withdrew from mining ventures, capital became exceedingly scarce. The pandemic requisitioning of mules by the military and a temporary interruption of the mule trade from Salta made transport to and from the isolated mining camps unreliable and expensive. Indian peasants, with less pressure from provincial elites on their labor and commodities in the agricultural and textile sectors, felt little compunction to accept wage work at the mining camps. In fact mining, like textile manufacturing, increasingly became a sphere of autonomous peasant activity. When Paul Marcoy traveled through the altiplano in 1860, his elite informants told him in frustration that the Indians knew of many rich silver and gold lodes but refused to reveal them for fear of renewed mining labor drafts, an apt metaphor for the sense of impotence that the elite felt in face of peasant autonomy.[108]

The other commodity that assumed great importance for southern Peru's exports after independence was chinchona bark. Although the largest amount of this raw material for the nineteenth-century cure-all medicine, quinine, was gathered in the Bolivian ceja de la selva provinces of Apolobamba and Larecaja, just south of the border with Peru, the Tambopata valley of Carabaya province rendered the highest-quality chinchona bark from its Calisaya trees. Foreign interest in the plant led to various expeditions into the region: in 1846 by the French natural scientist Hugues Algernon Weddell, who had been commissioned by the Museum of Natural History in Paris, and in 1860 by Clements Markham, who was instructed by the British government to collect seedlings of the tree in Carabaya and transplant them to Ceylon, an apparently successful operation.[109]

Many hacendados from the altiplano participated in the chinchona bark trade, among them Mariano Riquelme, a wool trader and owner of Hacienda Checayani in Muñani, and José Manuel Torres, owner and renter of haciendas in the same district. In the mid-1850s Torres received large advances for the delivery of bark from merchants in La Paz and Puno town and repeatedly had difficulties fulfilling his contracts because of the primitive production arrangements in the forests.[110] He operated in the Bolivian ceja de la selva, a region to which both traders and Indian peasants from Azángaro frequently traveled until the 1920s, either for commercial purposes or for work.

Chinchona bark exports fluctuated wildly from year to year because of the primitive nature of collection and the remoteness of the Calisaya forests. In 1835 exports from Peruvian ports reached the large volume of 14,000 quintales (valued at 440,000 pesos), more than two-thirds of which came from Carabaya or Bolivia. Peruvian bark exports still exceeded those of wools.[111] This proportion changed in the following years with the rapid expansion of both alpaca and sheep wool exports. Between 1850 and 1859 Islay's bark exports underwent a steady decline, initially caused by an adulteration of the high-quality Calisaya bark, which made it unsalable.[112]

For elite altiplano traders and landholders, the years between 1842 and the early 1850s witnessed perhaps the most frustrating phase in the long and tortuous transition from a mining supply economy to one of raw material exports. These years simultaneously saw the failure of attempts to revitalize the colonial commercial patterns based on silver mining and sale of woolen textiles in Upper Peru and the dashing of hopes for a rapid acceleration of raw wool sales in Europe as exports plummeted and prices deteriorated. In an analysis of southern Peru's agricultural crisis Francisco de Rivero in 1845 expressed the puzzlement of the region's livestock interests. He called at one and the same time for increased exports of improved wool at higher prices and the protection of "some factories of crude cloth," for whose products "the consumer might pay a price equal to that which today he is satisfied to pay for similar products of the European industry."[113] In this difficult conjuncture the altiplano elite looked to the montaña of Carabaya, hoping to exploit not only its export commodities, such as gold and chinchona bark, but also a wide variety of products that could strengthen their position in the domestic markets. But this was a frontier region, in which all the familiar problems that plagued them in their home base on the altiplano—high transport costs, lack of capital, and scarcity of labor—were exacerbated to the extreme.

In 1851 Agustín Aragón, a hacendado and wool trader from San Antón in the province of Azángaro, owned a coffee plantation in the Quebrada de Ayapata, some eighty kilometers north of San Antón across the Cordillera de Carabaya.[114] Thirteen years later his brother-in-law Simeon Rufino Macedo, son of Colonel Macedo (who led the conspiracy to adjoin Puno, Cuzco, and Arequipa to Bolivia in 1829) and owner of several estates in the districts of Potoni and Asillo in Azángaro, formed a company with a Frenchman to construct a "*finca cocal* [coca farm] for all types of fruits and edible plants in the montaña of Inambari or any other point of the valleys of the Province of Carabaya." Despite elaborate preparations, including the construction of a still for cane alcohol and the use of peón labor from Macedo's estates in Azángaro, the project failed. The meager starting capital of 4,000 pesos, all that an altiplano hacendado such as Macedo could muster, proved insufficient to overcome the very grave transport and communication problems posed by Puno's jungle region.[115]

Stimulated by the acquaintance with this region that men such as Riquelme, Aragón, and Macedo had gained in the chinchona bark trade and in gold-mining ventures, the efforts to develop Carabaya's tropical agriculture were aimed at capturing Puno's own market for such goods as coca leaves, fruits, and rice, until then supplied by neighboring ceja de la selva regions in Bolivia and Cuzco. These men also hoped to tap into the sizable earnings from the export of crops such as coffee and tobacco, the potential of which regions such as the Yungas of La Paz had already demonstrated. But after prospects for the altiplano livestock economy brightened with sustained export demand for wool in the mid-1850s, efforts by the region's hacendados and traders to exploit the potential riches of the adjacent montaña valleys slackened. For Indian peasants from the altiplano and for occasional adventurers, Carabaya remained accessible on their own terms, as they independently searched for gold, planted a few patches of coca bushes, maize, and fruits, or collected chinchona bark. The altiplano elite now largely contented itself with profiting from these goods by purchasing them from the peasants and adventurers at fairs in Crucero or Rosaspata or at their warehouses in Azángaro town when they returned to the altiplano at the end of the dry season.

The relative failure of strengthening both the regional and export trades through colonization of Puno's ceja de la selva during the mid-nineteenth century contrasts starkly with the success of such efforts by commercial and landholding elites in the central sierra. There regional trade intensified between the late 1840s and 1879 because of the sale of sugar and alcohol produced on newly established plantations in Junin's Amazonian piedmont. The difference highlights the greater availability of capital and greater population densities in the central sierra.[116] Puno's ceja de la selva could become an important commercial producer of agricultural products only with the construction of access roads, first by a foreign mining company in the 1890s and, in the 1920s, by the Peruvian government, a period when pressure on land in the altiplano had notably increased.

The Commercial System until Mid-century

During the first three decades after independence, as landholder and merchant elites in southern Peru desperately tried to adjust their economic activities to the new political, commercial, and social circumstances, new trading patterns were gradually constructed, incorporating distinct spatial circuits, new groups of traders, and changed modalities of trade. By the mid-nineteenth century the various livestock and agricultural products from the northern altiplano and surrounding, ecologically distinct regions all fed into a complex trade based to a large degree on reciprocity. Trade for export and trade for local consumption were closely intertwined.

After 1824 European and North American merchants rapidly gained control over southern Peru's foreign trade, taking up residence in the cities of Arequipa and Tacna, from where they handled both the export of Peruvian and Bolivian goods and the import of European and North American manufactured goods.[117] Despite its strategic importance the foreign mercantile community in southern Peru was small until mid-century. In 1827 Arequipa had at most forty British residents, and merchants from other nations could be counted on one hand. By the late 1850s Arequipa's foreign community had grown to only about eighty members, thirty-six of whom were Germans and the majority of the rest English.[118] Many of the foreign commercial houses in Arequipa were branches of larger companies established in Lima or Valparaiso. They often had partnerships or even closer ties with firms in London, Liverpool, Hamburg, or Le Havre.[119]

Before the last quarter of the nineteenth century Arequipa's merchants relied on three channels for purchasing wools and other export commodities: direct delivery to Arequipa by producers, purchases from various types of independent Peruvian traders, and contracts at yearly trade fairs. Some Indian peasant wool producers from the altiplano carried their clip directly to the stores and warehouses of the foreign merchants in Arequipa, combining these sales with their annual trip to purchase necessary provisions from the coastal valleys, such as sugar, aguardiente, and dried chile peppers. But it was the producers of larger amounts of wool, owners of haciendas, who took greatest advantage of direct sales to the foreign exporters in Arequipa. The hacendados realized higher prices when they sold their wool in Arequipa, and the added cost of transport was minimal as they could rely on pack animals belonging to either their estates or their shepherds. The shepherds were obligated to accompany the wool transport without additional compensation, a service known as *alquila*. The only added cost for the hacendado lay in provisions for the accompanying shepherds and fodder for the pack animals, mostly the frugal llamas. Furthermore, direct sale to exporters in Arequipa spared the hacendados the inconvenience of having to deal with muleteers, considered troublesome and unreliable.[120]

Far more frequent than direct delivery of the wool by producers to an exporter in Arequipa was the bulking of wool by one or more levels of Peruvian traders, who then sold large amounts to the export houses. These local, provincial, and regional wool purchases were often based on established clientele networks and involved credit transactions as well as sales of other commodities. The bulking of wools in the production zone and their transport to the coast was controlled to a large degree by altiplano hacendados and traders in this early phase, a pattern that was to change significantly only after the War of the Pacific. The atomistic nature of production—with thousands of Indian peasants supplying more than half of all raw wools as late as the 1870s—and all the expenses, uncertainties, and delays in communication and transportation made it difficult and potentially unprofitable for foreign merchants to attempt to control the trade circuits connecting the entrepôt and port cities with the interior. Newly emerging Peruvian merchants were left with much space to expand their own commercial operations in the interior and maintain a high degree of autonomy vis-à-vis the export merchants. This constellation changed only during the last quarter of the century.[121]

Juan Paredes was an important provincial wool bulker in Azángaro between the 1840s and early 1870s. Born in 1804 as the son of a muleteer, he inherited a string of mules and a modest liquid capital of two thousand pesos. By the 1840s Paredes had progressed from being a mere transport entrepreneur to undertaking varied trading activities on his own account. Based on a medium-sized estate inherited by his wife, he also began to move into landholding, parleyed his role as a trader and hacendado into political power in the province, and in turn used his power and influence during the last three decades of his life for a vast expansion of his family's landholdings.[122]

Paredes bought wool throughout the province either directly from producers, such as owners of small and medium-sized haciendas and indigenous peasant landholders, or from district-level wool bulkers, themselves frequently estate owners. In the four to six months prior to the wool clip in March or April, contracts were drawn up specifying how much wool a given producer or trader would deliver to Paredes once the new wool was available. The purchaser usually advanced a large percentage of the total price at the time of concluding a contract. The advances had the function of assuring supply and making it more difficult for the seller to demand a higher price for his wool at the time of delivery.[123] Quantities purchased by provincial wool bulkers ranged from two quintales (200 pounds) to fifty quintales (5,000 pounds). Paredes in turn sold the wool to regional bulkers who handled larger volumes of wool, but at times he also sold directly to Peruvian or foreign merchant houses in Arequipa. These traders made contracts with Paredes in much the same way as he did with his smaller suppliers. They also advanced him a considerable share of the total purchase price months before delivery, funds that Paredes needed for advances to his suppliers. To function as higher-level, greater-volume wool bulkers, men such as Agustín Aragón from San Antón, Hermenegildo Agramonte from Cabanillas, and Mariano Riquelme from Azángaro needed access to greater amounts of liquid capital and possessed installations to wash the wool. Large sums of metallic currency, always scarce in the altiplano, were needed to purchase 500, 1,000, or more quintales of wool, since cash advances down the commercialization chain were vital to the business. Having facilities to wash wool strengthened the trader's bargaining position with the exporters.[124]

Business relations were imbued with a sense of obligation, trust, and friendship because they were a natural extension of broader clientalistic ties permeating altiplano society. In his letters to Paredes the businessman José

Mariano Escobedo, an Azangarino native living in Arequipa and probably Paredes's most important wool-trading partner, routinely used the endearing address "My dear countryman and friend."[125] The more-than-businesslike nature of the relationship between Paredes and his wool suppliers from the haciendas and pueblos of the province is evident in a letter that he received in 1845. Manuel Mestas, a small hacendado from Caminaca, informed Paredes that he would not be able to deliver the contracted 100 arrobas of wool. The supplier tried to placate Paredes as follows:

> I ardently beseech your good heart that as a good friend you may
> consider the best way of extricating me from the stated problem
> for now because I find myself incapable of complying [with
> the contract] I seek with all satisfaction your kindness offering
> in my insignificance although I am not worth anything maybe I
> will be able to serve you some day in compensation for the favor
> for which I am asking you now, for which favor I hope by
> means of your angelical heart; the eighty arrobas and a bit more
> is soon ready to have them conducted to that capital [Azángaro] at your disposition according to the contract.[126]

Mestas was clearly worried about consequences much graver than the simple loss of a business partner should Paredes take any serious steps about the impending breach of contract. Mestas belonged to Paredes's clientele and depended on him for goods and services that may have included access to foodstuffs from Cuzco and Arequipa as well as to imported goods, otherwise attainable only with difficulty or at higher prices; support in the pursuit or retention of local offices such as governor, mayor, or justice of the peace in his district; and intercession on Mestas's behalf in courts. Wool trade constituted only one aspect of the multifaceted relationship of men such as Juan Paredes and Manuel Mestas.

Economic benefits varied greatly according to the level on which a producer or trader entered the commercialization chain. The more directly one could sell wool to the exporters in Arequipa, the higher the price one could achieve.[127] Scattered figures indicate that during the 1850s and 1860s provincial wool bulkers paid only between 28 and 38 percent of the FOB price of sheep wools in the port Islay to their suppliers in Azángaro. In 1862 Juan Paredes received 100 percent more for unwashed wool delivered in Arequipa than he paid for it in Azángaro and 160 percent more if he delivered it washed.[128]

It was mostly the smallest wool producers, especially Indian peasants, and local traders who sold wool at the levels of the commercialization chain furthest removed from Arequipa. Owners of haciendas and large-volume traders could take advantage of wool sales directly to Arequipa or at least to regional wool bulkers. The hierarchical trade system allocated greater benefits to large landholders and wealthy traders in the altiplano than to peasant landholders, marginal hacendados, and petty traders.

Annual fairs held in a number of altiplano towns combined religious celebrations around a patron saint with popular revelry and multifold trading activities. The most important of these, attended by tens of thousands of peasants, muleteers, wool traders, import merchants, and shopkeepers, was the fair at Vilque, a small town some thirty kilometers west of Puno on the road to Arequipa.[129] Others were held at Pucará, on the road to Cuzco; Rosaspata, strategically located northeast of Lake Titicaca for the trade with Bolivia; and Crucero, a crossroad in the eastern cordillera whence the most important llama paths departed to the rich ceja de la selva of Carabaya.[130]

The Vilque fair, established during the colonial period, possibly under the auspices of the Jesuits who owned nearby Hacienda Yanarico, was celebrated for two to four weeks around Pentecost in May to venerate "a Holy Christ whose miracles are famed even in the remotest places."[131] Clements Markham has left us a colorful description of the fair in 1860:

> Outside the town there were thousands of mules from Tucuman
> waiting for Peruvian arrieros to buy them. In the plaza were
> booths full of every description of Manchester and Birmingham
> goods; in more retired places were gold dusts and coffee from
> Carabaya, silver from the mines, bark and chocolate from Bolivia,
> Germans with glassware and woolen knitted work, French
> modistes, Italians, Quichua and Aymara Indians in their various
> picturesque costumes—in fact all nations and tongues. . . . The
> road was crowded with people coming from Arequipa to the
> fair at Vilque: native shopkeepers, English merchants coming
> to arrange for their supplies of wool, and a noisy company of
> arrieros on their way to buy mules, and armed to the teeth with
> horse-pistols, old guns, and huge daggers, to defend their
> money-bags.[132]

The volume of business conducted at the fair during the late 1840s may have reached anywhere between 750,000 and 2 million pesos.[133] As British Consul Wilthew wrote to the Foreign Office in 1859, the "success or failure of the fair is a matter of no small consequence for the commercial community," and "numerous contracts for the delivery of wool" were concluded.[134]

The rise of the fairs in the decades after independence demonstrates the changes and continuities in southern Peru's commercial economy. On the one hand, the gatherings at Vilque, Pucará, and elsewhere of people of "all nations and tongues," including mule traders from Argentina and a variety of Bolivian businessmen, demonstrated that transnational trade in the Andes had by no means disappeared entirely. But when the Andean commercial space had been in its heyday between the late sixteenth and mid-eighteenth centuries, there had been no need for fairs with such an enormous radius of participation as Vilque had in the mid-nineteenth century. The link between seller and buyer, even when it covered distances as vast as that between Cuzco and Potosí, had been secured through force (as in the repartos) or through tight-knit corporate or familial relations. The fairs responded to a tendency toward more individualized trading patterns and incipient competition, while personal, face-to-face contact and the establishment of relationships of trust was still deemed an essential element of trade. The rise of the fairs was thus intimately tied to the new import and export trade and the establishment of a group of foreign merchants outside of the long-established social fabric in southern Peru and at the apex of the postindependence commercial hierarchy. In an environment of highly insecure and expensive transport and communication the fairs constituted virtually the only means for these merchants to establish direct links to the great number of small producers and petty traders who controlled the major part of export commodities, especially wools.[135] The fairs introduced an element of competition into a commercial environment in which large landholders and altiplano wool bulkers sought to monopolize the trading relationships of their local populations.

For the Indian livestock herders the possibility of selling their wool clip to competing national and foreign merchants at one of the yearly fairs offered a significant alternative to its sale to local traders and hacendados in their own district. The very existence of a distinct group of merchants with as yet no strong social ties to large landholders and other local elites in the altiplano damaged the stranglehold over trade exercised by such local elites. The loud protest of Puno's political authorities in the late 1820s over wool purchases by foreign merchants should thus be understood as more than mere concern about possible scarcities of the fiber. More important, it expressed the fear of losing local trading monopolies that had allowed hacendados, corregidores, or priests to impose their own terms of trade on the peasants. The repeated difficulties of local traders during the 1840s and 1850s to deliver the contracted quantity of wool may have arisen because small producers, especially Indian peasants, could afford to withhold their wool clip in the hope of selling at the next fair, probably for a better price.

Nevertheless, this competitive aspect of the trade fairs should not be exaggerated. The hierarchy of middlemen was absolutely indispensable for the Arequipa merchant houses to achieve the bulking of export commodities and the bulk breaking of imports. It was with larger-volume wool traders that the exporters concluded the most significant contracts at Vilque and Pucará. The peasant producers usually did not have the cash reserves to hold their wool clip until the fairs and routinely saw themselves forced to sell to local mestizo or creole traders and hacendados. In fact, the web of obligations created by the wool trade was one of the processes through which the newly arising mercantile and landholding elite in the northern altiplano sought to reestablish a higher degree of control over the region's peasantry. Still, this elite control had become fragile in the postindependence decades, and the competitive elements introduced through the fairs contributed to greater peasant autonomy. The newly rising mercantile and landholding elite of the altiplano would consolidate their control over peasant commercialization only in the decades between the 1860s and 1890s.

The interrelationship between the export and import trades and the purely domestic exchanges, apparent in the business conducted at the annual fairs, can be explored in greater depth through the web of Juan Paredes's commercial transactions (fig. 2.2). His trade consisted of both the export and local sale of goods either produced on his own estates or purchased within the province and the purchase of goods from neighboring regions or imported from Europe for his own consumption or for resale in the province. Because the sparsely populated province of Carabaya had no group of locally resident traders, it depended on traders in the altiplano for goods from third regions. Thus, in Carabaya, Paredes sold not only the range of goods produced in Azángaro but also commodities bought in Arequipa or Cuzco.

Often Paredes's trade was triangular. For example, when Juan Bautista Zea from Arapa contracted to sell Paredes fifty arrobas of wool in early 1847, he also asked him to remit a *carga* (four to five arrobas) of maize. Although the wool would ultimately be sold for export in Arequipa, Paredes was purchasing the maize in Cuzco or Carabaya. There in turn he sold animals on the hoof, dried meat, or tallow in exchange for cereals or coca leaves.[136]

The reciprocal nature of trade had much to do with the clientalistic, highly personal relations of business. But there was another powerful motive for reciprocity of trade relations—the scarcity of currency. By establishing long-term commercial partnerships in which one essentially paid for goods bought from a trade partner with other goods, the need for cash was reduced to a minimum. This practice was crucial in a society in which "we find ourselves very poor; such is the scarcity of coins that there is no money for anything," as the hacendado Andrés Urviola from Muñani

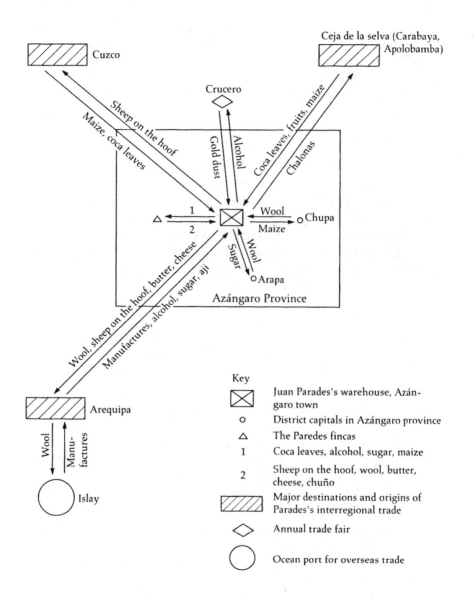

Key

⊠ Juan Parades's warehouse, Azángaro town

○ District capitals in Azángaro province

△ The Paredes fincas

1 Coca leaves, alcohol, sugar, maize

2 Sheep on the hoof, wool, butter, cheese, chuño

▨ Major destinations and origins of Parades's interregional trade

◇ Annual trade fair

○ Ocean port for overseas trade

FIGURE 2.2. Trading Network of Juan Paredes, Around 1850

wrote in 1867.[137] Technically, reciprocal trade relied on current accounts kept by both trade partners about the goods purchased and sold to each other, and these accounts were normally adjusted once every year. Only a fraction of the total value of trade conducted between the two partners ever had to be paid in cash.

The commodity flow in Azángaro's interregional trade around 1850 was not all that different, then, from what it had been in the eighteenth century: maize, wheat, and coca leaves from Cuzco for livestock on the hoof from Azángaro. Wool shipments to Cuzco were now much diminished. Coca leaves, maize, and fruits from the ceja de la selva of Carabaya and Bolivia were traded for dried meat and chuño from Azángaro. The province's traders also profited from their position as middlemen in the export of such goods as chinchona bark and gold dust from Carabaya and in supplying that region with alcohol, sugar, and other provisions from Arequipa and Cuzco. For its own consumption Arequipa received dried meat, livestock on the hoof, tallow, butter, and cheese from Azángaro, while supplying the altiplano province with cane alcohol, wine, sugar, peppers, dried fruits, oil, and other agricultural products. But the new element in Azángaro's trade relationship with Arequipa lay in the fact that the latter city was becoming the entrepôt for the altiplano's exports of wool as well as for the import of European goods. The Peruvian altiplano's declining trade with the Bolivian urban and mining centers, the centerpiece of the region's commercial circuit during the colonial period, was gradually being replaced in a restructured circuit in which Arequipa functioned as the funnel for the region's production for export. Although not yet apparent to many contemporary observers, by the early 1850s Arequipa was on its way to becoming the hegemonic urban center of a reduced southern Peruvian space, a position the city fully achieved between 1870 and 1890, while Cuzco's decay continued.[138]

Jean Piel has suggested that the first two or three decades after independence saw the Peruvian altiplano enjoying "a certain measure of regional prosperity based on agriculture."[139] His view is founded on the rise of the region's wool exports beginning in the late 1830s, a period during which most other Peruvian agricultural regions remained stagnant. But earnings from wool exports did not represent an additional source of income for the altiplano above an otherwise steady level of earnings. Rather, these earnings had to replace income lost from trade in woolen textiles and other livestock products with High Peru and from raw wool sales to Cuzco. It is suggestive that in 1791 the sale of 7,500 quintales of sheep wool from the northern altiplano to the Intendency of Cuzco alone represented close to 50 percent of sheep wool exports from Islay in the very favorable year of 1840, and these exports include production from provinces in Cuzco and Arequipa departments! If, for 1791, we add the substantial woolens woven in household production and obrajes in the northern altiplano and sold in High Peru, it is probable that the total volume of marketed wool in 1791, a year when southern Peru's colonial commercial circuit was already experiencing a crisis, may have reached or surpassed the volume exported in 1840.

But Piel's assertion of regional prosperity in the department of Puno during the early independence period might be closer to the mark with regard to the peasant economy. The demise of the obrajes, stagnating production of precious metals, increasing difficulties of access to the Bolivian markets, rising costs of transportation and credit, and flat commodity and land prices affected the landholding and commercial elites of the altiplano but had much less effect on the peasants. The production and peddling of their traditional wares, foremost among them woolen textiles, continued to be a viable source of monetary income for their peasant household economy. Their greater autonomy minimized the effects of price declines for their textile wares, as price impositions by local or provincial power holders diminished. The opening of the wool trade and the appearance of a distinct social group of foreign merchants added further competitive elements into regional trade, as long as the exporters and the rising Peruvian trading hierarchy still eyed each other with as much distrust as cooperation. The rapid rise of alpaca wool exports, produced to a much higher degree by Indian peasants than was sheep wool, was especially important for indigenous livestock herders. In short, as altiplano elites struggled to recover prosperity within trading circuits undergoing major changes, the peasant economy was growing in autonomy.

During the eighty years between 1775 and 1855 the patterns of trade in the northern altiplano underwent a complex transitional crisis that affected the region's elites and the peasantry in notably different ways. It touched every major aspect of elite-controlled trade: commodity flows, the commercial space, the social composition of all commercial intermediary groups, and the way business was conducted. During the mid-eighteenth century the colonial commercial circuits based on the supply of High Peru's silver mining centers had brought modest prosperity to the interconnected elites of hacendados, kurakas, priests, and crown officials in Azángaro and neighboring provinces. But between the 1780s and the 1840s these circuits decayed. The late colonial recovery of silver mining bypassed the intendencies of Puno and Cuzco as the "Andean space" increasingly frayed, pulled apart by the growth of two poles, the Potosí–Buenos Aires axis and the urban and mining economy of central and northern Peru, with southern Peru dangling in the middle.

These problems were exacerbated as silver mining went into a slump after 1800 and brief attempts at revitalization after independence definitely failed during the 1840s. In various waves since the 1780s, European industrialization intruded into the markets for the mainstay of the altiplano's livestock economy, woolen textiles. External price competition hastened the demise of the inefficient obrajes, as rebellions, the Wars of Independence, and succeeding civil wars disrupted trading routes and made markets insecure and capital and transport more expensive. Merchant and landholding elites tried to save as much as possible of the old trades in the decades after independence while eagerly grasping the opportunities afforded by export demand for wool, chinchona bark, and silver. But new trade circuits proved unstable at first. By the mid-1840s the old textile trade, the Bolivian markets, and the new export trade were all in crisis simultaneously. For a brief instant the only salvation seemed to lie in the difficult commercial exploitation of the montaña frontier to the east.

There is a certain irony about the economic situation of the northern altiplano elites during the decades after independence. On the one hand, their autonomy grew with the decay of the colonial trading circuits in which traders, muleteers, and estate owners from the Intendency of Puno depended on merchants from Cuzco, Arequipa, and Potosí or La Plata for their business. As the Andean space frayed, the northern altiplano became less of an "internal space." One might even say that the region's elites for the first time became visible historical subjects, distinct and separate from the merchants, hacendados, and officeholders residing in the cities of Cuzco or Arequipa. On the other hand, this increased autonomy did not coincide with growing prosperity; rather, it arose in an era of stagnating or falling commodity prices, insecure markets, expensive transport and capital, recurrent warfare, and the beginning of competitive trading practices introduced by foreign merchants. Most important, the temporary "liberation" of northern altiplano traders and hacendados from the colonial mercantile elites in the surrounding urban centers coincided with the growing autonomy of the region's peasantry. In contrast to creole merchants and hacendados, the northern altiplano's peasants continued to find sufficient markets in Cuzco, Arequipa, and even Bolivia for their cheap woolens and other artisanal and livestock products, as they were less affected by price competition. The peasants also profited initially from the introduction of competition in the emerging export trades for wool and chinchona bark.

By the mid-1850s high prices for Peruvian alpaca and sheep wools was signaling the beginning of a period of booming wool exports. At this time, then, Azángaro and the northern altiplano had completed the readjustment from a colonial mining-supply economy to an economy based on exports. The region's landholding elite, intertwined with the traders and political authorities, sought alternative strategies of reestablishing their control over the indigenous population in order to maximize their exploitation of the peasantry. The expansion of haciendas and the concomitant integration of ever more Indian peasants into the estate economy was—among other causes—rooted in this attempt by hacendados to regain control over the peasant economy.

3 Colonialism Adrift

Azángaro and the whole of the northern altiplano had participated in market exchanges in the framework of Spanish colonial political economy since the second half of the sixteenth century. But by the late colonial period it was not a "market economy," much less a "market society." Indeed, even in the early twentieth century these terms would remain inappropriate; that is, there existed nothing close to a self-regulating market in which the values of all traded or bartered commodities were determined primarily by the equilibrium between supply and demand. Nor were people's social positions determined primarily by the exchange value of their skills or the goods they offered on the market. Rather, custom, privilege, and power all exerted strong influence on market exchanges and social chances of individuals, families, and groups.[1] The changes in Azángaro's agrarian society during the waning decades of the colonial regime took place against the background of this interdependence between commerce and the social, cultural, and political relations of production.

Spanish colonialism affected various regions in America differently and penetrated Indian societies at different times. Azángaro was located in one of the two cores of the Spanish Empire in the Americas—Mesoamerica and the central Andes—that became centers of European colonization between the 1520s and 1550s. Yet, although the northern altiplano's colonial experience differed greatly from that of frontier regions, such as the nearby Amazonian piedmont, the Araucanian-controlled territories of southern Chile, or the *tierra adentro* (inland) of northern Mexico, it remained something like an internal, dominated space until the very end of the colonial era. Distant from major Spanish urban centers—Cuzco was three days away by horse—the region was unpopular among Spaniards because of its frosty climate and the fierce autonomy of the Indian herders.[2]

Although geographically and socially furthest removed from Spanish colonial centers, rural society in provinces such as Azángaro was characterized most dramatically by colonialism. A handful of direct representatives of the colonial state and a few Spanish or culturally hispanized landholders, miners, and traders here clashed and—at the same time—lived together with an overwhelming majority of indigenous peasants, who adjusted as little as necessary in order to save what they could of their ethnic identity.[3] The dual function of any colonial regime—to control the conquered population politically and socially and to exploit it economically—left an indelible imprint on the structure of Azángaro's rural society. But even for the late colonial period the sources suggest that the extraordinary power of the private, crown, and church representatives of the colonial regime contrasted markedly with the precarious Spanish settlement of Azángaro and neighboring altiplano provinces.

The Formation of Livestock Estates up to 1750

Between the 1540s and 1573 all Indians in the region of Azángaro were distributed to ten *encomenderos*, who were entrusted with both rights of tribute from the Indians and responsibility for their welfare. Despite the legal separation between encomienda and landholding, these men established some of Azángaro's first estates.[4] In a number of cases encomenderos combined grants of Indians in the temperate valleys near Cuzco with those in the higher and colder livestock zone of Azángaro, suggesting an early integration of both regions dominated by colonists residing in the city of Cuzco.[5]

A detailed account of the early formation of haciendas in the northern altiplano lies outside the scope of this study. Suffice it to say that the mechanisms employed in the transfer of lands from Indians to Spaniards were the same here as in other, well-studied parts of Spanish America: land grants (*mercedes*) by the crown to worthy settlers, with a legally prescribed residence in a Spanish city; de facto appropriations of land from Indian peasants using largely illegal and deceptive procedures; and the reaffirmation of de facto possession by itinerant crown judges during recurring evaluations of land titles (*composiciones*).[6] For Azángaro, we have evidence of *visitas de tierras* (judicial evaluations of land titles) in 1595, 1607, 1655, and 1717.[7]

The precarious and slow entrenchment of direct Spanish exploitation in the northern altiplano may be detected in the timing of estate formation. Just as elsewhere in core Spanish America, the process got underway in Azángaro during the late sixteenth and, particularly, the seventeenth

TABLE 3.1. Livestock Estancias in Azángaro
Province, 1689 and 1825/30

Owner	1689	1825/30
Spaniards	33	} 68
Kurakas	5	
Church	4	34
Communities	4	8
Owner unknown	2	—
Total	48	110

Note: These figures exclude Poto, Pusi, and Taraco.

Sources: Villanueva Urteaga, *Cuzco 1689*, 111–26; Choque-huanca, *Ensayo*, 15–53.

centuries as the growth of colonial towns and a complex mining economy stimulated the development of Spanish livestock ranches supplementing goods extracted from the Indian peasant economy. But in contrast to other regions of the empire, in the northern altiplano the formative phase of estate building did not conclude or slow down at the end of the seventeenth century. Rather, more estates were incorporated between 1689 and the end of the colonial era than before (table 3.1); probably the greatest part of the post-1689 estates were formed before 1780.

In 1689 most Spanish livestock ranches in Azángaro were located in two widely separated clusters. The fertile valleys around Munañi and Putina, in the eastern part of the province close to the Cordillera de Carabaya, had the greatest concentration of estates. Most of these belonged to Spaniards who were working the gold and silver mines in the adjacent cordillera and piedmont of Carabaya; as one contemporary source noted, "The said estancias serve to dispense the supplies for the sustenance of the miners." As late as 1819 abandoned mines in the mining district of Aporoma were appurtenances of Estancia de Guasacona in Muñani.[8] The other cluster of estates was located on the western fringes of the corregimiento, in the parishes of Asillo and Santiago de Pupuja, close to or directly on the camino real from Cuzco to Upper Peru. These livestock ranches were owned mostly by Spaniards residing in Cuzco or, less often, Arequipa, among them descendants of the original encomenderos who still carried the title. For example, during the late seventeenth and early eighteenth centuries San Francisco de Purina in Asillo belonged to the encomendero Don Gerónimo de Costilla, Marqués de Buenavista, a citizen of Cuzco.[9] In Santiago the Jesuits' Colegio Grande of Cuzco owned two estancias from the early seventeenth century on. Proximity to the camino real, offering easier communication both with Cuzco and Upper Peru, was essential for making the formation of estates by powerful absentee lords feasible and profitable. These ranches supplied Cuzco with wool, dried meat, and other livestock products and may also have shipped such goods directly to the mining centers in Upper Peru.

Outside of these two clusters of estates Azángaro's parish priests mention only a handful of ranches in their reports to Bishop Mollinedo of Cuzco in 1689: one, owned by the kuraka Don Manuel Chuquiguanca, a few miles outside the pueblo of Azángaro; another four owned both by Spaniards and Indian communities in the vicinity of Lake Arapa; and another two further south on the camino real in the annex Achaya of Caminaca parish, at least one of which was owned by the Indian community. Until the end of the seventeenth century, then, a vast central corridor through Azángaro province, from the slopes of the Cordillera de Carabaya around Potoni in the north, through the modern districts of San Antón and San José, the wide plains around the pueblo of Azángaro, and all the way to the southern extreme of the province close to Lake Titicaca at Saman and Caminaca, was essentially free of Spanish estates. Virtually all this land still belonged to Indian peasants, their communities, and their kurakas. Spanish authority here was represented directly only through one parish priest, the corregidor, and their assistants.

Why was the Spanish presence in the core of what was to become one of Peru's premier livestock-raising provinces so precarious before the eighteenth century? It cannot have been due to the natural environment. As developments in the later nineteenth and early twentieth century demonstrate, much of the land in this central corridor of Azángaro constituted good pastures propitious for the formation of livestock haciendas. Location certainly influenced the spatial patterning of Spanish enterprises during the seventeenth century. Proximity to the mining region and to the main commercial artery of the viceroyalty drew two different types of Spanish entrepreneurs and landholders: relatively modest miners, residing on their estates when they were not in the seasonally operated mining camps, and powerful absentee landlords linked to Cuzco's aristocratic families. But the Spaniards' slowness in establishing agrarian enterprises in the central part of the province may also have had something to do with the cohesion of Indian society, the power of the kurakas, and the smaller population loss in that part of Azángaro. Indian societies based on raising large domesticated animals before conquest may have been in a better position to defend against Spanish encroachments onto their lands than were societies based on intensive crop agriculture. The dispersed settlements of the pastoralists slowed down the spread of deadly epidemics, and the need for extensive grazing lands for the cameloid herds allowed the Indian communities to claim large areas as indispensable for their livelihood. By physical occupation of extensive pastures, the herds of the Indian communities helped protect their land.[10]

With the large increase in the number of estates between the 1690s and the 1770s, their spatial and ownership patterns shifted. Whereas the two clusters (around Putina-Muñani and Asillo-Santiago) accounted for 85 percent of all estates in 1689, by the late colonial period only 53 percent were located there. The church, which owned less than 10 percent of the estates in 1689, controlled close to one-third by the late colonial period. More than half of the new church estates incorporated after 1689 were located in the core area of the province, where previously there had been hardly any estates. The rapid expansion of church lands in areas controlled by Indian communities and their kurakas suggests the parish priests' growing power over, and involvement with, the peasant economy during the early decades of the eighteenth century.[11]

Parishes had come into possession of some land early in the colonial period, perhaps by taking over some community lands assigned to the priests of the Inca religion.[12] But most of the land that appeared as church estates after 1689 had previously belonged to the kurakas or Indian communities. In the late sixteenth century Kuraka Diego Choquehuanca, founder and financial backer of the Church of Nuestra Señora de la Asunción de Azángaro, had donated extensive landholdings to the parish to help defray construction costs and administrative expenditures.[13] Communities may also have donated land to their parishes; in other cases they probably lost control over it unwittingly through the priests' administration of the lay fraternities' property or through failure to pay certain fees.[14] In contrast to other areas in Spanish America, in the altiplano parish churches held much more land than did orders, convents, or the Cuzco diocese. This was to make church lands more resistant to liberal legislation in the nineteenth century.

Among Azángaro's wealthiest landholders were some of the province's important kuraka families.[15] Between the mid-sixteenth and the mid-eighteenth century many kurakas increasingly "incorporated themselves into the group of provincial merchants, administrators, and landholders."[16] They used their position of authority over the Indian communities not only as brokers of the peninsular and creole elite but also in their own favor as private entrepreneurs or landholders. Such behavior represented a break with modes of social interaction of the prehispanic Andean society and led to tensions between Indian commoners and kurakas.

The Choquehuancas, the wealthiest and most powerful kuraka family, traced their lineage back to a son of Inca Huayna Capac.[17] The family had held the *cacicazgo* (office of cacique) of the parcialidad Anansaya of Azángaro nearly uninterruptedly throughout the colonial period, although their control of this lucrative office was challenged several times. In the mid-sixteenth century Diego Choquehuanca was declared an hidalgo and granted the title Marqués de Salinas by the Spanish crown. By 1780 the Choquehuancas possessed eleven estancias in Azángaro, among them such large and valuable estates as Picotani, Checayani, and Nequeneque in Muñani and Puscallani, Ccalla, and Catacora around Azángaro. Joséf Choquehuanca's account of the services that the family rendered the crown during the Túpac Amaru Rebellion underscores the family's self-esteem and sense of social exaltation. He stressed the generosity and goodwill that the family had always shown to Spaniards, to the extent that Josef's sisters "were even married to Europeans out of the love that we profess for the Nation." They owned properties "sufficient to maintain a splendor that corresponds to the honor and birth of our lineage"; in Azángaro "no house was more comfortably situated."[18]

Of the forty-six kurakas appearing in the 1754 tribute lists for the province, none came close to the wealth and power of the Choquehuancas. Although most probably lived as relatively affluent peasants submerged in the indigenous society of their communities, a few other families held wealth comparable to that of Spanish landholders, among them the Mango Turpos, probably kurakas of the parcialidad Urinsaya of Azángaro.[19]

During the first three quarters of the eighteenth century the incorporation of lands into livestock estates occurred at an accelerated rate among all groups of landholders, the church, private Spaniards and mestizos, kurakas, and also the Indian communities, which increasingly used rental fees from communal estancias to help pay tributes and church fees. As the textile production of the southern Peruvian region boomed, interest in livestock production grew.[20] Because this interest came at the nadir of the northern altiplano's population density, the crown made it easy to acquire "excess" Indian lands.[21]

A royal cedula of October 15, 1754, facilitated the process of hacienda expansion by simplifying the bureaucratic process of sale and composition of crown lands.[22] In 1762 the family of Kuraka Diego Choquehuanca occupied large tracts of land in the area of Muñani, leading to a legal battle with three Indian communities, or *ayllus*. In his deposition before the commissioner of the Audiencia de Charcas, Andrés Hanco, an *Indio origi-*

nario from ayllu Picotani, testified that Doña María Choquehuanca, daughter of the kuraka, had taken possession of the lands belonging to Indians of the ayllu Nequeneque, constructing a building with three large rooms "at the cost of the Indians, without paying them anything," precisely on the spot where the cottage of one of the expelled community peasants had stood. The "many plots of land" taken by Diego Choquehuanca from the three ayllus in total "might amount to about forty leagues of land." The kuraka was depriving the community peasants "from raising livestock and sowing the fields, saying that these are his lands by purchase of his ancestors."[23] The Choquehuancas may indeed have held legal title to at least some of these lands since the late sixteenth century, but they attempted to incorporate them into effective estate operations only in the second half of the eighteenth century, severely infringing on the legally tenuous but real possession of these lands by the three ayllus. Nevertheless, the Audiencia of Charcas confirmed the kuraka's rights to these lands on November 21, 1762, and the formal procedure of taking possession was carried out on May 6, 1765.

Scarcity of labor was one of the main reasons inducing the altiplano's elites to establish estates rather than to rely exclusively on the extractions of surplus from the peasant economy. But the settling of a permanent labor force on Andean livestock haciendas was a long-term process that had far from concluded by the second half of the eighteenth century. According to Karen Spalding, this process began on a large scale only during the mid-seventeenth century, considerably lagging behind the process of land absorption. Previously the estates had relied primarily on labor in the form of mita and tribute obligations of Indian communities.[24] With increased *repartos de bienes* (forced distribution of goods) by corregidores, Indians saw themselves less and less capable of paying for the goods heaped on them. Poor peasants began to pay off their debts by working on haciendas, whose owners paid the corregidor for this supply of labor.[25] Moreover, the very process of land acquisition by the estates frequently brought peasants into the ranks of labor tenants, or yanaconas. Indian families stayed on their land being incorporated into an hacienda.[26] Some families preferred to flee from the obligations imposed on the communities—tribute payments, mita labor, and repartos by corregidores—into the relative security of hacienda *yanaconaje.*[27]

Throughout the colonial period owners attempted to fix increasing numbers of indigenous peasants on their haciendas as a permanently servile labor force. Yanacona labor was cheaper since it could be paid largely in usufruct rights to grazing and agricultural land. Settling a yanacona on the estate also gave the hacendado access to the labor of his wife and children. Control over permanently settled workers reduced monetary payments for labor by a variety of manipulations, such as overcharging for foodstuffs and buying the yanaconas' own livestock products (hides and wool) at low prices.[28] But even more important may have been the quest for a secure labor supply. As the indigenous population declined until the first quarter of the eighteenth century and labor remained scarce long thereafter, hacendados worried whether sufficient numbers of mitayos and wage laborers could be drafted for their estates after the needs of the priority mining sector had been satisfied. Estates with few or no yanaconas had to rely on wage labor (*gente de ruego*) and thus diminished in value.[29]

Although copious and repeated crown decrees—notably the labor tariff of Viceroy Duque de la Palata of 1687—regulated the colonos' pay on livestock estancias, the stipulated monetary wages were paid mostly in goods.[30] Moreover, administrators frequently managed to minimize payment in any form. The yanaconas' tribute was deducted from their pay, and they were charged for every head of livestock that was lost, a frequent mishap under conditions of open range herding.[31] The prices that they had to pay to the hacienda for foodstuffs, beyond the short rations (*avíos*) received as part of their wage, were higher than those found in urban markets, sometimes by as much as 100 percent.[32] As a result of these practices, yanaconas frequently received only a small fraction of their monetary wage in any form. Payment for labor consisted of the limited avíos and the usufruct rights to pastures and agricultural lands of the hacienda.[33] By exempting yanaconas from mita labor and the repartos of corregidores, and by establishing special tribute rates for them (to be paid by the hacendado), the colonial administration legally defined their status as that of a caste.[34] When, in the early eighteenth century, the crown ordered that yanaconas should not be inhibited from leaving a hacienda, opposition to this measure was so strong in the Audiencia of Charcas that the royal decree was not published there.[35]

The economic operation of livestock estates remained haphazard. Three consecutive instructions for the administrators of the Jesuit ranch Ayuni y Camara between the 1690s and 1730s indicate that the order was attempting to institute more efficient exploitation of its stock and greater labor productivity, albeit with little success. Flocks of fertile ewes, rams, yearlings, and old sheep for slaughter were to be separated in order to regulate the reproductive cycle of the animals and diminish exorbitant mortality rates among newborn lambs, routinely reaching 50 percent. But the repeated admonitions in the Jesuit instructions to implement such improved ranching methods make it clear that on their own estancias they met with little success. They were never even attempted by most ranchers in the altiplano.[36]

On the whole, land remained abundant in the northern altiplano during the last century of the colonial period, even if access to it by specific social groups was increasingly contested. When estates were leased, the annual rental fee reflected only the value of its livestock capital. An estancia with 1,000 sheep usually brought the same 100 pesos rental fee per year as a flock of equal size without pastureland. This conventional rate remained unchanged between 1689 and the end of the colonial period.[37] Land by itself had as yet little value;[38] what counted was the livestock capital and the possibility of exploiting it in a secure fashion with a minimum of monetary operational expenditures. From the perspective of Spanish commercial interests, land in the northern altiplano was still in an incipient phase of being *mise en valeur*. Control of land in itself could not, in contrast to a mature feudal society, secure power or wealth.

How then are we to explain the accelerated incorporation of livestock ranches during the first three quarters of the eighteenth century? After 1720 human population increased and livestock populations seem to have followed suit, particularly in the face of Cuzco's textile boom and rising demand for meat. The exploitation of livestock herds outside of estates, however, became increasingly difficult. As early as 1689 Azángaro's parish priest complained about the great difficulty that the parish had maintaining its sheep flocks grazing on land informally set aside for this purpose by the Indian communities. The parish had not been granted mita laborers, "who can be reckoned with." Thus, the parish had to solicit Indians "from various parts" as shepherds "by pleading or through the power of money." These free workers, "whenever they want, leave the flock out in the pasture to fend for itself and abscond, and in most cases they do so for having stolen or killed [some of the livestock]."[39] Such insecurities multiplied as the flocks roaming the unincorporated community pastures grew. During favorable periods for livestock products that coincided with human and livestock population growth, the only way to safeguard the flocks and to secure a reliable work force was to incorporate estates. Only then could one petition the crown for mitayos or establish yanaconas on the land. But the estancias that developed in this mid-eighteenth century conjuncture remained rudimentary in their internal organization.

Land Tenure in the Indian Communities

The landholding pattern in the indigenous peasant communities was highly interrelated with the development of the colonial hacienda complex. The communities suffered directly from any expansion of surrounding estates, and there were labor linkages between both institutions. Toward the end of the colonial era Spanish concepts of property increasingly infiltrated peasant communities.[40]

By the eighteenth century the Indian ayllu or parcialidad differed in many respects from the preconquest Andean institutions. The ayllu of the Inca empire and the pre-Incaic ethnic kingdoms was constituted by extended family groups, which controlled the individual's access to material and spiritual resources and mediated the obligations and privileges of its members in the wider society.[41] Prior to Spanish colonization, ayllus belonged to one of two moieties, the Incaic parcialidades of Anansaya and Urinsaya, in which every level of society from the local kinship groups of agriculturalists to the Inca nobility was organized. During the centuries of colonial rule the ayllus underwent a gradual transformation into settlements defined by geographic location and their claims to land, often sanctioned by the crown. Although kinship ties, real or symbolic, continued to be important, they became less rigid, and the ayllus were increasingly inhabited by Indian peasants from different regions.

Viceroy Toledo's program of *reducciones*, initiated in the 1570s,[42] and the migration of large parts of the Indian population, particularly in the jurisdiction of the Audiencia de Charcas, contributed to these structural changes within the indigenous communities. In part these migrations were imposed by the colonial administration, the Potosí mita offering the most massive and notorious example.[43] In part they also represented a defensive reaction of Indian peoples against the exactions of Spanish colonial society: flight to areas outside the reach of the crown, church, or private entrepreneurs or to the anonymity of other communities and towns. The demographic development after conquest also proved a formidable obstacle to the maintenance of cultural and institutional continuity. The decline of the indigenous communities' population led to increasing encroachments on their lands from various sectors of Peruvian colonial society throughout the seventeenth and eighteenth centuries.

Legally all community lands were claimed by the crown, which granted their usufruct to the Indian families of the communities in exchange for tribute payments and mita labor services. This legal notion has been viewed as the basis of a long-lasting compact between colonial state and Indian communities.[44] It is certainly true that the crown had a keen interest in preserving the communal peasant economy, as it remained the crucial underpinning of private affluence and fiscal liquidity throughout Peru's colonial period. Since Toledo's time a whole body of protective legislation and institutions had grown to safeguard this interest, among them the *protectores de Indios*, attached to the audiencias, and the *corregidores de Indios*.[45] Nevertheless, Spanish entrepreneurs, clerics, church institutions, and kurakas found ways to appropriate crown land from communities, particularly since the shrinking number of peasants could not effectively work all lands the crown had granted them in usufruct.[46]

During the eighteenth century, with the growing impact of enlightened notions of property and efficient agricultural production, the colonial administration's protective policy toward Indians became conflictive and may very well have contributed to the diminution of communal landholdings. On the one hand, the crown became increasingly concerned that the communities should have sufficient land for their member families to subsist and to fulfill their fiscal and labor obligations. Between 1710 and 1780 composiciones de tierra in favor of communities became more frequent, improving the title by which communities held their land.[47] But at the same time historical claims to land tended to be given less validity. Rather, enlightened bureaucrats and jurists wanted to base the right of community landholders on the principle that "the parcels assigned to the members should be all the same and adjusted to what one family needed and could exploit," as Joaquin Costa paraphrased the Count of Campomanes's ideas.[48] During the middle decades of the eighteenth century such precepts gradually permeated Peruvian colonial juridical practice. Crown officials began to carry out periodic land redistributions in the communities. Each Indian family of fully recognized community members received a uniform amount of land, varying from region to region. "Excess" community lands were to be sold in auctions, creating one more source of revenue for the exchequer of the Spanish king.[49]

Because this policy came during the decades just following the nadir of Peru's Indian population, it produced severe problems when the population rebounded in the second quarter of the eighteenth century. Soon remaining lands could not supply all Indians living in communities with enough agricultural and pastureland for feeding their families and fulfilling their obligations toward the various civil and religious authorities.[50] As early as the mid-eighteenth century Jorge Juan and Antonio de Ulloa, authors of the *Noticias secretas*, noted that "at present the lands that remain for [the Indians] are much reduced and many of them have none."[51]

The difference between community peasants with and without land was to a certain extent institutionalized by the colonial administration. In the altiplano the distinction between originarios and forasteros, the former paying a higher rate of tribute, was based not so much on the geographic origin of the Indians as it was on their privileges in the corporate communities.[52] Although the term *forastero* originally described an Indian residing in a community that was not his or her place of birth, it continued to be used for forasteros' descendants over several generations, people who were born and continued to live in the same community without achieving full usufruct rights of communal lands. Many forastero families possessed a small parcel of land, but it was always their goal to join the ayllu to obtain a share of communal land and thereby become full members of the community, or originarios.[53] In the meantime they survived by working on nearby estates, becoming clients of wealthier originarios, or renting land from the community or one of its members.[54] In 1761, for example, Juan Calsina, a notable from the ayllu Anansaya of Azángaro, brought suit against two forastero families, Nicolás and Sebastian Catari and the Amarus, before the Audiencia of Charcas. Two years earlier he had given in to their pleas and permitted them "to fallow and sow"—presumably as renters—a plot within his estancia Calaguala Hallapise, which his family had owned since the time of his great-grandfather Francisco Aiaviri Calsina. Now the Cataris and Amarus had extended the sections on which they were sowing until they had reached the house of Calsina. Calsina asked the audiencia to expel the two forastero families from his lands; the court ruled accordingly.[55]

Throughout the eighteenth century the problem of community peasants with no or insufficient land seems to have become more serious. In Azángaro the number of originarios declined by 37 percent between the recounts of 1758–59 and 1786, while the number of forasteros increased by 239 percent (table 3.2). In 1786 nearly two-thirds of the forasteros in 1786 possessed some land. During the last quarter of the eighteenth century originarios often wanted to be registered as forasteros in order to avoid mita service in Potosí and pay lower tribute rates. In brief, the number of community peasants who held enough communal lands to maintain their family subsistence and support the various levies by crown, church, and private entrepreneurs seems to have declined during the decades preceding the Túpac Amaru Rebellion.

But this cannot have been the whole picture with regard to land property of Indian peasants. What about more affluent peasants? Was it impossible for them to increase their landholdings even though they possessed the economic means to do so? Within the framework of the communities such expansion was indeed impossible since the colonial authorities undertook periodic redistributions of land with the particular goal of equalizing the plots of all originarios.[56] But peasants could acquire land outside the communities in fee simple by purchases from private landholders or by composition with the crown. Such must have been the case with the lands of the Turpo family in Asillo, for example. In 1900 Gabino Turpo applied

TABLE 3.2. Composition of Azángaro's Tributarios, 1758/59–1825/26

	1758/59		1786		1825/26	
	Number	%	Number	%	Number	%
Originarios	1,242	44.3	779	13.2	1,542	18.5
Forasteros	1,510	53.9	5,126	86.8	6,809	81.5
With land	n.a.	n.a.	[3,611]	[61.1]	n.a.	n.a.
Without land	n.a.	n.a.	[1,515]	[25.6]	n.a.	n.a.
Uros	49	1.7	—	—	—	—
Total	2,801	99.9	5,905	100.0	8,351	100.0

Note: These figures exclude Taraco, Pusi, and Poto.

Sources: Macera, Tierra y población, 161–62; Choquehuanca, Ensayo, 15–54.

for the registration of various plots of agricultural land in the ayllu Silluta of the parcialidad Urinsaya in Puno's departmental property registry. He explained that his title went back through several generations to Mateo Turpo, who had acquired the land sometime in the colonial period by composition before the Protector de Indios Francisco de Mina in Potosí.[57]

As the crown interfered more and more with communal land tenure, only land held outside the community guaranteed relatively safe possession to the peasant. Private ownership of land among Indian peasants was one of the signs of the penetration of Spanish property norms and concepts of the individual's position within society into the indigenous Andean world. At times peasants acquired land and herds as a basis for challenging a kuraka for office.[58] It appears that the peasants accumulating land in fee simple often came from the ranks of the principales, the highest communal officeholders, or the kurakas.[59] Private landholding by Indian peasants must have reached considerable proportions in late colonial Azángaro.[60] Only thus can we explain the paradoxical combination of low population density, incipient hacienda formation, and the scarcity of communal land. Private landholding introduced a new type of socioeconomic differentiation into the ranks of the Indian peasantry.[61]

The Exploitation of the Indigenous Peasantry

The system of colonial exploitation in rural provinces such as Azángaro continued to be "indirect" until the end of the colonial period. Surplus was extracted from the indigenous peasantry in the form of payments in kind, of money, and of labor while leaving the majority of the colonial subjects in their own agrarian society. All members of the provincial elite, from the representatives of the crown to priests, kurakas, and private entrepreneurs, used their authority over the Indian population to benefit personally. Civil and ecclesiastical administration was inextricably intertwined with private appropriation. At the same time, only a minority of Indians suffered "direct exploitation" as servile laborers on the rural estates, in the mines, or in manufactories.

The two major ways by which the colonial administration extracted surplus from the Indian community peasants were the head tax and obligatory labor services. During the eighteenth century tribute rates continued to vary from province to province.[62] The tribute rate of the *corregimientos* of the northern altiplano was relatively low. In 1779 the Protector of Indians of the Audiencia of Lima, Dr. Baquijano, pointed out that the Indian communal lands there were extremely scarce—much below legal allotments—and that "because of [the land's] sterility and frequent floods [*irrupciones*]" it was "nearly useless and infertile." As a result, Indians in the province of Paucarcolla were suffering scarcities, and "far from being able to harvest the crops in order to trade with them, in most instances they are lacking them even for their own sustenance, so that they are forced to maintain themselves with wild herbs." Concurring with the Indians' petition, he suggested reducing their tribute rates.[63]

Tribute collection was the responsibility of the kurakas, who were to turn over the moneys semiannually to the corregidores. This system resulted in a great number of abuses against both crown and commoners. In 1762 the Indians from three ayllus in Muñani, province of Azángaro, complained that their Cacique Diego Choquehuanca had hidden various Indians from being entered into the tribute list so that he could collect the tribute for his own account, that he was charging up to two pesos tribute per semester from twelve-year-old boys (legally exempt), and that he took a tribute of three pesos per semester from his yanaconas, whom he temporarily declared to be originarios.[64]

The other major obligation imposed on community Indians by the crown consisted of forced labor services, or mita. The Spanish colonial administration justified the continued and, indeed, much expanded use of this Incaic institution by reference to the supposed tendency of the Indians to idleness and the assumed need of forced labor for the realm's "public good."[65] Sanctioned and administered by the colonial government, mita labor mostly benefited private economic enterprises. It was used in mines, agricultural and livestock estates, and textile sweatshops. Employment in public activities, such as public construction, the postal service, and *tambos* (way stations and inns), was of secondary importance.[66] In the mining mita one-seventh of the adult male population of an Indian community served one-year turns as mitayos. Beginning in the sixteenth century, Azángaro belonged to the sixteen corregimientos, which sent mitayos to the silver mines of Potosí.

The Potosí mita had a tremendous social and economic impact on the Indian peoples of the altiplano. After the mournful *kacharparis* (dances of parting) had been performed, the several hundred mitayos assembled in the provincial capital set out on their two-month, 600-kilometer trek to the mines. Accompanied by their wives and children, they took along llamas to transport household utensils, corn, and potatoes and some alpacas for meat. George Kubler has estimated that the Potosí mita from Chucuito province alone involved the movement of thirty thousand to fifty thousand animals each year. At the end of their turn many mitayos did not return to their communities, some having died while others stayed in Potosí.[67] During the seventeenth century the number of mitayos arriving in Potosí declined sharply, recovering somewhat following the 1730s. Many peasants now paid a fee to the mine owners in lieu of their labor obligations.[68]

By the eighteenth century parish priests had become powerful figures in the altiplano, benefiting greatly from their authority over Indian parishioners. They charged for every service performed—baptisms, marriages, and funerals—and forced individual members of the Indian communities to take charge of fitting out the yearly celebrations in honor of the patron saints. The Indian who received this responsibility had to pay for some new ornament for the patron saint, to provide food and drink for all celebrants, to hire musicians, and, last but not least, to pay a fee to the priest.[69] Such exactions often indebted the peasants, a situation from which they could extract themselves only by selling some of their lands or animals or by obliging themselves to work for the priest. Priests also operated as merchants, using their Indian parishioners as a captive market, although these practices were outlawed by the church. Priests often came from poor families, and their legal sources of income did not suffice to afford them a comfortable living, particularly if they had to support an illegitimate family.[70]

The unique position of kurakas in Peruvian colonial society—privileged leaders of indigenous society and representatives of Spanish colonial authority—offered them many opportunities to enrich themselves legally and illegally through various extractions from the Indian communities. Nicolás Sánchez Albornóz has noted that as early as the end of the seventeenth century the indigenous population of the altiplano showed particular frustration and anger about the exploitation it suffered at the hands of its own ethnic lords.[71] During the eighteenth century community Indians from Azángaro frequently brought suit against their kurakas before the Audiencia of Charcas.[72] Their accusations show the breadth of economic roles of a powerful kuraka in the altiplano, ranging from owner of estates, to local official imbued with authority by the viceroy to collect tribute and to dispatch mitayos, to merchant trading in locally produced and imported goods. Diego Choquehuanca's extraordinary ability to accumulate private wealth depended on his access to and control of the indigenous peasantry, both in the communities whose spokesperson he was supposed to be and on his own estates. By the mid-eighteenth century Choquehuanca's authority was not based solely on ties of kinship and reciprocal trust any more. Community Indians brought litigation against what they felt to be excessive exactions by their kuraka and routinely sought to escape compliance with these exactions, resistance for which they often received brutal punishment. Many kurakas behaved toward the indigenous peasantry in some ways as entrepreneurs, employing their crown-sanctioned authority for private ends, just as other members of the colonial provincial elite did.[73]

The infamous repartos de bienes by corregidores, which became such a heavy burden on Peru's indigenous peasantry during the eighteenth century, were by no means an unparalleled abuse. Still, corregidores practiced the reparto and other mercantile transactions forced on the indigenous peasantry on a larger scale than kurakas or priests did. As early as 1649 the revenues of the corregidor of Azángaro accruing from his commercial activities—sale of wine in the province and of locally produced sheep and saddle bags in High Peru—amounted to thirty thousand pesos for a two-year period.[74]

The eighteenth century saw a tremendous increase in the amount of goods distributed among the Indian peasantry. Recognizing that the salaries that the viceregal administration could afford to pay the corregidores were insufficient, the reform of the *repartimiento* system in 1751–56 for the first time legalized the practice, limited and defined by specific schedules.[75] The schedule for Azángaro permitted sales amounting to 114,500 pesos during a five-year term of office.[76] This meant an expenditure of about ten pesos for every Indian man, woman, and child every five years, or about 45 pesos per family. In comparison, such a family might have been paying anywhere from thirty-six to eighty pesos in tribute payments during a similar five-year period.[77] Corregidores, however, were not content to sell goods limited to the amount and price established by the schedule.[78] In 1771, before the completion of his term, the corregidor of

Azángaro, Fernando Inclán y Valdez, had already distributed "Castilian clothes, locally produced clothes, and mules" for 43,293 pesos in the parish of Asillo alone. When on top of these sales he carried out another distribution of forty-five mules for a further 1,440 pesos, the *cacica y gobernadora* of Asillo, Polonia Fernández Hidalgo, petitioned the Audiencia of Charcas to order the corregidor to take back this last reparto because the Indians still owed 23,000 pesos on the previously distributed goods. The excessive forced purchases had made it impossible for the Indians to pay their tribute on time. The cacica also reminded the authorities that Asillo's population was much smaller than that of the parish of Azángaro. The Audiencia of Charcas admonished the corregidor to limit his repartos to the amount permitted by the schedule and not to sell the Indians anything against their will.[79] But it is doubtful that this order changed his practices. Even the previous distributions of goods in Asillo, a parish accounting for about one-sixth of the province's Indian population, meant that Inclán had probably sold goods for about 260,000 pesos in the whole province of Azángaro, more than twice the amount permitted by the tariff.

The repartos de bienes were particularly odious to the Indians because of some of the ways that they were carried out: the very high prices of the goods sold by the corregidor against the low prices of the goods that the corregidor bought from the peasants; the uselessness of some articles that the Indians were forced to buy (even the mules, the most important article in the Azángaro distribution, were of rather dubious utility to them, well equipped as they were with the cheaper llamas as transport animals); and the use of distributed mules for transporting the merchandise of the corregidor without compensation.[80] In the course of the eighteenth century Azángaro's peasants repeatedly fought against the obligations imposed on them by the corregidores' forced sales. In 1741 this struggle led to a rebellion against corregidor Alfonso Santa.[81] In 1780, when Gregorio de Cangas classified all corregimientos in Peru according to their profitability, he commented that, although Azángaro was a first-class corregimiento, it was among the worst of the viceroyalty because of the cold climate and the "bellicosity of its inhabitants."[82]

Kurakas, priests, corregidores, and owners of estates all based the economic foundation of their elite status on the extraction of surplus from the community Indians. Because all of these provincial elites were relying on the same Indian peasants as "economic resource" and frequently proceeded illegally in their dealings, it was essential for the functioning of the whole system that they cooperate among each other. There is much evidence for such collusion between corregidores, kurakas, and priests.[83] It could take many different forms—for example, "profit sharing" between kuraka and corregidor from the tributes they retained by falsifying tribute lists.[84] If for any reason cooperation between the various elite sectors broke down, their control and exploitation of the indigenous peasantry was endangered.

The Late Colonial Crisis

After the second quarter of the eighteenth century, with the renewed growth of the altiplano's Indian population, many forastero families faced a mounting land shortage. Originarios became more reluctant to share their communal land base with growing numbers of newcomers or second and third sons of originario and forastero families already settled in the communities. Colonial administrators in charge of the periodic redistributions of community lands agreed with the originarios that the lands were too scarce to include all landless Indians in the redistribution. During the 1770s and 1780s concern over scarcity of land as a cause for the Indian peasants' impoverishment became widespread.[85]

Even though conflicts over land had been on the rise during the preceding decades both among the various groups within the communities and between Indian peasants and the expanding hacienda sector, claims of land scarcity in the altiplano of the late eighteenth century remain puzzling from today's perspective. After all, Azángaro's population density was still quite low, and land in and of itself continued to be of little value. Furthermore, despite the establishment of new estates during the first three quarters of the eighteenth century, their numbers and total acreage remained modest compared to the situation in the early twentieth century. Indeed, conservative estimates would suggest that the peasantry controlled at least 50 percent of the agriculturally useful land in Azángaro until the end of the colonial period.

The puzzle can be disentangled only if we consider the effects of the growing level of exploitation to which most groups of peasants were subjected in the course of the eighteenth century. Payments and services owed to the representatives of crown and church as well as to other members of the provincial elite forced Indians to sell or slaughter increasing numbers of their animals.[86] By the 1770s the reliance on livestock for paying tribute, debts from corregidores' repartos, and other exactions, inevitable for peasants whose primary income came from animal husbandry, impeded the natural growth of the herds and may have depleted them. Royal officials, in any case not too intent on seeing those causes of the Indians' poverty linked to the socioeconomic system that they represented, attributed the stagnation of livestock herds to the "infertility" of the altiplano's soil and assumed that the pastures simply could not support more animals. From there it was only a further step to conclude that the peasants' access to land had become dangerously insufficient.

In the decades prior to the Túpac Amaru Rebellion of the early 1780s, Azángaro's provincial elite—corregidores, priests, kurakas, and hispanized large landholders—had increased the extraction of surplus from the indigenous peasant economy just when the viceregal administration levied new taxes on Indians and extended their incidence. This apparent tightening of the squeeze led to what might be termed "overexploitation," with serious consequences for the whole fabric of society. The collusion between the various sectors of the elite was breaking down in the scramble for the limited income that could be derived from indigenous labor, land, and production. In the report to his successor, written in 1776, Viceroy Amat y Junient expressed his concern over the damages caused by the actions of corregidores:

> Not only the Indians but also the respectable citizens
> who . . . possess haciendas in the provinces suffer much
> damage [from the repartos of corregidores], because the greed
> of the corregidores reaches their mayordomos and workers; the
> corregidores oblige them to make considerable payments for
> their servants and yanaconas and if they don't follow suit,
> they bother them, apprehend them and separate them from
> their work . . . and if they complain bitterly, the corregidores
> treat them as rioters.[87]

In Azángaro a severe conflict between the family of kuraka Diego Choquehuanca and the corregidor, Lorenzo Sata y Zubiría, surfaced immediately after the repression of the Túpac Amaru Rebellion. In December 1782 the corregidor was using the provincial militia to stop the Choquehuancas from requisitioning from several Indian communities thousands of heads of livestock that the kuraka family claimed to have been stolen from its estates during the rebellion. The kuraka's son, Joséf Choquehuanca, called the corregidor "our capital enemy" and refused to carry out further repartos; he was imprisoned but was later cleared of all charges by the Audiencia of Charcas.[88]

This type of struggle between various sectors of southern Peru's colonial provincial elite tended to destabilize control over and exploitation of the indigenous peasantry. The Indians could appeal—with some hope of being heard—for help against abuses by one authority to another authority. Fights between corregidores, kurakas, priests, and other members of the provincial elite allowed the audiencia to uncover illegal practices, hitherto hushed up by the collusion between all those profiting from them. This weakening of elite cohesion facilitated the Túpac Amaru Rebellion of

1780–1782. In the altiplano, peasant participation in the rebellion was directed as much against abuses by corregidores, kurakas, and hispanized large landholders as it was against the heavier burden of taxation that the viceregal administration attempted to impose on most sectors of Peru's society.[89]

One of the first steps that authorities in Lima took to contain the rebellion in 1780 was to outlaw repartos de bienes by corregidores.[90] After initially allowing the corregidores to stay in office until the end of their five-year terms, a decree of August 5, 1783, ordered their immediate removal.[91] Nevertheless, in Azángaro repartos continued until the end of the colonial era, albeit on a diminished scale, under the officials replacing the corregidores, the *subdelegados*. In 1789 the subdelegados of Azángaro, Lampa, and Carabaya misused funds from the royal treasury to distribute mules and cloth for 60,000 pesos among the Indians of their provinces.[92]

In spite of its military defeat, the Túpac Amaru Rebellion ushered in a number of lasting changes in the altiplano. The position of the kurakas was weakened, a measure taken by the viceregal administration not so much to control abuses by the indigenous Andean nobility of their subjects as to prevent these privileged members of colonial society from ever leading an uprising again. The office of cacicazgo was no longer to be hereditary; instead, crown officials were ordered to appoint "men of good character" known to be loyal to the Spanish king; they might even be Spaniards.[93] In many communities kurakas were also to cede their official powers, including the collection of tributes, to *alcaldes y recaudadores de tributo*.[94]

In Azángaro the clan of the Choquehuancas now saw the beginning of the decline of its power and wealth. This decline was probably caused as much by the destruction the rebellion wrought on their properties as it was by the new legal restrictions placed on their office. Most of the family's livestock haciendas had been burned and looted by the rebels, and several family members were killed. Beginning in the 1790s, even before the death of Diego Choquehuanca in 1796, the family had dissipated its energy in lawsuits between the numerous descendants of the old kuraka.[95] The Mango Turpo family also suffered losses during the rebellion. After a long bureaucratic process the Viceroy of Buenos Aires named Tomas Mango kuraka of the parcialidad Anansaya of Asillo some time between 1786 and 1790. But already in July of that year another principal Indian from Asillo contested his appointment on the ground that the Mango Turpos were practicing "extortions, abuses, and outrages" against the community Indians.[96]

The rebellion had an impact on land tenure in the altiplano that has not been fully recognized by scholars.[97] Túpac Amaru's troops and independent peasant bands occupied many haciendas during the fifteen months of uninterrupted control of Azángaro and neighboring provinces.[98] In some instances—for example, during the uprising in Oruro in February–March 1781—the Indian peasants forced the owners of haciendas to sign notarial contracts making the peasants the legal owners of such hacienda lands.[99] In Azángaro the titles of private and church estancias were burned.[100] Of course, much land spontaneously occupied by Indian peasants during the rebellion was taken back afterward by the previous holders. But many Spanish residents of the region had been killed or had permanently left the altiplano. The gaps in the ranks of Azángaro's landholding elite began to be filled by new landholders, of creole and mestizo origin, as early as the last four decades of the colonial era; in contrast, in those regions of the viceroyalty not affected by the rebellion this process took place only in the decades following the Wars of Independence.

At the same time, some of the land occupied by rebelling peasants was never reclaimed. A report on the Intendency of Puno from 1803 still described the whole Collao as "very depopulated of Spanish people and of other castas [mixed races] since the time of the rebellion by Túpac Amaru and the Cataris."[101] Only eight peninsular or creole families resided in Azángaro town in 1813.[102] Both private and ecclesiastical estates were affected by the rebellion. In 1799, nearly two decades after the defeat of Túpac Amaru, Indian peasants still occupied land in the northern altiplano that had been claimed by parish churches and convents before the rebellion. Many church estates were reduced to half their previous size. The livestock capital of the estates was now suffering "great losses each year" because of scarce pastures. One contemporary source noted that even though royal judges repeatedly had ordered peasants to return these lands to the church, "it has not been possible to confine them to their just borders. This toleration of the abuse is gradually spreading so much that in a short while those estancias will cease to exist and with them the Divine Worship and the spiritual guidance offered for the benefit of the same Indians."[103] Peasants used the chaos of the long months of rebellion and the disarray into which Azángaro's church fell during the following years (with at least one parish priest tried as an accomplice of the rebels) to undo what had happened throughout much of the eighteenth century: the incorporation of communal lands informally granted to parishes and lay brotherhoods into livestock estates.

The rate of legally sanctioned sales and compositions of crown lands, including the lands in usufruct of the Indian communities, slowed down after the Túpac Amaru rebellion. Applying enlightened notions of landed property and productive, independent farmers, the Ordenanza de Intendentes of 1782 gave the intendants the power to investigate land titles and correct abusive appropriations of communal lands. The intendants were to name judges and land measurers in each partido, and their decisions could be appealed to the Junta Superior de Real Hacienda in Lima. But given the great amount of de facto land appropriations during the eighteenth century, these regulations caused so many complaints and protests that Viceroy de la Croix suspended them.[104] Consequently, between the late 1780s and at least 1816 the viceregal administration expedited legal titles of sale or composition of crown lands only in "very rare cases."[105]

Nevertheless, during the administration of José González y Montoya as intendant of Puno between 1801 and 1806, new sales of community lands were carried out, some of them in Azángaro. In November 1802 Nicolás Montesinos, Alcalde Recaudador de Tributos of Asillo, petitioned the intendant for the composition and sale of Estancia Caiconi in his favor. Montesinos claimed that this estancia, located some forty kilometers northeast of Asillo in the foothills of the Cordillera de Carabaya, constituted unoccupied crown land (*baldíos*). Witnesses supported his claim. They explained that "by custom" the land had been held by the "caciques y recaudadores de tributos" of Asillo as long as they could remember. Whenever a new man occupied that position, he assumed possession of Caiconi as appurtenance of the office, without any claims of hereditary rights by the heirs of his predecessors. The witnesses, all Spanish residents of Asillo, were a bit vague about the rights of the Indian community to the estancia lands. One flatly declared that "the *común* of the Indians of ayllu Hila where said estancia is located never possessed it." But according to another witness, "The community Indians never benefited from [the lands of Caiconi], although it is said that it belongs to the community." All witnesses agreed, however, that a change in the "property regime" of Caiconi would not hurt the community Indians, since they never benefited from it in the first place; moreover, they owned enough crop and pasture lands. On the contrary, they emphasized, the composition and sale of Caiconi would remove the detriment that the Royal Treasury had suffered because taxes had never been paid on the land.

The royal authorities in Azángaro and Puno accordingly went through all the customary steps of conferring title over Caiconi to Montesinos, including a public offering of the land by a town crier in loud voice on the plaza of Asillo on nine different occasions. After Montesinos had paid the determined value of the estancia into the royal treasury at Chucuito some time in 1803, the matter was sent on to Lima for the expedition of the title by the Junta Superior de Hacienda. There, however, it was held up, and although Montesinos was in possession of Caiconi, by 1807 he still had not been granted title.[106] A decree of the Junta Superior of August 19, 1809, declared the sales and compositions expedited under Intendant González in Puno null and void. Nevertheless, by April 1813 the cabildo of Azángaro, "composed mostly of loyal Indians that have grown old in the service to the Sovereign," complained that many of the communal lands sold illegally under the auspices of González had still not been returned to the community Indians.[107]

These struggles over land during the decades after the Túpac Amaru Rebellion present evidence for the changes occurring in the notion of property and the rise of a new quality of conflicts between Indian and Spanish sectors of altiplano colonial society. Parishes, kurakas, and even private creole or mestizo residents had initially received usufruct rights to pasturelands from Indian communities for circumscribed and well-defined purposes: parishes were allowed to use the products from the sheep, cattle, or cameloids that would be pastured there in support of a hospital, a special parish fund, or the outfitting of a patron saint; a kuraka would be granted lands as appurtenance of his office in recognition of the reciprocal services that he was assumed to render for the community; creoles and mestizos might build rural chapels whose upkeep would naturally be supported by the surrounding lands.[108]

For the Indian communities land-use rights had not been based on universalistic notions of property but rather on highly specific arrangements that tied material control over land to the maintenance of mutual obligations between the community and the person or institution benefiting from the usufruct.[109] In the course of the eighteenth century this notion of land use was challenged by the colonial authorities and the provincial elites, a development that originated both in the attempt to achieve more effective control over livestock operations and in enlightened property concepts. If the beneficiary of traditional use rights began to construct a building complex on the land and treated the shepherds, whom the community had customarily dispatched as part of what it perceived as mutual obligations, as yanaconas, the community would consider this a breach of the customary use rights and initiate measures to restore the old status. Peasants would drive livestock onto the now disputed pastures, and the community would file petitions and suits with the authorities.

Before the 1780s communities in the altiplano seem to have had little success with such measures. The provincial elites were relatively united, and the authorities were as yet not overly concerned about presumed scarcities of land for the peasants and instead saw every composition in favor of an individual property holder as a step toward a more rational economic order. By the 1780s this situation had changed. Infighting between corregidores or subdelegados, priests, kurakas, and estate owners created opportunities for the communities to recover land against an enfeebled opposition. They could hope to find a receptive ear at court and among higher-level officialdom. Fear about the explosive consequences of a presumed peasant land shortage led to the curtailment of alienations of community lands.

Of equal importance for turning the tide may have been the fact that the interest in expanding livestock estates or incorporating new ones dropped off considerably after the 1780s as demand for livestock products stagnated or even declined. Around 1810, for example, the hacendado Gregorio Choquehuanca, son of the deceased kuraka Diego and canon at the cathedral chapter in Chuquisaca, allowed several indigenous families to enjoy the usufruct of estancias that he considered "integral parts" of his hacienda Ccalla in Azángaro parish without forcing these families to lend their services as yanaconas.[110]

Nevertheless, for the poorest Indian peasants, forasteros, and younger children of originarios, access to land remained precarious during the remainder of the colonial period. A growing number of them abandoned their communities in which they had lived for generations. In part this was the consequence of a series of social and natural calamities. Following on the heels of the rebellion, the northern altiplano was struck by a drought between 1782 and 1784 that led to crop failures, further reduction of livestock herds, and death by starvation of many people.[111] In 1784, more than a year after the effective pacification of the region, the prices of several staple foods—including corn, flour, and legumes—reached all-time high levels in the Collao.[112]

As food became scarce, Indians sought opportunities to earn a few reales through engaging in petty trade, working as servants, or attending to travelers on the roads.[113] The new century brought no relief. An angina epidemic in 1802–3 killed one-tenth of the province's population, and the Wars of Independence saw massive recruitments of Azángaro's Indians, mostly by the royalists, as early as 1810–11. In conjunction with harsh frosts throughout southern Peru, in 1814 and 1816 the disruptions of the military campaigns brought about food shortages so severe that, according to José Domingo Choquehuanca, Azángaro's streets and countryside were filled with corpses of starved people.[114]

Vagrancy, as contemporary authorities called the increasing mobility among the indigenous population of the altiplano, had other causes as well.[115] According to one source, during the negotiations of Diego Cristóbal Túpac Amaru with Mariscal del Valle about a general pardon in late 1781, "the people of Azángaro were filled with so much despair when they heard that the corregidores were returning" that many families left for the eastern escarpment of the Andes in Carabaya and Apolo (modern Bolivia) with their livestock and belongings.[116] Fleeing to the rims of the Spanish colonized realm had always been a method of evading excessive burdens heaped on the Indians by colonial authorities. Some crown officials had long expressed their fear that abusive repartos, increased crown taxation, and church fees might induce Indians to withdraw to the "barbarous and disloyal nations."[117]

But there existed another and probably more frequent expression of "vagrancy" among the poorest peasants in the altiplano: precarious squatting on underutilized lands. In his description in 1790 of the bishopric of Cuzco, of which the partido of Azángaro formed the southernmost part, Pablo José Oricaín described this phenomenon with dramatic detail:

> No less painful is the fact that many Indians move about, astray
> in the steepest and most arid mountain regions, together with
> their families and livestock, under the pretext of bringing the
> animals from one pasture to the other. They wander around
> carrying some short sticks; wherever they find a source of water
> and sufficient pasture, they build a temporary shelter until the
> residents of that place oblige them to render services or rents;
> when they perceive any formal obligations, they take apart their
> hut and move on to another jurisdiction, and in this manner they
> migrate from one place to the next.[118]

A growing number of forasteros and children of originarios with no or insufficient land took precarious possession of any pastures not fully or permanently used by those individuals or institutions deemed to have rights to them. These could be lands which communities considered to belong to them but which the crown considered *baldíos*, or outlying stretches of estates recently formed by private landholders, kurakas, or the parishes, which were underutilized and had uncertain titles. Squatting allowed the poorest peasants to escape, albeit in a fragile and precarious fashion, the two conditions that threatened their livelihood most seriously: lack of land and the heavy burden of taxes and fees.

The weakening of various sectors of the southern sierra's colonial elite beginning in the early 1780s may have decreased the control over the Indian peasantry as a labor force, in spite of stringent antivagrancy decrees.[119] With the abolition of the repartos de bienes, continued on a smaller scale and with less regularity by the subdelegados, one of the most powerful mechanisms of obliging peasants to work outside of their communities or sell commodities to hispanized traders had ceased to be effective. That the abolition of repartos would lead to less production and labor by the Indians for the benefit of hacendados, merchants, caciques, and priests was precisely the concern that prompted Visitor General Escobedo to advocate a renewal of official trade with the Indians under the euphemistic label of *socorros*, a plan soon abandoned for fear of leading to new revolts.[120] Crown policy toward the Indians had to steer a course between the Scylla of overly heavy surplus extraction, leading to the partial or total withdrawal of Indians from the colonial order, and the Charybdis of limiting such extractions too severely, allowing the peasantry too much autonomy to the inevitable detriment of the interests of the primary constituents of the colonial regime in the rural Andes, the provincial elites. But under the critical conditions that had arisen by the early 1780s the crown felt forced to adopt a path out of this dilemma that aimed at establishing a stronger direct cash nexus between the Indian peasantry and the crown and limiting surplus extractions by the provincial elites.

While the burden of repartos and extractions by kurakas was reduced, tribute payments in the northern altiplano rose dramatically, especially in the second half of the 1780s (fig. 3.1).[121] These increases can be attributed only in part to Indian population growth. Tribute revenue in the region's treasury districts grew fifteenfold between the 1750s and the mid-1820s, several times the rate of Indian population growth. The difference finds its explanation in improved and more systematic means of collection, an effort that began in the 1750s but culminated in the 1780s, when alcaldes y recaudadores de tributo in many cases took over from the kurakas.[122] Legally barred from carrying out repartos, the subdelegados, who had replaced the corregidores as the highest authorities in the provinces, had a keen personal interest in maximizing tribute collections, as they retained 3 percent of the taxes paid. It seems no mere coincidence that tribute payments should dramatically increase precisely during the decade after the forced trade with Indians had been outlawed and legal trade in the altiplano—in contrast to other areas of Peru—stagnated, as evidenced by the leveling off of alcabala receipts.

In sum, the decades between the outbreak of the Túpac Amaru Rebellion and the demise of the Spanish colonial regime represented the first phase of a long era of transformation for the agrarian economy and society of the altiplano. It had its origins in a multifaceted crisis that undermined the viability of the colonial order firmly established since the Toledan reforms of the 1570s. This order had largely been based on the "indirect" exploitation of the community peasantry, the extraction of surplus in the form of commodities, labor, and money from their formally autonomous economy through the mediation of the colonial authorities. The disruption of the regional trade circuits; the weakening cohesion of the provincial elite;

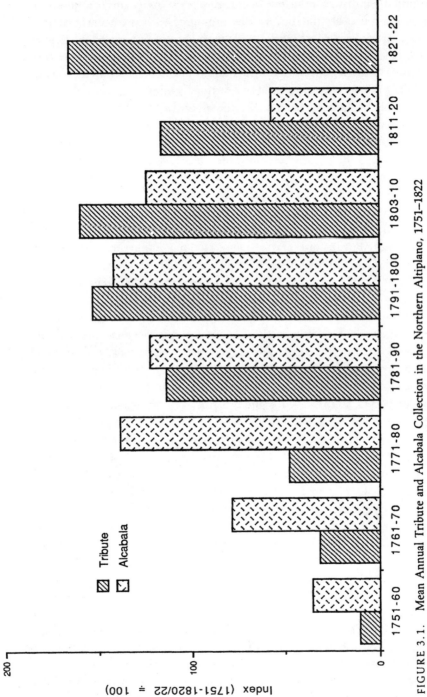

FIGURE 3.1. Mean Annual Tribute and Alcabala Collection in the Northern Altiplano, 1751–1822

Note: Up to 1800: cajas reales of Carabaya and Chucuito; from 1803: caja real of Puno.

Source: TePaske and Klein, *Royal Treasuries* 1:88–101, 446–52; 2:86–99.

the population increase in the Indian communities and the concomitant internal conflicts over land; the shift from informal exploitation of peasant lands through kurakas, priests, and private mestizos and creoles to their growing incorporation into formalized estate operations; and the impact of the Bourbons' "enlightened despotic" fiscal and agrarian policies—all contributed to undermine the established colonial order.

Beginning in the 1780s, members of all social groups in the altiplano were groping to redefine their economic operation and the relations among each other, while the outlines of the new order remained blurred. Estate owners, kurakas, priests, and hispanized traders entered a phase of difficulty and instability as their trade with High Peru shrank, their control over the peasant economy weakened, and the Bourbons increasingly blocked the consolidation of their landholdings.

For the peasants of the altiplano the decades between the 1780s and the early 1820s must have appeared as perplexingly "chiaroscuro," as Eric Van Young has noted for New Spain. For them this era brought increasing bureaucratic interference in such communal affairs as the appointment of kurakas and the disposal of communal pastures and crop lands. With the connivance of colonial administrators, properties belonging to the old community chests were often appropriated by mestizos and creoles who had rented them,[123] and the collection of tribute among those peasants who had not left their communities continued at a very high level until the beginning of the Wars of Independence.

Yet in many ways the onset of the crisis also strengthened the autonomy of the altiplano peasantry. The forced repartos de bienes, a crucial aspect of the colonial order at least since the late seventeenth century, had been greatly reduced, and private entrepreneurs found it more difficult to harness the peasant economy for their own advantage. The ambiguous agrarian policy of the Bourbons finally stopped the consolidation of newly formed private estates and the incorporation of further communal lands into entrenched ones; and although the crown policy of limiting communal landholdings to a specified amount per household had contributed to serious land shortages within the communities, the blockage of further hacienda expansion into what authorities declared to be baldíos indirectly favored the temporary appropriation of such lands by peasant squatters. There were also serious limits to the effectiveness of the attempted greater control of the peasantry through colonial authorities. Their removal from lands that the crown deemed to belong to the royal domain or private and church owners largely failed, and during the critical years of the "Napoleonic captivity" of Spain's monarchy, Azángaro's Indians successfully exploited new legislation to stymie tax collection for over a year.[124]

In rural areas such as the northern altiplano, then, the order that Bourbon reformers in Lima and Madrid hoped to create began to be choked by the contradictions of their own policies. These were epitomized by a legal scarcity of land for peasants in a region of low population density, a region where land was so plentiful that it had no exchange value distinct from the livestock flocks that it could nourish. Before the contours of the new, "liberal" order could emerge under commercial and political conditions more favorable to hispanized estate owners, traders, and the new provincial authorities of the republic, it was the peasants who benefited most from the uncertainty. Achieving, for the time being, an equilibrium with the colonial elites that had pressed on communal resources, their broadened autonomy gave them a brief breathing space that was to prove vital to their capacity to cope with the intense pressures of the rejuvenated provincial elites after 1850.

4   The Oligarchization
of Liberal Visions

A few years after Peru's independence, José Domingo Choquehuanca drew a somber picture of the decay and impoverishment of Azángaro province. Most adobe houses in the towns were in bad repair, "and if one tried to sell, there would be no one to buy, which results from the depopulation and the poverty of the area." All but a handful of mines were abandoned. And the "very few" estates dedicated to ranching, "the wealth of the province," were languishing, and nobody would undertake their improvement "because of ignorance, insufficient capital, or lack of application."[1]

In part Choquehuanca was expressing the frustration of one who loved his homeland in the face of the crisis that had befallen the economy and the very social order of the altiplano during the preceding decades. But a new element also colored his perception: he portrayed the state of the province from the vantage of his liberal convictions. He reported on the natural wealth of the altiplano and on its impoverishment due to flawed human institutions. The tyranny of the recently defeated Spanish regime, the heavy and still growing burden of the church on the livestock industry, and the ignorance and superstition of the Indian peasantry were to blame for the pitiful state of affairs. If these obstacles were removed, then the virtuous propensity toward self-improvement of estate owner, artisan, trader, and peasant alike would surely lead to affluence in Azángaro, as promised by the province's rich natural endowments for mining, livestock raising, fishing, industry, and commerce. Indeed, Choquehuanca noted that some of the better citizens were already beginning to adopt the customs of enlightened society.

Choquehuanca's treatise on Azángaro, published in 1831, aptly reflected the historical moment. In the thrall of an epochal crisis that touched most aspects of the social, political, and economic order of the northern altiplano,

107

the leading citizens of the region were beginning to envision more clearly the direction in which they wanted things to move in order to achieve stability and affluence. But it would take another quarter century before a liberal agrarian regime was firmly established in the Peruvian altiplano, freed from the hindrances and ambiguities of the late colonial order yet distant from the hopeful visions of the immediate postindependence years. In the meantime, under the deceptive surface of political chaos and economic stagnation, important shifts were affecting the patterns of land tenure and social stratification in the region.

The Languishing Estates

During the period immediately following independence hacendados and other members of the hispanized elite showed little interest in acquiring lands from Indian peasants. Rather, the greatest activity of sales and purchases, as well as leases, occurred within the estate sector.[2] For many old, established families in the altiplano and in Cuzco, economic difficulties caused by commercial dislocation and war-related losses had become so pressing that they could not hold on to their estates. The composition of Azángaro's landholding elite changed considerably during the decades following the termination of the Wars of Independence. By 1825 those creole hacendado families who had accumulated landholdings in Azángaro on the basis of sixteenth-century encomiendas had disappeared from the province.[3] Of the thirty-eight families represented among the fifty officers · of Azángaro's militia regiment in 1806, by midcentury at least nine had vanished from the ranks of provincial hacendados.[4] Among the owners of large estates it was especially members of the colonial Cuzqueño patriciate who were giving up their haciendas in the altiplano, a process that had begun even before independence. Other families, while remaining residents of Azángaro, lost estates or saw their holdings splintered through inheritance to numerous heirs. Notable among these were the Choquehuanca and Mango families, who suffered from the abolition of the office of cacicazgo on July 4, 1825, and from interminable legal struggles over inheritance.[5]

Between the 1810s and 1840s individuals or families from outside the province acquired estates in Azángaro. Most of these newcomers could rely on income from a military position, an administrative office, or an ecclesiastical appointment or had accumulated some wealth as traders before becoming landholders in the altiplano.[6] Francisco Lizares, for example, a creole born in Urubamba near Cuzco before the turn of the century, was a sergeant major in the royal army well into the Wars of Independence.[7]

He appeared in Azángaro sometime during the early 1820s. During the following three decades Lizares managed to lay the foundations for two separate lineages of Azangarino hacendado families. At the time of his death around 1850, his wife, Juliana Montesinos, a native Azangarina, and their three legitimate daughters—Maria Dolores, Augustina, and Antonia Lizares Montesinos—inherited four small to medium-sized haciendas in the districts of Azángaro and Arapa stocked with more than 1,700 head of sheep and 140 cows. Lizares had been granted two of these estates in emphyteusis for 150 years by the church between 1829 and the 1830s.[8] Like other men of limited means, Lizares was taking the first step toward building up sizable landholdings: the short-term rental or, preferably, long-term lease of a church hacienda.

Building on the inheritance from Francisco Lizares and his mistress Josefa Quiñones, Lizares's illegitimate son, José Maria Lizares Quiñones, became one of the wealthiest and most powerful men in Azángaro during the second half of the nineteenth century. The origin of the possession of most of his numerous estates is clouded, but as early as 1840 Francisco Lizares was expanding the small hacienda Muñani Chico—owned by Josefa Quiñones, a woman of some notoriety in Azángaro's provincial society—by purchases from neighboring peasants. This hacienda was to become a sprawling estate during the late nineteenth century and the centerpiece of the vast landholdings of the Lizares Quiñones.[9]

Another newcomer, Manuel Ruperto Estévez, had worked as a merchant in Arequipa during the final years of colonial rule. From there he conducted a substantial trade in European goods and coca leaves with Cuzco and the altiplano. He became administrator of Puno's departmental treasury during the 1830s and in 1846 purchased Hacienda Huasacona, district Muñani, from Juliana Aragón vda. de Riquelme, whose family had acquired the estate only during the 1830s.[10] The livestock capital of Huasacona, which had been one of the province's important estates since the seventeenth century, amounted to 15,000 *ovejas madres en reduccion*, or units of sheep. (Abbreviated OMR, this figure was the basic unit for tallying livestock.) For such a sizable purchase Estévez relied on his own wealth as well as lines of credit from outside the province.[11] Like most affluent hacendados, he never resided on his estate or even lived in the province. Two years after purchasing Huasacona he leased it to a notable from Muñani, who operated it for decades.[12]

During the two decades following the occupation of Lima by San Martín in July 1821, successive Peruvian administrations confiscated property belonging to peninsular Spaniards as well as religious and civil institutions. It has long been assumed that the early Peruvian state played a significant role in changing the composition of Peru's class of large landholders by distributing confiscated estates through donations, sales, or adjudications to private citizens. This redistribution presumably helped the public treasury and created "a new republican landholding aristocracy" indebted to particular administrations.[13] Although such redistribution may have been frequent on the coast, in Azángaro only a few haciendas were transferred through state interference. The institutions that suffered most loss of land were the community funds. In 1821 the Caja de Censos de Indios in Lima, the umbrella organization for all community funds, was incorporated into a newly created Dirección de Censos y Obras Pías.[14] In the following years the payments by tenants of the ancient caja's properties were neglected, forgotten, or suspended. In 1825 the interest on the credits granted by the caja were lowered from 5 percent annually to 2 percent for rural and 3 percent for urban properties. Debtors were allowed to amortize these credits by paying with documents of the public debt at their nominal value, although their market value was much lower. Many properties of the caja were simply usurped by those who happened to be holding them.[15]

In Azángaro, Hacienda Payamarca of the community fund of Asillo was adjudicated to the Sociedad de Beneficencia Pública of Puno some time after its foundation in the 1830s. In 1853 the beneficencia sold the estate to José Mariano Escobedo. A wool merchant and at that time one of Puno's two senators to the Peruvian congress, Escobedo had been in possession of Payamarca by virtue of a lease (*censo*) granted by the fund to Escobedo's mother in the early years of the century. Escobedo, perhaps a nephew of subdelegado Ramón Escobedo, whom Azángaro's peasants had accused of illegally appropriating community lands in 1813, paid the purchase price of 6,000 pesos with internal debt bonds, redeemable at the Caja de Consolidación, established by President Echenique's notorious scheme of consolidating the internal debt.[16]

The church suffered little loss of land through confiscations in Azángaro. During the liberal administrations of Luis José de Orbegoso and Andrés Santa Cruz, between 1834 and 1839, such confiscations were frequent in many parts of the republic.[17] In 1835 President Orbegoso ordered José Rufino Echenique, the future president, "to capitalize and sell all properties held in mortmain existing in [Puno] with the goal of procuring resources for the army." After learning how much corruption this process entailed and how the temporary holders of many estates saw it as a convenient means to obtain full property titles, Echenique decided that such "violent expropriations" were "contrary to [his] principles" and renounced the commission.[18] Indeed, in Azángaro province most church haciendas remained untouched by government expropriation during the early decades after independence.[19]

Tax lists on rural property for the neighboring province of Lampa for 1843 and 1850 give a rough idea of the size distribution of altiplano estates. The number of haciendas in that province grew modestly from 154 in 1843 to 184 in 1876; however, this increase may merely reflect a change in terminology.[20] The size of most estates was not measured in the altiplano until after 1900; thus, we have to rely on livestock capital—expressed in OMR—as an index of the size of estates.

In 1843 Lampa province counted twenty-one large estates with 5,000 or more sheep, somewhat less than one-seventh of the total number of estates.[21] Of Lampa's 154 estates, 54 percent were mid-sized (between 1,000 and 5,000 OMR), and 32 percent were small (fewer than 1,000 OMR). Only nine haciendas held 10,000 or more units of sheep. In 1843 the largest estate, Hacienda Miraflores in the district of Cabanillas, a property of the Beneficencia Pública of Cuzco, maintained on its pastures 16,000 OMR of its own plus 2,000 OMR belonging to the long-term tenant. From what we know about carrying capacity of altiplano pastures, we can estimate that an hacienda such as Miraflores required anywhere from 6,000 hectares to 18,000 hectares to maintain these sheep flocks.[22] Although such haciendas were many times larger than the majority of small and medium-sized estates, they did not reach the dimensions of the vast livestock latifundia of northern Mexico or even some of the mixed livestock and crop-raising estates of the Bajío, described by David Brading for the eighteenth and early nineteenth centuries.[23]

The tax rolls assessed the net income produced by an estate as a flat rate of 10 percent of its livestock capital. For example, in 1843 Hacienda Miraflores, with its 18,000 OMR, was assumed to generate 1,800 pesos income per year for its leaseholder. But tenants of estates throughout the 1840s and 1850s also routinely paid leases set at 10 percent of the livestock capital if the flocks fully used the carrying capacity.[24] The actual ratio of income to livestock thus must have exceeded the fictitious ratio of 1:10 used as a basis of tax assessment.[25] Even so, few haciendas could have generated an annual income of 4,000 or 5,000 pesos. The majority of Lampa's estates, holding from 1,000 to 5,000 OMR, must have produced annual net incomes of below 1,000 pesos.[26] Small estates generated at most an income of 200 pesos annually.

Even the largest altiplano estates did not produce an income that by itself made their owners wealthy men or women by any but narrow regional

TABLE 4.1. Haciendas in Azángaro with 5,000 or more OMR, Mid-Nineteenth Century

Estate	Location	Owner or Enfiteuta	Tenant	Livestock (OMR)	Value (pesos)	Size (has.)	Year of Information
Puscallani	Azángaro	María del Rosario Choquehuanca	Modesto Basadre	6,776	n.a.	n.a.	1852
Calcala	Chupa	Martina Carpio vda. de Urbina	Bonifacio Ramos	10,000	n.a.	n.a.	1853
Checayani	Muñani	Juliana Aragón de Riquelme	—	14,000	n.a.	n.a.	1854
Huasacona	Muñani	Manuel Ruperto Estévez	José Manuel Torres	15,000	34,565	9,654–12,594	1854
Payamarca/Pumanota	Asillo	José Mariano Escobedo	—	11,000	n.a.	n.a.	1856
Pachaje	Putina	Virginia Urviola	Andrés Urviola	1,000/5,000[a]	n.a.	n.a.	1858
Nequeneque	Muñani	María A. Vieyra y Choquehunaca	—	n.a.	Above 20,000	n.a.	1862
Muñani Chico	Muñani	José Luis Quiñones	José Manuel Torres	5,000	n.a.	n.a.	1855
Quelviri	San José	Santiago and Carmen Riquelme	Miguel Bueno, José Pastor	6,000	n.a.	n.a.	1859
Tarucani/Sirasirani	Putina	José Manuel Calle	Andrés Urviola	6,000	n.a.	n.a.	1863
Potoni	Potoni	Rufino Macedo[b]	—	5,200/6,000[a]	n.a.	2,680	1849
Purina y Viscachani	Asillo	Dionicio Zevallos[b]	—	5,500	n.a.	2,321	1828
Picotani	Muñani	Juana Manuela Choquehuanca	—	n.a.	n.a.	15,000–20,000	1855

[a]The owner planned to restock the estate up to the higher number. [b]Enfiteuta; owner was the parish church.

Sources: REPA and REPP, 1852–64; RPIP, vols. 3–4.

standards. Unlike many of the coastal vineyards and sugar haciendas, one of the dozen or so very large estates in the department of Puno did not constitute sufficient property and income to place its owner among Peru's fluid upper class. Ownership of a small finca provided for only an extremely modest life-style, in which being able to afford certain dietary items and some European garb and household furnishings took on great importance for maintaining the distinction between one's own social position and that of Indian peasants.

The size range of Azángaro's estates in the middle years of the past century was similar to that of Lampa province. In Choquehuanca's opinion, of the seventy privately owned estates, fifty-seven were "only some small properties, the products of which hardly suffice to subsist on."[27] Of the thirteen large haciendas with 5,000 or more units of sheep (table 4.1), eight were nearly contiguous; from Puscallani in the northeastern corner of Azángaro district to Picotani, Huasacona, Checayani, Muñani Chico, and Nequeneque in the district of Muñani and, continuing southeastward, to Tarucani/Sirasirani and Pachaje in the district of Putina. This had been one of the two core regions of estates in the province as early as the seventeenth century. The medium-sized and small estates were more dispersed, although they thinned out considerably in the southwestern corner of the province.

The value of Azángaro's livestock haciendas was low. Huasacona, one of the largest and best-capitalized estates, sold for 25,040 pesos in 1854, not counting mortgages for a total of 9,525 pesos owed various establishments and persons in Cuzco. This price included all livestock and installations.[28] In 1862 José Mariano Escobedo asked his business friend Juan Paredes to try to sell Hacienda Quichusa, district Azángaro, for him. "If somebody would buy it, capitalized with 2,000 sheep, for 4,000 pesos cash down, you could sell, by which you would do me a favor."[29] During the severe slump of the mid-1840s estates often could be sold only at a loss, if buyers could be found at all.[30]

The value of land in the altiplano stood in close relation to the livestock capital that it could maintain. It had probably not changed much since the late colonial period, although evidence for this claim remains tenuous.[31] During the mid-eighteenth century the Jesuits charged a rate of 10 percent of livestock capital as lease for their haciendas Llallahua and Titiri. This same conventional rate prevailed for rentals one hundred years later. As late as the mid-nineteenth century many appraisals of estates still neglected to differentiate between the value of livestock capital and the land itself. Such differentiation became necessary only in those cases in which an estate had excess pastures over its present livestock capital—that is, when it was undercapitalized.[32]

The appraisers of land (*peritos agrimensores*), often estate owners themselves, based their assessments on land quality and other factors determining how many livestock units an estate could maintain throughout the year. Visual inspections served them in arriving at this judgment. The same criteria used to evaluate Hacienda Llallahua in 1771 were applied nearly one hundred years later, in 1869, on the occasion of a dispute over the adequate rental rate for the small Hacienda Achoc, property of the parish church of San Miguel de Achaya. The prospective renter, Casimira Zea vda. de Hidalgo, cited these criteria:

> One has to find out the extension of the estate, the quality and
> type of its pastures, its livestock capital, both regarding sheep and
> cattle; if an estate is good in all respects, [and] contains a large
> livestock capital, there is no doubt that one could well pay 15
> percent rent on it, because in this case the income it produces
> [*utilidad*] is real or of a regular level. But in the contrary case, as
> happens when I try to lease a small finquita, a rent of 15 percent
> results highly excessive and the estate would hardly bring any
> income. . . . [Achoc is] small in size, dry, has few pastures . . . ,
> has no waterholes, nor a comfortable building complex, nor
> does it have its own Indians or shepherds so that for the
> necessary services one has to entreat and beg people from out-
> side the estate, who don't stay forever. Its livestock capital is
> extremely small, as it has no more than 1,000 head, and with
> this capital one can get only a very small income from the estate,
> which might possibly reach the 15 percent that has been indicated
> as rent by the treasury of the bishopric.[33]

In appraisals all factors influencing the quality and profitability of an altiplano livestock estate were subsumed conventionally in one figure: the value of a unit of livestock capital, including its necessary pasture.[34] Put differently, even by the 1860s land in the altiplano continued to be of little value in and of itself. Just as in the colonial period, it was treated as an appurtenance of the livestock, the "lead commodity" determining the exchange value of land.[35]

The wealthiest landholders, who could be said to belong to southern Peru's regional elite, often owned several estates, aside from urban properties and investments in mines or commerce. María Rivero vda. de Velasco, born in the small market town of Vilque, west of Puno, was one of the wealthiest persons in the department of Puno by midcentury (table

4.2). Not atypically, a significant part of her properties—Hacienda Añavile, the mine Jesus María, and the house in Arequipa—were sold on her death to pay for various private and public debts (including arrears of taxes); the remaining proceeds were to be distributed among the poor of Puno town.[36]

The Lampa tax lists of 1843 and 1850 reveal another important aspect of altiplano hacienda structure in that era.[37] In 1843 nearly half of all estates were not operated by their owners. Eleven of the seventy-one estates were held in emphyteusis for the standard three "civil lives" (150 years). Such long-term leases were used mostly by corporate landowners, such as parishes and convents, to receive a steady flow of income from their property. Many of the other sixty estates operating under short-term rental contracts belonged to corporate holders as well, mostly parish churches.[38] But there was also a considerable number of private hacienda owners who preferred to rent out their estates rather than to operate them directly.[39] This tendency was most pronounced for the largest haciendas. In 1843 an amazing 80.9 percent of all large haciendas in Lampa province were not operated by their owners. The percentage declined for medium-sized estates to 55.9 percent and to only 14.3 percent among the small estates. The sample of large haciendas from Azángaro at midcentury (table 4.1) suggests a similarly high share of indirect hacienda operation (nearly 70 percent of the total). In the Lampa tax list for 1850 the percentage of estates operated by their owners had already begun to climb appreciably to just under two-thirds, with the shift most marked among mid-sized estates. This shift may be an early indication of the improving conjuncture.

Many hacienda owners in the altiplano were unwilling to exploit their estates by themselves during the difficult postindependence years. While risks and uncertainties had increased, it had become more difficult to bring outside laborers onto the estates for the wool clip and the slaughter of the old animals, and the cost of transport and credit had gone up. Yet rents had stagnated or even declined since the 1770s. Under these circumstances many owners of estates preferred the relatively secure and steady income from lease fees to operating the hacienda directly, even though this approach diminished the absolute level of income. Owners of small estates could ill afford to give up part of their income to a renter since they usually needed every peso to make ends meet. The greater revenues of the owners of larger estates, often multiplied through ownership of several haciendas, gave them more leeway with regard to the manner of operating an estate. Absenteeism among large estate owners also favored leasing out haciendas to tenants, as difficult transport and communication conditions rendered adequate supervision of the estate's management nearly impossible. In

TABLE 4.2. Property of María Rivero vda. de Velasco, 1854

A. Livestock Estates	Livestock capital
Hda. Toroya, Dist. Cabana	8,000 sheep
Hda. Añavile, Dist. Cabana	5,000 sheep
Hda. Tolapalca, Dist. Vilque	660 sheep
	25 llamas
Hdas. Cochela Tango and	3,300 sheep
Chijollane, Dist. Atuncolla	50 cows
	5 bulls
Hda. Buenavista, Dist. Caracoto	3,300 sheep
	50 cows
	5 bulls
Hda. Chujura, Dist. Vilque	2,200 sheep
	25 cows
	5 bulls
Hda. Qquera, Dist. Vilque	2,200 sheep
Estancias Taccara and Quillora	550 sheep
Total Livestock Capital	25,210 sheep
	125 cows
	15 bulls
	25 llamas

B. Other Real Estate[a]

3 houses in Vilque
4 houses in Puno
1 house in Arequipa
3 crop fields, with cottage, in the outskirts of Puno
1 mill for silver ore, in the outskirts of Puno
Hacienda mineral Jesús María, Dist. Tiquillaca

[a]Missing from this list: Hacienda mineral Poto, located in the Cordillera de Carabaya, northeast of Muñani. In early 1854 Rivero had leased the famous gold mine to Juan Bustamante, the traveler and later leader of an Indian uprising, for 2,450 pesos annually (REPP, año 1854, Cáceres [Jan. 25, 1854]).

Source: Will of María Rivero vda. de Velasco, REPP, año 1854, Cáceres (Jan. 24, 1854).

contrast, the majority of owners of medium-sized estates lived in Azángaro town or in the capital of the district where their hacienda was located. Owners of small estates often lived on the land itself.[40]

The low revenue-generating capacity of altiplano livestock haciendas around 1850 had one further cause, undercapitalization. The 1843 Lampa tax list contains several haciendas *en casco*, without any livestock. In 1854 Manuela Cornejo vda. de Collado gave her Hacienda Quisuni, district Putina, in rent to Gaspar Deza for twenty pesos annually. The estate, probably rather small, had no livestock capital at the time; not only did this lack reduce income from the estate to a negligible amount, but it also encouraged invasions by neighbors.[41] Numerous estates held less livestock capital than their pastures allowed. Owners strove to increase stock, at times without much success. Years, sometimes decades, after estate owners had commissioned the tenant or the administrator of the estate to refurbish its livestock, haciendas often continued in the same condition of under-capitalization.[42] The undercapitalization of estates constituted a graver problem for the owners of small haciendas than it did for the wealthiest landholders, who could afford to use the income from one estate for increasing its stock while relying on other sources of income for day-to-day living expenses. Yet the apparent difficulties in capitalizing estates contributed to the depressed condition of livestock enterprises of any size.

Statistics for various altiplano provinces from the last decades of the colonial era and the first years after independence suggest low levels of livestock populations (table 4.3). The figures for Azángaro during the late 1820s, probably more accurate than those for Lampa and Huancané, translate into an average livestock density of just over one OMR per hectare of pasture. By 1920 livestock density in the province had doubled.[43] The growth of livestock populations outpaced that of the province's human population by more than 50 percent during the next century. Whereas the ratio between livestock and human population stood at about 15:1 in 1825–29, it stood at 24:1 in 1940–45.

Unfortunately, we cannot make reliable estimates about the altiplano's livestock population for periods before 1800. Given the smaller human population, however, it seems unlikely that during the early or mid-eighteenth century livestock density lay at or even above the low value for 1825–29. Ecological conditions in the altiplano, as well as the nature of domesticated sheep and cameloids, do not allow these animals to fend for themselves; these stocks follow the human settlement frontier rather than precede it. Consequently, in the long run a certain correlation between human and livestock populations would prevail in the altiplano, as long as the maximum carrying capacities of pastures had not been exceeded and

TABLE 4.3. Livestock Populations in Three Altiplano Provinces, 1807–29

	Huancané, 1807[a]		Lampa, 1808[b]		Azángaro, 1825/29[c]	
	N	%	N	%	N	%
Sheep	139,862	81.6	142,444	92.7	316,568	87.9
Cattle	5,999	3.5	3,748	2.4	17,326	4.8
Llamas	15,426	9.0	5,125	3.3	7,125	2.0
Alpacas	3,257	1.9	601	0.4	—	—[d]
Horses	1,200	0.7	574	0.4	8,510	2.4
Mules	343	0.2	92	0.1	1,030	0.3
Donkeys	1,200	0.7	342	0.2	1,870	0.5
Pigs	4,113	2.4	653	0.4	7,850	2.2
Total	171,400	100.0	153,579	99.9	360,279	100.1

Sources and Notes:

[a]Macera, *Mapas coloniales de haciendas cuzqueñas,* lxi–lxii.

[b]"Partido de Lampa de la provincia é intendencia de la Ciudad de Puno: Estado que manifiesta en primer lugar el numero de pueblos y habitantes clasificados, y en segundo lugar los valores de todos los frutos y efectos de agricultura, de industria y minerales que ha producido este partido en todo el año de 18..[*sic*], distinguido por el numero, peso o medida de cada clase," Lampa, May 23, 1808, BNP.

[c]Choquehuanca, *Ensayo,* 15–53; excludes Poto, Pusi, and Taraco.

[d]Possibly lumped with llamas.

society remained overwhelmingly agrarian. Nevertheless, circumstantial evidence suggests that the ratio between livestock and human populations was considerably higher during the early and mid-eighteenth century than it was fifty to seventy-five years later.[44] In other words, during the decades between the 1780s and 1840s livestock populations, still growing sluggishly in absolute numbers, lagged behind the growth of human population in Azángaro. The recurring civil wars and military campaigns "contributed not a little to diminish the capital of estates," a knowledgeable author commented in 1845.[45] Moreover, modern long-range climatic analysis has found that these decades were in the center of a secular period of below-average precipitation in the Andes, leading to recurring scarcity of pasture and an associated decline in natural livestock population growth rates.[46] In the five years from 1825 to 1829 "there was not one year of plentiful pastures," José Domingo Choquehuanca tells us.[47]

Choquehuanca also attributed much importance to the extensive church property in Azángaro. The church owned thirty-four livestock haciendas

TABLE 4.4. Livestock Capital on Azángaro's Haciendas, by
Ownership, 1825–29

	Sheep			Cattle		
Ownership	Total	%	Average per Estate	Total	%	Average per Estate
Private	55,940	44.0	823	3,749	71.8	51
Owned by communities	11,225	8.8	1,403	—	—	—
Church or chaplaincies	60,000	47.2	1,765	1,470	28.2	43
All Estates	127,165	100.0	1,155	5,219	100.0	47

Note: These figures exclude Poto, Pusi, and Taraco.
Source: Choquehuanca, *Ensayo*, 15–53.

in the province in 1825–29, about 31 percent of all estates;[48] 8.5 percent
of the province's cattle, corresponding to 28.2 percent of the cattle of all
livestock estates, belonged to the church, as did 19 percent of the province's
sheep, or 47.2 percent of sheep on estates (table 4.4). The overwhelming
majority of church estates belonged to individual parishes and were administered by the bishopric of Cuzco. Only two estates, both located in the
district Santiago de Pupuja, still belonged to religious orders in the early
republican era—Hacienda Quera of the convent of Nazarenes in Cuzco and
Hacienda Achosita of the convent of Santo Domingo in Cuzco.

A true nineteenth-century liberal, Choquehuanca found in the church
a convenient explanation for the ills the province was suffering. Because
the parishes were often giving their haciendas in short-term rentals to
people who were not residents of the province, the number of affluent
estate owners who otherwise might have populated the towns was naturally reduced.[49] Even more harmful, church estates were not receiving the
improvements that any private owner would have undertaken. Their livestock capital never grew since the short-term renters were eager to sell all
increments of livestock to make a high profit during the few years of the
lease. Presumably, such profits were often taken out of the province since
many tenants left after terminating the rental term.[50]

It is true that church estates given in short-term lease were frequently
left in a worse state by the tenants than they had received them, with a
diminished livestock capital and run-down installations. But the church
gave its largest and most capitalized haciendas in emphyteusis for 150
years.[51] Of the twelve estates given in emphyteusis during the three

decades after independence, five were given to members of old families of the province (the Macedos and Riquelmes). Another four estates were given to Cuzqueños (Francisco Lizares and José Joaquín de Tapia), who founded families in Azángaro. Only the holders of the three remaining estates seem not to have been long-term residents of Azángaro. Safe in their possession for 150 years, the emphyteutic leaseholders, of course, had no reason to plunder them. Within eleven years of taking Hacienda Potoni in emphyteusis in 1849, Rufino Macedo had nearly doubled its livestock capital to ten thousand ewes, declaring that he had carried out "valuable improvements . . . on the finca, consisting of two houses of sufficient comfort on its borders, enclosed corrals for slaughtering, barley fields adjacent to these, and two ditches, constructed at high cost to irrigate the *ahijaderos* [moist pastures]. All these improvements have cost us much more than 4,000 pesos."[52]

In short, Choquehuanca's critique of the church as landholder can be accepted to only a limited degree. The major explanation for the depression of the province's livestock economy during the early years of Peru's republican era still has to be sought in the effects of the commercial crisis that had hit the southern Peruvian Sierra since the 1780s and in the destruction wrought on the region by the Túpac Amaru Rebellion and the Wars of Independence, social and economic conditions exacerbated by a secular cycle of below-average precipitation.

Just as in other Spanish American republics, liberal politicians in independent Peru sought to limit the economic influence of the church and to free property from encumbrances. As early as 1823 a "constitutional declaration" abolished all colonial fetters, such as chaplaincies, censos, and entails, to the free exercise of property rights. The civil code of 1852 prohibited donations of land to mortmain and the foundation of new chaplaincies, censos, and pious works; it also allowed the liquidation of existing encumbrances.[53]

But in Azángaro church-related encumbrances and credit facilities played a minor role; I have found only three cases of chaplaincies in the province.[54] How are we to explain this apparent near absence of chaplaincies, censos, and other land-related credit operations by the church, which contrasts with what is known about other regional hacienda complexes in Spanish America up to the mid-nineteenth century?[55] First, the value of most estates was too low and their owners often too poor to afford a sizable encumbrance. A chaplaincy of 3,000 pesos came close to the value of most of the province's haciendas prior to 1850 and would have resulted in the complete transfer of their annual net utility from the owner to the ecclesiastic beneficiary. The isolated cases of chaplaincies or other encumbrances pertained to the very largest estates in the province, such as Picotani or Huasacona, or indeed represented the transfer of the complete estate to an ecclesiastic beneficiary, as with "Hacienda Capellania" Loquicolla Grande.[56] Second, Puno became the seat of a diocese only in 1866. Before then negotiations for church loans, as well as the administration of donations to church beneficiaries, took place in Cuzco, some three to four days on horseback from Azángaro.[57] Azángarino landholders naturally suffered much inconvenience in conducting business in such a distant center; moreover, hacendados from the immediate vicinity of Cuzco must have had an advantage in applying for credit from the diocese or a convent, since they could maintain closer contacts with the hierarchy.[58] With a weak competitive position in the attainment of loans, altiplano landholders may well have checked their zeal in granting donations such as chaplaincies, since the return on such investments—in terms of added leverage vis-à-vis the church hierarchy in Cuzco—was low.

The Agrarian Reform of the 1820s and the Altiplano Peasantry

The explosive mixture of depressed conditions for livestock estates, strong reactions of peasants to earlier land losses, and the liberal reformist decrees and laws had a great impact on landholding among the altiplano peasantry. Initially, the ignorance of the Bolivarian leaders about the diverse realities in the Peruvian countryside limited the effectiveness of their agrarian reform measures. In the end a law that struck a curious balance between liberal property concepts and Bourbon enlightened reformism contributed greatly to shaping the country's rural property regime for decades to come.

Late Bourbon thinking on rural property regimes had been hampered by insurmountable contradictions. On the one hand, it aspired to a broad distribution of landed property as the most promising path to increased agricultural production. On the other hand, for reasons of fiscal necessity and social order, the Bourbons could never quite relinquish the peculiar relationship between crown and Indian peasantry that they had inherited from the Hapsburgs. Even during the early nineteenth century they depended on the peasantry for the fiscal solvency of the colony and for regulated access to Indian labor. In return, they had to guarantee minimally the continuity of social hierarchies and customs within the Indian communities, even though crown policies became more contradictory in this regard after 1780. As a consequence of this special relationship, symbolized by the tribute nexus, the Bourbons felt constrained in disposing of established usufruct patterns of communal lands that might upset the originarios' capacity or willingness to pay higher tribute rates and hold onerous offices in their communities. As much as they were concerned about a broad distribution of productive property, the Bourbons saw no way of converting Indian peasants into freeholders with full title to their land, along the lines of liberal property concepts, without jettisoning the special relationship that was the indispensable fiscal and social basis of their colonial regime in the Andes.

Viceroy José Fernando Abascal y Sousa, as critical of liberalism as he was pragmatic about shifting policy options, clearly perceived the linkage between the special status of the Indian and the limits of agrarian reform. Only after the liberal Cortes of Cadiz, much to his chagrin, had abolished tribute and mita in 1812, thus critically undermining the stability of the colonial regime, did Abascal consider a distribution of lands to landless and impoverished families of mestizos, whose condition he blamed for much banditry and crime. In his report of 1816 he suggested that "the property of these lands [previously reserved to the originarios] belongs by right of return to the state; the great amount of surplus lands among them present a most welcome opportunity to settle infinite families of mestizos, liberating them from the misery in which they have been living."[59]

From this perspective the renewed abolition of tribute by José de San Martín by a decree of August 27, 1821, was the crucial prerequisite for the first agrarian measures taken by the republican regime. On April 8, 1824, when the altiplano was still under royalist control, Simón Bolívar decreed from Trujillo that all state lands were to be sold at a price one-third below their assessed value. Indians were to be considered owners of the lands that they then possessed. The decree further ordered the distribution of community lands to those Indians presently without any parcels of land so that "no Indian should remain without his respective plot." Surplus community lands should be sold under the same conditions as other state lands. In every province commissioners should be named in order to distribute land "with the necessary exactitude, impartiality, and justice."[60]

Bolívar's first foray into the maze of Peru's rural property structure pursued a dual goal: (1) to use the sale of state lands below value as a means to raise urgently needed cash for the liberation, and (2) to increase agricultural production through the creation of an industrious class of Indian and mestizo yeoman farmers. This was the most liberal but also the most unrealistic of the major agrarian laws of the 1820s. It placed no restrictions on the resale of distributed lands, thus fulfilling the precept of liberal writings on land according to which only its untrammeled circulation could assure optimal use. But Bolívar and his advisers failed to realize that the sale of state lands, even one-third below market value, effectively excluded those poor, landless Indians and mestizos whom it was meant to benefit. In many provinces, as in the altiplano, there would also be no communal lands left for free distribution above and beyond granting full title to those presently in possession. Finally, entrusting the distribution to commissioners named in the provinces virtually assured that only local elites and their limited clienteles would benefit. In short, it was impossible for the weak insurgent authorities to achieve an agrarian reform that would at one and the same time produce income for the struggling state, significantly broaden the distribution of land, and assure its free circulation.

As Bolívar and his advisers gained a better understanding of Peru's agrarian structure, they weakened the philosophically liberal contents of their agrarian policies and moved closer to Bourbon reformist positions articulated since the mid-eighteenth century. A decree of July 4, 1825, stipulated limits on the amount of community land to be distributed to landless Indians, according to which caciques were entitled to considerably more land than commoners. The holdings of caciques and tax collectors based on their office, which had caused so much conflict during the late colonial era, were not to be recognized, whereas those of *caciques de sangre*, the descendants of Andean nobility, were. Indians who had become owners of community lands by the decree of April 1824 could not sell them prior to 1850. The decree also sought to strengthen the central government's control over the selection of provincial land commissioners.[61] While favoring caciques one last time based on their social position rather than on privileges stemming from their office, Bolívar proceeded on the very same day (July 4, 1825) to extinguish the title of cacique altogether.[62]

The dilution of liberal contents in the agrarian legislation became more marked during the following year. Because of mounting fiscal pressure, in August 1826 the Bolivarian council of government, in which Bourbon reformists such as Hipólito Unanue and José de Larrea y Loredo held prominent positions, reintroduced Indian tribute under the euphemistic denomination of *contribución de indígenas*, a measure that replicated most of the modalities of its predecessor tax. The inevitable consequence for the agrarian program followed on the heels, when in December 1826 Bolívar instructed provincial authorities to prefer originarios, who paid the full rate of the contribución de indígenas, to forasteros in the distribution of community lands.[63]

As things stood by December 1826, the Bolivarians had removed any legally fixed privileges from Indian communities but had recognized existing stratification based on social prestige and wealth, ratifying the greater claims of former caciques and originarios to communal lands. Having understood the scarcity of communal lands in many regions of the country, their concept had reverted to the Bourbon practice of distributing strictly limited amounts of communal lands in a manner reaffirming social hierarchies within the communities, albeit with the decisive difference that the plots now were to be held in fee simple.

Yet these principles of distribution within the communities clashed with the most liberal plank of the original agrarian decree of 1824 that had been retained, namely, that every Indian was to own whatever land he or she held at the moment without contradiction. This provision could not be applied to land within the communities but only to lands that Indians possessed outside the communities, often under the precarious conditions of the late colonial period. Moreover, for all lands that Indians were to own in fee simple, the Bolivarians now had taken back the key liberal property concept of unfettered circulation by imposing a twenty-five-year prohibition on land sales. Apprehensive about Indian peasants' capacity to compete with powerful provincial elites in the ideally envisioned free market, the Bolivarians had sacrificed the liberal notion of unfettered property circulation in order to safeguard the older Bourbon goal of broad distribution of productive land.[64]

As the Bolivarians understood full well, especially after the Liberator's triumphant tour through the southern highlands in mid-1825, the implementation of their agrarian reform measures depended on power constellations in the provinces. Because their program went beyond the mere conversion of usufruct rights and precarious, insecure tenures of Indian peasants into full property rights, aiming as it did also at the redistribution of community lands, they needed to rely on the willingness of local authorities to carry out these measures "with impartiality and justice." Here Bolívar's agrarian reform measures appear to have floundered completely. The land commissions in the provinces either failed to carry out the measurement and registration of community lands or committed "the most pernicious abuse" of unjustly granting land titles to their favorites, although they lacked authority "to expedite property titles, or to confirm titles of those in possession, and especially to distribute lands or carry out compositions; they were merely authorized to inform [the government]."[65] In August 1827 a congressional resolution reiterated that no community lands should be sold until the land commissions had delivered their reports to the central government.[66] Thus, the realization grew that in order to achieve anything concerning the agrarian problem, the provincial authorities, closely tied to the elites, had to be largely removed from the process.

The law that was to have lasting impact on the landholding pattern, at least as far as Azángaro is concerned, was that passed by the congress on March 27, 1828. It again declared Indians, but now also mestizos, to be proprietors of the lands that they presently occupied on the basis of the periodic distributions of communal lands, or—in the case of land outside the communities as defined by the Bourbon authorities—"without contradiction," that is, without other claimants coming forth to dispute their possession. The only limitation on their right to sell this land now consisted in the stipulation that they be able to read and write. Landless Indians and mestizos were to receive the remaining lands belonging to the state once the Juntas Departamentales had gathered the corresponding statistics. Should there be any surplus lands left after this operation, they were to be assigned to schools to provide revenues.[67]

During the following decades this law must have circulated even in the remotest corners of Peru. Indian peasants considered its provisions as the basis of their title to an estancia. When, for example, on May 10, 1859, María, Carmen, and Sebastián Carcausto sold Estancia Ccatahui Sencca in the ayllu Urinsaya, district Azángaro, to Juan Paredes, they stated that they had inherited the land from their father, "whom the law of the year '28 found in possession and since that time we are owners [of the estancia].'"[68]

The crucial difference between the law of 1828 and the preceding Bolivarian measures lay in the influence that commissioners or any provincial authorities could exert over its execution. Now the granting of full property rights to land presently held by Indians or mestizos was to proceed immediately, independent of and prior to any land registrations and assessments by authorities. The distribution of community or other state lands to landless Indians and mestizos was to occur separate from and subsequent to the mere extension of property rights to any lands now held in usufruct or precariously.

In the altiplano this extension of property titles had the effect of an agrarian reform. Besides reaffirming peasants' rights to community lands, it strengthened their title to the lands that they occupied and worked precariously but that had been in limbo during the last decades of the colonial regime: lands that had been claimed by private hacendados, the church, kurakas, or their successors as tax collectors but that the crown had increasingly refused to grant in fee simple through compositions since the 1780s; or lands that had never been claimed as property by members of the colonial elite and that the crown had considered *tierras realengas* (crown lands) but were habitually occupied by forasteros and others without sufficient access to lands in the communities.

In the face of the weakened position of elite landholders the law of 1828 in Azángaro managed to undo in one stroke the paradoxical late colonial condition of land scarcity among the peasantry in an era of abundant land and low population densities. The national government ceased its attempts to dislodge peasants from lands that they occupied in 1828, as the Bourbons had done by repeatedly declaring all community lands and much of the land precariously worked by peasants outside the communities to be realengas. Hacendados and the church lost the legal battle over much of the land that they had attempted to integrate into their estates in the decades before 1780 and in some cases even later.

To be sure, the law of 1828 failed, just as the Bolivarian measures had, to redistribute any lands. In Azángaro "there was not an inch of land without somebody in precarious possession, . . . and thus article 2 of the law [referring to distribution of surplus state lands] has been inapplicable."[69] Provincial authorities did manage illegally to sell or reaffirm through composition some state lands considered *sobrantes* or *tierras de oficio* after the abolition of the office of cacique and the earlier Bolivarian land measures.[70] But there can be no doubt that in the altiplano the primary beneficiaries of the law of 1828 were the thousands of peasant families who had precariously held lands outside of the communities since the late eighteenth century. It thus legally solidified the temporary stalemate between peasant and hacienda sectors in the northern altiplano. Any future attempts to take control of peasant lands could not be based on colonial title claims. In the decades of a rapidly accelerating land transfers after 1850 notaries routinely recognized the peasants' property titles based on the 1828 law.

This interpretation does not refute the notion that the agrarian laws of the 1820s legally facilitated the onslaught on Indian lands in the late nineteenth and early twentieth centuries, but it does demonstrate that the measures of the 1820s did not simply constitute the ill-advised application of abstract liberal property notions. The goals of the agrarian reformers of the 1820s—increasing revenues, a broad distribution of land, and its free circulation—could not be attained at once.

In the political battles over defining a realistic policy, waged between various factions in Lima and provincial authorities and elite groups, the liberal impulse was tempered and modified in such a fashion that in the end the agrarian measures showed as much Bourbon reformist continuities as they showed new liberal departures. The effect that the replacement of confusing land-use rights and precarious tenures by individual property titles was to have on the development of an ideally free land market would become apparent only after 1850. Indeed, this long-term effect was of secondary importance for the reformers of the 1820s. Their foremost concerns were directed at securing state revenue collection among Indian and mestizo smallholders and stimulating agricultural production through a broad distribution of land.

The renewed reliance on an Indian head tax brought with it the recognition of social hierarchies in the Indian communities, albeit without the colonial corporate privileges and associated official powers.[71] Indeed, fiscal interests led early republican governments to keep a watchful eye on the preservation of the Indians' land base. As late as 1847, just two or three years before the explosion of guano revenues, Manuel del Rio, minister of finance during Ramón Castilla's first administration, called for a law that would allow Indians to sell their land only to other Indians. He feared that a widespread use of the Indians' right to sell their land freely to whomever they wished would lead to a serious depletion of revenue collection, as Indians with no or too little land would pay only half the rate of the contribución de indígenas.[72]

The critics of nineteenth-century Peruvian liberalism have asserted that the agrarian laws enacted during the 1820s caused an immediate cycle of land grabbing by hispanized large landholders.[73] Yet between the late 1820s and the 1850s the transfer of land from Azángaro's peasant sector to the estate sector proceeded at a rather slow pace. Indeed, peasant land only trickled into the estate sector during the 1850s (see chapter 6), and there is no reason to believe that during the two preceding decades hacienda expansion had proceeded at a more dramatic pace, particularly given the depressed level of the wool market during most of the 1840s.[74] Although some early republican hacendados—most notoriously Francisco Lizares in Muñani—did expand their holdings onto peasant lands, these remained isolated cases. During the three decades after independence Azángaro's Indian peasants held their lands, which they had just been granted in fee simple, with fewer challenges and threats of being dislodged than they had faced during the last century of the colonial era.[75]

It has often been assumed that the legislation of the 1820s legally abolished the communities.[76] Yet, although the reforms of the 1820s legally privatized all communally held land, no law or decree went so far as to positively outlaw Indian communities. This remained true for the rest of the century. Not even the civil code of 1852 abolished communities; it merely followed the legislative tradition, well established by then, of disregarding the institution altogether.[77] By the mid-nineteenth century the indigenous community had become, in Jorge Basadre's words, "a submerged juridic patrimony, alive in the soul and customs of the peasants, although invisible and strange to the formal mentality of legislators, magistrates and authorities."[78]

Because the national state had withdrawn its legal protection and ceased to enforce the standard functions that had given all communities certain common characteristics during the colonial era, their continued vitality depended primarily on local circumstances, the most important being the relations of production, type of production (particularly the contrast between stock-raising and agricultural communities), degree of market integration, power constellations between the Indian peasants and the local elite, and the cohesion within the communities. Consequently, after the 1820s the Indian communities in the distinct regions of Peru underwent a process of increasing differentiation, particularly regarding their systems of land tenure.[79]

In many parts of Cuzco department, community lands continued to be redistributed annually and were not treated like private property in terms of inheritance. But in the altiplano the law of 1828 did create individual peasant landholders and reduced communal landholding to a minimum. However, this change did not signify the disappearance of Azángaro's communities. In February 1844, for example, the community Tiramasa accused one Juan Arpita before the justice of the peace of Azángaro of invading the plots called Moroquere, Calasacsani, and Chijurani. The representatives of the community explained that "the lands in question belong to the community and are *mandas* on which annually at the proper time they planted their crops." Arpita objected that Chijurani was his own property. The justice of the peace settled the dispute by ordering each party, the community and Juan Arpita, not to transgress into the other's property. A dividing line was plowed, satisfying both sides.[80] The community of Tiramasa, then, was alive enough to defend itself against incursions. The land in question served as agricultural plots, the so-called mandas or *levas* of the community, which formed the surviving nucleus of communal land in Azángaro well into the twentieth century. But these plots were minute—no more than a few hectares—compared with the vast pastoral lands that had come to be considered the private land of the peasant families since the decrees of the 1820s.

When describing the gradual process of privatization of communal lands in Peru, most authors claim that pastures remained communal property longer than agricultural fields did.[81] In Azángaro, though, the opposite occurred. Why did the land tenure pattern of communities evolve so differently there than in other Peruvian regions? The answer to this question lies in the economic basis of particular communities. As the concept of private property penetrates traditional community structures, it will find acceptance first for that part of the peasants' economic operation that constitutes their primary income-earning activity, particularly if it links them to the market. The concept of individual gain, which a long-term interaction with the market fosters, will strengthen the peasant's desire to have exclusive and irrevocable control over the land that enables him or her to produce a marketable surplus. Competition will be keen for the lands employed in the production of these goods. Conversely, those lands used for the production of goods consumed only by the peasant families within the community will be less subject to the pressures of privatization because no market value will be attached to those goods. Hence, individual competition for these resources will tend to be weaker. In Azángaro Indian peasants first began to abandon communal landholding patterns on the pasturelands since animal husbandry was the economic activity of overwhelming importance for every family. Although competition for pasturelands was keen, the peasants left the small agricultural plots to be worked under a communal regime.

Just as in the land question, the effectiveness of labor recruitment, taxation, and various schemes to exploit Indians' resources ultimately depended on power constellations at the provincial and local level.[82] In August 1821 a decree by San Martín had abolished all types of forced labor services, including mita and *pongueaje* (domestic service).[83] But such decrees could not automatically change long-entrenched practices of the landholders and the civil and ecclesiastic authorities accustomed to dominating provincial society. In December 1828 the Junta Departamental of Puno, with José Domingo Choquehuanca and José Ignacio Evia as representatives for Azángaro province, denounced the "infractions of the constitution" by which Indian peasants were routinely victimized. The long list of abuses included forced labor for civil and church authorities, arbitrary and excessive fees charged by judges and priest, levy of illegal local taxes, and requisitioning of peasants' livestock and other property without compensation. Such abuses had been routinely practiced under the colonial regime, but Puno's Junta Departamental found it particularly deplorable that "under a *liberal* government the injustice of the stronger should prevail [my emphasis]."[84]

Yet, while lamenting the "illiberal" practices of local authorities in Puno's provinces, the Junta Departamental almost simultaneously, in December 1828, agreed on a draft of a departmental mining code (Reglamento de Minería) that included an elaborate scheme for recruiting labor almost identical to the colonial mita. District governors were to determine the number of vagrants and "harmful" *(perjudiciales)* persons in their areas. A supervisory committee on mining, elected by all mine owners in the department, would apportion labor contingents to be sent to each mine. Subprefects were to be responsible for delivering the workers to the mine operator, who had to pay the workers a salary and a mileage fee for their trips to and from the mines and provide them with "comfortable and healthy" accommodations. The code contained a provision for contracting "voluntary workers" through district governors against advance payments. The Junta Departamental thus proposed to entrust the recruitment of Indian mining labor, an operation that by definition and necessity involved force, to the same local authorities whom they had just accused of serious abuses against the freedom and property rights of the Indians.[85]

We do not know whether this mining code ever became effective. The small numbers of mine workers that the silver and gold mines in the various districts of the department of Puno required for their struggling operations in the decades after independence were certainly recruited by some type of coercion.[86] Yet until midcentury such measures were of limited success. During the brief mining flurry of the early 1850s authorities complained about the scarcity of mining labor in the Cordillera de Carabaya. Azángaro's peasants refused to work in the gold-washing operations in Poto belonging to Señora Rivero vda. de Velasco, even though there they could "earn substantial wages."[87] The machinery of coercion, now lacking the sanction of the central state, had become more haphazard. With the opening of export trades in wool and cascarilla, the peasants had alternative means of generating the cash they needed to pay the various taxes and fees and to acquire Manchester shirting cloth.

After its reintroduction in 1826 the contribución de indígenas continued as the second most important source of revenue for the central government until a few years before its abolition in 1854 by Ramón Castilla.[88] Although collection of the tax was higher, in absolute terms, by 1850 than tribute revenues were during the 1790s, the amount taken in per tributary was lower.[89] For the department of Puno collection per Indian tributary declined by one-fifth, from an average of 5.29 pesos during the 1790s to 4.22 pesos in 1846.[90] In Azángaro province the mean amount owed per tributary according to the tax lists declined from 5.92 pesos annually during the late 1820s to 5.55 pesos in 1843. The nominal rate of the head tax remained unchanged between its reintroduction in 1826 and its abolition in 1854, ten pesos annually per originario and five pesos per forastero.

Several factors might account for this declining effective taxation of Indians in the altiplano—indeed, across the nation—between the late colonial period and the mid-nineteenth century. As Nicolás Sánchez Albornoz has argued for the Bolivian altiplano,[91] the ratio of originarios to forasteros (or *sobrinos*) might have continued its long-term decline through the mid-nineteenth century, thus increasing the weight of the lower tribute rate for forasteros in the mean rate. But in Azángaro and neighboring provinces of the northern altiplano the decline in the number of originarios bottomed out as early as the tribute recounts undertaken by

Visitor General Mariano Escobedo during the mid-1780s in the wake of the Túpac Amaru Rebellion.[92] As the total number of Indian peasants enrolled in the tax lists grew during the early independence period, the number of originarios grew proportionately. In the tax lists of the mid-1820s the number of originarios grew more rapidly even than that of forasteros, suggesting that some of the forasteros who had long held less than the full allotment of land within the communities temporarily switched to the category of originarios, perhaps in order to maintain the distinction from those peasants, who only now received title to land through agrarian reform measures.[93]

Confusion reigned among the provincial commissioners charged with drawing up the tax lists for the contribución de indígenas. After each peasant's land had been confirmed by the laws of the 1820s, how much sense did it still make to differentiate between originarios and forasteros? Although the distinction might still reflect different amounts of land held by members of the two groups within the old communities, there now existed many forasteros with as much land outside the colonial communities as originario families held within them. The tax list of 1830 for Huancané province lumped all Indian tributaries under the category *"con tierras"*; the same province's list for 1850 again differentiated between originarios and forasteros, stressing, however, that the members of both groups held land. The lists for Lampa, Carabaya, and Azángaro provinces differentiated mostly between tributaries "con tierras" and "sin tierras," with the latter category holding between two-thirds and four-fifths of all tributaries. And the last list for the contribución de indígenas drawn up for Chucuito province in 1853, a year before the abolition of the tax, adopted a much more differentiated categorization of tributaries into originarios, forasteros, *uros*, *sacristanes*, mestizos, and *yerbateros*, an atomization of categories that also characterized Indian tax lists across the border in Bolivia during the mid-nineteenth century.[94]

These various categorizations no longer reflected different access to land by various groups of Indian peasants: the land tenure patterns of neighboring provinces such as Huancané and Azángaro were much too similar to lend credence to figures in the tax lists according to which all peasants in Huancané owned land, whereas some three-fourths of those in Azángaro owned none. Rather, the lists now reflected deeply ingrained status differences among Indian community peasants, coupled with the interest of the treasury to keep up the number of peasants paying the full tax rate as originarios.[95]

The major cause for declining per capita collections of the Indian head tax lay in the *quiebras*, the failure of provincial and district authorities to make all Indian tributaries pay. In 1846 Indians in the department of Puno failed to pay more than one-fourth of the head tax they owed; this was no isolated incident, as debts of more than 450,000 pesos had accumulated for previous years by then.[96] During his tenure as prefect of Puno between June 1834 and March 1835, Ramón Castilla pleaded continuously with subprefects in the provinces to submit long overdue taxes to the departmental treasury, apparently with little success. After Castilla had repeatedly reminded the subprefects since late June that they should speedily remit the sums still owed on the tax for the San Juan term (to be collected on or around June 24), by October 18 he threatened that they would be deposed if they had not rendered the accounts for that term by the end of the month. But by November 17 he was cajoling them, saying that "displaying all [their] energy, influence, and authority in the province," they should now undertake the collection of the head tax for the Christmas term and start remitting "the greatest possible sum" to the departmental treasury "without omitting any measure to effect the payment of outstanding past tax debts."[97]

Subprefects changed at brief intervals because of patronage appointments by the revolving national administrations; often they remained in office for less than a year. They had great difficulties in regularizing tax collection in their provinces, and their performance was seldom scrutinized through subsequent *residencias*, as was prescribed by law.[98] No doubt the subprefects just as frequently appointed new district governors who actually oversaw the collection of the head tax. Instability of local and provincial administration debilitated the authorities' capacity to collect the head tax and gave individual governors and subprefects greater opportunities for cheating the treasury by retaining part of the taxes. On the one hand, in this situation the Indian peasants may have found it easier to evade payment. On the other hand, collection became more arbitrary, for much depended on the attitudes and enforcement powers of each local official, often an affluent Indian or a small mestizo landholder himself.[99]

Although the peasants of the northern altiplano enjoyed greater stability during the early republican era in their control over land and faced less severe and effective labor drafts and declining rates of taxation, the frequent civil wars brought disruption of a type that had arisen only since the campaigns between royalists and insurgents in 1810. As many of these struggles were fought in southern Peru, the department of Puno again and again saw itself as the arena for recruitments and provisioning of both contending sides, especially between 1834 and 1844.

During early 1834 the country was embroiled in the contest for power between the former president Agustín Gamarra and the elected President Orbegoso. In Puno the French traveler Etienne, comte de Sartiges witnessed how soldiers of a regiment supporting Gamarra during the night went out and surrounded the hamlets in the vicinity of the city. In the morning they fetched the fit men out of the peasant huts, tied their hands, and led them to Puno. "There they proceeded to cut their hair and mark their ears so that they could be recognized and executed in case of desertion. The conscripts were locked into a church turned into barracks. They were let out only twice per day for exercises." A few days later, when de Sartiges passed through Lampa, troops belonging to a division under Colonel Miguel San Román "acted as if they were in enemy country: horses, mules, livestock, fodder, foodstuffs—everything they claimed in the name of the patria."[100]

The impressment of fathers or adult sons and the requisitioning of livestock (the infamous *chaqueo*) and foodstuff inevitably affected the income of the peasant family, especially when these depredations occurred at crucial periods during the agricultural cycle. It is likely that peasant communities close to the main roads, such as those in Santiago de Pupuja, suffered these abuses more frequently than did the more remote communities in the central and easterly parts of Azángaro province. In general, this type of exploitation at the hands of caudillo armies was marked by its arbitrary and haphazard nature, making it worse for those affected but perhaps affecting only limited numbers of communities during limited periods of time. It was a far cry not only from the more systematic annual recruitment drives of the early twentieth century, during which the army scoured the countryside of the altiplano from one end to the other, but also from the fairly bureaucratic application of the mita during the colonial period. The exploitation of the Indian peasantry by the caudillo armies is further evidence for the increasingly incidental and personalistic structures of power in the rural altiplano during the early postindependence decades.

Some sixty years ago José Carlos Mariátegui flatly affirmed that with Peru's independence "a regime was inaugurated which—whatever may have been its principles—to a certain degree worsened the condition of the Indians instead of improving it."[101] Nevertheless, during the postindependence decades the Indian peasantry of the altiplano enjoyed increased autonomy. Released from the most disruptive colonial measures, such as the Potosí mita and the strict Bourbon limits on the extent of the community holdings, the peasants could consolidate their control over land and rebuild communal institutions in those settlements where forasteros had moved up from being precarious squatters to proprietors. The agrarian legislation merely provided the legal space for this consolidation. The fledgling central state did not automatically back the interests of provincial elites, as the Bourbons had done until 1780. The increased breathing space of the Indian peasants was the result both of their own assertiveness since the days of the Túpac Amaru Rebellion and of the continued weakness of provincial elites, in the midst of a semisecular commercial crisis and a major social recomposition.[102]

Increasing autonomy did not necessarily bring growing material well-being, however. Peasants were also affected by declining prices for their home-produced textiles. The decrease of surplus extraction had not raised their income above what might be called the subsistence level for all to withstand bad years without suffering. A drought in 1848 immediately produced a famine in Puno because of crop failure, and the typhoid epidemic of the mid-1850s devastated the altiplano's population.[103] But for better years I am inclined to agree with the observation of Modesto Basadre y Chocano, subprefect of Azángaro during the early 1850s, that "the Indian peasantry of Azángaro with their small crop fields and their livestock had enough to cover their limited necessities."[104]

Azángaro's Society During the Early Independence Era

As late as 1810 Azángaro had been a province in which only a few royal officers, priests, and creole or mestizo entrepreneurs lived as intruders and exploiters in an Indian world. By the 1860s the non-Indian elites had confidently begun to see themselves as the legitimate masters of this world, firmly entrenched at the top of a provincial society becoming more structured and differentiated even though the legal barriers of the colonial caste society were disappearing.

Until the mid-nineteenth century no settlement in the province had reached the status of a town. Azángaro had been a corregimiento de Indios during the colonial period, and the colonial regime did not recognize urban centers that were not Spanish. The small population centers that did exist by the mid-eighteenth century had sprung up around parish churches, mining camps, or even particularly important estancias.[105] As late as the 1820s no settlement counted more than 550 residents, and several had fewer than 100. Together these small nuclei accounted for about 6 percent of the province's population.

The three largest centers were Putina, Azángaro, and Asillo. Whereas Azángaro and Asillo had been centers of some importance in the prehispanic period, Putina had been founded by Spanish miners and estancieros around 1600. By the early nineteenth century Putina still had considerably more Spanish residents than did the other parishes of the province.[106] As an "Indian province," without a Spanish town, the pueblos should have had cabildos de Indios. But by the late colonial era the intromission of creoles and mestizos into erstwhile corregimientos de Indios had become so routine that some of them occupied positions as *alcaldes* and *regidores* on the cabildos. Still, as late as 1813 the majority of councillors in the pueblo of Azángaro continued to be Indians.[107] In smaller nuclei probably no corporate bodies beyond the Indian communal authorities existed until the establishment of the republican administration during the late 1820s.

The physical appearance of these pueblos underscored their social distance from Spanish colonial cities. At most two hundred low adobe houses with thatched roofs were huddled around the parish churches, the only imposing buildings to be found in the province. In most pueblos a plaza faced the church; there, market stalls were put up and processions held on the days of the patron saints. The streets were laid out "without any order," a mix between a rudimentary Spanish colonial grid and Indian conceptions of nucleation, albeit now agglutinated by the Christian church.

Most houses in the pueblos belonged to peasants. These were humble, rectangular adobe cottages, mostly with a single room of about six by three meters. They had no windows and no ceiling below the thatched roof; the hard-stamped ground served as floor, and the low door frame was usually closed by a hide, as timber was expensive in the treeless altiplano. Behind this cottage there lay a plot of some three hundred to four hundred square meters enclosed by an adobe or stone wall; in this enclosure animals were guarded and fodder, fuel, agricultural implements, and other tools stored. Quite a few of these houses remained empty during most of the year, as they belonged to Indian peasants who lived on their estancias in the surrounding countryside and spent time in the pueblos only during market days or the weeks of the major festivals or while engaged in official business. Other cottages, on the perimeter of the pueblos, were permanently inhabited by peasants who owned lands close by. The distinction between "urban" space and the countryside was fluid.

The residences of notable citizens were larger and better furnished than those of the peasants, but they shared the same types of building materials and domestic utensils. The "complete houses," as José Domingo Choquehuanca called elite residences, were distinguished by having "a door to the street, a courtyard, and all the other features of convenience and security expected of a house."[108] They were equipped with wooden floors, plastered walls, some furnishings, and silverware and plates, produced locally or in one of the many towns in the southern Andes with a reputation for a particular craft. European goods were rare and prized possessions even among affluent citizens. For Choquehuanca, the notable citizens of Azángaro still lived "a la rústica" as late as the 1820s, in houses that left much to be desired from the standpoint of modern comfort, let alone luxury.

Whereas the residences of merchants, miners, and the more substantial landholders in towns such as Puno, Arequipa, or Cuzco were valued at 3,000 to 6,000 pesos or more, hardly a house in Azángaro province was worth more than 900 pesos, with simple peasant cottages costing as little as 20 pesos. Even these modest and rustic elite residences were rare in Azángaro until after independence. Choquehuanca counted thirty in Putina, twenty-three in Azángaro, and only six in Asillo; several pueblos had no house with a patio and a wooden door.[109]

In style, size, and comfort there was little difference between houses in the pueblos and building complexes in the countryside. There the peasants lived in small clusters of the same type of cottages, often intricately grouped together in a manner revealing the relationship between the nuclear family and the patrilineal descent group. The caseríos (building complexes) of altiplano estates had nothing of the grandeur of many colonial Mexican haciendas or even of Cuzco's great estates. The caseríos of the most established haciendas might be two courtyards deep, with the rooms around the second courtyard used to store potatoes, wool, hides, and dried sheep carcasses or to produce cheeses. Off to the side there might be a small chapel, "indecently plain and lacking the necessary adornments," dedicated to a local patron saint celebrated for a certain miracle or apparition;[110] however, most haciendas lacked such a chapel. To give the caserío a grander, more dignified appearance, the driveway leading to the main door was often lined with graceful kkolli trees. Whereas peasant estancias were dispersed throughout the landscape, in the middle of broad plains, on the banks of a river, or on hillsides, hacienda building complexes tended to be constructed at the foot of hills, slightly elevated from the pampa they faced. Perhaps such a location was chosen for easier defense against rebelling peasants.

Until the 1820s Azángaro was as yet too rustic a society for patterns of consumption to serve as a major criterion of social distinction. "Before the present regime [i.e., independent Peru] most people dressed in baizes and other rough materials," Choquehuanca observed, and "while our fathers heaped up gold and silver, they lived sadly, without enjoying the comforts of a civilized society."[111] Social hierarchies were shaped by the privilege and authority that came with the modest civil and ecclesiastic offices and through one's position in the caste system. Distinction was underscored and reenacted by the place and honor accorded to families in religious festivities and civil ceremonies, such as the homages for arriving dignitaries.

But in the unstable environment of the early nineteenth century privilege and authority appear to have been shaky underpinnings of social hierarchy. By 1806 Azángaro's recently formed Dragoon Militia Regiment, which should have offered creoles and mestizos an arena of social distinction, was experiencing gaps in its command ranks. Adjutant Cayetano Castro had left the province, and no one knew his whereabouts; Captain Nicolás Montesinos of the Second Company had been residing for two years in Cuzco; Captain Mariano Cáceres of the Eleventh Company was absent and served as substitute mayor of a town in the province of Apolo in the Viceroyalty of Buenos Aires; Lieutenant Juan Balenzuela of the Twelfth Company had fled after committing acts damaging to the royal interests; Grenadier Lieutenant Carlos Velarde had left for Cuzco and married an Indian woman without permit.[112] After independence things got worse. The provincial militia unit, now renamed the Civic Cavalry Regiment, was "purely nominal." Officers commissioned to lead units in neighboring districts refused to go so that "they would not have to neglect the attentions of their house, nor incur burdensome expenses." The list of regulars included old men and invalids. Limited to the province's mestizos, the manpower pool was too small. The regiment existed only on paper.[113]

More disconcerting from the perspective of the privileged, the forms of submission and devout respect routinely expected from Indians by the provincial elite during colonial times were temporarily relaxed with the egalitarian ideological affectation of the incipient republic. "In the five years since independence it has been notable that such servile submission is beginning to disappear; for this reason those accustomed to see the Indians tremble, find that the world is lost and there is no respect and subordination any more."[114]

For liberals such as José Domingo Choquehuanca, the crisis of authority and privilege was desirable. He stressed other criteria of stratification, more akin to his belief in the perfectibility of the individual through education and application. For Choquehuanca the distribution of income and property, while still reflecting the inequities of Spain's tyrannical regime, became of central importance. The liberal institutions and norms of the republic would allow all to better their stations. In 1830 Azángaro's distribution of wealth demonstrated both the enduring effects of the colonial caste society and the impoverishment the province had suffered during preceding decades.

Choquehuanca divided Azángaro's population according to a combined income and property index, apparently based on the physiocratic notion of net revenue, into three basic "classes": "rich," "well-off," and "poor." Relative to the "poverty of the province," he considered as rich those "who hold values up to 50,000 pesos and who can live in abundance as their consumption is smaller than their revenues." By this vague definition he found only three rich persons in the province, two of whom were priests and the third an owner of estates.

The well-off were defined as those "who can live without want and who thus can pay all the taxes they owe and defray all other necessary expenses." Choquehuanca subdivided this "class" into three groups of people according to their "savings and material comfort." The top layer consisted of the remaining parish priests, about ten men, who were in a position to accumulate funds through the sometimes substantial parish fees. They were followed by the "old proprietors, commonly called hacendados. These only amount to thirteen [families], although the tables show seventy privately owned estates. . . . The other estates are merely some small properties, whose products hardly suffice to subsist." The lowest strata of the well-off consisted of the "new proprietors"—the Indians who had benefited from the agrarian laws of the 1820s—and some mestizos who owned land or exercised a "commercial industry." Among these must have been the owners of small estates. Choquehuanca placed two-thirds of the province's Indian population in the ranks of the "new proprietors."

The poor encompassed the remaining Indians and "other inhabitants." "They suffer every manner of privation for lack of nourishment and other necessities of life; they are so poor that in years of scarcity they eat roots and many starve to death." Choquehuanca stressed that these were hard-working people trying to pay their taxes and parish fees, an eloquent comment on the weight of state and church exactions on the rural poor.[115]

Choquehuanca's classification replicates old schemes of the relative well-being of people that differentiate between those who become wealthier, as their "rents" exceed their needs; those who lead a secure, more or less comfortable life, neither accumulating riches nor threatened by starvation; and those who are constantly threatened by want. During the early years after independence Azángaro was, in economic terms, a comparatively homogeneous society, with very few "wealth-accumulating" people and a broad majority of people living more or less well, without want. But there existed a substantial minority of poor peasants, some of them landless, whose well-being was seriously endangered in years of scarcity. Choquehuanca emphasized this problem to demonstrate the heritage of exploitation and ignorance bequeathed by Spanish colonialism. Declining prices for craft goods and the shrinkage of long-range marketing networks hit hardest those peasants who had either no land or too little land and livestock capital for family reproduction. Yet this group was perhaps smaller than the author suggested, and it was certainly not growing during the early decades after independence.

It is striking that the parish priests stood at the apex of Azángaro society in terms of income. Choquehuanca might have exaggerated this point because of his anticlerical inclinations. Nevertheless, this situation underscores the relatively modest proportions of landed wealth in the altiplano of the early postindependence period and suggests that priests survived wars and commercial dislocation more unscathed than other elite groups did. Parish priests purportedly earned between 2,000 and 4,000 pesos annually from baptisms, funerals, weddings, ceremonies for patron saints, and altar offerings.[116] These figures may be unrealistically high, but even the 1,500 pesos that Father Bonifacio Deza (parish priest of Azángaro town, the most lucrative benefice in the province) earned according to the tax list for 1850 represents an enormous sum of money for the altiplano society of the time. Parish priests continued to find ways to extract resources from their Indian parishioners.[117]

The economic situation of estate owners need not be dwelt on here. Choquehuanca merely confirms what was suggested earlier, namely, that there existed only a dozen or so large estates in the province and that all were experiencing hard times, reducing the rent their owners could hope to derive. However, the lowest stratum of the well-off requires further scrutiny. Here Choquehuanca placed not only the owners of small fincas and the great majority of Indian peasants but also those following some trade. In other words, he suggested that diverse groups were, in terms of economic well-being, quite undifferentiated. Income and living standards did not carve a great chasm between the small finca owner, the trader, and many Indian peasants.

Artisanal activities and commerce consisted in two more or less distinct sectors in Azángaro during the early decades after independence. A small number of traders, shopkeepers, and artisans in the provincial capital and the larger pueblos earned a modest income sufficient in itself to place them among the well-off, this vague middle sector of a rather poor rural society. The great majority of those practicing trades, however, were peasants. In their case the sale of a few bundles of coca leaves, a bushel or two of maize, some homespun baizes, or pottery added but a small amount of cash to households otherwise based on agriculture and livestock raising.[118]

A tax list for the *contribución general de industrias* from 1850 confirms the slim numbers and exiguous economic position of full-time "urban" artisans, traders, and professionals. The tax was levied at a flat rate of 4 percent on annual income above 50 pesos derived from commerce, artisanal production, professions, operation of rented estates, and nongovernment employment (e.g., hacienda administrators).[119] Among sixty-seven households primarily dedicated to these pursuits in the district of Azángaro, only twenty-three were drawing incomes of more than 50 pesos from their "industry." Their earnings ranged from 88 to 200 pesos, with the highest income listed for one lawyer, the provincial tax farmer for tithes, and one trader. Twenty-seven heads of households were declared to be "without lucrative occupation" or "without property." These must have been traders, artisans, shopkeepers, and possibly a few employees with monetary income so small as to be exempted from the tax.[120]

Yet the number of households supplementing their incomes through crafts or commercial activities continued to be large. In the 1862 population census nearly 50 percent of all persons in Azángaro town for whom an occupation was listed were traders, shopkeepers, or artisans (including textile workers; see fig. 4.1). Among general artisans, such as masons, bakers, candlemakers, carpenters, dyemakers, and silversmiths, no whites appeared; most were Indian men. Crafts played a particularly prominent role for the small population classified as mestizo. Except for a few white male tailors, the still important textile trades were the domain of women from all ethnic backgrounds. Nearly all white women in this sector worked as seamstresses. They were widows or wives in households of relatively poor finca owners or traders. Whereas mestizo women in this sector were evenly divided between seamstresses and spinners or weavers, nearly all Indian textile workers were spinners or weavers. Except for a few mestizos, crafts provided only a supplementary income for households, and even the handful of full-time artisans in Azángaro probably relied on access to some land for their livelihood.

Trade and storekeeping were the only other occupations in the 1862 census to which large numbers of persons from all three ethnic groups had access. The spread of incomes from trade was larger than that among artisans. Some of the most affluent families of Azángaro's provincial society practiced trade, usually in conjunction with owning estates. Juan Paredes belonged to the small group with considerable income from trade, 200 pesos annually according to the tax list of 1850. This type of operation required a far-flung network of contacts and access to credit, allowing the exchange of many different commodities. At the other extreme of the trading hierarchy were many Indian peasants who made one or two journeys each year to the montaña or the valleys around Cuzco or Arequipa after completing their harvests. Their trade was small in volume and specialized as to goods exchanged. Nearly all women active in trade were either shopkeepers or operated small inns. These activities, if not associated with proper trade in livestock products, alcohol, maize, sugar, or imported goods by another member of the household, produced little monetary income, as pure retail stores sold only small quantities of commodities. Although mercantile endeavors could net respectable returns by provincial standards, practitioners of trade were stratified fairly rigidly along ethnic and gender lines, just as artisans were. But this was not a neat "urban"-rural divide, as many peasant artisans and peasant traders lived in the pueblos.[121]

Azángaro's Indians, who continued to make up about 90 percent of the province's population throughout the nineteenth century, were internally differentiated by multiple dimensions: differing status between kurakas, originarios, and forasteros or between colonos on estates and community peasants; varying levels of honorific offices within the communities and parishes; and the purely economic dimensions of income and wealth. Status and economic condition still overlapped to a considerable degree in the position of many families, yet Azángaro's Indians had long ceased to be part of an integrated, one-dimensional social hierarchy.

As late as the 1870s over three-fourths of the province's Indians lived outside of livestock estates and were in some way associated with an ayllu or parcialidad. The economic differentiation among this community peasantry depended primarily on access to land, which determined the size of livestock herds a family might own. The agrarian reforms of the 1820s had, as noted above, diminished differences between kurakas, originarios, and forasteros in terms of their access to land, but over the next few decades these differences had not fully disappeared. Although many forasteros now owned sufficient land for the subsistence of their families, the poorest peasants with the least land were still likely to come from their ranks, and the most affluent Indian landholders were still to be found among the now officially disestablished kurakas. Kurakas continued to command respect from Indian commoners and may still have received labor services and goods from their communities, although the surviving ancient lineages of noble kurakas were now fully integrated into the provincial landholding elite.[122] Lesser kuraka families who had held power in individual parcialidades, such as the Carcaustos and Zecenarro Mamanis in Azángaro, the Callohuancas in Asillo, the Amanquis in Arapa, and the Carlosvisa in Achaya, continued to own impressive landholdings during the mid-nineteenth century, with livestock herds of up to a thousand sheep.[123] The originarios apparently also continued among the ranks of the more affluent peasants; by the 1820s they were largely identical with the principales, those occupying the higher, more honorific communal offices and exempted from the "mechanical services." Many sent their children to live in Arequipa for a number of years so that they would learn Spanish, often living as domestic servants in well-to-do households.[124]

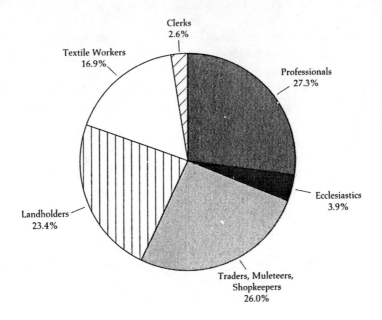

Clerks
2.6%

Textile Workers
16.9%

Professionals
27.3%

Ecclesiastics
3.9%

Landholders
23.4%

Traders, Muleteers,
Shopkeepers
26.0%

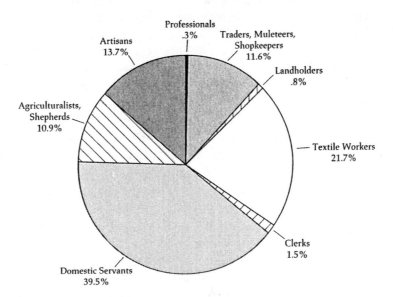

Professionals
.3%

Artisans
13.7%

Traders, Muleteers,
Shopkeepers
11.6%

Landholders
.8%

Agriculturalists,
Shepherds
10.9%

Textile Workers
21.7%

Clerks
1.5%

Domestic Servants
39.5%

FIGURE 4.1. Occupations in Azángaro Town, by Ethnic Group, 1862. *Top:* Whites. *Bottom:* Indians.

Source: Manuscript census of 1862, BMP.

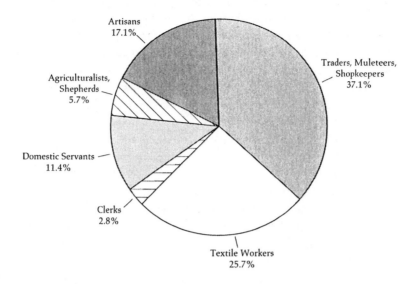

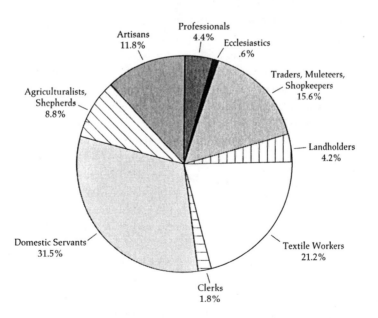

FIGURE 4.1 continued. *Top:* **Mestizos.** *Bottom:* **All ethnic groups.**

About one-seventh of Azángaro's Indian peasantry worked as colonos on livestock estates, a percentage that increased after midcentury.[125] As hacendados made no effort to control the colonos' peasant economy, their livestock herds varied between a dozen and five hundred or more head of sheep. Besides usufruct rights in hacienda pastures and a plot of cropland, their remuneration depended on the size of hacienda livestock herds entrusted to them; four reales per month for each one hundred sheep was a conventional rate during the 1840s.[126] Yet the relative affluence or poverty of the colonos depended primarily on their own peasant economy, the amount of livestock products they could sell or barter, the size of their own crops, and their artisanal production. The internal differentiation among labor tenants was great, certainly much greater than the income difference between this group as a whole and the community peasantry. Given that estates were frequently understocked and that control over colonos was lax, we have no reason to assume that their economic situation differed greatly from that of community peasants. The real difference between the two groups had more to do with questions of status and honor than with material well-being.

In sum, between the 1820s and 1860 the span between the wealthiest and poorest strata of Azángaro's income and property distribution was—compared to other Latin American estate complexes—relatively small. About twenty priests and hacendados, some of whom were also active in commerce, drew an annual income of between 500 and 1,500 pesos. The majority of estate owners, however, earned no more than 100 to 200 pesos per year. The few professionals in the province did not earn more than this. Among traders, a small elite with far-flung nets of mercantile connections earned about 200 or 300 pesos per year, while most Indian and mestizo peddlers, shopkeepers, and muleteers earned anywhere from 20 to 80 pesos for their exertions. Among the artisans the scale was lower. Here again a small group, mostly mestizos practicing their craft in the pueblos, earned considerably more than did Indian artisans, urban or rural. The multi-layered peasantry, finally, bracketed the whole range between intermediate income groups and absolute poverty, with most peasant families earning well below 100 pesos.

Such an income scale should nonetheless be treated with caution. As Lewis Taylor has observed about the area of Cajamarca during the nineteenth century, "Occupational categories as applied to particular individuals and social groups—landowners, miners, peasants, laborers, artisans, muleteers, merchants, etc.— . . . tend to disguise the complicated nature of the populace's working existence."[127] During the mid-nineteenth century, and for a long time thereafter, Azángaro's population—Spaniards and Indians, urban and rural folk alike—relied on multiple activities, combining stock raising and agriculture with trade, shopkeeping, craft production, and mining.

Hierarchies of occupation, property, and income had not as yet changed much between the late 1820s and 1860. Still, after midcentury Azángaro's society was showing a subtly different texture. This shift cannot be characterized simply as the change from a caste-oriented society to a class society, as suggested by much of the recent literature.[128] It is true that one's place in the colonial hierarchy of ethnic castes, reaffirmed by the legislation of the 1820s, lost its legal definition and backing as a yardstick for honor and status after Ramón Castilla abolished the contribución de indígenas in 1854. In its place the provincial elite increasingly defined its excellence in terms of life-style, income, and property. These were the liberal notions of a civilized society that José Domingo Choquehuanca had stressed in 1831 as the path along which Azángaro would overcome the colonial heritage of racial inequality and exploitation. Full of hope that the liberal institutions and laws of the republic would allow all citizens to share the benefits of civilization and affluence, he perceived "the civilized part" of Azángaro's population, composed primarily of public authorities and hacendados, as slowly adopting this new life-style. They were taking up "decent and agreeable manners and modes of behavior" and "modern customs, as for example in the good taste and arrangement of the dinner table and in fashions."[129]

After the national government withdrew its support of caste society during Castilla's second administration (1854–62), provincial elites began to use such liberal notions to buttress a reconstructed ideology of stratification. But this ideology merged with the older ethnic prejudices to create a new, more polarized vision of society. This polarization was reflected in the censuses. In 1798 only 561 persons in Azángaro were considered españoles, a mere 1.5 percent of the population. In that year 3,106 persons, or 8.6 percent of the provincial population, were classified as mestizos, and nearly 90 percent were classified as Indians. The 1876 census counted only 1,293 mestizos, 2.8 percent of Azángaro's population, whereas the white population had increased to 1,308. Already in the 1862 census the category of mestizos had become limited to a few muleteers, shopkeepers, artisans, and hacienda administrators.[130] They were turned into a vague, residual ethnic group whose lifestyle, income, and property qualifications could not be easily placed in the emerging polarized ethnic vision of society: on the one hand, the "civilized" hacendados, civil and ecclesiastic authorities, and better merchants, considered whites, who flouted a "modern" lifestyle, and on the other, the overwhelming majority of "barbaric" Indians persisting in their "anachronistic" habits.[131]

In the practice of the republican provincial elites, liberal notions turned from a moralizing, hopeful call for emancipation of all social groups from the strictures of Spanish "medieval" tyranny into the justification of exclusionary pretensions to social excellence and political power.[132] The agrarian laws of the 1820s, the abolition of the Indian head tax in 1854, and the passage of a largely liberal civil code in 1852, designed to strengthen and clarify property rights, did nothing to improve the situation of Indians in terms of their social treatment and recognition of their rights by local power holders. Those few individuals in the altiplano who at midcentury continued to fight for the emancipation of the Indians were appalled by the pseudo-liberal practices of their peers. In 1867 Juan Bustamante, a businessman and politician from Lampa province who had been an eyewitness to the French revolution of 1848 and was shortly to promote an Indian rebellion, lamented the "horrible condition to which the Indian caste is subjected":

> The generous efforts of enlightened authorities to alleviate the
> nefarious burdens which weigh down three-fourths of our
> population have been sterile and impotent. The Indian does not
> resist becoming civilized, nor is he incapable of turning into
> an educated, laborious, moral, and independent citizen. . . . The
> persons opposed to the regeneration of the Indian and frustrating
> every well-intentioned effort . . . enrich themselves by abusing
> the ignorance, humiliation, and abandonment of the Indian. They
> don't want the Indian to open his eyes to the light of the truth
> so that he may not know his rights and emancipate himself from
> his oppressors.[133]

By the mid-nineteenth century a new paradox was beginning to characterize altiplano society. While most families in the province continued to live off modest incomes and properties, with a mere handful of affluent citizens and a considerable minority of poor folk at the ends of the economic scale, the new republican elite defined itself through an increasingly polarized vision of social status and prestige that was embodied in their treatment of Indians. Until the 1860s one could still find cases of prestigious affluent Indians treated as equals by notables, for example, in the role of bondsmen or as trusted allies of prominent Azangarinos in political undertakings.[134] In subsequent decades such equality became rare, as hacendados, merchants, and officialdom associated "Indianness" with backward peasants or estate colonos. Henceforth, relatively well-to-do Indians aspiring to prestige outside their own community had to demonstrate their worthiness and civilization through Spanish speech, European garb, residence in town, and the role they were willing—and allowed—to play in religious and civil ceremonies.

It was not coincidental that the notable citizens of Azángaro now applied for the provincial capital to be elevated to the status of *ciudad*, a petition finally passed into law by the congress in 1875. Putina received the same honor in 1889.[135] Azángaro town had firmly established its "urban primacy" in the province by the time of the 1862 census. Its population had tripled since the late 1820s to reach 1,595, while other pueblos had grown more slowly. During the administration of José Rufino Echenique in the early 1850s Azángaro received a municipal building, and a canal was constructed from Lake Lolanta, one kilometer from town, to supply drinking water "of good quality."[136] By 1862 two schools for boys functioned in the province. Ninety-three of the ninety-five students at Azángaro's Colegio Municipal were classified as white.[137] Although the province was far from undergoing a process of urbanization, the distinction between town and countryside became more marked as rudimentary amenities of urban life appeared.

The number of state officials and authorities, still small in absolute terms, had also grown significantly after independence. The Judge of First Instance and his subaltern scribes and doormen, the justices of peace in every district, the governors in the districts, and, at the top, the subprefect and the provincial deputy to congress were positions now open to the provincial and local elite, a multiplication of positions of power and authority through which services and goods could be extracted from the Indian peasantry. The municipal councils ceased to be cabildos de Indios, and the councillors and mayors were now elected from the ranks of the provincial elites; only councils in districts with few haciendas and a particularly small "urban" nucleus, such as Saman or Achaya, still had Indian peasants among its members.[138]

By the 1850s, then, a new republican elite was well on its way toward redefining the patterns of dominance and domination in the altiplano. It appropriated liberal notions of civilization as the basis for its preeminence vis-à-vis the vast Indian majority. A process of "traditional modernization" had begun. The newly emerging elites selectively grafted notions of a constitutional political culture, liberal legal norms, and bourgeois cultural values and patterns of consumption onto old hierarchical norms of social conduct, in which the honor of the family and a harsh patriarchal order of domination and subordination maintained their uncurtailed validity and legitimacy.[139] In contrast to the early hopeful and moralizing liberal conceptions of a Choquehuanca, by midcentury Azángaro's elites relied on their self-righteous conviction of representing progressive civilization in a backward Indian province to justify innumerable forms of exploitation and abuse of the peasantry. As might be expected, few elite members in the altiplano dared to embrace the anticlerical planks of European liberalism; the church was to remain a major pillar of their superficially modernized yet still patriarchal order.

For the casual observer, the altiplano at midcentury might have appeared unchanged. The towns were still unattractive agglomerations of thatched adobe buildings. Estates continued to operate the same way they had one hundred years earlier. Many of the elite families who considered themselves as whites, imbued with modern values and life-style, might have been looked on as rather rude mestizo bumpkins in Lima or even Arequipa. Yet the new republican landholders, traders, and officials had found a way to adapt their domination over the vast majority of Indian peasants to the changed patterns of commerce, law, and politics emanating from Lima and Europe. The stage for the rise of gamonalismo, that peculiarly violent Andean version of bossism, was set. Azángaro's elites were ready to grasp the opportunities presented by expanding markets for their livestock products.

II THE WOOL EXPORT CYCLE, 1855–1920

5   The Symbiosis of Exports and Regional Trade

Most Latin American economies went through a period of rapid growth between the 1850s and 1920 as the extension of steamship services and the construction of rail lines from major ports to agricultural and mineral production zones allowed raw materials from the region to supply the burgeoning industrial economies of Western Europe and North America. Peru certainly participated in this experience of rapid growth, but more than any other nation in Latin America, its economic development during these seven or eight decades was punctured by a devastating depression lasting from 1873 to the late 1880s. The depression was brought on by the collapse of the lucrative guano export business, the destruction and loss of resources inflicted by Chilean troops during the War of the Pacific (1879–83), and the particularly severe cyclical crises simultaneously wrecking the European economies.[1] Growth of foreign trade, capital investment, and government revenues was impressive in the decades after the crisis.[2] But growth came with considerable costs: increasing dependence on the performance of key export sectors; a decline in "autonomous development" and in the growth of domestic industrial output; increasing foreign ownership of enterprises; intensifying regional and social income disparities; and the concentration of the modern sector of the economy in Lima and a few enclaves along the north coast and in the central highlands.[3]

In this chapter I examine the degree to which southern Peru shared the paradoxical national experience of strong growth with few lasting benefits. I argue that growth of foreign trade, although significant by regional standards, was less impressive in the south than it was in the north and center. Before 1920 the trade cycles were not as disruptive for the region as they were for Peru as a whole, and the growth of wool exports was associated with an expansion of domestic regional commerce. In great parts

151

of southern Peru, especially in the altiplano, trade continued to be shaped by low per capita incomes, the strength of the peasant household economy, and a neocolonial, clientalistic sociopolitical structure.

Southern Peru's Export Performance

By the 1850s the export of wool to Europe had come to constitute the altiplano's most important source of income. After the slow demise of the colonial mining-supply economy, producers and traders adapted to the new commercialization system. Yet it is difficult to speak unequivocally of an overpowering wool export boom for southern Peru during the following sixty-five years. Evaluation of wool export performance during this period depends on specific variables: the volume or value of exports; sheep or alpaca wool exports; and, most important, the currency used as a basis for measurement. The task is further complicated by the fact that, in spite of wool's strategic importance for the region, Peru never became a major source of supply in the world markets: during the first quarter of the twentieth century the country's wool exports constituted between one-third and one-half of one percent of world wool production.[4] Most international trade publications did not bother to list data on Peruvian exports, so that on such matters as the FOB price of wools in a Peruvian harbor, the disposition of the wools in the consumer nations, and even the volume of exports, statistics for Peru remain less reliable than they do for major producers such as Argentina or Australia. Although the data for the years between 1855 and 1920 are more reliable than those for the immediate postindependence period, the statistics discussed below should be viewed with caution, particularly regarding year-to-year fluctuations.[5]

Five countries with high land/labor ratios—Australia, New Zealand, South Africa, Argentina, and Uruguay—rose to dominate the world trade in wools during the second half of the nineteenth century. As the modern woolen industries grew rapidly, first in England between 1850 and the late 1870s and thereafter in other European countries and the United States, these overseas suppliers controlled a growing share of world trade in animal fibers. The shifting pattern of the wool trade was accelerated by the diminution of sheep herds in most of the major West European wool consuming nations.[6]

Peru also benefited from this rapid growth of demand for overseas fibers. But it could not keep pace with the five major wool exporters because its wool-producing regions, notably the altiplano, lacked the one condition allowing them to augment production for export in close correlation to rising demand: plentiful land not employed in production for domestic

TABLE 5.1. Annual Averages of Sheep Wool Exports from Islay
and Mollendo by Five-Year Periods, 1855–1929

Period	Volume (kg.)	Index	Value (pounds sterling)[a]	Index	Value (soles m.n.)[a]	Index
1855–59	1,001,910	100.0	106,275	100.0	532,585	100.0
1860–64	1,216,358	121.4	149,069	140.3	779,390	146.3
1865–69	1,297,899	129.5	153,275	144.2	798,197	149.9
1870–74	1,006,346	100.4	120,011	112.9	646,088	121.3
1875–79	1,040,944	103.9	110,291	103.8	622,092	116.8
1880–84	959,926	95.8	84,463	79.5	581,440[b]	109.2
1885–89	984,747	98.3	72,060	67.8	494,618	92.9
1890–94	1,173,084	117.1	85,171	80.1	687,983	129.2
1895–99	1,137,954	113.6	76,394	71.9	803,325	150.8
1900–1904	1,140,540	113.8	81,856	77.0	808,572	151.8
1905–9	1,159,626	115.7	107,275	100.9	1,057,019	198.5
1910–14	1,458,014	145.5	136,524	128.5	1,363,569	256.0
1915–19	2,069,163	206.5	456,815	429.8	3,983,198	747.9
1920–24	1,448,162	144.5	220,949	207.9	n.a.	n.a.
1925–29	1,532,578	153.0	225,787	212.4	n.a.	n.a.

[a]At British port of importation.
[b]Excluding 1882.
Source: Jacobsen, "Land Tenure," 815–33, app. 1.

markets or for peasant household subsistence. While countries such as
South Africa and Australia increased their sheep wool exports more than
tenfold between the late 1850s and 1911–15, Peru merely doubled its
exports. As early as the mid-1860s Peruvian sheep wool exports reached
a peak volume not surpassed until the boom years between 1916 and 1919.
The volume of national alpaca wool exports rose somewhat more steadily,
growing by about 150 percent between the late 1850s and 1910–14 (tables
5.1, 5.2). Yet, although the elasticity of wool supplies for export markets
was much lower in Peru than it was in the major export nations, it was not
altogether absent. In the short run, merchants, large landholders, and
peasants adjusted their wool remittances to foreign demand. Furthermore,
for many decades Peruvian wool production increased more rapidly than
did exports. Thus, growing domestic consumption must be considered as
one factor that limited export expansion.

TABLE 5.2. Annual Averages of Alpaca Wool Exports from Islay
and Mollendo by Five-Year Periods, 1855–1929

Period	Volume (kg.)	Index	Value (pounds sterling)	Index	Value (soles m.n.)[a]	Index
1855–59	978,332	100.0	271,025	100.0	1,367,861	100.0
1860–64	1,018,446	104.1	303,931	112.1	1,564,604	114.4
1865–69	1,143,945	116.9	343,617	126.8	1,782,383	130.3
1870–74	1,427,770	145.9	395,782	146.0	2,135,593	156.1
1875–79	1,537,059	157.1	330,523	122.0	1,860,059	136.0
1880–84	1,446,472	147.8	195,206	72.0	1,167,078	85.3
1885–89	1,693,528	173.1	176,202	65.0	1,206,593	88.2
1890–94	1,994,276	203.8	225,045	83.0	1,833,829	134.1
1895–99	2,137,266	218.5	253,815	93.7	2,660,655	194.5
1900–1904	2,286,133	233.7	264,502	97.6	2,614,000	191.1
1905–9	2,351,060	240.3	279,155	103.0	2,750,776	201.1
1910–14	2,211,559	226.1	255,984	94.5	2,497,405	182.6
1915–19	2,648,845	270.8	701,093	258.7	6,088,178	445.1
1920–24	2,247,466	229.7	415,424	153.3	n.a.	n.a.
1925–29	2,445,344	250.0	482,368	178.0	n.a.	n.a.

[a]At British port of importation.

Source: Jacobsen, "Land Tenure," 815–33, app. 1.

Sheep wool exports from Islay, the port on Arequipa's coast that handled most of southern Peru's maritime trade until 1870, expanded vigorously from the mid-1850s until 1867 in terms of both volume and value (table 5.1). In the latter year nearly two thousand metric tons were exported, close to double the amount of average yearly exports during the quinquennium 1855–59, a period of record wool exports itself. As prices rose vigorously in reaction to the cotton famine and the rapid growth of Britain's woolen industries, total value of sheep wool exports climbed by nearly 200 percent between 1855 and 1867 (figs. 5.1, 5.2).[7] Expansion was interrupted in individual years, such as 1857 and 1865, because of civil wars, when the road to the port was blocked and transport animals became scarce.[8]

Sheep wool exports contracted briefly between 1868 and 1870, with prices declining by up to 30 percent and total export value plummeting to below half of its mid-1860s peak level (from 1,151,318 to 413,241 soles

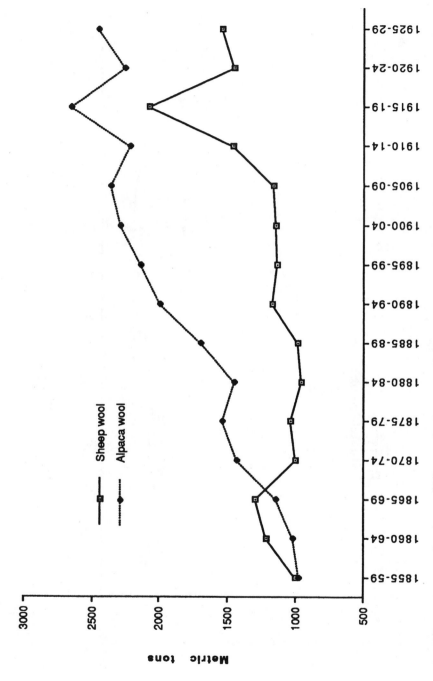

FIGURE 5.1. Annual Volume of Sheep and Alpaca Wool Exports from Islay and Mollendo, 1855–1929 (Five-Year Averages)

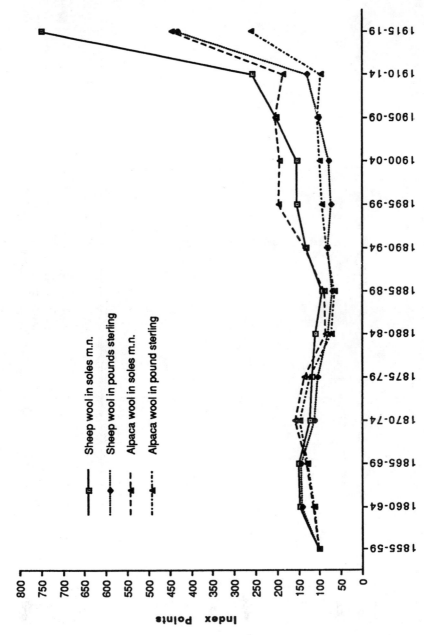

FIGURE 5.2. Value of Sheep and Alpaca Wool Exports from Islay and Mollendo, in British Pounds Sterling and Soles m.n., 1855–1919 (Five-Year Averages; 1855–59 = 100)

m.n.). When trade recovered again during most of the 1870s, sheep wool prices in Britain (CIF prices [that is, the price including cost, insurance, and freight]) for the first time showed the effects of overproduction of wools in Australasia and the Río de la Plata.[9] After 1873 the British woolen industry, the all-important consumer of Peruvian sheep wools, was hit hard by shrinking export markets in continental Europe and the United States, the effect of both a severe cyclical crisis there and a change in fashion, when consumers began to abandon Bradford worsted goods in favor of soft, all-woolen fabrics, often made with merino wools; this branch of the industry was more developed in France, where Peru sold little wool.[10] Even in the best year of the 1870s (1877) total value of sheep wool exports (Peruvian currency) lay about 25 percent below the record value of 1867.

During the 1880s the double blow of an industrial crisis in Europe and the War of the Pacific in Peru produced the most severe depression of southern Peru's wool export for the whole period under consideration. As early as 1879 British CIF prices had dropped 20 percent below the 1855–59 average. In 1880 the Chileans blockaded the port of Mollendo and destroyed port installations. Although there was no fighting in southern Peru's wool-producing zone, pack animals required to get the clip to railroad stations became scarce, and the army placed large orders for uniforms with shops and the one existing woolen mill in Urcos (department of Cuzco), diminishing exportable wool surpluses.[11] By 1882 the quantity of sheep wool exports through Mollendo had declined to just over half of the average amount for the years 1855–59. Although the restoration of peace in 1883 permitted the sale of stocks accumulated during the war years—sheep wool exports nearly tripled in 1884 from the preceding year—the slump continued, perhaps because of the civil war between Mariano Iglesias and Andrés Avelino Cáceres, until 1887.[12] Even so, southern Peru suffered less from the war and its aftermath than did central and northern Peru, where the 1880s produced the most severe economic and social crisis between the Wars of Independence and the Great Depression of 1929–32, causing the bankruptcy of many hacendados and endemic social unrest.[13]

The recovery of southern Peru's sheep wool exports coincided with a difficult period for international trade. The volume of exports from Mollendo increased moderately from the late 1880s until 1897, reaching a peak 25 percent higher than the average for the years 1855–59 yet still substantially below the level of the boom years of the mid-1860s. But through the early 1890s prices in Liverpool and London continued their long decline, begun in 1873, to less than two-thirds of the average price during the late 1850s.[14] World production of wools increased by more than a third between 1887 and 1895, affected especially by the dizzying growth of sheep herds in Australia.[15] This surge of supply coincided with a severe slump of demand during the depression of 1890–95. The cyclical crisis intensified the structural crisis of the British woolen industry—still by far the most important customer for Peruvian wools—which saw its markets eroded by the growing success of foreign competition.[16] The total value of sheep wool exports from southern Peru in terms of pound sterling at British ports thus recovered only slightly from the nadir of the 1880s.

After 1895 international wool markets began a long period of prosperity. As global wool production stagnated, prices increased steadily until the end of World War I, except for brief recessions in 1907–8 and 1911–12.[17] Peruvian sheep wool exports did not immediately benefit from this price increase. Southern Peru exported mostly coarse wools consumed by the mills around Bradford, which turned out traditional worsted fabrics whose market share continued to decline.[18] Thus, in contrast to average wool prices on the international markets, CIF prices for Peruvian sheep wool began to recover only after 1904; 1915 was the first year since 1878 during which they surpassed the average level for the years 1855–59. Export volume may have reflected these specific market conditions for Peruvian sheep wool. It stagnated through 1902 at between 900 and 1,200 tons, about the same level as during the second half of the 1850s. But after 1903 exports expanded vigorously, reaching over 2,000 tons in 1911, a volume slightly above the previous peak of 1867. Shipments from Mollendo dipped briefly but sharply in the recession years of 1907–8 and 1912.

After a brief crisis in southern Peru's wool business during the early months of World War I, brought on by the country's financial woes, Europe's wartime scarcities produced a wool export boom of unprecedented dimensions between 1915 and the first postwar year of 1919. At more than 2,500 tons, the volume of sheep wool exports in the peak year of 1917 was more than two and a half times larger than the average for the years 1855–59. Although only a modest increase over previous peak years such as 1867 or 1911, this growth of exports demonstrates the responsiveness of merchants and producers to favorable market conditions.[19] By 1918 a kilogram of average Peruvian sheep wool sold for 79.4 pence at an English port, over three times the average for 1855–59. The combination of extremely high prices and record export volumes brought a bonanza of earnings for the five-year period 1915–1919. In the following year, 1920, prices and export volumes plunged precipitously, with severe repercussions for southern Peru's economy (discussed further in chapter 9).

Overall, the record of southern Peruvian sheep wool exports between the mid-1850s and 1920 is not one of impressive growth. Prices and total

TABLE 5.3. FOB and CIF Prices for Peruvian Sheep Wool, 1861–1929 (in soles m.n. per kg.)

	FOB Islay and Mollendo	CIF British Ports	Difference, CIF − FOB	FOB as % of CIF
1861–66	.50	.68	.18	73.5
1886–92	.41	.51	.10	80.4
1928–29	1.79	1.93	.14	92.7

Sources: FOB prices: Bonilla, *Gran Bretaña* 4:164–256, 5:2–94; Dir. General de Aduanas, Sección de Estadística, *Estadística* 1928:378–79, 1929:372–74. CIF prices: Bonilla, "Islay," 43–44, table 5; Behnsen and Genzmer, *Weltwirtschaft der Wolle*, 84.

value in terms of British currency went through two growth periods, 1855 to 1867 and 1903–4 to 1919–20. Although World War I briefly led to an export bonanza of much greater proportions than that during the first cycle of expansion, export volume had grown only modestly from the first to the second peak. In between there lay a period of decline, from 1867–72 to 1882–95 (depending on whether one looks at price or volume), and another of halting recovery, from the late 1880s to the early 1900s.

The picture looks different if transport costs and currency exchange rates are considered. The dramatic decrease in maritime freight charges between the 1850s and the early decades of the twentieth century—brought about first by steel-hulled sailing clippers and, beginning in the 1870s, by regular steamship lines—contributed, as Berrick Saul has put it, "to the steady decline of import prices for Britain during the 'Great Depression' [of 1873–95], whilst reducing the impact of unfavorable terms of trade for primary producers."[20] In other words, an increasing share of CIF prices accrued to exporters. The reduction in transport costs varied greatly according to specific commodities and routes, with high-bulk/low-value goods hauled over the longest distances generally benefiting most.[21] Rory Miller has suggested that between 1863 and the late 1880s shipping rates for wool from Peru to Liverpool declined by at least 50 percent. By my own calculations (table 5.3) nearly half of the precipitous decline in the international wool prices between the early 1870s and mid-1890s was absorbed by the reduction in the cost of overseas shipping, insurance, and other incidental charges. For Peruvian producers the effects of declining CIF prices were much less drastic and more short-lived than it appears at first sight.[22]

A compensatory effect of similar proportions was achieved through currency devaluation. As silver became demonetized in one nation after another beginning in the early 1870s, it lost 50 percent of its value in terms of gold until the mid-1890s. Peru's adherence to the silver standard led to the devaluation of the silver *sol* by the same ratio from the 1860s, an expression of the agricultural exporters' power, especially between 1887 and 1895.[23] When the Piérola administration switched Peru to the gold standard between 1897 and 1900, the exchange rate stabilized at about twenty-four pence per sol.[24] This parity was maintained with only slight fluctuations until Peru's export boom during and immediately after World War I led to a brief appreciation of her currency by about 20 percent, only to slide below the gold parity during the early 1920s.

This currency devaluation made the slump of sheep wool prices during the last quarter of the nineteenth century less severe and shorter in terms of soles (fig. 5.2). As early as 1889 the price lay above the average for 1855–59, and in 1894 it surpassed the previous peak of the mid-1860s. In 1897 the CIF value of sheep wool exports through Mollendo lay only 21 percent below the best year of the 1860s in terms of soles, and by 1905 it had surpassed the previous peak of 1867 by nearly 30 percent.[25] If we take FOB prices into consideration, the whole decade between 1892 and 1902 (before the renewed expansion of export volumes) appears as one of growing affluence for southern Peru's sheep wool trade.[26]

But the role of currency transactions in southern Peru was more complex than this analysis suggests. At least until 1910 the department of Puno relied primarily on Bolivian coins as a medium of circulation, whereas Peruvian currency remained scarce. By one calculation, between the first emission of debased coins under President Santa Cruz in 1829 and the termination of this practice after the overthrow of the Melgarejo regime in 1869, some thirty-four million pesos were minted in Bolivia, of which ten million circulated in Peru.[27] Repeated attempts by both the Peruvian and Bolivian governments to withdraw this debased coinage from circulation proved insufficient, and the debased *quintos* and *arañas*, coins valued at one-fifth and one-fourth of a Bolivian peso, were still the most common currency in the Peruvian altiplano decades after their last coinage.[28] In 1890 the Peruvian government once again undertook to convert all "bad money" circulating in southern Peru; this effort was opposed by merchants and the general public, burned by losses sustained in the conversion of paper money during the late 1880s. Although the operation seemed to succeed in Cuzco and Arequipa, the minister of finance and trade had to admit that "since [in Puno] the Bolivian pesetas called arañas are the only circulating money, it will be somewhat more difficult to let it disappear soon."[29] As Indian livestock herders insisted on being paid in coins for their wool and hides, the withdrawal of Bolivian currency without replacing it with Peruvian coinage of small denominations would have led to a collapse of the wool export business.

Monetary confusion in Peru's altiplano was greatest between the mid-1880s and 1905. Debased Bolivian peso denominations and coins of the more recent decimal *boliviano* currency, dubbed *soles moneda boliviana* in Azángaro, predominated, but gradually circulation of Peruvian *soles moneda nacional* (soles m.n.) increased. As late as the 1890s some "strong" pesos continued to change hands, probably official Peruvian coinage from before the introduction of soles in 1863. Bolivian currencies constituted a widespread medium of payment in the Peruvian altiplano as late as 1920. At that time many stores in towns such as Puno, Juliaca, and Ayaviri and even farther north in Sicuani and Cuzco considered money exchange an important part of their business, prominently displaying the service in advertisements.[30] Throughout the wool-producing area Bolivian currency was the lubricant of trade at least until 1910.

The predominance of Bolivian currencies is important for calculating regional earnings from exports because their exchange rate fluctuated vis-à-vis Peruvian currency. Bolivia fully adopted the gold standard only in 1908, eleven years after Peru had taken this step.[31] During this period Bolivian silver currencies depreciated against Peruvian soles m.n. proportionately to the declining value of silver on international markets, just as the Peruvian currency had done vis-à-vis the pound sterling up to 1897 (fig. 5.3).[32] Because producers were paid overwhelmingly in debased Bolivian pesos or bolivianos, their devaluation resulted in higher earnings from wool exports for several years between 1898 and 1910.

But fluctuations in the value of Bolivian coins in the Peruvian altiplano show another influence: that of demand fluctuations for wool. "Coinage is becoming scarcer every day and the prices [for wool] in silver are reduced, as is natural," one trader in Ayaviri noted at the beginning of the World War I boom in mid-1915.[33] The demand for coinage—and this meant mostly Bolivian coins until the 1910s—in the altiplano was determined primarily by the export conjuncture: an export boom led to appreciation of the Bolivian coins vis-à-vis soles m.n., and trade crises, such as those of 1901–2 and 1907–8, brought the value of the coins down. Such currency fluctuations attenuated the price paid to producers in boom periods and diminished the rate of decline during crisis years while making imported goods more expensive. The free currency market of the altiplano worked as a buffer—especially for Indian peasants, who relied most on Bolivian currency—against the gyrations of the export commodity cycle.

Alpaca wool exports from Islay and Mollendo developed differently than did those of sheep wool (see table 5.2, figs. 5.1, 5.2). During the late 1850s export volumes for both fibers, at about one thousand tons, were nearly equal. But between 1869 and 1920 alpaca exports exceeded those of sheep wools in every year except one. During the first decade of the twentieth

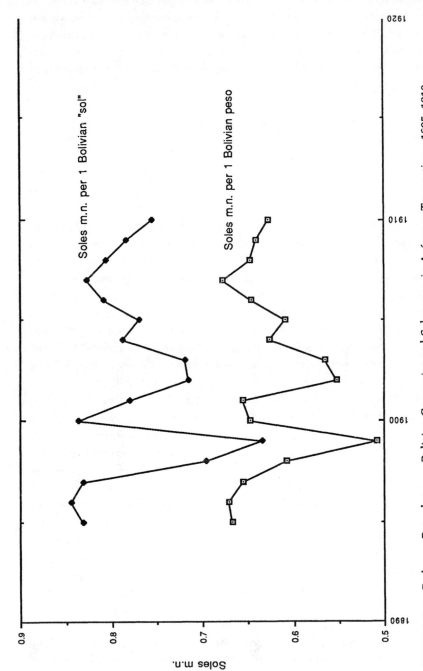

FIGURE 5.3 Exchange Rates between Bolivian Currencies and Soles m.n. in Azángaro Transactions, 1895–1910.

Sources: REPA and REPP, 1895–1910.

century, with exports of up to 2,600 tons, alpaca export volumes often were double those of sheep wool. The former increased rather steadily during the whole period from 1855–59. Only the averages for two five-year periods, 1880–84 and 1910–14, show moderate declines. However, the steady growth in the volume of alpaca wool exports failed to translate into an equally strong growth in their value, as prices went through a longer and deeper slump than did sheep wool prices. Alpaca wool was produced by only three Andean countries (with the lion's share coming from southern Peru); until quite late in the nineteenth century the totality of industrial consumers consisted of a small number of manufacturers located mostly in the West Riding, and demand for the precious fiber was highly dependent on fashions. Thus, market conditions for alpaca wools differed greatly from those for sheep wools.

Because production of alpaca wool was widely dispersed among a large number of Indian smallholders with no organization and little information about market conditions, Andean producers had little control over prices. On the contrary, for many years a few processors were able to impose low prices. The three manufacturing companies that were "overwhelmingly dominant" as consumers of British alpaca wool imports until the early 1870s—Fosters, Titus Salt, and G. and I. Turner—frequently colluded to keep down the price of their raw materials.[34] In the United States, a market of increasing importance since the closing decades of the nineteenth century, the preeminent consumer, the Farr Alpaca Company, successfully sought to discourage the entry of new competitors into the market.[35]

Such evidence for oligopsonistic control over the alpaca wool market, in addition to cyclical and structural weaknesses of demand, must be taken into consideration as a factor underlying the particularly severe and long-term depression of alpaca wool prices. The much finer and longer alpaca fiber had always fetched considerably higher prices than sheep wool had. The premium for alpaca peaked during the 1850s and 1860s, with prices of two-and-one-half times those for sheep wool. When international wool prices began their long-term decline in the mid-1870s, alpaca wools were hit considerably harder and longer than sheep wools were. A fashion change in the 1870s exacerbated the cyclical crises over the following fifteen years, sending CIF alpaca prices from a peak of 96.8 pence per kilogram in 1864 to a nadir of 22.3 pence in 1888.[36] In terms of pounds sterling the price did not reach the average level of 1855–59 in a single year between 1876 and 1917, and during most years of this period it was less than half the average price for the late 1850s. In spite of continued growth in export volumes five-year averages of total value remained below or barely above the par value for the 1855–59 period until the boom years of World War

I (sheep wool export values in pounds sterling had witnessed a more steady recovery since 1905). Alpaca wool prices profited from the boom of World War I, but less so than sheep wool prices did.[37]

Of course, because of the Peruvian currency devaluation, the slump of alpaca wool export values in terms of soles m.n. during the 1880s was also less severe than if it were measured in pounds sterling. As early as 1895 the total value of alpaca wool exports in soles m.n. surpassed the previous peak of 1866. By this measure, for the remainder of the period alpaca export values grew parallel to those for sheep wool, in spite of the stronger growth of volume. However, the alpaca trade benefited less from reductions in overseas transport costs than did sheep wool.[38]

Although the longer-term trends for wool prices and export volumes (table 5.4) underscore the responsiveness of southern Peruvian producers and traders to external demand, two problems need special consideration:[39] (1) Why did sheep wool export volumes stagnate between 1892 and 1902 when, as early as 1893–94, CIF prices in soles m.n. had reached levels comparable to the previous peak of the mid-1860s? (2) By contrast, why did alpaca wool export volumes continue to grow so vigorously between the mid-1880s and 1905–6 when prices in pounds sterling were depressed throughout this period and even prices in soles m.n. failed to return to the level of the mid-1860s? To answer these questions, we need to consider the development of domestic production of both fibers, changing ratios of domestic consumption to exports, and the impact of foreign demand on different groups of wool producers.

Information on these issues is fragmentary. It seems unlikely, however, that a strongly differentiated development in the production of both fibers caused these phases of countercyclical export volumes. During the century after independence sheep populations in the altiplano and neighboring livestock zones grew approximately threefold while alpaca herds may have grown somewhat faster. As noted in chapter 2, around 1840 a higher percentage of total alpaca wool production than of sheep wool production was exported. Given the trends for export volumes and total production of both fibers, this situation did not change over the next eighty years. All estimates from the early twentieth century suggest a considerably larger production of sheep wool than of alpaca wool, although alpaca wool exports continued to outpace those of sheep wool.[40] Production ceilings thus cannot explain the stagnation of sheep wool exports during the years of improving market conditions between 1892 and 1902. If anything, the expansion of alpaca wool exports might have been hampered by short supply, especially in years of rapidly growing demand. The British engineer A. J. Duffield, who claimed to have studied Peruvian wool production methods for four

TABLE 5.4. Major Trend Periods for Peruvian Wool Prices and
Export Volumes, 1855–1919

CIF Prices for Peruvian Sheep Wool at British Ports

Pounds Sterling		Soles m.n.	
1855[a]–1872:	Rise	1855[a]–1872:	Rise
1872–1897:	Decline	1872–1885:	Decline
1897–1902:	Stagnation	1885–1894/95:	Rise
1902–1918/19:	Rise	1894/95–1903:	Stagnation
		1903–1918/19:	Rise

CIF Prices for Peruvian Alpaca Wool at British Ports

Pounds Sterling		Soles m.n.	
1855[a]–1875:	Rise	1855[a]–1875	Rise
1875–1888:	Decline	1875–1888	Decline
1888–1914:	Stagnation	1888–1895/96:	Rise
1914–1918/19:	Rise	1895/96–1914:	Stagnation
		1914–1918/19:	Rise

Volume of Wool Exports from Islay/Mollendo

Sheep Wool		Alpaca Wool	
1855[a]–1867:	Growth	1855[a]–1876:	Growth
1867–1882:	Decline	1876–1883:	Decline
1882–1892:	Recovery	1883–1905/6:	Growth
1892–1902:	Stagnation	1905/6–1914:	Stagnation
1902–1917/18:	Growth	1914–1918:	Growth

[a]Or earlier.

years, wrote in 1877 that "all the wool of the alpaca, the llama and the
vicuña is sent to England. No Peruvian of any social standing has had the
pluck or the sense to do anything towards extending the cultivation of
alpaca wool." Had its production been expanded, Peru might have derived
"a net annual income of £20,000,000."[41]

Although this figure certainly was poetic exaggeration, designed to
underscore the Peruvian elite's failure during the "age of bird dung," other
evidence also suggests that Indian peasants routinely sold most or all of their

TABLE 5.5. Composition of Exports From Islay and Mollendo by Value, 1863–1930 (in percent)

	1863[a]	1886–92	1897–1901	1902–04[c]	1909–14	1915–19	1920–24	1925–30
Wool	76	41	40	62	61	81	65	66
Hides	—	1	2	6	5	4	3	4
Live Animals	—	—	—	—	1	1	—	—
Pergaminos	—	—	1	—	1	1	2	4
Cascarilla	13	8	1	—	—	—	—	—
Coca	—	2	4	7	2	1	1	1
Coffee	—	—	1	—	—	—	—	1
Rubber	—	—	8	2	10	2	—	—
Cotton	—	—	—	—	—	1	8	9
Sugar	—	—	—	5	—	2	7	2
Gold	3	—	—	—	—	—	—	2
Silver	6	16	11	9	1	2[e]	4[e]	4[e]
Copper	—	18	15	3	2	2	4	4
Petroleum	—	—	—	—	—	1	—	—
Borax	—	—	6	5	6	—	1	—
Coinage	1	8	8	1	1	—	—	—
Other	[b]	6	4	1	[11][d]	2	4	2
Total	99	100	100	101	101	98	99	99

[a]1863–1901 figures include Bolivian exports through Mollendo.
[b]Arithmetic error in source: "Total" is smaller than sum of exports; thus no residual.
[c]From 1902 onward figures only include South Peruvian exports.
[d]Arithmetic error in source: "Total" is too large by about 2,000,000 S./m.n. "Other" has to be reduced accordingly.
[e]Includes combined silver and gold ores.

Sources: Bonilla, Gran Bretaña vol. IV; Dir. General de Aduanas, Sección de Estadística, Estadística, annual.

alpaca wool crop during the second half of the nineteenth century.[42] As late as 1927 the Indian peasantry in Chumbivilcas, a livestock-raising province in the department of Cuzco, owned about 72 percent of domestic cameloids; during the preceding sixty years this percentage would have been even higher.[43] As hacendados remained reluctant to enter the alpaca-raising business, supply of this fiber was highly dependent on peasant production. With the exception of a few items of ceremonial clothing, peasants appear to have substituted sheep and llama wools for their home consumption of alpaca wool. This substitution was prompted both by the price premium paid for alpaca and by the strong pressures wool traders exerted on them. Traders could still earn handsome profits even during the long phase of declining demand for alpaca wools by passing on the lion's share of price reductions to the peasant producers. Thus, the role that alpaca wools played in peasants' household economy and the exploitive commercialization practices into which they were tied help explain the failure of alpaca wool exports to respond to the long-term downturn in international demand.

Sheep wool exports, by contrast, responded more closely to international demand fluctuations. A higher share—probably above 50 percent by the 1890s—was produced on estates. The stagnation of exports during the mid and late 1890s corresponded to a phase in which, because of the devaluation of the currency and increasing levels of industrial protection, the terms of trade favored domestic processing over exports. A number of woolen mills were founded both in the south and in Lima.[44] Wool producers and traders must have sold a growing albeit still minor share of the clip to these new mills. By 1902 the output of the Cuzco mills may have begun to affect peasant demand for cheap imported cloth in the south, as the British vice consul in Mollendo reported a sharp drop in sales of Bradford serges over previous years.[45] But in the following years the terms of trade again favored raw material exports, a result of declining tariffs for textiles, currency stabilization, and the stagnation in international wool supplies. Industrial wool processing in Peru seems to have stagnated while exports increased again.[46]

Even if wool dominated the region's foreign trade, southern Peru never became a single-export economy between the 1850s and 1920. The long-term share of wool in the total value of exports from Islay and Mollendo hovered around 60 to 65 percent (table 5.5). It briefly increased to as much as 80 or 90 percent in boom years during the 1860s and 1910s and may have fallen below 60 percent in the decades of declining wool prices between the mid-1870s and mid-1890s.[47] After the turn of the century other livestock products, especially cowhides, contributed up to 7 or 8 percent to southern Peru's exports.

A wide range of mineral and agricultural commodities complemented southern Peru's wool exports. Most of these contributed to the region's foreign trade in appreciable amounts only for a decade or two, but as one product was displaced from international markets others grew. Cascarilla (chinchona bark) remained the region's second export commodity through the 1880s but dwindled to insignificance during the next decade as aspirin replaced quinine as a cure-all. During the 1890s coca leaves, rubber, and borax began to be exported from Mollendo in large amounts, each contributing briefly between 7 and 20 percent to total southern Peruvian exports. But by the early 1910s these trades had withered, displaced by substitute products, more efficient foreign producers, or conflicts with the Peruvian government.[48] Beginning in the mid-1910s cotton and, more briefly, sugar, both produced in the valleys between Arequipa and the coast, became important export commodities for southern Peru.

Minerals such as silver, gold, and copper were, of course, the other major exports from the region. However, although as late as 1840 about one-half of regional exports came from mineral ores, concentrates, and bars (especially silver) or specie, mining in the southern sierra appears to have undergone a long decay between the 1850s (after the boomlet in gold exploration in Puno's montaña) and the 1880s, perhaps because of lack of capital, scarcity of labor, and especially the remoteness of many deposits, resulting in exorbitant transport costs.[49] The extension of the rail link from the port of Mollendo to the northern altiplano by the late 1870s, greater political stability after 1886, and the rapid fall of exchange rates between 1890 and 1893 led to an upswing of mining activity in the southern sierra. Between the early 1890s and 1907 British, American, and native capitalists made substantial investments in machinery for the extraction and processing of silver and gold ores in Arequipa's Cailloma province and in Lampa, Carabaya, and Sandia provinces in Puno.[50] The high share of minerals in Mollendo's global exports during the 1890s was due largely to increasing Bolivian transshipments of silver, copper, and tin. But during the years 1902–4, when statistics for Peruvian and Bolivian exports through Mollendo are separated for the first time, gold, silver, and copper still contributed 17 percent to Peruvian exports from that port. Yet during the 1910s mineral exports declined. Gold was marketed mostly within Peru; a temporary turn to the domestic market might also account for the temporary decline of silver exports.[51]

This broad range of secondary exports regularly contributed about one-third of foreign trade earnings. Not only did they buffer cyclical fluctuations in the wool trade, but they also extended the geographic reach of monetarized trade to diverse and distant districts, from the valleys of

Arequipa to its highland mining zones and the broad eastern escarpment of the Andes. This diverse range of exports strengthened the network of regional trade conducted by hispanized and foreign traders. Although regional commerce, outside of the circuits maintained by the peasantry, had atrophied during the long decades of declining markets between the late eighteenth century and 1850, it now rose to new vitality in close but complicated interrelationship with the export trades.

Imports, Domestic Production, and Regional Trading Circuits

Southern Peru's balance of trade with foreign countries conducted through Islay and Mollendo stayed positive for most years between the mid-1850s and 1919.[52] Trade surpluses were especially impressive during the mid-1860s and the years of World War I but were large in most years since the 1890s. In part such surpluses flowed out of the region to Lima in the form of import duties and direct and indirect taxes. The south, like other provincial regions of Peru, helped to pay with its balance-of-trade surplus for the higher level of imports consumed in the capital, whose port, Callao, consistently garnered a share of imports much beyond its hinterland's share of national population and its export capacity. But part of these surpluses must have been retained in the south and contributed to the growth of expenditures for consumption or investment satisfied with regionally produced commodities.

"At least 60 percent of the population of Peru is practically negligible so far as the purchase of foreign goods is concerned," wrote William E. Dunn, the commercial attaché of the United States embassy in Lima, in 1925. In his opinion the Indian peasants, living in their "bare and desolate mud or stone huts in the Andean heights" and lacking "the remotest ideas of comfort in life," limited their purchases of manufactured goods to "a few cheap tools or an occasional novelty that strikes their fancy." They spent the "petty sums" they earned from the sale of wool and other products on the purchase of alcohol and coca leaves. Dunn viewed "mestizos of the lower class," with their "dilapidated houses, . . . furnished with only a few indispensable household articles," as only slightly better customers of imported goods. In fact, he thought that "the combined purchasing power of the Peruvian people might well be compared with that of the average American city of about 650,000." (Peru had about five million inhabitants at the time.) Demand for a broad range of upscale consumer goods, especially important for U.S. foreign trade by the early twentieth century, was concentrated in Peru's major cities, especially Lima.[53]

Although Dunn's cultural prejudices are striking, there is no reason to accuse him of underestimating the Indian peasants' propensity to consume imported goods. It was, after all, his job to identify potential markets for U.S. products. Southern Peru, with its great concentration of Indian peasants, consumed relatively few imports in relation to its population. During the first two decades of the twentieth century the region, with close to one-third of the country's population, accounted for 10 to 15 percent of Peru's total imports.[54] Without major urban centers the disproportion between population and consumption of imports was, of course, greater yet in the altiplano. As early as 1850, a few years after the terminal crisis of southern Peru's textile manufactories, the important trade fair at Vilque saw wholesale purchases of regional products for export of 490,000 pesos, while the sale of imported wares to altiplano traders and consumers amounted to only 300,000 pesos.[55] And for the period between 1920 and 1935 the Arequipa export and import house of Guillermo Ricketts y Compañía "bought much [primarily wools for export] and sold little [imports]" in Puno.[56]

Among the fifty-two different articles of wearing apparel imported into Peru in 1913, imports through Mollendo accounted for 10 percent or more of national imports for only fifteen articles.[57] Ready-made imported apparel did not sell much in southern Peru, either because its high price limited demand to two or three retail stores in Arequipa, or because the cheapest grades of standard clothing items were already being produced in small domestic clothing manufactories, or because most of the "better" families in the provinces continued to rely on seamstresses and tailors for major items of their wardrobes such as dresses and suits.[58] Similar problems were faced by a wide range of imported consumer goods in southern Peru. Domestic and artisanal production continued to supply many of the traditional items of consumption. At the same time, many items in the broadening range of commodities newly added to consumption patterns in southern Peru, especially since the 1890s, were produced by a growing number of small factories and artisanal shops in Arequipa and Cuzco or in Lima and other coastal towns.

To be sure, an ever-broadening range of imported goods did circulate throughout the southern highlands, integrating the remotest hamlet and the humblest peasant family into a commercial chain that had its other end in mighty factories in Bradford, Limoges, or Essen. As early as the 1830s and 1840s certain imported textile materials, hardware, glassware, and foodstuffs were consumed in altiplano provinces. Consumption patterns changed considerably after the coming of the railroad, and especially after the late 1880s.[59] The range of goods available in altiplano stores and markets expanded rapidly, and many of the newly offered items were imports. The dry-goods store of José Pantigoso Chavez on the Plaza Mayor of Puno town in 1858 carried a total of 74 items, of which 21 can be identified as likely imports, 36 as domestically produced, and 15 as either imported or domestic goods.[60]

By comparison, in 1890 the Casa de Comercio de Efectos Ultramarinos y de Abarrote Moller and Compañía, also located in Puno town, carried 241 different articles, of which 148 were probable imports, 35 were domestic goods, and a further 58 were of uncertain origin.[61] The more affluent of Azángaro's hacendados purchased imported furniture, household goods, apparel, and luxury food items. For example, in February 1873 the hacendado Manuel E. Paredes from Azángaro received special foods, beverages, and glass and china ware from a general and dry-goods store in Puno. Of the bill, which came to 142 pesos, 5 1/2 reales, items amounting to at least 56 1/2 pesos corresponded to imported goods, among them Norwegian beer and Spanish canned fish.[62] In the 1909 will of the hacendado Mariano Wenceslao Enríquez, long-time parish priest of Azángaro, appear such imported items as "one new French piano," a typewriter, and a sewing machine.[63]

Indian peasants also spent some money on imported goods. In the early 1860s, probably the apex of the relative strength of imports in southern Peruvian markets, the English traveler Clements Markham claimed, with considerable exaggeration, that "almost all the woolen clothing of the Peruvian Indians is now imported from Yorkshire, and their shirtings from Lowell."[64] Beginning no later than the last decade of the nineteenth century, peasants and poorer urban folk in the altiplano purchased such imported wares as basic tools (e.g., scissors and plowshares), needles, mirrors, and aniline dyes.[65] For southern Peru as a whole, the composition of imports underwent a major shift between the 1860s and the 1910s. In 1863 at least 52.3 percent of total imports through Islay were textiles, but their share had declined to an average of 34.9 percent between 1913 and 1916. By the mid-1910s, 40.5 percent of imports through Mollendo consisted of metal goods, ceramics, glass, cement, timber, paints, oil, rubber goods, tools, and machines, a broadened range of consumer and investment goods difficult to disentangle.[66]

But the weight of such imports in the overall expenditures of the altiplano's population, from community peasants to large, hispanized landholders, should not be exaggerated. With the exception of certain textiles, purchases of imports by hacendados or Indian peasants constituted occasional, extraordinary expenditures and did not belong to their day-to-day consumption. The items of the normal diet not only of peasants but also of hacendados, when they did not stem from the livestock growers' own production, originated mostly in regions adjacent to the altiplano.[67] Outlays for domestically produced maize, rice, noodles, flour, salt, fresh and dried fruits, and sugar occasioned considerable expenditures, particularly for the peasants. A great deal of income was spent on stimulants such as coca leaves and alcohol (aguardiente de caña for the peasants, *pisco* [brandy from Peru's coastal vineyards] and wine for the hacendados). Candles and fuel (if the dung of one's animals was insufficient), locally produced pots and silverware, and other domestically produced household items had to be purchased on a regular basis. Although the construction of a peasant's adobe hut required the purchase only of timber—not a cheap item in the woodless altiplano—the building of a hacendado's urban residence and, more generally speaking, investments in urban real estate swallowed up much money. Both hispanized hacendados and indigenous peasants invested savings from the sale of wool or other livestock products in land and livestock. There were expenditures for transportation, for the education of children in the case of more affluent landholders, and, last but not least, for numerous national, municipal, and church taxes and fees. In short, altiplano wool producers, after selling their wool to merchants, did not immediately turn around and spend all their returns on imported goods. This fact was obvious to Clements Markham, who wondered what alpaca herders did "with the enormous sums of money thus received." He suggested that they routinely buried such cash income.[68]

Among the altiplano peasantry, burial may indeed have been a common method of saving money for large, special expenditures (e.g., baptisms, marriages, and funerals), a type of deferred consumption. More generally, the increasing revenue brought into the region by wool exports and associated activities stimulated regional trade with domestically produced goods. Since the 1850s the export of wools had become the lead sector of the southern Peruvian economy. As export earnings grew, demand for regionally produced goods rose. Wools were now fueling the economies of the southern highlands just as silver had during much of the colonial era. As Manuel Burga and Wilson Reátegui observe, wool exports helped to form an economic region that became dynamic through that trade.[69]

What had changed since the mid-eighteenth century was the spatial definition of the economic region, the social composition of commercial networks, and the distribution of benefits from trade. The symbiotic relationship between the conjuncture for the major export commodity and the conjunctures for a broad range of regionally exchanged goods did not change, however. The strengthened foreign trade nexus had undermined or even destroyed specific processing activities and commercial flows by the

TABLE 5.6. Wool Production in Southern Peru (Estimates)
and Exports From Islay and Mollendo, 1840–1917
(1,000 metric tons)

	Production		Exports		% Retained Domestically	
	Sheep	Alpaca	Sheep	Alpaca	Sheep	Alpaca
1840	2,152.0	925.7	904.7	598.1	58.0	35.4
1867	3,432.9	1,664.7	1,985.0	1,337.4	42.2	19.7
1917	5,804.9	3,033.3	2,560.5	2,247.0	55.9	25.9

Sources: Exports based on Jacobsen, "Cycles and Booms," 490–500, tables 3–6; Jacobsen, "Land Tenure," 815–33, app. 1. For wool production, I constructed baseline estimates for 1830 and 1929. For 1830 see chap. 2, n. 76. In the other baseline year, 1929, the first national agricultural and livestock census was carried out; see Dir. de Agricultura y Ganadería, *Estadística general agro-pecuaria.* Its figures are unreliable. For the department of Puno, it calculates a sheep population nearly identical to that for 1959, while for cameloids it indicates about one-fifth of the 1959 population. Given that by 1959 southern Peruvian livestock herds had just been decimated by the catastrophic drought of the mid-1950s, I have estimated net growth of livestock populations and wool production between 1929 and 1959 of 10 percent. I arrived at estimates for 1840, 1867, and 1917 by calculating the linear absolute growth between the two base years. Of course, this renders only rather rough estimates.

mid-nineteenth century, but over the next seventy years it did not have the strength or the explosive impact to completely eliminate trade in artisanal goods and other regionally produced processed commodities. On the contrary, indications are that the share of regionally or nationally produced goods among the total goods consumed in southern Peru rose after about 1870.

Take the crucial case of wools. As late as 1840 close to 60 percent of sheep wool and over a third of alpaca wool produced in southern Peru was not exported but was processed in the region, either on looms in peasant households or in the remaining obrajes. Most obrajes finally collapsed during the mid-1840s, a new wave of cheaper imported textiles entered the region, and the price for wool rose dramatically during the 1850s and 1860s. Because of these developments, the share of wools that was exported appears to have risen sharply. By 1867 only about 42 percent of sheep wool and 20 percent of alpaca wool may have been retained domestically (table 5.6), confirming the frequent complaints by British consuls that the exports of alpaca wools were limited by tight supply. But over the following fifty years this trend was reversed as livestock herds grew faster than wool exports. For the whole period 1830–1917, southern Peru's sheep population may have grown nearly three and a half times, whereas sheep wool exports grew 2.8 times between 1840 and 1917. Alpaca herds may have grown more than four and a half times, with exports expanding by a factor of 3.7 between 1840 and 1917.[70] Between 1867, when the ratio of wool exports to wool production probably reached its highest point, and 1917, sheep wool production may be estimated to have grown by nearly 70 percent, while exports increased by only 30 percent. The share of domestically retained wool thus was elevated to at least 55.9 percent in the case of sheep wool and a more modest 25.9 percent in the case of alpaca wool.[71]

Two reasons account for the growing domestic consumption of raw wools. One is the opening of modern woolen mills in southern Peru that processed the regionally produced raw materials. The first opened in 1861 on Hacienda Lucre, site of an old obraje close to Cuzco, by the Garmendia family, a prominent family of large landholders since colonial times. After a mere twenty years of nearly complete prostration of elite-controlled textile production, this was the first step in the reversal of that trend. But southern Peru's modern textile industry grew very slowly. Between 1895 and 1910 two more mills began operations in Maranganí and Urcos, in the colonial centers of Cuzco's textile production in Canchis and Quispicanchis provinces, and one opened in Arequipa. The Maranganí factory, "one of the most progressive and up to date enterprises in South America," had modern English, German, and Belgian machinery installed. It relied on Indian community peasants and colonos as workers, something that remained true for all textile factories in Cuzco before 1920.[72]

These factories were small in terms of capital, installed capacity, and work force in comparison with the woolen mills in Lima and especially with the cotton mills in the capital, owned by powerful foreign enterprises such as W. R. Grace and Duncan Fox and Company. The south Peruvian market for manufactured woolens was now disputed by three sets of producers: factories located in the region itself, in Lima, and in Europe. By the second decade of this century more nationally produced textiles were sold in the region than imports. And although the large Lima factories dominated the market for cotton goods, the southern factories were relatively strong in woolens up to the end of World War I, especially in highland departments such as Cuzco, Apurimac, and Puno, but briefly also in Arequipa. The Cuzco factories specialized in baizes, cashmeres, flannels, and blankets aimed at peasants and other downscale consumers, a market segment for which their lower transport costs and intimate knowledge of regional styles and marketing arrangements gave them the edge.[73]

Nevertheless, according to one report, by 1918 Peru's factories still absorbed only some 680 metric tons of sheep wool, below 10 percent of national production and just under 20 percent of exports.[74] Although this industrial use of wools clearly contributed to the shifting balance between exports and domestic consumption, the surprising fact is the continued weight of wool processing in peasant households. Even during the height of the wool export boom toward the end of World War I, nearly one hundred years after the opening of direct foreign trade with England and more than fifty years after the installation of the first modern woolen mill in the country, cloth woven on the simple looms of the peasant households must have consumed between 45 and 55 percent of all sheep wool and close to one-fourth of all alpaca wool produced in southern Peru.[75] Estimates are too rough to indicate with confidence whether the *relative* share of peasant household production in the disposition of southern Peru's total wool clip had begun to decline during the first century after independence, when consumption of wool by obrajes was replaced by wool exports and modern factory processing. But it is clear that with the strong growth of livestock populations the *absolute* quantity of wools processed in peasant households continued to increase until 1920. Although southern Peru's rural folks and the poorer strata of the towns had purchased certain imported textile items since the 1830s or 1840s and had begun to use domestically manufactured woolens since the 1860s, the attendant reduction in the per capita consumption of household-produced textiles was more than offset by the increase in the region's population that continued to rely on some home-woven fabrics. To reiterate this crucial point: the absolute amount of woolens produced in peasant households continued to grow during the century after independence, even if per capita consumption began to decline.

This increased output of homespun woolens would not have been unusual as a relatively brief transitional phenomenon accompanying the formation of an integrated domestic market in conjunction with the emerging dominance of the capitalist mode of production, as Emilio Sereni has shown for the Italian case. For a period of some thirty years following the onset of the formation of a large-scale textile industry in the 1860s, the processing of linen and hemp in rural households in Italy continued on a high level, and the number of looms in the countryside continued to increase even until the early 1890s. But the opening of Italy to massive foreign trade, the liberal policies of the *resorgimiento*, and, after 1880, a policy of industrial protection created a national market in which rural producers increasingly succumbed to the large factories in the northern cities, industry and agriculture became thoroughly separated, and the mezzogiorno was made into a "dependent territory" of the northern industrialists.[76]

In the comparative perspective of Western Europe, Sereni considered the Italian transition toward a capitalist national market excruciatingly slow, held back by "feudal remnants." But the Peruvian case was quite different.

Before 1930 no national market emerged; foreign trade and modern industry, rather than functioning as battering rams bringing down the walls
of southern Peru's traditional modes of production and exchange, accom-
modated themselves to regional interests; agriculture and industry remained highly linked, and domestic household production grew along with
foreign trade and modern industry, whose capacity to expand thus remained limited.[77] Low productivity in agriculture and artisanal production,
as well as the neocolonial structure of the society, made the southern
Peruvian highlands resilient to the forces of change.

The money circulating in southern Peru through export activities thus
stimulated a broad range of domestic production and processing for regional trade without drastically changing the mode by which these commodities were produced. The demand for many of these commodities
moved together with the export economy. Maize in Cuzco became scarce
in 1917 when demand from the core livestock area between Sicuani and
Lake Titicaca rose in conjunction with the wool export boom.[78] Sheep and
cattle on the hoof from Puno and maize from Cuzco briefly encountered
strong markets in Chilean-occupied Tarapacá during the 1910s, when that
region's nitrate export peaked.[79] Since the 1850s the consumption of grape
alcohol from the valleys of Moquegua and around Arequipa had increased
in the rural areas of the altiplano. After the railroad facilitated access from
the coast to the southern highlands, cane alcohol from the rapidly modernizing north coast sugar estates pushed out the southern grape alcohols,
and peasant consumption of aguardiente de caña grew in close relation to
conjunctures of the wool market.[80]

Besides the various woolen goods, a broad range of artisanal products
found strong demand throughout southern Peru. Artisans from the altiplano and workshops in Arequipa or Cuzco did not merely continue to
produce standard items of long-standing demand but adjusted their production to shifting urban consumption patterns. Potters in Santiago de
Pupuja and Pucará diversified from the plain jars and pots used for cooking
in most of the altiplano, creating vases, ashtrays, and ornamental pieces
sought after by urban middle-class families. Leather workshops, especially
in Arequipa, also adjusted their production to new urban demands in
footwear, clothing accessories, and household furnishings.[81]

Southern Peru took on its contours as a distinct trading region during
the second half of the nineteenth century as a consequence of this artic-
ulation between foreign and regional trade. From Desaguadero to Abancay,
from Huancané to Camaná, and from Quillabamba to Moquegua, dozens
of trading circuits transmitted the impulses from the export activities to
remote valleys and mountain slopes that produced commodities for the

regional market. While regional interchanges intensified along with foreign trade, commerce with Bolivia, which had been the major pole of the erstwhile colonial pattern of exchange, lost in relative weight. Southern Peru became a distinct region for which the links with Liverpool were more important than those with Lima. Since the early 1870s the railroad line connecting the port of Mollendo and the entrepôt Arequipa with the highland zone had become the backbone of this trading region, erecting new commercial hierarchies, fostering new urban centers, and relegating others to a marginal position within those hierarchies. The creation of a new spatial hierarchy in southern Peru's commerce as a result of the rise of the wool exports and the construction of a modern transport funnel went hand in hand with the renovation and intensification of social hierarchy in trade: the growing centrality of the import and export merchants, benefiting most from the advantages of improved means of transportation and communication; the establishment or, in some towns, the expansion of several layers of middlemen, from wholesalers, regional bulkers, and owners of well-stocked general stores in important centers along the rail line to itinerant peddlers and wool purchasers; and the dependent incorporation of mestizo and Indian traders into the bottom rungs of these hierarchies. As Gordon Appleby has argued persuasively, trade in southern Peru became organized into a "dendritic" model, akin to a tree in which the life of even the remotest twig in the crown depends ultimately on the main stem.[82]

But this was not the whole story. Much of the regional trade continued to flow outside of the channels of this "dendritic" system, even if it did not escape its influence in terms of demand fluctuations. Many points of conflict and tension marked the attempts by merchants entrenched in the export- import hierarchy to impose their trade routes, their prices, and their commercial intermediation on peasants, muleteers, and others who continued to ply older, more autonomous trade circuits based on intraregional complementarity. The conflicts erupting in southern Peruvian trade since the late nineteenth century were not primarily between groups attempting to impose foreign trade against the maintenance of intraregional exchanges or vice versa. Especially in the altiplano there were few traders who did not have a foothold in both types of activity. At stake was the social distribution of benefits within a regional trading system made up of heterogeneous elements.

Two studies on other Andean regions have emphasized that between the 1870s and 1880s regional commercial circuits were disrupted through the corrosive effects of economic liberalism and war. Tristan Platt has pointed to the "internal market" for maize and wheat in Upper Peru and Bolivia up to the 1860s. Cochabamba and, after independence, Chayanta supplied the northern Bolivian altiplano and adjacent regions in southern Peru with these staples. The community peasantry of Chayanta played a prominent role in the "internal market" as long as the Bolivian state pursued a protectionist trade policy and maintained its alliance with the Indians symbolized by the tribute nexus. This "internal market" was destroyed within little more than a decade, when between the late 1860s and early 1880s the Bolivian national elite turned to a free-trade policy, allowing Chilean grains to flood the national market, and simultaneously attempted to institute a liberal land policy, which, had it been successful, would have destroyed the Indian ayllu and replaced it throughout the republic with large estates.[83]

The other case concerns the central Peruvian sierra, analyzed by Nelson Manrique. Since the 1840s a dynamic, relatively autonomous regional market had developed, based on the rising demand for livestock products in Lima and an intensive trade in locally produced cane alcohol. This regional market conjuncture, in contrast to the picture drawn by Platt for Chayanta, primarily benefited large landholders and merchants. It entered into crisis through the destruction and social mobilization wrought on the region by the War of the Pacific. As most families of the central sierra's regional oligarchy saw their properties destroyed, sources of credit withdrawn, and markets challenged, they lost control over the regional economy first to better-capitalized businessmen from Lima and, after 1900, to "imperialist capital" taking over the copper-mining industry. In Manrique's view the formation and demise of the central sierra's regional market were inevitable steps toward the formation of Peru's national market.[84]

Southern Peru underwent a different development. After painful adjustments to the displacements of certain domestic goods by imports between the 1780s and 1850s, the regional market became tied to the growth of foreign trade. The liberalization of imports during the 1850s and 1860s helped to establish foreign trade as the strategic, lead sector of southern Peru's economy, favored the formation of new mercantile hierarchies dominated by the foreign houses of Arequipa, and in this way fostered the growth of the "dendritic" trading pattern that defined the south as a region in and of itself. But this trade liberalization did not lead to a general crisis of intraregional trade, as Platt has described for Chayanta. The crucial difference between the two cases concerns the commodities involved and the producers. In Chayanta the strategic products for peasant participation in the "internal market"—cereals—could easily be replaced by imports once the tariff and transport conditions favored such replacement. In southern Peru the strategic export commodity was produced to a considerable part by peasants. The same activity of livestock raising that involved the peasantry in the export nexus simultaneously produced a broad range of goods for regional trade, from wool and hides to meat, tallow, butter, and cheese. Wool bulkers could hardly have wanted the peasants to cease barter and trade in such commodities, as it would have made them totally dependent on income from wool sales for export, inevitably leading to demands for higher prices for peasants' wool.

Other commodities from different parts of southern Peru, such as coca leaves, tea and coffee, cane and grape alcohols, chile peppers, raisins, and olives, had little to fear from overseas imports. Between 1888 and 1897 higher import tariffs and exchange rate devaluation led to increased levels of effective protection, but this situation did not automatically benefit regional trade controlled by peasants; rather, it led to modest import substitutions through a few new factories, such as the woolen mills discussed above, iron foundries, and breweries, which merely shifted the origin of manufactured goods confronting some of the peasants' domestic goods. Industrialists and merchants were either identical or the former were highly dependent on the latter before 1920. For this reason the national debate over import tariffs during the 1890s does not appear to have split the region's business elite. Until the end of the World War I export boom most members of that elite, in Cuzco and Puno as much as in Arequipa, remained free traders.[85]

The Altiplano's Commercial System Between the 1850s and 1920

Until the late 1850s the export of wool through Islay was controlled by only four companies of foreign origin operating from Arequipa—two British, one French, and one German.[86] For them, the import of manufactured goods from Europe was as important as their export business. In both activities the foreign houses still operated mostly in Arequipa itself. As importers they worked as wholesalers; as exporters they bought wool from middlemen directly in Arequipa or made a yearly venture to one of the annual fairs on the altiplano.[87]

In these circumstances independent Peruvian merchants had a considerable role to play in all stages of wool bulking prior to final exportation. Affluent men such as José Mariano Escobedo, an Azangarino resident in Arequipa, or the Arequipeño José María Peña often entered the wool trade only as one line of business among many.[88] Escobedo owned a number of haciendas in Azángaro and received large public works contracts from the government. In 1851 he began the wool trade as a partner of the German merchant Guillermo Harmsen.[89] Peña had owned gold mines in the Cordillera de Carabaya since before 1850.[90] Sometime before 1865 he had formed a company with Eusebio Prudencio, a Bolivian, "for the purchase of chinchona bark and alpaca wool and the sale of merchandise in Soraicho," located in Huancané province from where the trade with the Bolivian lakeshore as well as the ceja de la selva could easily be organized. Prudencio was to take care of business in Soraicho while Peña arranged for the sale in England as well as the purchase of Peruvian and imported goods finding demand on the eastern rim of the altiplano.[91] Peña probably held similar contracts with traders from other wool-producing regions, and his mercantile operation spanned the whole altiplano.

Merchants with the necessary capital joined together with persons who could ensure a supply of wool from their own extensive estates. This was the case in the company founded by Manuel and José María Costas and Antonio Fernández, all of Puno, on April 15, 1853.[92] Fernández saw himself incapable of paying his share of the company's capital, so it was paid in by the Costas brothers as credit. The Costas brothers found it advantageous to join in a common enterprise with Fernández because he was owner and renter of numerous livestock estates and promised "to cede to the Society all sheep wools proceeding from his haciendas." These haciendas happened to be located west of Puno in the geographic funnel of the altiplano leading to the main mule road to Arequipa and thus could well serve as warehousing, washing, and packing points for the wools purchased by the company prior to their transport across the western cordillera.[93]

Only six years after the founding of the company Fernández admitted owing his partners the amazing sum of 53,832 pesos, 4 reales, a sum corresponding to more than 10 percent of the total value of average annual sheep wool exports from Islay during the 1850s and more than the value of the largest altiplano estates during those years. This debt represented cash withdrawals from the company's funds as well as sales on Fernández's own account of sizable quantities of company sheep wool as payment of private debts to the Arequipa export houses.[94] The size of such transactions suggests that a relatively small number of Peruvian wool traders, either individuals or companies, must have supplied a large share of all wool subsequently exported by the Arequipa houses. Despite the heavy debts incurred by their early partner Fernández, the Costas family continued its wool-trading business at least until 1925.[95]

Before the 1870s the tendency of the foreign houses to limit their mercantile operation largely to Arequipa and the concomitant strong position of Peruvian merchants such as Escobedo, Peña, and Costas also had consequences for the structure of southern Peru's credit network. During the 1850s and 1860s altiplano wool traders and hacendados depended on the Arequipa export houses for credit—for example, for their wool purchases or investments in real estate—considerably less than they would toward the end of the century. The large regional wool bulkers apparently possessed sufficient working capital not to require advances from the exporters for purchasing large amounts of wool; thus, they could operate independently and decide when and to whom they would sell their wools. It seems to have been these regional bulkers who extended credit to their suppliers.

Another important source of credit existed in the altiplano during the third quarter of the past century. A small group of merchants, who partially overlapped with the regional wool bulkers, had become something like specialized bankers extending credit to dozens of shopkeepers, landholders, and magistrates. Antonio Amenábar was one such "merchant banker." Born in Córdoba, Argentina, between 1824 and 1826, he pursued a great variety of business ventures in Puno and Tacna, including transportation (he invested in the first metal cargo ship operating on Lake Titicaca) and collection of government taxes.[96] In 1865 his Puno stores contained goods, including imports, worth 40,839 pesos. At the same time he had outstanding credits, extended since 1860, amounting to 46,675 pesos (including interest). Among his fifty-four debtors, who owed him between 70 and 6,000 pesos principal besides interest, were members of the department's wealthiest and most powerful families—the Macedos, the Pinos, the San Romans, the Núñez, the Aguirres, the Tovars, and the Arésteguis. Some of them owned haciendas in Azángaro province.[97] Nine years later, in 1874, his will no longer listed merchandise from a store, which by then was possibly the property of his wife through a legal "division of goods."[98] But he still had outstanding credits amounting to 36,500 pesos, extended to twelve clients since 1871.[99]

On a smaller scale, some provincial traders also seem to have attempted a measure of specialization into such credit operations. A case in point is Pedro Palazuelos, hacendado and trader from Putina in Azángaro province. After his death, sometime before May 1865, his wife and son attempted to collect some 5,800 pesos in outstanding credits extended to nine clients, most of whom were prominent Azangarinos. Besides further, probably minimal debts by another nine clients, Palazuelos's heirs also tried to recover rented livestock and 6,000 pesos given as advances to Indian peasants for purchases of wool and slaughter animals.[100] The amount of general-purpose monetary credits extended by Palazuelos and the number of his debtors justify calling him a specialized creditor. But the borderline to the more general phenomenon of small money loans, practiced by many landholders and traders in the altiplano, seems blurred.

The scarcity of cash threatened vital routine commercial transactions for many families. A dense network of small, reciprocal credit transactions, organized through ties of kinship and trust among friends, sprang up in the towns and hamlets of the altiplano in an era of increasing trade. Such petty credit exchanges could shift imperceptibly into more hierarchical, asymmetric credit relationships, constructed by provincial traders who had somewhat more cash and were eager to profit directly from the cash scarcity or to build up a dependent clientele for mercantile endeavors.

With the increase in southern Peru's exports of wool and other raw materials, demand for transport animals rose during the middle decades of the nineteenth century. At least until the late 1860s a lively trade in mules from Salta kept up the supply of these animals. In June 1857, for example, the merchants Juan Bautista Coret and Telesforo Padilla from Salta and Simón de Oteira from La Paz passed through Puno with some sixteen hundred mules, which they hoped to sell on their march to Lima, a good part of them probably in the vicinity of Arequipa.[101] In Puno, de Oteira purchased another 540 mules from Fernando del Valle, a local hacendado and "merchant banker."[102] It appears that del Valle regularly acquired mules in order to let them regain their strength on his estates in Acora after their long trek from Argentina. He resold some of these animals to passing traders and kept enough for his own trains, with which he transported pisco from Moquegua to La Paz.[103]

During the third quarter of the nineteenth century the transport business concentrated in Arequipa and adjacent valleys as this city became the entrepôt for southern Peru's exports. Markham considered Arequipa's muleteers, whose increasingly numerous mule herds had taken over much of the city's fertile *campiña* from food crops, to be a "wealthy class of men" during the 1860s.[104] Of course, these mule trains did not enjoy a monopoly over southern Peru's transport requirements. Peasant landholders and hacendados transported much of their products on their own llamas. Specialized transport entrepreneurs in the altiplano working with llamas also continued to ply the trans-Andean routes.[105]

One of the reasons why the foreign merchants limited their activities largely to transactions in Arequipa itself lay in the extreme difficulties of transport between the coast and the altiplano. In the words of one foreign traveler, "Most of the roads are merely mule tracks and they are taken over passes of the Andes from 14,000 to 17,000 feet above the sea amidst snow and ice."[106] The regularly established mail covered the distance from Arequipa to Puno in three days, and pack trains needed at least five days for the same route.[107]

Between about 1860 and 1875 changes in the commercial structure of southern Peru began to affect the balance between the various social groups involved. The boom of wool exports and generally favorable commercial conditions during the 1860s led to the establishment of many new export houses.[108] As early as 1862 the mercantile community of Arequipa and Islay was clamoring for a railroad connection between the Ciudad Blanca and its port.[109] On December 18, 1869, the Peruvian government commissioned Henry Meiggs, an American engineer involved in the nitrate business, to construct a railroad line from the Pacific coast via Arequipa to Puno. Choosing a termination point a few kilometers south of the established port of Islay, the line connecting Arequipa with Mollendo was opened for traffic on January 1, 1871. By 1873 the whole line of 351 kilometers to Puno, crossing the western cordillera at an altitude of about forty-five hundred meters at Crucero Alto, was completed.[110] From Puno regular boat services across Lake Titicaca connected this line with Bolivia, and by the early years of this century, a number of cargo ships had established regular links with a whole string of small ports, including Moho and Huancané in the north and Ilave, Juli, Yunguyo, and Desaguadero in the south.[111]

The northern section of the altiplano began to be integrated into this modern transportation funnel to and from the coastal port with the construction of the railroad line ultimately linking Cuzco to the Puno–Arequipa line. Meiggs received the government contract to build this line in December 1871. Branching off from the previously constructed line at Juliaca, about forty kilometers north of Puno, it pursues a northerly course and for some sixty kilometers straddles the border between Lampa and Azángaro provinces. This course, necessitated when powerful citizens of Lampa rejected the track's passing through their town,[112] gave rise to four railroad stations—Calapuja, Laro, Estación de Pucará, and Tirapata—conveniently located for large parts of Azángaro's livestock-raising zones. By the mid-1870s, before the financial crisis halted further construction, the railroad line had been completed for 131 kilometers to the town of Santa Rosa, close to the northwestern rim of the altiplano. All of the Peruvian altiplano had now been put into reasonable proximity of rail or boat transport; except for isolated hamlets in both cordilleras most locations lay within two days' journey on muleback from railroad stations or ports.[113]

Traffic on the line remained thin until the 1920s. One passenger train a day traveled in each direction between Arequipa and Mollendo, and only two per week ran between the entrepôt city and Puno, covering the distance of 350 kilometers in ten to twelve hours. Freight trains were no more frequent, and schedules changed often in accordance with traffic conditions. These frequencies remained basically unchanged until the mid-1920s.[114] The railroad operated at a loss during its first years. It was built not to accommodate already existing trade but to produce its own business through a major reduction in transport costs and an anticipated expansion of trade. Such expectations by the government and southern Peru's business elite proved optimistic at best. In contrast to Mexico, where the shift from a slow and inefficient transport system to railroads contributed to strong economic growth,[115] southern Peru's growth of trade and production remained relatively modest. The modernization of the transport system failed to transform the relations of production in the countryside or to deepen the market. Railroad freightage grew primarily by concentrating commercial flows through the consolidation of the dendritic system, drawing business from muleteers. Railroads accelerated economic growth in Latin America most when the commodities to be moved were bulky items, such as minerals or grains, and when there were virgin resources (land, major untapped mineral deposits) in the production zone accessed by the rail link. Neither of these conditions prevailed in the case of the altiplano. Moreover, since transport costs represented only a small part of the FOB values of wools—no more than 15 percent by one estimate—a reduction in freight rates through the switch from mules and llamas to rail could produce only small savings for the producer.[116]

Paradoxically, when trade flourished, the modern transportation funnel rapidly reached its full capacity. British consuls repeatedly complained about bottlenecks caused by shortages of boxcars, the inefficient steamer service across Lake Titicaca, and insufficient warehouses in the port of Mollendo.[117] The Peruvian Corporation, the British proprietor of the Ferrocarril del Sur and the lake steamers since 1890, apparently adapted to southern Peru's business environment by keeping transport space scarce.[118] Yet railroad freight rates appear to have been relatively low compared to those of other lines in Peru.[119]

Nevertheless, traders and livestock growers in the altiplano frequently complained that the Peruvian Corporation's transport rates favored imports and Bolivian transit commodities over goods from the Cuzco and Puno highlands shipped to the coast.[120] During the first forty years the railroad, to be marginally profitable, depended on cargo to and from Bolivia, especially ores but also wool from the departments of La Paz and Oruro as well as imports for the urban market of La Paz. Despite wool's great importance for the regional economy, shipments of it from the Peruvian production areas, the core zone of the railroad's operation, never brought enough business for the down trips to break even. When the new La Paz–Arica line opened in 1914, Bolivian business on the Ferrocarril del Sur was sharply reduced, with "catastrophic effects" for the line's profitability. To compensate, in 1919 the Peruvian Corporation began a series of rate increases in excess of rising costs. In the following decade the company attempted to increase the tonnage of wool shipped by railroad from the altiplano to Mollendo. Until the mid-1920s it unsuccessfully sought to establish a huge wool-production syndicate under its control in Puno and Cuzco, an undertaking meant to ensure increased wool shipments on the rail line. As late as 1932 the Ferrocarril del Sur drew only 7.4 percent of its total freight income from the transportation of wool.[121]

Llama and mule transport was not replaced by the railroad overnight. Pack trains were still needed to take wool and other livestock products from the estates and offline urban bulking centers to the warehouses at railroad stations and lakeside ports and bring back domestic and imported supplies, hauled up to the altiplano from the coast or Arequipa by railroad. Nor did transport animals disappear immediately from the old mule paths crossing the western cordillera. As late as the 1920s as much as 20 to 25 percent of exported altiplano wool was transported to Arequipa by llama or mule trains.[122] In particular, many owners of small and medium-sized haciendas, who wanted to benefit from direct sales to the export houses in Arequipa but were in no position to profit from day-to-day fluctuations of wool prices, preferred to use their own or their shepherds' llamas as inexpensive means of transport.

The new extractive enterprises that developed in the department of Puno beginning in the 1890s—gold mining in the cordillera and piedmont of Carabaya and rubber collection further down in the rain forest—brought muleteers and llama drivers additional business on the roads and trails that fed into the railroad line. The supply of mining and rubber companies in Carabaya and Sandia provinces proved profitable both for altiplano estate owners, who dispatched their own transport llamas or those of their colonos, and for professional muleteers, mostly from Arequipa, who plied these new circuits with strings of up to a hundred mules.[123]

After the mid-1890s, construction of improved roads, passable by four-wheeled vehicles, began in the Peruvian altiplano. The foreign-owned Inca Mining Company constructed a road from the Tirapata railroad station toward its gold mines at Santo Domingo on Río Inambari. For over ninety kilometers this road passed through Azángaro province, connecting its northern and eastern districts (Asillo, San Antón, and Potoni) more comfortably with the rail line.[124] Public road construction projects connected the capital, Azángaro, to the railroad station Estación de Pucará (a distance of some thirty kilometers) as early as 1896, and Azángaro with Asillo (about twenty kilometers) by 1916. During the 1920s the eastern part of the province around Muñani and Putina was incorporated into the road network both by a link to Azángaro town and through a more southerly direct connection to Juliaca via Huancané (see map 1.1).

By the late 1920s Puno's road network, with about two thousand kilometers of improved roads completed, was the most extensive in the whole republic. One observer explained this comparatively rapid progress as the consequence both of the favorable terrain—the broad pampas of the altiplano—and the abundance of Indian labor pressed into the heavy chores of road building by local authorities and estate owners. These factors were important, but the new roads also underscored the departmental elite's influence in national politics during the first third of this century. Paradoxically, although the condition of altiplano roads was described as "excellent" as early as 1913, there still hardly existed any motorized vehicles. Only during the 1920s did trucks begin to assume an important role in transport to and from railroad stations. Just as in the case of railroads, construction of roads largely preceded effective demand.[125]

In spite of its modest impact on the scale of trade and on relations of production, the modernization of the transport system has to be considered the most important motor behind changes in the spatial patterning and the social and economic structure of trade in the altiplano.[126] Previously the role of towns in the bulking of wool and other commodities for export, as well as in the distribution of imported goods, had been relatively small since in a "landscape of uniform, primitive transportation" much wool could be transported from the producer to the entrepôt city, Arequipa, without being handled in towns, even though it passed through several layers of middlemen.[127] The switch of the predominant transport mode from llama and mule train to railroad and lake steamers brought about the rise of commercial centers, strategically located on the rail line or the lakeshore, where merchants handled the transshipment of goods flowing in both directions through the funnel. Puno, Juliaca, and Ayaviri benefited most from this new spatial pattern. Other important commercial centers owed their very birth to the railroad, among them Estación de Pucará and Tirapata in Azángaro province.[128] Some urban centers that did not share the advantage of being located on the rail line or the lakeshore managed to hold on to and even intensify commercial activity. This was true of Azángaro town and Putina in the eastern part of the province, which remained secondary centers of wool bulking because of their distance from railroad stations or ports.[129]

A growing number of traders, shopkeepers, and commercial establishments now set up business, and the penetration of trade by the Arequipa export houses intensified. These changes were already becoming noticeable by the mid-1870s, though the crisis and dislocation caused by the War of the Pacific retarded their full development until about 1890. Some of the new traders and shopkeepers had long been residents of the department of Puno; many others came from Arequipa, Cuzco, Tacna, and other parts of Peru, and quite a few came from overseas. Except for the entrepreneurs and engineers at the newly opened mines, foreigners settled in the largest towns, principally Puno and—after the turn of the century—Juliaca, rapidly becoming the major wool-bulking center in the department because of its strategic location at the hub of the new transport lines. Combining wholesaling and retailing activities, many foreigners established well-stocked stores with adjacent warehouses where they sold imported and Peruvian merchandise and purchased "country products," mostly wool and hides but also gold, rubber, and coffee.[130]

Rodolfo Möller may stand as an example of foreign retailers in Puno. His Casa de Comercio de Efectos Ultramarinos y de Abarrote Möller y Compañía carried a great variety of foreign and domestic merchandise: ten bottles of "eau de Cologne, best grade," some hundred cans of different aniline dyes, 26 cases of Lion brand Norwegian beer, 27 varas of white narrow cotton flannel, 221 packages of white thread for "Chardio" sewing machines, kerosene from Tumbes, paper, silverware, scissors, and knives.[131] Möller had bought most items on credit from the import and export house of Enrique W. Gibson y Compañía in Arequipa.

The Peruvians, from both inside and outside the department of Puno, who had swelled the ranks of altiplano traders and shopkeepers since the 1870s spread more evenly through the towns of the region. In Azángaro newcomers settled especially in the capital of the province, some of the larger district capitals such as Asillo and Putina, and, of course, at the railroad stations Tirapata and Estación de Pucará, where warehouses and shops sprang up around the railroad tracks on what previously had been pastures.

Many of the newcomers first appeared in the altiplano as muleteers or itinerant traders from Arequipa or other surrounding regions with which Puno traditionally had maintained an active commercial interchange. One such man was Manuel Sixto Mostajo Yáñez. His father, an itinerant peddler from Arequipa, had frequently passed through Azángaro on his sales trips to Sandia, the piedmont region northeast of the province. Manuel continued this business. Sometime during the 1890s he married Victoria Enríquez, who belonged to an old hacendado family from Azángaro and was the niece (or even daughter) of the town's long-time parish priest, Mariano Wenceslao Enríquez. Mostajo now established his residence in the provincial capital, built—apparently with financial aid from Father Enríquez—a large house on the Plaza de Armas, and established a store, where he sold such goods as cloth, window glass, and the like.[132] He became wool-buying agent for the Arequipa export house of Ricketts and in 1903 received a contract from the Peruvian postal service to transport baggage and parcels from Azángaro to Sandia.[133] As early as 1901 Mostajo was so well integrated into Azángaro's provincial society that he became treasurer of the town's municipal council.[134] But he maintained his itinerant trading expeditions to the ceja de la selva and to the annual fairs at Pucará, Rosaspata, and Cojata until the end of his business career. In 1930 Mostajo ordered for such a peddling circuit items including woolen shawls, cheap felt skirts, cheap hats, Italian borsalino hats, cotton cloth, thread, aniline dyes, and even unassembled bicycles.[135]

Among long-time residents of Azángaro a growing number of hacendados diversified into wool trading and shopkeeping just as the Paredes family had done since the 1840s. Around 1890 the half brothers Bernardino Arias Echenique and José Sebastián Urquiaga inherited Hacienda Sollocota, a small livestock estate of colonial origin, around which they built a vast landholding complex. At the same time they went into business as alcohol merchants in Azángaro town, and at least Urquiaga also operated as a wool trader.[136]

Owners of strategically located haciendas were able to use their locations to purchase the production of smallholders in the surrounding area. This tendency was already observed by the Italian naturalist Antonio Raimondi in 1864 regarding an estate in Azángaro's district of Potoni, on the slope of the Cordillera de Carabaya: "Hacienda Potoni has as its object the collection of the sheep wool of the surrounding countryside and of the much more valuable alpaca wool produced in the immediately neighboring province of Carabaya."[137] In 1904 Mariano C. Rodríguez, a landholder and trader from Rosaspata, Huancané province, offered to sell altiplano products to Ricketts y Compañía in Arequipa. He explained that his Hacienda Huaranca Chico was located close to the Bolivian border and that there, on the estate, "one can easily buy all these products [wool, rubber, and chinchona bark]."[138] Access to smallholder production was a more crucial qualification for altiplano traders than was formal knowledge of commercial operations.[139] Rodríguez explained to Ricketts that his family used the income from livestock ranching "to comfortably supply our needs." For his business he spent no money on rent and little on wages because "we have Indians who work for us nearly free of charge. In this way I can utilize the profit from the business to capitalize [it] and to attend to unforeseen business losses."[140] While the operation of livestock haciendas was to provide the income for a comfortable life-style, Rodríguez hoped to use his commercial business as a source of capital accumulation.

Below the ranks of mestizo merchants and specialized itinerant traders flourished a complex and fluid world of peasant barter and trade. Exchange between altiplano peasant herders and agricultural producers of different ecological levels had been an important part of the structure of Andean society since prehispanic times. Trips by owners of livestock estancias from Azángaro to the ceja de la selva regions of Carabaya, Sandia, or the adjacent valleys of Bolivia ordinarily served the purpose of exchanging wool, dried meat, hides, and other altiplano products for coca leaves, maize, and medicinal herbs for the herders' own consumption. But it was only a small step to trade more of such goods than one needed for family subsistence, particularly when the terms of trade developed favorably for livestock products.[141] If such a trip went well, the peasant from Azángaro could profit from the barter or sale of his or her products in the ceja de la selva and again on return to the altiplano from the sale of the surplus maize or coca leaves.

Tomás Lipa, a peasant from Putina, seems to have engaged in this kind of trade, frequently making trips to Caupolicán province in Bolivia. In 1888 he rented one sector of estate pastures of Hacienda Chamacca, district Azángaro, and promised the owners, Josefa González and her husband Lorenzo Aparicio, to take one mule loaded with goods on their account with him on each trip to Bolivia.[142] Nineteen years later, in 1907, his son Pablo Lipa extended a credit of 1,200 soles to the notary Filiberto Aparicio González, son of Lorenzo, who then handed the whole estate over to Lipa as security for a contractual period of four obligatory and five voluntary years.[143] Trade had permitted the younger Lipa to accumulate this large amount of cash and, with it, the temporary possession of a hacienda. Other peasants found an avenue to trade by opening tiny stores in their rural communities—selling a few pounds of coca leaves, sugar, and so on—or by selling to urban bulkers not only their own wool clip but also that of relatives and neighbors. As Benjamin Orlove has noted, such bartering and trading peasants "shade[d] imperceptibly into the traveling buyers."[144]

As trading networks in the altiplano became denser, the Arequipa export and import houses strengthened their position vis-à-vis the other groups involved.[145] The marketing of Peruvian wools overseas continued in the same manner for the whole period under consideration. Sheep wool was sold for the Arequipa export houses at auctions in London and Liverpool, whereas alpaca wool was disposed of "through the even more archaic system of private deals between handlers and manufacturers" in England.[146] In contrast, by the turn of the century Australia and New Zealand had established national wool auctions, and Argentina had developed an intermediate system in which export houses shipping directly to French manufacturers, purchasing agents of European houses, and consignment agents competed with each other.[147] In the Peruvian system prices were least responsive to local supply conditions, whereas the position of the exporters vis-à-vis the producer was strengthened.

Improved transport conditions and fast communication links (the telegraph) between the coast and the altiplano permitted the Arequipa houses to bring to bear their advantages—greater capital resources, links with the

European wool importers, and up-to-date information on prices and market conditions. Since the 1870s and particularly during the economic recovery after the War of the Pacific, companies such as Gibson, Stafford, Ricketts, and Braillard had established purchasing and sales outlets in the commercial centers and at key railroad stations of southern Peru's wool production zone, from Desaguadero in the south to Sicuani in the north and from Conima (Huancané province) in the east to Santa Lucía (Lampa province) in the west.[148]

Specific arrangements of market penetration varied greatly. In the most important centers the export houses opened branch offices. Some traders in the altiplano became their exclusive agents, handling all their sales and purchases through one Arequipa house. Among independent traders some concluded long-term contracts with the Arequipa houses, whereas others concluded contracts with varying export firms in Arequipa. Branch offices, agents, and large independent wool bulkers depended on three sources for their fiber purchases. Owners of small and medium-sized haciendas frequently offered their clip to the agents on a yearly basis and delivered it to agents' shops and warehouses on their own pack animals. Many peasant smallholders and colonos brought small amounts of wool to traders' shops on an irregular basis. And last, hundreds of itinerant traders, usually working firmly established circuits, combed the weekly markets in district capitals and communities as well as the yearly fairs for as much wool as they could find or could afford to buy and then sold it to the agents. Many small traders worked for only one agent and one export house.[149]

The owners of the largest haciendas preferred to deal directly with the Arequipa companies. José Guillermo de Castresana, an Arequipeño businessman and, from 1906, owner of Hacienda Picotani in Muñani district, regularly instructed the administrator of his estate when to expedite the wool clip to the railroad station Estación de Pucará and on to Arequipa.[150] Through social ties with one or the other export house, Castresana possessed information on wool price fluctuations and adjusted the transport schedule of the wools accordingly.

The Arequipa houses regularly extended credit for wool purchases to their agents and independent traders, who did likewise with their suppliers. In 1920 the roughly ten wool-buying agencies in Santa Rosa every week received between six thousand and fifteen thousand soles in coins from their respective export houses in Arequipa.[151] By advancing a large share of the total value of wool, the traders hoped to secure supply. Wool buying was highly competitive on each level, between the Arequipa exporters, between agents, and between itinerant traders. The Arequipa houses attempted to gain complete control of local producing zones and were willing to have their agents pay considerably higher prices for wool to the itinerant traders during an interim phase in order to ward off competition.[152]

The Arequipa houses exercised the predominant influence over short-term wool prices in the altiplano. Every week they cabled price quotations to the traders there, refusing to purchase any wool above that figure. The trader then calculated the cost of handling and freight as well as his profit margin to determine the price that he could afford to pay his suppliers. Although price quotations generally had to follow the prices established at the London wool auctions, the exporters could afford to vary the margins between the world market quotation and the price at which they purchased wool, particularly in a declining market.[153] In 1921, for example, the Sociedad Ganadera del Departamento de Puno, organized by hacendados at the height of the postwar crisis, complained that the prices for wool paid to them by the Arequipa merchants not only had declined precipitously since the boom years of the war but were even low compared with the prewar levels—for old clients, eleven pesos per quintal compared with thirty-five pesos before the war.[154] Yet prices paid for average Peruvian sheep wool at a British port stood at nearly the same level in 1921 as they had in 1913. The key to the exporters' strong position vis-à-vis their suppliers lay in their relatively plentiful working capital, which permitted them to accumulate stocks in their warehouses. Thus, as Appleby has observed, "In a falling market the Arequipa house might either suspend purchases or set extremely low prices until it could dispose of its stocks of high-priced wools."[155]

Producers and small traders were not totally defenseless against the price dictates of the exporters. Lively competition between houses such as Gibson, Ricketts, and Stafford permitted them to sell their wool to the highest bidder.[156] Nevertheless, many hacendados and wool traders preferred to maintain lasting commercial ties with one house because the exporters could bestow a number of advantages on long-time clients, including better credit terms, banking services, preferred treatment in the supply of imported goods, and guaranteed prices for wools during the three to six months between the contract and actual delivery.[157]

With the penetration of the wool trade in its primary bulking stages by the Arequipa export houses, direct credit links between these houses and the owners of larger haciendas, traders, and shopkeepers in the department of Puno became more frequent. Hacendados selling their livestock products directly to the exporters maintained current accounts with them by which they purchased imported goods on credit against the security of their next wool clip. Wills of hacendados often listed debts to the import and export houses.[158] Between the mid-1870s and early 1880s this growing credit dependence led to a number of sales of urban real estate in the department of Puno by local traders and hacendados to the export houses in payment of debt, probably a consequence of falling wool prices.[159] However, prior to the 1920s merchants in Arequipa, Juliaca, and Puno rarely gained control of important landholdings in Azángaro province through debt foreclosures.

With the foundation of the Banco de Arequipa in 1871, modern bank credit made its appearance in southern Peru. Based on the capital of the regional oligarchy, the bank extended its operations to Cuzco and Puno.[160] Together with the increasing importance of the large import and export houses, banks slowly supplanted merchant bankers such as Amenabar or del Valle as credit institutions in the altiplano. This process is symbolized in a credit contract from 1875 in which a Puno shopkeeper received a credit of 1,700 pesos from the Banco de Puno—presumably a branch of the Banco de Arequipa—but relied on the merchant banker Fernando del Valle as cosigner for the loan, who in turn received a mortgage on real estate as security for his potential obligations against the bank.[161]

The Banco de Arequipa and its Puno branch fell victim to Peru's financial collapse of 1876. Only in the late 1880s did another bank begin to operate again in Arequipa, and Puno had to wait until the early 1920s before a branch of the Banco de Perú y Londres opened its doors.[162] Between the late 1890s and World War I Peru's reconstituted banking system remained cool toward agro-exporters; the banks pursued a stable money policy in opposition to export interests and considered agricultural mortgages a bad risk. In 1902 Wenceslao Molina, a professor of animal husbandry at San Marcos University in Lima and the heir to Hacienda Churura in Putina, outlined a program of measures necessary for the establishment of a modern livestock industry in Peru. Reflecting a general frustration of large agro-exporters with the credit system after the adoption of the gold standard, Molina demanded the establishment of agricultural mortgage banks, "which could fill the void left by the presently [existing banking institutions], which grant credits only to the merchants and keep them from the hard-working rancher."[163]

Alfonso Quiroz's recent work on Peru's financial institutions confirms Molina's critique. Yet despite their unwillingness to finance agricultural improvements, banks did play an increasing role in export financing. With the help of the banks, bills of exchange finally became common in the wool export business, a first step in alleviating the chronic cash shortage in the altiplano. But only large traders and producers benefited from the introduction of this financial tool.[164] The hacendados' reliance on credit from the export houses increased their multifaceted dependence on these merchants, and they inevitably resented their relative weakness.[165] Whenever earnings from wool exports declined, hacendados experienced the uneven distribution of the benefits from the trade particularly keenly and—as after the brief slump of 1901–2—called for measures "to throw off the yoke of the export houses."[166] This conflict of interest intensified in the period of the sharp slump of the early 1920s.[167] Prior to this date, however, long periods of improving market conditions muted the conflict and left the hegemony of the export houses untouched. In the words of the owner of a small hacienda in Azángaro, "the wholesalers were in charge."[168]

If hacendados had reason to complain about the uneven distribution of benefits from the wool trade, the indigenous peasants entering the market with small amounts of wool found themselves in a much more disadvantageous position. Although competition sometimes led wool exporters and their agents in the altiplano to outbid each other to secure the production of a large hacienda, the indigenous smallholders rarely received this benefit.[169] This was just one of the economic consequences of the sociocultural domination of the Indian smallholder by the social groups controlling the commercialization of wool.

Wool traders in the altiplano automatically classified sheep wool into "estate wool" and "common wool." Estate wool was presumed to have longer and finer fibers, to be of a uniform white color, and to contain less hay and dirt. The wool bought from Indian estancia owners was automatically downgraded as being dirtier and having shorter fibers and a greater admixture of black wool.[170] Thus, peasants received considerably less for their wool than did estate owners. In 1920, for example, wool-buying agents in Santa Rosa paid five soles less per quintal of sheep wool to peasants than they did to hacendados, at a current price of fifty-five soles per quintal, a discount of nearly 10 percent.[171] When buying wool from Indians, the traders at times used rigged scales. They discounted one pound in every quintal for dirt, wetness, and the weight of the rope holding the bales together, although such weight losses were calculated in the basic price for unwashed wool. When peasants wanted to sell wool or hides to merchants, they were often met at the outskirts of town by *alcanzadores*, who sought to persuade the approaching Indians to sell their goods to a particular merchant, a persuasion that could take the form of money advances, alcohol, or brute force.[172] Once in the store, they were obliged to buy alcohol, sugar, or maize at inflated prices.[173]

In some parts of the southern highlands, the bulking of wools produced by peasants could be organized in a fashion similar to the colonial repartos de bienes. In a village of Chumbivilcas province in Cuzco department, peasants protested in 1882 that "in certain seasons of the year [wool traders] from different towns come to our huts . . . and force an excessively small price for this commodity on us. At the time of the wool clip they capriciously snatch [the wool] from us, weighing a quintal as an arroba. When for this very reason we are incapable of paying the whole debt which they force us to contract, they double our losses by charging usurious interests, and end up secretly taking all our livestock from us."[174] In Puno's Chucuito province the authorities themselves practiced a forced system of wool bulking as late as 1920. A few weeks before the shearing season, in December or January, the district governor would distribute money, lent to him by wool traders, to the Indian livestock herders, obliging them to deliver a specified amount of wool. If they refused to accept the conditions, the governor employed the communal authorities to deposit the money for the wool at the peasants' hut, and the latter knew that they "had to come up with the equivalent amount of wool."[175] Mayors and subprefects entered the wool business precisely because they had power over Indian herders and thus could guarantee supplies to exporters.[176]

Imposing low prices and securing supplies for specific traders and authorities were the goals of these methods of deceit and force. Such schemes were practiced again and again by those with leverage over Indian peasant producers. They subverted an intrinsically competitive market into a myriad of monopolistic relations of appropriation. But they were no longer the very precondition of peasant market participation, as repartos de bienes still might have been during the eighteenth century.

Between the 1850s and 1920 Indian livestock herders increasingly came to view market transactions with hispanized traders as important regular parts of their household subsistence economy. Their margin of autonomy in exchange relations was diminishing as the dendritic system matured after the War of the Pacific. As late as the 1850s and 1860s a legend flourished among Puno's elite that Indian peasants had buried about ten million Bolivian pesos, their receipts from increasing wool sales, money that thus "vanished from circulation."[177] In other words, there existed a sphere of monetarized circulation among the peasants that lay outside the control of the altiplano traders.

Over the next sixty years both pull and push factors brought the peasants into increasing dependence on hispanized traders. The ever-denser network of itinerant traders and wool-buying agents, especially after 1890, made it more difficult to escape their purchasing pressures. The diminishing land base in the parcialidades, caused by hacienda expansion and population increase, led to smaller average livestock herds for most peasant families. Fiscal measures sought to capture more of the peasants' monetary income from wool sales. Between 1867 and the 1890s governments in Lima undertook repeated attempts to collect the contribución *personal,* a new head tax that replaced the contribución de indígenas. A new alcohol consumption tax established in 1887, excise taxes on alcohol, sugar, and tobacco introduced in 1904, and the broadened collection of the contribución de predios rústicos after 1902, which in Azángaro primarily affected peasants, were at once means and expression of a more effective control over the peasantry, especially after the 1890s. The railroad and telegraph and the establishment of rural police posts in each province after 1895 made it easier to quell uprisings or discourage them before they were undertaken.

But this greater reliance on market transactions did not mean the abandonment of the traditional goals of the peasant economy: subsistence of the family in the context of communal solidarity. Cash received for livestock products from traders paid for the considerable expenses of festivities, such as those for a community's patron saint, a baptism, a wedding, or a funeral. Indian livestock herders from the northern altiplano perhaps made cash purchases of commodities such as salt, pottery, or alcohol with which to maintain long-standing barter relationships in neighboring areas as the montaña in Bolivia's Larecaja province. As the parity of exchange values between bartered goods remained constant for longer periods of time, during phases of increasing prices for wool and hides it was advantageous to purchase barter goods with cash received for livestock products.[178]

Indian peasants held back much wool from the export trade even during boom years. Other livestock products, including tallow, sheepskins, and dried meat, entered the dendritic system of monetarized trade in even smaller proportion. Besides direct consumption in the peasant household, these goods continued to serve as means of exchange in traditional barter relationships. For example, each May after the shearing season the colonos of Hacienda Picotani abandoned their estate and went down to the valleys of Sandia to provision themselves with maize, coca leaves, and other foodstuffs in exchange for livestock products and homespun baizes.[179] During the World War I boom peasants from around Juliaca refused to sell any serge to the merchants to whom they sold raw wool, as they were taking increasing amounts of this home-woven cloth 150 kilometers farther north to Sicuani, their traditional spot for provisioning with maize.[180]

Indian livestock producers did not object to being integrated into the market, as they had come to rely on cash as part of their family subsistence strategy. What they objected to was the force and deceit that traders and authorities routinely imposed in the "marketplace." However, they did not accept such exploitation fatalistically. Indians "give life to business in this region," as wool trader Francisco Rodríguez of Santa Rosa wrote to Ricketts in 1918, and this market position allowed them to use ruses, tricks, and plain common sense to countermand and limit their exploitation at the hands of unscrupulous traders.[181] Indians mixed hay and dirt into the wool, moistened it, and even poured sugar water over it to increase the weight.[182] In 1932, when Bolivian customs agents began to collect export duties on wool, alpaca herders from south of the border ceased to sell their wool to Peruvian traders in border towns such as Cojata and Moho, instead establishing relations with merchants in Puerto Acosta on the Bolivian side.[183] Peasant herders sought to adjust their sales both to the rhythms and requirements of their household economy and to market fluctuations.

During the 1920s, a period of unstable wool prices, traders again and again complained about "the absence of the Indians" from weekly markets or annual fairs. "The Indians held back [their alpaca wool] in expectation of price improvements, they only sold amounts indispensable for satisfying their most pressing needs," wrote the Ricketts's agent Hipólito Sanchez from Moho in Huancané province in September of 1926.[184] They tried to sell the wool during the season of highest prices, September through December, coinciding with the months of the agricultural cycle when last year's harvested food began to get scarce. Before celebrations such as carnival or patron saints' festivities, wool sales increased, as did alcohol purchases.[185]

Peasants considered trading a complex skill entrusted only to the most experienced and honored family members, an activity in which sons were trained from a tender age, when they accompanied their fathers on expeditions to distant market towns or subtropical valleys. To give some stability and predictability to trading in those alien environments, the peasants sought long-lasting trading relationships with *compadres* (their children's godparents, whom they sought out as protectors). A trader might have as many as six hundred compadres among peasants selling him wool.[186]

But resistance always proved fragile. The very compadre to whom the peasant had entrusted himself over many years for his wool sales might exploit that dependence. And the attempt to hold the wool clip until prices were high collapsed when there was a prolonged price slump or when food was scarce because of crop failures. Then the reverse pattern was set in motion: peasants had to market their wool as fast as possible, whatever the losses. They sheared the animals before term, bringing shorter fibers to market; the price they received would be doubly low on account of the inopportune season of sale and the low quality of their wool.[187] Of course, poor peasants, with scarce resources of land and animals, faced these problems more frequently than did affluent comuneros and colonos. And alpaca herders, such as those high up in the Cordillera de Carabaya, with their undisputed control over the know-how of producing the cameloids' precious fiber, may have had a more stable market position than did sheep-wool producing comuneros from the altiplano proper.

Through the tremendous intensification of the competition for land, the wool market may have driven forward this type of social differentiation among the peasantry. But comuneros and colonos had a number of countervailing strategies at their disposal that assuaged such effects of the wool market before 1920. For better or for worse, the prosperity of the altiplano's indigenous livestock herders—as well as of hacendados, transport entrepreneurs, traders, and administrators—had become linked to the vagaries of international demand for wool, just as they had depended on the fortunes of the mining centers in Upper Peru until the end of the colonial era.

6   The Avalanche
of Hacienda Expansion

The early decades of the republican period were marked by a relative equilibrium between the hacienda and peasant sectors of the altiplano. This situation began to change during the 1850s. As early as 1867 Colonel Andrés Recharte, subprefect of Azángaro, could write that "most of the damages and abuses suffered by the Indians have stemmed from the mestizos' covetousness for their land."[1] After the slow decay of the colonial mining-supply economy and the dislocations caused by the Wars of Independence, a newly emerging landholding elite gradually adapted to the wool export economy. By midcentury, as the prospects of wool exports became brighter, they sought to control the important peasant sector more thoroughly in order to capture a greater share of regional income. In this chapter I discuss central aspects of Azángaro's changing property relations between the mid-1850s and 1920.[2]

Methodological Considerations

I devised a methodology to answer questions as the following: How did the "flows" of land between various social groups evolve over time? How did the size distribution of land parcels offered for sale vary between different social groups? The notarial contracts render bits and pieces of information, permitting the judicious construction of a scheme for categorizing all participants in transactions. They normally list occupation, place of birth and residence, capacity to speak Spanish, and—less dependably—the socioethnic origin and any public offices held by each party. I gathered these data in an index of all participants in notarial transactions, containing some eight thousand cards, and assigned each party to a notarial transaction to one of the following categories:

1. Indigenous peasant
2. Hispanized large landholder
3. Intermediate group (including persons of indeterminable social status)
4. Church
5. Beneficencia pública

Internal consistency of assignments was maintained through the use of clear criteria in the evaluation of the social indicators. Some values placed the person into category 1 ("indigenous peasants"): for example, the occupations *labrador* and *pastor*, the socioethnic labels *indígena* or *indio*, lack of knowledge of Spanish, and residence in a parcialidad or ayllu. Other values indicated that a person belonged to category 2 ("hispanized large landholders"): for example, occupations such as *hacendado* or *abogado*, knowledge of Spanish, and holding of offices such as *gobernador, subprefecto,* or *juez de primera instancia.* Certain terms were used so indiscriminately that I considered them to be neutral. Some notaries applied the occupational labels *propietario* and *comerciante* as an insoluble pair to all individuals, the peasant selling a parcel for 50 soles m.n. as well as an hacendado selling an estate for 5,000 soles m.n.

At least two social indicators had to point unequivocally to category 1 or 2 to make an assignment. For example, in order to assign a person to category 1 ("indigenous peasant"), he or she had to be described as indígena *and* labrador, as a non-Spanish speaker *and* living in a parcialidad. If the social indicators showed any ambivalence, or if there was only scanty information on a party to a contract, I placed the case in category 3. Thus, two subgroups constitute the members of this category: persons for whom information was insufficient, and persons for whom the social indicators seemed ambiguous, truly an intermediate group on the range from indigenous peasant to hispanized large landholder.

This problem brings us to the conception underlying the categorization scheme. Azángaro's social stratification was considerably more complex during the late nineteenth and early twentieth centuries than this scheme implies. However, what mattered here was to choose a scheme that reflected an underlying structural element of Azángaro's society while allowing the categorization of most contract parties despite limited information on their social backgrounds. Thus, the scheme strikes a compromise between the exigencies of an all-too-imperfect source and the issues that I sought to investigate.

The categories are viewed as lying on a continuous scale in which the various status groups in Azángaro's society grade imperceptibly into each other. The scale is bounded on both ends by ideal types formed by a total clustering of all social indicators capable of defining a category. Categories 1 and 2 are meant as such ideal types at polar ends of Azángaro's social scale: on the one hand, the indigenous peasant who was born and lives in an Indian community, lives poorly from the income derived from herding and crop raising on small parcels of land, is a monolingual Quechua speaker without any schooling, is labeled as "Indian" by members of all other social groups (including notaries), wears rough, self-made baize clothes, and derives supplementary income from working on nearby haciendas, from artisanal home production, or from petty trade activities that remain secondary and do not break through the predominantly agrarian pattern of his life. On the other end of the scale is the hispanized large landholder, the ideal type of category 2, who speaks Spanish, has enjoyed formal education, owns one or more large estates employing dozens of peasant families as colonos, usually lives in a townhouse in the provincial capital, might even own a house in Puno, Arequipa, or Lima, dresses in European garb, consumes imported goods, holds important administrative, legislative, and judicial positions in the province or the department, and maintains close contacts with higher strata of regional and national society. This construction of ideal types describes both the fluidity and the stark polarity in the socioethnic stratification of Peru's sierra.[3]

Most individuals appearing in notarial transactions were not ideal-typical "indigenous peasants" or "hispanized large landholders" but rather approximated one of the two polar constructs. I felt justified in including most merchants and officeholders in category 2, since they were pulled toward the ideal type of the hispanized large landholders. This, after all, is why they appeared so often before the notary as land purchasers. Socially they had more in common with the largest hacendados of the province than with the Indian peasantry. Category 2 thus encompasses all sectors of Azángaro's provincial elite, of which the large landholder was the dominant figure.

Category 3 includes petty traders, owners of minimal estates (perhaps employing two or three colonos) imperceptibly shading into peasant estancias, persons about whose knowledge of Spanish the notarial records waver back and forth, and persons who generally lived in the district capitals but who may also have resided on their modest landholdings. The distinction between this intermediate group and impoverished hacendados on the one hand, and affluent peasants on the other, is minimal in most cases. For this study the distinction is based on an arbitrary cut in the continuous scale by requiring two social indicators, the minimal sign of "clustering," for assigning an individual to one of the two polar categories.

Although information on the economic situation of the contracting parties (e.g., the amount and type of land property held *prior* to their participation in notarial transactions) has influenced their assignment to one of the social categories, the transactions themselves were not used for this purpose. To be sure, a person buying or selling a large estate was excluded ipso facto from category 1. But because the accumulation or loss of landed property has to be viewed as one important indicator for social mobility in Azángaro, consideration of the notarial transactions for determining an individual's social category would have resulted in a circular argument. Thus, a person who in early contracts shows all the traits of an indigenous peasant will be treated as such for all subsequent contracts, even though he might purchase such an amount of land that at the end of his "career" he might more meaningfully be placed in category 3 or even category 2.

Hacienda Expansion

The enormous upsurge of sales constituted the single most important factor influencing the provincial landholding pattern between the 1850s and 1920. Sales of rural landholdings represented the overwhelming majority of contracts recorded by notaries. Their annual number and total value grew from a trickle during the 1850s to an avalanche during the first and second decades of this century.[4] Nearly three-fourths of all sales contracts concluded between 1851 and 1920 were transacted during the last two decades of that period (table 6.1).

This growth of land sales did not proceed in a linear fashion. A first cycle of sales activity reached a peak in 1867 with forty-seven sales contracts evaluated at 35,549 soles m.n.; then their frequency and value declined until about the early 1880s. Only after the end of the War of the Pacific did a recovery begin, and during the early and mid-1890s a level close to the previous peak year of 1867 was reached. A quantitative leap occurred in 1898–99, when within two years the frequency of sales roughly tripled, accompanied by a smaller increase in total value. After 1904 the frequency of sales climbed again to reach 297 sales during 1908, five times more than in the peak year of 1867 during the first cycle. Between 1908 and 1913 the number and value of land transactions reached their peak for the whole period under consideration. In 1914 there followed a brief but sharp slump.

TABLE 6.1. Number and Value of All Land Sales in Azángaro Province by Ten-Year Periods, 1851–1920

	Value (soles m.n.)	%	Number	%	Mean Sales Price (soles m.n.)
1851–60	39,002.62	2.5	26	0.6	1,500.10
1861–70	97,460.40	6.3	197	4.2	494.72
1871–80	65,786.78	4.2	187	4.0	351.80
1881–90	75,128.63	4.8	255	5.4	294.62
1891–1900	171,307.98	11.1	606	12.9	282.68
1901–10	523,995.73	33.8	1,789	37.9	292.90
1911–20[a]	[576,724.95]	[37.2]	[1,655]	[35.1]	[348.47]
Total	1,549,407.09	99.9	4,715	100.1	328.61

[a]Estimate based on the values for 1913–14 and 1918–19.

Sources: REPA, 1854–1920; REPP, 1852–1920.

The recovery during the remainder of the decade failed to bring back the frantic rhythm of sales of the prewar years.[5]

A breakdown of all sales according to price allows a clearer understanding of the types of land property changing hands in Azángaro. In over 88 percent of all sales the price lay below 500 soles m.n., and for nearly two-thirds of all cases the price was below 200 soles m.n. In contrast, only 2.9 percent of all priced transactions concerned pieces of land for which a buyer paid 2,000 soles m.n. or more. But how much land could one buy for 200, 500, or 2,000 soles m.n.? There was no easily discernible correlation between the price of land and its size. Beyond factors such as quality and location of the land, the social positions of buyer and seller often influenced price. Powerful hacendados might force a peasants dependent on them for credit and work to sell their ancestral estancia for a price much below its "market value."[6]

If we differentiate sales contracts according to property categories, the preponderance of the estancia is overwhelming. But what did contemporaries understand by *estancia*? During the colonial period the term had referred to livestock ranches.[7] For some areas of Spanish America, notably Argentina, *estancia* even today refers to sizable livestock estates. In the altiplano, however, it ceased to have that meaning by the mid-nineteenth century. Just as David Brading has described for west-central Mexico, the term *hacienda* began to be used for a particular type of landholding in the altiplano only during the eighteenth century. It took one hundred years, from the mid-eighteenth to the mid-nineteenth century, for it to replace the term *estancia* in the semantic field of "livestock estate operating with semi-servile labor."[8] By the 1850s such properties were usually labeled *haciendas* or *fincas*, but on occasion *estancia* was still used with this meaning.[9] In 1849 the Puneño Juan Bustamante, while speaking of the region's "haciendas" still referred to their owners as "estancieros," a term soon to be supplanted by "hacendado."[10]

After the 1860s the term *estancia* was not used any more when speaking about livestock estates in the Peruvian altiplano. In its new semantic field it referred to the Indian peasant's rural "farm," with its adobe huts, a corral enclosed by a stone wall, pastures, and some parcels planted with potatoes, quinua, and other crops. *Estancia* became equivalent to "agricultural units of family or sub-family size," in recent social science terminology.[11] Writing in 1947, Juan Chávez Molina, the heir to Hacienda Churura, district Putina, flatly affirmed that "the estancia today is a small property."[12] The term had lost the connotation of livestock ranch. In an analysis of Puno's social stratification in 1931–32, Oswaldo Zea asserted that "in the area of crop farming [*zona de chacarismo*] small properties are widespread and are called estancias."[13] The predominance of estancias in Azángaro land transactions thus offers a first indication that land of the peasantry formed the lion's share of the rural property passing hands in the province.[14]

Haciendas and fincas together accounted for just over 5 percent of the total number of sales.[15] On average, fewer than three estates were bought and sold each year between the 1850s and 1910. Size was not a sufficient criterion for differentiating fincas and haciendas from lesser landholdings (fig. 6.1). Attempts to rely on quantitative criteria for defining what constitutes a finca or hacienda, such as minimum size, minimum number of livestock, or minimum production of the property, remain unsatisfactory.[16] By these criteria there was considerable overlap between small fincas and peasant estancias.[17] What distinguished the hacienda from peasant estancias or other family smallholdings was its internal social organization: a stable, hierarchically ordered population resided on its land, and its members were "directly tied to the owner or his representative through a number of personal obligations, of both a material and symbolic nature."[18]

Thus, beginning in the 1850s the same paradoxical constellation of continuity and polarity crystallized in the altiplano's land tenure regime that we observed for the region's social structure: on the one hand, a continuous spread in the size of holdings, from large estates to smallholdings; and on the other, a stark juxtaposition between hacienda and Indian

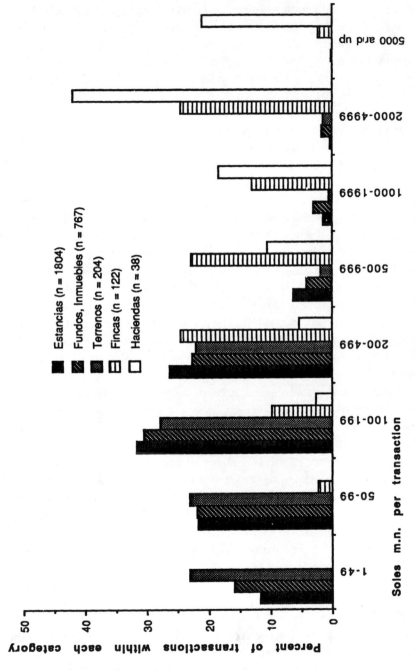

FIGURE 6.1. Land Sales in Azángaro, by Category of Property and Price Range, 1852–1910

peasant estancia. This dichotomy was based on the neocolonial division between hispanized rural elite and an indigenous peasantry, a division more deeply rooted in the perceptions of the two groups than in different rationalities of their economic operations.

Did the accelerating tempo of land transfers alter Azángaro's landholding pattern or merely represent increased exchange of property within the same categories of landholdings and proprietors? To answer this question, we have to differentiate land sales according to the social origin of sellers and buyers. Among the three social categories of the scale, only members of the category of hispanized large landholders appear as net purchasers of rural property in Azángaro. Only for this group do number and value of land purchases exceed sales (fig. 6.2). By value, some 70 percent of all land transfers into the holdings of this group represent land of indigenous peasants; by number, these transfers are nearly 86 percent. The intermediate group of landholders contributed about 27 percent of the value and 13 percent of the number of land parcels purchased by large landholders.

Land purchases by hispanized large landholders were more markedly cyclical than were overall provincial sales transactions. After negligible amounts of land purchases from peasants and members of the intermediate group during the 1850s, hispanized large landholders expanded their landholdings by more than 140 notarized purchases during the 1860s, with transactions peaking in 1867. During the next two quinquennia these purchases steadily declined to a low of 35 transactions for the period 1876–80, roughly 60 percent below the level of 1866–70.

Land purchases from indigenous peasants continued at a low level through the early 1880s and began to pick up again only in the quinquennium 1886–90 (table 6.2). The brief surge of purchases by hispanized large landholders during the early 1880s resulted exclusively from an increase in transactions with persons assigned to the intermediate group. These transactions during the difficult years of the War of the Pacific may point to the problems faced by impoverished owners of marginal fincas. The double crisis of the early 1880s, in which war-related disruptions of livestock production and commercialization of wool were added to the problem of sliding wool prices, perhaps caused some concentration of landholding *within* the estate sector while expansion of haciendas into peasant land slowed down.[19] On September 10, 1881, for example, the brothers Felipe and Manuel Figueroa Obando sold Finca Antocollo y Antaña in Putina district without livestock capital for 3,600 pesos (2,800 soles m.n.). At least one of the brothers had been in debt for five years; during the war years they apparently saw no way of extricating themselves from this debt other than selling their land.[20] After 1881 the Figueroa Obandos disappeared from the ranks of estate owners in Azángaro.

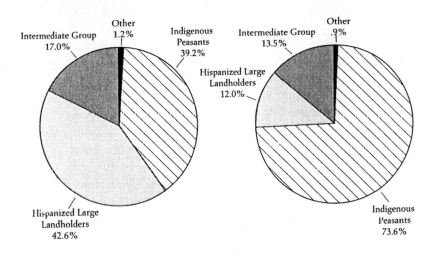

FIGURE 6.2A. Social Categories of Sellers in Azángaro Land Sales, 1852–1910. *Left:* By value of sales. *Right:* By number of sales.

Sources: REPA and REPP, 1852

The net transfer of land from indigenous peasants to hispanized large landholders (purchases minus sales) accentuates the nadir of the curve for hacienda expansions between 1876 and 1885. For the long run, this measure can best depict the cyclical nature of hacienda formation in parts of Latin America or, as Eric Hobsbawm has put it, how "in the course of post-colonial history haciendas have been formed, expanded, split up and reformed, depending on political change and economic conjuncture."[21] Sales to peasants increased during this decade of severe commercial, fiscal, and political crisis, just when purchases by hispanized large landholders decreased. As in the quarter century after independence, peasants benefited from the crisis of the hispanized landholding elite, at least with regard to retaining their land.[22]

During the early 1890s land purchases by hispanized large landholders recovered, and from the second half of the 1890s onward their purchases grew at such rapid pace that all previous land transactions are dwarfed by comparison. The value of their acquisitions increased by 160 percent from 1891–95 to 1896–1900, followed by a further jump in 1901–5 of over 50

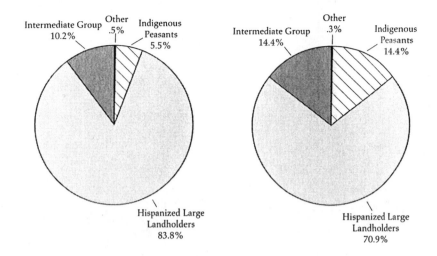

FIGURE 6.2B. Social Categories of Purchasers in Azángaro Land Sales, 1852–1910. *Left:* By value of purchases. *Right:* By number of purchases. *Sources:* REPA and REPP, 1852

percent and another rise of 125 percent from the first to the second quinquennium of the present century. The peak of hacienda expansion was reached between 1908 and 1913. During 1908, with a total of 212 purchases, the frenzy of land purchases by hacendados and other members of the provincial elite approached two transactions every three days.[23]

How are we to account for the accelerating rhythm of hacienda expansion between the late 1850s and 1913? Both contemporary observers and modern scholars have pointed to the favorable conditions thought to prevail in southern Peru's wool export trade as the most important incentive for many hispanized large landholders to expand their estates and found new ones.[24] In 1916 José Sebastián Urquiaga—who, through one of Azángaro's most spectacular land-purchasing campaigns, had turned the small maternal finca Sollocota into one of the province's largest estates—explained this context as follows:

> About 25 years ago [i.e., 1890–91] the haciendas of the
> department of Puno passed nearly unnoticed as profitable estates;

TABLE 6.2. Land Purchases by Hispanized Large Landholders from All Other Categories, 1852–1919

	A Purchases from Indigenous Peasants		B Purchases from Intermediate Group		C Purchases from Others		D All Purchases (A+B+C)		E Mean Annual Purchases			
	Value	N	Value	N	Value	N	Value	N	Value	Index[a]	N	Index[a]
1852–55	387	2	160	1	120	1	667	4	167	2	1	3
1856–60	1,219	5	1,867	3	1,867	1	4,953	9	991	14	2	6
1861–65	5,178	33	1,946	8	—	—	7,124	41	1,424	19	8	25
1866–70	12,577	80	8,938	22	—	—	21,515	102	4,303	58	20	61
1871–75	9,455	52	2,684	14	—	—	12,139	66	2,428	33	13	41
1876–80	6,559	28	1,561	6	240	1	8,360	35	1,672	22	7	22
1881–85	5,771	31	9,469	19	—	—	15,240	50	3,048	41	10	31
1886–90	6,917	47	2,058	11	53	1	9,028	59	1,806	24	11	31
1891–95	12,894	81	8,335	16	228	1	21,457	98	4,291	58	20	61
1896–1900	37,274	230	17,891	35	800	3	55,965	268	11,193	150	54	165
1901–5	66,768	385	17,963	33	1,645	6	86,376	424	17,275	231	85	261
1906–10	143,873	672	48,451	85	3,910	5	196,234	762	39,247	526	152	469
1913	28,517	140	760	3	22,208	8	51,485	151		690		465
1914	3,005	24	2,200	7	3,000	1	8,205	32		110		98
1918	14,144	81	3,650	8	5,803	2	23,597	91		316		280
1919	16,410	53	11,477	8	—	—	27,887	61		374		188

[a]100 = Mean annual value and N of purchases, 1852–1910.

Sources: REPA, REPP, 1852–1919.

their products, such as livestock, wool, dried meat, cheese, butter, etc., were sold at extremely low prices, less than half of what they are today. And as the price improvement has made itself felt year after year, the interest in acquiring fincas in the interior was awakened. But since the owners with very few exceptions did not sell their estates, people thought of buying estancias from the ayllu Indians.[25]

Land purchases by hacendados followed export market conditions for wool as the single most important product of the altiplano livestock estates closely enough to reflect cyclical swings of wool prices and export volumes (fig. 6.3).[26] The year 1914 confirms the close correlation between trade conditions and land purchases by hispanized large landholders. The brief dislocation of commercial and credit circuits in southern Peru brought on by the outbreak of World War I coincided with a sharp reduction of land acquisitions by hacendados.[27]

But by the late 1910s something had changed. In these years the value of wool exports reached unprecedented heights, and hacendados were more prosperous than ever before. Yet, although in 1918 and 1919 they again acquired much more land than they had in the crisis year of 1914, acquisitions from peasants lay considerably below the levels of 1908–13. Just when the wool market reached its peak, the correlation with land acquisitions broke down. One mighty reason discouraged many hacendados from attempting to acquire more peasant lands: the Rumi Maqui Rebellion, which had swept through several livestock districts of Azángaro province since mid-1915, lifted the level of peasant resistance to encroachments on their lands to a level not seen in the altiplano since the late colonial period. Resistance by community peasants against hacendados continued for the rest of the decade, becoming broader and more ideologically charged during the early 1920s.[28] The tide of hacienda expansion thus began to turn even before the wave of prosperity brought on by rising wool exports had crested.

Other authors have explained the drastic and rather sudden increase of land purchases by hispanized landholders since the mid-1890s as the result of political constellations. Karen Spalding suggested that hacendados required strong military backing in order to shift the balance of landholding in their favor. The conditions for extending such military support were created only when the Civilista oligarchy effectively took power in Lima after Piérola's victory over the Cáceres forces in 1895. The growth of altiplano livestock haciendas thus "was primarily the product of the alliance between the serrano [highland] political elite and the nouveaux riches of the coast, who themselves were dependent on their alliance with foreign capital."[29]

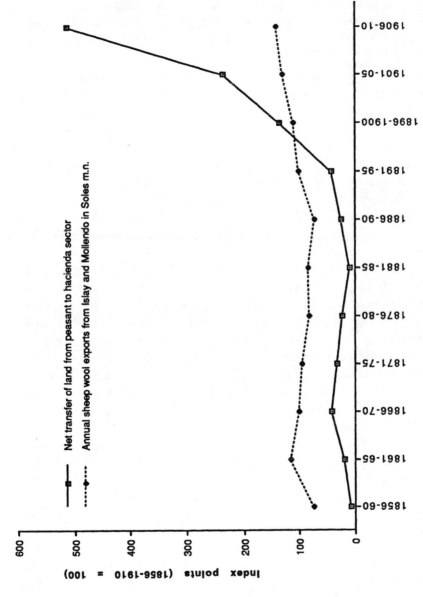

FIGURE 6.3   Annual Averages of Land Transfers to Hacienda Sector and of Sheep Wool Exports, 1856–1910, in Soles m.n.

There are two serious problems with this thesis. (1) There is no evidence for the development of such a general class alliance between altiplano hacendados and the ruling coastal oligarchy. Azángaro's politically active hacendados were split along party lines, and many of them fought the local and regional representatives of Lima's ruling Civilista party. (2) Under normal circumstances hispanized landholders in the altiplano did not require military or police contingents supplied by the central government to expand their estates onto peasant lands.[30] As early as 1874 Azángaro's subprefect Daniel Rossel y Salas, a native of Putina who later became judge of Puno's Superior Court and, by marriage, co-owner of Hacienda Huasacona in Muñani, had vividly portrayed how the province's large landholders could carry out armed raids totally independent of, and indeed against the will of, the national police.[31]

In 1931 José Frisancho—who was the offspring of a prominent landholding family from the altiplano town of Pucará and whose judicial career took him from the position of prosecutor in Azángaro's Court of First Instance to the presidency of Peru's Supreme Court—presented an argument similar to Spalding's.[32] As he saw it, the centralism of Lima's "pseudo-aristocracy" after 1895 subverted the political and moral fiber of serrano society, making it servile and corrupt.[33] This subversion had a sudden and dramatic impact on landholding in the highlands. Between independence and 1895 the upright, patrician landholders of the sierra were "mere conservers of the colonial haciendas," and "not a single case" existed in which indigenous community lands were incorporated into a latifundium. "After 1895 occurred the rapid transformation of the communities into latifundia, to such a degree that in some provinces the ayllus have disappeared."[34]

In Frisancho's view the new political regime established by Piérola brought a class of persons to the surface of altiplano society who had no scruples about appropriating peasant lands. In reality, however, there was no sudden qualitative break in the relations between hacendados and Indians and, more specifically, in the methods of acquiring peasant lands. The whole panoply of a paternalistic, neocolonial society—from entrapment through debt to legal ruses and sheer force—became gradually entrenched during the decades before 1895.

But Frisancho's analysis contains one important observation: after the end of the War of the Pacific, and increasingly during the 1890s, many newcomers to the altiplano began to form estates from strings of peasant estancias. These new residents were attracted to the economic opportunities linked to the short-lived mining and rubber collection boom in the ceja de la selva of Carabaya and Sandia but also to the growth of commercial networks in the altiplano. The military campaigns during the War of the Pacific and the subsequent civil war may also have led some soldiers and officers to settle in the altiplano.[35] Among the 436 men entered in Azángaro's electoral register for the year 1897, 96 were born outside the province.[36] The influx of these newcomers during the late 1880s and early 1890s accounts for a good part of the increased land purchases in Azángaro following 1895.

The two decades between Piérola's civil war victory in 1895 and World War I marked the high tide of gamonal power over the Indian peasantry of the altiplano. The consolidation of Peru's oligarchic regime during what has come to be called the Aristocratic Republic set the stage allowing the region's elite of large landholders, traders, and officeholders to take full advantage of the favorable commercial conjuncture that whetted their appetites for pastoral resources and peasant labor. The penetration of a modern network of transportation and communication through the southern sierra, fueled by exaggerated hopes of economic development, and the expansion of the infrastructure and fiscal means of the central state helped to strengthen the altiplano's elite after 1895.

But the path on which this elite had come into being, in an incipient and contradictory fashion between the 1820s and 1850 and in a first moment of ebullient power between the late 1850s and early 1870s, was unique to the south. This newly forming elite was indebted to the central government only through its relative weakness in the southern highlands. The bases of the large landholders' power, independent of any alliance with oligarchic groups on the national level, were their favorable insertion into the expanding commercial circuits centered on Arequipa as well as the consolidation of clientele systems, a process made easier by the commercial expansion. It is true that beginning in the 1890s the provincial elite of the altiplano expected increasing support from the central government to consolidate their gains vis-à-vis the peasantry, both through distribution of funds and offices derived from Lima among their clients and through strengthened police and military contingents in the countryside. Yet the gamonales never saw themselves as junior partners of Lima's oligarchy. They insisted on maintaining independent power in the provinces against what they perceived as the threat of subversive modernization pushed by the central government.

The Value of Land

If indeed an improvement in the economic conjuncture for altiplano livestock products constituted the major motivation for the rapid increase of land purchases by Azángaro provincial elite, then this improvement should be reflected in rental rates of estates and the price of land itself. Rental rates paid for Azángaro livestock haciendas, in spite of problems with the data base,[37] show a remarkably clear development.[38] From just over 8 percent of productive capital in soles m.n. (just over 10 percent in pesos) during the 1850s, the mean rate jumped to just under 10 percent in soles m.n. (just over 12 percent in pesos) in the 1860s. During the following twenty years it stagnated, and only during the 1890s does a new rise become visible. The rate climbed from 12 percent in soles m.n. during the 1890s to 15.6 percent in the following decade and 22 percent between 1910 and 1917, nearly three times as high as during the 1850s. The average annual lease paid on a hacienda fully capitalized at 1,000 OMR jumped from 80 soles m.n. in the 1850s to 220 soles m.n. during the boom years of World War I.[39] At that time an hacienda produced as much in annual leases without any livestock capital as it had done sixty years earlier when fully capitalized.[40]

The increased profitability of operating a livestock estate during the 1860s, expressed in rising rental rates, coincided with the first postindependence push toward hacienda expansion in Azángaro. When southern Peru's wool export economy went through its phase of retraction, from about 1873 until the mid-1880s, rental rates stagnated and hacendados scaled down land purchases, reaching an extremely low level between the mid-1870s and 1885.[41] Growing income from wool exports after the mid-1880s—preceding the recovery of the international conjuncture for wool by about ten years because of the devaluation of the Peruvian currency—was reflected in renewed increases in rental rates beginning in the early 1890s. These increases in turn set the stage for the new wave of land purchases by new and old hacendados, which climaxed during the five years preceding World War I.

Continuous sets of rental contracts for one and the same estate spanning the greater part of the period from the 1850s to the 1910s exist only for small, usually church-owned fincas.[42] Soñata, one such small, church-owned finca, was located in the parcialidad Cacsani in Arapa. Because of its favorable situation on a bend of Río Azángaro, the finca in 1913 could dedicate 100 of its total 668 hectares to crops. On the remaining second- and third-class pastures it could maintain about 1,070 sheep.[43] Surprisingly, the rent charged by the church on Soñata reflected the general rise of rental rates with a considerable lag. After neglecting even to charge the tenant for excess pastures in 1860, the rate stayed unaltered at 10 percent (in terms of pesos) until the 1890s. Only after 1901 and then again in 1914 did the annual rent paid for Soñata participate in the general upward trend of rental rates.

The explanation for this "unorthodox" finding has to be sought in the slower-than-average rise of minimum rental rates. Small fincas, often undercapitalized and equipped with an insufficient colono labor force, too little water, and inferior pastures, did not partake in the growing profitability of hacienda operations during the 1860s and the years between 1890 and 1920 to the same extent as large ones did. For such estates the church could find renters only at below-average rates.

It proves more difficult to determine the development of land values during this sixty-five-year period. The most obvious problem consists in the scarcity of information on the size of landholdings, mentioned in notarial contracts only since the early twentieth century. The measurement of property, carried out primarily by nonprofessional agrimensores, was required for the inscription of landholdings into the departmental land register, established in 1889. Although these measurements purported to be exact down to the last square meter, their reliability is rather low, and they could vary by 25 percent or more.[44] Until the 1890s the rare mention of a landholding's size merely gave its approximate perimeter or its length and width by kilometers. Thus, it is not possible to determine the development of the average hectare prices over a longer period of time.

The only way to use the large data base of notarial sales contracts for measuring changes of land prices consists in determining the average price of land per transaction. For most categories of sales the mean purchase price per transaction declined from the 1860s or 1870s to the 1880s and 1890s. In all cases it grew between the 1890s and the first decade of this century. These changing average price levels can be interpreted in two ways: either land prices fell between about 1870 and 1890, or the mean size of land parcels offered for sale went down. Individual property histories suggest that even during the difficult years between the late 1870s and early 1880s land prices did not decline. Thus, it would seem that the mean size of land parcels offered for sale tended to decline between the 1860s and the 1880s or 1890s, an early indication of the impact of population increase on Azángaro's landholding pattern. Of course, we cannot exclude the possibility that land values had already begun to climb in the 1860s or 1870s and that these increases merely failed to show up in mean sales values because of the reduction of the mean size of land parcels. It is equally possible that the size reduction continued after the 1890s but was now covered up by a stronger increase of prices for land. One might interpret the peculiar development of the mean purchase price per transaction as the outcome of a scissorlike configuration between land values and mean size of land parcels offered for sale: until the 1880s or early 1890s decreasing average size had a stronger impact on mean purchase prices than did the increasing land value; this relation was reversed after 1900.

Prices for land organized in estates underwent sharp increases between the 1850s and 1920, generally by between 100 and 200 percent (table 6.3). Increases occurred both in the early phase, from the late 1850s to the 1880s, and in the second half of the period, from the 1890s. Haciendas whose value temporarily declined (Loquicolla Chico, Huañingora) had experienced a decline in their livestock population.[45]

The crucial variable in the appraisal of pastureland was its livestock carrying capacity. We can piece together a set of figures covering a longer time span for the value of the unit of land required to feed one sheep year-round *plus* the value of the sheep itself (table 6.4). This had been the conventional measure in the appraisal of estates since the colonial period. Of course, the actual size of this unit varied according to the carrying capacity of the land. In all, the price of a unit of top-quality pastureland required to feed one sheep plus the sheep itself increased by about 250 to 300 percent between the 1850s and the second decade of the present century.[46] One can again discern two waves of price increases, one prior to the 1890s, probably during the 1860s, and a second, showing a considerably greater rise, between 1902 and World War I.

This price development for land was closely linked to prices for live sheep, which rose at about the same rhythm as land values (table 6.5). Livestock prices were the key factor directly influencing the value of pastoral land in the altiplano. The values of sheep and cattle, in turn, are directly related to the prices of the products derived from them, and here wool is crucial for the altiplano. The two phases of price spurts for sheep occurred when wool prices rose between the late 1850s and early 1870s and again between the mid-1890s and World War I. Livestock prices did not, however, participate in the slump of the 1870s and 1880s; they merely stagnated. This stagnation probably reflected domestic inflation in Peru but might also indicate that the tradition of price conventions, immune to short-term market forces, still had some influence on livestock prices. The impetus for increases in the price of land, during the 1860s and again between about 1895 and the end of World War I, came, transmitted by livestock prices, from heightened demand for the altiplano's most important commercial product, wool.

The preceding discussion of rental rates and prices for land is based on information concerning haciendas or land in the hacienda sector. The development of market prices for peasant lands is much less clear. Moreover, the very notion may be flawed. Consider the constitution of Hacienda

TABLE 6.3. Prices of Selected Estates in Azángaro, 1854–1963

Date of Appraisal	Price (soles m.n.)	Context of Price Setting
Huasacona, Dist. Muñani		
July 7, 1854	27,652.00	Sale
May 9, 1889	40,000.00	Sale
May 20, 1925	181,073.00	Evaluation
Apr. 24, 1937	287,437.00	Sale
Checayani and anexo Quesollani, Dist. Muñani		
Oct. 23, 1902	54,000.00	Evaluation
May 31, 1904	44,777.40	Evaluation
Nov. 5, 1963	443,992.80	Evaluation
Checca, Dist. Santiago de Pupuja		
Jan. 3, 1863	10,400.00	Exchange
July 21, 1899	20,000.00	Evaluation
Loquicolla Chico, Dist. Putina		
Mar. 11, 1862	8,000.00[a]	Sale
Apr. 30, 1882	6,000.00[b]	Sale
Ichocollo, Dist. Putina		
July 3, 1859	5,308.00	Evaluation
Jan. 10, 1875	10,032.00	Sale
May 28, 1917	20,450.00	Evaluation
Calacala, Dist. Chupa		
July 3, 1859	15,344.90	Evaluation
Feb. 9, 1867	24,000.00	Sale
June 4, 1872	19,200.00	Promise of sale
July 22, 1893	19,200.00	Sale
Apr. 25, 1899	19,200.00	Sale

(continued)

TABLE 6.3 continued

Date of Appraisal	Price (soles m.n.)	Context of Price Setting
Quichusa, Dist. Azángaro		
Sept. 20, 1862	3,200.00	Sale
Dec. 5, 1912	8,000.00	Evaluation
Huañingora, Dist. Achaya		
June 23, 1866	4,800.00ᶜ	Evaluation
July 23, 1893	3,200.00ᵈ	Sale
Dec. 4, 1901	15,600.00ᵉ	Evaluation

ᵃIncluding 2,000 head of livestock.
ᵇWithout livestock.
ᶜIncluding 2,000 OMR.
ᵈIncl. 1,000 OMR.
ᵉIncl 1,000 OMR.

Sources: REPA and REPP, 1854–1902; RPIP, vols 1–3; Min. de Agricultura, Zona Agraria 12 (Puno), Expediente de Afectación: Huasacona.

Lourdes in Potoni district between 1880 and 1901.[47] The eight distinct estancias and fincas making up the new estate had been purchased by Adoraida Gallegos for no more than 4,600 soles m.n. Yet in 1901, less than ten years after most of the parcels of land were purchased, an appraisal gave Hacienda Lourdes' value as 12,156 soles m.n., not at all unlikely for an estate extending over 11,719 hectares. Only a small part of this jump of nearly 200 percent in the value of the integrated landholding over the purchase price of the individual estancias reflects the general price trend. The greater part resulted from the higher unit value of land organized in estates, with a stable resident labor force and its own livestock capital, compared with unincorporated peasant land. The formation of Hacienda Lourdes illustrates the economic advantages enjoyed by Azángaro's owners of estates over peasant landholders.

Repeated sales of peasant lands reveal rather peculiar price developments. On April 24, 1908, for example, the peasant woman Teresa Quispe Huarcaya from parcialidad Curayllo in Arapa sold Estancia Collini Accohuani to José Albino Ruiz, politician and owner of the large Hacienda Checayani in Muñani, for 200 pesos. "More than twenty years" earlier she had bought the estancia from Marta Huarcaya for the same price.[48] In a

TABLE 6.4. Prices for Estate Pasture Lands, 1850s–1916
(in soles m.n.)

	Unit of First-Class Pasture Necessary to Feed 1 Sheep (including cost of the sheep)[a]	Price per Hectare (without sheep)	
		Lowest	Highest
1850s[b]	1.50–2.00		
1895[c]	3.00		
1902[d]	3.00	0.75	5.40
1908[e]		3.20	7.20
1912/13[f]	5.00	1.80	11.25
1916[g]	5.50		

[a]The carrying capacity per hectare of the best pastures was variously estimated at between 3.0 and 4.5 OMR.

[b]Estimate, in appraisal of Hacienda Huancarani, Azángaro, Apr. 12, 1845, MPA; REPA, año 1863, Patiño, F. 53, No. 18 (Apr. 22, 1863).

[c]Appraisal of Hda. Sollocota in REPP, año 1895, San Martín, No. 83 (Nov. 9, 1895).

[d]Jiménez, Breves apuntes, 83. Hectare values are my own calculations based on Jiménez, using higher carrying capacities, between 1.5 and 4.5 units of sheep per hectare.

[e]Cisneros, Frutos de paz, 262.

[f]Appraisals of various haciendas between Sept. 4, 1912, and May 1, 1913, in REPP, 1912–1915.

[g]Urquiaga, Sublevaciones, 24.

TABLE 6.5. Prices for Adult Criollo Sheep in Azángaro,
1850s–1915

	Conventional Price[a] (soles m.n.)	Price Range (soles m.n.)
1850s–early 1860s	0.40	—
Mid-1860s–Mid-1890s	1.00	.67–1.20
Late 1890s–1908	1.50	.56–1.75
1909–1913	2.00	1.50–3.00
1915	3.00	—

[a]This is the price most often found during a specific period; it is not necessarily the statistical mean, however.

Sources: Juan Medrano to Juan Paredes, Caira, Nov. 1857, in MPA; 24 notarial contracts, REPA and REPP, 1863–1915.

similar case, the Indian peasant Marcelo Sacaca in 1888 had purchased estancia Pachaje Chico in Putina for 1,600 *soles en quintos bolivianos* (soles q.b.) with money inherited from his mother-in-law Juliana Quenallata. Nearly twenty years later, on June 22, 1907, two granddaughters and coheirs of Juliana Quenallata, Jacoba and María Mejía Machaca and their husbands, sold their share in Pachaje Chico to Manuel Esteban Paredes Urviola, a member of one of the largest landholding clans and the only medical doctor of the province, on the basis of the 1888 transaction, without any price increase.[49] But in other cases peasant land underwent surprisingly large price increases over short periods. On June 25, 1910, Francisco Adrián Toro Nafria, a merchant and hacendado from Asillo, bought Fundo Quisini, located in parcialidad Jila or Supira (the notarial contracts are contradictory) of the San Antón district, from the peasant Damaso Hispanocca Vilca for 50 soles m.n. Two months later, on August 13, 1910, Toro Nafria resold the land to Pablo Anco Turpo and his wife Victoriana Turpo Ccallasaca, peasants from San Antón, for 150 soles m.n., a 200 percent gain, diminished only slightly by the fees for title deed and sales tax.[50]

Such contradictory price developments for individual peasant landholdings reflect the social position of both parties to the transactions. Where the landholding was resold without any price increase even after several decades, the seller was an Indian peasant and the purchaser a hispanized large landholder. The speculative gains, by contrast, were realized by hispanized large landholders reselling (or trading) a property to peasants. These price developments, then, have their common explanation in the social dominance of one contracting partner over the other.

The nature of prices for land changed slowly in the altiplano. Around 1850 prices for land, like rental rates and livestock prices, still had a strongly conventional character. Short-term economic fluctuations did not easily disturb this pricing structure. Within the region all people involved in transactions over land or livestock shared a common understanding about these pricing rules. Phrases such as "according to the conventions used in this department" or "customarily fixed at" appeared often in notarial contracts. This is not to say that land values and livestock prices bore no relation to market conditions; rather, major secular economic changes were required to prompt readjustments in those conventional prices. Thus, for example, the conventional price for one adult sheep remained at four reales between the beginning of the nineteenth century and the 1850s.[51] Rental rates for estates continued to be calculated on the same basis of 10 percent of livestock capital during the 1850s just as they had in the 1770s.[52] The few examples at our disposal to analyze land values in this early period suggest the same type of stability.[53]

During the following sixty years the impact of market conditions on land values became more pervasive, and convention gradually lost strength as the basis for determining prices and lease fees on land and livestock. This development was aided by the growing technical capacity to measure the quality and extension of land. But it had its causes in the increasing awareness of the impact of market fluctuations on land values and income levels among some of the region's landholders, itself a consequence of the link to the world market for wool. This process, by which prices for pastureland came to reflect market conditions for the altiplano's livestock products, was far from complete by 1920. Azángaro's pricing structure for land remained ambiguous during the early years of this century, leading at times to seemingly erratic prices for one and the same landholding. This ambiguity allowed members of the socially dominant groups to draw extra profit from land transactions with peasants and tradition-bound landholding institutions such as the church.

To summarize the development of land values in Azángaro: The value of estates generally rose between 100 and 200 percent from the 1850s to about 1920, with prices for top-quality pastureland rising by up to 300 percent. First-class haciendas, endowed with the best pastureland, sufficient resident labor, and, most important, extensive acreage, experienced a steeper rise in their value than did smaller estates with scarcer natural and labor resources. By contrast, the price for peasant land does not reflect market conditions because in most cases it was shaped by the social constellation between buyer and seller rather than general price trends. Still, for estates the link between wool exports, livestock prices, and land values explains why old and new landholders adjusted their purchases of land to the rhythm of the regional wool export economy: earnings from estate operations followed this rhythm.

The Geography and Ecology of Hacienda Expansion

The enormous expansion of estates onto peasant lands between the late 1850s and 1920 affected Azángaro's districts and communities unevenly. Whereas the four districts in which indigenous peasants sold the most land to hispanized large landholders and members of the intermediate group accounted for more than 60 percent of all transactions, the four districts with the fewest sales by peasants accounted for only 8.5 percent.[54] In Azángaro, by far the district with most sales by peasants to other groups of landholders (nearly 30 percent of the total number), peasants alienated land valued at over 96,000 soles m.n. in 563 transactions until 1910. At the other extreme, for Caminaca district the notaries registered only 18 such transactions for a total of under 2,700 soles m.n.

Distinct ecological and land-use zones in the province had a bearing on the spatial distribution of land sales. Caminaca and Saman in the south of the province experienced only a limited expansion of haciendas onto peasant lands. On the plains between Lake Titicaca and Lake Arapa agriculture played a relatively more important role than it did in other parts of the province. Until the mid-nineteenth century only a few small estates had been established there, and land was more evenly distributed than it was in the pastoral areas of the province. The comparatively equal distribution of lands and the absence of powerful hacendados inhibited the subsequent advance of estates into peasant communities since large agglomerations of land could not serve as points of departure for acquisition schemes. When a few small estates were finally formed in Saman after 1900—among them Finca Santa Clara, owned by the hacendado and livestock trader Ildefonso González from Arapa, and Finca San Juan, owned by the local merchant and livestock trader Mariano Abarca Dueñas—peasant resistance was particularly adamant.[55] After 1912 bloody clashes ensued between these gamonales and the peasants.[56] In the short run gamonales could inflict losses of land, material belongings, and even life on peasants. But in Saman the balance of power between peasants and haciendas was such that after 1940 no hacienda survived.[57]

The four districts in which hacienda expansion had the greatest impact in relation to population lay in the predominantly pastoral zone of the province to the northeast of Azángaro town. In three of these, San José, San Antón, and Potoni, ecological conditions favored livestock raising, but only a handful of haciendas had existed in the early republican period, perhaps because of their isolation from trade and communication circuits of that time. There hacienda expansion had particularly dramatic consequences for the land tenure pattern. Although by the early independence period a considerable number of estates had existed in the fourth district in this group, Azángaro, it was also the location of the greatest number of peasant parcialidades. The combination of a strong estate base and plentiful peasant lands, as well as the advantages offered by the provincial center with its commercial and administrative opportunities, accounts for Azángaro's predominant share in land acquisitions by established or aspiring large landholders.

Muñani and Putina, with their fertile valley pastures and their arid cordillera slopes unfit for crops, belonged to the areas most suited for livestock raising in Puno department. Yet in proportion to population both districts experienced a low rate of peasant land sales to other groups of landholders. Here a great part of peasant lands had already been absorbed by haciendas by the early republican period. By the 1870s little peasant land remained in Muñani. In Putina a number of parcialidades survived at least until the early twentieth century, and peasant land sales were rather frequent in absolute terms. Transactions among hacendados and intermediate landholders had a greater weight in Putina than in any other district, corroborating the existence of numerous haciendas and smaller nonpeasant landholdings since before 1850.

In contrast to what happened in the seventeenth and eighteenth centuries, Azángaro's "hacienda frontier" now moved outward from the center of the province. During the 1850s and 1860s more than 80 percent of peasant land sales to hacendados and intermediate landholders concerned land in Azángaro district, with only a sprinkling in all other districts. The bulk of purchases can be attributed to purchases by Juan Paredes and José María Lizares, the most dynamic hacendados in the province between independence and the War of the Pacific. Both men came from families that arrived in Azángaro after independence, and both held administrative offices and participated in trade in the provincial capital. They could build up a clientele system most easily in the immediate vicinity of their residence, seat of business and of official power, and thus began their land purchases in Azángaro district.

Even though the market for livestock products had become favorable, most hacendado families in the rest of the province did not expand their landholdings onto peasant lands during this period. Until the late 1860s it remained relatively easy to find estates for lease, and despite the wool export boom, a sufficient number of hacendados and owners of smaller nonpeasant landholdings were still willing to sell land. Apparently not all established landholders were profiting from the favorable market conditions, and some saw themselves forced to give up their estates. Such sales occurred even during the second boom phase after the 1890s.

Supply and demand for pastoral land were still largely balanced during the 1860s. Aside from the situation in Azángaro and Muñani districts, potential land buyers had no need to resort to peasant estancias. After 1890, by contrast, mushrooming demand for land could not be met any more by nonpeasant landholdings offered for sale. During the first boom period in the 1860s Azángaro's land tenure pattern was still affected as much by changes in the composition of the hacendado class as it was by outright hacienda expansion, whereas after 1890 the weight shifted decidedly to the latter mode.[58]

From 1870 to 1890 the "hacienda frontier" moved into some of the districts in which relatively many haciendas had existed before, including

Putina, Arapa, and Santiago. Some of the districts that were to become central locations for hacienda expansion between the 1890s and 1920, such as San José, San Antón, and Potoni, still saw no or only minimal land transfers from peasants to hacendados and intermediate landholders. Until 1890 the purchases of peasant lands served mostly to enlarge well-established estates rather than to constitute new ones. Although a few new estates were formed during the 1870s or before, most were founded after 1890. Only the increasing demand for land beginning in the last decade of the past century—coinciding with the entry of a substantial number of newcomers into Azángaro's land market—prompted aspiring estate owners to penetrate hitherto unaffected Indian communities. It was easier to acquire peasant lands in districts with a long-established hacienda-community complex, since there peasants were more closely tied into patterns of dependence and paternalism. By contrast, in areas such as San Antón and Potoni the majority of peasants had traditionally lived and worked outside the sphere of influence of estates.

In these areas the advance of the hacienda frontier was aided after 1890 by the opening of the road from railroad station Tirapata via Asillo, San Antón, through Potoni district to Macusani and from there to the ceja de la selva of Carabaya. The trade connected with the rubber and gold exploitations in Carabaya province, which now passed through these districts, and the growing network of itinerant wool buyers regularly visiting every parcialidad multiplied the opportunities for intricating peasants into clientele systems as the prelude to land acquisition schemes. During the thirty years following 1891 the tide of land transfers from peasants to hacendados and intermediate landholders engulfed nearly the entire province. Only Muñani, with little peasant land remaining, and Caminaca were largely untouched by the avalanche. This period saw particularly rapid growth of old and new estates in the northeastern districts of Potoni, San Antón, and San José. It may not have been mere coincidence that the most serious peasant rebellion, the Rumi Maqui Rebellion of 1915–16, centered on San José district.

Sales of peasant land to hacendados and intermediate landholders varied greatly from parcialidad to parcialidad. The data must be interpreted with great caution, as parcialidades or ayllus could change their boundaries over time.[59] In seven of Azángaro's ten districts with six or more parcialidades, more than 50 percent of all peasant land sales occurred in just two parcialidades. In five of these districts, the two communities with the heaviest sales activity accounted for more than 70 percent of all such transactions. Of the five parcialidades in Saman, one, Chejachi, accounted for 82 percent of all peasant land sales to other categories of landholders (88.6 percent by value). Chejachi is located on Saman's northern border, next to Arapa district. Hacendados who owned landholdings in Arapa extended their land purchases into the neighboring district. The two districts in which peasant land sales were least concentrated in a few parcialidades, Azángaro and San José districts, were those with the highest number and value of sales. Here the expansion and new foundation of haciendas spread over most areas of the districts so that no parcialidades stood out.

Different size and population of individual communities may account for some of these variations. In the absence of information on the extension of parcialidades I tested the relevance of population by selecting two districts, Caminaca and San Antón, for which the parcialidades listed in the censuses of 1862, 1876, and 1940 remained the same and were nearly identical to those appearing in the notarial registers. Population does make a difference in the ranking and spread of land sales activity in various parcialidades. But great variations remain unexplained by population. Using the average population from the three censuses, in Hila, San Antón, one sale was transacted by every seven community members, whereas in Sullca one sale was concluded by every thirty-three persons. In terms of value more than ten times as much land per capita was sold in Sillota as in Sullca. In Caminaca, with only a few peasant land sales, per capita sales differed little in three parcialidades, but there were none in a fourth community.[60]

What accounts for this great variation of per capita land sales in different parcialidades? Just as between districts, the varying weight of agriculture and livestock raising probably played an important role. So did more specific locational conditions, such as the proximity of a parcialidad to established haciendas and the availability of water, good pastures, and collpares. The ten parcialidades with the highest number or value of peasant land sales to hacendados or intermediate landholders (map 6.1) together accounted for about one-third of all such sales. Specific locational factors help explain the heavy losses of land in most of these communities. Parcialidad Jayuraya, for example, was located in the hilly and broken terrain southwest of the pampa of Río Tarucani between Muñani and Putina. For many of the estates clustered around these two towns, and particularly for Hacienda Checayani, Jayuraya formed the only potential area of expansion, since they were hemmed in by other estates on all other sides. Similarly, we can detect locational reasons for limited alienation of lands in some communities. Between the 1850s and 1910 parcialidad Sillota, in Asillo, lost only one-third as many parcels of land to hacendados and intermediate landholders as did Collana (in the same district) between the 1850s and 1910, although Collana had 50 percent fewer inhabitants.

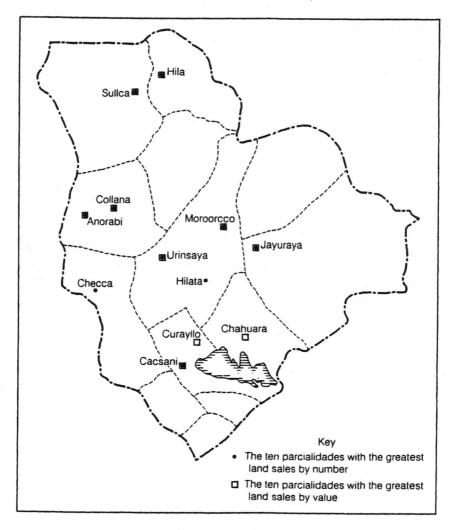

MAP 6.1. The Ten Parcialidades with the Greatest Number and/or Value of Land Sales by Peasants to Hacendados and Intermediate Landholders, Azángaro Province

Much of Sillota's territory, north of Asillo town, offered quite favorable conditions for agriculture in the low foothills on both sides of the Río Grande; only small fincas developed here.

But do locational factors suffice to explain why parcialidades were affected so differently by the process of hacienda expansion? It seems likely that the internal situation of the parcialidades played an important role in determining vulnerability to outside pressure. Factors such as community solidarity, the affluence or poverty of community members, demographic pressure on the land base, cleavages between rich and poor peasants, and the survival of autonomous cultural traditions could help or hinder access of aspiring outside landholders to the land of community members. Local cultural and ideological traditions and politics thus intervened in blocking or facilitating the avalanche of hacienda expansion.[61]

Expansion Strategies

Interpretations of the modalities of hacienda expansion in the altiplano cluster around two extremes, which might be called the myths of free will and brutal force. Apologists have stressed the legality of most land acquisitions by hacendados and described the purchases of peasant lands as a contract between free and—as far as the transaction goes—equal parties. This apologetic view was expressed by the first organization of Puno's hacienda owners in a petition sent to President Augusto Leguía in 1921. The hacendados claimed that estates were based either on colonial land grants and compositions or on "just and legal titles for land . . . purchased, without deceit and according to the law, from the Indians since the period in which these were declared owners of the land they had occupied and free to sell."[62]

The other extreme view regarding hacienda formation became widespread with the rise of *indigenismo* in the second decade of this century and has remained one of the points of accusation against the agrarian regime of the southern sierra before 1969. As the sociologist Jorge Lora Cam put it in 1976, "Haciendas in Puno were mostly formed by violent usurpation of the land of the community Indians, converting some of them into colonos enserfed to the gamonal power, while others were thrown out if they were not physically liquidated."[63]

Both characterizations of the process of hacienda formation and expansion fail to grasp the complexity of socioeconomic interaction patterns in the altiplano during the late nineteenth and early twentieth centuries. A sales transaction between free and equal economic agents and a violent usurpation of land have one thing in common: they are punctual actions. Both parties, seller and purchaser in the first case and aggressor and victim in the second, need not have interacted previously. This lack of interaction may be characteristic, on the one hand, of individualistic market societies in which all actors at least ideally have the freedom to make economic choices and, on the other hand, of societies in which social cohesion has utterly broken down, as in conquest or civil war. But in a society such as that of Azángaro, built on long-standing ties of family, religion, and community and on neocolonial hierarchies, sales transactions between free and equal economic agents and violent usurpations of land were merely the extreme modes of land acquisition on a scale in which most cases were characterized by a mixture of volition and coercion.[64] The social positions of the contracting parties, their economic resources, the existence or nonexistence of kinship ties between them, and other factors gave special significance to each individual transaction.

Land purchases, the most frequent form of estate formation and expansion, varied greatly as to type and size of land, social status of seller and buyer, and circumstances leading to the transaction. Those with sufficient capital or access to credit facilities tried to purchase small fincas as a central building block in the process of forming a large new estate. The most spectacular example of this strategy was the formation of Hacienda San José in the district of the same name. Sometime during the mid-1880s the half brothers José Sebastian Urquiaga Echenique, born in 1857, and Bernardino Arias Echenique, born in 1860, inherited Hacienda Sollocota, located in the border area of districts Azángaro and San José, from their maternal family.[65] During the eighteenth century the estate had belonged to Miguel de Echenique, a Spanish miner working veins in Carabaya and an ancestor of President José Rufino Echenique. Although gradually decaying, Sollocota remained in control of the family during the early republican period.[66] In the decade after Carlota Echenique, mother of José Sebastian and Bernardino, had assumed the administration of the largely decapitalized estate, sometime around 1860, she undertook to restock Sollocota with cattle and sheep.[67] The family's landholdings expanded only after José Sebastian and Bernardino inherited the finca. Between 1891 and 1905 the two together bought sixty-five separate properties; nearly all were located in the general vicinity of Hacienda Sollocota, some in the northern part of Azángaro district, but most in San José. Among the properties were several small to medium-sized fincas, such as Finca Parcani, with a livestock capital of 1,800 sheep, and Finca Unión. Although Parcani was an older estate, Unión had been recently formed by the previous owner, José Guillermo Riquelme, through agglomerating at least thirteen peasant estancias.[68] In February 1903 Urquiaga and Arias Echenique bought Finca Quimsacalco, an estate of colonial vintage with a capacity of 4,000 sheep, from three brothers and sisters of José Guillermo Riquelme for 12,000 soles m.n.[69]

Beginning in 1905 the two half brothers began to purchase land separately, and we may assume that around that year they effectively divided their property.[70] Urquiaga received the old maternal Finca Sollocota, now greatly expanded by some of the landholdings purchased since the early 1890s. Arias Echenique became exclusive owner of the majority of the purchased property, including the three Fincas Quimsacalco, Parcani, and Unión. All of this land was incorporated into a new estate called San José. The narrow Río San José now formed the border between the two estates for some fifteen kilometers. Both Urquiaga and Arias Echenique continued to expand their separate haciendas through the 1910s and succeeded in integrating further estates (the colonial Hacienda Puscallani became part of Sollocota) besides dozens of peasant estancias. By 1925 Hacienda San José, according to one measure, extended for 40,000 hectares in the districts of San José, San Antón, and Potoni.[71] After years of legal fights it passed into possession of the Sociedad Ganadera del Sur in 1944, a corporation owning a dozen large estates in the department of Puno and controlled by the Gibsons from Arequipa, the largest southern Peruvian import, export, and banking house.[72] Some of the land of San José, within half a century, had been exploited through four different levels of landholdings. Original peasant estancias had been integrated into a small finca (Unión), which became part of the large estate of San José; this hacienda in turn was purchased by the largest corporate landholding company of southern Peru. The formation of the new Hacienda San José, accomplished in thirty years at most, relied on the integration of a number of older estates besides the purchase of dozens of peasant estancias. Without the older estates, in themselves extending over several thousand hectares, San José would have remained a medium-sized finca like most new fincas incorporating only peasant estancias.[73]

This type of agglomeration was an option only for the wealthiest and most powerful large landholders of the province.[74] In most cases the expansion or new formation of estates depended entirely on the incorporation of peasant estancias. This was a slow and tedious process, requiring contact with numerous Indian peasants, some of whom might hold rights to only minuscule plots. Given the advancing fragmentation of the original peasant landholdings since the colonial and early republican periods, potential purchasers frequently had to carry out genealogical inquiries to locate all persons with rights to an estancia.[75] José Albino Ruiz proceeded in this manner in 1908 when acquiring a number of peasant landholdings in the border area between Azángaro and Arapa districts, "with the aim of forming a small finca called Calahuire."[76] This had been the name of the original landholding owned by the Indian Carlos León Huarcaya in the mid-eighteenth century. Ruiz now was purchasing some ten different shares from third- and fourth-generation descendants who all traced their lineage to that common root, the "stem" of the family.[77]

Most transactions over land between hacendados and peasants do not mention the circumstances under which they were concluded and, in their formalistic language, give the impression of a totally free agreement between the two parties. But a sufficient number of contracts grant us glimpses into the great variety of means designed to coax peasants into relinquishing control over their land. Frequently a peasant had received food on credit from a hacendado "for the subsistence of his family" over a period of several years. The creditor would finally present the bill and, if the peasant were incapable of repaying the debt in money or some commodity as wool or livestock, demand payment in form of land. I found 165 cases in which land was explicitly sold as payment of a debt. But in reality the number was higher, as many notarial contracts lacked precision to list such circumstances. Debts leading to the sale of land could arise out of a great variety of situations. The purchase of sheep on credit or monetary obligations in connection with church festivities at times led to land sales by peasants.[78] More frequent were cases of debts incurred to defray the expenses of a proper funeral.[79]

Old people often relinquished their land in exchange for future material benefits, including the payment of their funeral, rather than as payment for past debts. Juliana Ramos, a small shopkeeper of peasant origin in Asillo, whose husband and only son had died, in January of 1893 sold her "Hacienda" Viluyo with the adjoining estancias Misquichuno and Hulquicunca and her small store on the plaza of Asillo to Lieutenant Colonel Juan Manuel Sarmiento, a Cuzqueño military officer, for 140 soles. She explained that the properties might be worth a bit more but that she considered the difference a donation to Sarmiento for the services "which I have received from the buyer and for those which I will receive given that Sr. Sarmiento pledges to feed and dress me, to cure me when I am ill, and to bury me when God calls me."[80]

The sale of land was coupled with the expectation of material aid and protection by a strong hacendado. Often a peasant had no choice but to become integrated into such clientalistic dependencies. For hacendados intent on expanding their landholdings, such transactions brought important advantages. It was easier to persuade Indian smallholders who had come to depend on a hacendado to relinquish legal title to their land than it was to deal with fiercely independent peasants with sufficient economic means to reject any purchase offer or to have to resort to costly legal battles or coercive measures.

Acquiring land from an indebted peasant often reduced the effective purchase price. Although the notarial bills of sale usually stated that the seller had received the full price to his "entire satisfaction," in many cases it was paid only later or not in its entirety at all.[81] If the seller was a client peasant, the purchaser might pay a considerable share of the total price in goods, such as foodstuffs, the price of which could be fixed to his or her advantage.[82] In many cases hacendados withheld a part of the purchase price in order to pay it later to a co-owner of the property not present at the transaction; this money was often retained for good by the purchaser. In other cases hacendados had to pay only part of the purchase price in recompense for services already rendered or to be rendered to the seller in future. In 1867 Juan Paredes acquired an estancia in ayllu Hilahuata from a peasant widow, paying cash for only one-fourth of the property and receiving usufruct of the rest free of charge in recompense for raising the woman's minor child in his household, surely more of a benefit than an expense for the hacendado.[83]

Cases in which hispanized landholders paid only a small share of the purchase price for a parcel of land after having given legal counsel— commonly without professional qualifications—have become notorious.[84] In 1899 Lieutenant Colonel Victor Gregorio Rossello, descendant of an old Azangarino landholding family and veteran of the War of the Pacific, was forgiven four-fifths of the purchase price of 500 soles m.n. for Estancia Callapani in district Santiago de Pupuja in recognition of his judicial efforts on behalf of the sellers, a group of peasants and weavers from the par- cialidad Mataro in the same district. On top of this, Rossello was forgiven the remaining one-fifth of the purchase price as "indemnification for all the damages which we [the sellers] have caused him through repeated attacks on his properties."[85] Rossello thus acquired legal title to Callapani without paying one centavo to the previous owners.

This contract demonstrates the ambivalence of paternalism in the con- text of an expanding hacienda complex and neocolonial social relations. How can we believe that the peasant owners of Estancia Callapani sought out Rossello as their spokesman in court cases when they had had conflicts with him serious enough to lead to recurring attacks on his estate? The notarial contracts cannot directly reflect what the mostly illiterate and Quechua-speaking peasants stated. We hear only what the notary put in their mouths. In the present case direct statements by the peasants prob- ably would have revealed that they were coerced or tricked into the deal with Rossello. The establishment of clientalistic relations here was a one- sided strategy by the hispanized landholder to gain access to the land and labor of Indian peasants.

But such clientalistic links by no means needed to be based on deceit or coercion. Although the dominant partner was likely to benefit most, the reciprocal benefits for the dependent peasant, in the form of protection, credit, and foodstuff in times of need, could constitute significant assets. Some peasants accepted dependence on a paternalistic gamonal as a prudent course of action without being a victim of specific entrapment beyond that constituted by the structure of society.[86]

These underlying social relations are indicated by the long delays that often occurred between the conclusion of an informal contract and the entry of the title deed in the notarial register. The original contract might be celebrated before the justice of the peace of the local district or in the residence of the hacendado. It was common knowledge that many justices of the peace were corrupt. An Indian peasant could be induced to sign over land rights without even realizing the impact of the action.[87] It was simple enough to make up an informal contract through trickery or forgery, since most peasants could not sign their names and one of the witnesses signed for them.[88] Only years later would the interested party bring the transaction before the notary to elevate it to a fully recognized title document. In the intervening time the peasant might have become a colono on the purchaser's hacienda while continuing to live in his or her old estancia. In other instances the original peasant owner had died in the meantime. Only then did the hacendado approach the heirs to demand the reaffirmation of the original sale, often claiming that part of the purchase price had been paid already to the deceased person as an advance (*arrás*). The heirs, unfamiliar with the informal contract as documentary proof of the hacendado's assertions, could often do nothing—short of risking legal actions with all their expenses and delays—but to consent to the notarial reaffirmation of the sale.[89]

Of 3,060 sales contracts between 1854 and 1910, 278 were protocolizations, with an average lag of nearly eight years between the informal conclusion of the sale and its entry in the notarial register as a title deed.[90] In another 460 contracts the purchaser was stated to have been in possession of the property for at least four weeks and up to forty years prior to the notarization. In all, there was a lag between the informal conclusion of a sales contract and its notarial registration in a minimum of 24.1 percent of all sales transactions.

The peculiarity of the altiplano land market is illustrated by the importance of a transaction called *anticresis* or *prenda pretorial*. It involved the extension of a credit to a landholder, who, rather than mortgaging his or her land as security for the credit, would turn it over in usufruct to the creditor for a period of between five and ten years, at the end of which the loan was to be repaid and the land returned to the owner. The rent of the land and the interest on the loan were considered to be of equal value, so that the debtor did not pay interest and the creditor did not pay rent. An anticresis contract, then, fulfilled two functions, extension of credit and medium-term land transfer, with a minimum of cash transactions.

Which of the two functions was primary for the transaction depended on the social relations between the contracting parties. If the creditor was a hispanized large landholder and the person turning over a plot of land an indigenous peasant, the contract's primary function mostly lay in the appropriation of land by the large landholder. For five to ten years the hacendado was getting a piece of land for extending a sum of money considerably below its sales price. If the peasant failed to return the credit at the appointed time, the creditor could demand the formal sale of the land, for which he or she paid only a minimal additional sum. In this way unfulfilled anticresis contracts represented a variety of the "delay strategy" discussed above.[91] Adoraida Gallegos, for example, systematically employed anticresis contracts over fifteen peasant estancias to gain control of land at the fringes of her Hacienda Lourdes.[92]

But anticresis contracts were more important for peasants than for hispanized large landholders.[93] Nearly one-third of all anticresis contracts were concluded between peasants, a rate much higher than that for sales. The popularity of anticresis contracts with peasants and intermediate landholders reflects two important traits of Azángaro's rural society, the scarcity of cash and the uncertainty of loan repayment.[94] They affected the poorest people most heavily, so that wherever possible, they recurred to transactions minimizing the flow of cash. For poor landholders in need of a substantial amount of cash, the anticresis contract was preferable to mortgaging their land, since it freed them from regular interest payments. Creditors, especially peasants and other small landholders, preferred to take over the possession of a land parcel as tangible security until repayment of their loan rather than risking the uncertainty and trouble of collecting interest and principle on a loan. Anticresis contracts, then, reflected the fragility of the altiplano's credit market, the weakness of the legal framework for enforcing contracts, and the high level of material protection against losses from transactions demanded especially by the poorest landholders.

The anticresis contract constituted an alternative to renting or buying land. Renting peasant land, although involving smaller cash transactions, was not a real option, as peasants were reluctant to relinquish control of land in exchange for a small rental fee. For the purpose of providing day-to-day subsistence, it was obviously more economical to work the land by oneself rather than to rely on a rental fee, which had to lie considerably below the gross value of goods produced by the land. Only when peasants needed major sums of money in extraordinary or critical situations, such as family celebrations, funerals, crop failures, or livestock epidemics, were they willing to relinquish control over land. From the perspectives of both the owner and the person with limited cash resources wishing to acquire land, an anticresis contract could be preferable to an outright sales transaction. The owner could hope to regain control of the land on repayment of the loan. For the person with limited cash wanting to acquire land, anticresis was cheaper than outright purchase and also kept that option open.

The contrast between the use of anticresis contracts and rentals in Azángaro is striking. Land rentals from peasants or members of the intermediate group played only a minimal role among the strategies of hispanized large landholders to gain access to more land. In only 7.3 percent of all rentals did indigenous peasants lease land to hispanized landholders. Rental contracts were overwhelmingly concluded over landholdings belonging to hacendados (50.0 percent) and the church (20.1 percent). In most cases these holdings were rented out to hispanized large landholders. The parishes and Cuzco convents never leased their fincas to peasants, an important fact for evaluating the economic role of the church in the province. Intermediate landholders, by contrast, did have some access to land for rent both from hispanized large landholders and from the church.

Newcomers to the province—mestizo and white traders, transport entrepreneurs, administrators, lawyers, and priests—often lacked sufficient capital to purchase an incorporated estate or had not yet established strong clientalistic links that would enable them to form a new hacienda; these newcomers often began their ventures as renters of small or medium-sized fincas. In one-fifth of all rental contracts the renter was born outside Azángaro province. For example, sometime during the mid-1880s Felipe R. López, a trader born in 1851 on the peninsula of Capachica near Puno town, came to Azángaro with his wife, the Arequipeña Petronila Butiler, and established a small dry-goods store.[95] By 1889 they were renting the small Finca Upaupani, two miles outside of the provincial capital, from a member of the Paredes clan for a yearly rental fee of 32 soles q.b.(26.66 soles m.n.). At the time Upaupani had no livestock capital.[96] In 1899 López and his wife rented the small Finca Pumire, probably with livestock capital, for five years for the annual rental fee of 100 soles q.b.(63.37 soles m.n.).[97] Only in the following year, after more than ten years of residence in Azángaro, did López begin to purchase land.

The majority of renters, however, were well-established landholders. Even the greatest hacendados of the province, such as the Paredes clan or the Lizares Quiñones, found it advantageous to rent additional estates, because, as one landholder stated, it could "advance the productivity [*industria*] of their estates."[98] Renting estancias or fincas adjacent to their own estate could bring about economies of scale, allowing them to run more sheep per flock or to form more flocks for different categories of sheep so as to obtain better breeding results.

But the number of properties offered for rent did not keep up with expanding demand for land; the number of contracts concluded between hispanized large landholders declined slightly, from thirty-four between 1851 and 1870 to thirty-one between 1871 and 1890 and another thirty-one contracts during the following twenty years. As new estates were being formed and old ones expanded at a rather spectacular rate, the possibility of leasing land from hispanized large landholders became more limited. The interest of hacendados in managing their own estates was increasing.

When a hacendado failed to acquire a landholding by one of the contractual procedures outlined above, he or she could resort to the judicial system. In 1916 José Frisancho, Azángaro's state attorney during much of the second decade of this century, published a scathing indictment of the administration of justice in the province.[99] It climaxed in the oft-cited assertion that "in spite of having been victim of frequent crimes, in not one case has the Indian achieved justice against some hacendado." In Frisancho's view, Azángaro's judicial personnel, from the judge of first instance to the district justices of the peace, the scribes, the court-appointed experts, and the witnesses, had become subservient to the interests of the large landholders, interests that found their strongest expression in the rapid appropriation of the land of the Indian peasantry.[100] This development largely explained why in Azángaro "latifundism has reached an extreme degree of preponderance, much more so than in any other Peruvian altiplano province." Frisancho resigned in his struggle against the "forensic denaturalization" in Azángaro and found that any reform effort had to collapse "before the impenetrable resistance of the social environment, zealously guarding its vested interests."[101] Because of such indictments, it is commonplace to characterize the sierra's judicial system during the first century of republican Peru as serving the class interests of the hacendados, a tool for the exploitation of the Indian peasantry.[102]

In reality, courts fulfilled a more complex role in serrano provincial society. They functioned as an arena for testing the power of the litigants. The outcome of a case did not necessarily rest on which party had the law on its side but rather on who could bring to bear more influence on the court. Such influence could take the form of better legal preparation, more money to spend on the suit—not necessarily for bribes but for lawyers and appeals to higher courts—and more leverage for concluding quid pro quo deals with court personnel, requiring bargaining chips of value outside the court system.[103] In a legal contest between a hispanized large landholder and an Indian peasant, the outcome may indeed have been a foregone conclusion. But often peasants were backed by another hacendado whose client they had become. The suit thus became a contest between two hacendados, and the outcome was by no means certain. Litigation over land between hacendados or between peasants occurred just as frequently as legal battles between a hacendado and peasant.

Viewing the judicial system as an arena for power contests between gamonales and their clients helps to explain why many court cases over land were never concluded. Of every hundred cases over land brought before courts in the department of Puno in 1893, only five were concluded within the year.[104] Many suits dragged on for years or even generations. Often the litigants decided to abandon the judicial struggle and settle out of court. The economically weaker party had been exhausted by the high cost of litigation and was now willing to accept the terms of the stronger party. In the context of hacienda expansion strategies, such cases constituted the continuation of economic means of land acquisition within the judicial arena.[105] In some cases even the threat of litigation could be sufficient to force poor landholders to relinquish their claims.[106]

In the absence of title to a claimed property, an interested party could initiate proceedings of *formación de titulos supletorios*. Witnesses were heard to verify the legal and undisputed possession of the petitioner, and notices calling for any opposition to the granting of judicial title were published and affixed in public places. Of course, neither the witnesses nor the public call for opposition presented an effective palliative against abuse. Supportive witnesses could easily be found among the claimant's clients and friends, and the peasants whose land was mostly at issue in these proceedings could not read the public notices. In 1903 Adoraida Gallegos initiated proceedings on Estancias Ccaramocco, Chuantira, and Pisacani in Potoni district. She claimed to have inherited these lands from her father, Geronimo Gallegos, but no will existed to prove it. Four witnesses, all Indian peasants from Potoni, confirmed her claim, the justice of the peace had the notices affixed in the small population center for thirty days, and they were printed nineteen times in Puno's newspaper, *El Ciudadano*, which was not likely to be read by anybody in Potoni, 220 kilometers farther north with only a handful of literate residents. When no opposition was voiced, Gallegos was granted judicial title to the estancias by Puno's judge of first instance, and they became part of her Hacienda Lourdes.[107]

Judicial procedures such as the formación de titulos supletorios, the *queja de desahuicio*, and the *interdicto de adquirir* played a notorious role in the surreptitious appropriation of land by members of the provincial elite.[108] In 1913, when the wave of hacienda expansion was cresting, the president of Puno's superior court admitted that the "interdicto de adquirir greatly facilitates the usurpation of land." Not infrequently, the Indian owner of an estancia, unaware of any legal proceedings, "sees a judge approach his cottage accompanied by a person whom he does not know and to whom the judicial personage formally hands over the land that he [the real owner] had inherited from his ancestors."[109]

The departmental property register is filled with examples from Azángaro, in which such judicial procedures led to the desired end without any public opposition.[110] Cases in which peasants successfully resisted such procedures were rare, although not unknown.[111] But more than any concrete judicial procedure, the venality and partiality of the judges, scribes, and witnesses made the use of the judicial system appear promising to persons attempting to gain control of some parcel of land, a problem particularly severe at the district level.[112]

Last, hacienda expansion could proceed through violent usurpation of neighboring landholdings. José Avila, himself a judge in Azángaro during the 1960s and 1970s, has given us an ideal-typical description of sequences of violent actions aimed at land usurpation:

> The grabbing of land from Indians begins with the act of daily placing cattle and mules belonging to the usurper in the pastures and cultivated fields of the Indian. In this the colonos and employees of the latifundista use force, and they proceed to kill the few head of livestock of the Indian for their own consumption. Alternatively they drive the Indian's livestock to the latifundia's central building complex, [kill the animals there], and distribute most of the meat and hides among themselves, while reserving the carcasses of the best-fed animals for the patrón or as gifts to the provincial authorities. . . . In the following days the looting of the Indian's hut begins with the object of weakening his economic situation. This goes on until, under the pressure of this display of force, the owner decides to sign the bill of sale. As sales price they receive a small sum in money or kind according to the whim of the land grabber.[113]

This account includes different violent actions against landholders that were recurrent themes in legal proceedings as well as in indigenista literature of the time.[114] Avila places the individual episodes of aggression in the framework of escalating use of force in an overall usurpation strategy, but each of these episodes could occur separately. If peasants yielded to a neighboring estate owner after repeated trampling of their planted fields and consumption of their pastures by the gamonal's livestock, an escalation of force would be unnecessary.

Competing claims over the same parcel of land were common in the altiplano during the nineteenth and early twentieth centuries. Labyrinthine title histories and vague border definitions could justify competing claims on innumerable holdings. Border demarcations usually relied on natural landmarks such as hill crests, creeks, and even trees or shrubs and at best on easily changeable ditches or border stones. Many usurpations could be justified as recovery of land properly belonging to the invader.[115] Even complete knowledge of all relevant title deeds does not always make it clear which landholder held the legally more valid claim since titles themselves could overlap. Violent usurpations occurred not only in the context of hacienda encroachments onto peasant lands but also in interactions among hacendados as well as among peasants.[116] Display of force was the other side of Azángaro's clientalistic society. It permeated relations between members of all social groups in the altiplano, although peasants became victims most frequently.

It is difficult to estimate how important violent usurpations of peasant lands were for the overall process of hacienda expansion in Azángaro between the 1860s and 1920. Although petty harassment, such as introducing livestock onto the pastures of a neighboring landholder, occurred regularly, the use of more serious levels of force, such as destruction of peasant residences, never lost its character as an extraordinary event. Nevertheless, the huge wave of land purchases by hispanized large landholders between the 1890s and 1920 led to endemic open violence in Azángaro's countryside, an expression of the critical impasse that the altiplano's neocolonial society was approaching.

Hacienda expansion strategies were further differentiated by a number of economic variables, including size of the parcels acquired, capital available for hacienda operations, and the dispersion or concentration of parcels acquired. Land purchases by relatively poor, marginal large landholders differed considerably from those by the wealthiest and most powerful families in the province.[117] Itinerant traders, small retailers in the district capitals, small-time muleteers, pettifoggers, and other *mistis* (members of the local elite, usually of mestizo background) desperate to distance themselves from the ranks of the Indian peasantry commanded exiguous funds sufficient only for purchasing a few small parcels with which to enlarge their small fincas, establish themselves as marginal finca owners, or enlarge their scattered estancia holdings.

For example, Cesar Salas Flores, an orphan born in the capital of the neighboring province of Lampa, came to Azángaro as an unskilled worker with a band of muleteers sometime during the late 1880s or early 1890s.[118] He married Isabel Mango, a descendant of an impoverished kuraka family who brought only a little property into the marriage. Salas himself had no capital and did not establish any trade or transport business in Azángaro;[119] rather, his main occupation consisted in working as a *tinterillo*, or petti-fogger, and acquiring small peasant properties in the process. By 1909 Salas had agglomerated six to eight peasant estancias around the two largest properties. He had acquired one of the two central properties, Vilquecunca, located five kilometers northwest of Azángaro in the plains of the Río Grande close to the road to Asillo, in December 1892 for 520 soles q.b. (433 soles m.n.) from the peasants José María and Juan Quispe.[120] The newly forming finca lay within the territory of the parcialidades Jallapise and Urinsaya and stretched—as did many estates—from the banks of the river to the hillsides of Cerro Mamanire, the northeastern edge of the gently sloping massif separating the Azángaro and Pucará rivers. Although Vilquecunca was referred to as a "finca" after 1899, effective estate operations took longer to establish. In 1900 Salas gave Vilquecunca and its seven or eight cabañas, the agglomerated estancias, in anticresis to Norberto Vásquez, another newcomer trader busy forming estates, for a credit of 240 soles m.n., obviously without livestock capital.[121] In late June 1907 he reclaimed Vilquecunca from Vásquez, only to conclude another anticresis contract with him two and one-half months later. This time, however, Salas gave Vásquez only one of the finca's constituent estancias, Cangallo Llinquipata Quilinquilini, for a credit of 200 soles m.n.[122] Salas apparently now needed the major part of the finca for himself, and we may assume that it had taken him that long to build up a livestock capital commensurate with the pasturelands of Vilquecunca. To operate the estate himself without a minimally sufficient livestock capital would have been both uneconomical and dangerous, as estates with no or too little stock invited usurpations by neighbors. Just one year before resuming direct control over most of Vilquecunca, Salas gave the second finca that he was in the process of constituting, Anccosa, about fifteen kilometers west of Azángaro in Asillo district, in anticresis, also without livestock capital.[123] He was perhaps pooling all of his livestock capital to use the larger finca's carrying capacity to the highest degree possible. The formation of effectively operating fincas, then, merely began with the agglomeration of a sufficient land base.

Such nominal new estates went through a transitional phase in which their operation differed little from their situation as independent peasant estancias. The former peasant owners, obligated to stay on as colonos of the new estate, now had to plant a few *masas* (a traditional land measure equal to 760 square meters) of potatoes or quinua for the patrón and render transport and domestic services. But lacking the requisite capital, the marginal estate owner may have been unable to make full use of the labor and pasture resources for quite some time. This process contrasts with the formation of haciendas by some of the wealthiest families in the province. In the cases of haciendas San José and Sollocota, the owners counted on a preexisting core of one or more older estates and had sufficient capital to stock the expanding pasturelands with additional sheep and cattle. The transition from loosely agglomerated peasant lands to well-integrated, fully stocked estate must have been briefer here.

Marginal large landholders such as César Salas had just sufficient means and influence to build an estate within a narrowly circumscribed area, perhaps only within one parcialidad. But most of the wealthiest hacendado families acquired land throughout the province, in some cases even in several provinces. When José Angelino Lizares was born in the mid-1860s, his family had already achieved affluence and power in Azángaro, since both his father, José María Lizares, and his grandparents, Francisco Lizares and Josefa Quiñones, had persistently increased the family's landholdings.[124] When José María Lizares Quiñones passed the administration of his estates to his sons José Angelino and Francisco in 1895, the family owned seven fincas in Muñani and Azángaro (Muñani-Chico, Arcopunco, Calla-tomasa, Ticani, Tintire, Quichusa, and Cayacayani) and several smaller estancias in Azángaro and Santiago de Pupuja, with a total livestock capital of 28,000 OMR.[125]

José Angelino continued the acquisition of landholdings in Santiago, Azángaro, and Muñani and expanded further into San Antón, Arapa, and Chupa. His landholdings now were scattered over some six thousand square kilometers of territory. He succeeded in forming new estates in widely dispersed parts of the province because he not only had sufficient monetary resources but could also call on numerous social ties extending beyond the provincial capital and the family bailiwick in Muñani. These ties derived in part from family connections and in part from broader client networks. His purchase of land in San Antón followed his marriage to Leonor González Terrazas, daughter of the judge of first instance, Federico González Figueroa, who had been putting together Finca Cangalli in San Antón since around 1900. Given as a dowry to Lizares Quiñones's wife, Cangalli became the core of Lizares Quiñones's new Hacienda Esmeralda.[126] In Chupa, Lizares Quiñones's formation of new estates against the determined resistance of community peasants proceeded with the support of one of the most influential local families, the Salas. Both Lizares Quiñones and Nicomedes Salas had received military titles during the Cacerist administrations between 1886 and 1895.[127]

Lizares Quiñones's provincewide influence owed much to his political career, which he began as mayor of Azángaro's provincial council during the early 1890s. He held the congressional representation of the province for many years between 1908 and 1929, followed by a short term as senator for Puno until the overthrow of the Leguía regime in 1930.[128] These positions allowed Lizares to ingratiate himself with some of the notables of the districts and to influence the distribution of administrative positions on the provincial and district levels to serve his interest. By developing this sociopolitical "infrastructure" throughout the province, he enhanced his capacity to induce local landholders to sell him land and to apply pressure in case they refused.

The majority of large landholders in Azángaro followed Lizares Quiñones's strategy of building up dispersed estates throughout the province, but a few affluent land purchasers whose biographies suggest economic and political resources similar to those of Lizares chose not to form dispersed estates. Some of the most prominent were Arias Echenique and Urquiaga (discussed above) and José Albino Ruiz, the owner of large Hacienda Checayani in Muñani district. They concentrated on developing single, very large estates, whereas most of Lizares Quiñones's fincas, like those of other hispanized landholders owning dispersed properties, such as the Paredes clan, González Figueroa, and the Rossellos, were merely medium-sized. Specific local circumstances may have influenced such divergent patterns: Lizares Quiñones's Hacienda Muñani-Chico, for instance, was totally surrounded by other estates, precluding further expansion. But they may also reflect the first appearance of somewhat divergent goals. For a minority of hacendados, the formation of efficient livestock haciendas took on growing importance, and they emphasized maximum size. Yet most hacendados expanded their landholdings primarily in order to enhance their power and influence in the province. Here a broad geographical spread of the estates could only be advantageous. In other words, Lizares Quiñones's acquisition and expansion of fincas in six different districts not only built on his already considerable sociopolitical power but served to increase and fortify it.

For the department of Huancavelica in the central sierra, Henri Favre has noted that the process of hacienda expansion between the end of the War of the Pacific and 1919 proceeded in three different ways: (1) expansion of existing estates through incorporation of surrounding landholdings, (2) constitution of totally new haciendas by purchases of a large number of small properties, and (3) reconstitution of colonial haciendas that had splintered since the late colonial period.[129] The first two forms of expansion also characterized the landholding development in Azángaro. Reconstitution of splintered colonial estates, however, occurred only rarely in the altiplano. Not many haciendas had splintered by the late nineteenth century. The few reconstitutions in Azángaro province took place in Putina and Muñani, districts whose livestock economy had been closely linked to mining enterprises during the colonial period.[130] The more pronounced discontinuity of land tenure patterns of some estates in Putina and Muñani, as in Huancavelica, was perhaps a consequence of the integration of mining enterprises with livestock haciendas. Once the mining operations had decayed, some associated haciendas also decayed, and the impoverished owners were unable to prevent their physical disintegration.

But the expansion of Azángaro's estate sector was a much more complex process than suggested by Favre's classification. Variations in the mode of land transactions, the mean value of acquired landholdings, the concentration or dispersion of properties, and the number of sellers per transaction gave each expansion project a different social and economic significance. This complexity contributed to the emergence of a landholding pattern by the second decade of this century that was far from a uniform landscape of large estates.

Inheritance and Sale: The Stability of Landholding Families

Fifty years ago Emilio Romero, the distinguished Peruvian geographer who was born and raised in Puno, wrote that "toward the end of the nineteenth century . . . property in the sierra became somewhat divided."[131] For Azángaro, Romero's assertion cannot be maintained in this general fashion. Although parcelization began to affect peasant estancias and properties of other small landholders, haciendas survived the crisis of inheritance surprisingly intact. Hacendado families, fully aware of the dangers that any splintering of the family estate entailed, pursued elaborate strategies for countering the centrifugal tendencies of inheritance. But more than any of these strategies, it was the expansionary environment in trade and livestock raising that forestalled the atomization of family estates before 1920.

Property was transferred from one generation to the next in three ways: (1) owners passed on property before their death; (2) wills specified how goods were to be distributed by the executor after the testator's death; (3) the goods of a person dying intestate were distributed strictly in accord with legal prescriptions governing inheritance. The first form of property transfer was known as *antícipo de legítimo*. Used when the owner could not properly take care of his estate, mostly because of old age, such transfers commonly took the form of a donation. But at times parents also sold landholdings to their children. This form of generational transfer offered the greatest degree of discretion to the owner, who could favor a preferred heir without coming into conflict with Peru's inheritance laws. Moreover, distributing the estate during the lifetime of the testator allowed continued exercise of parental authority to quell discord between heirs, who often had to promise "to conserve the good family relations."[132]

The generational transfer of property through wills imposed greater strictures on the testator. Peruvian inheritance law, inscribed in the civil code of 1852, was based on the two Spanish principles of equal inheritance and bilateralism. By law and practice the testator's direct descendants, his or her children and their offspring, enjoyed precedence as heirs. Property that husband and wife brought into matrimony (*bienes raices*) always remained the separate estate of each spouse. A married testator could dispose only of the goods that he or she brought into the marriage and 50 percent of the property that the couple had accumulated during matrimony (*gananciales*), with the other 50 percent automatically belonging to the spouse.

Given the rapid expansion of many family holdings, the weight of gananciales vis-à-vis bienes raices could be great, and the surviving spouse's share of the total estate might approach 50 percent. Furthermore, it frequently was the wife who brought in the bulk of bienes raices when marrying. Although Peruvian law treated wives as minors who needed the consent of their husbands for legal transactions, after her husband's death the widow often found herself as owner with full control of the major part of the family estate.[133] A widow thus might come to hold the controlling shares of large estate complexes, particularly when she was considerably younger than her husband (as in second marriages), when the couple had had no children, or when the husband had died young and the children were still minors. In many cases widows were declared executors of their husbands' estates and legal guardians of their children, controlling their property until they came of age. Juana Manuela Choquehuanca, for example, controlled the parental Hacienda Picotani in the cordillera above Muñani for some twenty years after the death of her husband, Mariano Paredes, in the mid-1870s.[134] Carmen Piérola, a native of Bolivia, managed to be married to three sons of Juan Paredes in a row between the late 1870s and 1904, surviving them all and in the process managing—and expanding—a large part of the clan's landed estates.[135]

The legal minority of wives and Azángaro's social norms assigning a domestic role to women in hacendado families kept them from managing estates during their married lives. After the husband's death, the widow had to face unaccustomed tasks made difficult by a society in which the exertion of authority was tied to the threat or application of force. Not surprisingly, widows frequently entrusted the management of the family estate to a friend or relative, left more decisions to the finca's administrator, or even rented it out. All of these options risked the estate's deterioration through neglect or willful overexploitation.[136]

Family estates in more than one case entered a critical phase when they passed into the control of a widow or a young, unmarried daughter of the deceased head of the family. In contrast to women from peasant and petty shopkeeper families, who were often used to economic decision making, women from the landholding elite had been socialized in such a way as not to be concerned with economic matters.[137] In several cases widows or young single heiresses could not hold on to family estates.[138] Contemporary society saw women as unfit to manage livestock estates. The "incapacity in which [female heads of households] find themselves to improve their lot" condemned their families to the fate of impoverishment, in the view of a priest in Saman.[139] But certainly there were women in Azángaro who had great success as landholders or traders.[140] Adoraida Gallegos, never having married, formed one of the province's greatest estate complexes between the 1880s and 1920. It is perhaps more than coincidence that she has become a legendary figure in the province, depicted as a fearless and haughty woman, riding around the frontiers of her estate with pistols on her hips, not hesitating to whip any neighbor who tried to appropriate her lands; she was, in short, a woman who acted "as a man."[141] Her very legend seems to confirm how exceptional such independent women were among the province's hacendado families.

Although Spanish and Peruvian law prescribed equal inheritance among all legitimate children, the testator had the possibility of improving the share of any child through a *mejora*, usually one-fifth or one-third of all property. Asunción Lavrín and Edith Couturier have suggested that in colonial Mexico mejoras served "to buttress the family's social position and prevent the deterioration of its economic status" or, in other words, to favor the heir who promised to hold the family estate together most efficiently.[142] In Azángaro the stated purpose of mejoras was to reward a child who had helped the testator during his or her old age with particular dedication or to secure the material situation of the heir facing the greatest economic uncertainties, perhaps a daughter who had married poorly or would probably stay single.[143] But mejoras appeared seldom in wills of Azángarino landholders.

Family strategic considerations may have played a larger role in the testator's disposition as to quality and type of property rather than its quantity. The heir whom the testator expected to be most capable of preserving and enhancing the family property and social position tended to receive the centerpiece of the landholdings, the best-established, largest, and most lucrative hacienda. In the settlement concluded by José María Lizares with his estranged wife Dominga Alarcón in 1905, a settlement that was to be his final will, he specified that, whatever the disposition of the remaining family fincas, his son José Angelino should receive for his "loyal services" Haciendas Muñani Chico and Nequeneque, the largest and best established of the family's estates. Notwithstanding an equitable distribution of the family estate in terms of quantity or monetary value among all heirs, the most trusted son was to receive the family's best haciendas.[144]

Following Spanish legal tradition, most testators attempted an equitable distribution of their property among their legitimate children, regardless of sex or birth order. The goal of providing each heir with equal material belongings took precedence over the goal of assuring the maintenance of the economic and social position of the family through accumulation of property in the hands of one heir. Although contradictory on the surface, these goals in fact were complementary. Testators knew full well that the single greatest danger to the maintenance of the family's economic and social position consisted in interminable legal squabbles. The need to sell land for defraying the costs of litigation damaged the fortunes not only of peasant families but of hacienda owners as well, as in the case of the Choquehuanca family (discussed below). Avoiding costly litigation constituted a precondition for preserving the social and economic position of the family; an equitable distribution of the family estate among all heirs could best assure this goal.[145]

If someone died intestate, the estate had to be divided according to legal norms between the heirs-at-law. The surviving spouse would receive his or her gananciales, one-fifth of the estate went to the recognized illegitimate children, and the rest would be divided in equal parts among the legitimate children. No mejoras or legacies could be granted, and normally none of the heirs-at-law could be disinherited. The division of the estate could then be carried out either through an out-of-court settlement within the family or by a legal procedure involving its judicial inventory, appraisal, and subsequent division. If the proceedings promised to be protracted, the estate was placed in judicial deposit. The court-appointed trustee was charged with insuring the integrity and continued revenue generation of the properties, which he often chose to lease out.[146]

On the surface these formal aspects of inheritance suggest that the generational transfer of estates led to dispersion of family landholding complexes, but to what degree this dispersal actually occurred depended on two factors, the number of heirs and the manner in which they chose to operate the estate. The number of children varied widely in hacendado families, from none to eighteen, including illegitimate children. In twenty-nine wills of Azángarino hispanized large landholders between 1854 and 1909, the mean number of children of the testator, from all marriages and extramarital relations, was 4.89. But on average only 2.17 children were still alive at the time of the father's or mother's last will. The figures were higher for the eight testators between 1854 and 1878 (an average of 8.125 children, with 3.75 surviving at the time of the parental will) than it was for the twenty-one cases between 1892 and 1909 (an average of 3.6 children, with 1.57 surviving at the time of the parental will).[147] The number of children surviving their parents on average was rather low. To be sure, in a few important hacendado families four, five, or even eight children had to share the parental estate. The large estate of Juan Paredes just sufficed to bequeath one finca to each of his six surviving legitimate children, leave Finca Lacconi to his two illegitimate sons, and set aside the small Finca San Juan de Dios for a beneficent institution.[148] But in many cases the family estate had to be distributed among only two heirs or passed in its entirety to a single surviving son or daughter.

Following the appeal of so many parents not to divide the family fincas, heirs frequently sought to operate the estates jointly.[149] In September 1893, for example, the four surviving children of Mariano Solorzano and Augustina Terroba, traders from Putina who had shifted their operation to the capital of the department, formally established a company to manage the undivided estate left by their parents. The capital of the company consisted of the family's real estate, including Haciendas Collpani and Loquicolla Chico in Putina and two large houses in Puno town, as well as livestock capital, household furnishings, and business credits. The object of the company was to "administer, improve, and increase the property that constitutes its capital" and to "dedicate itself to the customary businesses of the family, such as trade in wool, planting of potatoes, barley, and quinua, slaughter, trade in alcohol, and other transactions up to the value of 1,000 soles monthly."[150] The management of the company was to rotate between the four fraternal partners on a quarterly basis. The managing partner was to receive 55 percent of profits or losses on new business deals concluded under his management. Fifty soles monthly were to be distributed to each partner from company earnings for subsistence, and remaining profits would be reinvested. Company real estate could not be sold, and proceeds from the sale of other company property were to be reinvested into the purchase of further real estate.

The company did not last long. Ten months after its founding it was dissolved and the property divided among the five heirs, including the widow of the deceased brother Mariano Casto Solorzano. Each heir received a portion worth about 13,000 soles m.n. To effect an equitable division, three fincas were carved out of the two existing estates. The portion with the greater part of Hacienda Collpani fell to Adrian, and that containing most of Hacienda Loquicolla Chico's lands to Julio. The newly created Finca Pampa Grande, mostly on the lands of Loquicolla Chico, fell to Emilia Toro, the widow of Mariano Casto Solorzano, in representation of her daughter Natividad's rights. The two remaining heirs, Maria Manuela and Natalia, received the houses in Puno and several small chacras located in the outskirts of that town.[151]

In subsequent years only two of the five brothers and sisters continued the same type of economic operation the parents had exercised, ranching and trade. The other three heirs or their descendants shifted the source of their livelihood to Puno town. Adrian Solorzano, who had received the greater part of Hacienda Collpani, studied law in Lima and Arequipa and in July 1900 was accredited as lawyer in Puno.[152] He took out loans on Collpani, leased it to other family members, and in December 1905 consented to sell the estate for 10,500 soles m.n. without livestock to his brother Julio.[153] He effectively withdrew from landholding and trade and dedicated himself to work as lawyer, teacher, and journalist in Puno, becoming a prominent and trusted public figure in the capital of the department.[154]

Between 1896 or 1897 and 1904, Finca Pampa Grande, property of the deceased Mariano Casto Solorzano's minor daughter Natividad, was administered by Alberto Gadea, second husband of Natividad's mother Emilia Toro and director of Puno's Colégio Nacional San Carlos during the decade following Nicolás Piérola's civil war victory.[155] After Emilia Toro's death sometime before April 1904, Pampa Grande was leased jointly to Natalia Solorzano de Zaa and her brother Julio, who was still renting the finca during the 1920s. Natividad and her maternal family became urban rentiers.[156]

María Manuela Solorzano had married the Puno notary San Martín even before the establishment of the company in 1893. In the subsequent division of the paternal estate she received one of the large houses in Puno town. In the notarial registers she does not appear again as a landholder in Azángaro, and we may assume that she and her family lived off the income from her husband's business and any property he may have owned.

Natalia Solorzano had received the other urban property in the 1894 division, but she and her husband, Arturo Zaa, remained active traders in Azángaro province. By 1900 the couple was again acquiring landholdings by lease or anticresis in the same area where the family haciendas were located. In 1913 Zaa and his wife acquired Hacienda Loquicolla Grande, adjacent to the Solorzano family estate Loquicolla Chico, from the Puno diocese in exchange for urban property.[157] Natalia Solorzano and her husband thus were reestablishing their position as large landholders and traders.

Julio Solorzano, the fifth heir who had received most of Hacienda Loquicolla Chico in the property division, was soon able to expand his landholdings in Putina through leases and purchases from family members as well as other landholders.[158] After the dissolution of the family company, and probably taking up old family business connections, he established himself in trade selling wool to Arequipa export houses such as Stafford and Ricketts.[159] By 1902 he owned the most important dry-goods store in Putina,[160] and within a decade his position compared favorably with that of his parents in spite of the estate's division.

Thus, of the five heirs to the estate of Mariano Solorzano and Augustina Terroba, only two continued to own livestock haciendas and trade in a wide range of goods. Some ten years after the division of 1894 the rural landholdings were reconcentrated in the hands of one heir through Julio's purchase of Collpani and his long-term lease of Pampa Grande. Two heirs, Julio and Natalia, achieved an expansion of family holdings into adjacent estates and estancias. Heirs who relinquished control over their portion of the family landholdings preferred family members in their sales, as stipulated in many divisions of estates.[161] In the case of the Solorzano family, the three heirs who by choice or circumstances lost control over family estates did not suffer social descent. Through marriage or occupation they managed to transfer their social status to an urban base.

The majority of Azángaro's multi-estate complexes underwent a similar partition shortly after the death of the patriarch. These partitions rarely led to a long-term splintering of family estates prior to 1920. This was a period during which old haciendas expanded rapidly and new ones were formed. The paternal social status and client networks could usually be carried over to the next generation. This situation helped heirs in expanding their portion of the family estate through purchase or lease of adjoining landholdings, just as Julio Solorzano was doing. In a recurring pattern, some heirs withdrew from landholding altogether, while one or two heirs aggressively participated in the wave of expansions and new formations of estates. Children or grandchildren of the founders who had established or consolidated the family estate between the 1840s and early 1870s at times purchased as much or more land than their parents or grandparents had. Besides the Lizares family, we may cite the descendants of Juan Paredes, whose granddaughter Sabina, together with her husband Carlos A. Sarmiento, belonged to the five greatest land purchasers between the 1850s and 1920.[162]

Heirs tried to insure the territorial integrity of a single parental finca by any of three techniques: (1) operating it jointly (*pro indiviso*); (2) rotating the lease of the estate to each of the heirs while the other heirs drew rent corresponding to their share of the estate; or (3) leasing the whole estate to a third person and dividing the rent among all heirs. Joint operation of an estate tended to be adopted particularly by heirs of rather poor families who had always lived on the finca itself or in the district capital and had no other source of income. But these arrangements were fragile and did not resolve the principal problem of having a growing number of family members depend on the income from one estate. In most instances where such schemes were applied to medium-sized or large estates, they did not last longer than ten years. Heirs setting up a business, building a new house in town, or having some other urgent need for cash became interested in selling their shares. Again and again one heir succeeded in reuniting all shares of the estate, thus ending the danger of property splintering.[163]

A fascinating example concerns Hacienda Checayani in Muñani, where the estate was reunited only in the third generation. The hacienda had belonged to the Choquehuanca family during the late eighteenth century. By 1892 it had become divided among seven grandchildren of the last owner of the whole estate, Mariano Riquelme, who had acquired it sometime before 1844. By 1906, after fifteen years of intrafamily squabbles, a contest between two in-laws for control of the hacienda, a momentary decision to relinquish family control over it altogether, and more than twenty-five notarial contracts between family members, Natalia Riquelme and her husband, José Albino Ruiz, again were sole owners of Checayani, a condition last enjoyed more than fifty years earlier by her grandfather.[164] When Natalia Riquelme dictated her fifth will shortly before her death in childbed in 1908, she reflected on the tortuous property history of Checayani and admonished her heirs not to give up what had been reached:

> I declare . . . so that my children may know that the whole [title]
> documentation of Finca Checayani until its definite registration
> and the judicial possession has been a very difficult undertaking
> which cost many thousand soles and innumerable privations.
> All of this is owed to my husband, don José Albino Ruiz, to
> whom my children should be eternally grateful. Thus I recom-
> mend to them and their heirs never to sell Checayani to an
> outside person nor to divide it . . . in order to conserve the
> integrity of the finca and so that this estate which was acquired
> by my grandfather Mariano Riquelme and his wife Juliana
> Aragón may not disappear.[165]

In the 1980s the core part of Checayani, which was not affected by the agrarian reform during the early 1970s, was still owned and operated by Natalia's grandson, Martín Humfredo Macedo Ruiz, a fifth-generation owner from the same family. Indeed, none of Azángaro's large estates and relatively few mid-sized estates became divided through inheritance prior to 1920.[166]

The outstanding exception to this stability of family estate complexes concerned the Choquehuanca family. Legal quarrels occupied the numerous descendants of Cacique Diego Choquehuanca for a whole century following his death in 1796. Of the eleven estates that the family owned in Azángaro province at the time of the Túpac Amaru Rebellion, only five remained family property by the 1840s: Haciendas Catacora, Ccalla, and Puscallani in Azángaro district and Haciendas Picotani and Nequeneque in Muñani. By 1910 the family had definitely lost three of these (Catacora, Puscallani, and Picotani) and held on only to shares of the other two estates.[167] Each of four lines of Choquehuanca descendants with some claim to family property fought legal battles about all of these five estates against all other members of the family. Several of the cases were decided by the Supreme Court in Lima only after decades of litigation. Every generation brought new dissensions between heirs.[168] The endless and costly lawsuits must be viewed as the major cause of the ultimate loss of most Choquehuanca landholdings and the ensuing impoverishment of most family members. Successive generations of Choquehuancas took out large loans to defray court costs, promised their lawyers shares of estates in lieu of honoraria, and proceeded to sell portions of or complete estates, all to defray fees for lawyers and the courts.[169] By the first decade of the present century the family had lost its preeminence among Azángaro's landholders.[170] The Choquehuancas, who in 1780 had been the greatest landowners in the province, some 120 years later had become marginalized.

Intrafamily litigation about land was common among Azángaro's hacendado families, but the Choquehuancas hold the record for duration, frequency, and ubiquity of such fights, with about every branch of the family at some point suing every other line. To a degree, the lack of family cohesion, which produced such devastating effects, must be viewed as the consequence of losing the office of cacique. As long as one family member held the cacicazgo of Azángaro's parcialidad Anansaya, the Choquehuanca estate had survived intact.[171] The loss of the cacicazgo appears to have brought with it the atrophy of the intrafamilial structure of authority: no heir could claim any primacy over his or her brothers and sisters or cousins. As the Choquehuancas lost the economic benefits associated with the office of cacicazgo, such as the cacique's salary and the opportunity to exploit the Indian peasants, a chaotic scramble for the family's resources commenced.[172] What at first glance appears as the peculiar decline of a single family of large landholders may have been symptomatic for the decline of a social group, the affluent elite of colonial cacique families descended mostly from the prehispanic Andean nobility.[173]

Estates faced acute dangers of atomization among poor hacendado families when none of the heirs succeeded in acquiring other property or establishing themselves in some trade or business of equal prestige and income-earning potential. During a period when commercial opportunities blossomed and it was fairly easy to constitute new estates, this problem did not arise often. Not surprisingly, the few cases of long-term atomization of Azángaro estates had originated during the economically difficult period before the 1850s.

Fincas underwent a process of splintering in two different ways. The parcels of all heirs could be divided, resulting in independent estancias of diminishing size. This had been the fate of Finca Nuestra Señora de las Nieves de Chocallaca in Putina, last owned and operated as a whole by one Juan Ortíz in the late eighteenth century. One hundred years later, grand-children, great-grandchildren, and great-great-grandchildren of Ortíz all owned independent estancias or shares of such, connected by nothing but family ties among the owners and their memory of an "ancient and extinguished finca."[174]

In the other mode of estate splintering, heirs never formally divided the estate and continued to own and operate it pro indiviso. Despite the fragility of this construction, under certain conditions a finca remained common property of all heirs even over several generations. Although the integrity of the estate was preserved, in the long run its internal structure changed profoundly. In effect, the growing number of co-owners lost the characteristics of hacendados and gradually approached the status of members of a peasant community. This process occurred in Finca Carasupo Chico in Muñani. The estate had belonged to one Diego Vargas probably before the end of the colonial period. Around 1900 some twenty-five heirs—at least great-grandchildren of the common ancestor—lived on the estate with their families. Although all heirs continued to own the property jointly, each family individually worked a small segment, a cabaña. In negotiations with outsiders—for example, with neighboring landholders about border disputes—they acted as a group representing the whole estate. By 1900 the status of Carasupo Chico was becoming confused. Sometimes still referred to as a finca, in other documents it began to be called a parcialidad or comunidad. In an 1897 property tax register the owners of Carasupo Chico appeared as follows: "José S. Endara, Mariano Arizales, Felipe Serna, and the other *comunarios*." In July 1907 all the co-owners leased Carasupo Chico to a neighboring hacendado, Federico Gonzales Figueroa. Because they lived on the estate, we may assume that they became the tenant's shepherds. Most of the generation of owners in possession of Carasupo Chico around 1900 no longer spoke Spanish. Although some worked as rural weavers or cobblers, others were referred to as *agricultores*, an occupational label nearly always applied to peasants in

TABLE 6.6. Absolute and Mean Numbers of Sales of Thirty-Two Estates in Azángaro, 1850s–1920

	Intrafamily Sales		Extrafamily Sales		All Sales	
	N	Mean N per hda.	N	Mean N per hda.	N	Mean N per hda.
Large hdas. (N = 10)	7	0.7	3	0.3	10	1.0
All other hdas. (N = 22)	3	0.13	18	0.81	21	0.95
All hdas. (N = 32)	10	0.31	21	0.65	31	0.96

Note: These figures include exchanges of property.

Sources: REPA and REPP, 1852–1920.

the notarial contracts.[175] At the end of a process that spanned at least three generations, the heirs of hacendado Diego Vargas were becoming peasants.

The majority of families managed to hold on to their haciendas over two or three generations. Probably two factors contributed more to this stability than anything else: the replacement rate remained, on the average, relatively low during this period, as child mortality was still quite high, and the expansionary tendencies of southern Peru's wool export economy between the late 1850s and 1920 created income-earning alternatives in the regional economy for "excess heirs." Such heirs could form new estates, establish themselves in trade, or seek administrative positions. Expansion thus helped to keep down the burden of supporting growing numbers of descendants who encumbered family estates. Although the passage of landed property from one generation to the next often entailed a crisis, family estates were generally kept together, later to expand through reuniting most portions in the hands of one or two heirs and the acquisition of further landholdings.

The stability of estate ownership is confirmed by a sample of thirty-two fincas and haciendas with substantially complete information on title transfers between the 1850s and 1920 (tables 6.6, 6.7). On average there was nearly one sales transaction per estate during the seventy-year period from 1851 to 1920, with more than one-third (37.5 percent) not entering the market at all. In order to measure the continuity of estate possession by Azángaro's hacendado families, we need to exclude sales transactions within families. Half of the thirty-two estates underwent no extrafamily sales transaction between 1851 and 1920. Thirteen estates were sold once

TABLE 6.7. Frequency of Sales of Thirty-Two Estates in Azángaro, 1850s–1920

| | Estates with (N of Sales): | | | | | | | | | | |
| | Intrafamily Sales | | | Extrafamily Sales | | | | All Sales | | | |
	0	1	2	0	1	2	3	0	1	2	3
Large hdas. (N = 10)	5	3	2	7	3	—	—	5	1	3	1
All other hdas. (N = 22)	19	3	—	9	10	1	2	7	11	2	2
All Hdas. (N = 32)	24	6	2	16	13	1	2	12	12	5	3

Note: These figures include exchanges of property.

Sources: REPA and REPP, 1852–1920.

outside the families of the owner, but only three passed to different families two or three times.

These figures indicate a remarkable degree of stability of landholding in Azángaro's estate sector. For a comparable seventy-year period, from 1690 to 1760, seven of eleven haciendas in the area of Huancavelica were sold more than three times, and only one remained property of the same family throughout.[176] But the overall stability of landholding in Azángaro's estate sector masks rather significant differences between large haciendas and small and medium-sized estates: although seven of the ten large estates in this sample never were sold outside the family between the 1850s and 1920, the same held true for only nine of the twenty-two other estates, that is, just over 40 percent as compared with 70 percent for large haciendas. At the same time, only a small fraction of the small and medium-sized fincas were ever transferred by sale within the same family, whereas such sales occurred with half of the large haciendas. Large estates were sold much less often than were small and medium-sized fincas and were more likely to be purchased by another family member, perhaps an heir attempting to reunite all the shares. Small and medium-sized fincas showed a higher propensity to be sold and were less likely to be purchased by other family members. Put differently, heirs to shares of small or medium-sized fincas found it more difficult to reunite the parental property than did families owning large haciendas. This confirms that the generational transfer of landholdings presented a more critical situation for poor hacendados than it did for Azángaro's landholding elite.

The Lands of the Church

In spite of repeated attempts by liberals and military caudillos to expropriate church estates in Azángaro, they survived nearly intact until the early twentieth century.[177] None of the estates was operated directly by church organizations. Except for two or three estates—Purina and Posoconi in Asillo and Potoni in the district of the same name—church fincas were relatively small, with a mean size slightly below the average for all estates in the province. With the establishment of new haciendas, the church's share of estates declined from close to a third in the early 1830s to between 10 and 15 percent by the second decade of this century.

Some church estates were rented by newcomers as an affordable first step toward becoming hacendados, but most were rented or held in emphyteusis by established families of large landholders from the province. Often a hacendado leased a church estate immediately adjacent to a finca of his or her own and integrated both into one livestock operation. In the case of Hacienda Posoconi in Asillo, around 1840 Coronel Rufino Macedo sold the emphyteutic rights, acquired in 1829 for 150 years, to José Mariano Escobedo, the Azangarino merchant and politician residing in Arequipa. Posoconi, with 1,568 hectares, had a livestock capital of 4,080 head of sheep and brought rental fees of 400 pesos annually for the church of Asillo.[178] Because the estate had no adequate water supply, it made eminent sense to integrate it with some neighboring landholdings. Since 1805, through a *censo*, Escobedo's family had been in possession of the adjacent Finca Payamarca, property of the Indian community of Asillo, and, since the early 1830s, of the Sociedad de Beneficencia Pública in Puno.[179] Between the mid-1830s and 1857 Escobedo bought another three substantial landholdings, all bordering on Payamarca and Posoconi. Although the church continued to hold the property title to Posoconi and its livestock capital, the whole complex by the late 1850s was operated as one single estate with the considerable livestock capital of 16,600 sheep. Escobedo bequeathed all these landholdings to his illegitimate daughter Teresa O'Phelan,[180] whose husband, Arequipeño Manuel Velando, purchased further adjacent peasants estancias and one finca during the 1870s. Another adjoining finca, Rosaspata, was added to the complex during the early 1910s.[181]

By the 1910s Posoconi had become the center of a sprawling private estate complex of some 4,673 hectares, which surrounded it on all sides.

In 1915 the Velando O'Phelans finally consolidated the property title to the hacienda when the church sold Posoconi in fee simple to the family for 4,800 soles m.n., roughly one-fourth of its appraised value.[182] Unable to repay massive debts contracted during the boom years of World War I, the Velando O'Phelans in 1923 had to sell Posoconi, with more than 36,338 head of sheep, for 13,500 libras peruanas (135,000 soles m.n.) to the Arequipeño merchant house Enrique W. Gibson. In 1926 the estate became part of the newly founded Sociedad Ganadera del Sur.[183]

Throughout the first century after independence, liberal critics continued to blame the church's mortmain property for its retrogressive influence on Peruvian agriculture, much as Choquehuanca had done in 1830. Failing to see the effect of changed commodity markets, the French agriculturalist J. B. Martinet erroneously blamed mortmain holdings for increased land prices and rental rates during the 1860s.[184] As late as 1930 Julio Delgado, a Cuzqueño social scientist, leveled the same charge against the church properties as Choquehuanca had done one hundred years earlier, claiming that in short-term leases of church fincas their productivity declined since "the tenant does not concern himself with improvements, but only with drawing the greatest possible gain by extracting the maximum from the land."[185]

For the approximately twenty church haciendas in Azángaro that were actually operated under short-term leases, Delgado's charge is correct. But the overall importance of these estates was limited, as they were mostly small, comprising a few hundred hectares and with a livestock capacity rarely exceeding 1,000 sheep. Tenants often overexploited these fincas during their five- to nine-year leases. Again and again the estates had less livestock at the end of the lease than at the beginning.[186] For the parishes in Azángaro and the Puno diocese that shared the income from the estates, the recurring losses of capital translated into a diminution of their revenue. Because of undercapitalization and the insecurity of their borders, these church estates regularly were rented out at lower rates than were privately owned haciendas, and the church saw itself forced to cede part of the annual rental fee to the tenant for restocking. Hacienda Ocra in Muñani lost three-fourths of its livestock capital between 1870 and 1890 during its lease to Luis Paredes; the church had to accept a corresponding decline in its effective lease fee when it handed the estate over to a new tenant, José Angelino Lizares Quiñones, in 1890.[187] But low rental rates were not limited to the church estates leased for short terms. As annual fees for emphyteutic haciendas were fixed for the 150 years' duration of the contract, after about 1860 they lay considerably below rising lease fees paid for private estates.

The church undertook only feeble efforts to recover losses from over-exploitation of its estates. Rather than itself taking legal steps against the responsible tenant, it merely obligated the following tenant to pursue the recovery of embezzled livestock. Judging from the chronic undercapitalization of many small church fincas, these endeavors generally met with little success. It proved difficult for the church to press charges against former tenants, who blamed the shepherds for the decline of the estate's livestock capital, left Azángaro after terminating the lease, or pleaded poverty and incapacity to pay the debt.[188] The only real alternative consisted in leasing all estates by long-term emphyteusis contracts. But few tenants could be found willing to take over small, undercapitalized, and unstable fincas for more than a few years.

But why could the church not avoid such despoliations of its estates to begin with? It was improbable that a priest would mobilize the colonos of one of the parish estates in order to stop invasions by neighboring hacendados by force, an action routinely taken by private landowners. More important, the parish priests were firmly tied to the local society of their parishes through commercial contracts, friendship, and family relations. Because the tenants commonly belonged to the same small group of district notables as did the priest, the latter usually pursued the repayment of lost or embezzled church livestock capital rather half-heartedly and recommended to the diocese to lease estates at low rental rates.[189] It thus appears that the church could neither avoid despoliations of its small fincas nor hope to recover most of its losses from short-term leases.

The decapitalization of the small church fincas allowed the tenants, often owners of haciendas themselves, to improve their income, increase their own livestock capital, and lease pastures at low rates in order to supplement fodder for their animals. Contrary to the church's critics, church estates in themselves cannot be seen as a major factor impeding economic progress in the Peruvian sierra. They were part and parcel of an agrarian system that for a number of reasons failed to stimulate the development of the rural economy. In brief, until the early twentieth century the landholding regime of the church contributed to the economic stability of the altiplano's seignorial livestock regime. It subsidized the interests of those new and old hacendado families who continued to rely on capital-extensive relations of production for sustaining their privileged socioeconomic status.

On November 7, 1911, law number 1447 went into effect, obligating the owners of all real estate held in emphyteusis to sell their title (*dominio directo*) to the persons enjoying the usufruct right of such property, the *enfiteuta*. Coming half a century after the peak of anticlerical land legislation throughout Latin America, the law was a major step in reducing mortmain landholdings; it seems not to have led to heated public debates about the role of the church in civil society. According to a complicated formula, it prescribed the share of the property's assessed value that the enfiteuta had to pay, a share that declined the longer the emphyteusis contract had been running. Puno's Bishop Valentín Ampuero immediately began to implement the law, ordering assessments of all church estates in question. In Azángaro the first emphyteutic finca, Hacienda Cancata in Santiago de Pupuja, was consolidated on September 11, 1912. By the end of 1918 eleven emphyteutic church fincas in Azángaro, among them such valuable large estates as Purina and Posoconi, had been alienated through consolidation (table 6.8). But Bishop Ampuero, for reasons not entirely clear, went one step further and, without legal necessity, initiated the outright sale of church fincas operated under short-term leases, a decision that earned him severe criticism within the church.[190] Between April 1912 and March 1914 the diocese sold six fincas in Azángaro operated under short-term leases. They were mostly acquired by the tenants actually in possession. Altogether the church alienated seventeen estates in Azángaro in the seven years following the consolidation law, half of all its land-holdings in the province. By value and acreage the reduction of church property was considerably steeper, since most of the large haciendas were consolidated or sold. Thereafter, the role of the church as landholder, with 5 to 7 percent of all estates, became insignificant in Azángaro.

The holders of emphyteutic haciendas profited greatly from consolidation. After having enjoyed bargain lease fees for decades, they now had to pay only a fraction of the estate's assessed value. In May 1913 Elena Landaeta, widow of José Luis Quiñones, paid 3,786.42 soles m.n. for the consolidation of Hacienda Parpuma, assessed at 9,351 soles m.n. Two months later she sold the finca and a few small adjacent estancias to Pio León Cabrera, a notorious land grabber from Sandia province, for 18,000 soles m.n.[191] With the law of consolidation the landholding elite in the altiplano—and presumably elsewhere in Peru—benefited one last time from the church as a major player in the region's agrarian ancien régime.

The church's importance for the agrarian structure of Spanish America is thought to have rested on three factors: (1) its role as landholder; (2) the "huge amount of encumbrances"—such as chaplaincies and pious works—that weighed on privately owned estates; and (3) its role as creditor to private estate owners. In Arnold Bauer's view, church influence sig-nificantly declined throughout Spanish America during the century from 1750 to 1850 because of anticlerical action by the Bourbon reformers, by political and military leaders in the era of the Wars of Independence, and again by mid-nineteenth century liberal politicians.[192] In the Peruvian

TABLE 6.8. Church Estates in Azángaro Alienated through Consolidation or Sale, 1912–20

Date of Alienation	Estate	Location	Size[a]	Enfiteuta or Purchaser	Year of original contract	Appraised Value[b]	Price Paid[b]	Type of Transaction
4-11-1912	Occra	Muñani	"10 km. around"	M. E. Paredes	—	9,000	9,000	Sale
9-11-1912	Cancata	Santiago	601	J. Bustinza vda. de Dianderas	n.a.	n.a.	5,742	Consolidation
11-29-1912	Purina y Viscachani	Asillo	2,321	M. J. Cabrera vda. de Rios	1851	25,127	7,131	Consolidation
12-4-1912	Ninahuisa	Putina	358	J. A. Ruiz	—	1,487	1,487	Sale
4-22-1913	Huntuma	Azángaro	111	D. La Rosa and F. Luna	1829	2,054	1,149	Consolidation
4-23-1913	Cuturi y Soñata	Arapa	1,172	D. La Rosa and F. Luna	1830s	8,347	1,149	Consolidation
5-2-1913	Cantería	Asillo	170	M. F. Macedo	1875	1,994	697	Consolidation
5-23-1913	Parpuma	Azángaro	1,763	E. Landaeta vda. de Quiñones	1829	9,351	3,786	Consolidation
6-4-1913	Llancacahua	Putina	999	J. A. Ruiz	—	5,019	5,019	Sale
6-6-1913	Loquicolla	Putina	1,203	N. Solorzano and A. Zaa	—	7,715	7,715	Sale
8-16-1913	Conchilla	Caminaca	290	C. Santisteban	—	3,000	3,000	Sale
8-20-1913	Potoni	Potoni	2,680	A. Toro Nafria	1849	18,000	8,066	Consolidation
3-27-1914	Ahijadero	Caminaca	n.a	J. M. Fernández Maldonado	—	3,000	3,000	Sale
1-21-1915	Qquera	Santiago	1,293	J. Avila	1879	16,863	5,348	Consolidation
6-26-1915	Posoconi	Asillo	1,568	Velando O'Phelan	1827	20,400	4,800	Consolidation
4-24-1918	Quequerana	Azángaro	895	M. A. Manrique, J. L. Astorga, J. B. Paredes	1826	16,495	3,773	Consolidation
9-17-1918	Tahuacachi	Azángaro	n.a.	M. Manrique	1829	12,000	2,031	Consolidation

[a]In hectares. [b]In soles m.n.

Sources: REPP, 1912–1920.

altiplano, however, church influence on the agrarian structure declined much more slowly during the first century after independence, perhaps because the region was distant from the centers of civil and ecclesiastic power. Church encumbrances on land had never been extensive there, and by the nineteenth century there is not much evidence for the church as a source of credit either. Legislation to abolish chaplaincies and censos before the War of the Pacific did nothing more than prevent new donations or encumbrances. As late as 1877 Martinet found that "the chaplaincies in Peru still exist nearly in their entirety."[193] In Azángaro the few chaplaincies finally ceased to exist by the early twentieth century; church credit to private landholders remained as rare then as it had been in 1850 or even 1820.[194] But the role of the church as a landholder remained strong for nearly a century after independence, at last virtually disappearing with the execution of the law of consolidation.

Communal group preparing fallow land for sowing, Melgar province.
Photograph by Pedro Condori, Talleres de Fotografía Social (TAFOS),
1989.

Members of a cooperative (ex-hacienda) near Ayaviri sack and weigh
alpaca wool for dispatch to wholesalers. Photograph by TAFOS, 1989.

Central building complex of Hacienda Muñani Chico of the Lizares Quiñones family. Note the watch tower at the right. Photograph by the author, 1976.

The end of an era: the cooperative (ex-hacienda) Quisuni in Orurillo, Melgar province, after it was burnt and destroyed by a Sendero Luminoso detachment. Photograph by Damaso Quispe, TAFOS, August 16, 1989.

Adoraida Gallegos, owner of Hacienda Lourdes, circa 1910. Photograph from the private archive of Mauro Paredes, Azángaro.

José Angelino Lizares Quiñones, one of the most powerful hacendados and politicians in Azángaro during the early twentieth century. Photograph from an electoral pamphlet, 1924.

Electoral rally in Azángaro town for José Angelino Lizares Quiñones, 1924. Photograph from the private archive of Mauro Paredes, Azángaro.

Founding meeting of Azángaro's Fraternal Society of Workers in 1929. Some hacendados were members. Seated, second from the right, is the subprefect of the province. Photograph from the private archive of Mauro Paredes, Azángaro.

7 Communities, the State, and Peasant Solidarity

The history of the Andean peasant community during the century after independence remains largely unwritten.[1] Ignored by the laws, the courts, and the administration of the Peruvian republic, the community took on a bewildering variety of forms and functions. Property regimes, the extent and nature of economic cooperation and of autonomous local cultural and ritual traditions, relationships with hierarchies of authority and power—all developed differently in various regions and shifted over time. By 1920 an observer would have been hard pressed to say what the communities of the north coast, the Mantaro valley, and the altiplano had in common.

In this chapter I focus on the property and usufruct of land, social inequality, and the rise of new communities in Azángaro between the mid-nineteenth century and 1920. During this era the autonomy of the communities faced the greatest challenge since the Toledan reforms of the late sixteenth century. As their resource base came under growing external and internal pressure, the communities readjusted the meaning and scope of communal solidarity. The rise of numerous new communities, based on family descent groups, testifies to the continued vitality of this crucial Andean institution, even in times of adversity.

Land, People, and Animals in the Communities

A first impression of the extraordinary complexity and shifting meaning of the altiplano peasant community can be gained from a discussion of the three terms employed to denote aspects of it during the nineteenth and early twentieth centuries: *parcialidad, ayllu,* and *comunidad.* By far the most frequent term in contemporary usage was *parcialidad.* Usually the term referred simply to all landholdings within a geographic area demarcated more or less clearly along customary lines. Even estates owned by hispanized large landholders were described as being situated within a parcialidad.[2] Parcialidad was also the preferred term for the institutional aspects of the community, the hierarchies of religious and civil offices that gave form to the organization of communal solidarity and articulated the relations with governors, justices of the peace, and parish priests in the districts.

The term ayllu, although less popular with hispanized officialdom, was used with essentially the same meanings as parcialidad. Usages such as "parcialidad Urinsaya, ayllu Cullco" (1869) might be thought to express the ancient moiety structure. However, the prehispanic notion of moieties seems to have largely disappeared; other references to the same communities reversed the two terms. Such encapsulation probably reflected the recent formation of subdivisions within peasant communities.[3]

As parcialidad and ayllu were increasingly used to denote the territorial and institutional aspects of communities, usage of the third term, comunidad, became restricted. Until the end of the colonial period the term usually signified three aspects viewed as widely overlapping: a crown-sanctioned corporate institution, its territorial base, and usufruct of the land controlled in common. This third semantic field set usage of the term comunidad apart from parcialidad and ayllu in the century after independence, leading to its diminished employment in notarial transactions and administrative documentation. Whenever the term was used in connection with land, it referred to common property or usufruct.[4] Whenever parcialidad or ayllu was employed in connection with land after 1850, it was a statement about the geographic location of the land, not its title or use.

After the agrarian reform legislation of the 1820s the community as an institution and whatever common property regimes survived within it had become divorced from each other. As communal property was alien to republican legislation, this notion was reflected in the semantics and the usage of the terms referring to the community. Comunidad, the term signifying common property or usufruct over land, ceased to be used when referring to the community as an institution.

When Peruvian intellectuals, especially in southern Peru but after the 1910s also in Lima, began to espouse the Indian heritage of the country, they were particularly fascinated by the indigenous peasant communities. Here many indigenistas hoped to find the social organization that, without disrupting Andean society, could best move Peru's serrano countryside toward "socialistic cooperativism," as Hildebrando Castro Pozo wrote in 1924. For the indigenistas the most important feature of the communities consisted in the alleged continued predominance of communal property of land.[5] The growing political strength of the indigenista campaign was first codified in the constitution of 1920, elaborated as a consequence of Augusto Leguía's seizure of power. Article 58 brought the first official recognition of what was now called the *comunidad de indígenas* since independence. Underscoring the close link between comunidad and property, article 41 proclaimed that "the property belonging to the State, to public institutions and to the comunidades de indígenas is unalienable and can only be transferred by public title in the cases and in the form prescribed by law."[6]

In 1925 the government began to register parcialidades and ayllus that had been granted official recognition. This was the starting point for the emergence of a legally uniform category of communities in which geographical boundaries, internal institutions, and the communal property of the land again coincided as they had during the colonial period.[7] All of the lands within the boundaries of the community constituted communal property, and none could be alienated to outsiders, a legal concept strengthened by articles 208 and 209 of the constitution of 1933 and by the Peruvian Indigenous Community Statute of 1936.[8] But in contrast to the colonial era, only a minority of communities sought and achieved this official recognition. As late as 1958 only 24.6 percent of the 5,986 known communities in Peru had been registered. In the vast majority of communities without recognition the transfer of land remained unrestricted. By 1958 a considerably lower proportion of known communities—only thirty of 1,396, or 2.1 percent—had chosen and achieved recognition in Puno than had done so in any other department of Peru.[9] Their reluctance to seek official recognition suggests how far property regimes and institutional aspects of communities had drifted apart in the minds of the altiplano peasantry.

All this points to a tenuous survival of communal landholding in the altiplano up to the present century. Generally four types of property continued to be subject to some degree of common control by larger groups of community peasants: (1) agricultural land with a fixed crop rotation, the *manda, lihua, suyo,* or *aynoca;* (2) lands set aside for the payment of fees to civil and religious authorities; (3) special appurtenances of communities, such as access to lakes, watering holes, springs, and mineral deposits, as well as customary rights of groups of peasant families (e.g., rights of passage through private plots); (4) communal pastures. Not every community comprised all four types of common property, and their extent varied from district to district. The frequency, extent, and location of the fourth type of common property, communal pastures, is the critical issue for the pattern of land tenure of agrarian communities dedicated primarily to livestock raising.

The lihua landholding pattern strengthened communal institutions through its fixed obligatory rotation system, much like open field systems in ancien régime Europe. Every family received a strip within the field dedicated to one crop. In the relatively fertile soil of the lakeshore belt around Lakes Titicaca and Arapa, a rotation of three or four different annual crops was practiced. Nearly always begun with potatoes, it continued in years two to four with barley, oats, quinua, ocas, or lima beans in varying orders, after which the plots were left fallow for one or two years.[10] In more arid parts of the altiplano, such as San José's parcialidad Llaulli, lihua plots might be planted only once every seven years.[11] After the harvest the lihua was opened for the livestock of all co-owners to feed on the stubble or remaining foliage.[12]

Lihuas or mandas in which many, but not necessarily all, families of a parcialidad held parcels existed in communities of most districts in Azángaro around 1900. In some communities—for example, the newly formed comunidad San José—annual rituals of distributing the strips of land within the lihua continued until the mid-twentieth century, even if each family always received the same strips.[13] Title belonged to individual families.[14] Lihua plots seem to have been small and unevenly distributed. In a community in Salinas, south of Azángaro, twenty-eight peasants in 1932 owned 101 agricultural parcels of one *masa* (760 square meters) each, amounting to a total of 7.676 hectares, or 0.274 hectares per person. One comunario held ten masas (0.76 hectares), whereas some only held one masa (0.076 hectares).[15] Besides their parcels in the lihua, most peasants also planted crops on their own estancia lands, usually in the immediate vicinity of their residence.

Some communities set aside special parcels of land called *yanasis*, "which have to be cultivated exclusively and free of charge for the governor."[16] One of the duties of the highest community officials was to supervise the timely plowing, sowing, weeding, and harvesting of these plots and to see to the care of the sheep that the community maintained on its own pastures for the authorities.[17] Yanasis plots were limited to Huancané province and the adjacent districts in Azángaro, especially Chupa and Saman.[18] But even where no yanasis plots were set aside, local authorities received agricultural and livestock products from communities. Year after year the communal authorities selected some of the best plots of the lands of individual family estancias on a rotating basis for this purpose. One contemporary author estimated that each community in

Azángaro annually dedicated between 80 and 120 masas (6.08 to 9.12 hectares) of private croplands for the governor, which took sixty peasants four to six days to fallow with their digging sticks (*tacllas*).[19]

Special resources were often held as common property. Springs, creeks, ponds, and shores of rivers and lakes could be used by many (although not necessarily all) of the peasant families of a community for irrigating garden plots, watering the animals, feeding them on semiaquatic plants, and fishing. Paths to such places, even if they traversed private land, were considered appurtenances of all adjoining lands. These resources, however, do not seem to have been considered common property of communities as institutions; rather, they went along with the ownership of specific plots or residence in their vicinity. When estancias or parcels of land were sold, leased, or transferred in any other way, rights to appurtenances were noted. Adjoining haciendas might share in them.[20]

When such specific resources held a preponderant weight for the peasants' economy, common rights tended to disappear. The outstanding example in Azángaro province was the exploitation of the Lake of Salinas, some twelve kilometers southeast of Azángaro town. Until the 1870s community peasants owned practically the whole lakeshore. It was divided into small, privately owned stretches of shoreline, between twenty and one hundred meters wide, called *entradas de sal*. Only title to such an entrada gave a family the right to scrape salt from the dried lakebed between June and December, when the water had receded. The amount of salt that a family could gather apparently depended on the width of the entrada.[21] In 1896 the Piérola administration established the state salt monopoly and instituted a tax on salt "for the rescue of Tacna and Arica," occupied by Chile since the War of the Pacific. At Lake Salinas, as at other sierra salines exploited by peasants, these measures led to a price increase of some 400 to 800 percent—from between five and ten centavos to between fifty-one and fifty-six centavos per quintal of salt—and to the peasants' loss of control over its commercialization. The ensuing cycle of militant peasant protests was repressed militarily.[22]

How frequent and extended were pasture commons in Azángaro's parcialidades between the 1850s and 1920? In 1921 Carlos Valdéz de la Torre evaluated land tenure patterns in altiplano communities: "In the department of Puno the evolution of indigenous agricultural property has reached a greater degree of specificity than in Cuzco; in Huancané, Chucuito, Azángaro, Lampa, and possibly in the other provinces every individual is proprietor of his plot and can sell it freely. There are no regularly redistributed plots and *property remains undivided only concerning pastures and hills.*"[23] This evaluation by Valdéz, a Cuzqueño with limited knowledge of local circumstances in Puno, is paradoxical: while stressing that by the 1920s privatization had advanced further in Puno's communities than in those of Cuzco, he told his readers that "only" pastures and hills remained common property. But over 90 percent of all lands in the altiplano were pastures!

References to "common parcels" or "community properties" appear often in notarial contracts, but in only a few instances are common pastures mentioned. One case concerns the plots Incacancha, Cuncapampa, Patapampa, and Coparciopata in parcialidad Yanico of Arapa district. Around 1870 Melchor Quispe, a fifty-year-old peasant from Yanico, claimed these plots as private property, whereas a large group of other peasants from the same parcialidad considered them as common lands. To terminate the costly legal battle, in March 1871 both sides agreed to an out-of-court settlement. These lands were to be "common usufruct [*disfrute comun*] of all persons referred to [Quispe and thirty-three other community peasants] so that they may benefit from its pastures as before without forming cabañas and other obstacles." If for any reasons cabañas needed to be built, construction was to be undertaken only with the approval of all families with rights to the land. Land could be rented out only to one of the contract parties and never to third persons. All agreed to sustain costs for litigation over this land against outsiders.[24]

These lands were undoubtedly an example of pasture commons, and the contract sought to block their internal division, privatization, and alienation. The requirement that permission be sought before constructing residences on the land foresaw the formation of new households from within the group of participating families; however, such permission was to be closely controlled by all interested parties. Each subscriber's rights in these plots hinged on his or her willingness to rally to their defense against potential outside claimants, particularly, if need be, by contributing to court costs. Failure to share in the costs of defending communal property was often considered as forfeiting one's title claims.[25]

The number of peasants who held rights in the pasture commons is crucial for interpreting this case. In 1876 parcialidad Yanico had a population of 764 persons, constituting at least some 150 nuclear families.[26] Even if we assume that each of the thirty-four male peasants holding rights to the pasture commons, subject of the 1871 agreement, represented a different nuclear family, fewer than one-fourth of all families in Yanico shared these rights. In other words, these were not pasture commons of parcialidad Yanico but of a certain group of peasants who, though they lived within that parcialidad, were defined by some other criterion.

A second example helps to identify such specific groups inside communities. In April 1863 twenty-three Indian peasants from *parcialidades* Choquechambi and Caroneque in Muñani district initiated litigation against the owners of Hacienda Muñani Chico, José Luis Quiñones and his half-brother José María Lizares Quiñones, for usurping various parcels of land belonging to the community. Among other items they instructed their judicial plenipotentiary to take legal steps against the following loss of land:

> Equally he should reject the violent dispossession which the
> current Justice of the Peace of Muñani district, Don Juan Antonio
> Iruri, has perpetrated through the border demarcation . . . of
> the plots Accopata, *property of the Ccoris, integral part of the
> commons where all of us Indians used to peacefully maintain our
> livestock*, and today we suffer very grave damages . . . ; the
> pretext [for the border demarcation was that] Pedro Quispe had
> sold the lands of Accopata although it was clear that *all the other
> coheirs were owners* and through the said demarcation *a number
> of families also suffered dispossession*.[27]

When Pedro Quispe married Francisca Ccori, his parents-in-law assigned them part of their family estancia, namely the lands called Accopata, "with perfectly marked borders . . . so that we might live independently." After most of their children had died, "and finding our wealth [*fortuna*] in a decadent state after more than forty years of marriage," in February 1863 the couple signed a contract of promise of sale concerning Accopata and two other shares of the Ccori's family estancias now held by the families of Francisca Ccori's brother and sister, in favor of José Luis Quiñones and José María Lizares Quiñones. Pedro Quispe claimed to have received authorization for initiating the sale of those shares from his wife's family. But soon the Ccoris raised opposition to the proposed sale and demanded a legal division of the three parts of the Ccori estancia. In this situation the border demarcation must have occurred, by which Justice of the Peace Iruri, a half brother of the owners of Muñani Chico, adjudicated Accopata, Quispe's share in the Ccori family estancia, to the Lizares Quiñones as a consequence of the sales agreement. Although originally all shares of the estancia had been included, because of the resistance of the Ccoris and other community peasants only Accopata effectively became part of Muñani Chico. But the peasants fought even this loss of land. By 1872 the lawsuits, as well as the hatred between the Ccoris and their in-law Pedro Quispe, had not terminated.[28]

What, then, were the pasture commons among which the community peasants counted Accopata? This plot, along with the other parts of the

Ccori estancia, was used by all members of an extended family as pasture for their various livestock herds. The head of the Ccori family had assigned one sector of the estancia to his daughter and her husband Pedro Quispe, probably for establishing a residence and clarifying inheritance rights. Yet this assignment had not ended the practice of herding the livestock of various family members indiscriminately on the different parts of the family estancia. Accopata was thus both individual property and pasture commons for an extended family of community peasants.

Nothing in the documentation suggests that by the second half of the nineteenth century Azángaro peasant communities as corporate entities still held title to pasture commons. In fact, among all categories of property for which some type of common or group holding occurred, only the second category, the yanasis lands, clearly constituted corporate communal property. Rights to lihua plots, although shared by all members of a community in specific cases, were not derived from membership in the community as a corporation but rather through traditional title of families to the usufruct of certain plots. The same holds true for rights to appurtenances and to pastureland.

The Indian community as a clearly defined corporation existed only in relation to the civil and ecclesiastic authorities of the broader society. As long as the colonial state dealt with the Indian peasantry through communities on many levels, their function as corporate holders of property were strong in regard not only to the lands worked by individual peasant families in usufruct but also to the extensive holdings of community chests and *cofradías* (Catholic lay brotherhoods). In the later nineteenth century only local authorities dealt with communities as corporations, whereas demands of higher-level civil and ecclesiastic authorities largely ceased or were directed immediately at individual families. The corporate function of the communities vis-à-vis the local authorities still found its expression in the survival of specific plots maintained for the governor, priest, and justice of the peace, although even these burdens had been allocated to individual peasant family plots in most communities. Below the level of the weakened corporate community, groups of peasant families continued to use land jointly, even if individual family members were convinced of holding full property rights and were strengthened in this conviction by outside landholders applying pressure to purchase the land.[29]

In an effort to overcome the formalistic juxtaposition of community and hacienda, Benjamin Orlove and Glynn Custred have described one type of southern Peruvian social organization, which resembles conditions in Azángaro between the 1850s and 1920. The "localized descent groups," found among pastoralists of the high slopes of the western cordillera in Arequipa's Castilla province, consist of three to ten house-holds, which are

> linked usually through agnatic ties; frequently the household
> heads are brothers and patrilateral cousins. The residences are
> located in named population nuclei separated from each other by
> distances of over a kilometer. These groups are sometimes three
> generations deep. . . . Each localized descent group owns some of
> the scarce permanent pasture land along with huts and corrals
> located on it; . . . individuals have grazing rights both on these
> permanent pastures and on the rainy season pastures by virtue of
> membership in a localized descent group. . . . Each household
> uses a portion of the land for its own maintenance, but owner-
> ship remains corporate with the senior household head acting as
> executor. In such cases only sons and unmarried daughters may
> lay claim to the land.[30]

With some modifications, this model can be applied to altiplano com-munities. The relation between property title and actual land use could vary. A descent group might use some or all of its pastures and agricultural plots jointly, either while holding joint title to the land (pro indiviso) or even after having undertaken a formal distribution of all shares among coheirs. Joint title to ancestral lands did not automatically ensure that usufruct was not by individual families. In the majority of cases where a legal division of the ancestral lands had been carried out, at least some land was used by individual families. In contrast to the pristine social organi-zation of pastoralists of the cordillera, peasant descent groups in the al-tiplano tended to be more open; built-in mechanisms for self-perpetuation and defense against alteration from outside forces were usually weaker. There is little evidence to suggest that in Azángaro valuable dry-season pastures and arid hilltops were held in common by descent groups more frequently than other types of pasture were.[31]

As in the case of the Ccori family lands, common usufruct of land within Azángaro peasant descent groups was endangered and subverted by outside and inside pressures. In a clientalistic rural society with an accelerating demand for land, individual peasants within descent groups could find themselves forced to sell their rights in the ancestral estancia to a powerful outsider. This situation led to numerous instances of litigation in which a group of peasants fought the sale of one share of the family estancia by one of their coheirs. On one level, they reflect contradictory coexisting concepts of rights to peasant lands: even if nobody doubted that a peasant had inherited title to a specific share of a family landholding, it was by no means clear for the coheirs that this entitled him or her to sell that share to outsiders. On another level, such legal conflicts demonstrated that the degree of economic well-being could vary strongly within descent groups. Some members became indebted to outsiders by mortgaging their share of the family estancia, whereas others within the group remained economically independent. There is little evidence to suggest that descent groups in Azángaro attempted to prevent the transfer of a share of the family land to outside peasants by marriage to a female heir.[32] Such transfers constituted another source of external pressure on the joint usufruct of land by peasant descent groups.

Many potential causes for tension *within* such groups existed. After the death of the head of an extended family who had controlled all family lands, relations between brothers, cousins, nephews, and uncles frequently showed as much competition as solidarity. The senior member of the following generation often lacked the authority of the deceased patriarch.[33] Litigation between altiplano peasants, frequent by the late nineteenth century, was fed not to a small degree by intrafamily conflicts. It was incompatible with the maintenance of joint usufruct of a landholding by a descent group.

Even where land was used jointly by all nuclear families of descent groups, they usually operated their own livestock herds. Inevitably this independence led to a differentiation of wealth. As one peasant increased his herds by marriage, purchased some livestock, and was able to keep down the mortality of his animals, his relative might have lost sheep during a harsh winter or might see himself forced to sell animals to defray the costs associated with a communal office. Differences in the size of herds did not threaten the descent group's joint use of the ancestral land as long as pasture was plentiful, but once the herds pressed hard on the family's pasture resources, tensions were bound to build. In such a situation the more affluent peasants within the group sought to augment usage rights to the land in any way they could. If one parcel of the land had been purchased, or if expenses for its defense had been incurred, the peasants who paid these outlays would claim increased rights to the family lands against those group members who had been too poor to contribute.[34]

But when did pastureland become scarce in Azángaro's peasant communities? Writing in the 1940s, the anthropologist Bernard Mishkin suggested for the southern Peruvian sierra in general that "a sharp increase in the number of livestock, with the resultant competition for pasturage, has removed any vestige of pasture commons."[35] The animal/land ratio in the communities was determined by three factors: the amount of pastureland available, the size of livestock populations, and—a secondary

TABLE 7.1. Development of Azángaro's Community Freeholder Population, 1876–1940

	1876	1940	*Percentage increase, 1876–1940*	*Percentage increase, 1876–1940, total population of each district*
Achaya	1,672	2,099	25.5	53.6
Arapa	3,371	6,710[a]	99.0	148.1
Asillo	4,089	8,045	96.7	142.0
Azángaro	4,323	8,780[b]	103.1	134.7
Caminaca	1,731	3,293	90.2	88.2
Chupa	2,875	6,053[c]	110.5	184.6
Muñani	230	224	−2.6	93.1
Potoni	947[d]	547	−42.2	36.5
Putina	1,507	2,625	74.2	95.5
Saman	4,362	8,448	93.7	94.2
San Antón	1,439	2,509	74.3	107.9
San José	1,816	1,928	6.2	76.4
Santiago	3,770	5,541	47.0	92.7
Total	32,132	56,802	76.8	114.4

[a]Excluding Villa de Betanzos, classified as a pueblo in this census.
[b]Including San Juan de Salinas, part of Azángaro until 1908.
[c]Excluding Huilacunca-Ayrampuni, classified as a pueblo in this census.
[d]Excluding mining and construction camps.
Sources: See table 1.1.

factor with a strong bearing on the two primary factors—the population of the communities.

The growth of the human population is the clearest factor. In most districts the overall population grew faster than did its smallholder population (table 7.1). This increase is accounted for by population growth in the "urban" centers, mining camps, and, most important, haciendas. These data nicely confirm findings on the growth of the province's hacienda sector. In districts with a minimal growth of estates, such as Saman and Caminaca, the population growth rates for the whole district and for their community freeholders show the smallest difference. In districts with rapid hacienda expansion, for example, San José and Chupa, the growth rate for the total population was considerably larger than that for peasant free-holders. These figures, of course, suggest a transfer of population from the communities to haciendas or urban centers.

Some studies have claimed a correlation between hacienda expansion and the spatial distribution of population in the altiplano. A commercial guide to southern Peru for 1920 suggested that "the absorption of the communities and smallholdings of the Indians by the hacendados has much influenced the gradual depopulation of certain areas."[36] However, in most of Azángaro's districts hacienda expansion did not cause depopulation (table 7.1). According to a more specific notion, hacienda expansion would have caused a shift of the altiplano's population toward areas with a high concentration of peasant parcialidades and few estates, principally the belt around Lake Titicaca and the large pampas north and east of Juliaca, including some parts of Lampa province and Azángaro's districts of Achaya, Caminaca, and Saman.[37] But in Azángaro province such a pattern is also not discernible before 1940. Some districts—for example, Chupa—in which the estate sector swallowed much of the peasant lands experienced above-average overall population growth, whereas other districts with rapid hacienda expansion—for example, Potoni—saw their population increase only slowly. Saman and Caminaca, with minimal hacienda expansion, experienced below-average population growth. It appears likely that ecological conditions had a major impact on differential population growth between districts. In particular, the suitability of land for supplementary crop production may have influenced sustainable population levels in the communities.[38] This factor explains above-average population growth in Chupa, Arapa, Asillo, and Azángaro, the district with the most complex land-use pattern.

Community population increased by possibly 50 to 60 percent between 1876 and 1940,[39] but there were great variations from district to district. Lacking a measure for the extent of peasant lands sold to hacendados and intermediate landholders, we can present only a crude index of the increase of population pressure in each district's community sector by considering the combined effect of population growth and loss of land to outsiders. In the districts of Arapa, Asillo, Azángaro, and Chupa population density in the communities grew most since there peasants lost much land to haciendas while their population increased at a high rate. In Putina, San Antón, Caminaca, Saman, San José, and Santiago, communities experienced moderate increases of population density. In San José's communities, for example, a high rate of land sales had a diminished effect on density because of low population growth. Density increased least in the communities of

Achaya, Muñani, and Potoni districts because population growth or the rate of land sales to outsiders were low to intermediate. In Muñani the rudimentary community sector, which had survived the earlier expansion of estates, saw little change in population density; there density had probably approached its ecological limits even by 1870 or 1880 because of the communities' scanty remaining land base.[40] This case remained exceptional; before 1920 most communities had not reached the limit of their capacity to sustain human populations under prevailing land-use patterns.

Population density in most districts' communities thus increased at widely varying rates during the census interval 1876–1940. But whatever the local differences, the amount of land available to many peasant families diminished, confirming the declining mean size of land parcels sold by indigenous peasants. In many cases, by 1900 ten, twenty, or more related peasants owned shares of a landholding that all recalled having been the property of one common ancestor a few generations back. Fundo Chafani Choquechambi, for example, located in Arapa's parcialidad Ilata, had been the exclusive property of Vicente Ayamamani during the first half of the nineteenth century. It was extensive enough to be sold in 1906 for the considerable sum of 2,000 soles m.n. The purchaser, Luis Felipe Luna, renamed the fundo Hacienda Luisa, even without the addition of further peasant lands. By the time of this transaction the landholding had been parceled into nine cabañas, shared by twenty-five descendants (not counting husbands and wives) of Vicente Ayamamani.[41] Still, even by 1910 or 1920 in some localities large older peasant estancias remained undivided; in addition, sizable landholdings had recently been agglomerated by newly affluent peasants.

What impact did the diminishing size of land available to many peasant households have on the animal/land ratio in the communities? In chapter 3 I estimated that during the early years after independence livestock density lay below the carrying capacity of pastures both in the estate and peasant sectors. Despite unreliable earlier sources, there is little doubt that Azángaro's livestock population underwent long-term growth, increasing by some 300 percent between the 1820s and the mid-twentieth century (table 7.2). Herds could be expected to recover naturally after the repeated decimations between 1780 and the mid-1850s; this recovery was favored by the interests of hacendados and peasants alike in increasing their herds, as demands for wool and live animals increased after the 1850s. In the long run, the most important cause for the growing numbers of sheep and cattle must be sought in the growth of Azángaro's human population. A burgeoning number of families whose subsistence was based primarily on livestock resources attempted to build up their herds to the limit allowed

TABLE 7.2. Azángaro's Livestock Population, 1825–1959

	1825/29[a]	1911[b]	1920[c]	1929[d]	1945[e]	1959[f]
Cattle	17,326	18,526	[29,200]	22,268	54,750	76,400
Sheep	316,568	546,580	[883,558]	1,182,580	1,668,276	1,322,200
Cameloids	7,125	12,600	[26,301]	8,865	59,780	54,400
Equines	11,410	3,200	n.a.	6,332	n.a.	17,000
Total OMR[g]	632,041	795,340	[1,241,310][h]	1,502,812	2,365,226[h]	2,392,200

Notes and Sources:

[a]Choquehuanca, Ensayo, 15–55.

[b]Min. de Fomento, Dir. de Fomento, La industria, 15.

[c]Mean of high and low estimates, from Jacobsen, "Land Tenure," 871–81, app. 6.

[d]Dir. de Agricultura y Ganadería, Estadística . . . del año 1929, 394–96.

[e]Belón y Barrionuevo, La industria, 15–16. The author gives the livestock population for the department of Puno; I calculated the Azángaro figures by applying the proportion of the province's livestock in 1959 to the 1945 figures.

[f]Min. de Hda. y Comercio, Plan regional, vol. 28, Informe PS/G/59, Manual de estadística regional, 239–41.

[g]Based on conversion rates in Jiménez, Breves apuntes, 63–64.

[h]Without equines.

by the available pasture.[42] But when did this increasing livestock population begin to exceed the carrying capacity of pastures in communities? Livestock density in Azángaro's peasant sector reached a level of between 2.76 and 5.04 units of sheep per hectare by 1920, a range appreciably higher than the mean carrying capacity of about two units of sheep per hectare for natural altiplano pastures.[43] To place those values in historical perspective, by 1960 livestock density in Azángaro's peasant communities had reached seventeen units of sheep per hectare. Pastures could maintain considerably more animals than their assumed carrying capacities, and herds did not suddenly stop growing once pastures reached their defined capacities. But it should not be thought that the customary calculations of pasture carrying capacity were fictitious: too many practical ranchers and livestock technicians concurred on the extremely low nutritive value of altiplano pastures.[44] When livestock densities exceeded the carrying capacity of pastures, animals tended to become rickety, mortality rates shot up, and production of wool and meat declined.[45]

Peasants possessed certain means for diminishing these effects of overgrazing. Through limited irrigation works they could increase the amount of pastures that grew year-round. By making careful use of the moist winter pastures (moyas or ahijaderos), they effectively increased the carrying capacity of their overall pastoral land resources.[46] Moreover, community peasants placed some of their animals with the herds of hacienda colonos grazing on estate pastures, in return for which they would pay the colono in goods or services. This practice shifted livestock pressure on pasture resources from the peasant to the estate sector.[47] Community peasants could also legally rent pastures from neighboring estates, although in Azángaro such rental appears to have been rare. According to Mishkin, "a wealthy herder [from the community] must ultimately seek pasturage in the haciendas," an example of what Juan Martínez Aliér has called the "external siege" on hacienda resources.[48]

My estimate for the animal/land ratio in Azángaro's peasant communities lends weight to the notion that by the early years of this century the use of common lands by localized descent groups was coming under increasing internal pressure through growing conflict over limited pasture resources, in addition to the external pressure exerted by neighboring landholders. As Julio Delgado noted in 1930, landholding in southern Peru's peasant sector was passing through "the transition from family property to individual [property]."[49]

Inheritance patterns among peasants reflect this weakening of the descent group, associated with the diminishing role of a paternal head of an extended family. In 1916 José Sebastian Urquiaga still saw the majority of Azángaro's Indian peasants passing a much smaller share of goods to daughters; the first-born son, viewed as "representative of the family," became universal heir.[50] Nevertheless, peasant wills in which a male heir received all of the family's land to the disadvantage of sisters are exceedingly rare.[51] Children at times were disinherited for "disloyalty" or "lack of respect" against the parents, but male heirs suffered such ostracism just as often as female heirs did.[52] In most wills sons and daughters received equal shares of property. Indian women routinely appear as owners of parental landholdings in all types of notarial contracts, from wills to bills of sale. By the early twentieth century, then, inheritance of land among Azángaro's Indian peasants, at least among those affluent few who left notarial wills, approximated the pattern of equal inheritance among the province's hispanized residents.

Commercial Penetration, the State, and the Shifting Locus of Communal Solidarity

The crisis of common property and joint usufruct of land by descent groups of course did not lead to the disappearance of solidarity within such groups or within the larger parcialidades. Mutual labor exchange, common defense against outside land invasion, shared rituals and celebrations, and the myriad of everyday activities shared or undertaken jointly—all these continued, contributing to the trust binding such groups together.

Far from being stable, static entities, peasant communities in the altiplano were undergoing a process of complex metamorphosis by the early twentieth century, particularly by branching off or splitting into several new ones.[53] The dynamic elements in such subdivisions were the descent groups. In the 1940 census the term *estancia* for the first time denotes rural population centers that had developed out of peasant landholdings divided between a growing number of second- and third-generation heirs.[54] Often the "locus of solidarity" was shifting from the old parcialidad to smaller groups even while the scope of that solidarity was becoming more limited through the individualization of land-use patterns. The old parcialidades were not affected uniformly by this process, however, and in 1940 many still held considerably more population than did most of the recently constituted ayllus, parcialidades, or estancias. Of Arapa's eight parcialidades from the 1876 census, six continued to thrive in 1940 with populations of between 182 and 588 persons; one had disappeared totally and another one—the important nineteenth-century parcialidad of Yanico—had shriveled to a population of three. The transfer of solidarity from the older parcialidades to the new units based on descent groups probably began at their geographic rims. There the landholdings of descent groups could span several communities, and intermarriage with members of neighboring communities was more likely.[55] Such marriages contributed to a pattern in which peasants from one parcialidad held land in another parcialidad, weakening solidarity in at least one.[56]

But between the 1880s and 1920 most of the old parcialidades continued to provide some institutional cohesion to the various descent groups, sectors (*barrios*), or estancias that had sprung up inside them. This cohesion was engendered through a curious dialectic of exploitation by outside authorities and defensive assertion of autonomy and solidarity within the community. Along with the growing entrenchment of hispanized local and provincial elites, the extraction of labor and resources from the communities through their hierarchy of offices, not new in itself, reached its greatest scope and elaboration in this era. Yet such extraction also became more volatile and unstable; after 1920 this form of tributary exploitation would enter a phase of decomposition.

The number of offices in the communities grew with the variety and frequency of extraction practiced by the authorities. In some districts the governors, local representatives of the central government, had sixty to eighty communal officers at their disposal, apart from those designated to serve the parish priest and the justice of the peace. Most communal officers were chosen for a term of one year in elaborate ceremonies held each January 1. Every parcialidad chose one *segunda*, the highest communal authority, who was "obliged to present himself before the governor every Sunday and on days of festivities together with his subordinates . . . in order to give account of the projects carried out since the last meeting." The segunda coordinated all the work and obligations of the whole parcialidad toward the governor, priest, and justice of the peace. He distributed duties to and collected goods from his immediate subordinates, *alcaldes* and *hilacatas*, who represented the various barrios, estancias, and descent groups within the parcialidad. They in turn fulfilled the same function within their sector, supervising the lower officers, *alguaciles* (guards), *propios* (messengers), *pongos*, and *mitanis* (men and women doing domestic service in the authority's household).

The duties toward the governors were broad in scope, time consuming, often costly, and mostly uncompensated. Either personally or collectively, the officers and their parcialidad planted and harvested fields for the governor's private use; rendered fixed quantities of sheep, wool, and other livestock products; spun and wove wool that the governor had distributed among them; disbursed within the communities the money with which the governor purchased additional wool at a fixed price; transported his goods to and from urban markets with their own animals; served in his household; and collected taxes in the communities.[57] The authorities used the community officers to recruit laborers for the *faenas* (public work projects). In 1893 Azángaro's mayor requested the subprefect and district governors to provide Indians from parcialidades to make adobes for the "urgently needed" construction of a new prison; one year later the mayor requested twenty Indians per week to pave the provincial capital's Plaza de Armas, suggesting that they be paid "the same daily subvention as the prison laborers," ten centavos.[58]

According to Nelson Manrique, this heightened and systematized use of traditional communal authorities meant that in southern Peru "they ended up being reduced to a condition of servants of priests and local functionaries of the central government and unpaid helpmates of the state."[59] Yet the most affluent and respected families in the parcialidades, from whom the highest communal authorities were recruited, were hardly pliable dupes in this apparent subversion of their venerable offices. They were generally willing to play along, in part because this shabby remnant of the colonial "compact" between crown and community might still afford some protection of the communal domain against outside intrusions. In part they were pursuing their own interests against other peasants.

Francisco Mostajo, the eminent progressive liberal intellectual from Arequipa, observed in 1923 that

> the Indians of Huancané province gladly work in the construction of roads and the repair of churches, the only public work projects in those parts. They have internalized the social concepts of the Inca Empire or of still earlier societies so much, that they believe that these collective labor projects give them title to the property and usufruct of the land on which they live and plant crops. I build roads, I repair the church—the Indian will tell you when he is drunk or when he perceives a threat of being imprisoned—and this is my land: nobody can take it from me. When Protestant Indians refused to participate in the repair of the church, the other Indians said: you should not have any land then, you may not use "our" roads.[60]

In part this view reflected the indigenista reinterpretation of Andean collective work customs that Mostajo hoped to harness for a "wise social legislation." But the notion that a link existed between fulfilling one's public duties in the parcialidad and the claim to land was alive among some altiplano peasants during the early twentieth century. In a will of 1910 Tiburcio Choquehuanca, a seventy-five-year-old peasant from parcialidad Jallapise with sufficient means to have purchased a dwelling in Azángaro town, espoused this view. He thought that his title to Estancia Parajaya, acquired in part through inheritance and in part through purchase, was reaffirmed because he and his wife had "rendered for this parcel the communal services or offices of mitani, pongo, alguacil, alcalde, and segunda, services that my children have also rendered for the custom that is common in these districts and that gives title to assure the possession of property."[61]

Peasants thus appealed both to notions of private property and to the older notions of reciprocal obligations and rights as legitimizing their possession of land. It was a kind of insurance policy in the face of threats against their land resources arising from various quarters of the local hispanized elite. As long as private property rights to peasant estancias continued to be threatened by neighboring estate owners through their predominance in the courts and use of force, appeal to the legitimacy of possession of land through the "compact" with the authorities of state and church might provide a modicum of protection. The segunda, alcaldes, and hilacatas could rally the whole parcialidad to defend land and to reject demands by outsiders that went beyond customary obligations.

At the same time, however, the communal authorities were involved in the complex contests over political power between the various gamonales, the provincial and local bosses using patronage and clientalism to advance their family's own interests. Depending on specific local power constellations, segunda and alcaldes in some cases were allies of the governor, receiving a share of the taxes they collected, entering into commercial deals with him, or pursuing common strategies to appropriate municipal or communal land.[62] Such alliances heightened centrifugal forces on the cohesion of old parcialidades, persuading peasants in its various sectors to transfer the "locus of solidarity" increasingly to the descent group or to strengthen the private property claims to the family's land.

In 1900 the contribución personal, the disguised Indian head tax that President Castilla had abolished in 1854 but that continued to lead a spurious life during the second half of the nineteenth century, was abrogated for good in the department of Puno, five years after its abolition by Peru's national congress. This ended the long history of tribute and its various successor taxes, which had formed one of the key links between the state and the Indian communities.

For the national congress and the executive in Lima, increasingly under the sway of coastal financiers, merchants, and agro-exporters after the revolution of 1895, the tax had become a dispensable embarrassment, too reminiscent of the crude extractions by the Spanish crown. The Indian community had ceased to be important for the financial well-being of the central government. For the notable citizens and authorities in the sierra, however, the abrogation of the contribución personal was a matter of concern, since it was the major source of income of the departmental councils. Established in 1886 by President Andrés Cáceres to oversee fiscal decentralization, these bodies demonstrated the political power of the serrano gamonales and hacendados during the decade of Peru's "New Militarism" after the War of the Pacific. The tax's abolition weakened their political autonomy, making them more dependent on the treasury in Lima. Puno's Prefect Manuel Eleuterio Ponce, himself a notorious land grabber in Arapa, lamented that departmental tax income had plummeted by two-thirds in 1901. But far from helplessly accepting this shrinkage of regionally controlled funds, authorities in the altiplano reacted by shifting the tax burden on the Indians to increased collection of property tax (*contribución de predios rústicos*) on their estancias.[63] During the following decade the mean tax assessment grew more rapidly in districts with relatively few estates and a predominant peasant sector, such as Saman and Achaya, than in those with high concentrations of estates (table 7.3).

For Puno's peasantry, the meaning of the shift from contribución personal to the property tax was ambiguous. During the 1880s and 1890s communities in Bolivia's altiplano had successfully resisted this shift,

TABLE 7.3. Mean Property Tax Assessment per Landholding, 1897 and 1912 (Ranked by Rate of Change)

	1897 (soles m.n.)	1912 (soles m.n.)	Percentage Change, 1897–1912
San Antón	11.04	7.75	−29.8
Santiago	9.70	9.56	−1.4
San José	5.53	7.72	39.6
Muñani	15.10	23.44	55.2
Asillo	4.72	7.68	62.7
Potoni	6.89	13.59	97.2
Putina	5.09	10.35	103.3
Azángaro	5.29	12.06[a]	128.0
Caminaca	2.42	5.95	145.9
Arapa	3.13	8.39	168.0
Achaya	2.43	8.57	252.7
Chupa	1.72	7.95	362.2
Saman	1.32	6.44	387.9
Provincial average	4.41	9.27	110.2

[a]This figure excludes Salinas.

Sources: Matrículas de contribuyentes, 1897 and 1912; BMP.

designed by that nation's liberal oligarchy as the cornerstone of a radical policy of breaking up communal property by administrative fiat. The communitarian ideology of Bolivia's altiplano peasantry saw "both the 'servicios forzosos' and the payment of tributo, in accordance with traditionally accepted norms, . . . [as] the communal counterpart of a *pact of reciprocity* with the state."[64] But in Puno no tear was shed by community peasants when the contribución personal was finally abolished, and by 1900 they had accepted payment of property tax *in principle*. Here the tax was applied to peasants gradually, with a few appearing in matriculas as early as 1850. Instead of imposing a completely alien notion of property, the slowly advancing incorporation of the department's peasantry into the property tax rolls paralleled rather than preceded the advance of notions of private property. The connection of this shift with changes in the institutional corporate character of Puno's parcialidades is crucial. The abolition of the contribución personal weakened the position of the traditional communal officers, who had collected the tax from every adult male in their jurisdiction for the district authorities.

The increasing collection of the contribución de predios rústicos among the communal peasantry coincided with the establishment of a new tax collection agency, the Compañía Nacional de Recaudación, independent of district and provincial authorities. Because many families in the communities did not have to pay property tax, the Compañía's agents may have dealt directly with the heads of those households that did.[65] They may also have approached the hilacatas of relatively affluent descent groups or barrios, where many families were entered in the tax rolls. In any case, tax collection ceased to be an issue for the parcialidad as a whole. Descent groups opposed to the impositions by communal authorities now grasped the opportunity to strengthen title to their own land by willingly cooperating with the collection of property taxes, in the process furthering the transfer of solidarity from the old parcialidad to their own smaller groups.[66]

This is not to say that Puno's peasantry did not resist the increased collection of property tax. The massive revamping of Peru's tax structure under Presidents Nicolás Piérola, Eduardo López de Romaña, Manuel Candamo, and José Pardo in the decade after the revolution of 1895 coincided with a new wave of peasant mobilization in the altiplano. The salt tax and monopoly introduced in 1896, the new excise taxes on sugar and alcohol of 1904, and the increases in property taxes amounted to a completely new program of fiscal extraction from the country's still mostly rural population. The tax system was now based on a notion of individual consumers rather than on corporate groups of producers. But in contrast to Bolivia, in the Peruvian altiplano property taxes, which strengthened a landholding regime based on private title by individuals and their families, never became the dominant issue of peasant resistance.[67]

At least two-thirds of all landholdings enrolled in the property tax registers between 1897 and 1912 belonged to peasants. It was public knowledge that assessed peasants paid a proportionally higher rate than did most hacendados. Not only did estate owners frequently underreport their livestock capital, resulting in a low assessed tax rate,[68] but tax commissioners also liberally estimated stocks for many landholdings of illiterate peasants, who had little chance to do anything against this abuse. The 600 to 1,200 peasants enrolled in the tax registers between 1897 and 1912 represented only a small share of all peasants owning land in the province. By legislative resolution of October 30, 1893, all landholding units producing income below 100 soles m.n.—equivalent to a livestock capital of up to 500 head of sheep—were exempted from paying property tax.[69] Most peasants owned smaller livestock herds. Nevertheless, until 1907 tax commissioners entered many peasants with annual incomes of below 100 soles m.n. in the rolls; in the 1897 rolls more than 80 percent of all assessed peasants fell into this category. Even so, most peasants were not assessed for the property tax. Nobody paid who had an estimated annual income below 20 soles m.n., equivalent to a livestock capital of 100 OMR; in some communities, and even entire districts, hardly any peasants were entered.

A law of December 4, 1908, reaffirmed the exemption of property producing less than 100 soles m.n. in annual income, and this time it stuck in Azángaro. It had the curious effect that the presumed livestock capital of many peasant holdings, from which the estimate of annual income was calculated, doubled or tripled in subsequent tax rolls, from 200 or 300 OMR to 500, 800, or even 1,000 OMR. At the same time the number of peasants assessed declined by half from the 1902 rolls. Although tax assessments clearly reflected widely different levels of income derived from livestock operations among the peasants, who paid and how much he or she paid evidently depended in good measure on power constellations and on the client networks of the tax commissioners.

Social differentiation in Andean communities is not a new phenomenon of the past century. Even the often repeated claim that it has increased immensely with advancing commercial penetration or the "transition to capitalism" is difficult to prove because of the lack of comparable income and property statistics for the nineteenth and earlier centuries. Migration and the need to pursue income-earning activities outside of agriculture have characterized generations of Andean peasants in previous centuries as well. All we can say is that these phenomena became more massive (and thus more visible) during the twentieth century and that the criteria and mechanisms for social differentiation gradually underwent important changes.

During the colonial period, and to a certain degree even during the decades immediately following independence, wealth and prestige in the communities had been closely tied to lineage. The families of kurakas and many originarios maintained a higher level of access to community resources by birthright, even if they increasingly used the privileges of their offices and the opportunities in the marketplace to enhance their position vis-à-vis commoners. Although they had lost their privileges during the agrarian reforms of the 1820s, the descendants of minor kurakas remained among the wealthiest peasant families as late as the 1850s. Some owned estancias with a thousand head of sheep or more, not unlike small to mid-sized fincas. This was the case with the Puraca family and their Estancia Buenavista de Conguyo in parcialidad Moroorcco, or the Zecenarro Mamanis' landholding San Antonio de Lacconi.[70] Without relinquishing their Indian identity, affluent community peasants during the middle decades of the past century still had enough social standing to be called on as guarantors in contracts between hispanized landholders, pledging their estancias and livestock capital as security.[71]

In the more complex and fragmented economic and political environment of the altiplano around 1900, social differentiation within the peasant communities also became more complex, and families relied on a broader range of strategies to ensure reproduction of their household economies. A cautious interpretation of the 1897 property tax rolls, raised before political and fiscal pressures introduced the massive distortions of the subsequent decade, allows us a glimpse of the more affluent peasant families of that time. Perhaps as many as 8 to 10 percent of the families in the communities, between 600 and 800 families, owned livestock herds of 100 or more animals.[72] The wealthiest among them, possibly 2 percent of Azángaro's community peasantry, had herds of 500, 1,000, or even 2,000 animals. They were prevalent especially in cordillera communities on the northeastern rim of the province, between Putina and San Antón, where few crops could be grown. Population pressure tended to be lower there, and perhaps communal institutions remained stronger, blocking competition by new families for scarce resources such as moyas.[73] The wealthier descent groups thus could fully benefit from increased demand for sheep and especially alpaca wools.

In communities with stronger pressures from neighboring landholders or from internal population growth, especially in the plains and valleys and on lakeshores, accumulation of wealth required additional strategies. In some cases prominent families in the parcialidades relied on political assets to get more land, pay less taxes, and avoid being hindered in their commercial activity. Such ends could be achieved through patronage with the local authorities or a powerful hacendado. In districts with a weak elite of hispanized large landholders and traders, the dividing line between mistis and affluent community peasants was quite fluid, and here prominent comuneros might become justices of the peace or serve on the town council.[74]

Purchase of additional land from other peasants or, less frequently, from hispanized large landholders became increasingly important for families with large herds. Whereas for the whole period 1852–1910 purchases by peasants accounted only for 14.4 percent of all sales transactions by number and 5.5 percent by value, between 1913 and 1919 they constituted 24.9 percent by number and 6.9 percent by value. The boom of the wool export economy propelled affluent peasants in the altiplano to expand their landholdings, secured by notarial title deed.

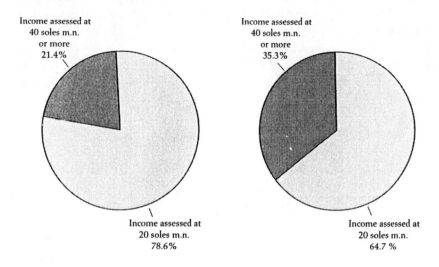

Income assessed at
40 soles m.n.
or more
21.4%

Income assessed at
20 soles m.n.
78.6%

Income assessed at
40 soles m.n.
or more
35.3%

Income assessed at
20 soles m.n.
64.7 %

FIGURE 7.1.   Annual Income of Peasants in Chupa in 1897, by Age. *Left:* 49 years or younger. *Right:* 50 years or older.

Source: Matrículas de contribuyentes, 1897, BMP.

In many cases peasants were buying from relatives parcels of lands that had formed part of the estancia of the descent group.[75] Thus, the pattern so frequent among hacendado families repeated itself among a minority of affluent peasant families. The most entrepreneurial son or grandson attempted to reunite the original holding, increasingly splintered through equal inheritance. Possession of land was also linked to the life cycle of peasant families in the altiplano, something first suggested by A. Y. Chayanov for Russia. In 1897, in three districts with numerous affluent peasants, Arapa, Asillo, and San José, nearly 60 percent of peasant landholders paying property tax were in their fifties, sixties, or seventies, a much higher proportion than in the population at large. In Chupa the proportion of peasants with a relatively high annual income, an expression of the amount of livestock and ultimately of the land they possessed, was considerably higher among older peasants than among the younger ones (fig. 7.1). In other words, over the years well-to-do peasant families were often able to expand their landholdings as the labor power of the grown children allowed them to keep larger herds. But in contrast to Chayanov's model, no automatic shrinkage of the family domain occurred during the parents' old age. To be sure, old age presented a crisis for many peasant families. Adult children established their own households based on parcels of the family estancia. Aging parents were often swayed to accept dependence on a neighboring hacendado in the hope of receiving protection and material benefits, from food supplements to payment of funeral expenses. But among affluent peasants in the tax rolls, many were in their seventies, veritable patriarchs controlling the family domain. After their death the heirs continued to operate the estancia jointly (pro indiviso), manifested in the tax rolls by dozens of entries such as "heirs of Juan Quispe" or "Andrés Maldonado and co-owners." Where descent groups continued joint ownership of the family estancias, the Chayanovian down phase of the landholding cycle of peasant families could be avoided.

But such traditional family strategies do not suffice to explain growing land purchases by peasants. In many communities transfers of land among peasants remained negligible as late as 1910. For the entire sixty preceding years a total of nine land sales between the peasants of Saman's five parcialidades were recorded by the notaries of Azángaro and Puno. By contrast, the ten parcialidades with the greatest sales activity between peasants accounted for nearly half of all such land transfers in Azángaro. Most of these parcialidades were not identical with those that lost a great deal of land to hispanized large landholders. For some parcialidades the correlation between strong peasant purchase activity and numerous affluent peasants in the tax rolls is striking. Families such as the Callohuancas, the Sucaris, and the Huaricachas in Asillo's parcialidades of Sillota, Anoravi, and Hila or the Sacacas and Quenallatas in Putina's Huayllapata appeared as owners of five hundred head of livestock or more in the tax rolls and as active land purchasers in the notarial registers. There were, then, a few communities in which the land market was considerably more active than in the rest and which had a particularly vigorous group of kulak peasants.

Commercial activities played an important role for many affluent peasants. The sale of rural crafts and of livestock products from their own estancias were part of the survival strategies of most peasant households, an expression of their precarious subsistence. But real trade, with goods acquired from neighboring peasants, from other traders, or from producers in distinct regions, could be more than that. It allowed dozens of affluent peasants to accumulate funds for the purchase of additional lands or livestock or for social investments in outfitting festivities in the communities. Although rural crafts largely remained an expression of peasant poverty, trade often was associated with affluence. Peasants were especially active as traders of livestock, coca leaves, and alcohol; some worked as itinerant wool buyers. Just as with land purchases, peasant traders were concentrated in a few districts and in specific communities.[76]

In the absence of detailed ethnohistorical information, we can only conjecture about what distinguished communities with an active land market and numerous peasant traders. No single factor can account for all communities in which market forces seem especially strong. Some, such as those in Asillo, Putina, Chupa, and Arapa, benefited from a broad mix of resources, with relatively plentiful croplands, riverine, or lakeshore pastures propitious for cattle grazing and sufficient higher pasture grounds to maintain numerous sheep and alpacas. The social differentiation in these communities was more complex than it was in the cordillera or on the broad plains in the center of the province. The intensity of peasant trading owed much to the location of communities. For example, many families were active as coca leaf traders in Chupa and Putina communities, from where peasants regularly undertook barter trips across the nearby cordillera to Larecaja province in Bolivia, an old center of coca estates. Livestock trade, by peasants as well as by hispanized traders, was strong in Saman and Arapa, strategically located for driving herds to market in Juliaca and Puno.

But the nature of commercial penetration, the relation between communal resources and household economy, and the prevalence of a stratum of kulak peasants also depended on politics and on the effectiveness of solidarity in each and every parcialidad. The correlation between incipient market-based stratification in the communities and ecological, demographic, and commercial factors was never perfect. It should also be stressed that Azángaro's kulaks largely continued to be well-integrated members of their respective communities, drawing advantages from the exercise of high office, relying on relations of asymmetrical reciprocity and clientelage to receive cheap labor services, and prepared to rally the whole parcialidad in defense of "communal" property.[77]

Most peasant families faced a more precarious existence. Perhaps as many as 80 percent of Azángaro's peasants owned between twenty and a hundred sheep, a cow with its calf, and perhaps two or three transport animals. They could sell only a few livestock products before diminishing their herds, with devastating consequences over several difficult seasons. Any crisis could seriously upset their livelihood: droughts or livestock epidemics, increasing the mortality of the animals; crop failures; a protracted fight over land; theft of animals; onerous impositions by the governor or the priest; recruitment into the army; and the expenses and difficult adjustments required by major events in the life cycle, especially marriages and deaths. The limited amount of surplus livestock products that they could sell made other sources of income more important: crops; rural crafts, such as spinning and weaving, pottery making, cheese making, and rope making; occasional labor for neighboring hacendados or for hispanized residents in the district and provincial capital; seasonal work in the mines in the Cordillera de Carabaya or further down the eastern slope of the Andes in gold-washing camps, coca plantations, or rubber tree forests, or in construction projects and as day laborers in cities such as Puno and Arequipa.

This is an unexceptional picture of a traditional middling and poor peasantry, facing the cyclical crises in their precarious family subsistence with a great variety of strategies. Perhaps "proletarian" forms of seasonal supplementary labor had increased somewhat by 1900 from fifty years earlier, with growing needs for workers during the brief mining boom in the Cordillera de Carabaya as well as the beginning expansion of employment opportunities in southern Peru's cities. But such types of seasonal wage work for altiplano peasants were not totally absent during the early years after independence. In any case, they remained the income sources of last resort; peasants preferred to supplement their farm income through peddling and barter, rural crafts, and occasional labor in nearby towns and estates.

Indeed, it seems unlikely that the average income of Azángaro's peasants declined significantly between the early decades after independence and World War I. A rough estimate suggests that the number of livestock held by every man, woman, and child in the province's communities stayed roughly the same between 1825–29 and 1920 at ten OMR.[78] With prices for animals and livestock products during the 1860s and perhaps again between the mid-1890s and 1917 outpacing the price of comestibles, stimulants, and manufactures typically purchased by peasants, it cannot be ruled out that their real income rose during those years.

Yet the old and familiar cyclical crises of peasant households could take on new and drastic consequences. The heightened volatility of prices for pastoral goods, demographic pressure, and a consolidated hispanized elite with more power and money all contributed to force thousands of poor and middling peasants to relinquish control over their lands and become colonos on estates. In most cases the sale of land was not the consequence of long-term impoverishment but of a relative loss of autonomy. The capacity of many peasants to minimize the effects of the cyclical crises on their household economy through the solidarity of the community was diminished. An increasing share of their exchange relations were with the hierarchy of hispanized traders, shopkeepers, and commercial agents. The value of their marketable surplus of livestock goods underwent sharper cyclical swings than had been common until midcentury.

The land resources in the communities were often becoming too scarce to provide the buffer that would allow amiable settlements of conflicts arising out of greater pressure of livestock populations on available pastures within the descent groups. In such situations, blurred pro indiviso title rights to the estancia of an extended family became the wedge by which hispanized landholders broke into the land of community peasants. Those avid to expand their estates now had sufficient cash or credit, and often the political backing, to exploit any crisis of a peasant household's subsistence economy. After gradually tightening peasant's dependence through loans of money or foodstuffs, through labor exactions, or through protection before the courts, the police, or the local administration, an estate owner would finally force the peasant to give up title to his or her parcel of land and incorporate it, together with the former owner's household, into the hacendado's estate. This process of increasing dependence often had little to do with impoverishment.[79]

The multiple pressures on the community peasantry thus resulted in a rapid and vast growth of the ranks of colonos in the estates. This status, in which the household economy of the former community peasant remained intact, was an ambiguous and ill-defined halfway point between peasant autonomy and the complete loss of "peasantness" experienced by landless peasants who left their native communities. The hacienda thus functioned as a kind of forced catchment basin, a depository for a peasant reserve army. With the disintegration of some newly formed estates during the decades after 1920, numerous colonos would revert back to a fully autonomous status as community peasants.

But how many peasants lived in the communities without land or even without livestock? Such poor peasants appear in the manuscript census as early as 1862, living as dependents in the households of more affluent peasants, who had often taken them in as young children.[80] Their situation approached that of colonos on estates. Their main task consisted in herding a flock of their patrón. In return they were allowed to keep animals of their own and possibly build a residence in the center of a sector of the patrón's pastures.[81] In such cases landless dependents could form households and families. This may also have been the situation of landless or near-landless rural artisans earning the overwhelming share of their livelihood through their craft. In communities where families relied primarily on craftwork, such as the potter communities in Santiago de Pupuja, the availability of this alternative helped to keep on the land dozens of poor families who might otherwise have migrated or sought employment in a nearby hacienda.

More frequently, however, a landless peasant would stay as a single retainer in the household of his or her patrón, assigned whatever jobs needed to be done—from herding to spinning or weaving, to construction and repair of the patrón's cabaña and transport of some products to market—against the sole recompense of food and lodging. In this position he or she could not accumulate resources sufficient to form an independent household. This type of retainership probably corresponded to specific phases in the life cycle of poor peasants. As children they were given as dependents into the households of more affluent peasants to strengthen clientalistic ties. When they reached adulthood they attempted to form independent households, either as shepherds on an estate, as artisans, or as muleteers. But some—especially women, for whom the lack of a dowry formed a serious obstacle—might be forced to remain as dependents in their patróns' households throughout their lives. Widowed older peasants without descendants, unable to maintain their own household economy, also attached themselves to more affluent peasant households. The social structure within communities was characterized by clientalistic relations similar to those between peasants and hispanized large landholders, albeit on a smaller scale of exchange between economic resources and labor services.[82]

Landless peasants had a few avenues to establish independent households tied into the agrarian economy. If they owned some animals, they could turn them over to one or more peasants with sufficient pastures. Either the owner of the land would pay rent on the animals and keep all of their products, or owners of land and animals would share in the products, a contract known as *waqui* in some parts of southern Peru.[83] In 1910 Casimira Mamani, a sixty-year-old widow, owned and lived in half a house in Azángaro town. She possessed no land but had eight cows, two young bulls, one riding horse with two colts, one donkey with its colt, and thirty sheep, maintained on the pastures of six different peasants.[84]

In rare cases landless peasants were granted vacant plots in the communities by a process of petitioning district authorities with the concurrence of communal officers.[85] Some were assigned plots of families extinguished in one of the severe epidemics, such as the typhoid fever epidemic of 1856–58.[86] Of course, theoretically landless peasants could lease, take in anticresis, or purchase land from other landholders. But it is my impression that most peasants buying land or taking up a plot in anticresis were affluent peasants.[87]

Despite growing pressure on land resources landless peasants seem not to have formed an increasing share of community population in the early years of this century.[88] There are two reasons for this situation. Many landless peasants living as retainers in households of other peasants did not found families and had fewer children than did peasants with sufficient resources or income for sustaining households. Consequently, their status tended not to be inherited; rather, this social stratum was renewed from generation to generation. Second, with growing demographic pressures in the communities it became preferable for impoverished peasants to become colonos on estates, where they could maintain their own household economies. Others emigrated to the ceja de la selva, the Cuzco valley system, or Arequipa. But before 1920 the number of families permanently leaving the countryside was dwarfed by those who continued to work as peasants in the estates.

8 Gamonales, Colonos, and Capitalists

The decades between the late 1850s and 1920 were the heyday of the altiplano livestock estate. In an increasingly hectic drive toward expansion, old and new landholding families came to claim a greater share of the region's resources than they had since the conquest: the proportion of land, livestock capital, and labor held in the hacienda sector reached a peak during the first third of the present century. For this offensive against the Indian peasantry to bring long-term success, the control over the expanded resource base needed to be secure and effective. As hacendados tried to set down stable and profitable relations of production in their expanding domains, imperceptibly slow but no less real developments began to change both labor relations and technical aspects of livestock operations. By the early twentieth century the long-term stability of yanaconaje, with its seigneurial overtones, was giving way to a labor tenancy that was, at its edges, more mobile and took on contractual overtones. Modest capital investments showed the path toward more intensive livestock production. But this was not a transition from feudal haciendas to capitalist livestock ranches. Most hacendados were unwilling, and the few who tried were unable, to change the fundamental traits of the labor tenancy system and convert to modern, capital-intensive methods of production. This traditionalism was to have long-term implications for the power constellations in the region's agrarian structure.

Labor Recruitment

Beginning in the late 1850s, the number of colonos on Azángaro's estates grew rapidly. In 1829, just after independence, at most some 5,600 persons lived as colono families on the province's estates, no more than 14 percent of Azángaro's rural population. By 1876 this number had nearly doubled to more than 9,800, accounting for just under one-fourth (23.4 percent) of Azángaro's rural population. Between 1876 and 1940 the number of colonos and their families grew more than threefold to 31,651. In the latter year colonos made up 35.8 percent of Azángaro's rural population; their share may have been higher during the 1920s.[1] The resident population on some of Azángaro's largest estates grew even more spectacularly between the 1860s and 1920s (table 8.1).

This wave of new colonos was the last phase in a process of "fixing" an adequate, stable labor force on altiplano livestock estates that began in the late sixteenth century. For the 350 years before the early 1900s, the number of *yanaconas*, as labor tenants were still often called even after independence, had been insufficient. During the colonial period hacendados had to rely on supplementary mitayos even for routine tasks such as herding and shearing. As late as the 1860s estates drafted nominally free laborers from neighboring communities.[2]

Until after 1900 hacendados jealously guarded their colono labor force. Administrators and renters were admonished by the owners not to do anything that might cause colonos to abandon the hacienda; rather, if possible they should procure additional labor tenants. But by the early twentieth century an expanded colono labor force had greatly diminished the need for outside labor. Most estates could now carry out all routine tasks of the livestock cycle as well as their limited agricultural operations with the resident labor force. Hacendados employed only small numbers of outside wage laborers for special projects, such as constructing sheepfolds or digging irrigation ditches.[3] Until 1920, then, the tendency was toward diminution of old forms of wage labor on the estates.

Some of the increase in the number of colonos was due to population growth among earlier hacienda residents: the children of colonos staying on the hacienda and establishing new households as shepherds. But between 1876 and 1940 population growth on Azángaro's haciendas was nearly three times larger than that of the peasant communities, pointing to the incorporation of people from the outside. The lion's share of these newly incorporated colonos were peasants and their families from adjacent communities whose land the haciendas had acquired. Routinely the notarial bills of sale legalizing these land transfers noted that the sellers had promised "to serve the buyer as yanaconas."[4] The peasant families stayed on their land, converted into a cabaña of the estate, but now had to fulfill the labor obligations associated with their new status as colonos. Most colono families were incorporated into the estates with their land. At the peak of hacienda expansion around 1910 some thirteen thousand to fifteen

TABLE 8.1. Permanent Residents of Haciendas, 1862–1972

	Sollocota		Picotani		Llallahua		Ccalla		Muñani Chico		Pachaje Grande	
	A	B	A	B	A	B	A	B	A	B	A	B
1862			20	122			28	164	28	133	21	95
1876		41		116		44		531		400		138
1906	50ᵃ											
1909			70									
1918	54ᵃ											
1924			61ᵇ									
1927			43ᵇ									
1928–29	91											
1931			55ᵇ									
1935			66ᵇ									
1940	122	699	44	196	185	807	98	468	105	705	27	183
1960							50					
1961	70	402	29	186	25	141	40	286	61	421	20	82
1972			39	116							17	93

Note: A = number of colonos; B = number of hacienda residents.
ᵃActual number slightly higher.
ᵇColonos with *cargo* only; total number slightly higher.
Sources: AFA-P; AFA-S; censuses of 1862 (MS.), 1876, 1940, 1961, and 1972; Aramburú López de Romaña, "Organización," 54; Diaz Bedregál, "Apuntes."

thousand persons belonged to such first-generation colono families, more than a third of the total population of the hacienda sector.

But not all colonos settled in an estate with a family, nor did all stay there for the rest of their lives. By the early twentieth century a complex pattern had developed in which a core of colono families resided in one and the same hacienda for a lifetime, perhaps for generations, whereas other colonos worked on an estate for a few years and then moved on to another estate. On Hacienda Picotani in 1909 six patronyms accounted for forty-one of the sixty-eight shepherds employed by the estate. Fifteen years later, in 1924, only ten of the twenty-seven patronyms from 1909 were still present, but the core six still accounted for more than 50 percent of all shepherds.[5]

Long-term colono families usually belonged to a few kin groups contributing numerous shepherds to the estate, whereas individual colonos without strong family ties came and went over the years. Mobile colonos were often unmarried young men with little livestock of their own who switched estates in search for the best working conditions. As many of the small, newly formed haciendas had only scarce pasture resources, and their owners, with little capital, tended to pay the lowest wages and meager food subsidies, fluctuation of colonos was strongest there.[6] By the early twentieth century, then, a group of colonos—still quite small—emerged who were highly responsive to different labor conditions. They had probably come from landless or land-poor families in the communities and remained poor on the estates. Until the 1920s haciendas functioned as a catchment basin for these rural poor, whose only alternative consisted in migrating to urban or mining areas.

The mechanisms by which hacendados induced peasants to work for them included a complex mix of coercion and economic and ideological elements.[7] This mix largely reflects the ambiguous bases of land sales by peasants to hispanized landholders, characterized in chapter 6 as a blend between a free contract and imposition by force. Certainly force or the threat of force could play an important role in turning peasants into colonos. Community peasants at times explicitly rejected "being turned into yanaconas," taking legal steps to block the maneuvers of powerful hacendados.[8] Evidence for such campaigns comes largely from the 1860s and 1870s, when pressures on community resources had not reached a critical level. Rather than a deterioration of their economic condition, they feared a loss of status, suggesting that colonial corporate caste stratification still influenced peasant thinking during the decades before the War of the Pacific. At least until that date peasants judged the condition of yanacona as lower in relation to hierarchies within the communities.

Toward the end of the nineteenth century economic reasons began to play a greater role in peasants' resignation to becoming hacienda colonos. Sale of their land often stood at the end of a series of debts. Dependence on the cyclical wool export trade, tighter political control exercised by local gamonales, and growing scarcity of land in the communities made peasants more vulnerable to debt entrapment strategies. Once a hacendado had succeeded in affecting their land, acceptance of the status of colono, with continued usufruct of at least part of that land, was preferable to staying on as landless peasants in the community or searching for wage labor in distant places. What mattered most to peasants was the continued usufruct of their land; hence their transformation into labor tenants was perhaps less drastic than it seems from our vantage point, fully accustomed as we are to thinking in terms of private property and the sanctity of contract. The peasants-turned-colonos who continued to work their erstwhile land for their families' subsistence certainly did not conceive of this transformation as ceding absolute dominion over the land to the new patrón.

As Gavin Smith has observed for the central Peruvian sierra, even communities "with a long history of confrontation and independence" were shaped by "an equally long history in which Andean peasants have been expected, in their turn therefore expected to offer services to superiors who often went under kin terms or pseudo-kin terms as taita or padrino/patrón."[9] Indeed, the fact of being incorporated as colonos into a hacienda did not automatically alter the type of services that the peasant previously had to render in his community. He and his family had been obliged to herd sheep, plant crops, transport goods to market, and work as domestic servants for the governor or the priest, just as they now would be expected to do for the patrón of the hacienda.[10] Gamonal exploitation was not exclusive to the estates; it was replicated in the authority structure that tied communities to local officialdom. Acceptance of the colono status ideologically signified a switch of patrón, not a totally novel form of subordination.

On the surface, the drive of altiplano hacendados to expand their labor force appears overwhelmingly successful. But a closer look at the *colonato*, as it had evolved by the early twentieth century demonstrates how fluid, fragile, and unwieldy this labor regime had become. Rather than a broad-based transition to a more tightly controlled regime of wage labor, the struggles over the nature of colonato presaged a new stalemate between the social forces in the rural altiplano.

The Colonato and Paternalism

The settlement pattern on estates closely resembled that of the rest of the province. Even today the traveler has difficulty distinguishing between territories belonging to haciendas and those forming parcialidades. The caserío constituted the estate's nerve center; here orders to shepherds originated, and central functions and labor processes were carried out. By 1900 caseríos had changed little in their physical appearance since the early years after independence. Improvements usually took the form of enlarging the building complex without changing its essential features. More rooms were added around a second or third patio. Some "progressive" hacendados invested in corrugated tin roofs to replace the old thatch. In a few instances special quarters were built for preparing cheese and butter, without, however, any notable investment in modern dairy-processing equipment.

Although many small fincas were managed by the owner, most large haciendas were under the direction of a *mayordomo* or, after 1900, an *administrador.* Until the 1870s most mayordomos were recruited from among trusted shepherd families on the estate itself, but after the War of the Pacific a growing share of administrators were sons of small estate owners and other members of the altiplano's middle strata whose families belonged to the network of friends and clients of the hacendado. In a few cases large haciendas employed natives of Arequipa or other coastal towns or foreigners as administrators. Besides free room and board in the caserío, their remuneration consisted of a salary perhaps ten times that of shepherds and a fixed percentage of the hacienda's yearling sheep, which they could sell or raise on estate pastures at will.[11] With few expenses on the estate, some administrators accumulated savings that they invested in land themselves. While administrator on the Molina family's important Hacienda Churura in Putina during the early years of this century, the Arequipeño Luis Gutiérrez put together a finca of his own through purchases of land from a nearby peasant community.[12]

Hacendados usually left their administrators considerable freedom in the daily management of the estates, partly because they had limited understanding of the intricacies of livestock raising and partly because the wealthiest among them increasingly preferred to reside in fine houses in Puno, Arequipa, or Lima, pursuing political or administrative careers, engaging in liberal professions, or tending to business interests. They personally took charge of the disposition of the hacienda products, of land purchases and sales, and of other legal matters; but the administrator controlled the timing of major tasks in the annual livestock cycle, the assignments and hiring of shepherds, and the rudimentary ledgers registering the livestock capital and accounts with the colonos. Inevitably all kinds of conflicts developed between owners and administrators. The belief that "the administrators did not have any interests in the prosperity of the hacienda and cared only for their prosperity" was widespread.[13] Where a relation of personal trust between owner and administrator did not prevail, the position could become volatile. During his first five years as owner of Hacienda Picotani, the Arequipeño Manuel Guillermo de Castresana hired and fired four administrators.

At times an administrator could function as lightning rod for the owner. In his daily contact with the shepherds the administrator would discipline them, at times with cruelty, while in the estimation of the colonos the hacendado remained the *taita* (father), the final arbiter over right and wrong, the dispenser of protection. When the administrator was socially close to the Indian colonos, he could become a broker who might transmit the interests of the "hacienda community" to the owner. In 1925 one mayordomo penned the complaints of colonos, who could not write, against the administrator of Picotani, an act that promptly cost the mayordomo his job.[14] Mayordomos helped organize the celebration of the haciendas' patron saint and partook in the devotion to them. "I have promised to become *ccapero* [one of the officials] for the fiesta, I am going to serve our Lady of the Rosary in Toma and am daily asking her blessings for your health, my Sr. Patrón," wrote Pedro Balero, the mayordomo of Hacienda Toma, to its owner, Juan Paredes, in 1874. "I sure hope you'll also come to see our fiesta."[15]

Below administrator and mayordomo every hacienda employed a number of subaltern officials drawn from among the shepherds. The *quipu*, "generally the shepherd with the greatest knowledge and best behavior," was directly in charge of many livestock operations—selection, classification, assignment of pastures, slaughter, and wool clip.[16] The quipu continued to work as shepherd, leaving the care of the flock to his wife and children. He received a salary about twice that of shepherds and rations of food and stimulants during his presence at the caserío; he was also assigned some laborers, perhaps young sons of other shepherds, to harvest his fields. Haciendas further employed *rodeantes*, sons of colonos who still had not received a flock of their own and normally lived in their parents' household. Paid rations and a salary up to twice that of shepherds, they took orders from the quipu. A type of circuit riders, they guarded moyas and external hacienda boundaries from intruders and conveyed orders to the shepherds.[17]

In 1928 Emilio Romero remarked that "generally, the Indian organization [of the estates] has continued. All the positions are Indian and they have their prerogatives and jurisdictions within the territory of the hacienda."[18] A certain similarity with the hierarchy of offices in the Indian communities may indeed be noted. Even though quipus and rodeantes were handpicked by the administrator or owner, they had to enjoy the respect of most shepherds to be effective. In Picotani, for example, all three quipus in 1909 belonged to the preeminent kin group, the Mullisacas.[19] In contrast to most large estates on Peru's coast, altiplano livestock haciendas had not yet developed a clear separation between "white-collar" employees, identified with management, and manual workers. The day-to-day functioning of the estate rested on the smooth cooperation of a hierarchy of Indian supervisory officers mediating between owner or administrator and the colonos, just as communal officers did vis-à-vis district authorities.

The colono family formed the basic unit of production of the altiplano livestock estate.[20] They lived far removed from the caserío in the center of their cabaña or *tiana*, the sector of pastures assigned to them for herding hacienda flocks. Families were rarely switched from one cabaña to another, and some, on the older estates, may have lived in the same spot for generations. Their residences, one or more low, windowless, thatched-roof adobe cottages, differed in no way from those of community peasants.

Once or twice a year the head of the colono family was assigned a *cargo*, the flock of hacienda livestock that he would drive to his sector of pastures. He would be responsible for the flock's well-being until he had to render accounts six to twelve months later. In the meantime supervision by the hacienda administration was sporadic. Once every week or two the quipu or one of the rodeantes would visit the cabaña, check whether the estate's flock was doing well, and pass along instructions about upcoming tasks and events in the caserío.

Besides the year-round work of herding, the colono family was obligated to provide labor for a broad range of other tasks during the annual production cycle. The head of the household or an adult son had to participate in the wool clip in February and March and the slaughter in June and July at the caserío, the two major annual labor tasks lasting up to a month each. At least one family member had to take part in the agricultural labors of the estate: plowing, sowing, weeding, and harvesting tubers, quinua, and barley, produced on most haciendas as provisions for the shepherds and the owner's urban household and as fodder for cattle and pack animals. They were obligated to transport hacienda products to merchants in towns or to warehouses at railroad stations and to bring back provisions on the return trip. Such trips could remove the colono for a week or more from his own household labors. Colonos commonly had to use their own llamas or mules for this service, without any recompense for loss or damage. Men and women of the colono family had to work as pongos and mitanis in the caserío or the urban residence of the owner for up to one month per year. In that function they were the general-purpose servants, cooking, washing, cleaning, running errands, and fixing things around the house. The colono family had to send one worker to the estate's extraordinary projects (faenas), building or repairing irrigation ditches or fixing the stone walls around corrals and moyas.[21]

All labor services were unregulated. There were no written contracts.[22] This vagueness of the quantity and quality of labor obligations presented opportunities for both the labor tenants and the hacendado to interpret obligations in their favor. Conflicts could develop on a wide range of issues. By the early 1900s, an era in which the colonato expanded so rapidly that on many estates the majority of labor tenants had arrived during the previous decade, the weight of custom began to lose strength in the definition of rights and obligations.

The remuneration of the colonos theoretically consisted of three distinct elements: rights to the usufruct of hacienda resources, wages, and gifts and subsidies. The first of these was by far the most important for the colonos, constituting the basis of what Juan Martínez Alier has called their income as peasants.[23] They had the right to maintain their own livestock (*huacchos*) on the pastures of the cabaña they occupied, and they could plant crops for their own family subsistence. Traditionally no limitations had been placed on huaccho flocks and crops of colonos, and this remained the case on most estates in 1920. The huacchos and the colono's flock of hacienda animals were pastured together, convenient for the colono but loaded with problems for the hacendado. It was easy to exchange animals between the two flocks; frequent crossbreeding kept huaccho and estate animals equally scroungy and unimproved; and the size of estate flocks was limited by the simultaneously pastured huacchos, since losses on flocks of more than a thousand animals grew exponentially.[24]

Huaccho flocks consumed a significant share of the haciendas' pasture resources. The labor tenants' livestock accounted for 25 to 50 percent of all animals maintained within an estate's borders, in some cases even more.[25] This was perhaps the strongest indication of the limited control of a hacendado over the colonos. Colonos might collectively produce as much wool and other livestock products as the hacendado did. It was on some of the smaller estates, put together since the 1880s, that pastures remained scarcest and the weight of huacchos was strongest. Some small fincas appeared to be little more than agglomerations of peasant estancias loosely held together by the authority of the gamonal owner, who extracted just enough commodities and labor from his "domain" to underwrite his social aspirations.[26]

With little control exercised by the hacendado, the size of huaccho flocks varied substantially, both within one estate and between estates. They were the most important factor determining the well-being and social status of colono families. On some estates in Muñani and Putina a few families owned as many as one thousand or even two thousand OMR, including herds with hundreds of alpacas, making them no less affluent than kulak families in the communities.[27] The most prominent colono families, such as those of Guillermo and Aniceto Mullisaca in Hacienda Picotani, had resided on their estates for generations; the clan of the Mullisacas had been members of the ayllu Picotani, which Kuraka Diego Choquehuanca transformed into an estate during the 1760s.

But in contrast to such "kulak colonos" most colono families owned between twenty and one hundred head of livestock; some may not have owned any. Because well-being depended largely on the strength of their "peasant economy," colonos with little stock and scarce opportunities to trade were poor. "Generally the pay for the shepherd is not sufficient to satisfy the most pressing needs of his family and he finds himself forced to steal the products of the hacienda," commented one agronomist as late as 1932.[28] Administrators of Hacienda Picotani regularly worried about the estate's "poor colonos" whose families did not have enough to eat. Women shepherds, widowed or single, and young single male shepherds were found most often among the poor on the estates.

What allowed this tremendous differentiation in the ranks of the colonos? We can only speculate. Affluent colonos needed to have access to plentiful pastures from the hacienda and sufficient labor from their kin group. This condition in turn required mutually reinforcing privileges and respect from the hacendado and fellow colonos. The situation of affluent colonos, mediating between the patrón and other shepherds, may have been akin to that of high communal authorities.[29] Poor shepherds, in contrast, lacked access to sufficient labor power and thus found it difficult to maintain sizable huaccho herds, grow enough crops for family subsistence, and dedicate time to produce craft goods for home consumption and barter. Perhaps their condition was made more permanent by being assigned a cabaña with pastures of limited extent and poor quality.

Wages and subsidies and gifts remained secondary and merely supplementary for the colono families' subsistence economy, yet they had important implications for the nature of the labor regime. Differentiation between wages and gifts and subsidies was largely fictitious before 1920. Wages for yanacona shepherds had been decreed at least since the ordinances of the Viceroy Duque de la Palata in 1687.[30] By the mid-nineteenth century some estates were calculating remunerations to colonos based on the number of livestock herded, although payment was mostly in the form of subsidies (*avíos*) of food and stimulants. Other estates alotted avíos as a fixed monthly amount, without reference to a wage.[31]

This ambiguity continued into the twentieth century. A slowly increasing number of haciendas nominally paid wages, now calculated on the basis of the length of the colono's service per year.[32] But payment continued to be largely in chuño, maize, coca leaves, alcohol, and dried meat. The national debate about the "feudal exploitation" of Andean "serfs" led to a series of protective laws by congress beginning in 1916, largely reasserting legislation on the books from the 1820s prohibiting forced labor and requiring payment of wages.[33] These laws only made the duplicity of altiplano landlords more of an open secret, however, without changing the basic practice of payment in kind for some thirty years after the first law's passage in 1916.

During the early twentieth century, then, two issues remained confused and unresolved: whether wages would be paid, and, if they were paid, whether they would take the form of avíos or of money. As estates were expanding rapidly and commercial interchange intensified, the very nature of the labor regime began to be at issue. Would the altiplano haciendas move toward rural wage labor or see a continued evolution of the seigneurial, paternalistic regime of labor tenancy? Every attempt by hacendados to alter a particular obligation, privilege, or form of payment of colonos and every demand or defiant stance of resistance by colonos formed part of the evolving definition of this labor regime.

Nominal wages increased between the mid-nineteenth century and the early decades of the twentieth century. During the early 1840s Juan Paredes paid an average of 27.5 pesos annually to the shepherds of Hacienda Quimsachata in Azángaro, most of it in foodstuff and stimulants.[34] In 1908–9 Hacienda Picotani, which had recently passed into the possession of the Arequipeño financier and businessman Manuel Guillermo de Castresana, paid between 38.40 and 62.40 soles bolivianos annually, equivalent to between 48 and 78 pesos. In 1917–18, at the height of the wool boom, Hacienda Sollocota, owned by the heirs of the recently deceased José Sebastian Urquiaga, still paid a uniform 38.40 soles (presumably bolivianos) annually, or 48 pesos.[35] The increase in nominal wages since the 1840s amounted to between 74.5 and 157.8 percent. However, with prices for chuño, maize, and coca leaves rising by more than 100 percent during this period, in real terms Picotani's highest wages of 1908–9 lay only some 50 percent above those paid in Quimsachata in the early 1840s, while the lowest wages lay below those of the 1840s.

Disbursements of wages in the form of goods or cash were made on an irregular basis, as the colonos needed them, although on some estates a pound of coca leaves and an arroba of maize were distributed to each shepherd every month. Once a year, in September, after the slaughter and the recount of the estate's livestock capital, the administrator settled accounts with each shepherd. Advances drawn during the previous twelve months were added up, and the shepherd then received the remainder of his or her annual wage. If the shepherd had drawn more than the allotted wage, the difference would be carried over to next year's accounts. On Hacienda Sollocota, in 1918, the colonos on average took more than half of their annual wages at the September settlement of accounts, mostly in the form of chuño and other foodstuffs. Although the timing and composition of their pay varied according to family size and the strength of their own peasant economy, cash disbursements were insignificant for most. The Sollocota data suggest that the major function of wages was to help tide colono families over during the six months prior to harvest, when food reserves from their own previous harvest were running low.[36]

Advances included not only goods or money received by the colonos toward their annual wage but other debts to the hacienda as well. The major source of such debts concerned *fallas de ganado*, the animals from estate flocks for which shepherds could not account at the annual recount in August or September.[37] Unless the colono brought the hide or carcass of a dead sheep to the caserío shortly after it had died, he or she was held responsible for its loss. Its value would be subtracted from the yearly wage, and the colono was expected to pay with wool or a sheep from his or her own flocks as compensation. Fallas were a constant bone of contention between colonos and hacienda administrators. Shepherds claimed, with good reason, that on the open range losses to wild animals or rustlers were unavoidable. Administrators and owners, perhaps with equal justification, were convinced that colonos took better care of their own animals than they did of those of the estate and occasionally slaughtered hacienda sheep for their own consumption. They also accused colonos of appropriating hacienda lambs for their own flocks before they could be marked and of handing over dead huaccho lambs as belonging to the estate flock.[38]

Debts from fallas could be considerable, and estates found it difficult to collect them from the shepherds. Between September 1907 and September 1908 the administrator of Hacienda Picotani charged colonos with losing 846 sheep, mostly lambs from one day to six months old. Some colonos were responsible for up to 100 fallas. The shepherds disputed most fallas, and Picotani's administrator Adrian Fischer was concerned that if he did not manage to take huaccho animals in recompense for the lost hacienda sheep, the shepherds would "laugh [at me] and never comply [with orders]." One year later Fischer had received only 274 sheep and nine soles bolivianos cash in payment of these fallas.[39]

On Picotani colonos were regularly in debt not only for fallas but also for extraordinary avíos, such as the gallon cans of alcohol that they bought during festivities. The administration used such debts to gain access to the colonos' own wool production. In special ledgers, separate from the wage accounts, the administration entered the amounts of wool equivalent to the value of such debts, according to fixed barter ratios between alcohol, maize, or falla stock and wool. For example, for one can of alcohol (probably a gallon) the shepherd would owe two quintales of sheep wool. On October 1, 1909, the end of the agricultural year 1908–9, fifty-six colonos of

Picotani owed the estate 118 quintales of sheep wool, 4 quintales of alpaca wool, and 12.5 pounds of llama wool. Two well-off colonos with substantial huaccho herds owed about 11 quintales of sheep wool each, whereas colonos whom the administration classified as poor owed from a maximum of 4.5 quintales down to 12.5 pounds of sheep wool. Only ten of the colonos employed at the time owed no wool. In two cases the debts had been contracted during the preceding agricultural year, 1907–8. Although one of these cases involved the substantial amount of over 8 quintales sheep wool, Fischer considered them as "lost in the balance for 1908, deducting them from the profit for that year." Such debts, then, were to be paid with the wool clip from the following year; if still unpaid after twelve months, they were written off.[40]

"You cannot imagine how much labor it is costing to get the *indiada* [Indian shepherds] to pay up the fallas and wool debt," Fischer wrote to the owner, Manuel Guillermo de Castresana, on August 30, 1908. "I have given them until the tenth of the coming month to cancel their wool accounts and bring in the fallas." Three weeks later, on September 20, less than half of the wool debt had been paid up in one sector of the estate. Fischer found that much of the credit granted by his predecessor was recorded inaccurately and amounted to absurd charges, with several colonos disputing their debts.[41] It was unlikely that he would be able to collect the totality of the substantial wool debts arising from credits granted during the preceding year. Two years earlier his predecessor had managed to collect just over half of the amount Fischer now hoped to collect.[42]

Debt peonage was not a feature of labor tenancy in altiplano livestock estates by the early twentieth century. Hacendados systematically used credit to force peasants to relinquish their land and become colonos on their estates, but once this end was achieved, credit served more limited goals in the correlations of power within the estate. Some hacendados used it, with limited success, as a lever to gain control over the labor tenants' own wool production. More generally, credit was required to stabilize the livelihood of colono families and thus increase their willingness to stay on the estate year after year.[43] In the altiplano the hacienda store, the notorious *tienda de raya* of Mexican cereal estates, was unknown. To be sure, some hacendados used the exchange of goods with their colonos as an extra source of income, charging dearly for foodstuffs and paying little for the colonos' wool; in effect such hacendados replicated the relations between wool traders or urban shopkeepers and community peasants.[44] But other hacendados charged their colonos at cost for maize, coca leaves, and alcohol and paid prices for colonos' wool on a par with those paid by itinerant traders in the communities or in district capitals.[45] Debts were not used systematically as a tool to retain colonos by force; rather, owners and administrators were constantly bothered with the difficulty of collecting debts. As José Sebastian Urquiaga, owner of Hacienda Sollocota, wrote in 1916, the shepherd could "withdraw from the estate at his convenience; all he has to do is turn over the hacienda flock as he received it."[46]

Hacendado control over the labor and resources of their colono families was strictly limited. Indeed, the colonos' strategies to assure their families' subsistence involved virtually the same range of activities as those of the community peasants. The colono's wife and minor children fulfilled the most time-consuming obligation toward the estate, herding the sheep entrusted to them. They perhaps bore the brunt of any increased work requirements imposed by the transition from community peasant to colono. The father was free to pursue more autonomous income-earning activities and to cultivate social ties with fellow colonos and friends and relatives in nearby communities. Colonos marketed a wide range of rural crafts, the most important being textiles; pottery, hats, and other items were also marketed. But their premier commercial activity concerned sale or barter of wool and other livestock products from their own huaccho flocks.

Even hacendados who sought to capture these goods to enhance the trade with their estate's direct "demesne" production failed to cut off the colonos' market ties. In Picotani, for example, the hacienda hardly received any of the valuable wool from their large alpaca herds (amounting to 7,741 heads in 1929), and the labor tenants exchanged as much as half of their sheep wool directly with third parties.[47] Where hacendados sought to force colonos to sell them their livestock products, colonos still found ways to entrust the wool to friends and relatives in nearby communities for later sale.[48] Itinerant traders, buying up wool, tallow, and hides and peddling alcohol, coca leaves, aniline dyes, and borsalino hats, included stops at colonos' cabañas on their circuits.

Most colonos periodically left the estate to barter or sell their livestock and crafts products for family provisions. One of Picotani's well-to-do shepherds, Benito Mullisaca, on one occasion sold the estate 200 quintales of salt, a crucial commodity for livestock operations; he had brought the salt from Lake Salinas, in the central plains of the province.[49] Just as in the communities, then, exchange activities of colonos shaded into trade proper. In some cases colonos maintained fields in distinct ecological zones to produce the maize needed to supplement the avíos. Many of Picotani's shepherds left the estate after the conclusion of the wool clip for one or two weeks in April to harvest their maize in the ceja de la selva of Sandia, at times causing considerable delays to hacienda work projects.[50]

Yet this impressive autonomy of colono households was only one side of the coin. Hacendados sought, with varying degrees of success, to tie their labor tenants into a hierarchical, paternalistic order of authority. As was true for paternalistic authority in most premodern agrarian structures, it relied both on benevolence—generosity and protection—and on malevolence—punishment and withdrawal of favor.[51] In altiplano livestock estates paternalism was cast in the idiom of Andean asymmetric reciprocity, with its emphasis on festive common labor and gifts, as well as in the idiom of Catholic patriarchy, stressing the concern of the father for the spiritual and material well-being of his children.[52]

The patrón's generosity and protection was designed to succor the colonos' life from birth until death, at work and in celebrations, on the estate and in their dealings with outsiders, much like an invisible shield. Hacendados became godfathers of the labor tenants' children at the occasion of their baptism. They loaned money or directly contributed to the costs of funerals and, at least until 1880, were asked to give their blessing to marriages between children of colonos. Hacendados sought amicable relations with parish priests so that they would attend to the spiritual needs of the hacienda's residents and officiate at baptisms, marriages, funerals, and the annual celebrations for the estate's patron saint.[53]

When all colonos worked together at the caserío or in the fields, they expected and received a copious, warm meal and perhaps a handful of coca leaves and a swig of alcohol. During the slaughter some estates allowed their colonos to keep part of the innards, reason enough for the whole shepherd family to attend this task. Colonos in charge of cows were allowed to keep the milk one day every week. And on certain occasions the administrator distributed gifts in the name of the patrón, a vara or two of cloth, for example. When colonos conducted business outside the confines of the estate, transporting hacienda products to town or the railroad station, exchanging goods for their own household economy in markets or the ceja de la selva, they were under the protection of their patrón. The hacendados used their influence and connections, as well as their lawyers, to free colonos grabbed by the Guardia Nacional or the army on their recruitment sweeps and to get them out of jail when accused of minor infractions. When colonos were attacked or livestock was stolen from them, the hacienda administration pressed charges and sought restitution on their behalf. Conflicts between labor tenants were routinely settled by the hacendado rather than before courts.[54]

But such protection and favors were always conditional and could be withdrawn at the whim of the hacendado. Administrators could give troublesome colonos difficult or time-consuming assignments, impound animals from their huaccho flocks, or fail to intervene on their behalf before the authorities. Some hacendados and administrators resorted to floggings against colonos who had failed "to show respect" or refused to carry out an order. And numerous estate owners and administrators did not stop short of sexually abusing the wives and daughters of their labor tenants, on the estate or when they served as mitanis in their townhouses.[55] In case of resistance or negligence by colonos "the reprisals are immediate and consist of material punishments and exactions," as the Cuzqueño indigenista Francisco Ponce de León noted. Mayordomos and foremen were well armed, and "with such constant threats, the patrón maintains his real and effective authority over the submissive and defenseless Indian."[56]

No doubt, colonos viewed their hacendado as a powerful personage whose protection they needed and whose wrath it was prudent to avoid. Many of the more traditional hacendados, the gamonales, adapted the construction of their power to the cultural and material environment of the Andean peasant world. They practiced and championed a traditional Catholicism and showed a certain respect for peasant ritual. Celebrations of the estate's patron saint, weddings, and funerals served to reenact and actualize the paternal ties binding the patrón to "his men." The colonos rendered homage to their *taita* (father), who in return demonstrated generous affection for his *hijitos* (sons). Alberto Flores Galindo and Manuel Burga have shown in the case of Azángaro's José Angelino Lizares Quiñones how legends and rumors could imbue a gamonal with an aura of magic, associating him with supernatural events and shamanistic powers. Use of violent force, although vital for such all-encompassing visions of the patrón, constituted merely a tool of last resort in the construction of his authority.[57]

At the same time hacendados viewed themselves as outposts of modern, European, civilization in a sea of Indian barbarians. In communications among themselves, with their staff, and with public authorities, the Indians were "lazy," "shameless," and "abusive" in their appropriation of hacienda resources and "refractory to learning." One administrator repeatedly referred to the incorporation of community peasants into the hacienda as "conquests." Often, although by no means always, such images of the Indian colono were suffused with a vicious racism. Andrea Pinedo, widow of the uniquely powerful and abusive gamonal Pio León Cabrera, embittered about the brutal sacking and destruction of her husband's Hacienda Hanccoyo in 1917 by colonos and political enemies, a few years later referred to Indians as "cannibals" and "helots," overcome "in the lair of their ancestral vices by slovenliness and their innate apathy."[58]

There was, to be sure, an overlap between the visions of the hacendado as traditional, quasi-magical lord and as representative of modern civilization. In both constructs it was his right, even his duty, to rule the Indian colonos with a "firm hand." An owner of a livestock estate in Cuzco's Quispicanchis province admonished his administrator in 1904 that he should "correct [the colonos] with toughness so that they mend their ways and cease being rascals."[59] Both constructs formed part of the traditional hacendado's self-image. Fully versed in the Andean peasant world, their language, customs, norms, and codes of behavior, he felt superior to them by dint of his education (even if slight), his modern life-style, his social intercourse with the notable citizens of the province, or even birth.

His persona, the Janus-faced construct of his power, was at once a product of the Andean peasant world, one contemporary version of accepted forms of domination and subordination, and the representation of Western civilization, whose mission it was to conquer the barbarian Indian peasants and convert them into "industrious laborers." Authority derived from such constructs, even if all encompassing on the surface, was highly fragile. For the colono the generous and protective taita could easily be unmasked as the exploitive gamonal. Both images were "true." On one level at least, what Eugene Genovese has written of antebellum Southern masters may be applied to altiplano hacendados at the apogee of their power: "The most flattering self-portraits of the slaveholders and the harshest and most exaggerated indictments of their critics have much in common. . . . They were tough, proud, and arrogant; liberal-spirited in all that did not touch their honor; gracious and courteous; generous and kind; quick to anger and extraordinarily cruel. . . . They were not men to be taken lightly, not men to be frivolously made enemies of."[60]

Paternalistic authority, even if claiming to hold sway across all domains of the subjects' lives, is inherently limited and ill defined. So much more so in the setting of altiplano livestock estates, with their dispersed settlement and labor patterns and the long history of peasant autonomy. In the relation of domination and subordination between hacendado and colono part of the "transcript" was hidden, to use the language of James Scott. Both needed to get along with each other on a daily basis and were aware of the roughly defined customary boundaries of reciprocal obligations and rights. Hacendados could not afford to lay bare their contempt for the Indian labor tenants in their day-to-day dealings as they did when among themselves. Colonos, while "investing" in demonstrations of deference and respect toward the patrón, and, in principle, accepting their subordination, sought to "hide the track" of their resistance and, on most days, kept anger or contempt felt toward administrator or hacendado to the relative safety of conversations with family and friends.[61]

Hacendados, eager to stabilize their expanding work force, needed to limit the severity and frequency of punishments and other measures of social control. Picotani's administrator Adrian Fischer, when reporting his success in recruiting new shepherds, noted the dire consequences of neglecting such caution: "Pascual Miranda from Tarucani also has a flock [on our estate] already. That finca increasingly finds itself without Indians, just as Sollocota, and I believe the reason is that both Don Victor and César Ballón apply the stick with cruelty."[62] And Juliana Garmendia, owner of Hacienda Ccapana, a livestock estate in Cuzco's Quispicanchis province, repeatedly admonished the administrator "to treat the Indians with prudence; I notice that they are desperate because, they say, you beat them, and they want to leave the finca; I am alerting you to this, because that would be against our interest."[63]

The Economics of the Estate

The altiplano livestock hacienda operated at a low level of productivity, and efforts at improvement remained feeble during the early decades of this century. Most owners sought to maximize the net income derived from their estates by minimizing monetary outlays for production and commercialization.[64] In some regards such a strategy was exactly the opposite of that of modern capitalist agrarian enterprises seeking to optimize the return on invested capital. The labor regime, with its stress on minimizing the wage bill, was merely one, albeit central, aspect of this strategy. The same low productivity–low capitalization approach characterized the quality and pasturing of the estate's stock, its installations, and its means of transportation.

Most of the sheep roaming altiplano pastures around 1900 were descendants of the Spanish merinos brought to Peru during the sixteenth and seventeenth centuries. Contemporary observers agreed that Puno's sheep population, degenerate through lack of selective breeding, combined many of the characteristics in the species most undesirable for efficient ranching operations: low weight; coarse, irregular, and short fibers; and little wool. To boot, many sheep came in hues from black to shades of brown and gray, "dirty colors" that at times found no market in Europe.[65] Whereas purebred merinos or Corriedales or South Downs, typical of Australian or Argentine flocks, weighed 60 to 112 kilograms and easily produced 7 kilograms of wool annually, Peru's criollos weighed about 15 kilograms and produced 1 kilogram of wool.[66] Obviously these sheep also produced little meat, a less important product for altiplano ranchers. Descriptions of Puno's cattle were no more flattering.[67]

One of the advantages of large estates was that they could aim at economies of scale through the efficient separation of flocks and herds and their optimal rotation through different pastures. A typical small to mid-sized finca, with a livestock capital of 1,500 OMR and six or seven colonos, perhaps employed one labor tenant each in charge of one cattle herd and one flock of alpacas, undifferentiated as to age and sex. The remaining four or five shepherds employed to watch the stock of sheep would not be sufficient to form optimally differentiated flocks. In contrast, a large estate such as Sollocota, with some fifty colonos, maintained highly differentiated flocks: ewes placed with rams for fertilization; ewes with lambs up to six months old; yearlings separated by sex; rams; ewes between weaning of their last lamb and new fertilization; one- and two-year-old wethers; lambing flocks (pregnant ewes after separation from the rams); slaughter animals (three-year-old wethers and five- to six-year-old ewes). In addition, Sollocota kept fourteen differentiated cattle herds, two flocks of alpacas, one flock of transport llamas, and two colonos in charge of the riding horses.[68]

Ideally such a careful regime of flocks and herds differentiated according to annual reproduction cycles should have produced certain productivity gains—through higher rates of reproduction and efficient use of pastures—even without any further investments. Thus, ideally, agglomeration of land into large estates should have brought productivity increases. But the gains seem to have been small. In 1909 Picotani's 20,844 adult sheep produced about 2.5 pounds of wool per head, only slightly more than the average for all estates.[69] No estate could easily escape the complex set of conditions that kept productivity low. They were inextricably intertwined with the logic, or the "rules of play," of altiplano society.

Hacendados pursued a strategy of maximizing their livestock even to the point of risking fodder shortages.[70] Ranchers relied nearly exclusively on unimproved natural pastures,[71] and availability of fodder fluctuated sharply from year to year and from season to season. Many estates strove to bring their livestock capital to a level at which the carrying capacity of the pastures would be fully used during the season with plentiful fodder. Toward the end of the dry season, between September and November, fodder became scarce and mortality rates increased. In Sollocota's ledgers the following entries appeared for the animals entrusted to the shepherd Agapito Montesinos in 1906: "October 15, 2 ewes dead (because of weakness [por flacas])"; "November 19, 2 ewes dead (because of weakness)"; "November 22, 1 ewe and 2 rams dead (because of weakness)"; "December 10, 4 ewes and 1 ram dead (because of weakness)."[72]

Haciendas set aside some of the best pastures, those maintaining moisture longest, for the dry season and constructed stone fences around these moyas. Some pastures produced fresh fodder months after the last rains in March or April through small irrigation works.[73] But these moyas had "only a small extension," often insufficient to tide all animals over the long months without rain.[74] And the shepherds did not always respect the moyas. They had the "shamelessness," lamented one administrator, to put their own huacchos on the fresh pastures, leaving the grazed, exhausted pasture for the estate animals.[75]

Agronomists and livestock technicians had no doubt that hacendados "preferred quantity to quality." "Don't we see here livestock ranches with numerous flocks of animals that are nearly always skinny and little developed?" the veterinarian A. Declerq from Peru's National Agricultural School asked in a lecture before the Sociedad Nacional de Agricultura in 1907. "What is the cause of this state of affairs? It is only the disproportion between the number of animals and the quantity of fodder."[76] This choice of "quantity over quality" both expressed and reinforced a vicious circle like those encountered by other Third World economies, from which it is so difficult to escape: because the productivity of each animal was low, hacendados aimed for maximum stock, which in turn perpetuated low productivity. To choose significantly lower levels of stock heightened the danger of invasions of temporarily vacant pastures by neighboring hacendados and community peasants, initiating a downward spiral of hacienda resources: a further need to reduce livestock capital, in its turn inviting further invasions, and so on. Under conditions of high risk, insecurity, and disputed rights to resources, the efficient estate maximized livestock capital, even if this approach lowered productivity.[77]

This rationality informed the strategy of stock reproduction adopted by most hacendados. The German agronomist Karl Kaerger calculated from the livestock inventory of an estate near Juliaca, a few kilometers southwest of Azángaro province, that only forty live lambs were produced per one hundred fertile ewes annually.[78] Statistics for several estates in Azángaro confirm these low rates of reproduction (table 8.2). By comparison, on the Hacienda de Hermanas, one of the vast ranches belonging to the Sanchez Navarro family in the state of Coahuila, Mexico, even in 1847 more than ninety lambs were born to one hundred ewes. In the western United States lamb crops of range-herded sheep averaged nearly 80 percent by the early

TABLE 8.2. Composition of Sheep Flocks on Three Estates
(percentages in parentheses)

	Picotani, 1909		Picotani, 1915		Sollocota, 1928		Huito, 1896	
Rams	786	(3.0)	1,970	(5.8)	139	(1.1)	58	(4.3)
Ewes	11,782	(45.3)	16,845	(49.6)	5,974	(45.4)	625	(46.0)
Wethers	3,770	(14.5)	6,104	(18.0)	1,902	(14.5)	185	(13.6)
Yearlings	4,506	(17.3)	3,985	(11.7)	2,632	(20.0)	281	(20.7)
Lambs	5,143[a]	(19.8)	5,071[b]	(14.9)	2,499	(19.0)	209	(15.4)
Total	25,987	(99.9)	33,975	(100.0)	13,146	(100.0)	1,358	(99.9)
Lambs as a percentage of ewes		43.7[a]		30.1[b]		41.8		33.4[c]

[a]Includes 1,774 *crias de vientre* (unborn lambs). If a 50 percent mortality rate is assumed for these lambs, the rate of live lambs as a percentage of ewes declines to 36.1 percent.

[b]Includes 1,376 crias de vientre. With the same assumption as in the previous note, the rate of live lambs declines to 26.0 percent.

[c]Six-month-old sheep were counted as yearlings. If counted as lambs, the rate of live lambs as a percentage of ewes increases to 52.2 percent.

Sources: Aramburú López de Romaña, "Organización," 15; AFA-S; REPA.

twentieth century, and those of farm sheep, tended in enclosed paddocks, could be as high as 130 to 150 percent.[79]

The major cause for low lambing crops on altiplano estates was mortality among lambs.[80] As many as 50 percent of lambs died during the first six months after birth, most of them during the first few weeks. Another 25 percent of lambs fell to loss or theft.[81] The lambs were born in the open range, during day and night, during lambing periods that lasted for a month or more. Sheepfolds to protect pregnant ewes and newborn lambs from frosts and hail were virtually unknown. Administrators complained that the shepherds "completely neglected" to care for the newborn lambs or appropriated unmarked lambs for their huaccho flocks. Some lambs were not accepted by their mothers, others were accidentally separated from them, and many ewes were too weak to feed their lambs. Lacking intensive supervision, many of these lambs died of starvation, if they were not too sickly to survive in the first place.[82]

With such meager results in each lambing period, altiplano hacendados attempted to maximize the increase of their stock by scheduling up to four lambing seasons each year: the Christmas, March, San Juan's Day, and

Lapaca (Quechua for "stealthy") lambings. Ewes that had not produced a lamb at one of the two major lambings, Christmas and San Juan, were again placed with rams three months later. Many hacendados tried to get two lambs per year from each ewe, expecting at least one lamb to die. They were continuing a practice that the Jesuits had already sought to abandon— without clear success—on their ranches two hundred years earlier. Livestock technicians were advocating only one annual lambing season, around Christmas when the weather was more benign. Experience in Australia and Argentina had shown that this was the way to maximize lambing crops, allowing the shepherds to concentrate attention on each lamb and permitting the ewes to recover their strength.[83]

Stock reproduction was further hampered by the failure to practice selective breeding, by diseases and adult livestock mortality, and by the short life span of sheep. Not only did most hacendados fail to introduce new blood through the purchase of purebred or improved rams, but they also neglected inbreeding through selection of the best ewes and rams from their own flocks. Ewes were culled only because of old age, thus keeping unproductive and infertile animals that depressed the lamb crop. Some 10 percent of adult sheep died annually on most estates because of both malnutrition and diseases.

Bacterial infections were rare in the dry and cold altiplano climate, but parasites such as the ovine ticks (*garrapata*), scab mites (*sarna*), and various species of worms attacking the sheep's lungs and stomach were endemic, stunting growth, reproductive capacity, and the weight of fleeces. In 1924, after nearly twenty years of striving for improvements on Hacienda Picotani, one of the altiplano's most "reformist" estates, its new administrator was shocked to discover that nearly all its sheep were infected with up to four varieties of worms in addition to being "covered with garrapatas." He warned the owners that if nothing was undertaken immediately, much of the stock might be lost.[84] A number of widespread poisonous weeds, especially the "*zenkalayo*, of mortiferous effects for the animals," contributed to the precarious health conditions of many flocks.[85]

"The tough and nutrient-poor fodder" that dominated Puno's pastures meant that sheep had to be slaughtered at five years, "at most at six, but sometimes even at four years," because they had lost their teeth.[86] This meant that ewes, first served by rams at eighteen to twenty-four months, could be used only three to four years for reproduction. With annual lambing crops ranging from 20 to 50 percent, each ewe on average produced as few as 0.6 and no more than 2 surviving lambs during its entire life span. These were dangerously low rates of reproduction, which toward the lower end of the range did not guarantee replacement of culled sheep. For example, the mid-sized Hacienda Huito in Santiago de Pupuja, belonging to Dr. Alejandro Cano Arce, judge on the bench of Puno's superior court, in May 1896 had two flocks of old ewes and two-year-old wethers, altogether 287 animals, which would be slaughtered in July. At the same time the estate had 326 lambs born since the previous June. With a comparatively high lambing crop of 52.2 percent Huito barely managed to increase its stock by less than 3 percent over the year.[87] Lambing crops below 40 percent could be insufficient to replace existing stock.

The stability of estate livestock capitals was precarious in the altiplano. On average, the region's aggregate sheep, alpaca, and cattle population grew at a slow rate of perhaps 3 percent annually during the century after independence. But many estates saw their stock decline over several years, as did peasant smallholders. Lax management of the flocks, instability of borders, endemic livestock rustling, years of drought, sharp frosts, and hail, a livestock epidemic—all could disrupt the precarious balance of flocks and herds. A downward spiral could result, at the end of which small and mid-sized estates remained without livestock capital and the largest estates lost up to two-fifths of their capital during a span of several years. Such unstable, downward-spiraling livestock operations explain the frequent cases of estates sold without stock or with stock considerably below their pastures' carrying capacity. The need to restock was common for the precarious, low-productivity economy of altiplano estates.

Multiple annual lambings required frequent and highly complex movements of sheep between various flocks. Under these conditions rudimentary accounting and lax maintenance of livestock ledgers made optimal disposition of the flock nearly impossible. "The majority of estates," wrote Vicente Jiménez in the first practical guide for altiplano ranchers, published in 1902, "keep only sporadic annotations without system or order. The owners are . . . satisfied with lambings irregularly registered by the mayordomo, or with a verbal report by a mere quipu and at times even with the declarations by the shepherd himself, never complete or precise. As a result the livestock capital remains stationary, if it does not suffer losses."[88] Multiple lambings, scarcity of fodder, diseases, high mortality rates, the pervasiveness of livestock rustling, and border insecurity tended to cancel out productivity advantages theoretically achieved by large estates through economies of scale.

But low productivity was not identical to inefficiency. Under the precarious, low-productivity conditions of the altiplano livestock economy, efficient operations made the difference between flourishing estates with high income-earning potential for the owner and decaying, disintegrating estates. Efficient livestock estates were characterized by a stable or growing livestock population making full use of available pastures; enough colono families to minimize the need for external labor; enough food production for supplying the colonos; well-established marketing networks, including cheap sources for food supplements (maize, coca leaves, alcohol), preferably through barter for the estate's own surplus crops (potatoes) and livestock products; control and supervision of the labor force through at least minimal bookkeeping; and, last but not least, safe and stable borders.

The two major threats to efficient operation of seigneurial livestock estates were posed by rising costs of production and by disintegration. Costs reached critically high levels if the estate failed to produce sufficient crops to feed its resident labor force, if it needed to hire outside labor on a permanent basis, if flocks could not be kept stable and needed to be replenished through purchases, or if disputes over land required expensive litigation. Estates were threatened by disintegration when they were considerably understocked, when control over shepherds was especially weak, and when serious disputes about hacienda lands arose either within the owners' family or with neighbors. All these factors, often interrelated, could cripple estate operations and lead to a serious decline of its income-generating capacity. The owner might be forced to sell, or the hacienda might shrink in size or become atomized. Clearly then, a great difference existed between efficient and inefficient seigneurial livestock estates. But the criteria for efficiency had little to do with capitalist, profit-optimizing modes of operation.

Available sources do not allow us to calculate the rate of return on altiplano livestock estates with any degree of confidence. It varied according to the conjunctures for livestock products and from one estate to the next. Returns depended on the estate's efficiency, on the type of tenure (that is, whether the hacienda was held in fee simple or emphyteusis or was rented), and on the level of debt incurred in the acquisition of land and livestock capital. Large estates usually rendered a greater rate of return than small ones did, not because they were more productive through economies of scale, but because they could more easily achieve the kind of efficiency described above. Their owners were more powerful and could protect their colonos more effectively against abuses by authorities, traders, and the military, crucial for stabilizing a resident labor force. They could use their considerable labor power to fight border incursions and livestock rustlers; on many large haciendas the ratio between resources used for "demesne" production and those given over to the colonos also tended to be more favorable to the owner. Because power was such a vital ingredient in the altiplano's livestock economy, large landowners faced fewer risks of seeing their stock decline or control over land diminish through external and internal siege, with obvious consequences for the rate of return.

The very notion of profit or rate of return renders misleading results for the type of economy prevailing in the altiplano during the early twentieth century. Labor and land were not fully commodified, and the goods produced on an estate did not all enter the market.[89] Calculating market prices for capital, inputs, and labor, as well as for the output of the hacienda, thus exaggerates the amount of capital invested, the costs of production, and the total value of production.[90] If, by contrast, calculations are based merely on the money actually paid and received by the hacendado for the various factors of production and for the estate's output, the results for individual haciendas are no longer comparable. (For example, one hacendado may have purchased his or her estate, whereas another may have inherited or agglomerated land through trickery.) Because the notion of rate of return continued to be so inappropriate for altiplano estates, it is not surprising that accounting for profits and losses was practiced hardly at all. What hacendados cared about in 1910—just as they had in 1830, when José Domingo Choquehuanca differentiated Azángaro's social classes according to wealth—were net revenues, the difference between current gross revenues produced by the estate and the current costs of production.

The meaning of the following widely differing estimates of rates of return, then, should not be exaggerated. In the first years of this century the French traveler Paul Walle visited livestock haciendas in the central sierra, where some hacendados had undertaken considerable efforts to improve their estates. In spite of the high mortality and low productivity of the livestock, ranchers there claimed rates of return (*intérêt*) of up to 25 percent and not below 10 percent.[91] Altiplano estates rarely reached Walle's maximum rates of return, except perhaps during the boom years of World War I. During the decade before 1915 they may have hovered around 10 percent. In 1909 Hacienda Picotani was worth about 80,000 soles m.n., more than any other estate in Azángaro province. It sold about 8,000 soles m.n. of wools that year, and additional sales of animals on the hoof, dried meat, tallow, hides, butter, and cheese probably totaled about 4,000 soles m.n. The estate paid wages and salaries, mostly in kind, of 3,498.93 soles m.n. to its permanently employed colonos and administrators. Other expenditures—for livestock medicine, salt, a small number of new stock, legal fees, and incidental wages for special construction projects—were small, perhaps no more than 1,000 soles m.n. Thus, total costs of about 4,500 soles m.n. represented slightly more than a third of the value of production, 12,000 soles m.n. Picotani's net revenues of 7,500 soles m.n. for 1909 would have brought a rate of return of 9.4 percent.[92]

José Sebastian Urquiaga, the large landholder from Azángaro, calculated that in 1916, early in the World War I export boom, an altiplano hacienda of "ten square miles" (about 25,000 hectares) with a livestock capital of 10,000 head of all types and ages, or 7,500 OMR, and average quality pastures, would have cost between 33,750 and 41,250 soles m.n. He suggested that its "net rent" at that moment, "when wool achieved its highest price due to the European war," would amount to 5,000 soles m.n. annually, a rate of return of between 12.1 and 14.8 percent.[93] Because Urquiaga sought to downplay hacendado exploitation, this was perhaps a conservative estimate. In any case, such an average hacienda's "net rent" would have increased over the next two years as a result of even steeper increases in the price of wools.

Ten years later, in 1929, when costs had increased while prices had not recovered high wartime levels, Carlos Barreda, an agronomist and spokesman for reformist ranchers in Puno department, suggested much lower rates of return. "Rigorously calculating the production of a mid-sized estate which is managed by the owner, . . . the utility barely reaches 6 percent of the capital employed." Even this low rate of return was possible only by paying "extremely low" wages to colonos. If shepherds were paid the legally mandated minimum wages, "no hacienda would produce a utility or interest on capital," and at a "rational wage" of 30 soles m.n. per month, "most haciendas would go bankrupt." Barreda concluded that the profit of most altiplano estates "is due . . . to the work of the Indian shepherds converted into utility."[94]

These widely divergent estimates of rates of return, from 6 percent in 1929 to perhaps 15 percent in 1916, in part reflect different conjunctures. More important, however, they demonstrate the imprecision of the measure. With accounting continuing at a rudimentary level in most estates, hacendados simply did not think in terms of capitalist rates of return. It is worth repeating that it was the notion of net revenue that mattered to them, the simple calculation of the difference between the value of the estate's marketed commodities and the cost of production and other regular expenditures. The data confirms for the altiplano the notion well established for Andean estates and haciendas in other parts of Spanish America, that low labor costs were crucial for maintaining large net revenues.[95] Other costs were even lower. Expenditures for tools, improved stock, seeds for pasture, and building materials were so small that they rarely figure in estimates of hacienda production costs.[96] Thus, the fixed capital of the estates remained minimal, limited largely to the simple adobe constructions of the caserío.

Under such conditions rising wage bills would have an immediate, devastating effect on net revenue. Greater outlays for labor allowing a more controlled, regularized work process and making use of increasingly specialized skills made economic sense only if they went hand in hand with capital investments, such as fencing and improved stock and pastures, assuring higher productivity per unit of labor. Initiating such a process was out of the question for most hacendados. They lacked sufficient capital, the credit system was not designed to proffer it, and their control over the estate's resources remained strictly limited. Endemic land invasions and livestock rustling by neighboring hacendados and community peasants and the colonos' stubborn defense of their autonomy made it less than certain that improving landholders could reap any benefits from capital investments. Under the circumstances most old and new hacendado families adopted the least risky strategy for increasing net revenues: they expanded their haciendas, ran more livestock on them, and settled additional colono families, while keeping outlays for land, labor, and inputs of production at a minimum. They did so by making full use of kinship networks, clientalism, and especially their strengthened position vis-à-vis large segments of the altiplano peasantry resulting from many peasants' dependent insertion into dendritic commercialization channels and the provincial elite's greater power of repression.[97]

It would be too simple, however, to identify the low-productivity, "seigneurial" operation of most altiplano livestock estates during the early twentieth century as mere traditionalism, a continuation of how things had been in 1850 or even 1780. Ironically, it was the very structures blocking the emergence of capitalist livestock enterprises that offered the opportunity to hundreds of modest families of mestizos, whites, and even a few affluent Indian peasants to acquire small to mid-sized haciendas. Given the economies of scale in highly productive, capitalized ranching operations, a tidy transition to agrarian capitalism, with secure and well-defined property rights, skilled rural wage laborers, and improved stock grazing on fenced pastures would have resulted in a predominance of latifundism in the altiplano perhaps akin to the vast estancias of Argentina's fertile pampas. The continued and indeed enhanced strength of clientalism, paternalism, and violence as sources of power paradoxically fostered the emergence of middling landholders—owners of small to mid-sized haciendas as well as affluent peasants—rather than blocking it. While locked in a fierce contest over the distribution of resources that reproduced the main colonial divide between Hispanic conquerors and a subordinate Indian peasantry, most gamonal hacendados and Indian peasants joined in rejecting attempts to transform the altiplano along the lines of agrarian capitalism.

Attempts to Modernize Livestock Haciendas and the New Stalemate

So far I have stressed how during the two phases of expansion between the late 1850s and 1920 altiplano estates continued to be marked by low productivity and reliance on highly autonomous labor tenants. But after 1900 politicians, intellectuals, agronomists, veterinarians, and even a few practical ranchers wrote and spoke about the need to modernize technical, economic, and social aspects of livestock ranching in Peru. Until the 1920s those not too familiar with the day-to-day problems and the brutal conflicts in the altiplano showed great optimism about the possibility of achieving such modernization in a relatively short time, and they were encouraged by a brief spate of government interest in improving stock raising between 1917 and 1923. The height of the modernizers' enthusiasm was reached during the early 1920s, just when the altiplano haciendas had entered a severe crisis.

In December 1920 Colonel Robert Stordy, a retired colonial officer, delivered a lecture before the Royal Society of Arts in London. He had been tapped by the Peruvian Corporation and President Augusto Leguía to direct an experimental sheep ranch to be established in the department of Puno and had just returned to England after a six-month inspection tour of Peru's livestock raising zones. Stordy fired the imagination of his illustrious audience about the future potential of wool production in this distant land that conjured up "visions of unbound wealth, mystery and fable." "I venture to assert that the breeding and rearing of livestock should prove more valuable to the Republic than its mines," Stordy told the listeners. "In the great Peruvian Cordillera there lies a future pregnant with possibilities; . . . in the practice of sheep husbandry and the conservation and scientific development of the alpaca and vicuña hair industry there are commercial prospects of considerable extent and value." Stordy envisioned the investment of foreign (especially British) capital in altiplano ranches and land, with a core labor force of "a large number of ex-officers and men of the British Army who might be glad to avail themselves of the amenities of an outdoor life, . . . whose habits of discipline and appreciation of work would make them desirable members of the community, and who could . . . do much to raise Peru to that position among the wool and hair producing countries of the world which her natural advantages dictate." All that was needed to set this vast transformation in motion was for the

Peruvian government "to advance her best interests by throwing open large tracts of land for colonization on an extensive scale."[98] In advancing this ingenious plan to solve Britain's problems with unemployed veterans and develop Peru's economy in one stroke, Stordy failed to appraise his audience of the fact that, at the very moment when he spoke, a bitter conflict over increasingly scarce land was raging between hacendados and Indian community peasants in the region that he wanted opened for colonization. Based on racist stereotypes, his insistence on British (especially Scottish) colonists as shepherds because of their "habits of discipline and work" implied the need to remove the Indian peasants from their land to achieve his bountiful vision.

Others, although not sharing Stordy's racist calls for European colonization, foresaw a no less grandiose transformation of Peru's sheep and alpaca industry. Professor L. Maccagno, a zootechnician at Lima's National School for Agriculture and Veterinary Sciences, reported in 1924 on what he believed to be a growing disparity between world wool production and consumption and concluded that "Peru is the country best equipped to resolve the crisis. . . . No region in the world presents greater advantages than Peru [for increased wool production]." Maccagno believed that massive investments in ranching, both by national and foreign capitalists, was favored by the "existence of many estates of enormous extension" with "excellent conditions . . . for systematizing and improving pastures and stock."[99]

Confidence in a rapid and profound transformation of Peru's livestock estates into highly productive capitalist enterprises was fueled by the collapse of the wool market in 1920–21. This crisis both demonstrated the vulnerability of the seigneurial estate and the exhaustion of its growth potential and encouraged radical indigenistas to put forth the opposite vision of a rejuvenated Andean peasant community recovering its dominance (see chapter 9). During the first two decades of this century, however, calls for change had a less visionary ring to them, advocating instead gradual improvements toward the desired transformation. To be sure, fundamental critiques of the "semifeudal" hacienda had been voiced even before World War I, and highly productive agrarian enterprises employing proletarianized shepherds were already seen as the solution by many upper-class commentators on rural affairs. But during the heyday of the altiplano estate, politicians and professionals fully expected the hacendados themselves to undertake the required transformation.[100]

Against such expectations, change in the altiplano came painstakingly slow, and by the late 1920s it was evident that it would not soon touch the great majority of livestock estates. The following discussion of investments in improved livestock operations and attempts to change the labor regime thus concerns only a handful of haciendas in Azángaro and, out of more than a thousand estates, a few dozen in the whole Peruvian altiplano. A tiny minority of "improving landlords" sought to limit colono autonomy and to increase their reliance on wages, strengthen the administrative-supervisory structure of their estates, and invest in more productive stock, pastures, and tools.[101]

Encouraged by the intensifying national debate about feudal exploitation on serrano estates, colonos demanded payment for extraordinary services such as pongueaje and alquilas. When such payments were legislated in 1916, hacendados responded by charging *yerbaje,* a pasturage fee for the colonos' huaccho flocks, designed to cancel out the need for additional cash payments. Although such fictitious wages and countervailing fees lent a more contractual aspect to labor tenancy, they did not change the estates' day-to-day labor process.[102]

The "improving landlord" needed to be willing and have sufficient capital to increase the shepherds' wages in order to tackle the crucial issue in the transition to modern, productive livestock operations: a significant reduction in the colonos' use of hacienda resources and a complete separation of estate and huacchos flocks. A 1926 report about Hacienda Huacahuta in Melgar province, owned by the Bedoya and Revie Company, clearly indicated this nexus. The present difficulties could be overcome "through the system of enclosed paddocks. . . . Under this new system the Indian will be obliged to pasture his own flock on his own land, leaving the patrón free to improve and develop his hacienda for the benefit of the country and himself. The rancher will be able to pay much higher wages to the Indian, freeing him from the state of semislavery in which he finds himself today."[103]

After 1906, when Manuel Guillermo de Castresana acquired Hacienda Picotani, he began a slow and cautious campaign to limit the usufruct of estate pastures by colonos. In 1908 a differential wage scale was introduced according to which the poorest colonos earned nearly two-thirds higher wages than the richest colonos, a bonus for running only small huaccho flocks on hacienda pastures. The colonos with the largest flocks of huacchos were obliged to sell some of their slaughter animals to the estate at low prices "in order to compensate a bit for the pastures that they use."[104] In September 1911 administrator Carlos Esteves proposed to give the estate's critical lambing flocks to the poorest shepherds, rewarding them "according to their needs, with a bit more avíos. . . . They are more careful in shepherding the flocks and have less need for extensive pastures [for huacchos]." Castresana and his administrator systematically favored poorer shepherds over the entrenched colonos with large huaccho flocks by shifting the composition of their remuneration toward wages and avíos. Esteves suggested to Castresana that they follow this approach "to subdue the rich colonos a bit, or rather to punish them. It would not matter to you if two or three [rich] shepherds get annoyed; it will be much worse if the advance of your interests continues to suffer. The stock of the hacienda will never increase if they [the rich shepherds] keep on utilizing estate pastures and oppressing [sic] the estate's animals as they do until today."[105]

Despite Esteves's bravado, Castresana had to walk a tightrope in his endeavor to recover hacienda resources from the colonos and instill greater attention to the estate's livestock in them. As Picotani was expanding rapidly between 1906 and the war years, it needed more shepherds. The richest colonos formed the most stable part of the work force, and alienating them could undermine the stability of Picotani's livestock operation. Although Castresana taxed the shepherds' use of hacienda pastures, he never ordered an actual reduction of huaccho flocks.

The rhythm of change on Picotani picked up only after Castresana's death in 1924, when the hacienda passed into the possession of his nephews and nieces, the children of Eduardo López de Romaña, Peru's president between 1899 and 1903. On the recommendation of the Gildemeister family, owners of Peru's largest sugar estate, they hired a German agronomist as Picotani's new administrator. Having previously worked on a large corporate ranch in the central highlands, this man was in a hurry to make Picotani more productive. Eager to expand the estate's stock, he doubled the average number of sheep in each colono's flock by 1927. He required additional labor from the colonos, increased falla charges against them, and tried to abolish the food supplements. Shepherds unwilling to comply were routinely flogged. The colonos repeatedly protested against this erosion of their customary rights and working conditions to the owners, who warned the foreign administrator about the danger of an "Indian uprising," especially in Picotani where "the colonos formerly enjoyed consideration and good treatment." They ordered him "to change those radical extreme measures of punishment for prudent measures that defend the interests of the hacienda and at the same time are not abusive of the Indians."[106] But by 1928 the situation had come to a head. More than a third of the shepherds abandoned the estate, animal mortality increased, and the quality of wool and meat declined because of overgrazing. The remaining colonos plotted to blow up the caserío. The owners now agreed that the German administrator had to go, bitterly complaining to the Gildemeisters for recommending a man so inappropriate for the delicate task of directing an altiplano livestock estate.[107]

By the early 1930s Picotani had managed to recover its work force, achieve more stable flocks averaging about seven hundred animals, and improve productivity per shepherd and per sheep.[108] But the crucial matter of reducing huaccho flocks and strictly separating them from those of the hacienda had still not been achieved. In fact, huaccho flocks continued to grow, from 11,648 sheep and 7,741 llamas and alpacas in 1929 to 9,971 sheep and 14,722 llamas and alpacas in 1943. In that year the owners, after delaying for over a decade for fear of the colonos' reaction, finally approved a plan to castrate huaccho rams and designate a special flock of hacienda rams to breed huacchos. The goal was to improve the blood of huacchos so that accidental crossbreeding would be less damaging to improved hacienda flocks. During the years until the agrarian reform in the early 1970s, huacchos were reduced to about one-eighth of their number in 1943. Although the number of colonos declined by nearly 50 percent, from 66 in 1935 to 35 in 1969, the estate's stock was reduced by no more than 20 percent, and productivity per animal probably continued to rise.[109]

As early as the 1920s some colonos acquired specialized skills, for example, sheep shearing or supervising of lambings.[110] Basic medical service had been provided to the colonos since before 1920, but Picotani established a primary school for colono children only in 1946, more than three decades after the first schools opened in peasant communities.[111] As the owners sought to push back the colonos' peasant economy and create a more skilled work force, they increased wages, first between 1908 and 1911, then during the late 1920s, and again after World War II. Between 1906 and 1948 nominal wages went up elevenfold, perhaps double the increase for retail food prices.[112] As cash wages became more important, Picotani's owners had to relinquish their attempts to block direct commercial ties between the estate's work force and outside traders.

Efforts to change the traditional colonato regime, with its high degree of autonomy of shepherd families and their lack of modern sheep-ranching skills, began in earnest only during the years of the World War I bonanza. Colonos resisted these efforts almost immediately, seeking to block any erosion of their autonomy. In 1917, with the bloody attack on Pio León Cabrera's Hacienda Hanccoyo in the mountainous border region between Azángaro and Sandia provinces and a little-known uprising in Hacienda Huasacona, Muñani district, colonos rose up against their patrones for the first time.[113] During the 1920s they organized militant protests on numerous haciendas in Azángaro and adjacent provinces in Puno and southern Cuzco. Often in contact with the broad movement of community peasants sweeping the southern highlands, the colonos nevertheless pursued their own agenda. They protested against limits on huaccho flocks, steep fees for hacienda pastures, forced breeding programs designed to change the quality and color of their huacchos, and restrictions on the sale of their livestock products. "Unionist" demands, typical for rural workers, were not absent but secondary. They included limits on the size of flocks, no reduction of food subsidies, and compensation for special services such as alquila and pongueaje.[114]

Riots, protests, and participation in rebellions by colonos began to block and channel changes in the labor regime. By 1930 the grand designs for transforming the region's sheep and alpaca industry into a high-productivity business based on wage labor had failed. The direction and speed of change on modernizing estates became steadier, slower, and more predictable. The colonato would not be abolished, but use rights of the shepherds would gradually be limited and huaccho flocks reduced and separated from hacienda flocks. The weight of wages in shepherds' total remuneration increased, and colonos acquired special skills. By the 1950s the labor system on modernizing estates had become contractual. On a few estates, such as Posoconi in Asillo, labor unions submitted lists of demands to management in the name of all colonos. There the old paternalism, if it survived at all, degenerated to mere folklore.

This gradually evolving contractual colonato retained some basic features of the old while removing obstacles for highly productive, capital-intensive ranching.[115] Not unlike other labor-tenancy regimes on modernizing estates, such as its namesake on Brazil's coffee *fazendas*, it continued to keep the cost of labor down and reduced the hacendado's risks during cyclical crises caused by declining commodity prices, livestock epidemics, or harsh weather. These landlord gains were achieved after decades of gradual, piecemeal changes and then only by a small group of modernizers. Before 1920 they had hardly made a dent in reforming the altiplano estates' labor regime.[116]

Isolated technical changes preceded reforms of the labor regime on modernizing estates, but their effectiveness necessarily remained limited. Attempts to improve the breed of sheep through the importation of rams from Europe and Argentina began as early as the 1840s, and after the 1890s they became more regular.[117] But before 1920 they showed minimal results. The few imported purebred animals quickly died from diseases, and no infrastructure existed to keep their improved-breed offspring separated from the great majority of degenerate animals.[118] Prodded by the experimental sheep ranch that began operating in Chuquibambilla, Melgar province, in 1921, some modernizing estates, among them San José, Sollocota, and Picotani, began to import large numbers of purebred rams from Argentina. By the early 1930s Picotani maintained a few flocks of purebred

Corriedale and Rambouillet sheep and larger numbers of three-fourths and half-blooded sheep; even these animals produced 70 to 150 percent more wool than did the unimproved criollos.[119] During the 1920s some estates finally altered reproductive cycles to one annual lambing season, devoting special care to the survival of the newborn lambs.[120]

Beginning in the early years of this century, a few improving hacendados invested in technical facilities, such as sheepfolds, shearing knives or scissors or, on one estate, even a hydraulic machine for the wool clip, sheep dips to combat parasites, and wool-washing installations and presses.[121] Use of trucks to transport hacienda products to railroad stations, eliminating conflicts with colonos over alquila services, began only in the 1920s. During the mid-twentieth century truck transport revolutionized the altiplano's marketing system, benefiting haciendas and peasant communities alike.[122]

Some hacendados undertook to increase the efficiency of their estate's administration, indispensable if they hoped to tighten control over colonos and introduce more regulated, "scientific" methods of livestock raising. Instead of the rudimentary ledgers registering avíos and the livestock added to or subtracted from the shepherds' flocks, modernizing haciendas now kept numerous accounts, meticulously recording the disposition and productivity of the different types of stock, the results of the annual wool clip and slaughter, the dispatch of hacienda products to market, remaining products and supplies on hand in the warehouse, the disposition of the flocks, and payments to and debts of the colonos.[123] Improving landlords hired more quipus and rodeantes from among their colonos. A handful of administrators now had some training in agronomy; others at least possessed basic skills of reading, writing, and arithmetic, a far cry from the semiliterate mayordomos still the norm on altiplano estates as late as the 1870s. It remained rare for an owner's son to study agronomy before taking over the parental estate.[124] Increasingly, sons of large landholders from the altiplano sought an education preparing them for urban careers, as they were loath to be directly associated with the management of their parental estates, deemed feudal and antiprogressive by public opinion even before the onset of the crisis in 1920.

Technical change came slowest where it most directly interfered with the labor regime. This was true especially of the introduction of artificial pastures and of fencing, measures of strategic importance for increasing productivity yet also inimical to the colonos' autonomy. Around the turn of the century Alberto Gadea, the director of Puno's Colegio San Carlos, experimented with new, more nutritive strains of pasture, and more hacendados planted barley as additional livestock feed.[125] But these examples did not catch on. Any serious effort to tackle the increasing problem of insufficient feed required fencing in order to protect the young shoots of improved grasses or barley until they matured. Indeed, during the war boom several altiplano hacendados began to fence in pastures, preparing to plant high-nutrition grasses.[126] They encountered immediate and adamant resistance by the colonos, who understood full well that fences would lead to exclusion of their huaccho flocks from the estates.

As late as the 1960s fences remained exceptional in the altiplano. The great majority of hacendados, of course, had never even attempted to invest in seeds for high-nutrition grasses or in fencing, in part because they lacked funds or credit to do so. The obstacles to augmenting fodder by these means presented the most immediate motivation for hacendados to acquire additional land during the years of rising demand for wool, allowing them to keep larger flocks. Lack of fencing also forced hacendados to keep the size of flocks within conventional limits to avoid loss or predation. With increasing livestock capital, estate owners inevitably had to employ more shepherds.

The Andean Hacienda Revisited

Our current understanding of the Andean estate as it operated between the late nineteenth century and the 1960s owes much to the pioneering work of three economists, Juan Martínez Alier, Shane Hunt, and Geoffrey Bertram.[127] All three rejected the widespread image of Andean seigneurial estates as feudal or semifeudal enterprises whose inefficiency and apparent waste of resources reflected the social parasitism and lack of entrepreneurial spirit of the hacendados, latifundists who relentlessly and brutally exploited their Indian "serfs." All three authors sought to demonstrate that the persistence of labor tenancy made economic sense from the perspective of both hacendado and colono as long as certain assumptions prevailed. In concluding this chapter, I summarize Bertram's discussion of the hacienda, which draws and expands on the work of Keith Griffin, Martínez Alier, and Hunt, and then highlight how my own discussion goes beyond the 1970s revisionism.

Bertram suggests that because of sociopolitical conditions the opportunity costs of land were lower for the large landholder than they were for the peasant. Andean hacendados attempted to monopolize land in order to manipulate other markets, especially those for labor and credit. Wage labor does not automatically represent a more advanced type of relations of production than labor tenancy does. Because both hacendado and colono were rational actors, the choice between the two systems "rests upon the efficiency and profitability in production for external markets, in the case of the landowner, and the comparison between the cash wage offered and the value of usufruct access to land for the colono." Labor tenancy will prevail as long as the value of a year's access to a plot of land for the colono is higher than the cash wage for a year's labor on the hacienda, and the value of a year's labor is in turn higher than the opportunity cost of the same plot for the hacendado. Under these conditions both hacendado and peasant are better off than they would be in a system based exclusively on payment by means of a cash wage.

The peasant enterprise, employing the labor of the whole family and redistributing the output, constituted the underpinning of the Andean hacienda. Colonos preferred it to wage labor also because it provided security and employment to all members of the family and a safety cushion in difficult times. "Unless there is full employment in the wider system," guaranteeing "any member of the peasant enterprise employment at the prevailing wage rate," the peasant enterprise will use its members' labor even when its marginal product is substantially below the prevailing wage rate and will tenaciously defend the access to land on which it is based. Bertram, following Martínez Alier, saw proof for this assertion in the fact that expulsion of a colono from a hacienda was often considered punishment.

This system comes under pressure through exogenous change, especially through increases in the price paid for hacienda products. The hacendado will seek to raise productivity and to work more of the land directly, in "demesne." With a sufficient increase in the value of estate lands, the hacendado will try to abandon the labor tenancy regime altogether in favor of wage labor. In an open economy—one in which the landlord does not automatically possess the type of power requisite for keeping his or her opportunity costs for land and labor stable—the balance of class forces ultimately determines the capacity of the landlord to carry out such changes. "The same forces which led the hacienda to seek to expand could also produce a countervailing (though not equal) strengthening of the peasantry's motive and ability to resist." The notorious slowness with which innovations such as enclosures, specialization of labor, new crop types, improved pastures, and new stock breeds have been introduced on serrano estates during the twentieth century was due not to the "feudal" mentality of the large landlords but rather to the strength of Indian opposition. Bertram concludes that the "hacienda has thus been an agent of progress (in the sense of modernization of the rural sector) while the peasantry has been conservative." Peasants calculated that the benefits of modernization would accrue primarily to other groups while they would have to bear the costs. [128]

How does this analysis fit into the preceding discussion of altiplano livestock estates? In order to stress the economic rationality of the Andean agrarian structure, Bertram and Martínez Alier confound and conflate the issue of the incorporation of peasants into the estate with the issue of alternative labor regimes, labor tenancy or wage labor. The expansion of the hacienda would be explicable by the same shift of relative factor costs as the expansion of hacienda demesne production. Indeed, these authors see both processes as essentially one and the same thing: in reaction to increasing commodity prices hacendados reclaimed old lands of the hacienda to which they possessed titles dating to colonial times but which they had not worked because of a lack of a market. This construct clearly does not explain the great majority of land transfers from peasants to hacendados in the altiplano during the late nineteenth and early twentieth centuries. It allows the authors to disregard issues of ideology and culture involved in the incorporation of peasants and their land into haciendas. From the perspective of the peasants, this process represented a totally distinct and much less cataclysmic change than did any attempt to switch from labor tenancy to wage labor, even though, from the perspective of the hacendado, both could be understood as reactions to changing relative prices.

Most authors writing on the Latin American hacienda, including Bertram, Hunt, and Martínez Alier, assume that estates held land far in excess of productive needs, primarily as a mechanism to pry loose labor from the Indian community sector. But this assertion is difficult to prove, and the case of the altiplano seems to contradict it. Land not regularly used by its putative owner was likely to be invaded by peasants or neighboring hacendados. When the market improved for livestock products after the 1850s, hacendados required both more labor and more land. The acquisition of land cannot be explained simply as a ploy to incorporate more labor into the estate. At the same time, the incorporation of more labor cannot be said to have been the *consequence* of the monopolization of land by hacendados. In fact, by the late 1910s, when the extraordinary expansion of the hacienda sector had largely run its course, additional labor requirements were, it appears, met less by transfers from the communities to the haciendas and more by shifts of colonos from one estate to another.[129]

During the phase of expansion the willingness of community peasants to work as colonos on estates should not be explained primarily by hacienda monopolization of land. More important factors were the increasing commercial dependence of peasants on gamonales eager to use their credit and compadrazgo relationships as a means to incorporate both the land and the labor of their clients into new or expanding estates; demographic pressures from within the peasant communities, which did not automatically derive from hacienda expansion itself; and finally the greater concentration of effective force in the hands of provincial hacendado elites. Altogether the significance of the shift from freeholder to colono, from the ideological perspective of the peasant, was perhaps less dramatic than commonly assumed. When peasants passed into the sphere of hacienda control, together with their families, their livestock, and their land, they were changing one patrón, the district governor or some other authority, for another, the hacendado. Gavin Smith has captured this shift aptly for the central Peruvian highlands by suggesting that hacienda expansion may be understood as part of a community coming under the sway of an hacendado, while not necessarily severing ties with and participation in the trunk community.[130]

Not only did hacienda colonos and community peasants have more in common and, indeed, show a greater overlap than usually assumed, but they also showed a similar kind of internal differentiation. The minority of colonos with no or very little livestock, and no or very little family labor to rely on, enjoyed considerably fewer benefits from their peasant enterprise than most others did. They were more open to the lures of modernizing estate owners when these sought to shift the balance of remunerations from usufruct rights to wage payments. Poor colonos relativize the notion of Martínez Alier and Bertram that dismissal from the estate was considered punishment. A small number of colonos in the altiplano were quite mobile by the early twentieth century, moving between estates in search of the best remunerations. Martínez Alier's argument that the situation of labor tenants was more favorable than that of community freeholders thus has to be specified both in terms of the period and the specific strata of colonos and types of estates.[131]

Only the massive transfer of land from the peasant sector to the estate sector between the late 1850s and 1920 created more favorable animal/land ratios in the estate sector than existed in communities of peasant freeholders. But even by 1910 or 1920 peasants integrated as colonos into newly formed small estates often had no more pastureland available for their own flocks than they had controlled previously as community freeholders.[132]

To understand the resilience of seigneurial livestock estates based on labor tenancy, we need to go beyond a consideration of commodity, labor, and land markets. Changes in these markets were a necessary condition for the transition toward capital-intensive agrarian enterprises using wage labor. But they were never sufficient to bring about these changes. The cost of capital, the high-risk environment, the neocolonial mode of constructing power, and peasant resistance to such power "explain" the reluctance of owners of seigneurial estates to undertake their modernization even when other relative factor costs favored such change.

Long-term credit for capital improvement projects continued to be unavailable in the altiplano during the early twentieth century, except for small amounts raised locally at usurious rates. Hacendados constantly feared attacks on their livestock, invasions of their pastures, and destruction of their installations. The massive transfer of land from peasant communities heightened these risks. Although the Peruvian state had sought to strengthen the legal guarantees for private property after the 1850s, this attempt proved largely ineffective in the altiplano. The same landholders who demanded guarantees for rural property owners relied on clientalism, the peasants' acceptance of charismatic authority, and, as an ultimate resort, violence to expand their holdings.

What Bertram called "class constellations" were closely connected to this high-risk environment; indeed, such constellations underlay the lack of definition of rights in resources. Most colonos resisted the improving landlords' attempts to banish their huaccho flocks and turn them into rural proletarians, and not merely because their own peasant enterprise generated more income than they could trust wages to do. Wealthy colonos such as the Mullisacas in Picotani, original residents of the place who for more than a century had raised their alpacas and sheep and exercised far-flung trading activities under the umbrella of the hacienda, but also many of the thousands of peasants recently incorporated into estates, did not consider the hacendados to be owners of the land they were working. They accepted the right of the hacendados to exploit the resources of their estates and to their family's labor, as long as the hacendados respected their rights to the usufruct of hacienda pastures and crop lands. The hacienda sector was highly successful in expanding its share of resources, including land, between the 1860s and 1920, but estate owners did not have the same free disposition over these resources that a capitalist entrepreneur enjoys.

It is misleading to speak of the hacendado as the progressive, modernizing element in the altiplano's rural economy of the early twentieth century, and the peasant, either in the community or on an estate, as the conservative force. Most hacendados, like most of the peasants, clung to labor-intensive, low-productivity methods of production not because they were intrinsically conservative but because they offered the most secure way to keep a tenuous hold on resources, especially land. Eventually, a minority of peasants, like their counterparts among the large landholders, sought to invest in more intensive exploitation of their estancias. There was no iron law that condemned them to becoming either proletarians or increasingly archaic peasants on shrinking plots of poor lands; they were not automatically condemned to exemplify the notions of either Lenin or Chayanov, as David Lehman has remarked. [133] The blocked development of productivity on the altiplano's haciendas, just as among the community peasants, cannot, in the last instance, be explained in terms of relative factor costs. It was the consequence of a neocolonial society in which rights to resources were contested and fragmentary and in which liberal notions of property and contract did not become fully accepted. As long as this colonial heritage remained strong, hacendados and peasants alike would waver between a profit-optimizing, high-risk strategy of investing into more intensive livestock production and the conventional risk-averting path of capital-extensive production embedded in social relations of hierarchy (patron-client relationships) and solidarity (within networks of family and friends). The seigneurial hacienda and the communal peasant economy formed two sides of the same coin.

The implementation of modern stock-raising methods on a broad scale presupposed their acceptance by the majority of hacendados, colonos, and community peasants alike and required multifaceted changes on individual estates. The successful introduction of such improvements as selective breeding, fencing, artificial pastures, and reductions of stocks in order to achieve optimal productivity per animal implied not merely technical changes but a major reorientation in the relations of production, intimately tied to the system of social stratification. Questions concerning the capital intensity of production were intertwined with the labor regime and the land tenure pattern. Selective breeding made sense only if hacendados could separate their own livestock from that of colonos. Providing sufficient fodder for hacienda livestock implied, at a minimum, limiting access of the colonos' huaccho flocks to estate pastures or even switching to a system of wage labor without usufruct rights. Reducing stock capital presupposed a land tenure pattern with universally recognized and respected borders.

Tied up with the capital-extensive agrarian complex of the altiplano was a whole sociopolitical system of domination, a value system and a life-style that gave even rather marginal hacendados a favorable place in provincial society. A livestock economy in which market forces reign unimpeded would have undermined this world, in which hacendados commanded respect as much for their family origin, social status, public office, and patterns of consumption as for their economic resources. [134] Introducing a system of wage labor would weaken the clientalistic, paternalistic structure of Azángaro's estates and society at large. Although the most affluent hacendados might have benefited from agrarian capitalism, the majority of estate owners would have seen their social status threatened.

Recently historians writing on large landed estates in Latin America during the "age of export economies" have sought to stress how much the institution changed during the decades between the continent's more intensive insertion into world markets through railroad and steamship and the Great Depression of 1929–32. Simon Miller concluded an article on Mexican cereal estates by arguing that "far from being a 'feudal' anachronism of artificial and foreign origins, the arable hacienda of the Mesa Central was in fact a dynamic and appropriate adaptation to nineteenth century Mexico and capable of significant capital accumulation."[135] Likewise, Michael Jimenez suggests that before 1930 coffee hacienda owners in Colombia's Cundinamarca state were "travelling far in grandfather's car" by consolidating recently formed or expanded estates and adapting them to changing labor and market conditions.[136]

We have certainly come a long way since the first third of this century, when indigenista, populist, liberal, or Marxist critics of the Spanish American hacienda decried it as feudal and archaic, an obstinate, anachronistic remnant of a long-passed colonial age. I have tried to show how the altiplano estate of the early twentieth century was the product of struggles over land and labor between various strata of hispanized landholders, community peasants, and labor tenants. It adapted to changing markets, transportation systems, commercial hierarchies, and power constellations in the province and nationally. It would not make much sense to view the altiplano hacienda at its apogee, the boom years between the 1890s and the end of World War I, as a mere remnant of the colonial regime. After all, half of the haciendas in 1920 had not existed a hundred years earlier. Most of their owners did not come from a closed, preexisting stratum of colonial large landholders; rather, they were the recent beneficiaries and protagonists of struggles with the peasantry, a self-made group of hacendados who skillfully and often ruthlessly exploited newly arising commercial and political opportunities.

Yet if we look inside the hacienda, at its labor regime and technical-economic aspects, we cannot avoid the conclusion that change came exceedingly piecemeal and slow, that hacendados adapted to new commercial opportunities primarily by expanding the scope of long-standing practices. Why did altiplano livestock ranchers travel less far in grandfather's car than did owners of Colombian coffee fincas or central Mexican cereal haciendas?

Part of the answer may lie in the nature of the production process. Altiplano ranching was highly decentralized, with different flocks and colonos' cabañas often miles apart. Centralized or centrally coordinated labor processes occupied no more than eight to ten weeks every year. Entrenched decentralized production processes such as these would have been difficult to turn around under any circumstances. Altiplano ranchers also had a certain amount of bad luck. In contrast to their Colombian colleagues, they were hit with a severe crisis and a period of volatile markets immediately on the tails of the great expansion of their landholdings, leaving them little time for internal consolidation and modernization. Hacendados were also hampered by the high cost of capital and difficulties of transportation, even though by the 1920s more roads had been constructed in Puno department than just about anywhere else in Peru.

But the fundamental problem was the very nature of the altiplano's hierarchical and segmented neocolonial society. By *neocolonialism* I am not referring primarily to any dependence that might have continued to tie the altiplano, now by strings of commerce rather than sovereignty, to an overseas metropolis. Rather, I am referring to the revitalized strength of a colonial mind-set polarizing society into Indians and Spaniards or whites; to the ambiguity, among all social groups in the altiplano, between clinging to the security in hierarchical or communal associations and taking advantage of new commercial opportunities; and to the willingness, or perhaps the perceived inevitability, of actors among all social groups to rely on force and violence in the pursuit of personal or group interests.

This neocolonialism of the altiplano's late nineteenth and early twentieth centuries socioeconomic and political matrix allowed large landholders to expand the land formally under their control but blocked the universal recognition of property rights and, hence, full rights of disposition for the hacendados. It allowed hacendados to integrate Indian laborers into their expanding domains at minimal costs but blocked the transition toward a wage-labor regime. Neocolonialism facilitated the cycle between the 1860s and 1920 in which hispanized landholders came to control an increasing share of altiplano resources, but it also constituted the basis of Indian peasant resistance against that expanded control.

The practices of paternalism, coercion, and violence, through which the hispanized provincial elite defined the community peasants and colonos as Indian and subordinate, reinforced the Indians' own perception of their identity as distinct and taught them the continued usefulness of communal solidarity and of maintaining their peasant livelihoods. In a real sense neocolonialism informed both the strength of the landlord offensive and the strength of peasant resistance against it. The peak of hacienda expansion nearly coincided with the hacendados' attempts to initiate internal transformations on their domain and the peasants' "internal" and "external" resistance against both. When this resistance was followed, in 1920, by the collapse of the booming market for wools, hacendados and peasants, the minority of modernizers and the majority of "traditionalists" among both groups, entered a new phase of stalemate.

9   Conclusion

Gamonales Aren't Forever

The Main Threads of the Story

We have now followed the winding and interwoven trails of Azángaro's history for some one hundred and fifty years, and it is necessary to seek high ground allowing us to look back and discern the major direction of these trails. Several turning points mark the trajectory of the region's society and economy: the 1780s, the 1850s, and the 1920s. The middle decades of the eighteenth century were a period of growth for the northern altiplano, fostered by the recovery of silver mining in High Peru and Cuzco's booming woolen industry, which drew its raw materials from livestock herders in Azángaro and neighboring provinces. Encouraged by Bourbon enlightened notions about property, provincial elites sought to convert informal exploitation of Indian communal land and labor, hitherto justified by notions of reciprocity, into formalized estates with a resident labor force. Hacienda formation continued strongly for much of the eighteenth century. Although the altiplano's population recovered vigorously from the epidemics of the late seventeenth and early eighteenth centuries, population density remained low. Land was not scarce in absolute terms; it had monetary value only in conjunction with livestock. Nevertheless, conflicts over land rose sharply after midcentury, both among community peasants and among the communities, their kurakas, and other sectors of the hispanized provincial elite. Bourbon policy limited the lands each community could hold according to its population and sold "excess lands" to private landholders. Affluent peasants increasingly relied on landholdings in fee simple. But the major challenge for the livelihood of the communal peasantry was posed by the growth of forced surplus extractions, in the form of repartos de bienes, and taxes and fees levied by crown and church. During the 1760s and 1770s the peasant economy was threatened primarily through harsher terms of the colonial tributary mode of production.

The era of crisis and gradual realignment began during the 1780s and lasted until the mid-1850s. Competition from European textile imports, the semisecular decline of Upper Peru's silver production, and, after independence, rising transport costs coincided with depressed prices. Elite-controlled trading circuits between Upper and Lower Peru gradually decayed. The division of the former "Andean space," first into separate viceroyalties and later into distinct republics, drove the disruption of commercial circuits forward. Complementary exchange relations between peasants fared better during these decades.

The Túpac Amaru Rebellion marks the onset of the era of crisis and realignment for the northern altiplano, as it exacerbated the contradictions of the Bourbons' political economy. The colonial authorities relied both on repression and limitations of elite surplus extraction to regain control over the communal peasantry in the Andean highlands. They sought to halt the consolidation of haciendas but could not bring themselves to implement their protoliberal property notions on disputed crown lands or in the peasant communities. Estates of kurakas, the church, and private hispanized entrepreneurs lost land to peasant squatters. In the last decades before independence a sense of uncertainty permeated social and property relations in the altiplano. To say that the peasants lost the Túpac Amaru Rebellion is only half true.

The agrarian reform laws of the 1820s helped to consolidate the gains that peasants had achieved through land occupations and lifted the corporate character from the communities. But early republican governments did not challenge social hierarchies in the communities, as they sought to stabilize revenue collection from the head tax. With demand for labor stagnant, elite-controlled trade in disarray, the land base more secure, and per capita collections of head tax and of other forms of surplus extraction diminished, the Indian community peasantry enjoyed a brief interval of enhanced autonomy, crucial for its capacity to withstand the gamonal onslaught that was to come.

During the first three postindependence decades a new provincial elite gradually took shape and sought to set the criteria for social stratification. The disintegration of the colonial system of domination, based largely on state-sanctioned surplus extraction, laid bare a social landscape that was "Indian" to a surprising extent. Except for parish priests and a handful of large landholding families of colonial origin, the emerging provincial elite thus pulled itself up by its own bootstraps from modest backgrounds. The tools to do so were provided by opportunities in trade and control over public office, avenues to power intertwined in broadening clientele networks. It was only during the early 1850s that traders and large landholders in the northern altiplano relinquished all hopes of reconstructing colonial trading circuits and fully embraced the exportation of wools as the inevitable base for provincial trade. And only the upswing of the export economy during the 1850s provided the fiscal wherewithal to stabilize political power on the provincial and local levels. The emerging hispanized elite relied on notions gleaned from the ascending European bourgeois civilization—the importance of private property, education, and "modern" patterns of consumption—to establish its difference from the vast majority of Indian community peasants and estate colonos and to buttress its claim to exclusive exercise of political power and leadership in the province. The Indians now became those "barbarians" who did not embrace the hallmarks of a progressive civilization, and by the late nineteenth century their distinctness was increasingly described in racial terms. Although income and property distribution was gradated between the most affluent large landholding families and the poorest peasants, with a considerable overlap between marginal finca owners, small traders, and affluent peasants, altiplano society became polarized sociopolitically.

The redefinition of the Indians from a historic corporate group to an intrinsically distinct racial group outside of the pale of civilization came to form the basis of the neocolonial relationship between the peasantry and the provincial elite. It justified enhanced surplus extraction by local authorities and the increasing incorporation of community peasants into estates as colonos. The self-made gamonal elite invested its growing power to convert the Indian peasantry into directly dependent clients in the spheres of both commercialization and production. But this was a dialectical process. One could equally say that it was the growing gamonal control over Indian land and labor and over the peasants' commodities in the marketplace that constituted the essence of the provincial elite's growing power. The gamonales, rural bosses in the districts and the province, constructed their own position in society both through intimacy with the peasant world, from whence many had come themselves, and through difference from that world.

Between the 1850s and 1920 the wool export trade was the motor of the economy of the altiplano and of much of southern Peru, just as silver mining had been during the colonial period. Although export volumes grew only modestly, rising international prices delivered growing incomes to producers and traders. Decreasing costs of international transport and the devaluation of Peruvian and Bolivian currencies augmented regional returns on the export trade. Articulated through the rail line between the altiplano and the port of Mollendo, the wool export business created a dendritic pattern of trade throughout much of southern Peru. It fostered a new spatial pattern of commerce centered on the entrepôt Arequipa and slowly marginalized exchanges with the Bolivian altiplano. The wool export economy helped define a common southern Peruvian identity that had first appeared in the political struggles during the Túpac Amaru Rebellion and Peru's postindependence civil wars. After an interim phase in which prominent altiplano merchants acted quite autonomously as wool bulkers, merchant bankers, and distributors of European imports, in the late 1880s the Arequipa export houses began to extend their influence in the production zone through a hierarchical system of agencies and itinerant wool buyers. Traders and producers alike became increasingly dependent on credit from the Arequipa firms. Although competitive on each level of trade, wool buyers sought to create local monopolies and firmly tie producers to themselves. By the early twentieth century peasants were eager to participate in trade but bitterly resented and resisted the ruses and violence of hispanized traders and local authorities that greatly diminished their returns on every deal.

Regional trade in foodstuffs, stimulants, textiles, household goods, and building materials grew in tandem with wool exports. Although imports gradually led to a restructuring of processing industries, artisanal production did not vanish; in fact, local processing of wools grew more rapidly than wool exports did during the late nineteenth and early twentieth centuries. Low productivity, in both the agrarian sector and processing, in association with the neocolonial system of domination, kept income levels low for most people in the region and precluded an advancing division of labor. In addition, high transport costs, even after the establishment of the rail link, and maintenance of localized fashions and tastes and of long-standing personalized exchange relations among peasants in various ecological zones contributed to keep regional artisanal production competitive with imports and the modest beginnings of import-substituting industries.

Fueled by the rise of the wool export trade, old and new hispanized large landholders acquired an unprecedented amount of land from community peasants to found new livestock estates and expand old ones. Land purchases were correlated with fluctuations in the demand for wool and the price of livestock. Only as an outcome of this massive process of hacienda expansion, swallowing between one-fourth and one-third of Azángaro's usable lands in the short span of some sixty years, did livestock haciendas come to control the majority of land in the altiplano. The number of haciendas and fincas in Azángaro province more than doubled between the 1820s and 1940, with most new estates founded since the 1850s. Most of the new foundations remained small, cobbled together by traders, officials, and established landholding families through the acquisition of small strings of peasant estancias. Some two dozen haciendas had become very large indeed by World War I. All large haciendas had their origin in colonial estates, expanding rapidly during the late nineteenth and early twentieth centuries by incorporating other estates and numerous peasant holdings. Church property, much of it operated through long-term leaseholds, survived virtually undiminished until the second decade of the present century.

The distance between the income and wealth of families owning large estates and most other hacendado families had grown since the mid-nineteenth century. Most affluent hacendado families could hold on to their landholdings for three or more generations and found ways to avoid splintering their properties through inheritance. Indeed, revisionist writers on Latin American haciendas may have overemphasized the rate of sales of haciendas, as they failed to consider frequent intrafamily contracts. Hacendados realized the central importance of family cohesion for holding on to the family's estate and social position.

Despite the enormous upswing in land transfers, it would be misleading to speak of a land market in the altiplano around 1900. There was no open marketplace for land. Perfect strangers, without social or family ties, political power, or business connections in the province, normally had no way of knowing what was "for sale" and virtually no chance at all of buying rural property. In most cases the notarial bill of sale, which purported to be a contract between free and equal agents, in fact inscribed a long-standing relation of dependency or, worse, a fait accompli based on deceit or violence. Over the sixty-five years of the wool export economy, prices for haciendas gradually came to reflect market conditions, and the custom of "conventional prices," changing only with major long-term economic shifts, gave way. But as late as 1920 prices for peasant lands still reflected specific social constellations between seller and buyer rather than supply and demand.

A fully developed land market is intimately connected to the notion of private property, as defined by laws and sanctioned by the state's law enforcement and judicial agencies. Such a notion was not unequivocally accepted in the altiplano. Land invasions, vague land boundaries, and livestock rustling remained pandemic. The ambivalence toward private property was shared by community peasants and large landholders. Members of the provincial elite made fine speeches about the "defense of private property," which was, after all, one of the key planks of the worldview through which they hoped to distinguish themselves from the Indian peasantry. Yet in moving border posts, leading their livestock onto neighbors' fields, impounding neighbors' livestock, and, *manu militari*, occupying lands claimed by others, they were ready to disregard precepts of private property if in doing so they could broaden their own control over land. The courts, the notaries, and the land registry office in Puno functioned not as indisputable arbiters and guarantors of property rights but as arenas for contesting power between various gamonales and their clients. A title deed, highly prized by peasants and landholders alike, served not as a symbol of indisputable rights but as one of various tools or weapons wielded in the struggle over land. Possession of land required its unchallenged, habitual use or the effective projection of power up to the borders one claimed. A property title, without use or power over the land, did not guarantee possession.

In parcialidades and ayllus corporate communal landholding became rare after the agrarian reform of the 1820s. During the following century it was largely the patrilineal family descent groups, embedded within the communities, that continued the practice of common usufruct of pastures. With higher livestock and population densities and the growing market opportunities for livestock products, however, the sharing of pasture commons came under pressure in the family descent groups. Communal solidarity remained important on other levels. As gamonales increasingly used the parcialidades' hierarchy of officeholders to extract labor, commodities, and money, the locus of that solidarity often shifted to sectors of peasants within the old communities, the family descent groups, for example.

The number of autonomous rural peasant settlements grew sharply during the early decades of the twentieth century, and the principales were losing their grip on the community population. These shifts were closely connected to the penetration of market forces in the communities' social stratification. Inequality, nothing new in the communities, increasingly came to be based on economic factors. But that did not diminish the need or the practice of communal solidarity, in defense of land, in resistance to arbitrary demands by authorities, in common work projects, and in celebrations. As long as provincial and local elites construed their power in juxtaposition to an Indian peasantry marked as inferior and different, communal organizations, expressions of ethnic identity and defense, would remain strong.

The number of colonos residing on livestock estates increased greatly between the late 1850s and 1920. Most were the former owners of the estancias that new and old estates were incorporating. Because the colonos maintained their autonomous peasant economy, often even continuing to reside on their former land, the change in their way of life and their income was less dramatic than has often been assumed. The majority of hacendados did not have the capital resources required to attempt a change to capital-intensive methods of production. Like the officeholders in the districts, they continued to exercise a paternalistic authority, all encompassing and fragile at the same time. In most of the small fincas and some of the largest haciendas the owner's control over resources remained strictly limited, and often the colonos together held as much livestock as their patrón. The minority of hacendados who sought to build highly productive livestock enterprises based on wage labor encountered massive colono resistance. Change to a wage labor regime here occurred in a painstakingly slow process between the 1920s and the 1950s.

The Crisis of the 1920s

The years around 1920 mark a sea change for the rural society of the northern altiplano, a change in the constellation of forces no less important than that initiated by the Túpac Amaru Rebellion 140 years earlier. Three strands of development, entangled in their causes and effects, brought about this epochal shift: a crisis in the wool trade and its economic repercussions for the estates; the mobilization of community peasants, estate colonos, and certain urban middle-class sectors; and population growth. When the Great Depression hit the altiplano economy during the early 1930s, it merely reaffirmed what had become clear during the preceding decade: the exportation of wools and other livestock products had ceased to be the motor of growth; the transfer of land from peasant communities into the hacienda sector had diminished and in some cases had even begun to be reversed; the years of prosperity and upward social mobility were over for many hacendado families; and population pressures were beginning to hurt the majority of Indian peasant families in the diminished domains of their communities. Yet none of the social forces in the region was able to impose an alternative model of economic growth. Instead, the altiplano's economy and society entered a long phase of stalemate that held until the agrarian reform of 1969.

The decade between 1915 and 1925 witnessed the most widespread peasant movements in the altiplano since the early 1780s. This cycle of peasant unrest had actually begun during the mid-1890s, in the aftermath of fiscal and administrative reforms introduced by the Piérola administration. During the following decade community peasants protested and fought against the new state monopoly on salt, the increased collection of rural property taxes, and the myriad fees, fines, labor services, and forced sales imposed on them by local and provincial officialdom.[1]

A few years later, between 1909 and 1913, at the height of the land-grabbing frenzy, Azángaro's community peasantry adopted more militant forms of resistance to the expansion of estates. In 1911 peasants from neighboring communities attacked and sacked Hacienda Cuturi of Luis

Felipe Luna in Arapa. In 1909–10 Hilahuata community in Chupa district sought to resist its forced conversion into a livestock estate by José Angelino Lizares Quiñones, resulting in brutal reprisals at the hands of local authorities and troops called in from Puno. In 1913 community peasants from Saman and adjacent districts fought against the land grabbing and other abuses of a local gamonal, Mariano Abarca Dueñas, a small-time coca and alcohol trader who had cobbled together a livestock estate, San Juan, since the 1890s through violence and deceit. After threatening to take the little town of Saman, power base of Abarca Dueñas and his allies, the peasants attacked Hacienda San Juan. A few months later, encouraged by the central government's promise to send an investigative commission, they ceased to recognize the local authorities and again sacked San Juan and several haciendas in neighboring Caminaca district. Answering pleas of local authorities and large landholders, the prefect of Puno sent a detachment of soldiers and gendarmes to "pacify" the zone. More than a hundred peasants were killed in the ensuing unequal battles.[2]

These early movements remained local affairs, limited in their goals to the removal of a specific abuse or grievance. Yet they made use of strategies and advanced a type of awareness that would come to fruition after 1920. They seized on political openings on the national level, as during the mildly reformist administrations of Manuel Candamo (1903–4) and Guillermo Billinghurst (1912–14), or on the local level, encouraged by the appointment of a sympathetic district governor or subprefect. Peasant resistance was inserted into local power struggles between gamonales and their clients in which disputes over land became entangled with competition for elective and appointed offices. The altiplano's provincial elite of the early twentieth century was far from united. Divisions between gamonales deepened, and clientele systems to a certain extent solidified after 1895. Provincial and district-level branches of Peru's three major parties (Civilistas, Demócratas, and Constitucionalistas) inscribed vertical alliances in party rolls, from leading hacendados down to small finca owners, shopkeepers, and even Indian peasants. In the struggle for power gamonales allowed no quarter. If they were united, on principle, in despising the Indians and brutally repressing peasant resistance, they used and even quietly supported such acts of resistance against elite competitors.[3]

When petitions and court cases failed to stop land grabbers and exploitive authorities, communities dispatched "messengers" to Lima. Aided by sympathetic middle-class intermediaries, they sought to present grievances to representatives of the central government and publicized them in the national press. During the early years of the twentieth century the "Indian problem" began to attract growing attention among intellectuals and public figures in the capital, and even conservative politicians close to the Civilista oligarchy, such as Manuel Vicente Villarán, began to call for protective legislation for Indians.[4] Reformist administrations dispatched commissions to the highlands, especially to the department of Puno, to investigate reports of abusive or illegal practices and forced appropriations of lands committed by public authorities or powerful citizens.[5] In the altiplano a small but growing number of educated urbanites, among them young lawyers, journalists, schoolteachers, and even a few priests, were willing to defend Indians, to promote their rights, and to name the names of abusive gamonales. Not infrequently these budding indigenistas were themselves children of hacendados, swayed by the growing rhetoric denouncing "feudal" haciendas. Francisco Chukiwanka Ayulo, for example, a spokesperson for the Asociación Pro-Derecho Indígena in Puno and staunch defender of Indian peasants, was the son of Juana Manuela Choquehuanca, descendant of the ancient kuraka family and, until 1893, owner of Hacienda Picotani.[6]

The Rumi Maqui Rebellion of 1915–16 elevated the struggle to a higher level of integration, planning, and staying power. The rebellion erupted on the night of December 1, 1915, when several hundred peasants attacked first Hacienda Atarani, San Anton district, property of Alejandro Choquehuanca, and then moved on to Bernardino Arias Echenique's Hacienda San José. Forewarned by the drums, *pututos* (bullhorns), and screams of the approaching peasants, a handful of well-armed estate employees took up defensive positions in a small tower at the back of the caserío—probably constructed for this purpose. From there they randomly fired into the crowd of attackers who had surged into the patio of the building, seeking to plunder it and to set it on fire. When the peasants fled at dawn, the defenders had killed between 10 and 132 of them. More were killed when San José's employees hunted down fleeing peasants in the surrounding countryside. In mid-January 1916, after scouring the area's communities, the hacendado's bands apprehended José Maria Turpo, who had led the peasants and was wounded in the attack and whom Arias Echenique and his men had for years considered one of their most dangerous opponents among the peasants. On the spot Turpo was tortured and barbarously executed by being dragged by galloping horses over rocky ground for two miles.[7]

This rebellion was again inserted into the struggles between various gamonales, so much so that authors sympathetic to the cause of the Indians flatly denied that there had been a rebellion at all and saw the whole affair as a confabulation of one gamonal band, seeking to hurt their enemies and to justify the slaughter of peasants. Yet recent studies by Augusto Ramos Zambrano and Luis Bustamante Otero leave no doubt that a peasant movement of rather large proportions had indeed been organized.

Why was this rebellion so important? In the first place, it linked the coordination and ideological projection of an outsider with mounting resistance of local peasant groups. The outsider was Teodomiro Gutiérrez Cuevas, the man sent by President Billinghurst in 1913 to investigate the conflicts in Saman. A midlevel military officer with a checkered career, Gutiérrez Cuevas had held various administrative posts in Puno and other parts of Peru since the early years of the century. He combined a conviction in the need to "redeem" the Indian through education and legal reforms with a certain anarchist orientation. After the overthrow of Billinghurst he fled to Chile and became convinced that only a militant movement of the peasants themselves could bring the needed changes. In September 1915 he clandestinely returned to the northern altiplano and established contact with José Maria Turpo and other peasants who had been meeting locally since July to plan actions aimed at blocking further land appropriations in the parcialidades of San Antón and San José districts by Bernardino Arias Echenique. Because of Gutiérrez Cuevas's work, peasants from the districts of San José, San Antón, Asillo, Santiago de Pupuja, Arapa, Chupa, Achaya, Saman, and Taraco as well as from the neighboring province of Sandia took part in the December 1 attack. In the few letters and manifestoes found to date Gutiérrez Cuevas called himself "Rumi Maqui" (Quechua for "Hand of Stone") , "General and Supreme Director of the indigenous pueblos and armed forces of the Federal State of Tahuantinsuyo" (a Quechua term for the Inca Empire), "Restorer of the Indians," and "Supreme Chief of the Indian pueblos and Generalissimo of their armies."[8] He proceeded to appoint leaders (cabecillas) of this nascent federal state in a number of districts; these leaders did not come from the ranks of established community authorities.

Rumi Maqui stressed the autonomy of individual Indian pueblos within a federal state that was to reunite Peru with Bolivia. This federalism, with its Incaic overtones, had been suggested a few years earlier by Azángaro's powerful gamonal, José Angelino Lizares Quiñones.[9] Rumi Maqui intended to destroy the rule of the gamonales in order to restore justice and liberty for "my loyal friends, the Indians of Puno." From the perspective of the Indians, modern authors have seen the Rumi Maqui Rebellion as a new manifestation of millenarianism in the southern Andes, as the expectation of a pachacuti, the Andean notion of a turning point of cosmic dimensions and the beginning of a new era through which what was below would be on top and vice versa. Indians would supplant the hispanized population in positions of power, the communities would get back the lands appropriated by estates, and the Incas would return.[10] Or at least these were the goals imputed to the movement by the altiplano's elite, always ready to dramatize and ridicule Indian peasant resistance in order to underscore the hopeless distance between themselves and the "Indian barbarians" and justify the call for massive repression.

Gutiérrez Cuevas no doubt sought to invoke the peasants' memories of a mythic past remembered as just. During a time when educated serranos had begun to show pride in Peru's prehispanic civilizations, Indian communities themselves at times defended their interests by exalting selectively remembered traditions going back to the seventeenth century or earlier: from the insistence on real or fabricated colonial property titles, to the secret collection of a colonial fee to meet expenses in the protection of lands (*rama*), to renewed use of colonial communal offices (south of Lake Titicaca in Bolivia's Pacajes province).[11] But these memories were mobilized to serve new goals squarely arising out of early twentieth-century political, economic, or cultural conflicts. The peasants attacking Hacienda San José did not fight to strengthen the old parcialidades or ayllus that had claimed the solidarity of Azángaro's peasantry during much of the nineteenth century. In the extant documents Turpo, the recognized peasant leader of the attack, is referred to as coming from Estancia Soratira in San Antón district, the landholding of the Turpo linear descent group. The family had fought Arias Echenique's attempts to incorporate the estancia into San José for years.[12] There is no evidence to suggest that Turpo or any other peasant participating in the Rumi Maqui Rebellion held high office in the old parcialidades. On the contrary, in one communication from early 1916, in which peasants of San José and San Antón detailed the persecution to which they had been subjected since the previous December and enumerated their grievances, they bitterly complained about the actions of "principales y autoridades," a formula that would reappear in the peasant movement of the early 1920s.[13] The Rumi Maqui movement was fighting against not only gamonales appropriating peasant land but also segundas, hilacatas, and alcaldes in the parcialidades, perhaps because they belonged to the political clientele of the gamonal enemy. But the insurrectionists also wanted to be free from the extractions organized by principales and district authorities for their own benefit. Some of those participating in the attack were fairly affluent peasants who had previously bought land and owned large livestock flocks.

In brief, the Rumi Maqui Rebellion conjoined the struggle against land-grabbing hacendados and abusive local authorities with the emancipation of dynamic groups within the parcialidades from oppressive communal authorities. The fight against powerful hacendados and their political clientele at the onset of the World War I export boom expressed a heightened militancy in the struggle for resources of growing commercial value. As wool prices began their dramatic rise, many community peasants were less and less willing to see benefits from the windfall taken away by hacendados seeking to monopolize land and "principales y autoridades" seeking to monopolize trade.[14] The Rumi Maqui Rebellion coincides with the moment when land purchases between Indian peasants were increasing notably, further evidence for the strengthening of a group of affluent peasants eager to exploit market opportunities.

The Indian leaders of the Rumi Maqui Rebellion combined the drive for unimpeded control over their properties and commodities with an assertion of greater political autonomy, expressed in millenarian and Incaic terms. This discourse fit their political strategy perfectly. On the one hand, it was precisely what their urban indigenista allies expected from them and could easily translate into progressive-liberal or anarchist notions of equality and justice, federalism and local autonomy. On the other hand, it gave them an ideological lever to gain support from poorer families in the communities who were in less of a position to benefit from newly arising commercial opportunities. It would thus allow them to reconstruct solidarity around new communities, split off from the old parcialidades and freed from impositions by the old village authorities.

The importance of the Rumi Maqui Rebellion lies in its combination of concrete socioeconomic goals with a political agenda, of a millenarian discourse with the drive for more economic and political autonomy. In economic terms dynamic peasant groups wished to take advantage of opportunities offered by the market without obstacles interposed by large landholders and political authorities. At the same time they were seeking to strengthen their political autonomy and cultural identity by reconstructing communal solidarity on a new, more voluntary and associational basis.[15] Peasants invoked idealized memories of autonomous communities because power continued to be held by gamonales, at times supported by the central state. The reconstruction of community was the inevitable counterpart to the hispanized provincial elite's reconstruction of the colonial dichotomy of conquerors and conquered, now transformed into a simplified and racist dichotomy between civilized whites and Indian barbarians. The insistence on re-creating new community structures since the 1910s and 1920s should not be misunderstood as the reassertion of some innate, atavistic "Indianness" in which a specific form of communal social economy and Indian cultural identity are one and the same thing. Rather, Indian peasants insisted on communal solidarity, adjusting its form to shifting economic, political, and cultural conditions, as long as it offered a measure of protection against a harsh power structure erected and maintained by provincial elites in neocolonial, dichotomized terms. Gamonal-ismo and Indian communalism conditioned each other.

The Rumi Maqui Rebellion only began to express this reorientation of the altiplano peasantry's economic, political, and cultural thinking and acting, and it is likely that the majority of peasants still remained loyal to the old principales. But the rebellion began to shift the constellation of forces in Azángaro, and it lasted much longer than the frustrated attack on Hacienda San José suggests. Clandestine meetings and contacts between various communities were held as early as mid-1915, and in late August, Bernardino Arias Echenique's lawyer alerted the provincial authorities that a general rebellion was being planned by community Indians to "recon-quer" all hacienda lands.[16] After the attack on Hacienda San José two army battalions were dispatched to the northern altiplano to "pacify" the region. Dozens of peasants were killed in the sweep of the troops and police forces through the provinces of Azángaro, Huancané, Sandia, and Puno. New reports of peasants massing to attack haciendas came in from widely dispersed districts as late as mid-January 1916.

In the meantime the national press had begun to discuss the abuses committed by Bernardino Arias Echenique, José Sebastian Urquiaga, and other altiplano large landholders. For the first time these men, important members of provincial society who had access to the officials in the national capital, saw themselves as the objects of a campaign denouncing their life's work of building large estates as exploitive, feudal, and antiprogressive. Even as demand for their estates' principal products was reaching unprec-edented heights toward the end of World War I, the transfer of land from the peasants to estates began to slow down.

A sharp slump of the international wool market during much of 1920 and 1921 ushered in a period of economic instability in southern Peru.[17] Wool prices continued to rise in international markets until early 1920. Because of postwar demobilization and the reestablishment of prewar supply channels, prices on the Liverpool market then fell by some 55 percent over a one-year period. In Peru prices had begun to fall earlier, from 50.5 pence per pound for first-class sheep wool in September 1918 to 39.5 pence in March 1920. Speculating that still higher international prices could be achieved, Arequipa exporters had begun to stockpile wools in 1919 and reduced demand in the production zones. When the Liverpool market collapsed in the second quarter of 1920, the consequences in southern Peru were particularly severe. The exporters, with their warehouses filled to capacity, reduced purchases to an absolute minimum, and some ceased buying wools altogether. By 1921 southern Peru's sheep wool exports had fallen by nearly four-fifths of the peak volume in 1917, totaling under 600 tons; alpaca wool exports declined by nearly two-thirds from 1918 peak volumes to just over 1,100 tons. Prices for first-class sheep wool fell from 39.5 pence per pound in March 1920 to 20.5 pence in December and 11.5 pence by September 1921, just over one-fifth of 1918 peak prices. A modest recovery for sheep wool prices began only in late 1922, whereas alpaca wools stagnated at below 30 percent of 1918 peak prices for most of the decade.[18]

The commercial crisis affected all sectors of altiplano society—large and small traders, estate owners, and community peasants—and produced ripple effects throughout southern Peru. Many retail merchants and wool-buying agents withdrew from trade.[19] Hacendados had taken up loans from the Arequipa export houses during the boom years, to be repaid with the expected high-priced wool clip and secured by mortgages on their estates.[20] As wool prices plummeted, many hacendados could not repay their debts. Merchants from Arequipa and Juliaca foreclosed on overdue debts, and for the first time the regional mercantile oligarchy acquired altiplano estates on a significant scale.[21] Several of Azángaro's large haciendas, including Posoconi, Purina, Huasacona, and, a bit later, San José, passed into the hands of export houses in Arequipa and Juliaca.[22] Community peasants and estate owners alike sought to restrict wool sales and postpone the clip. But faced with reductions in cash income of up to 80 percent, such restriction was not always possible. Small and large livestock producers alike were outraged at what they saw as arbitrary price slashing by the merchants.[23] The rift between producers and middlemen, covered up in the long phase of trade expansion, now came to the surface.

The crash of the wool market in 1920 brought the crisis for hacendados, gamonales, wool merchants, and the system of domination they had gradually constructed to its head. "Major uprisings rocked the zone; general lawlessness peaked; Indians and landowners each banded together for defense and/or mutual aid; political agitators roamed the highlands."[24] A "seismic wave" of rebellions and other forms of peasant resistance engrossed nearly every highland province of Puno and Cuzco departments between 1920 and 1923.[25] Social tensions came to a boiling point through a compounding of crises. The long-standing conflicts of altiplano society became more explosive with the profound slump of the wool trade. During his first four years in office President Augusto Leguía (1919–30) sought support against the Civilista oligarchy among the middle class, university students, southern regionalists, and, briefly, organized labor. Employing reformist rhetoric, he effectively opened political space through which the deepening social conflicts could come to the surface. This political opening coincided with a radicalization among middle and popular classes, especially in the provinces, where students and professionals adapted the bewildering array of new European ideologies, from fascism to bolshevism, to the conditions of regional society and politics.

The "Indian problem" now rapidly emerged as the core issue in a growing debate about Peru's national identity. Rooted in deep-seated social and ideological tensions, indigenismo rose to center stage aided by Leguía's "official indigenismo," as expressed by the recognition of the Indian community in the 1920 constitution, the opening of a Bureau of Indian Affairs in 1921, and his sponsorship of a bombastic but largely ineffective national "Patronage of the Indian Race." Indigenista reformers in Puno pursued two goals. By insisting on legal reforms improving the condition of Indian colonos and community peasants, they hoped to weaken the gamonales' hold on political power. By focusing on Indian cultural heritage and the distinct make-up of regional society, explained in terms of the altiplano's racial composition and the "telluric forces" of its stark environment, they sought regional autonomy from Lima's centralism. Although fighting for their own agenda, urban professionals, artisans, and students who embraced indigenismo and were willing to speak out for the Indian peasantry were becoming more numerous and more vociferous by the early 1920s.[26]

In June 1920 President Leguía appointed a commission charged with investigating the rising tide of complaints from Indians in Puno. When the commissioners arrived in Azángaro, "8,000 Indians in military formation and carrying sticks and a few guns" were there to meet them, ready to present their grievances.[27] A frightened provincial elite accused the commission of fostering an Indian rebellion. Hacendados sent a barrage of furious telegrams to the central government in Lima, demanding the withdrawal of the commission and the dispatch of troops. Although the commission heard some ten thousand cases and documented the severity of the conflict over land, especially in Azángaro province, it did not have the authority to settle them, although often encouraging Indians to pursue their claims.[28]

For the first time Indian peasants throughout the southern highlands felt encouraged to organize openly. In 1921 migrant peasants from the sierra founded the Comité Pro-Derecho Indígena "Tawantinsuyo" in Lima, and local branches were rapidly established in the provinces and districts of the altiplano. From 1921 to 1923, before the organization lost its effectiveness, the Comité's national congresses passed detailed reform resolutions. They demanded the establishment of schools and medical services in each community and hacienda, the return of community lands, new local authorities under direct control of the communities, better wages and working conditions for colonos, separation of church and state, and abolition of forced labor for road construction, recently introduced by President Leguía. This reformist program was packaged in redemptionist discourse containing both millenarian and anarcho-syndicalist elements.[29] The Comité's vision was disseminated in many parcialidades of the altiplano through delegates returning from Lima and through indigenista and labor movement papers, apparently read aloud in community assemblies.[30]

Put on the defensive by the double crisis of a severe commercial slump and unprecedented peasant mobilizations, hacendados for the first time organized leagues and held congresses to discuss "the Indian problem." In a memorandum to President Leguía of February 15, 1921, the Sociedad Ganadera del Departamento de Puno, representing more than ninety owners of livestock estates, feigned absolute innocence and defenselessness in the wave of rural violence sweeping the altiplano. "Our shepherds and we are victims of the theft and the attacks by community Indians; but these employ every possible means and false promises to demoralize them [the hacienda shepherds], to incite them to rebellion, imbuing them with hate and rancor against us." They blamed outside agitators for the unrest and were especially bitter about the government commission for its "little tact and its imprudence" in favoring community peasants. They demanded that the government should disavow the commission report, station more police and military in the altiplano provinces, and conduct military trials for captured "ringleaders" of the peasants.[31]

Up to 1920 peasant resistance had been directed primarily against local officialdom and land usurpations by hacendados. After 1920 patterns of commercialization and the situation within the livestock estates also became focal points of the peasant movement, resulting in a broadening of its social base. Bands of peasants attacked strings of llamas and mules transporting wool belonging to traders or hacendados, something that had never happened before. The depressed wool trade made the use of deceit and force in the marketplace insufferable for many Indian stock herders. In one case they grabbed a trader's scales, symbol of such trickery. Some hacendados delayed their wool remittances for fear of losing their crop.[32]

Attacks on livestock estates multiplied between 1920 and 1923, at least eight distinct instances being reported in Azángaro province alone.[33] At times these attacks were carried out by peasants from nearby communities, the pattern that had prevailed during the previous decade, but colonos now joined in or even organized the actions on their own. In some cases, as when the colonos took control of the sprawling latifundium Lauramarca in Cuzco's Canchis province for over a year in 1922–23, they demanded the hacienda's transformation into a community.[34] In other cases colonos rejected attempts to cut back their usufruct rights and other customary privileges. Colonos demonstrated that they continued to prize their autonomous peasant economy and that no principal social barrier existed between them and community peasants.

The climax of the peasant movement came in late 1923 in events centering on a community in Huancané province, with repercussions through much of the northern altiplano. After long judicial procedures and representations before President Leguía in Lima, the comuneros of Huancho in Huancané, on the border of Azángaro province, began to boycott that urban market and refused to render any more labor services for the hispanized authorities. Led by local members of the Comité Pro-Derecho Indígena "Tawantinsuyo," they proceeded to build a new, politically autonomous urban center in their community, which they named Huancho-Lima because it was based on the street outlay of the capital. They allotted ample space for a school and the church, designated special streets for the various artisanal trades, appointed new political authorities and a committee of public hygiene, and prohibited the speaking of Aymara. Most important, they established a weekly market on the plaza of their new city. The idea caught on, with other communities in Azángaro and Huancané provinces holding their own autonomous markets and heeding the calls of messengers from Huancho-Lima to cease recognition of local authorities.

For reasons that are still unclear, in December 1923 the people of Huancho began an offensive. According to one author, an Indian congress with delegates from the whole department of Puno was held in the new town, demanding abolition of the *envarados* (the old communal authorities, now seen as tools for exploitive hispanized authorities), return of lands appropriated by haciendas, foundation of rural schools, and punishment of those assassinating Indian leaders. These concrete political goals were again capped by a call for restoration of the Tahuantinsuyo.[35] In mid-December the Huanchinos attacked the Lizares Quiñones's Hacienda Caminacoya in Azángaro's Chupa district, scene of bloody confrontations in 1909–10, and assaulted a string of mules transporting wool for a Juliaca merchant. They then besieged the provincial capital of Huancané, bastion of the political bosses and hispanized commercial monopolies they wished to shake off. Many communities throughout Huancané province and adjacent areas in Azángaro also rose up and supported the siege. The hispanized townspeople, led by a particularly ruthless cabal of gamonales, were prepared for this offensive; they broke the siege and by late December had begun a brutal campaign of repression and revenge in the communities. Huancho-Lima was razed, as were community schools, deemed centers of insubordination; many peasant cottages were put to the torch, and thousands of head of livestock were taken from the peasants. By the time an army contingent had finished its pacification campaign in January 1924, perhaps two thousand community peasants in Huancané and Azángaro provinces were dead.[36]

This type of "pacification" once again proved as persuasive as its instigators had hoped. It broke the back of the Huanchinos' drive for autonomy, disoriented the work of the Comité Pro-Derecho Indígena "Tawantinsuyo," and quelled surging peasant militancy in the altiplano. Yet indiscriminate banditry and livestock rustling, committed by peasants and gamonal bands alike, remained endemic for the rest of the decade. Many authors have spoken of a defeat of the altiplano peasant movement. This seems an inevitable conclusion for those who, like Manuel Burga and Alberto Flores Galindo, have labeled the cycle of rebellions between 1915 and 1924 as millenarian, pure and simple. The peasant movement, in their view, "lacked political orientation, tactical skills and immediate goals." Steeped in a "religious consciousness, it wanted to reach all or nothing"; the peasants remained isolated, incapable of forging lasting alliances.[37]

But if we take the peasants at their word, their goals seem considerably less illusory, and the outcome of the mobilization appears less bleak. In many ways "the reestablishment of the Tahuantinsuyo" served as a unifying metaphor of the movement. The phrase echoed and reaffirmed the worst suspicions of gamonales and the boldest dreams of indigenistas. The metaphor encapsulated all the concrete, realistic, down-to-earth demands that the altiplano peasantry advanced during the early 1920s: the return of lands to Indian peasants, uninhibited trade, better payment for labor services, prohibition and effective abolition of involuntary services—from those exacted by district authorities to Leguía's *conscripción vial*—construction of rural schools, and political autonomy for the communities. These demands coincided with the reform programs put forward by the peasants' middle-class allies.

Seen in this light, the peasant movement produced, in conjunction with broader structural shifts, considerable results. To be sure, political and economic domination by gamonales, hacendados, and merchants did not disappear overnight, and, as the case of Huancané demonstrated, these sectors could still muster awesome repressive force. But by raising the risks and the costs of further accumulations of resources, at a time when their value had diminished through the slump and subsequent stagnation of the wool market, the movement contributed to the containment and decay of the order based on gamonalismo and haciendas.

Beginning in the 1920s, the old communal office hierarchy, the centerpiece of the subordination of the communities to the whims and exploitive schemes of local and provincial officials, fell into disuse in Azángaro's parcialidades.[38] Henceforth they were governed by elected community councils and lieutenant governors appointed by the Ministry of Government. A growing presence of representatives of the central government, including teachers, officers of the newly established Guardia Civil, and engineers supervising road construction, modestly began to check arbitrary rule by gamonales in rural districts.[39] Rather than automatically backing gamonales against Indian protests, under Leguía the central government began to pursue a strategy of solving the "Indian problem" through economic and social development.

With the introduction of trucks and the extension of Puno's road system during the 1920s, the region's commercial structure began to undergo major changes. The number of marketplaces grew, and for the first time regular weekly markets were established in peasant communities, a development that accelerated after World War II.[40] As traders of wool and hides and of foodstuffs for the growing urban demand came to the communities, the peasants' control over their own commercial transactions increased. This development further weakened gamonal authorities in the district capitals.[41]

With the unstable international wool conjuncture of the 1920s and 1930s, the expansion of estates continued the slowdown begun in 1914–15 and came to a standstill at some undetermined point (probably during the 1940s). There even appeared signs of a reversal of the trend, as some haciendas lost land or disappeared altogether through peasant invasions or through voluntary sales to peasants by impoverished hacendados. By 1940 no hacienda survived in Saman district, and the land of estates such as San Juan had been acquired once again by community peasants.[42]

Between 1920 and 1940 the transfer of peasants from communities to the estate sector came to a halt. Blocked from further physical expansion, haciendas had absorbed as much labor as they could use, and now, no later than 1940, the process was reversed. The population of the estate sector began to decline again, even in absolute terms. A few modernizing estates managed to reduce the number of their colonos, and in some economically marginal estates colonos became smallholding peasants as a result of parcelizations or invasions. At the same time population growth in the peasant communities and in "urban" centers accelerated (table 9.1). Thus, only after 1920, when the most hectic phase of hacienda expansion had ended, did conditions match the often repeated claim that the altiplano haciendas' control of vast areas of land led to a disproportionate concentration of population in the peasant sector.

The commercial and political crisis of the early 1920s emboldened the visions of those entrepreneurs, ranchers, and agronomists who wished to overcome the extensive, seigneurial livestock hacienda based on labor

TABLE 9.1. Hacienda and Peasant Freeholder Share of the Rural
Population of Azángaro Province, 1876–1961

	1876		1940		1961	
	N	%	N	%	N	%
Hacienda population	9,818	23.4	31,651	35.8	20,385	21.0
Peasant freeholder population	32,132	76.6	56,802	64.2	76,536	79.0
Total	41,950	100.0	88,453	100.0	96,921	100.0

Sources: Derived from Dir. de Estadística, Resumen del censo . . . hecho en 1876, 93–108;
Dir. Nacional del Estadística, Censo . . . de 1940 8:104–19; Dir. Nacional de Estadística y
Censos, Censo de 1961 4:113–40.

tenancy and to begin a serious effort to develop modern, capitalist stock
operations.[43] Some owners of large estates, including merchants who had
recently acquired landholdings, imported purebred sheep, invested in fencing, and undertook measures against high animal mortality. Several
haciendas were incorporated into shareholding companies, among them the
Sociedad Ganadera del Sur, controlled by the Gibson family from Arequipa. The modernizers sought to change the labor regime of their haciendas, although before the agrarian reform of 1969 a labor regime based
preponderantly on wages appeared on only a few estates. They limited the
herds of colonos, separated the pastures to be used by hacienda and colono
livestock, worked toward a greater specialization and productivity of their
work force, improved housing, and established schools and medical facilities. As these haciendas attempted to achieve higher productivity levels,
they now were interested in reducing the number of shepherds in order to
save expenses and retain a greater share of pastures for hacienda animals.[44]

These changes led to the gradual appearance of a sector of quite modern
livestock estates between the 1920s and the 1950s, but they did not spread
to the overwhelming majority of small and medium-sized haciendas and
left even some of the largest estates untouched. The major blockages were
lack of capital to finance improvements and colono resistance to any limitation of their long-standing privileges. Most haciendas continued to
operate as best they could, yet commercial stagnation and the assertiveness
of colonos weakened them economically. Their owners ceased to incorporate further peasants into their haciendas but often lacked the power to

dislodge colono families and their adult children. Under conditions of stagnating markets and mounting obstacles to expand haciendas or found new ones, inheritance posed a greater threat for many hacendado families than it had done during the boom years. Heirs sought to establish themselves in urban trades or professions and became part of the urban-based lower middle and middle classes of Juliaca, Puno, Arequipa, or Lima. But divisions of estates became more frequent. Many families became impoverished, stubbornly clinging to a social status in Azángaro's provincial society that their parents or grandparents had reached in better times.

Cleavages and conflicts among southern Peruvian elites involved in the wool economy erupted on all levels during the critical 1920s—between merchants and hacendados, between foreign entrepreneurs and the established regional elites, between the major transport company and wool merchants and producers, and between modernizing "capitalist" large landholders and the majority of more seigneurial hacendados. The Peruvian Corporation, the British-owned railway company, sought to offset losses caused by the opening of the rival La Paz–Arica line in 1914 by increasing transport tariffs between 41 and 274 percent from 1919 to 1923. This increase produced a xenophobic outcry among all sectors of southern Peruvian society, and Arequipa's Chamber of Commerce unsuccessfully demanded the nationalization of the company.[45] The Peruvian Corporation sought to foster demand for its transportation services by fomenting altiplano livestock production. It supported the project of an experimental sheep ranch, planned since the World War I boom years. The ranch, financed by a fee on wool exports, finally began operation at Chuquibambilla, Melgar province, in 1920. Hacendados were enthusiastic, expecting it to distribute purebred or crossbred rams to the ranchers at minimal costs. Three years later they had become disillusioned and bitter about the Granja Modelo de Chuquibambilla, "which to date has not rendered one positive benefit to the livestock industry."[46] Rather than cheaply distributing improved stock to Puno's ranchers and introducing new livestock raising techniques, the ranch had become a commercially operating hacienda, supported by government funds and controlled by its British managers.

Allied with and instigated by Colonel Stordy, the blundering manager of Chuquibambilla, in 1923 the Peruvian Corporation sought to attract a large foreign sheep-breeding company, the Compañia Rio Negro of Argentina, with the aim of buying up huge tracts of pastureland and establishing a modern, capital-intensive sheep ranch on a Patagonian scale. When the Rio Negro Company, in spite of guarantees by President Leguía, became aware that this project would involve serious conflicts with the altiplano's communal peasantry over land rights and the implantation of wage labor, it withdrew and the plan came to naught.[47] This was only the most spectacular of a number of attempts to form large syndicates for the production and commercialization of wool.[48] Some merchants and hacendados initially showed interest, hoping to see their estates improved by foreign capital and to share in the prospective increase of trade. But they soon became hostile when their expectations were dashed and they saw the foreign entrepreneurs as potent competitors rather than as partners. Then chambers of commerce and hacendado leagues organized shrill nationalistic campaigns to block such projects, claiming to speak for all southern Peruvians, from peasants to large landholders, "in defense of the Peruvian sierra, bulwark of nationality."[49]

The trajectory of Carlos Belón is paradigmatic for the developing dissensions between corporate modernizers and traditionalist hacendados during the 1920s and 1930s. His family owned large estates in Santiago de Pupuja and adjacent Lampa province, among them Hacienda Checca. During the early 1920s Belón aggressively sought associations with foreign entrepreneurs, hoping to tap their capital for repaying the family's debts to merchant houses and modernizing the estates. He became partner of the Gibsons of Arequipa in the establishment of the Sociedad Ganadera del Sur. The Gibsons decided to use that corporation to gain access to the maximum amount of wool by purchasing more and more estates rather than investing in the improvement of the corporation's earliest holdings. Belón withdrew his estates from the Sociedad Ganadera del Sur, leading to a noisy legal battle with the Arequipa family during the early 1930s. In the late 1920s he championed Puneño resistance to the establishment of a huge foreign-controlled alpaca wool purchasing monopoly. In 1931 he campaigned for a congressional seat under the aegis of APRA, the radical populist party recently founded by Victor Raúl Haya de la Torre. Belón's electoral platform focused on the defense of Indian peasants endangered by hacienda modernization. Although not opposed to limited improvements of stock operations, Belón now became an outspoken adversary of any plans to introduce wage labor on altiplano estates. By 1945, when he wrote a treatise on the altiplano's livestock industry, he was fighting against those "big capitalists" who attempted to introduce "the salaried worker in Puno and who work toward the disappearance of the community of pastures in the haciendas."[50] In effect, a frustrated modernizer had become an advocate of the extensive, seigneurial livestock hacienda and the type of relations between estate owners, colonos, and community peasants developed during the late nineteenth and early twentieth centuries.

The 1920s, then, mark a turning point for the economy and society of Azángaro and the Peruvian altiplano. Hacienda expansion had largely run its course. The seigneurial hacienda complex henceforth failed to absorb the growing rural population, to augment marketable production of wool and other livestock goods, and to guarantee the social position of the hacendados who had formed the dominant social group during the nineteenth and early twentieth centuries. This new situation was observed by the American journalist Carleton Beals, who traveled through the southern Peruvian sierra during the early 1930s: "In remote parts of Puno and Cuzco the tide of land seizures by large hacendados is receding, even . . . turning the other way. In that region landlordism is bankrupt, technically, economically and morally."[51]

Some Final Thoughts

In a recent review of Victor Bulmer-Thomas's incisive work on Central America's export economies, E. V. K. Fitzgerald succinctly paraphrased that author's main hypothesis as follows: "Export agriculture has been the source of dynamism in the Central American economy, providing potential resources for industrialization and social infrastructure, while simultaneously generating institutions and incentives that make these strategic objectives difficult to obtain."[52] This statement epitomizes the frustrations of economic, social, and political development in many parts of Latin America and approximates one of the main theses of this study. To phrase this idea more broadly, favorable commercial conjunctures for major primary products lead to economic growth throughout entire regional economies. At the same time there was a strengthening of the social forces, modes of behavior, and institutions that undermine the possibilities for sustainable growth and many of the required structural transformations, from infrastructure to education and a more even distribution of income. In the southern Andes this notion applies as much to the colonial silver cycle as to the wool export cycle that began in the 1820s, flourished between the 1850s and World War I, and decayed after 1920.

I have suggested in this book that an incomplete and truncated transition to capitalism lies at the root of the frustrations suffered by the export economy in the altiplano. During the mid-nineteenth century the notable citizens of rural areas such as the altiplano embraced the possibilities of integrating their region into international markets dominated by European and North American capitalists. They espoused the notions of material progress, the values, and the institutions propagated by Europe's seemingly triumphant civilization: free trade, the sanctity of private property, investment in transport infrastructure, and modern education. But they did so from a position of weakness rather than strength. The disintegration of the Andean colonial commercial circuits and structures of authority had destroyed the fortunes of many an obraje owner, hacendado, and merchant. During the period of crisis and realignment Andean peasants had become more autonomous and solidified their hold on much of the land.

Under these conditions the espousal of European progressive civilization was associated with authoritarian, hierarchical, and paternalistic notions of social control over the vast majority of the altiplano's population, the Indian peasantry. Developing the export trade, insisting on the sanctity of private, individual property, and drawing broad distinctions between an enlightened, Europeanized elite and the Indian masses, said to persist in their "ancestral vices," became mere tools to foster the narrow interests of provincial gamonales. It was the only path open to the struggling provincial notables to improve their own economic situation and build a base of power. The colonial divide between Spaniards, now called whites, and Indians was reinvented—indeed, recast in starker terms—within an export economy and notions of European civilization. It legitimized the rising provincial elite's exclusionary claims to power and delivered the tools to incorporate increasing numbers of Indian peasants into dependent relationships through trade, acquisition of their lands, appropriation of labor in livestock estates, and the use of local offices for surplus extraction from the communities.

Thus, between the mid-nineteenth century and 1920 there occurred a deepening of the commercial web, of market exchanges and the "commodification" of social relations, and *simultaneously* a strengthening of dependency, paternalism, and subjection of the peasants to the designs of gamonales. The newly empowered provincial elites were not picky about the means they employed to foster their economic and political interests, and these means frequently were in direct conflict with the notions of bourgeois society and competitive market economy that they espoused themselves. In brief, exploitation along the reinvented colonial and ethnic divide was made harsher with the rise of the export economy, but this exploitation had at least as much to do with strongly polarized neocolonial power relations as it did with class interests. Consequently, many gamonales feared that the rise of agrarian capitalism, with its impersonal capital, commodity, and labor markets, might undercut their political and economic power, based on highly personal qualities of leadership and protection of their clients and toughness against competing gamonales and unruly dependents.

The rise of the wool export trade created similar ambivalences among the peasants. The new era of economic expansion brought tremendous hardships for the great majority of peasants, who suffered insertion into highly dependent trade relationships, the transfer of much land from communities to the new or expanding haciendas, and growing demands from local authorities. But it also created complex transformations and differentiations among the Indian peasantry. In the first place, as the provincial elites used notions borrowed from European bourgeois civilization to distinguish themselves from the Indian peasantry, so the Indian peasantry came to have a stronger sense of its own separate and subaltern identity. The same degrading, racist, and authoritarian images of the Indian so emphatically disseminated by the altiplano provincial elite to underscore their own exalted identity appeared in the indigenista literature after the turn of the century as evidence for the need to protect and "redeem" the Indian.

The effects of the wool export cycle on communal solidarity were not all deleterious. No doubt, commercial, demographic, and land-related pressures strained what was left of common usufruct of land, but solidarity flourished in other arenas of community life. At the same time some of the more affluent peasants took seriously the gamonales' sermons about market economy and sanctity of private property and began to acquire additional parcels of land and to clamor for unimpeded trade and the termination of unpaid labor services and other obligations. In other words, the economic and political ideologies associated with the export economy and the social differentiations engendered by that economy began to create challenges to gamonal domination on its own terms. In the cycle of social movements that swept the altiplano between 1915 and 1924, these affluent peasants combined Incaic notions, inevitable products of the neocolonial divide of the preceding decades, with anarchist and progressive-liberal demands for autonomous markets, return of community lands, rural schools, and so on. In calling for more autonomous, associational communities, they weakened the hierarchical community structures that ironically had become the very tool of gamonal domination. But it is crucial to stress once again that these new, commercial peasant leaders were not abandoning communal solidarity altogether. A mirror image of ambivalences among hacendados, they sought both to advance their own family interests in market terms and, as an insurance policy against continued gamonal abuses, to foster Indian communal solidarity.

The blockage of the full transition to capital-intensive and highly productive agrarian structures based on wage labor and yeoman farming in the altiplano can be explained through a number of discrete economic variables, such as specific factor endowments and high transaction costs, which I have discussed in various parts of this study. But there remains a residue, not easily captured in economic terms, that has to do with historical constellations of power between social groups, modes of conflict resolution between them, and the type of legal and institutional framework the state provides for economic actors.

After the disintegration of the colonial corporate order, the Peruvian state of the nineteenth century increasingly sanctioned the notions of free trade, private property, and the sanctity of contract. But the state had little power in faraway provinces such as Azángaro other than that exercised by the provincial elite in the state's name. Until late in the nineteenth century the state in the altiplano was little more than the resonance box for the ideological pretensions of the provincial elite, as well as the arena for battles between various gamonal factions. After the central state gained more autonomy in the mid-1890s, the provincial elites hoped to make it into their handmaiden in their drive to concentrate a growing share of resources under their control. It did play that role in numerous instances, but never dependably so. Just when the state began to gain autonomy, it also began to listen, sporadically and unreliably, to the indigenista critics of the provincial elites. Yet even then, as witnessed by the military campaigns of repression between 1915 and 1924, it was still far from setting a firm, dependable frame as guarantor of private property and the sanctity of contract.

There is a sad irony in this history. Until the agrarian reform of 1969 it was commonplace to note that the most severe exploitation in Peru occurred precisely in the "mancha india," the southern sierra, including the altiplano, where the Indian population share continues to be high. Exploitation and the conservation of Indian identity somehow seemed to have formed an indissoluble pair. Only when Indian identity can be construed without the heavy burden of repression, and when businesspeople and officials in Peru's sierra have ceased to rely on the crutch of the neocolonial construction of power, can we hope for sustainable economic growth *and* a more equitable distribution of resources.

Notes

1. INTRODUCTION

1. *¿He vivido en vano?* 38–39.
2. Ibid., 55–61.
3. Ibid., 67–68.
4. This type of cultural explanation, quite popular among Latin Americanists as late as the 1960s, underlies even the influential North American interpretation, ostensibly written from the dependency perspective, by Stanley and Barbara Stein, *Colonial Heritage.*
5. D. Platt, "Dependency," 113–31; Gootenberg, *Between Silver and Guano*; Mathew, "First Anglo-Peruvian Debt," 562–86.
6. Bushnell and Macaulay, *Emergence*, ch. 13; Lewis, *Evolution.*
7. Bagú, *Economía*; Frank, *Capitalism*; Wallerstein, *Modern World System.*
8. Stavenhagen, *Social Classes in Agrarian Societies*; de Janvry, *Agrarian Question*; Bartra, *Estructura agraria*; Duncan and Rutledge, *Land and Labour*; Bergad, *Coffee*; Roseberry, *Coffee*; Seligson, *Peasants*; Sabato, *Agrarian Capitalism.* For Peru, see Mallon, *Defense of Community*; Burga, *De la encomienda*; Piel, *Capitalisme agraire*; Gonzales, *Plantation Agriculture*; Macera, *Las plantaciones azucareras*; Caballero, *Economía agraria.*
9. On different systems of markets, not all of which are associated with capitalism, see Polanyi, *Great Transformation.*
10. For Latin America, see Bauer, "Industry." On Spain's path of agrarian transformation, see the magisterial work by Herr, *Rural Change*, esp. 712–54. On the persistence of ancien régime features after the presumed twin "revolutions," bourgeois and industrial, see A. Mayer, *Per-*

sistence; Weber, *Peasants into Frenchman*. On the specificity of each and every path of development, see Blackbourn and Eley, *Peculiarities*.

11.   For an eloquent recent statement, see Roseberry, *Histories and Anthropologies*.

12.   Cf. Veliz, *Centralist Tradition*.

13.   This is not to deny the truism that dominant trends during a given epoch benefit or hurt the interests of one social group in relation to another social group, a crucial element in my assessment of the cycles in altiplano development.

14.   See Jacobsen, "Between the 'Espacio Peruano' and the National Market."

15.   Cf. Trazegnies, *La idea de derecho*, esp. part 3.

16.   The issue has recently been taken up by Gootenberg, *Between Silver and Guano*, from the perspective of Lima, and for the immediate postindependence decades. For interior regions as the altiplano it remains significant after the consolidation of the liberal guano state, and even as late as the 1920s.

17.   G. Smith, *Livelihood and Resistance*, esp. ch. 2.

18.   Knight, "Mexican Revolution," 19.

19.   Romero, *Monografía del departamento de Puno*, 75–76; C. Smith, "Central Andes," 266; Romero, *Perú*, 188–91.

20.   Romero, *Perú*, 212–13; Romero, *Monografía del departamento de Puno*, 99–101.

21.   Romero, *Monografía del departamento de Puno*, 138; Salas Perea, *Monografía*, 168; Rossello Paredes, *Murales de Azángaro*, 5–6.

22.   Martínez, *Las migraciones*, 17.

23.   The lake may have covered a considerably larger surface in prehistoric times; see Romero, *Perú*, 190, 218.

24.   Ibid., 218; Min. de Hacienda y Comercio, *Plan regional* 27:12.

25.   Min. de Hacienda y Comercio, *Plan regional* 27:11; Romero, *Perú*, 218; Dollfus, *Le Pérou*, 37.

26.   Dollfus, *Le Pérou*, 36.

27.   Romero, *Perú*, 207; Min. de Hacienda y Comercio, *Plan regional* 27:5.

28.   Romero, *Perú*, 209–11.

29.   Some authors suggest that severe droughts occur in five- or seven-year cycles; see ibid., 211. Dollfus (*Le Pérou*, 37) describes the effects of the most devastating droughts in recent history, those of 1955–57; the massive development study of southern Peru from the late 1950s (the *Plan regional*, published by the Ministerio de Hacienda y Comercio) was undertaken in reaction to the economic, social, and demographic dislocations caused by the droughts. For the devastating effects of a drought from 1814 to 1816, see Choquehuanca, *Ensayo*, 59.

30. Choquehuanca, *Ensayo*, 62.

31. Romero, *Monografía del departamento de Puno*, 408.

32. Pulgar Vidal, *Geografía*, 92; Romero, *Perú*, 220.

33. Although leguminous pastures are rare in the altiplano, the cloverlike *layo (Trifolium amabile)* has been used as animal fodder in Azángaro at least since the early nineteenth century; see Choquehuanca, *Ensayo*, 11; Romero, *Perú*, 220; Lavalle y García, "El mejoramiento," 74–75. I would like to thank Marcel Haitin for pointing out this last work to me. For more information on grasses and pastures, see Jacobsen, "Land Tenure," 21–22.

34. Romero, *Perú*, 219; C. Smith, "Central Andes," 269. In 1831 Choquehuanca (*Ensayo*, 11) mentioned as important grasses *quisna, huaylla, sicuya* (used not only for fodder but also for thatches of roofs), *carhuayo* (particularly fitted as fodder for llamas), and *sora*, flourishing in humid spots of the pampas. I have not found any mention of these grasses in modern works.

35. Romero, *Monografía del departamento de Puno*, 236–37; for other semiaquatic plants not identified in modern works, see Choquehuanca, *Ensayo*, 11. The famous *totora (Malacochete totora)* is only rarely used as fodder because of its great versatility; it is used for constructing boats, mats, and roofs and is also a delicious food for humans.

36. On the relation between agriculture and livestock raising in the Andes, see Golte, *La racionalidad*; Figueroa, *Capitalist Development*; Caballero, *Economía agraria*; see also Crotty, *Cattle, Economics, and Development*.

37. For Azángaro's crop production, see Jacobsen, "Land Tenure," 24, table 1-3.

38. Romero, *Perú*, 218; Choquehuanca, *Ensayo*, 15–55.

39. The potatoes are spread in an open field during the time of sharp frosts in June to July. After exposure to night frosts for about eight days, they are stepped on to squeeze out liquids, left for a few more days to freeze overnight, and are then ready for long-term storage. A more desired and expensive variety of *chuño*, called *moraya*, is placed into running streams for a few days between frost treatments; see Choquehuanca, *Ensayo*, 9–10.

40. Pulgar Vidal, *Geografía*, 97–98.

41. Cobo, *Historia del nuevo mundo* 1:161–62; Choquehuanca, *Ensayo*, 9, 15–55; Romero, *Perú*, 222; Pulgar Vidal, *Geografía*, 95–96.

42. Romero (*Perú*, 221) reports that barley was widely grown during the colonial period as forage for the large mule herds. Yet as late as the 1650s it was hardly planted at all in the altiplano because people believed that it would not withstand the region's harsh climate; see Cobo, *Historia del nuevo mundo* 1:161.

43. Choquehuanca, *Ensayo*, 9.

44. A rather unreliable account of agricultural production for the early 1950s claims higher production of barley than of quinua and canihua; see Guevara Velasco, *Apuntes*, vol. 1.

45. Cobo, *Historia* 1:162; Choquehuanca, *Ensayo*, 9; Romero, *Monografía del departamento de Puno*, 412–13.

46. Romero, *Monografía del departamento de Puno*, 246–49; Choquehuanca, *Ensayo*, 12.

47. Romero, *Monografía del departamento de Puno*, 247, 250, 436.

48. Dollfus, *Le Pérou*, 37; Romero, *Monografía del departamento de Puno*, 247.

49. Ibid., 252–53, 438; Choquehuanca, *Ensayo*, 13.

50. Ibid., 14; Erickson, "Archaeological Investigation." On Alan Kolata's work at Tiwanaku, see Obermiller, "Harvest from the Past."

51. Cobo, *Historia del nuevo mundo* 1:163.

52. Villanueva Urteaga, *Cuzco 1689*, 114–15.

53. Tschudi, *Reisen durch Südamerika* 5:359; Tschudi, citing Juan Domingo Zamacola y Tauregui, a late eighteenth-century priest from Cayma near Arequipa, speaks of an implausible population decline from 23,000 to 2,000 in the doctrina of Azángaro. Choquehuanca (*Ensayo*, 57–58) says that the 1719–20 epidemic reduced the province's population by two-thirds. Wightman, *Indigenous Migration and Social Change*, 42–44, 67–73.

54. Personal communication from David Cahill, February 1989.

55. An analysis of parish registers for the parish of Yanahuara, near Arequipa, rendered a 2.4 percent natural population increase annually between 1738 and 1747; see Cook, "La población," 33.

56. On the drought of 1803–5, see Tandeter, "Crisis in Upper Peru"; Macera and Márquez Abanto, "Informes geográficas del Perú colonial."

57. Gootenberg, "Population and Ethnicity."

58. Miller, "Reinterpreting the 1876 Census"; C. Smith, "Patterns," 77–78.

59. Kubler, *Indian Caste*, 28, 34.

60. On Azángaro's index of masculinity as a gauge for migratory patterns, see Jacobsen, "Land Tenure," 38, table 1-7.

61. In 1887, for example, Petrona Mamani and her husband Antonio Poma from Arapa sold their land, since they had permanently moved to Patambuco, in the ceja de la selva of Sandia; see REPA, año 1887, Rodríguez, F. 136, No. 64 (May 24, 1887).

62. In 1861 an old peasant woman, the widowed Petrona Quispe from Muñani, gave her Estancia Chichani to hacendado Juan Antonio Iruri because her only surviving son, Pedro Nolasco Luque, had left with the army long before and nobody knew his whereabouts or whether he was still alive; REPA, año 1861, Manrique, F. 169, No. 79 (Nov. 30, 1861).

63. Tschudi, *Reisen durch Südamerika* 5:210–11.

64. Grandidier, *Voyage*, 196; report by British Consul Wilthew about Islay trade in 1856, in Bonilla, *Gran Bretaña* 4:102.

65. On the *ley del terror*, see J. Basadre, *Historia de la república* 4:1653; E. Vásquez, *La rebelión de Juan Bustamante*, 190–92.

66. On recruiting practices in Azángaro province and countermeasures by haciendas, see Fischer to Castresana, Picotani, July 25, 1909, AFA-P.

67. Martínez, *Las migraciones*, 79–90, 115–17.

68. REPA, año 1907, Jiménez, F. 456, No. 178 (Sept. 3, 1907).

69. "Informe del médico titular de Azángaro," Aug. 10, 1920, cited in Roca Sánchez, *Por la clase indígena*, 284–85.

70. "Memoria del médico titular de las provincias Azángaro y Ayaviri para el año de 1908," in *Memoria del Presidente de la H. Junta Departamental*, app. 21, 99–103; on the closure of the port of Mollendo for two months in 1903 because of the outbreak of bubonic plague, see Bonilla, *Gran Bretaña* 4:57; for the epidemic on Haciendas Checayani and Caravilque, see REPA, año 1904, Jiménez, F. 597, No. 235 (Jan. 9, 1904).

71. Jacobsen, "Land Tenure," 44, table 1-9.

72. This assessment follows Brading, *Haciendas*, 50–53.

73. Cf. Gootenberg, "Population and Ethnicity"; Glave, "Demografía."

74. Van Young, *Hacienda and Market*.

2. FROM THE "ANDEAN SPACE" TO THE EXPORT FUNNEL

1. Bueno, *Geografía*, 115; Alcedo, *Diccionario* 1:162–63.

2. Céspedes del Castillo, *Lima y Buenos Aires*, 65; Sempat Assadourian, *El sistema*.

3. Piel, *Capitalisme agraire* 1:132–33; Bueno, *Geografía*, 113–15; Cobb, "Supply and Transportation," 31–33; Glave, *Trajinantes*, 9–67.

4. Romero, *Historia económica del Perú*, 154–55; Alcedo, *Diccionario* 1:89.

5. Bueno, *Geografía*, 113–15; Alcedo, *Diccionario* 1:165.

6. Flores Galindo, *Arequipa*, 19.

7. Rivero y Ustáriz, "Visita a las minas del departamento de Puno en el año de 1826," in his *Colección de memorias* 2:36; Markham, *Travels*, 99–102.

8. Murra, "El contról verticál," 89–123.

9. Cephalio, "Disertación."

10. The livestock production of the southern altiplano supplied cities and mining centers between La Paz and La Plata.

11. Cephalio, "Disertación"; Barriga, *Memorias* 1:52–57.

12.   This enormous number of sheep must have served both for urban meat supplies and for restocking livestock ranches in Cuzco's pastoral zone thus also indirectly supplying wool for the obrajes of Quispicanichis and Canas y Canchis.

13.   Macera dell'Orso and Márquez Abanto, "Informes geográficos del Perú colonial," 229.

14.   Paucarcolla's obrajes produced blankets for the army as late as the War of the Pacific in 1879; M. Basadre y Chocano, *Riquezas peruanas*, 103; Romero, *Historia económica del Perú*, 138–40.

15.   Silva Santisteban, *Los obrajes*, 150; Mörner, *Perfil*, 82–88.

16.   Cephalio, "Disertación," table 2, between ff. 228 and 229; as late as 1780 the obraje of Chacamarca in the partido of Vilcashuaman near Huamanga (some five hundred kilometers northwest of Azángaro) received 80 percent of its raw wools from the Collao; see Salas de Coloma, "Los obrajes huamanguinos," 228, table I.

17.   Cephalio, "Disertación."

18.   For the great variety of European textiles sold in Arequipa during the 1780s, see Barriga, *Memorias* 1:96–99.

19.   "Partido de Lampa de la Provincia e Intendencia de la Ciudad de Puno," May 23, 1808, BNP.

20.   Macera dell'Orso and Márquez Abanto, "Informes geográficos del Perú colonial," 250.

21.   Estimating 1.5 male tribute payers per household; based on figures from 1786 tribute recount, in Macera, *Tierra y población* 1:162.

22.   See Kriedte, Medick, and Schlumbohm, *Industrialisierung*; for an excellent case study, see Mooser, *Ländliche Klassengesellschaft*.

23.   This view coincides with Emmanuel LeRoy Ladurie's view that in France during the sixteenth and seventeenth centuries population development—ultimately shaped by epidemiological regimes—is the independent variable and economy is the dependent variable; see his "Die Tragödie des Gleichgewichts," 40.

24.   O. H. Hufton, *The Poor of Eighteenth Century France, 1750–1789* (Oxford: Oxford University Press, 1974), 15, as cited by Mooser, *Ländliche Klassengesellschaft*, 48.

25.   See, e.g., "Información testimonial tomada por el corregidor de Potosí en 1690," in Sanchez Albornóz, *Indios y tributos*, esp. 128–30; O'Phelan Godoy, *Rebellions*, 99–108; O'Phelan Godoy, "Aduanas," 58–61; Spalding, *Huarochirí*, 200–204; ANB, EC año 1762, No. 144.

26.   See Sempat Assadourian, *El sistema*.

27.   Céspedes del Castillo, *Lima y Buenos Aires*, 65–66.

28.   Ibid.; Flores Galindo, *Arequipa*, 23.

29.   Rivero y Ustáriz, "Visita a las minas," in his *Colección de memorias* 2:21; Choquehuanca, *Ensayo*, 64; Glave, *Trajinantes*, 23–79.

30.   Glave, *Trajinantes*, 23–79; Sánchez Albornóz, *Indios y tributos*, esp. 130; complaints against Kuraka Diego Choquehuanca by Indians from

ayllus Nequeneque, Picotani, and Chuquini (1760–62), ANB, EC año 1762, No. 144.

31. Tandeter and Wachtel, *Precios*, 9–15, 23–30; Tyrer, "Demographic and Economic History," 97–98; Moscoso, "Apuntes," 67–94.

32. Céspedes del Castillo, *Lima y Buenos Aires*, 65–66; Kossok, *El virreinato*, 57–60, 68–79.

33. Haring, *Spanish Empire in America*, 315–16; Kossok, *El virreinato*, 57.

34. Céspedes del Castillo, *Lima y Buenos Aires*, 120–21; O'Phelan Godoy, "Las reformas," 342.

35. J. Fisher, *Commercial Relations*, 14.

36. Ibid., 46, 55; for the effects on Lima-based commerce, see Flores Galindo, "Aristocracia en vilo," 274–77, and Haitin, "Urban Market and Agrarian Hinterland," 284–86.

37. Tandeter, "Trabajo forzado."

38. Céspedes del Castillo, *Lima y Buenos Aires*, 185.

39. O'Phelan Godoy, *Rebellions*, 162–68.

40. Ibid. The literature on the Túpac Amaru rebellion has become vast; for divergent interpretations, see Campbell, "Recent Research," 3–48; Golte, *Repartos y rebeliones*; Cornblit, "Society and Mass Rebellion"; Vega, *José Gabriel Túpac Amaru*; Flores Galindo, *Túpac Amaru II*; and *Actas del Coloquio*. The best general account is still Lewin, *La rebelión*.

41. Angelis, *Colección* 4:347; for other royalist kurakas in Azángaro, see "Carta del Ilmo. Sr. Dr. D. Juan Manuel Moscoso, Obispo del Cuzco, al de La Paz, Dr. D. Gregorio Francisco del Campo, sobre la sublevación de aquellas provincias," in ibid. 4:443.

42. Sahuaraura Titu Atauchi, *Estado del Perú*, 14 n. 32; on the symbolism of massive violence during the rebellion, see Flores Galindo, *Buscando un Inca*, 133–39; for skepticism on the extent of violence and destruction during the rebellion, see Mörner, *Perfíl de la sociedad rural*, 123–29.

43. Sahuaraura, *Estado del Perú*, 116 nn. 28–29; L. Fisher, *Last Inca Revolt*, 254–55; Jacobsen, "Land Tenure," 70–71.

44. "Breve reseña historica," 9.

45. Paz, *Guerra separatista* 1:270–271.

46. Diego Cristóval Túpac Amaru to Juan Manuel Moscoso, Bishop of Cuzco, May 8, 1782, in ibid. 2:239; see also ibid. 1:284.

47. Petition by corregidores of Carabaya and Azángaro, Jan. 18, 1781, ANB, EC año 1781.

48. Sahuaraura, *Estado del Perú*, 10 n. 10.

49. Cephalio, "Disertación," 225.

50. J. Fisher, *Government*, 127–28; Glave and Remy, *Estructura agraria*, 442–43, 518–19, speak of a crisis of overproduction in the southern sierra for the 1780s to 1820.

51. J. Fisher, *Government*, 49–52.

52. "Nuevo plan que establece la perpetua tranquilidad del vasto imperio del Perú y produce sumas ventajas a todos los dominios de S.C.M.," in *Juicio de limites* 4:95–112.

53. Flores Galindo, *Arequipa*, 39–44.

54. Ibid., 44.

55. Roel, *Historia social*, 223.

56. Cornejo Bouroncle, *Pumacahua*, 369–70. In 1814 the five-year-old José Rufino Echenique, the later Peruvian president whose family owned estates in the provinces of Carabaya and Azángaro, escaped death by lynching from a mob in the town of Phara, Carabaya, only through the mercy of one of the Indian peasants; see Echenique, *Memorias* 1:4.

57. Cornejo Bouroncle, *Pumacahua*, 385–447, 487–90.

58. Abascal y Sousa, *Memoria de gobierno* 1:219.

59. Ibid. 2:193.

60. Halperin Donghi, *Revolución y guerra*, 79–80.

61. Pentland, *Informe*, 104; Charles Ricketts to George Canning, Lima, 1826, in Bonilla, *Gran Bretaña* 1:64.

62. Choquehuanca, *Ensayo*, 64.

63. Halperín Donghi, *Historia contemporanea*, 147.

64. Haigh, *Sketches*, 380–81; see also Gootenberg, "Merchants, Foreigners, and the State," 175–77.

65. Bonilla, "Aspects" 1:65.

66. Gootenberg, "Merchants, Foreigners, and the State," 44.

67. "Manuel Aparicio, Prefecto de Puno al Ministro de Estado en el departamento de Gobierno y Relaciones Exteriores," Puno, June 15, 1826, cited in Bonilla, del Rio, and Ortíz de Zevallos, "Comercio libre," 18. The classical formulation of the dependency position remains Cardoso and Faletto, *Dependencia*; for Peru, see Bonilla and Spalding, "La independencia en el Perú," 15–65; for an opposing view, see D. Platt, "Dependency," 113–31.

68. Rivero, *Memorias*, 27; Gootenberg, "Merchants, Foreigners, and the State," 206; Tamayo Herrera, *Historia social del Cuzco*, 36–43.

69. Langer, "Espacios coloniales y economías nacionales," 140–47; Mörner, *Notas sobre el comercio*, 10.

70. Gootenberg, "Merchants, Foreigners, and the State," 215–16; Tamayo Herrera, *Historia social del Cuzco*, 41–43; Bosch Spencer, *Statistique commerciale*, 50–51, 331.

71. During the 1790s Tadeo Haenke noted that the abolition of repartos had diminished the price of many goods for Indians by half or more; see his *Descripción del Perú*, 112–14.

72. Choquehuanca, *Ensayo*.

73. Ibid., 65; Krüggeler, "Sozial und Wirtschaftsgeschichte," 13–14; Krüggeler, "El doble desafío"; Rivero, Memorias, 12.

74. Choquehuanca, Ensayo, 69.

75. Bosch Spencer, Statistique commerciale, 50–51; on Indian apparel circa 1870–1900, see Plane, Le Pérou, 27, 40–44; Forbes, On the Aymara Indians, 37; Tschudi (Peru 2:174–75), despite racism in some passages, admiringly described how Indians in the early 1840s continued to weave "cloth of excellent fineness." For a surely exaggerated view of the Indians' almost total reliance on imports, see Markham, Travels, 76 n. 6.

76. Marcoy, Travels 1:79, 84–85, 103.

77. I estimate southern Peru's sheep population, circa 1830, to have been 2,242,799 head, and that of cameloids 380,423 head. These figures are based on the ratio between livestock population for a few altiplano provinces from the early nineteenth century, contained in table 4.3, and from 1959, contained in Min. de Hacienda y Comercio, Plan regional 28:239–59. I applied these ratios to the 1959 figures for total sheep and cameloid populations in southern Peru to arrive at the estimates for 1830. Southern Peru includes the modern departments of Apurímac, Arequipa, Cuzco, Madre de Dios, Moquegua, Puno, and Tacna. In estimating wool production in 1830 I used the mean production figure per animal from 1959, contained in Plan regional. This calculation results in estimates of 1,677.614 metric tons of sheep wool and 652.045 metric tons of cameloid wools produced in southern Peru in 1830. Mean exports of sheep wool from Islay, 1837–40, were 764.382 tons per year, or 45.6 percent of southern Peru's estimated sheep wool production. The peak year of 1840 saw exports of 904.767 tons of sheep wool, 53.9 percent of estimated production. Mean annual cameloid wool exports from Islay in 1837–40 were 345.125 metric tons, or 52.9 percent of estimated production. In the peak year of 1840, 598.117 tons of cameloid wools were exported, 91.7 percent of production. The rates of wools exported are upper-bound estimates.

78. Choquehuanca, Ensayo, 28, 37 n. 1, 64.

79. For Mexico between the 1820s and 1860s, see Tutino, From Insurrection to Revolution, 229.

80. Wittman, Estudios históricos sobre Bolivia, 174.

81. Pentland, Informe sobre Bolivia, 105; José Maria Dalence, Bosquejo estadístico de Bolivia (Chuquisaca, 1851), as cited in Peñaloza, La Paz 4:24.

82. Pentland, Informe sobre Bolivia, 105; Peñaloza, La Paz 4:24; Peñaloza, Historia económica de Bolivia 2:91–92.

83. On commercial relations between Peru and Bolivia from the 1830s to 1860, see Jacobsen, "Land Tenure," 88–90; on continuity rather than ruptures in cross-border Andean trade, see Langer, "Espacios coloniales y economías nacionales."

84. Langer, "Espacios coloniales y economías nacionales," 146.

85. Among Macedo's co-conspirators were notable landowners and politicians, including Pedro Aguirre and Pedro Miguel Urbina and perhaps the Azangarinos José Mariano Escobedo and José Domingo Choquehuanca; see Herrera Alarcón, *Rebeliones*, 13–44.

86. The Azangarino hacendados Juan Cazorla and José Antonio de Macedo were deputies to the Assambly of Sicuani, which on March 17, 1836, declared the creation of a south Peruvian state under the protectorate of Santa Cruz; see Valdivia, *Memorias*, 160.

87. Colonel Manuel José Choquehuanca, a cousin of José Domingo, held this opinion; see Luna, *Choquehuanca el amauta*, 51.

88. Amat y Junient, *Memoria de Gobierno*, 230–32.

89. Hunt, *Price and Quantum Estimates*, 38–40; Bonilla, "Aspects" 1:26, 33, 39, 45; Bonilla, "Islay," 31–47.

90. On wool export statistics and their problems, see Jacobsen, "Land Tenure," 93–102.

91. Ibid., 95–96; Haigh, *Sketches*, 380–81.

92. Gosselman, *Informes*, 76–77.

93. For the years from 1843 to 1851 only a few highly contradictory wool export statistics are available. See Jacobsen, "Land Tenure," 97–99; Hunt, *Price and Quantum Estimates*, 38–39; Bonilla, "Islay," 42–43; Esteves, *Apuntes para la historia económica*, 38–45.

94. Gootenberg, "Social Origins"; Rivero, *Memorias*, 68–69.

95. Deane and Cole, *British Economic Growth*, 192–210; Southey, *Rise*, 4; Dechesne, *L'evolution*, 140–41.

96. Jacobsen, "Land Tenure," 97–99; Hunt, *Price and Quantum Estimates*, 38–39; Bonilla, "Islay," 42–43; R. Miller, "Wool Trade."

97. Detailed wool export statistics, omitted here for reasons of space, can be found in my article "Cycles and Booms," 492–500, and in Jacobsen, "Land Tenure," app. 1, 815–33.

98. Southey, *Rise*, 35–37, 77.

99. Jacobsen, "Land Tenure," 99–102; Hunt, *Price and Quantum Estimates*, 38–40; Bonilla, "Islay," 42–44.

100. Haigh, *Sketches*, 381.

101. Choquehuanca, *Ensayo*, 13; Rivero y Ustáriz, "Visita a las minas," in his *Colección* 2:5–36; Romero, *Monografía del departamento de Puno*, 439–56; Deustua, "Producción minera."

102. Deustua, "Producción minera"; Romero, *Monografía del departamento de Puno*, 448; Markham, *Travels*, 99–102; Castelnau, *Expedition* 3:404–5; Rivero y Ustáriz, "Visita a las minas," *Colección* 2:36; Porras Barrenechea, *Dos viajeros franceses*, 55. On Puno silver mining after independence, see Deustua, *La minería*, 86–96.

103. Romero, *Monografía del departamento de Puno*, 441, 454–56; Markham, *Travels*, 99–102.

104. Deustua, "El ciclo interno," 23–49.
105. Ibid., 27; M. Basadre y Chocano, *Riquezas peruana*, 144; Herndon and Gibbon, *Exploration* 2:91–92.
106. Romero, *Monografía del departamento de Puno*, 444–50; Deustua, "El ciclo interno," 27, 31–35.
107. Ibid., 31–32; Markham, *Travels*, 206–11; J. Basadre, *Historia de la república* 2:848–49; Herndon and Gibbon, *Exploration* 2:91–92. On the embeddedness of mining in the Andean agrarian economy, see Contreras, *Mineros*, esp. chs. 9–11.
108. Marcoy, *Travels* 1:99–100.
109. Basadre, *Historia de la república* 3:1310; Dancuart and Rodríguez, *Anales* 3:41–42.
110. Dancuart and Rodríguez, *Anales* 3:41–42; Rivero, *Memorias*, 40; Romero, *Historia económica del Perú*, 344; REPA, año 1855, Oblitas (May 22, 1855).
111. Great Britain, Parliament, *Sessional Papers*, 1837–38, 47:401–2.
112. Reports by Consul Cocks about Islay trade in 1863 and 1864, in Bonilla, *Gran Bretaña* 4:140–44, 164; Markham, *Travels*, 206.
113. Rivero, *Memorias*, 27, 66.
114. M. Basadre y Chocano, *Riquezas peruanas*, 122.
115. Ibid., 144; REPA, 1864, Patiño, F. 133, No. 57 (Dec. 24, 1864).
116. On the central sierra, see Manrique, *Mercado interno*, esp. 108–41; Wilson, "Propiedad," 36–54.
117. Tschudi, *Reisen durch Südamerika* 5:167.
118. Ibid. 5:351; Haigh, *Sketches*, 380–81.
119. Tschudi, *Reisen durch Südamerika* 5:179–80.
120. Hermenegildo Agramonte to Juan Paredes, Cabanillas, Dec. 3, 1850, MPA.
121. Glade, *Latin American Economies*, 202–3; Gootenberg, "Merchants, Foreigners, and the State," 203–22.
122. Will of Juan Paredes, Dec. 8, 1874, MPA.
123. Juan Bautista Zea to Juan Paredes, Arapa, Mar. 10, 1847, MPA.
124. Hermenegildo Agramonte to Juan Paredes, Cabanillas, Dec. 3, 1850; Agustín Aragón to Juan Paredes, Checayani, Sept. 22, 1853; Aragón to Francisco Esquiróz, San Antón, Mar. 15, 1867; all MPA.
125. See, e.g., Escobedo to Paredes, Arequipa, Apr. 11, 1862; see also Agustín Aragón to Paredes, Checayani, Sept. 22, 1853; both in MPA.
126. Mestas to Paredes, Caminaca, July 12, 1845, MPA (my translation retains the errors in the original).
127. Appleby, "Exportation and Its Aftermath," 55.
128. See Jacobsen, "Land Tenure," table 2–1, 112–12a.
129. Porras Barrenechea, *Dos viajeros franceses*, 204; M. Paz Soldán, *Geografía del Perú*, 423.

130. On the fair at Pucará, see Marcoy, *Travels* 1:107–8.

131. Bustamante, *Apuntes*, 10; Markham, *Travels*, 284.

132. Markham, *Travels*, 284.

133. For the lower estimate, see M. Paz Soldán, *Geografía del Perú*, 423; for the higher estimate, see Bustamante, *Apuntes*, 10.

134. M. Paz Soldán, *Geografía del Perú*, 423; report by Consul Wilthew about Islay trade in 1859, in Bonilla, *Gran Bretaña* 4:247.

135. See Glade, *Latin American Economies*, 202–3; Flores Galindo, *Arequipa*, 75.

136. Juan Bautista Zea to Juan Paredes, Arapa, Mar. 10, 1847; Juan Medrano to Paredes, Caira (dept. de Cuzco), Nov. 1857; both MPA.

137. Andrés Urviola to Manuel E. Paredes (his son-in-law), Muñani, Nov. 9, 1867, MPA.

138. M. Paz Soldán, *Geografía del Perú*, 464; J. Basadre, *Historia de la república* 3:1290–91; Flores Galindo, *Arequipa y el sur andino*, 108–9; Marcoy, *Travels* 1:52.

139. Piel, "Place of the Peasantry," 120–22.

3. COLONIALISM ADRIFT

1. This distinction is based on Polanyi, *Great Transformation*, esp. chs. 4–6.

2. On core and frontier regions, see Schwartz and Lockhart, *Early Latin America*; Cangas, *Compendio histórico, geográfico y genealógico y político del Reino del Perú* (1780), as cited by Moreno Cebrián, *El corregidor*, 79. Alistair Hennessy's notion of a "frontier of inclusion," in which "ethnic, cultural and economic facets of the indigenous society are absorbed within Westernized society," may be applied to eighteenth-century Azángaro; see his *The Frontier*, 19.

3. See, e.g., Spalding, *De Indio a campesino*; Macera, *Instrucciones*; Macera, *Mapas coloniales de haciendas cuzqueñas*; Macera, "Feudalismo colonial americano"; Golte, *Bauern in Peru*.

4. Cook, *Tasa de la visita*, 87–110.

5. During the sixteenth and early seventeenth centuries proprietors of encomiendas in Azángaro or neighboring altiplano provinces held encomiendas and were owners of estates or prominent office holders in Cuzco; among them were Juan de Berrio, Martín Hurtado de Arbieto, Gerónimo de Costilla, and Doña Beatriz Coya, daughter of Inca Sayri Túpac. In all cases the primary power base was Cuzco. See Glave and Remy, *Estructura agraria*, 81–83, 112, 118, 120, 124, 128, 146–48; Cook, *Tasa de la visita*, 87–89, 107.

6. Piel, *Capitalisme agraire* 1:147–67; Glave and Remy, *Estructura agraria*, ch. 3; K. Davies, *Landowners*; the most thorough discussion

of elite landholding in colonial Peru is Ramirez, *Provincial Patriarchs*, esp. ch. 6.

7. For 1595: "Datos para un estudio monográfico," 3. For 1607: eight different manuscripts of *visitas de estancias* and *visitas de ayllos*, ANB, Materiales sobre tierras e Indios, año 1607, Nos. 5, 9, 12, 13, 14, 15, 16, 19, and 20. For 1655: litigation about *despojo* from lands Acañani and Viscachani, Putina; ANB, Materiales sobre tierras e Indios, año 1759, No. 102. For 1717: litigation over *deslinde* of Hacienda Purina, dist. Asillo, Mar. 13, 1915, AJA.

8. REPC, J. C. Jordán, 1819/20, F. 132–35 (Nov. 16, 1819); Villanueva Urteaga, *Cuzco 1689*, 112.

9. Villanueva Urteaga, *Cuzco 1689*, 118–19; litigation over *deslinde* of Hacienda Purina, dist. Asillo, Mar. 13, 1915, AJA.

10. See Jacobsen, "Livestock Complexes," 113–42. For peasant communities' use of livestock herds as a protective mechanism against Spanish land encroachments in central Mexico, see C. Gibson, *Aztecs*, 212, 262, 540 n. 33. Crotty (*Cattle, Economics, and Development*, 87–88) ventures the fascinating speculation that the great vulnerability of the prehispanic American civilizations to European conquest may have had much to do with the almost total absence of conflict between pastoralists and crop-raising cultures in the Americas; this conflict had, of course, had a major impact on military development in the eastern hemisphere.

11. O'Phelan Godoy, *Rebellions*, 53–57.

12. Spalding, *De Indio a campesino*, 50.

13. Luna, *Choquehuanca el amauta*, 81–98. Most of these estancias do not appear in the report of Father José de Moscoso, parish priests of Azángaro, to Bishop Mollinedo in 1689.

14. Cf. Celestino and Meyers, *Las cofradías*, 149–56.

15. See the case of the powerful seventeenth-century kuraka Bartolomé Tupa Hallicalla of Asillo, analyzed in Glave, *Trajinantes*, ch. 6.

16. Spalding, *De Indio a campesino*, 55.

17. On the Choquehuanca family history, see Luna, *Choquehuanca el amauta*; Salas Perea, *Monografía*, 18–19; Torres Luna, *Puno histórico*, 183–203.

18. Account of the Services and Losses of the Choquehuanca family during the Túpac Amaru rebellion, ANB, EC año 1782, No. 57.

19. For the properties of Cristóbal Mango Turpo in 1741, see Salas Perea, *Monografía*, 20–21.

20. In Cuzco it was also the livestock-raising provinces—Canas y Canchis and Chumbivilcas—where the number of estates increased notably between 1689 and the 1780s, while in all other provinces it stagnated or declined. See Mörner, *Perfil*, 32, table 17.

21. For example, Hacienda Ccalla, halfway between the pueblos of Azángaro and Arapa, in 1689 was said to belong to an Indian community,

but by the late colonial period it was claimed by the Choquehuancas; see Villanueva Urteaga, *Cuzco 1689*, 115.

22.   Roel, *Historia social*, 276–77; Viceroy José F. de Abascal y Sousa, in his *Memoria de gobierno* 1:286, affirmed that on the basis of this cedula much land was sold or confirmed by composition between 1754 and 1780.

23.   Complaints against Diego Choquehuanca by Indios from ayllus Nequeneque, Picotani, and Chuquini, ANB, Materiales sobre tierras e Indios, EC año 1762, No. 144.

24.   Piel, *Capitalisme agraire* 1:170.

25.   Spalding, *De Indio a campesino*, 144–45.

26.   Piel, *Capitalisme agraire* 1:170; Juan y Santacilia and Ulloa, *Noticias secretas* 1:321.

27.   Golte, *Bauern in Peru*, 64; Santamaría, "La propiedad," 261–62.

28.   Macera, *Mapas coloniales de haciendas cuzqueñas*, cxii–cxv; Piel, *Capitalisme agraire* 1:211.

29.   Macera, *Mapas coloniales de haciendas cuzqueñas*, lxvi–lxvii; evaluation of the formerly Jesuit livestock estancias of Llallahua and Titiri, parish of Santiago de Pupuja, of 1771, in ibid., cxlvii–cxlviii.

30.   "Arancel de los jornales de Perú, 1687," in ibid., 145–46; see also "Obligaciones que han de tener los Indios Yanaconas de esta estancia [Camara, May 12, 1693]," in ibid., 74–75.

31.   Ibid., xxi–xxii; Juan y Santacilia and Ulloa, *Noticias secretas* 1:295–96.

32.   Macera, *Mapas coloniales de haciendas cuzqueñas*, cxii–cxv.

33.   For the Peruvian hacienda of the eighteenth century there exists to my knowledge no thorough analysis of the issue of debt peonage comparable to those by Herbert Nickel, Herman Konrad, and others on Mexico. During the 1740s Juan y Santacilia and Ulloa observed that Andean cattle ranches often strove to put their mitayos in debt in an attempt to retain them permanently on the estate. Pablo Macera surmises debt peonage on Peruvian Jesuit estates during the eighteenth century. He reports that debts were considered such an integral part of hacienda operations that they were counted with capital investments. Some estates employed *guatacos* to capture peasants for the estate and *buscadores* to round up escaped colonos. However, the 1702 instructions for the Jesuit livestock estancias Ayuni and Camara in Cuzco ordered that colonos should never be given more money or goods than they were due for work done, "because the Indian, when he owes, flees and the hacienda loses him." See Juan y Santacilia and Ulloa, *Noticias secretas* 1:293–94; Macera, *Mapas coloniales de haciendas cuzqueñas*, lxxxv, cix–cxi. On prerevolutionary Mexico, see Nickel, "Zur Immobilität," 289–328; Konrad, *Jesuit Hacienda*, 232. For a reinterpretation of credit to colonos, see Bauer, "Rural Workers," 34–63.

34.   Macera, *Mapas coloniales de haciendas cuzqueñas*, xci–xcii.

35.   Ibid.

36. Macera, *Mapas coloniales de haciendas cuzqueñas*, 76–102; Juan y Santacilia and Ulloa, *Noticias secretas* 1:296–97; Jacobsen, "Land Tenure," 193–95.

37. Villanueva Urteaga, *Cuzco 1689*, 77, 112; Macera, *Mapas coloniales de haciendas cuzqueñas*, cxlvii–cxlviii; rent of Estancia Parpuma (Azángaro parish), REPC, J. C. Jordán, 1816–18, F. 384 (Mar. 3, 1818). In exceptional cases (very good pastures, sufficient water, plentiful permanent labor force) rental rates were higher by as much as one-fifth.

38. Flores Galindo, *Arequipa*, 17.

39. Villanueva Urteaga, *Cuzco 1689*, 112.

40. Piel, *Capitalisme agraire* 1:189.

41. Ponce de Léon, "Aspecto económico del problema indígena," 139–41; Spalding, *Huarochirí*, 48–53.

42. Spalding, *Huarochirí*, 156–67; Stern, *Peru's Indian Peoples*, 76–113.

43. Bakewell, *Miners of the Red Mountain*; Cole, *Potosí Mita*; Tandeter, "Trabajo forzado."

44. See, e.g., Sempat Assadourian, *El sistema*, 313; T. Platt, *Estado boliviano*, esp. ch. 1.

45. Kubler, "Quechua," 346.

46. Piel, *Capitalisme agraire* 1:182–83.

47. Ibid. 1:191–95; Spalding, *Huarochirí*, 183.

48. Costa, *Colectivismo agrario en España* 7:174; for enlightened Spanish notions on property, see Herr, *Rural Change*, esp. chs. 1 and 2; for use of such notions in the altiplano, see Jacobsen, "Campesinos."

49. Spalding, *De Indio a campesino*, 143; Spalding, *Huarochirí*, 205–8.

50. Spalding, *Huarochirí*.

51. Juan y Santacilia and Ulloa, *Noticias secretas* 1:318–19.

52. Santamaría, "La propiedad," 261.

53. Ibid.; Choquehuanca (*Ensayo*, 16 n. 4) says that forasteros or sobrinos, as they were called in Azángaro after independence, were assigned "estancias in the places which the originarios did not occupy"; for a 1772 grant by the cacique of a plot of community land not used by any member, see "Documento para la historia de Azángaro," n.p.

54. Wightman, *Indigenous Migration*.

55. ANB, Año 1761, No. 102 (Sept. 5, 1761).

56. Spalding, *De Indio a campesino*, 119–21.

57. RPIP, T. 2, F. 240, p. cv, A. No. 1, Dec. 15, 1900.

58. Personal communication from David Cahill, Feb. 1989. Indians holding land in fee simple were eager to maintain their status as members in communities in order to enjoy its protection and privileges.

59. Conjecture based on the surnames of affluent peasants in the early postindependence period.

60. Cf. Poole, "Qorilazos abigeos," 268–69.

61.   Spalding, *De Indio a campesino.*
62.   Santamaría, "La propiedad," 270–71.
63.   On Sept. 9, 1779, the Audiencia of Charcas ruled accordingly; ANB, Materiales sobre tierras e Indios, EC año 1779, No. 224.
64.   Complaints against Cacique Diego Choquehuanca by Indians from ayllus Nequeneque, Picotani, and Chuquini, ANB, Materiales sobre tierras e Indios, EC año 1762, No. 144.
65.   J. Basadre, "El régimen de la mita"; and Juan y Santacilia and Ulloa, *Notícias secretas* 1:289–90.
66.   J. Basadre, "El régimen de la mita," 334.
67.   Kubler, "Quechua," 372–73.
68.   Cole, *Potosí Mita*, ch. 2.
69.   Golte, *Bauern in Peru*, 74.
70.   Macera, *Iglesia y economía*, 29–30; for repartos de bienes by priests, see also Amat y Junient, *Memoria de gobierno*, 200.
71.   Sánchez Albornóz, *El Indio*, 94.
72.   See, for example, ANB, Materiales sobre tierras e Indios, EC año 1762, No. 18; EC año 1762, No. 144; and EC año 1783, No. 76.
73.   Spalding, *De Indio a campesino*, 55.
74.   Francisco Alvarez Reyes, "Descripción breve del distrito de la Real Chancillería de la Ciudad de la Plata" (Aug. 26, 1649), in *Juicio de limites* 3:216.
75.   Moreno Cebrián, *El corregidor*, 279–316.
76.   Ibid., 321.
77.   This figure assumes between one and two adult male family members paying a tribute rate as originarios of between six and eight pesos per year.
78.   Golte, *Repartos y rebeliones*, 105, calculated a per capita reparto of 9.92 pesos in 1754 for Azángaro province.
79.   ANB, EC año 1771, No. 113.
80.   For abuses of repartos in Azángaro, see Moreno Cebrián, *El corregidor*, 176, 203, 207, 222.
81.   L. Fisher, *Last Inca Revolt*, 254.
82.   Moreno Cebrián, *El corregidor*, 79.
83.   Ibid.; on p. 184 the author speaks of the "alliance cacique-corregidor."
84.   *Informe* by Diego Cristóbal Túpac Amaru, Oct. 18, 1781, in Angelis, *Colección de obras* 4:421.
85.   ANB, Materiales sobre tierras e Indios, EC año 1779, No. 224; Juan y Santacilia and Ulloa, *Noticias secretas* 1:232.
86.   Similarly, in various parts of Europe many peasants had sufficient land resources but during the mid-eighteenth century, faced with rising rents, taxes, and fees, scarcely kept enough of their products for simple

reproduction of their family. Cf. Harnisch, *Die Herrschaft Boitzenburg*, 219–21.

87. Amat y Junient, *Memoria de gobierno*, 193.

88. ANB, Materiales sobre tierras e Indios, EC año 1783, No. 76; Luna, *Choquehuanca el amauta*, 81–98; Lewin, *La rebelión*, 193; for intraelite conflicts between priests and kurakas in Coporaque, Cuzco, just before the Túpac Amaru rebellion, see Hinojosa Cortijo, "Población," 232–33, 255.

89. Vega, *José Gabriel Túpac Amaru*.

90. J. Fisher, *Government*, 78–79.

91. Ibid.

92. Ibid., 51; Fisher also lists (92–93) a case of abuses by Azángaro's subdelegado, Antonio Coello y Doncel, in 1801; Moreno Cebrián, *El corregidor*, 700–701; Cahill, "Curas."

93. L. Fisher, *Last Inca Revolt*, 223; Sahuaraura Titu Atauchi, *Estado del Perú*, 7 n. 4.

94. Roel, *Historia social*, 372–76. Cf. Cahill, "Towards an Infra-structure."

95. ANB, Materiales sobre tierras e Indios, EC año 1782, No. 57, and EC año 1783, No. 7; letter of Jan. 3, 1925, to Arequipa newspaper by Manuel Isidoro Velazco Choquehuanca in Luna, *Choquehuanca el amauta*, 100–102 n. 2; ibid., 81–98.

96. "Oficio del Señor Antonio Zernadas Bermúdez [Oidor of Audiencia of Cuzco] al Señor Gobernador Intendente de Puno," Feb. 18, 1791, in Cornejo Bouroncle, *Pumacahua*, 216–17; Salas Perea, *Monografía*, 22–23. For evidence of succesful legal battles by communities against newly imposed kurakas, see Walker, "La violencia."

97. But cf. Larson, *Colonialism*, 277.

98. Vega, *José Gabriel Túpac Amaru*, 29–30.

99. Lewin, *La rebelión*, 576. For rebel plans to distribute hacienda lands, see Vega, *José Gabriel Túpac Amaru*, 30–31.

100. Petition by parish priests of Orurillo and Santiago to Bishop of Cuzco, October 5, 1799, in Comité Arquidiocesano, *Túpac Amaru*, 368.

101. Roel, *Historia social*, 223.

102. "Expediente sobre la queja presentada por el pueblo de Azángaro para que el gobierno virreynal ponga término a los desmanes que comete el Subdelegado Escobedo," Apr. 2, 1813, BNP, MS. D 656.

103. Petition by parish priests, Oct. 5, 1799, in Comité Arquidiocesano, *Túpac Amaru*, 368.

104. Abascal y Sousa, *Memoria de gobierno* 1:286–87.

105. Ibid.

106. "Composición y venta de la Estancia Caiconi," Nov. 16, 1802, Archivo de la Prefectura, Puno.

107. "Expediente sobre la queja presentada por el pueblo de Azángaro," Apr. 2, 1813.

108. Sallnow, "Manorial Labour," 39–56.

109. Enrique Mayer, "Tenencia y control comunal," 59–72.

110. Only in 1870, in a phase of rapid hacienda expansion, did Choquehuanca's descendants reclaim the land from the descendants of those Indian families. See *Interdicto de adquirir* of fundo Caluyo-Oque-Chupa, Sept. 3, 1920, AJA. For steep declines in the number of yanaconas in maize-producing haciendas of Larecaja, Bolivia, during the late eighteenth century, see Santamaría, "La estructura agraria," 589.

111. Sahuaraura Titu Atauchi, *Estado del Perú*, 15 n. 37.

112. Ibid., 12.

113. Ibid.

114. Choquehuanca, *Ensayo*, 57, 59; for military recruitments in Azángaro, see "Expediente formado a consecuencia de la representación que los Indios de Pupuja hacen ante el Justicia Mayor de Azángaro para no volver a ser alistados para la expedición y dicho Justicia Mayor lo dirige original a la Exma. Junta Provincial," Cuzco, Oct. 9, 1813, BNP, MS. D 515.

115. Most intendants passed decrees against vagrancy. The intendant of Puno, Quimper, in his *Bando de Buen Gobierno* of December 30, 1806, imposed a punishment of a month's public work on vagrants; see J. Fisher, *Government*, 171.

116. L. Fisher, *Last Inca Revolt*, 358.

117. For Viceroy Amat y Junient's concern in the 1770s, see his *Memoria de gobierno*, 193–94. During the 1780s and 1790s mitayos from Azángaro stayed on in Potosí after the end of their term and established a small trade in tallow from their native province, despite new decrees obliging mitayos to return to their communities to prevent a further drain of scarce rural population. See Tandeter, "Trabajo forzado," 35.

118. Pablo José Oricain, "Compendio breve de discursos varios sobre diferentes materias y noticias geográficas comprehensivas a éste Obispado del Cuzco" (1790), in *Juicio de limites* 11:331.

119. For an opposing view see Cahill, "*Curas*."

120. J. Fisher, *Government*, 88–89.

121. Ibid., 112–13.

122. Ibid., 111–14.

123. Report of Dec. 31, 1791, by Pedro Antonio Zernadas Bermúdez, *oidor* of the Audienca de Cuzco and president of the Comisión de la Caja General de Censos de Indios del Cuzco, entitled "Razón de los principales censos perdidos, unos por haberse arruinado las fincas sobre que estaban impuestos, otros por haberse oblado, y no vuelto a imponerse, y otros por haberse perdido en los pleitos de concurso de acreedores y de mas seguidos contra las fincas en que estaban impuestos"; BNP, MS. C 1274. According to Zernadas, communal properties valued at 50,489 pesos were totally lost;

properties worth 120,138 pesos were in limbo and rent had not been paid for years; rental fees were currently paid only on further properties valued at 29,783 pesos.

124. José Victoriano de la Riva, Contaduría General de Puno, to Mariano Escobedo, Justicia Mayor of Azángaro, Puno, May 27, 1813, BNP, MS. D 456, about failure of subdelegado to collect "contribución provisional" after abolition of tribute in 1812. On the autonomy of peasants in Cuzco after the Túpac Amaru Rebellion, see Walker, "Peasants, Caudillos, and the State," chs. 2–3.

4. THE OLIGARCHIZATION OF LIBERAL VISIONS

1. Choquehuanca, *Ensayo*.
2. Romero, *Historia económica del Perú*, 241–42. On the land market in Cuzco during the early republican era, cf. Mörner et al., *Compraventas*, esp. 42, table 6.
3. Hacienda Purina in Asillo, for example, passed from the heirs of Asillo's encomendero into the hands of the church sometime between 1717 and 1828; Expediente judicial, Mar. 13, 1915, AJA; RPIP, T. 5, F. 453, p. clii, A. No. 1 (Mar. 9, 1914).
4. "Regimiento de Dragones del Partido de Azángaro, provincia de Puno," Oct. 6, 1806, BNP; information for midcentury based on my index of persons participating in transactions over land in notarial contracts since 1852 and on 1862 population census of province of Azángaro, BMP.
5. Dancuart and Rodríguez, *Anales* 1:222; Luna, *Choquehuanca el amauta*, 27, 56–64.
6. Cf. Ramirez, *Provincial Patriarchs*, 136, on the north coast during the seventeenth century. Sabato (*Agrarian Capitalism*, 61) finds the same preponderance of officeholders and merchants among owners of livestock estates in Buenos Aires during the 1830s.
7. Information taken from a portrait of Francisco Lizares in the possession of Sr. Armando Dianderas, Arequipa.
8. Will of Francisco Lizares's daughter, María Dolores Lizares Montesinos, of July 4, 1904; REPA, año 1904, Jiménez, F. 837, No. 319. Emphyteusis contracts for Fincas Huntuma and Cuturi: REPP, año 1913, González, F. 54, No. 20 (Jan. 14, 1913), and F. 224, No. 75 (Apr. 23, 1913).
9. Amiable settlement concerning land of Hacienda Nequeneque (district Muñani) between Hilario Velazco and José María Lizares Quiñones, Dec. 4, 1854; REPA, año 1854, Calle. For a vicious description of Josefa Quiñones and her descendents, see the vitriolic pamphlet by an anonymous author (thought to be Luis Felipe Luna), *Biografía criminal*, 4–11.
10. REPC, años 1823–25, Jordán, F. 328 (July 5, 1824); on earlier sale of Huasacona by aristocratic Cuzqueño families, see REPC, años 1819–20, Jordán, F. 132–34 (Nov. 16, 1819).

11.   Estévez had taken out large loans from his brother Pedro, a merchant in Tacna, to come up with the considerable purchase price for Huasacona and two smaller estates on the peninsula of Capachica close to Puno; REPP, año 1853, Cáceres (July 8, 1853), and año 1854 (July 7, 1854).

12.   REPP, año 1854, Cáceres (Feb. 17, 1854).

13.   Piel, *Capitalisme agraire* 1:261; see also J. Basadre, *Historia de la república* 1:182.

14.   Valdéz de la Torre, *Evolución*, 158.

15.   J. Basadre, *Historia de la república* 1:171–72; Valdéz de la Torre, *Evolución*, 158.

16.   REPP, año 1853, Cáceres (June 7, 1853); for the early history of the Escobedos in Azángaro, see Wibel, "Evolution," 189–90.

17.   A decree issued by President Ramón Castilla on August 6, 1846, facilitated the return of church estates, expropriated during the Orbegoso and Santa Cruz administrations, by the present owners to the original proprietors; see Valdéz de la Torre, *Evolución*, 172–73.

18.   Echenique, *Memorias* 1:94.

19.   The significant exception was the sale of the church hacienda Pasincha by the state on March 2, 1836, for 1,500 pesos to Juan Antonio de Macedo, a partisan of Santa Cruz.

20.   Between 1843 and 1850 nearly all newly listed estates were small, marginal fincas with between 600 and 1,000 OMR.

21.   "Padrón de contribución de predios rústicos . . . de Lampa, 1843"; "Padrón de contribuciones prediales . . . de Lampa, 1850" (both AGN).

22.   Romero (*Monografía del departamento de Puno*, 436) apologetically points out that "the extension of a hacienda is not always a sign of wealth and prosperity." Puno's latifundism, according to him, was a necessary consequence of the scarcity of pastures.

23.   Brading, "Hacienda Profits," 33.

24.   See, e.g., rent of Hda. Calacala, distr. Chupa, by Martina Carpio vda. de Urbina to Bonifacio Ramos in 1853, REPP, año 1853, Cáceres (Oct. 5, 1853).

25.   For those estates operated by their owners, the state levied rural property tax at 4 percent of assessed gain from hacienda operation. If operated by renters or emphyteutic holders, an additional 2 percent tax was levied. However, only in a few cases did the 1843 and 1850 tax lists from Lampa explicitly enter 50 percent more gain for haciendas held by lease or emphyteusis, i.e., a ratio of gain:livestock capital of 1.5:10.

26.   This estimate assumes a ratio of gain:livestock capital of 2:10, allowing for an equal share of income for owner and tenant.

27.   Choquehuanca, *Ensayo*, 60.

28.   REPP, año 1854, Cáceres (July 7, 1854).

29.   Escobedo to Paredes, Arequipa, Apr. 11, 1862, MPA.

30. Rivero, *Memorias*, 9.

31. The mean value per *topo* of land in the department of Cuzco increased briefly during the early 1830s and declined from the late 1830s to the early 1850s; see Mörner et al., *Compraventas*, 27–32, graph no. 1, 35. The greater short-term volatility of land prices arises in Cuzco's cereal and sugar growing areas.

32. See, e.g., sale of estancia Carpani, distr. Muñani; REPA, año 1863, Patiño, F. 58, No. 18 (Apr. 22, 1863). Evaluation of Llallahua in 1771, in Macera, *Mapas coloniales de haciendas cuzqueñas*, cxlvii–cxlviii; evaluation of Huancarani, Azángaro, Apr. 12, 1845, MPA.

33. REPP, año 1869, unnamed judge (Feb. 15, 1869).

34. Cf. Burga, *De la encomienda a la hacienda*, 111–12 for the north coast during the seventeenth century.

35. Cf. Manrique, *Mercado interno*, 86.

36. REPP, año 1854, Cáceres (Jan. 24, 1854).

37. Jacobsen, "Land Tenure," 411, table 5–15.

38. The exact number of rented haciendas in Lampa province in 1843 belonging to corporate holders cannot be determined because of lack of information on the owners of fifty-five rented haciendas.

39. Rivero, *Memorias*, 43.

40. For sale of an estancia because the owner lived far away and saw no way of managing it profitably, see REPP, año 1857, Cáceres (Nov. 10, 1857).

41. REPP, año 1854, Cáceres (June 3, 1854).

42. For long-term failure to replenish the stock of Hda. San Francisco de Pachaje, Putina, see REPP, año 1858, Cáceres (Sept. 29, 1858); REPP, año 1859, Cáceres (Apr. 5, 1859); "Matrícula de predios rústicos, provincia de Azángaro, año de 1902," BMP.

43. Jacobsen, "Land Tenure," 871–81, app. 6.

44. During the 1750s Azángaro's human population was only one-third that of 1825–29. Assuming the same mean number of OMR per estate and the same ratio between livestock in the estate and peasant sectors as in 1825–29, and estimating the number of estates in the province during the 1750s at 70, an increment of 23 over the number for 1689, the ratio between livestock and human populations for the 1750s might have been as high as 30:1. The associated estimate for the province's livestock population for the 1750s is 414,697 OMR. These are lower range estimates, since they do not account for the considerable herds of cattle and sheep belonging to the church and private members of the elite pastured on community lands. The human population estimate for the ratio is based on 8 percent provincial population being white or mestizo, above the Indian population calculated from the tribute recounts for 1758–59.

45. Rivero, *Memorias*, 43.

46. Thompson, Mosley-Thompson, Bolzan, and Koci, "A 1500-Year Record"; the authors suggest below-average precipitation beginning in the 1720s and lasting until 1860.

47. Choquehuanca, Ensayo, 62.

48. Jacobsen, "Land Tenure," 222, table 3-6.

49. Choquehuanca, Ensayo, 57.

50. Ibid., 62.

51. Jacobsen, "Land Tenure," 230, table 3-8.

52. REPA, año 1860, Manrique (Aug. 24, 1860); REPA, año 1865, Patiño (May 22, 1865).

53. Trazegnies, La idea de derecho, 188; García Jordán, "La iglesia peruana," 19–43.

54. During the late colonial period apparently a larger number of chaplaincies consisted only of livestock herds, without land. Personal communication from David Cahill, July 1988.

55. In the Intendency of Arequipa chaplaincies and loans played an important role at least until 1840 and were considered by landholders as a dangerous drain on their income; see Wibel, "Evolution," 114–15, 353.

56. On Loquicolla Grande, see REPP, año 1856, Cáceres (Oct. 31, 1856); REPP, año 1859, Cáceres (Jan. 10, 1856); REPP, año 1913, González, F. 363, No. 118 (June 6, 1913); on Picotani, see REPA, año 1879, Torres Nuñez, F. 25, No. 53 (May 7, 1879); REPP, año 1897, González, No. 11 (Feb. 7, 1897); RPIP, T. 3, F. 379, p. lxxxiii, A. No. 2 (Sept. 29, 1906); on Huasacona, see contracts listed in notes 10 and 11.

57. Piérola, Anales.

58. Properties that carried encumbrances from church loans in the archdiocese of Lima during the seventeenth century, with a few exceptions, lay close to the city; see Hamnett, "Church Wealth in Peru."

59. Abascal y Sousa, Memoria de gobierno 1:175–80. Originarios in this context probably means the autochtonous population. The crown had reintroduced tribute in 1815, but it may not have been implemented in Peru by the time Abascal wrote his report in 1816; in the remaining quinquennium before the occupation of Lima by the patriot troops its collection never recovered pre-1812 levels.

60. Valdéz de la Torre, Evolución, 145–46; J. Basadre, Historia de la república 1:170–71.

61. Valdéz de la Torre, Evolución, 147–48; T. Davies, Indian Integration in Peru, 21.

62. Dancuart and Rodríguez, Anales 1:272; Peralta Ruíz, En pos del tributo, 36–43.

63. Ibid. 1:277–78; Valdéz de la Torre, Evolución, 148.

64. Piel, Capitalisme agraire 1:281–82.

65. Circular of February 1827, as cited in Valdéz de la Torre, Evolución, 152.

66. Ibid., 149.
67. Dancuart and Rodríguez, *Anales* 2:136; J. Basadre, *Historia de la república* 1:227.
68. REPA, año 1859, Manrique (May 10, 1859).
69. Choquehunaca, *Ensayo*, 72.
70. Ibid.
71. See Langer, "El liberalismo," 59–95, on early republican land legislation in Bolivia.
72. Min. de Hacienda, *Memoria [1847]*, 3–4. See also the circular of Prefect Ramón Castilla to five subprefects of the department of Puno, Dec. 5, 1834, in Instituto "Libertador Ramón Castilla," *Archivo Castilla* 4:183.
73. See, for example, T. Davies, *Indian Integration in Peru*, 22; Sivirichi, *Derecho indígena*, 102; and Mariátegui, "El Problema de la tierra," in his *Siete ensayos*, 75.
74. Macera, *Las plantaciones azucareras*, cl, speaks of "equilibrium" in the "secular conflict between the Indian communities and haciendas" from the 1780s to the 1850s.
75. For similar interpretations on Mexico, see Coatsworth, "Railroads," 48–71; Tutino, *From Insurrection to Revolution*, ch. 6; González Navarro (*Anatomía*, 142–47) demonstrates that attempts by national, state, or provincial governments and by local authorities to privatize Indian community lands in Central Mexico failed before 1855 against unrelenting peasant opposition.
76. T. Davies, *Indian Integration in Peru*, 21.
77. Sivirichi, *Derecho indígena*, 210ff.
78. J. Basadre, *Historia de la república* 3:1309.
79. Valdéz de la Torre, *Evolución*, 159.
80. REPA, año 1892, Meza (Dec. 21, 1892, prot. of original proceedings of Feb. 23, 1844).
81. See, for example, Valdéz de la Torre, *Evolución*, 159, specifically on Puno's communities.
82. Hünefeldt, "Poder y contribuciones."
83. Valdéz de la Torre, *Evolución*, 143.
84. "Infracciones de la Constitución en el Departamento de Puno manifestadas por la representación departamental," Dec. 1828, in Puertas Castro, *José Domingo Choquehuanca*, 22–27.
85. Ibid., 28.
86. Paul Marcoy in 1860 encountered a group of Indians chanting and dancing "kacharparis," the parting ceremony for mitayos during the colonial period. The ceremony was intoned for "Indians from Pujuja [*sic*] or Caminaca who the subprefect of Lampa [*sic*] has sent to work in some mine in the Raya [a mountainous border area between the altiplano and Cuzco department]"; Marcoy, *Travels* 1:113.
87. M. Basadre y Chocano, *Riquezas peruanas*, 144.

88. J. Basadre, *Historia de la república* 1:178; Sivirichi, *Derecho indígena*, 121; Jacobsen, "Taxation," 311–39.

89. Jacobsen, "Taxation," 325, table 2, where I estimate per capita tribute collection to have declined from 1.35 pesos in 1795 to 1.04 pesos in 1850, a drop of 23 percent.

90. Mean tribute collection for the Intendency of Puno during the 1790s (190,691.2 pesos) calculated from the gross intake of the cajas reales of Carabaya and Chucuito, given by TePaske and Klein, *Royal Treasuries* 1:99–101, 2:97–99. The number of tributarios in Puno in 1793 was estimated as follows: according to "El Obispado del Cuzco Visitado por su actual Diocesano el Y. N. D. D. Bartholomé Maria Heras . . . que lo exercía el dho. Sr. pr. todo el [*sic*] en 5 años contínuos y se dio a luz el año de 1798," reprinted facsimile in Mörner, *Perfil*, between pp. 132 and 133, the percentage of Indians in total population of the three altiplano partidos belonging to the bishopric of Cuzco was 86.85 percent. To arrive at total Indian population in the Intendency of Puno, I applied this percentage to total population for the intendency according to the census of Viceroy Gil y Lemos of 1793 (186,682), given by Romero, *Monografía del departamento de Puno*, 225; I divided the total Indian population by the conventional factor 4.5 to arrive at the number of tributarios (36,030) in the intendency. Values for 1846 were calculated as follows: according to "Estado que manifiesta el valor anual de la contribución jeneral de indíjenas y sus gastos con distinción de lo que satisfacen los poseedores de tierras y de lo que pagan los que no las tienen," in Min. de Hacienda, *Memoria [1847]*, 53,612 Indian tributaries were registered in the latest rolls for the Indian head tax in Puno, who were supposed to pay a total 306,926.25 pesos in 1846. But according to "Cuenta general de la administración de las rentas de la república," drawn up by the Sección de Valores of the Tribunal de Cuentas, also appended to the *Memoria [1847]*, by May 1847 88,073 pesos and 2.5 reales of all direct taxes owed for 1846 were still not paid (although they were to be collected during the year of assessment). The likelihood that they would have been paid in subsequent months seems remote, as the treasury of Puno also listed debts of some 480,000 pesos on direct taxes from prior years. The overwhelming part of these "quiebras," or tax debts, had to stem from unpaid contribución de indígenas, as it accounted for more than 95 percent of total direct taxes in the department. Even if we assume that not one real was paid on all other direct taxes owed in Puno for 1846, the debt on the Indians' contribution for that year would still have amounted to 80,493 pesos and 4.25 reales. I subtracted this sum from the amount owed according to the matrículas and arrived at the sum of 226,432 pesos 5.75 reales actually paid in contribuciones de indígenas in Puno during 1846. Dividing that sum through the number of tributaries listed in the matrículas rendered the mean Indian contribution paid per tributary.

91. Sánchez Albornóz, *Indios*, 43.

92. In Azángaro the ratio of originarios to forasteros stood at 1:6.6 in 1786, 1:4.5 in 1825–29, and 1:7.3 in 1843.

93. Renewed decline in Azángaro's ratio betweeen originarios and forasteros from 1825–29 to 1843 is responsible for the declining mean per capita tax rate *owed* from 1825–29 to 1843.

94. Macera, *Tierra y población* 1:257–66. *Uros* were the remnants of an ancient altiplano ethnic group. *Sacristanes* (sextons) and *yerbateros* (collectors of fodder or herb?) were apparently community peasants whose families traditionally held certain offices.

95. As early as the 1790s Tadeo Haenke considered the distinction between originarios and forasteros as "ridiculous" because the forasteros "today are as originarios as those that carry that label and possibly more well off"; Haenke, *Descripción del Perú*, 111.

96. For precise figures and sources, see n. 90. Cf. Peralta Ruíz, *En pos del tributo*, chs. 3–4, for the case of Cuzco.

97. Circulars, Ramón Castilla to five subprefects of department of Puno, Oct. 18, 1834 and Nov. 17, 1834, in Instituto "Libertador Ramón Castilla," *Archivo Castilla* 4:146, 169.

98. By January 31, 1835, four former subdelegados or subprefects of Azángaro owed 28,703 pesos on unremitted taxes; this figure did not include debts considered uncollectable; Ramón Castilla to Ministro de Estado en el Departamento de Hacienda, Puno, Feb. 6, 1835, in ibid. 4:223–25; for the instability and contested nature of local administration, see Hünefeldt, "Poder y contribuciones."

99. See Choquehuanca, *Ensayo*, 60–61, on collection procedures.

100. Porras Barrenchea, *Dos viajeros franceses*, 53 n. d, 55; Markham, *Travels*, 177. Recruitment caused such horror among peasants that some young men committed suicide to escape; see Bustamante, *Apuntes*, 90–93.

101. Mariátegui, "El problema de la tierra," in his *Siete ensayos*, 69.

102. For the case of Cuzco, see Walker, "Peasants, Caudillos, and the State," chs. 5–6, and Peralta Ruíz, *En pos del tributo*, 67.

103. Min. de Hacienda, *Memoria [1849]*, 8. On the typhoid epidemic of the mid-1850s, see ch. 1.

104. M. Basadre y Chocano, *Riquezas peruanas*, 144.

105. Giraldo and Franch, "Hacienda y gamonalismo," 7–8; Urquiaga Vásquez, *Huella histórica de Putina*, 28–29, 46.

106. According to a "Padroncillo de confesiones de la doctrina del pueblo de Putina" from 1809, at least 117 *españoles* lived in the parish; see Urquiaga Vásquez, *Huella histórica de Putina*, 57–59. The *vecindario* (Spanish citizens) of Azángaro amounted to only eight families in 1813; see "Expediente sobre la queja presentada por el pueblo de Azángaro para

que el gobierno virreynal ponga término a los desmanes que comete el subdelegado [Ramón] Escobedo," Apr. 2, 1813, BNP, MS. D 656.

107. "Expediente sobre la queja"; Putina had creole mayors at least since 1792; Urquiaga Vásquez, *Huella histórica de Putina*, 104.

108. Choquehuanca, *Ensayo*, 15 n. 1.

109. Ibid., 15–52; the mean value for "complete houses" in the late 1820s was 417 pesos, and 24 pesos for "incomplete houses" (one-room peasant cottages).

110. Choquehuanca, *Ensayo*, 17 n. 2; Sallnow, "Manorial Labour," 39–56.

111. Choquehuanca, *Ensayo*, 65; for similar observations on a ranching community in mid-nineteenth century Mexico, see González, *Pueblo en vilo*, 104–5.

112. "Regimiento de Dragones del Partido de Azángaro, provincia de Puno," Oct. 6, 1806, BNP.

113. Choquehuanca, *Ensayo*, 16 n. 1, 60.

114. Ibid., 68.

115. Ibid., 60. Choquehuanca's implicit estimate of the size of the "class" of *pobres*—basically one-third of the Indian population—is high. Included in this group were truly landless peasants—less than 10 percent of Indian peasants according to my estimates—and colonos on estates, although it is difficult to see why their livelihood should have been any less secure than that of middling community peasants. But according to my estimates, these two groups together amounted to only some 23 percent of the Indian peasantry. If Choquehuanca's estimate of the province's poor population is not simply too high—a distinct possibility—perhaps the poorest of the "new proprietors" also suffered periodic life-threatening scarcities. Following are my estimates of Azángaro's Indian peasantry (excluding Poto, Taraco and Pusi) according to land tenure status and tax categories between 1826 and 1835: Colonos on estates, 13.8%; originarios, 22.3%; forasteros with land, 54.7%; forasteros (excluding colonos) without land, 9.1%. For sources and method of estimation, see Jacobsen, "Land Tenure," pp. 834–41, app. 2.

116. Choquehuanca, *Ensayo*, 15–48.

117. "Contribución general de industria, Padrón de contribuyentes del Pueblo de Vilcapaza, Capital de la Provincia de Azángaro que empieza a regir desde el semestre de San Juan de 1850," private archive of Augusto Ramos Zambrano, Puno; for priests' life-styles in the altiplano around 1850, see Herndon and Gibbon, *Exploration* 2:88; Mörner, *Andean Past*, 133.

118. Altamirano, "La economía campesina," 93–130, suggests a preponderant role of artisanal production for peasant subsistence.

119. See Dancuart and Rodríguez, *Anales* 2:134; Calle, *Diccionario* 3:324–26.

120. "Contribución general de industria," private archive of Augusto Ramos Zambrano, Puno.

121. See Orlove, "Urban and Rural Artisans," 209.

122. On a mountain road Clements Markham encountered an "active young vicuña hunter, well mounted, and provided with a gun," who claimed to be on a wool-purchasing expedition for "the cacique Choquehuanca of Azángaro"; *Travels*, 196.

123. For example, the Zecenarro Mamanis' Estancia San Antonio de Lacconi, Azángaro district, in 1862 had 100 cows, more than 1,000 sheep and a "substantial string of horses and mules." REPA, año 1862, Patiño, F. 332, No. 159 (Oct. 31, 1862).

124. Choquehuanca, *Ensayo*, 67. During the mid-nineteenth century established families in that city kept Indian "pages," young boys serving the lady of the house and admired as something exotic. They were "purchased for a few piastres and a supply of cocoa [*sic*] and brandy" from their families in the highlands; Marcoy, *Travels* 1:43–44.

125. For very similar rates of rural labor employed on estates in the department of Cuzco in 1845, see Peralta Ruíz, *En pos del tributo*, 60–61.

126. Bustamante, *Apuntes*, 19; "Cuaderno de la Hacienda Quimsachata que corre desde primero de Agosto de 1841 a cargo del Mayordomo Manuel Machaca," MPA.

127. Taylor, "Earning a Living," 103–4. For multiple artisanal occupations within one family, see Herndon and Gibbon, *Exploration* 2:69; Mörner, *Historia social latinoamericana*, 187–233.

128. See, e.g., Spalding, *De Indio a campesino*, 192.

129. Choquehuanca, *Ensayo*, 65.

130. "El Obispado del Cuzco . . . año de 1798," in Mörner, *Perfíl*, between pp. 132 and 133; Dir. de Estadística, *Resumen del censo [1876]*, 93–109; "Censo de población de 1862, provincia de Azángaro," BMP.

131. On mestizos in early republican Cuzco, cf. Remy, "La sociedad," 451–84.

132. On "exclusionary" liberalism in Peru, cf. Gootenberg, "Beleaguered Liberals"; for Argentine debates, see Halperin Donghi, "Argentina." On consumption as a determinant of social status in nineteenth-century Latin America, see Bushnell and Macaulay, *Emergence of Latin America*, 52–53.

133. Bustamante, *Los Indios del Perú*, 19–20.

134. See the bond posted by the affluent peasants Francisco Zecenarro for Manuel E. Rosello, REPA, Manrique, año 1859 (Feb. 26, 1859); and Francisco Puraca for Antonio Chávez, REPA (minutes), Patiño, año 1863, F. 72 (Nov. 11, 1863).

135. Calle, *Diccionario* 1:268, 3:633.

136. Echenique, *Memorias* 2:181.

137. Leubel, *El Perú*, 233; "Censo de población de 1862, provincia de Azángaro," BMP.

138. Urquiaga Vásquez, *Huella histórica de Putina*, 76.

139. Cf. Trazegnies, *La idea de derecho*, 30–36, 285–340.

5. THE SYMBIOSIS OF EXPORTS AND REGIONAL TRADE

1. Hunt, "Growth and Guano," 255–318; Bonilla, *Guano y burguesía*; Yepez del Castillo, *Perú 1820–1920*; for Latin America in general, see Glade, "Latin America" 4:1–56.

2. Exports rose fourfold between the nadir of 1883 and 1910, from 1.4 to 6.2 million pounds sterling, and may have doubled again until 1919; British and U.S. capital investments grew nearly tenfold between 1880 and 1919, from U.S. $17 to 161 million; Thorp and Bertram, *Peru 1890–1977*, 27, 338.

3. Ibid., chs. 3–7.

4. There are no reliable figures for total Peruvian wool *production* before the late 1930s. In 1921 estimated global wool production amounted to 3,003 million English pounds; in that year Peru exported about 14 million English pounds, including both sheep and cameloid wools. See Hamilton, *Statistical Survey*, 56, table 17; *Wool Year Book, 1930*, 29–30.

5. Margins of error for export statistics on Peruvian wool for most years between the mid-1850s and 1920 lay in the range of 10 percent, only exceptionally rising to 20 percent. See the careful comparison of Peruvian export and British import statistics in Miller, "Wool Trade."

6. Deane and Cole, *British Economic Growth*, 196–201; Mues, *Die Organisation*, 152.

7. Based on English import prices, for lack of a long-term series of FOB Peruvian wool prices. Given the importance of currency devaluations, I calculated the soles equivalent of pound sterling import prices. I converted the values for years prior to 1863 from pesos into the decimal soles m.n., applying the conversion 1 peso = 0.80 soles m.n. Detailed wool export statistics are in Jacobsen, "Cycles and Booms," 491–500.

8. Bonilla, *Gran Bretaña* 4:103, 105–7, 168–69; Tschudi, *Reisen durch Südamerika* 5:351.

9. Lewis, *Evolution*, 80–81; Sabato, "Wool Trade," 65.

10. Saul, *Studies*, 102.

11. Report by Consul Robilliard about Mollendo trade in 1880, in Bonilla, *Gran Bretaña* 5:5–7; Manrique, *Yawar Mayu*, 103–5.

12. Report by Consul Robilliard about Mollendo trade in 1886, in Bonilla, *Gran Bretaña* 5:9.

13. Miller, "Wool Trade," 299; Manrique (*Yawar Mayu*, 94–135) even speaks, mistakenly in my view, of the relative affluence of wool producers during the war because of increased domestic demand for the production of uniforms and other articles.

14. Sartorius von Waltershausen, *Die Entstehung der Weltwirtschaft*, 419; Lewis, *Evolution*, 280–81, table A.11.

15. For world production of wool, see Lewis, *Evolution*, 277, table A.10. Australia's sheep population nearly doubled between 1880 and 1895, reaching a peak of 100,940,405 in the latter year; see Mues, *Die Organisation*, 155, app. 9.

16. Sigsworth and Blackman, "Woolen and Worsted Industries," 142–44; Saul, *Studies*, 106–7.

17. Lewis, *Evolution*, 277–81, tables A.10, A.11.

18. Saul, *Studies*, 126–27.

19. For the early war crisis in Peru, see Albert and Henderson, *South America*, ch. 2. For mechanisms to increase wool production in response to strong demand, see Burga and Reátegui, *Lanas*, 47–48, 99.

20. Saul, *Studies*, 93.

21. Bairoch, *Economic Development*, 119, table 35.

22. Miller, "Wool Trade," 303–4.

23. Garland, *La moneda en el Perú*, 67; Quiroz, "Financial Institutions," 232–37; Thorp and Bertram, *Peru 1890–1977*, 26–30; Jacobsen, "Land Tenure," 277, table 4-1.

24. Moll and Barreto, "El sistema monetario del Perú," 146–48.

25. In terms of pound sterling, earnings for the best year of this period, 1890, lay 56 percent below the best year of the 1860s, 1864.

26. Mean value of sheep wool exports from Islay and Mollendo, FOB, in soles m.n.: 1861–66: 653,891 soles; 1892–1903: 616,654 soles. To calculate FOB prices for 1892–1903, I used the mean ratio between CIF and FOB prices for 1886–92.

27. Benavides, *Historia de la moneda boliviana*, 39–41.

28. For Peruvian attempts to deal with Bolivian *moneda feble*, see Garland, *La moneda en el Perú*, 33–35; Echenique, *Memorias* 2:202–3; J. Basadre, *Historia de la república* 3:1451–52; on Bolivian conversion schemes, see Benavides, *Historia de la moneda boliviana*.

29. Min. de Hacienda y Comercio, *Memoria [1890]*, lxii–lxvii.

30. *Guía general*; for a model of currency exchange circuits, see Burga and Reátegui, *Lanas*, 163–67.

31. Benavides, *Historia de la moneda boliviana*, 97–99.

32. Political developments in Bolivia (such as the war with Brazil over the Acre territory in 1902–3) also played a role in the depreciation of her currency. The adoption of the silver standard by China and India, and Great Britain's rush to buy silver to supply these countries, led to a brief appreciation of bolivianos and debased pesos beginning in 1904; ibid., 83.

33. Paco Gutiérrez to Ricketts, Ayaviri, May 8, 1915, Lb. 26-Interior, AFA-R.

34. Sigsworth, *Black Dyke Mills*, 237, 243–56; I am indebted to Gordon Appleby for this reference. Handling alpaca wool apparently be-

came a specialized businesses in Arequipa, increasing local oligopsonistic control; personal communication from Rory Miller, Aug. 1990.

35. Hutner, *Farr Alpaca Company*, 32–34.

36. Sigsworth, *Black Dyke Mills*, 254.

37. Burga and Reátegui, *Lanas*, 35, speak of an "alpaca cycle" for 1915–19. Although this description is accurate for Ricketts, for southern Peru as a whole the boom years were a "sheep wool cycle." Prices and export volume for this fiber rose faster than did those for alpaca wool.

38. FOB prices as a percentage of CIF prices for alpaca wools developed as follows: 1861–66: 68.7%; 1886–91: 74.0%; 1928–29: 74.7%. There were enormous fluctuations from year to year within these periods. This fact, along with the unexpectedly large difference between CIF and FOB prices, suggests that the alpaca market was more speculative than was the sheep wool market.

39. On the correlation between southern Peruvian wool exports and international Kondratieff cycles, see Jacobsen, "Cycles and Booms."

40. According to the National Wool Producers Association, in 1942 about 4,085 tons of sheep wool and 2,318 tons of alpaca wool were either exported or consumed by factories in all of Peru. A further 2,000 tons, undifferentiated as to type of wool, was estimated to be used by Indian household production or urban artisans. If we generously assume that 50 percent of household and artisanal consumption pertained to alpaca wools, then total national wool production would have consisted of about 58.2 percent sheep wool, 38 percent alpaca wool, and 3.8 percent llama and *huarizo* wool. (A huarizo is a cross between a llama and an alpaca.) In the south the share of alpaca was perhaps higher. See *Memoria . . . de la Industria Lanar*, 56.

41. Duffield, *Peru*, 15–16.

42. Forbes, *On the Aymara Indians*, 69–70.

43. See Burga and Reátegui, *Lanas*, 88. I estimate the community peasants' and hacienda colonos' share of cameloids in Azángaro province around 1920 at between 60 and 70 percent; see Jacobsen, "Land Tenure," 871–81, app. 6.

44. Thorp and Bertram, *Peru 1890–1977*, 33–35, 348–49 (tables A.4.2, A.4.3); Wright, *The Old and the New Peru*, 448; Yepez del Castillo, *Perú 1820–1920*, 171–72; Boloña, "Tariff Policies," 83, table 3.3.

45. Report by Vice-Consul Robilliard about Mollendo trade in 1902, in Bonilla, *Gran Bretaña* 4:52.

46. Thorp and Bertram, *Peru 1890–1977*, 124–27; Lewis, *Evolution*, 170–71.

47. Table 5.5 exaggerates that slump for the years 1886 to 1901, however, as mineral exports from Bolivia, not listed separately in available trade statistics until 1902, contributed a growing share to total Mollendo exports until the completion of the rail link from La Paz to Arica in 1914.

48. Jacobsen, "Free Trade," 153; Reports by British vice consuls about Mollendo trade for 1898, 1900, 1901, and 1908–9, in Bonilla, *Gran Bretaña* 4:32, 40–47, 79; Dunn, *Peru*, 464–65.

49. See reports by the British consuls on Islay and Mollendo trade for 1862, 1863, 1871, and 1878 in Bonilla, *Gran Bretaña* 4:133, 144, 190–91, 257; on the decline of silver mining between the late 1840s and 1890, see Deustua, "Producción minera." For the crucial role of transport costs for mining in the central sierra, see Contreras, "Mineros." For Bolivian and Mexican mining conjunctures, cf. Mitre, *Los patriarcas de la plata*; Urrutia de Strebelski and Nava Oteo, "La minería," 119–45.

50. Reports by British consuls about Mollendo trade for 1890, 1898, 1900, 1901, 1902, 1906–7, 1908–9 and 1910–11, in Bonilla, *Gran Bretaña* 4:17, 32, 40, 47, 52, 74, 79, 87; Wright, *The Old and the New Peru*, 357.

51. Export of coinage, considerable during some years, appears to have been linked not to balance-of-trade deficits but rather to the attempted withdrawal of Bolivian currency from circulation in southern Peru during the 1890s. Report by British Vice-Consul Rowlands about Mollendo trade in 1908–9, in Bonilla, *Gran Bretaña* 4:79; Deustua, "El ciclo interno," 23–49.

52. A table on Islay and Mollendo's balance of trade, 1853–1931, can be obtained from the author.

53. Dunn, *Peru*, 24.

54. Imports through Mollendo accounted for between 7.2 and 11.0 percent of national imports from 1909 to 1916. Total southern Peruvian imports were somewhat higher.

55. Appleby, "Exportation and Its Aftermath," 81.

56. Burga and Reátegui, *Lanas*, 151.

57. My own calculation, based on Montavon, *Wearing Apparel in Peru*, 16–21.

58. Montavon, *Wearing Apparel in Peru*.

59. Krüggeler, "Lifestyles in the Peruvian Countryside."

60. REPP, Cáceres, año 1858 (Aug. 17, 1858).

61. REPP, año 1890 II, San Martín, No. 18 (Apr. 30, 1890).

62. Mercedes Martínez to Manuel E. Paredes; Puno, Feb. 17, 1873, MPA.

63. Will of Mariano Wenceslao Enríquez, in REPP, año 1909, Garnica, F. 375, No. 187 (Oct. 27, 1909).

64. Markham, *Travels*, 76 n. 6.

65. Appleby, "Exportation and Its Aftermath," 84–85; see also the inventory of a Puno store, in REPP, año 1890 II, San Martín, No. 18 (Apr. 30, 1890).

66. Import substitution of textiles advanced faster for Peru as a whole than for the south. Between 1911 and 1914 textiles and clothing accounted

for only 19–22 percent of total national imports. See Thorp and Bertram, *Peru 1890–1977*, 119, table 6.4; Boloña, "Tariff Policies," 253–63.

67.   Southern Peru's imports of staple foods, primarily wheat flour from Chile, accounted for only 5–10 percent of total imports between the 1860s and the years of World War I, growing roughly proportionate to the general growth of imports. Before the 1920s there are no signs of serious longer-term food shortages in the region. Report about Islay trade in 1863 by Consul Cocks, in Bonilla, *Gran Bretaña* 4:140; and table on Mollendo imports, 1910–31, constructed by author. Vincent Peloso, in his article "Succulence and Sustenance," argues that price and availability of staple foods, especially bread, became a political issue in Peru first during the 1860s and especially after the War of the Pacific. It was an issue for working classes of Lima, not the altiplano peasantry.

68.   Markham, *History*, 498; Markham, *Travels*, 102–3.

69.   Burga and Reátegui, *Lanas*, 179.

70.   I chose 1840 as starting point since the small initial wool exports around 1830 would have distorted the picture.

71.   These are low estimates, especially for 1917. They refer to peak years of wool exports and are based on an assumption of linear absolute growth of livestock populations between 1830 and 1917. In fact, the absolute growth of flocks must have been considerably larger between about 1890 and 1917 than before. Thus the share of domestically retained wools in southern Peru by the end of World War I is likely to have grown back to about two-thirds in the case of sheep wool and one-third in the case of alpaca wool. For 1942 the Junta Nacional de la Industria Lanar estimated that of a total of 8,667.9 metric tons of wools of all types, 5,148,8 tons, about 60 percent, were retained domestically. See *Memoria . . . de la Industria Lanar*, 56.

72.   Wright, *The Old and the New Peru*, 448; Yepez del Castillo, *Perú 1820–1920*, 171–72; Burga and Reátegui, *Lanas*, 138–39.

73.   Burga and Reátegui, *Lanas*, 136–37; Wright, *The Old and the New Peru*, 448.

74.   Yepez del Castillo, *Perú 1820–1920*, 171–72; the author's claim that domestic industrial wool production was about 10 percent of wool exports is misleading, as he includes both sheep and alpaca wools in the export figures. Domestic factories consumed practically no alpaca wool.

75.   Even if all of the 680 tons of sheep wool consumed by domestic factories had been produced in southern Peru, the share of sheep wool processed in peasant households could be estimated at 52.2 percent in 1918. For alpaca wool I have assumed that nearly all fiber not exported was processed in peasant households.

76.   Sereni, *Capitalismo y mercado nacional*, 99–119.

77.   Cf. Jacobsen, "Free Trade," 145–75.

78. Burga and Flores Galindo, *Apogeo*, 121; Burga and Reátegui, *Lanas*, 37–39.

79. Burga and Reátegui, *Lanas*, 37; Dunn, *Peru*, 144–50.

80. Forbes, *On the Aymara Indians*, 57; *Guía general*, 213.

81. Romero, *Monografía del departamento de Puno*, 506–7.

82. Appleby, "Exportation and Its Aftermath," 100–107.

83. T. Platt, *Estado boliviano*, chs. 1–2.

84. Manrique, *Mercado interno*, esp. 139–41, 191–94, 265–70; Wilson, "Propiedad e ideología," 36–54; Burga, "El Perú central," 227–310; Mallon, *Defense of Community*, ch. 4.

85. Cf. Jacobsen, "Free Trade"; on effective protection during the early 1890s, see Boloña, "Tariff Policies," 91–92.

86. Grandidier, *Voyage*, 50; the four companies were probably Gibbs and Company, Jack Brothers, Braillard et Compagnie, and Guillermo Harmsen y Compañía.

87. Report by Consul Vines about Islay trade during 1870 and 1871, in Bonilla, *Gran Bretaña* 4:189.

88. The wool business of Peña and Escobedo was significant enough for their names to appear in a 1856 report sent to the manufacturer Foster in England together with those of the four foreign companies as principal alpaca wool buyers; see Sigsworth, *Black Dyke Mills*, 236–37.

89. Will of José Mariano Escobedo of Oct. 24, 1859, in REPAr, año 1870–71, J. Cárdenas, F. 811.

90. REPAr, año 1852, J. Cárdenas (Mar. 5, 1852); REPA, año 1863, Manrique, F. 10, No. 7 (Jan. 27, 1863).

91. REPAr, año 1867, J. Cárdenas (May 31, 1867).

92. REPP, Cáceres, año 1859 (Oct. 8, 1859).

93. Ibid.

94. Ibid.

95. Bedoya, *Estadísticas*.

96. REPP, año 1871, Cáceres (Apr. 27, 1871); REPP, año 1874, Cáceres (Oct. 7, 1874).

97. First will of Antonio Amenábar in REPP, año 1865, Cáceres (Nov. 17, 1865).

98. Second will of Antonio Amenábar in REPP, año 1875, Cáceres (Aug. 24, 1875).

99. Ibid.

100. REPA, año 1865, Patiño, F. 58, No. 22 (May 26, 1865).

101. REPP, año 1857, Cáceres (June 10, 1857).

102. REPP, año 1857, Cáceres (June 18, 1857); REPP, año 1861, Cáceres (July 12, 1861).

103. REPP, año 1881, Cáceres (July 18, 1881).

104. Markham, *Travels*, 77.

105. Tschudi, *Reisen durch Südamerika* 5:195.

106. Markham, *History*, 452.

107. Romero, *Monografía del departamento de Puno*, 468.

108. Report by Consul Cocks about Islay trade in 1862, in Bonilla, *Gran Bretaña* 4:136.

109. Ibid.

110. Bonilla, *Gran Bretaña* 4:235; Romero, *Monografía del departamento de Puno*, 514–15; Min. de Fomento, Dir. de Obras Públicas y Vias de Comunicación, *Economía*, 41 (with wrong date, 1876, for opening of rail line).

111. Romero, *Monografía*, 492–93; Appleby, "Exportation and Its Aftermath," 114–15.

112. Appleby, "Exportation and Its Aftermath," 111.

113. The extension of the rail line into Cuzco department was begun only in the early 1890s; it reached the Imperial City in 1908; Min. de Fomento, *Economía*, 41–42.

114. Report by British Consul Graham about Islay Trade in 1874, in Bonilla, *Gran Bretaña* 4:241; Dunn, *Peru*, 57.

115. See Coatsworth, *Growth Against Development*, ch. 4.

116. I am indebted to Rory Miller (personal communication, Aug., 1990) for these ideas. Cf his thesis, "British Business," 290–94; and his article, "Grace Contract," 324–28.

117. Report by British Consul Graham about Islay trade, 1875; report by British Vice-Consul Robilliard about Mollendo trade, 1900; both in Bonilla, *Gran Bretaña* 4:39, 244.

118. On the establishment of the Peruvian Corporation by former bondholders of Peru's foreign debt, see Miller, "Making of the Grace Contract."

119. Miller, "British Business," 350–52, app. A. Yet the French commercial attaché, Auguste Plane, claimed that in 1903 the Peruvian Corporation charged 7.04 soles m.n. per 100 kilograms of freight from Sicuani, the northernmost wool-trading center in Cuzco's Canas province, to Mollendo, while the freight charge for the same 100 kilograms would be about 3.80 soles m.n. if transported by llama; Plane, *Le Pérou*, 55; I calculated the freight by llama on the basis that the distance from Sicuani to Mollendo is 500 kilometers; freight charges for mule transport would have lain between the railroad and llama rates. In 1931 the Peruvian Corporation charged about 7.00 soles m.n. for just under 100 kilograms of wool from Estación de Pucará to Arequipa; see Manuel Paredes to Ricketts, Azángaro, Sept. 8, 1931, Lb. 601, AFA-R.

120. H. Sánchez to Ricketts, Cojata, Dec. 5, 1923, Lb. 381, AFA-R.

121. Bertram, "Modernización," 7–11, 17; Min. de Fomento, *Economía*, 43.

122. Interview with José Luis Lescano, long-time chairman of the Asociación Ganadera del Departamento de Puno, Puno, Nov. 25, 1975; Carlos Barreda, "Carneros: La industria de las lanas en el Perú y el departamento de Puno," *La vida agrícola* 6:65 (1929), 355–62, reprinted in Flores Galindo, *Arequipa*, 159, app. 6.

123. REPA, año 1910, Jiménez, F. 779, No. 337 (Aug. 12, 1910); REPP, año 1910, González, F. 42, No. 16 (Feb. 17, 1910).

124. Romero, *Monografía del departamento de Puno*, 477.

125. "J. A. Lizares Quiñones se presenta ante la consideración de su pueblo" (flyer; n.p., n.d. [probably early 1932]), in MPA; Paz-Soldán, *La región Cuzco-Puno*, 23, 68; Diez Canseco, *La red nacional de carreteras*, 118; Dunn, *Peru*, 76, 89. On other new communication infrastructure in Azángaro (telegraph line and postal serive), see REPA, año 1907, Jiménez, F. 483, No. 190 (Sept. 19, 1907); Romero, *Monografía del departamento de Puno*, 484; and REPA, año 1903, Jiménez, F. 536, No. 214 (Dec. 12, 1903).

126. Flores Galindo, *Arequipa*, 83.

127. Appleby, "Exportation and Its Aftermath," 110.

128. Ibid., 111.

129. Ibid., 115–16.

130. The brothers Edward and Thomas Sothers, for example, British residents of Puno in 1885, called themselves "merchants and miners." They were exporting alpaca and sheep wool by consignment to Henry Kendall and Sons, London; REPP, año 1885, Cáceres (Feb. 4, 1885).

131. REPP, año 1890 II, San Martín, No. 18 (Apr. 30, 1890).

132. Interview with Agustín Román (born 1892), Azángaro, May 15, 1977.

133. Appleby, "Exportation and Its Aftermath," 85.

134. REPA, año 1901, Jiménez, F. 336, No. 123 (Sept. 4, 1901).

135. Interview with Agustín Román, Azángaro, May 15, 1977; for similar life histories of newcomer traders in Azángaro, see Jacobsen, "Land Tenure," 327.

136. Lb. 19 (1912), AFA-R; interview with Agustín Román, Azángaro, May 15, 1977.

137. Raimondi, *El Perú* 1:132.

138. M. C. Rodríguez to G. Ricketts, Rosaspata, Dec. 1, 1904, unnumbered Lb, AFA-R.

139. Appleby, "Exportation and Its Aftermath," 57.

140. M. C. Rodríguez to G. Ricketts, Rosaspata, Dec. 1, 1904, unnumbered Lb., AFA-R.

141. Orlove, *Alpacas, Sheep, and Men*, 142.

142. REPA, año 1888, González Figueroa, F. 21, No. 12 (Mar. 14, 1888).

143. REPA, año 1907, Jiménez, F. 3, No. 2 (Jan. 8, 1907).

144. Orlove, *Alpacas, Sheep, and Men,* 49.

145. The operations of the wool-export houses have been studied thoroughly by Appleby, Burga and Reátegui, and Orlove, and the following discussion is largely based on their work: Appleby, "Exportation and Its Aftermath," esp. ch. 2; Appleby, "Markets," 27–34; Burga and Reátegui, *Lanas;* Orlove, *Alpacas, Sheep, and Men,* ch. 4.

146. Appleby, "Exportation and Its Aftermath," 55–56.

147. Ibid.; Sabato, "Wool Trade."

148. Appleby, "Exportation and Its Aftermath," 62–63.

149. Ibid., 58.

150. Fischer to Castresana, Picotani, Aug. 9, 1908, AFA-P. Large wool producers in Argentina also sold directly to exporters; see Sabato, "Wool Trade," 55.

151. *Guía general,* 207–9.

152. Olivares to Ricketts, Cabanillas, n.d., Lb. 273, AFA-R, as cited in Appleby, "Exportation and Its Aftermath," 60–61.

153. On marketing of South American wools in Europe, see Behnsen and Genzmer, *Weltwirtschaft,* 36–39; on Peruvian wools, see Orlove, *Alpacas, Sheep, and Men,* 35–37.

154. Sociedad Ganadera del Departamento de Puno, *Memoria presentado al supremo gobierno,* 5–6.

155. Appleby, "Exportation and Its Aftermath," 63.

156. See, e.g., Solórzano to Ricketts, Putina, June 8, 1902, unnumbered Lb., AFA-R, where Solórzano offered sixty-six quintales of alpaca wool to Ricketts and Ratti and would sell to the highest bidder; see also Burga and Reátegui, *Lanas,* 84–85.

157. Sociedad Ganadera del Departamento de Puno, *Memoria presentado al supremo gobierno,* 5–6; Appleby, "Exportation and Its Aftermath," 63.

158. See, e.g., will of Manuel Diaz Cano, REPA, año 1895, Meza, F. 148, No. 62 (Aug. 19, 1895); will of Adoraida Gallegos, REPP, año 1901, González, F. 639, No. 268 (Sept. 5, 1901).

159. REPP, año 1877, Cáceres (Dec. 8, 1877); REPP, año 1878, Cáceres (June 18, 1878); REPP, año 1881, Cáceres (July 21, 1881).

160. Flores Galindo, *Arequipa,* 91.

161. REPP, año 1875, Cáceres (Nov. 11, 1875).

162. Quiroz, "Financial Institutions," 54, table 3.

163. Universidad Mayor de San Marcos, *Discurso,* 18–19.

164. Quiroz, "Financial Institutions," 77–78, 249–50, 340–63.

165. Burga and Reátegui, *Lanas,* 58.

166. Universidad Mayor de San Marcos, *Discurso,* 21–23.

167. Burga and Reátegui, *Lanas,* 58.

168. Interview with Agustín Román, Azángaro, May 15, 1977.
169. Appleby, "Exportation and Its Aftermath," 61.
170. Orlove, *Alpacas, Sheep, and Men*, 49.
171. *Guía general*, 207–9.
172. Roca Sánchez, *Por la clase indígena*, 169; Lazarte to Ricketts, Santa Rosa, Feb. 12, 1930, Lb. 556, AFA-R, as cited by Appleby, "Exportation and Its Aftermath," 62. By the 1920s this practice had become so disruptive in towns such as Sicuani and Ayaviri that even some of the merchants themselves called for legal steps against alcanzadores, who were hated by the Indians and ultimately hurt the business of the towns; see Burga and Reátegui, *Lanas*, 105.
173. Burga and Reátegui, *Lanas*, 207–9, 213; Roca Sánchez, *Por la clase indígena*, 169.
174. Petition by Indians of parcialidad Quiñota, Chumbivilcas, May 12, 1882, cited in Manrique, *Yawar Mayu*, 113.
175. Report of Commission, in Roca Sánchez, *Por la clase indígena*, 219.
176. Nieto to Ricketts, Puno, Sept. 30, 1927, Lb. 493; Lazarte to Ricketts, Santa Rosa, Feb. 1, 1930, Lb. 556, AFA-R.
177. Forbes, *On the Aymara Indians*, 35–36.
178. See Molino Rivero, "La tradicionalidad," 603–36.
179. Medina to Castresana, Picotani, May 12, 1907, AFA-P. By 1920 a regular Sunday market functioned in Sandia, where peasants from communities and haciendas in Azángaro and Huancané province offered fresh mutton, dried meat, cheese, lard, butter, bread, baizes, and serge in exchange for maize and coca leaves; exchanges were becoming more impersonal, intensive, and perhaps monetarized in contrast to the annual barter expeditions often connecting specific communities and families over generations; see *Guía general*, 229.
180. Lazarte to Ricketts, Cabanillas, Nov. 1, 1919, Lb. 281, AFA-R.
181. Rodríguez to Ricketts, Santa Rosa, Sept. 8, 1918, Lb. 261, AFA-R.
182. Pujalt to Ricketts, Nov. 18, 1917, Lb. 229, AFA-R; Burga and Reátegui, *Lanas*, 106.
183. Saravia to Ricketts, Cojata, Apr. 13, 1932, Lb. 619, AFA-R.
184. Sánchez to Ricketts, Moho, Sept. 14, 1926, Lb. 452, AFA-R.
185. Arturo López de Romaña to Ricketts, Lagunillas, Feb. 21, 1918, Lb. 260, AFA-R; *Guía general*, 213; Burga and Reátegui, *Lanas*, 97. In November 1919 peasants refused to accept a contract to weave *cordoncillo* (round lace), "because it is time to sow the chacras and they are very busy"; A. Ratti to Ricketts, Nov. 19, 1919, Lb. 281, AFA-R. During celebrations wools could not be expedited for a week or more because "all the Indians . . . go back to their estancias and one cannot count on them for

sorting, packing, and hauling"; Francisco Mariño to Ricketts, Puno, Feb. 9, 1929, Lb. 540, AFA-R. The labor market, like the commodity market, was embedded into the agricultural cycle.

186.   Burga and Reátegui, *Lanas*, 104–5; on separation between long-distance trade and local trade provisioning urban elites, see Appleby, "Exportation and Its Aftermath," 185–86. Among peasants long-distance trade was a male activity, and local marketplace sales of small quantities of foodstuffs was a female activity.

187.   Saravia to Ricketts, Cojata, Aug. 1, 1924, Lb. 418, AFA-R.

6. THE AVALANCHE OF HACIENDA EXPANSION

1.   Recharte to Juan Bustamante, Azángaro, Feb. 17, 1867, published in *El Comercio*, Lima, Sept. 12, 1867, rpt. E. Vásquez, *La rebelión de Juan Bustamante*, 301–3.

2.   For a discussion of the sources, see Jacobsen, "Land Tenure," ch. 5.

3.   Fuenzalida, "Poder, raza y etnía," in Fuenzalida et al., *El Indio y el poder*, 63–64.

4.   For annual land sales statistics, see Jacobsen, "Land Tenure," app. 4.

5.   Giraldo and Franch, "Hacienda y gamonalismo," 51, place the peak of land sales in 1915.

6.   See the sale of Estancia Huilapata, ayllu Hurinsaya-Cullco of Azángaro district, by the forty-two-year-old widow Eugenia Umasuyo y Condori, a monolingual Quechua speaker living in the same ayllu, to Carlos Abelardo Sarmiento y Espinoza for 100 soles m.n. Umasuyo was shepherdess on Sarmiento's Finca Cullco and was indebted to her patrón over missing livestock. With an extension of one square kilometer, Huilapata would have brought considerably more if sold by a hispanized large landholder. See REPA, año 1903, Jiménez, F. 363, No. 165 (Sept. 15, 1903).

7.   Konetzke, *Die Indianerkulturen*, 51–53.

8.   Brading, *Haciendas and Ranchos*, 63. For an unsatisfactory attempt to explain the switch from the term *estancia* to *hacienda* for the large estates in Chile's central valley during the eighteenth century, see Borde and Góngora, *Evolución* 1:58. Any explanation will have to deal with an apparent shift in the *perception* of the socioeconomic differentiation between various rural properties and their owners. For the conventional use of *estancia* for large estates during the eighteenth century in the altiplano, see *deslinde* of Estancia San Francisco de Purina, Asillo, by Mateo de Suero y González, Juez Visitador de Tierras, of June 23, 1717, contained in Expediente Judicial on Deslinde of San Francisco de Purina, Juez de Primera Instancia J. A. Pacheco Andia, Azángaro, Mar. 13, 1915, AJA; Macera, *Mapas coloniales de haciendas cuzqueñas*, 21–25. For the early use of term

hacienda, see accusations against Cacique Joséf Choquehuanca, Dec. 1, 1782–Jan. 3, 1783, Materias Sobre Tierras e Indios, EC Año 1783, No. 76, ANB. Particularly striking is the persistent use of *hacienda* for Azángaro's estates during the early postindependence years in Choquehuanca, *Ensayo*.

9. For example, on June 23, 1855, Juan Paredes mortgaged his "Estancia Huancarani" in Azángaro, the same estate that ten years earlier in an evaluation had already been referred to as an hacienda. REPA, año 1855 Oblitas (June 23, 1855); evaluation of Hda. Huancarani, Azángaro, Apr. 12, 1845, MPA. For other late applications of the term *estancia* to properties soon to be referred to only as *haciendas* or *fincas*, see REPA, año 1855 (Jan. 22, 1855); REPA, año 1855, Manrique (Aug. 23, 1855); REPA, año 1859, Manrique (June 12, 1859).

10. Bustamante, *Apuntes*, 17–19.

11. Recent reports by governmental or international organizations tend to view "estancia" as a minimal settlement nucleus, below the level of "aldea," "pueblo," or nonnucleated "comunidad." See Comité Interamericano de Desarrollo Agrícola, *Tenencia de la tierra*, 128 n. 23. This use of the term first appears in the 1940 national population census. See Dir. de Estadística, *Censo nacional [1940]* 8:88–119.

12. Juan Chávez Molina, "La comunidad indígena," *Lanas y Lanares*, nos. 8–9, 1947, reproduced in Flores Galindo, *Arequipa*, 165.

13. Zea, "Constatación." A property that had passed from a peasant to a member of Azángaro's elite did not immediately cease to be an estancia. See the use of the term *estancia* for denoting the constitutive parts of Hacienda Rosario, Potoni district, in REPA, año 1899, Paredes, F. 53, No. 26 (Apr. 25, 1899). Well-established sectors of haciendas are called *cabañas* or *tianas* in the altiplano but *estancias* in Cuzco; see Burga and Flores Galindo, *Apogeo*, 21.

14. Use of the terms *inmueble* and *fundo* became common after the establishment of the Registro de la Propiedad Inmueble in Puno in the late 1880s.

15. The distinction between fincas and haciendas was blurred in contemporary usage, but fincas tended to be small estates.

16. For a definition using size as the criterion, see V. Jiménez, *Breves apuntes*, 10–12; for a definition based on minimal livestock capital, see Quiroga, *La evolución jurídica*, 68 n.; for a definition based on production, see Burga and Flores Galindo, *Apogeo*, 150 n. 3.

17. François Bourricaud noted that in Puno "the size of the hacienda varies, the very hacendado as social type is far from being homogeneous, and the agricultural activities to which the hacienda dedicates itself also vary"; *Cambios en Puno*, 128.

18. Favre, "Evolución," 347; see also M. Vásquez (*Hacienda*, 9–10), who stresses the large extension of haciendas.

19. For the opposite view—that is, that the War of the Pacific strengthened the position of gamonales vis-à-vis the peasantry in the southern sierra—see Manrique, *Yawar Mayu*, 116–24.

20. REPA, año 1881, González Figueroa, F. 140, No. 73 (Sept. 10, 1881); REPA, año 1876, Zavala, F. 7, No. 5 (Aug. 24, 1876).

21. Hobsbawm, "Peasant Land Occupations," 151.

22. Jean Piel claims a general inverse relation between the conditions of peasants and hacendados; see "Place of the Peasantry," 119–20.

23. This period coincides with one of the peak periods of land transfers from peasant communities to haciendas in the department of La Paz, Bolivia; see Grieshaber, "La expansión," 33–83; Rivera Cusicanqui, "La expansión del latifundio."

24. See Urquiaga, *Sublevaciones*, 36; Bertram, "Modernización," 7; Hazen, "Awakening of Puno," 20; Appleby, "Exportation and Its Aftermath," 42–43; Burga and Flores Galindo, *Apogeo*, 117–18; Chevalier, "Temoignages litteraires," 824–25. Chevalier erroneously believed that the main phase of hacienda expansion followed World War I.

25. Urquiaga, *Sublevaciones*, 36.

26. The year-to-year correlation (Pearson's r) between prices for Peruvian sheep wool in soles m.n. at British ports of importation and the *number* of land purchases by hispanized large landholders from indigenous peasant from 1855 until 1910 is $r = .66$ and $r2 = .44$ (significant at the .00001 level); for the same period the correlation between the same measure of prices for Peruvian sheep wool and the *value* of the same category of land purchases is $r = .63$ and $r2 = .40$ (significant at the .00001 level). Oscillations appear stronger for hacendado land purchases than for wool exports, particularly after 1895. Perhaps hacendados did not attempt to fine-tune their expansion strategy to a particular level of economic conjuncture, attempting instead to acquire as much pastureland as possible when demand for livestock products increased. Under opposite economic conditions, when falling wool prices or export volumes reduced their income and credit became tighter, individual hacendados perhaps did not consider slowly reducing their land purchases but halted them altogether, at least as far as they involved immediate outlays of cash.

27. Although during 1914–15 a slump in the quantity of wool exports through Mollendo is not noticeable, apparently wholesalers reduced their purchases in the production zone, and credit—in contrast to the classical cycle in industrialized capitalist nations—became tight. See Burga and Reátegui, *Lanas*, 34.

28. Hazen, "Awakening of Puno," 139–50; D. Mayer, "La historia," 291–92; Bustamante Otero, "Mito y realidad"; Ramos Zambrano, *Movimientos*.

29. Spalding, "Estructura de clases," 26. For the general model of a class alliance between the national oligarchy and the provincial serrano

elites, see Cotler, *Clases*, 128–29, 158–60, and Mallon, *Defense of Community*, 134–35; for Azángaro, see Avila, "Exposición," 13; for the case of La Paz, see Grieshaber, "La expansión," 42–53.

30. For a debate of Spalding's ideas, see Jacobsen, "Desarrollo económico"; for an alternative to the dependency–class alliance model of Peru's political regime during the "Aristocratic Republic" (1895–1919), see Miller, "La oligarquía costeña," 551–66.

31. "Memoria del Subprefecto," 74–65.

32. Frisancho, *Del Jesuitismo al indianismo*; on Frisancho's life, see Frisancho Pineda, *Album de oro* 4:153.

33. Frisancho, *Del Jesuitismo al indianismo*, 31–32.

34. Ibid., 29, 38.

35. Such a military man was Lieutenant Colonel Juan Manuel Sarmiento, born in Tacna, who was purchasing land in San José during the early 1890s. See, e.g., REPA, año 1891, Meza, F. 12, No. 6 (Feb. 3, 1891). In another case, César Rubina had apparently arrived in the province during the War of the Pacific, married the Azangarina Bernardina Hermosilla, and purchased land during the early 1880s. In 1883 or 1884 Rubina left Azángaro in the division of Colonel Remigio Morales Bermúudez, with whom he marched to Lima. After having received no information as to his whereabouts for several years, in 1888 Bernardina Hermosilla successfully petitioned for the right to act independently in legal matters. See REPA, año 1888, González Figueroa, F. 66, No. 34 (Sept. 28, 1888).

36. Peru, *Registro electoral [1897]*.

37. Often renters had to pay a lump sum (*juanillo*) at the beginning of the contract period, a nonrefundable deposit amounting up to several annual rental fees. This deposit has not been considered in calculating average rental rates. For methodology of arriving at this index see Jacobsen, "Land Tenure," 431–32.

38. Jacobsen, "Land Tenure," 427, table 5-21.

39. Jiménez, *Breves apuntes*, 84–85, quotes average rental rates for different classes of estates as follows: First-class fincas: 15 percent on productive stock and 6 percent on excess carrying capacity. Second-class fincas: 12 percent on productive stock and 5 percent on excess carrying capacity. Third-class fincas: 10 percent on productive stock and 4 percent on excess carrying capacity.

40. See the lease of Hacienda Cuturi, districts Arapa and Santiago, at 9 percent (in soles m.n.), REPP, año 1911, González, F. 543, No. 221 (Sept. 16, 1911); and the lease of Hacienda Cututuni, also Arapa district, at 8 percent (in soles m.n.), REPP, año 1917, Aramayo González, F. 235, No. 106 (July 8, 1917).

41. In some cases rental rates did decline during the 1870s. The prospective tenant of Hacienda Huatacoa, in Santiago de Pupuja, wrote in

1871: "If for six or seven years past there has been some increase in the rent of fincas in view of the increase [in the price] of their products, presently, since [the price of their products] has decreased again, . . . it is clear that the only reason that could . . . justify the increased rental rate has disappeared." He suggested, and was granted, a reduction of the rental rate to 10 percent (in pesos; 8 percent in soles m.n.); see REPP, año 1871, Cáceres (May 17, 1871).

42. Larger estates seldom appeared on the rental market after 1890.

43. REPP, año 1913, González F. 224, No. 75 (Apr. 23, 1913); Jacobsen "Land Tenure," 439, table 5-23.

44. Jacobsen, "Land Tenure," 440.

45. The decline and subsequent stagnation of the sales price for Hacienda Cala-Cala in Chupa, a large estate since colonial times, from the late 1860s to 1900 may be due to transactions between brothers and sisters, but decay of livestock capital and buildings and installations cannot be ruled out.

46. Slatta, *Gauchos and the Vanishing Frontier*, 143, reports a jump of land prices of 250 percent in the vicinity of Buenos Aires from 1852 to 1860 in response to rising wool prices in England; see also Sabato, *Agrarian Capitalism*, 53–56.

47. Jacobsen, "Land Tenure," 448, table 5-26.

48. REPA, año 1908, Jiménez, F. 801, No. 320 (Apr. 24, 1908).

49. REPP, año 1888, Cáceres (June 22, 1888); REPA, año 1907, Jiménez, F. 127, No. 48 (Mar. 27, 1907).

50. REPA, año 1910, Jiménez, F. 711, No. 306 (June 25, 1910), and F. 790, No. 340 (Aug. 13, 1910). For an even larger speculative gain on peasant lands, see the string of property exchanges (*permutas*) transacted by Ildefonso González, a gamonal and livestock trader from Arapa, with peasants; Jacobsen, "Land Tenure," 450–51.

51. "Partido de Lampa . . . ; Estado que manifiesta . . . "; Lampa, May 23, 1808, BNP; Juan Medrano to Juan Paredes, Caira, Nov. 1857, MPA.

52. Macera, *Mapas coloniales de haciendas cuzqueñas*, cxlvii–cxlviii; REPP, año 1853, Cáceres (Oct. 5, 1853).

53. Macera, *Mapas coloniales de haciendas cuzqueñas*, cxlvii–cxlviii; REPA, año 1863, Patiño, F. 53, No. 18 (Apr. 22, 1863).

54. Jacobsen, "Land Tenure," 458, table 5-28.

55. For the formation of Finca Santa Clara, see the sale of twenty-two different plots in parcialidad Chejachi of district Saman by some sixty to seventy peasants to Ildefonso González Abarca for a total of 1,229 soles m.n., REPA, año 1904, Jiménez, F. 631, No. 245 (Jan. 19, 1904). On Finca San Juan of Mariano Abarca Dueñas, see RPIP, T. 6, F. 52, p. clxxiv, A. 1 (June 8, 1914); although San Juan does not appear in the "Matrícula de contribuyentes de predios rústicos" for Azángaro of 1897, it does appear

in that for 1902. The above-cited 1914 *anotación preventiva* in RPIP refers to a demarcation proceeding between San Juan and adjoining peasant properties of July 5, 1901, precisely during the interval between the two matrículas. This conflict and Abarca Dueñas' delay in having the judicial demarcation entered in the property register until 1914 suggest that the formation of San Juan involved usurpation of lands.

56. Frisancho, *Del Jesuitismo al indianismo*, 39; Frisancho, *Algunas vistas fiscales*, 33; Mariano Abarca Dueñas seems to have been one of the main instigators of the clashes with peasants; see Francisco Chukiwanca Ayulo, "Relación de los hechos realizados en Azángaro el 1 de Diciembre de 1915," *El Deber Pro-Indígena, Boletín Extraordinario*, no. 40 (Jan. 1916), rpt. Reátegui Chávez, *Documentos*, 23.

57. Salas Perea, *Monografía*, 165.

58. See Jacobsen, "Land Tenure," 480, table 5-33.

59. As population increased, communities split into several new ones. One and the same community name appearing in various notarial contracts might refer to different entities. See Hobsbawm, "Peasant Land Occupations," 126, 143. For methodological problems, see Jacobsen, "Land Tenure," 483.

60. Jacobsen, "Land Tenure," 487, table 5-35.

61. Florencia Mallon has demonstrated the impact of such local factors on communities in the Mantaro valley in her study *The Defense of Community*.

62. Sociedad Ganadera del Departamento de Puno, *Memorial*, 8. See also the apologia of José Luis Quiñones, a hacendado and deputy for Azángaro in congress, against accusations of brutal and selfish repression of peasant demands in the wake of the so-called Bustamante rebellion; *El comercio*, Sept. 14, 1867, reprinted in E. Vásquez, *La rebelión de Juan Bustamante*, 305–6.

63. Lora Cam, *La semifeudalidad*, 132; I am indebted to Gordon Appleby for excerpts of this thesis. For the same view, see Giraldo and Franch, "Hacienda y gamonalismo," 63.

64. Cf. Giraldo and Franch, "Hacienda y gamonalismo," 55.

65. REPP, año 1888, Cáceres (Apr. 17, 1888); Giraldo and Franch, "Hacienda y gamonalismo," 141–42.

66. José Rufino Echenique, the later president, mentions Sollocota as belonging to his family in 1834; see his *Memorias* 1:90.

67. REPA, año 1871, Patiño, F. 399, No. 186 (Apr. 26, 1871).

68. REPA, año 1902, Jiménez, F. 631, No. 231, and F. 636, No. 232 (both Apr. 12, 1902).

69. REPP, año 1903, Jiménez, F. 48, No. 22 (Feb. 6, 1903). Increasingly indebted, the Riquelmes had become impoverished, and the livestock capital of Quimsacalco declined from 4,000 OMR in 1860 to 1,000 in 1881 and to zero by the time of the sale to Urquiaga and Echenique. REPP, año

1867, Cáceres (June 27, 1867); REPA, año 1881, González Figueroa, F. 120, No. 61 (June 4, 1881); REPA, año 1903, Jiménez, F. 66, No. 27 (Feb. 9, 1903).

70. We possess only a reference to a "recognition" of the division of their property from 1925, concluded between Arias Echenique and heirs of Urquiaga; see Min. de Agricultura, Zona Agraria 12, Subdirección de Reforma Agraria, Expediente de Afectación, Sociedad Ganadera del Sur.

71. This size was recorded by Leopoldo Lasternau in 1925; according to a measurement by Victor Molina A. and Sergio Dianderas L. from 1958, San José covered only 9,973 hectares. Although 40,000 hectares would make San José extraordinarily large for regional standards, the smaller measurement could be a deliberate underestimation due to a dispute with several Indian communities; see ibid.

72. Ibid.

73. In the north coast valley of Jequetepeque, estates newly founded between the 1850s and 1890s also tended to remain small; see Burga, *De la encomienda*, 196.

74. Compare the case of Hacienda Checayani (Muñani) expanded by José Albino Ruiz; Hacienda Picotani (Muñani), one of the vast colonial estates of the Choquehuanca family, owed its twentieth-century importance partly to the incorporation of Haciendas Toma and Cambría—with 3,500 and 5,600 hectares respectively—between 1898 and 1920.

75. Urquiaga, *Sublevaciones*, 37.

76. REPA, año 1908, Jiménez, F. 778, No. 311 (Apr. 20, 1908).

77. REPA, año 1908, Jiménez, F. 814, No. 324 (Apr. 25, 1908).

78. REPA, año 1858, no No. (Apr. 26, 1858); Avila, "Exposición," 16–23; REPA, año 1868, Patiño, F. 189, No. 96 (Mar. 12, 1868).

79. REPA, año 1909, Jiménez, F. 299, No. 120 (Aug. 28, 1909).

80. REPA, año 1893, Meza, F. 12, No. 8 (Jan. 18, 1893).

81. Urquiaga, *Sublevaciones*, 40; Avila, "Exposición," 16–23.

82. See, e.g., REPA, año 1907, Aparicio, F. 14, No. 9 (Sept. 11, 1907).

83. REPA, año 1867, Patiño, F. 181, No. 91 (Dec. 16, 1867).

84. Giraldo and Franch, "Hacienda y gamonalismo," 57.

85. REPP, año 1899, Toranzos, No. 74 (Oct. 16, 1899).

86. For a case of land donation by a peasant to an hacendado, see REPA, año 1910, Jiménez, F. 761, No. 329 (prot. of an *escritura privada* of 1895); for a legacy by a peasant to an hacendado, see will of Carmen Hancco, REPA, año 1899, Paredes, F. 60, No. 27 (Apr. 25, 1899).

87. Avila, "Exposición," 16–23; Frisancho, *Algunas vistas fiscales*, 17.

88. In 1906, for example, Alejandro Cano, a superior court judge in Puno and a rather ruthless land grabber, had induced Mariano Condori to sell him his Fundo Charquismo in the parcialidad Titire of District Santiago de Pupuja. Fourteen months later Condori decided to sell Char-

quismo to a third person, Juan Gualberto Dianderas Bustinza, a descendant of an old hacendado family from Santiago, and declared: "A year ago Sr. Dr. Cano had me come to him and in a deceptive way gave me forty-four soles q.b. and made me sign a document about the sale of the shares of Charquismo that I am selling today. Since I received that money against my will and in order to avoid reclamations and litigation by the said Dr. Cano, I promise to pay that money back to him without charging rent for that part of the property which he [Cano] has used for pasturing livestock and sowing crops." Nevertheless, Cano had the original document protocollized and instituted a series of legal procedures through which Azángaro's judge of first instance, Federico González Figueroa, granted him judicial possession of Charquismo on October 23, 1907. Although in the sales contract with Dianderas the sales price was listed as 448 soles m.n., a sum probably never paid, Cano paid only 230 pesos (166 soles m.n.); see REPA, año 1907, Jiménez, F. 71, No. 31 (Mar. 1, 1907), and F. 527, No. 208 (Oct. 23, 1907).

89. See, e.g., REPA, año 1873, Patiño, F. 43, No. 70 (Jan. 28, 1873).

90. The protocollizations of a few notaries are lost.

91. REPA, año 1871, Patiño, F. 389, No. 180 (Mar. 28, 1871); REPA, año 1881, González Figueroa, F. 132, No. 69 (Aug. 29, 1881); RPIP, T. 9, F. 497, p. cmiv, A. 1 (Aug. 10, 1921).

92. See transfer of anticresis on Estancia Moccopata Villacollo, parcialidad Llaulli, district Potoni, bordering on Hacienda Lourdes, to Adoraida Gallegos, REPA, año 1910, Jiménez, F. 756, No. 327 (July 23, 1910).

93. Jacobsen, "Land Tenure," 536, table 6-4.

94. Burga and Reátegui, *Lanas*, 156–70.

95. "Matrícula de contribuyentes de predios rústicos para el año de 1897, provincia de Azángaro," BMP.

96. REPA, año 1889, González Figueroa, F. 16, No. 7 (Jan. 29, 1889).

97. REPA, año 1899, Paredes, F. 25, No. 14 (Mar. 27, 1899).

98. REPA, año 1870, Patiño, F. 330, No. 150 (Oct. 13, 1870).

99. Frisancho, *Algunas vistas fiscales*.

100. Ibid., 8–17. For the use of judicial and administrative trickery in the appropriation of lands from frontier settlers in Colombia, see LeGrand, *Frontier Expansion*.

101. Ibid., 14, 19.

102. See, e.g., Mariátegui, "El problema del Indio, su nuevo planteamiento," in his *Siete ensayos*, 36–37; Golte, *Bauern in Peru*, 102.

103. Cf. Mallon, *Defense of Community*, 157.

104. *Memoria del año judicial de 1893*, 4.

105. REPA, año 1888, Giraldo, F. 89, No. 44 (Nov. 27, 1888).

106. REPA, año 1880, Torres Nuñez, F. 66, No. 39 (Aug. 31, 1880).

107. RPIP, T. 2, F. 337, p. vii, A. 6 (Jan. 5, 1907).

108. For details on these procedures, see Jacobsen, "Land Tenure," 551–60.

109.   *Memoria leida en la ceremonia de apertura del año judicial de 1913*, 11.

110.   See, e.g., judicial possession of Fundo Condoriri, district Potoni, by Paulina Portillo vda. de Santos and her five children, and the subsequent registration of her property title in RPIP, T. 8, F. 481, p. dclxxi, A. 1 (Apr. 22, 1919).

111.   For an example of successful resistance, see the Expediente Judicial of May 13, 1920, AJA.

112.   Frisancho, *Algunas vistas fiscales*, 17.

113.   Avila, "Exposición," 22.

114.   For litigation about the invasion of land by a neighbor's livestock, see suit brought by the owner of Hacienda Chictani, Manuel E. Rossello, against Julia Paredes de Cantero, owner of Hacienda Huancarani, Expediente Judicial of Dec. 4, 1918, AJA; for litigation on cattle theft, see the case between Celso Ramírez, colono of Hacienda Ocsani, and Simon Segundo Huanca, *quipu* (foreman) on Hacienda Sollocota, Expediente Judicial of Oct. 4, 1922, AJA; for litigation on looting and destruction of peasant huts, see power of attorney given by Indians from the ayllus Caroneque and Choquechambi, district Muñani, to Juan Manuel Martínez against the owners of Hacienda Muñani Chico, REPA, año 1863, Patiño, F. 157, No. 67 (Dec. 23, 1863); Roca Sánchez, *Por la clase indígena*, 242–43.

115.   See suit by Manuel E. Jiménez against various Indian peasants from the district (formerly parcialidad) Salinas concerning the plots Huancarani Llustaccarcca, Expediente Judicial of May 9, 1932, AJA.

116.   See power of attorney by peasants from the parcialidad Chacamarca, district Saman, to sue "the Indians from parcialidad Titihui, Huancané, for the crimes of breaking into houses, destruction of more than thirty huts, damages, theft of equipment and household furnishings and destruction of planted fields"; REPA, año 1882, Torres Nuñez, F. 25, No. 13 (Mar. 22, 1882).

117.   Only the most affluent and powerful hacendado families could acquire land from fifteen, twenty, or even fifty peasants at once. In 1908 José Angelino Lizares Quiñones bought twenty-nine different properties from forty-three peasants and one hispanized landholder in a single contract for 3,068 soles m.n.; it was noted that all these parcels "today form Hacienda Huancané." REPA, año 1908, Jiménez, F. 1275, No. 504 (Dec. 29 1908).

118.   Interview with Agustín Román, born 1892, Azángaro, May 15, 1977.

119.   Ibid.; inventory of the goods of Isabel Mango, REPA, año 1906, Jiménez, F. 963, No. 303 (Feb. 16, 1906).

120.   REPA, año 1892, Meza, F. 360, No. 202 (Dec. 27, 1892).

121.   REPA, año 1900, Jiménez, F. 566 (Aug. 3, 1900).

122. REPA, año 1907, Jiménez, F. 330, No. 121 (June 28, 1907), and F. 476, No. 187 (Sept. 18, 1907).

123. REPA, año 1906, Jiménez, F. 1203, No. 384 (June 30, 1906).

124. For a vitriolic account of the Lizares's land-grabbing practices, see the anonymous *Biografía criminál*; see also Lora Cam, *La semifeudalidad*, 150–53.

125. REPA, año 1895, Meza, F. 107, No. 48 (July 27, 1895).

126. On the formation of Hacienda Cangalli/Esmeralda, see REPA, año 1902, Jiménez, F. 879, No. 341 (Nov. 6, 1902).

127. José Angelino Lizares Quiñones had, according to his own claims, become colonel of the regular army by 1895 and professed to be an ardent Cacerista until the end of his political career in 1930, against accusations branding him as a political opportunist; see his flier "J. A. Lizares Quiñones se presenta." Nicómedes Salas was named Capitán del Batallón Azángaro No. 9 of the Guardia Nacional by the Cacerista president Remigio Morales Bermúdez on August 23, 1890. Although Salas was Pierolista in 1895, some ten years later both families continued to have close ties. See G. Salas, *Razgos biográficos*, 6.

128. Lizares Quiñones, "J. A. Lizares Quiñones se presenta."

129. Favre, "Evolución," 243.

130. Manuel Isidro Velasco Choquehuanca, for example, claimed that his father Hilario and he himself had been reconstituting Hacienda Nequeneque-Mallquine in Muñani since the 1840s, an estate granted through composition by the crown to their ancestors, the Caciques Choquehuanca, in 1596 and disintegrating through the misfortunes befalling the family after the Túpac Amaru Rebellion. Velasco's declaration, published in an Arequipa newspaper on Jan. 3, 1925, is reprinted in Luna, *Choquehuanca el amauta*, 100–102 n. 2.

131. Romero, *Historia económica del Perú*, 284; Giraldo and Franch, "Hacienda y gamonalismo," 132–37.

132. See the antícipo de legítimo on one half of José María Lizares Quiñones's estate, contracted between his wife, Dominga Alarcón, and her children; REPA, año 1906, Jiménez, F. 1427, No. 473 (Oct. 14, 1906). Dominga Alarcón's will is in REPA, año 1905, Jiménez, F. 517, No. 206 (Oct. 4, 1905).

133. Lavrín and Couturier, "Dowries and Wills," 287.

134. RPIP, T. 3, F. 278, p. lxxxiii, A. 1 (Oct. 27, 1905); REPP, año 1855, Cáceres (July 23, 1855).

135. See the wills of Carmen Piérola, REPA, año 1894, Meza, F. 275, No. 32 (Apr. 4, 1894), and Pedro José Paredes, REPA, año 1902, Jiménez, F. 882, No. 342 (Nov. 14, 1902); Jacobsen, "Land Tenure," app. 5.

136. For the deterioration of the large Hacienda Tarucani during its leases in the 1880s and 1890s, see REPA, año 1908, Jiménez, F. 893, No. 350 (June 4, 1908, prot.).

137. Wilson, "Propiedad e ideología," 52; on peasant and shopkeeper women, see Escobar, "El mestizaje," 159.

138. I cannot say with statistical certainty whether property sales by female heirs occurred more frequently than did those by male heirs. During the late seventeenth and the eighteenth centuries landed property of the English aristocracy inherited through the female line tended to be sold more frequently than did property that passed to male heirs. But English inheritance was not bilateral, and mortgages on estates inherited by daughters were higher. See Clay, "Marriage," 503–18. Two of the many examples from Azángaro are the sale of Picotani by Juana Manuela Choquehuanca in 1893 and of the Aragón estates in San Antón by Manuela Lasteros around 1910.

139. REPP, año 1870, Cáceres (Nov. 7, 1870). For a convincing picture of the bases of gamonal authority, see Burga and Flores Galindo, *Apogeo*, 104–13.

140. According to Bourricaud, women tended to dominate economic affairs in altiplano families of hacendados and shopkeepers during the mid-twentieth century; *Cambios en Puno*, 185.

141. Paredes, "Apuntes," 64.

142. Lavrín and Couturier, "Dowries and Wills," 286.

143. See, e.g., the mejora granted by Luis Choquehuanca to his son José in recompense for valuable services in his old age; REPP, año 1897, González, No. 11 (Feb. 7, 1897).

144. REPA, año 1905, Jiménez, F. 204, No. 78 (Apr. 3, 1905).

145. The inheritance of illegitimate children recognized by their father depended primarily on the family constellation (number of legitimate children, social distance between mother and father) and the whims of the father. Law prescribed that illegitimate children should receive one-fifth of their parent's estate. But in practice an illegitimate child might receive everything (as in the case of Santiago Riquelme's illegitimate and only daughter, Natalia) or just a minimal monetary bequest. REPA, año 1892, Meza, F. 337, No. 177 (Nov. 22, 1892); REPA, año 1895, Meza, F. 148, No. 62 (Aug. 19, 1895). Cf. Wilson, "Propiedad e ideología," 43.

146. See the judicial deposit of the estate of Cipriano Figueroa in the late 1860s. The trustee immediately leased out Figueroa's four fincas in Putina (Canco, Huancarani, Mihani, and Antacollo); REPA, año 1869, Patino, F. 130, No. 65 (Aug. 14, 1869), and F. 138, No. 65 (Aug. 15, 1869); REPA, año 1872, Patiño, F. 9, No. 31 (Sept. 2, 1872). By 1910 Fincas Huancarani, Mihani, and Antacollo had become property of Puno's Beneficencia Pública, apparently because of inconclusive intestate procedures; see *Memoria del Director de la Sociedad de Beneficencia Pública* [1910].

147. Diana Balmori and Robert Oppenheimer have considered such declining birthrates among the second generation of the consolidating Chilean and Argentinian oligarchies as an indicator of social distancing

against outsiders; "Family Clusters." Replacement rates for twenty-nine hacendado testators from Azángaro between 1854 and 1909 were 1.9 for the total number of children (2.24 during the period 1854 to 1878 and 1.67 from 1892 to 1909) and 0.85 for the number of children surviving at the time of the will (1.03 from 1854 to 1878 and 0.73 from 1892 to 1909). But this includes single testators. I included all spouses for testators married more than once as well as the partners of productive extramarital relations in the ratio parents/children.

148. Will of Juan Paredes, Dec. 8, 1874, in MPA.

149. Cf. Balmori and Oppenheimer, "Family Clusters," 245–46.

150. REPP, año 1893–94, Toranzos, No. 156 (Sept. 3, 1893).

151. REPP, año 1893–94, Toranzos, No. 337 (July 11, 1894).

152. Salas Perea, *Monografía*, 75.

153. REPP, año 1900, González, No. 218 (Nov. 12, 1900); REPP, año 1904, González, F. 148, No. 56 (Mar. 11, 1904); REPP, año 1905, González, F. 364, No. 137 (May 30, 1905); REPP, año 1905, González, F. 894, No. 324 (Dec. 12, 1905).

154. Salas Perea, *Monografía*, 75.

155. On Gadea's importance for Puno's educational institutions, see Romero, *Monografía*, 375.

156. REPP, año 1904, González, F. 254, No. 91 (Apr. 20, 1904); REPP, año 1917, González, F. 191, No. 94 (July 2, 1917).

157. See the anticresis contract on the part of Hacienda Collpani of Nov. 12, 1900, listed in note 153; lease of Finca Loquicolla Grande, REPP, año 1902, González, F. 658, No. 233 (Oct. 11, 1902) and renewal of that contract, REPP, año 1910, Garnica, F. 714, No. 331 (May 13, 1910); acquisition of Loquicolla Grande, REPP, año 1913, González, F. 363, No. 118 (June 6, 1913).

158. REPP, año 1904, González, F. 148, No. 56 (Mar. 11, 1904) and F. 254, No. 91 (Apr. 20, 1904); REPP, año 1905, González, F. 894, No. 324 (Dec. 12, 1905); REPP, año 1917, González, F. 191, No. 94 (July 2, 1917); REPA, año 1903, Jiménez, F. 399, No. 180 (Oct. 10, 1903); Julio Solórzano leased Finca Mihani in Putina, one of the fincas administered by his father Mariano as trustee of Cipriano Figueroa's estate, at least between 1909 and 1930; see REPP, año 1909, González, F. 179, No. 79 (May 14, 1909), and *Memoria leida por el director de la Beneficencia Pública [1930]*.

159. Solórzano to Guillermo Ricketts in Arequipa, Putina, Dec. 31, 1898, unnumbered Lb., AFA-R.

160. "Matrícula de contribución industrial para el año de 1902, provincia de Azángaro," BMP.

161. See, for example, the family agreement about Haciendas Carasupo Grande and Jayuni, district Muñani, between Trinidad and Juan Indalecio Urviola Riveros, REPA, año 1910, Jiménez, F. 605, No. 264 (Apr. 30, 1910).

162. Jacobsen, "Land Tenure," 861–70, app. 5.

163. On the central Peruvian sierra, cf. Wilson, "Propiedad e ideología," 42.

164. For a property history of Checayani, see RPIP, T. 1, F. 145, and T. 3, F. 142, p. xc, A. 4 (Aug. 10, 1904), and subsequent asientos.

165. REPA, año 1908, Jiménez, F. 778, No. 331 (Apr. 20, 1908).

166. Interview, Martín Humfredo Macedo Ruíz, Azángaro, July 1976. For similar cases of reunited property titles, see property histories of Hacienda Calacala, RPIP, T. 1, p. cxxi, F. 191–92, and T. 7, F. 428–29; and Hacienda Huasacona, Min. de Agricultura, Zona Agraria 12, Puno, Subdirección de Reforma Agraria, Expediente de afectación, Huasacona, 1969.

167. For the sale of Catacora, see REPA, año 1906, Jiménez, F. 1296, No. 422 (Aug. 10, 1906); for Puscallani, see REPP, año 1897, González, No. 157 (Sept. 20, 1897); for Picotani, see RPIP, T. 3, F. 278, p. lxxxiii, A. 1 (Oct. 27, 1905). Luis Choquehuanca, in his 1894 will, claimed ownership of three fincas. In fact he was in possession of none of these, maintaining his title claim through an unending stream of legal suits, mostly against his own relatives; REPA, año 1894, Meza, F. 405, No. 196 (Nov. 21, 1894). For important new documentation on the Choquehuancas, see Ramos Zambrano, *José Domingo Choquehuanca*.

168. Torres Luna, *Puno histórico*, 190; Luna, *Choquehuanca el amauta*, 27; REPA, año 1861, Manrique, F. 150, No. 71 (Nov. 8, 1861); REPP, año 1897, González, No. 11 (Feb. 7, 1897); REPP, año 1862, Cáceres (Mar. 7, 1862); REPA, año 1896, Meza, F. 316, No. 136 (Mar. 10, 1896). Particularly interesting is the unending litigation of Hilario Velasco and his son Manuel Isidro against all other descendants of Diego Choquehuanca; both claimed rights to all family estates, even those no longer property of the Choquehuancas, such as Hacienda Checayani. See REPP, año 1871, Cáceres (May 29, 1871); account by Manuel Isidro Velasco in Luna, *Choquehuanca el amauta*, 100–102 n. 2; RPIP, p. cv, A. 1 of Oct. 25, 1909, in T. 4, F. 374–76; A. 2 of Jan. 31, 1940, in T. 4, F. 376; A. 3 of Apr. 29, 1943, in T. 4, F. 376–78; A. 4 of July 1, 1943, in T. 4, F. 379; A. 5 of June 25, 1948, in T. 21, F. 307–8; A. 6 of Nov. 17, 1949, in T. 21, F. 307; A. 8 of Dec. 16, 1949, in T. 21, F. 308–11; A. 9 of Oct. 15, 1956, in T. 21, F. 311–12; A. 10 of Jan. 21, 1957, in T. 21, F. 312, and T. 29, F. 476; REPA, año 1904, Jiménez, F. 758, No. 302 (June 9, 1904).

169. In a codicil to his will of Oct. 21, 1897, Luis Choquehuanca declared that attorney Melchor Patiño was to receive one-third of Hacienda Ccalla in payment of his legal services in the ongoing litigation over the estate; see REPP, año 1897, González, No. 183 (Oct. 21, 1897). In 1892 Juana Manuela Choquehuanca, daughter of Colonel Manuel Choquehuanca, sold small Finca Chosequere in Azángaro district in order to finance litigation against her son-in-law Rafael Aguirre; see REPA, año 1892, Meza, F. 342, No. 180 (Dec. 3, 1892). In order to finance litigation over

Hacienda Puscallani, Luis Choquehuanca took out loans totaling more than 4,000 pesos from Juan Paredes some time between 1865 and the early 1870s, of which he still owed 2,300 pesos (Paredes's heirs claimed the figure was 2,905 pesos) by the late 1890s; see Choquehuanca's second will of Feb. 7, 1897, REPP, año 1897, González, No. 11 (Feb. 7, 1897); Juan Paredes' will of Dec. 8, 1874, in MPA; and the sale of a share of this credit by heirs of Paredes to J. S. Urquiaga and B. Arias Echenique, REPA, año 1899, Paredes, F. 14, No. 9 (Mar. 10, 1899).

170. Only one descendant, Manuel Isidoro Velasco, still owned a large estate, Hacienda Nequeneque-Mallquine in Muñani; Luna, *Choquehuanca el amauta*, 100–102 n. 2.

171. There is no evidence suggesting that the Choquehuancas had been granted an entail. It does not appear in the proceedings to prove the family's nobility pursued by Gregorio Choquehuanca in 1792; see "Extracto de las pruebas." Much of their land may have been considered *tierras de oficio*, appurtenances of the office of cacique, which passed into possession of the heir assuming the office without being divided.

172. The Choquehuancas may still have enjoyed informal recognition as caciques among peasants of their parcialidad during the mid-nineteenth century.

173. Cf. the fate of the cacique family Apoalaya y Astocuri of Jauja, one of the wealthiest landholding clans of the central Peruvian sierra during the seventeenth and eighteenth centuries, in Celestino, *La economía pastoral*, 48.

174. Following are all relevant notarial contracts on parts of Finca Chocallaca: REPP, año 1853, notary not given (Aug. 26, 1853); REPA, año 1894, Meza, F. 404 (Nov. 9, 1894, prot.); REPA, año 1895, Meza, F. 153, No. 63 (Aug. 28, 1895, prot.); REPA, año 1904, Jiménez, F. 892 (Aug. 6, 1904, prot.); REPA, año 1862, Patiño, F. 270, No. 128 (Aug. 2, 1862); REPA, año 1855, judge not given (Jan. 22, 1855); REPA, año 1855, Calle (Jan. 15, 1855); REPA, año 1870, Patiño, F. 218, No. 116 (May 21, 1870); REPA, año 1904, Jiménez, F. 891 (Aug. 6, 1904, prot.); REPA, año 1874, judge not given (Sept. 4, 1874, date of contract minutes); REPA, año 1884, Miranda, F. 64, No. 35 (Sept. 18, 1884); REPA, año 1885, Miranda, F. 178, No. 86 (Aug. 2, 1885); REPA, año 1887, Rodríguez, F. 138, No. 65 (June 3, 1887); REPP, año 1900, González, F. 438 (Sept. 17, 1900, prot.); REPA, año 1902, Jiménez, F. 543, No. 188, and F. 545, No. 189 (Jan. 18, 1902); REPA, año 1903, Jiménez, F. 113, No. 49 (Mar. 5, 1903). Attempts to reunite the estate within the family remained feeble and, undertaken only in the third generation, came too late.

175. REPA, año 1907, Jiménez, F. 339, No. 135 (July 5, 1907); REPA, año 1907, Jiménez, F. 416, No. 161 (Aug. 10, 1907); REPA, año 1908, Jiménez, F. 1145, No. 454 (Sept. 23, 1908, two prots.); REPA, año 1908, Jiménez, F. 1150, No. 457 (Oct. 13, 1908); REPA, año 1909, Jiménez, F.

378, No. 160 (Oct. 23, 1909); REPP, año 1909, Garnica, F. 407, No. 199 (Nov. 12, 1909, prot.); "Matrícula de contribuyentes [1897]," BMP. The national census of 1876 still referred to Carasupo Chico as a hacienda, that of 1940 labeled it an estancia, and in the 1961 census it appears as a parcialidad; see Dir. Nacional de Estadística y Censos, *Censo de 1961* 4:125.

176. Favre, "Evolución," 108–17; Favre does not distinguish between intra- and extrafamily sales.

177. Jacobsen, "Land Tenure," 658, table 6-13.

178. Will of Rufino Macedo, REPA, año 1865, Patiño, F. 35, No. 19 (May 22, 1865); appraisal of Posocconi from Dec. 1912 by Facundo Gilt, REPP, año 1915, González, F. 394, No. 154 (June 26, 1915).

179. REPP, año 1853, Cáceres (June 7, 1853); first will of José Mariano Escobedo, REPAr, año 1870–71, Cárdenas, F. 811 (Aug. 17, 1846).

180. Second will of José Mariano Escobedo REPAr, año 1870–71, Cárdenas, F. 811 (Oct. 24, 1859).

181. Min. de Agricultura, Zona Agraria 12, Puno, Subdirección de Reforma Agraria, Expediente de afectación, Sociedad Ganadera del Sur, vol. 1, Property Title History of Hacienda Posocconi, Oct. 17, 1967.

182. REPP, año 1915, González, F. 394, No. 154 (June 26, 1915).

183. Min. de Agricultura, Zona Agraria 12, Expediente de afectación, Sociedad Ganadera del Sur, vol. 1, Property Title History of Hacienda Posocconi, Oct. 17, 1967.

184. Martinet, *La agricultura en el Perú*, 38–39.

185. Delgado, *Organización*, 28.

186. REPP, año 1914, Garnica, F. 496, No. 245 (Apr. 23, 1914); Jacobsen, "Land Tenure," 650, table 6-12.

187. REPA, año 1890, Meza, F. 35, No. 41 (Oct. 13, 1890), and F. 39, No. 43 (Oct. 14, 1890).

188. In 1870, for example, the parish priest of Saman accepted 700 pesos as payment in full for a debt of 2,700 pesos owed by Manuela Urbina vda. de Toro on church livestock, presumably because the debtor could not pay more; REPP, año 1870, Cáceres (Nov. 7, 1870).

189. Delgado (*Organización*, 27) claims that estates of Cuzco convents were usually leased to relatives of the treasurer (*síndico*) of the institution.

190. Ampuero, an ultramontane cleric, seems to have been concerned with the expansion of Catholic education in the altiplano. He revitalized the seminary school of San Ambrosio in Puno and advocated the establishment of a "workshop school" for the "rehabilitation of the Indian woman through religion, morals, work, and hygiene." He maintained an active Catholic press. See Robles Riquelme, "Episcopológia de Puno," 87. Such activities, which required increased church finances, have to be seen in the context of Ampuero's violent campaign against the educational work of Adventist missionaries from Argentina and the United States in the altiplano since 1911. See Hazen, "Awakening of Puno," 39. Small fincas

leased out for short terms, bringing meager income every year, were becoming bad investments. Another institutional landholder, Puno's Sociedad de Beneficencia Pública, solicited authorization from the government to sell its five small fincas in Azángaro province in 1926, "because they produce minimal rent"; see *Memoria leida por el director de la Beneficencia Pública [1928]*, 13–14.

191. REPP, año 1913, González, F. 478, No. 156 (July 12, 1913).

192. Bauer, "Church," 70–98.

193. Martinet, *La agricultura en el Perú*, 38–39. The prohibition against creating new *censos* or emphyteutic landholdings was reiterated in the 1911 consolidation law; see Espinoza and Malpica, *El problema*, 207.

194. The chaplaincy on Picotani was redeemed in 1904; see RPIP, T. 3, F. 379, p. lxxxiii, A. 2 (Sept. 29, 1906); Jacobsen, "Land Tenure," 660–62.

7. COMMUNITIES, THE STATE, AND PEASANT SOLIDARITY

1. For important recent contributions, see Mallon, *Defense of Community*; Grieshaber, "Survival," 223–69; T. Platt, *Estado boliviano*; Hünefeldt, "Poder y contribuciones," 367–407; Contreras, "Estado republicano," 9–44; and the forthcoming study by Luis Miguel Glave about the Canas of southern Cuzco.

2. Finca Mihani, for example, was described as being located "in the ayllu Cura of district Arapa," REPP, año 1907, Gonzales, F. 238, No. 105 (May 20, 1907); as argued below, the terms *ayllu* and *parcialidad* were often used interchangeably.

3. REPA, año 1869, Patiño F. 32, No. 21 (Mar. 8, 1869); REPA, año 1910, Murillo, F. 218, No. 127 (Feb. 1, 1910). In rare cases one and the same peasant estancia was referred to as belonging to different parcialidades. For the view that parcialidad as moiety survived into the twentieth century, see Mostajo, "Apuntes," 752.

4. On the postindependence desarticulation of various "functions" of communities in Morelos, Mexico, see Warman, *Y venimos a contradecir*, 315.

5. Paradigmatic is Castro Pozo's *Del ayllu al cooperativismo socialista*. See also his *Nuestra comunidad indígena*, 16, where the author asserts that "all comunidades that I had the opportunity to observe to a smaller or greater degree rest on the foundation of common property of the land."

6. Sivirichi, *Derecho indígena*, 122.

7. Ibid., 123; Yambert, "Thought and Reality," 70.

8. T. Davies, *Indian Integration in Peru*, 117; Handelman, *Struggle in the Andes*, 31–33.

9. Handelman, *Struggle in the Andes*, 32. For the Mantaro valley, see Winder, "Impact of the *Comunidad*," 209–40.

10. Roca Sánchez, *Por la clase indígena*, 227–28; Bourricaud, *Cambios en Puno*, 111; for the district of Cuyocuyo, Sandia province, largely settled by peasants from Putina, Chupa, and Muñani, see Nalvarte Maldonado, *Cuyocuyo*, 30–31.

11. REPA, año 1867, Patiño, F. 120, No. 57 (June 14, 1867).

12. Bourricaud, *Cambios en Puno*, 112.

13. Min. de Hacienda y Comercio, *Plan regional* 5:38; L. Gallegos, "San José," 11.

14. See Bourricaud, *Cambios en Puno*, 112, on the disappearance of communal tenure in the aynocas by the 1950s. Land parcels in the lihua of parcialidad Cayacaya in Putina were freely sold by individual peasants to noncommunity members during the early twentieth century; see, for example, REPA, año 1908, Jiménez, F. 1219, No. 482 (Nov. 19, 1908). See also Perú, Ministerio de Hacienda y Comercio, *Plan regional* 5:38.

15. Litigation over plot Huancarani-Llustaccarcca, Azángaro, May 9, 1932, AJA; a *masa* is the amount of land that a work party of three men can plow, sow, or harvest in one day; see Mishkin, "Contemporary Quechua," 418–19; for the area of a masa as 760 square meters in Azángaro, see Avila, "Exposición," 43; L. Gallegos, "San José," 11.

16. Roca Sánchez, *Por la clase indígena*, 233; for the 1870s, see Martinet, *La agricultura en el Perú*, 40–41. For community parcels reserved for the church and the municipalities in Cuzco department, see Mishkin, "Contemporary Quechua," 421. I have found no evidence for common land property of religious lay brotherhoods in Azángaro's communities. For their importance in the central Peruvian sierra, see Celestino and Meyers, *Las cofradías*, 161–62, 186.

17. Urquiaga, *Sublevaciones*, 11–15.

18. REPA, año 1907, Jiménez, F. 480, No. 189 (Sept. 19, 1907); REPA, año 1907, Jiménez, F. 193, No. 61 [an error; should be 71] (Apr. 19, 1907). Many community schools in the border area between Huancané and Azángaro provinces during the mid-1960s at times owned extensive yanasis plots, which prior to the schools' establishment had been administered by the Caja de Depósitos y Consignaciones. See Martínez, *Las migraciones*, 28.

19. Urquiaga, *Sublevaciones*, 11–12.

20. For examples of appurtenances (*servidumbres*), see REPP, año 1909, Deza, F. 24, No. 11 (Feb. 10, 1909); REPA, año 1909, Aparicio, F. 48, No. 226 (July 23, 1909); REPA, año 1909, Jiménez, F. 279, No. 113 (Aug. 25, 1909).

21. REPA, año 1903, Jiménez, F. 564, No. 220 (Dec. 21, 1903).

22. During the following two decades several hacendados gained direct access to Salinas's salt deposits through the acquisition of entradas de sal from community peasants; see REPA, año 1900, Jiménez, F. 379 (Jan.

9, 1900); REPA, año 1909, Jiménez, F. 126, No. 51 (Apr. 29, 1909). On the state salt monopoloy and rebellions against it, see Kapsoli, *Los movimientos*, 19, 32–35; Husson, "1896—La revolte du sel"; Husson, *De la guerra a la rebelión*, pt. 2; Urquiaga, *Sublevaciones*, 43–48; *Memoria del Sr. Prefecto [1901]*, 31. In 1920 the community peasants who continued to exploit the salt from Lake Salinas had still not accepted the state Compañía Salinera; see Roca Sánchez, *Por la clase indígena*, 246.

23. Valdéz de la Torre, *Evolución*, 159, 169 (my emphasis); Roca Sánchez, *Por la clase indígena*, 227–28. For estimates of pasture commons in 1959, see Perú, Ministerio de Hacienda y Comercio, *Plan regional* 5:38.

24. REPA, año 1871, Patiño, F. 391, No. 181 (Mar. 29, 1871).

25. See forfeiture of rights in Fundo Japutira, parcialidad Cayacaya-Pichacani of district Putina, by heirs of Ambrosio Mamani for failure to participate in the cost of legal defense, REPA, año 1909, Jiménez, F. 68, No. 26 (Feb. 12, 1909).

26. *Resumen del censo [1876]*, 103. Number of families based on estimate of five persons per family.

27. REPA, año 1863, Patiño, F. 55, No 19 (Apr. 25, 1863); my emphasis.

28. REPA, año 1872, Patiño, F. 30, No. 17 (June 22, 1872).

29. Delgado, *Organización*, 14; Ponce de León, "Aspectos económicos del problema indígena," 139–41.

30. Orlove and Custred, "Alternative Model," 45–46; Orlove, "Native Andean Pastoralists." It is important to differentiate strictly between these geographically isolated herders, found at elevations between 4,200 and 4,800 meters above sea level, and the peasantry of the altiplano proper.

31. For *moyas* (dry-season pastures) and hilltops held by individual peasant families, see REPA, año 1897, Paredes, F. 20, No. 10 (Jan. 26, 1897); REPA, año 1908, Jiménez, F. 1222, No. 483 (Nov. 19, 1908).

32. At times descent groups jointly using the family land purchased the share of a female coheir married to an outside peasant; see REPA, año 1909, Jiménez, F. 279, No. 113 (Aug. 25, 1909).

33. For a typical conflict within peasant families between minor orphans and an uncle, instituted as their guardian, see REPA, año 1862, Patiño, F. 332, No. 159 (Oct. 31, 1862).

34. On legal battles between related peasants, see Bourricaud, *Cambios en Puno*, 116–17; Martínez, "El indígena," 182.

35. Mishkin, "Contemporary Quechua," 421.

36. *Guía general*, 211; Malaga, "El problema social," 32–34.

37. Min. de Hacienda y Comercio, *Plan regional* 5:6.

38. Cf. Grieshaber, "Survival," esp. 242, 262.

39. This estimate of growth is deflated, since the 1876 census likely undercounted population by some 15 percent, as suggested in chapter 1.

40. This could not have been the case, however, for Muñani's other surviving community, Chijos, located high in the cordillera, where rela-

tively affluent livestock herders continued to own extensive property well into this century.

41. REPA, año 1906, Jiménez, F. 1087, No. 340 (Apr. 24, 1906).

42. The growth of Azángaro's livestock population did not proceed in a linear fashion, as it was interrupted by animal epidemics and droughts. One epidemic reduced alpaca herds during the 1920s; see Burga and Reátegui, *Lanas*, 91. The decline of the sheep population between 1945 and 1959 was almost certainly caused by the severe drought of the mid-1950s.

43. Jacobsen, "Land Tenure," 880, app. 6.

44. For average carrying capacity of two units of sheep per hectare, see V. Jiménez, *Breves apuntes*, 83; according to Urquiaga (*Sublevaciones*, 25), Azángaro's pastures allowed between 400 and 1000 units of sheep per square mile, or—assuming a mile of 1.609 km—1.5 to 3.9 units of sheep per hectare. Lavalle y García ("El mejoramiento," 53) suggests for the sierra in general eight hectares of pastures per cow, or—assuming customary reduction factors—a carrying capacity of 1.25 sheep per hectare. I am grateful to Marcel Haitin for pointing this work out to me. In an interview held in Puno on November 25, 1975, José Luis Lescano, the last president of the Asociación Agropecuaria Departamental, suggested that on the best altiplano pastures one hectare is required to adequately feed one sheep. This ratio climbs to about three hectares in the Cordillera Oriental and to five to seven hectares per sheep in the very arid Cordillera Occidental of Puno.

45. Lavalle y García, "El mejoramiento," 53.

46. Personal communication from Benjamin Orlove; see also his paper "Native Andean Pastoralists."

47. Urquiaga, *Sublevaciones*, 32.

48. Mishkin, "Contemporary Quechua," 426; Martínez Alier, *Los huacchilleros*, 3–7.

49. Delgado, *Organización*, 14.

50. Urquiaga, *Sublevaciones*, 22.

51. By will of Sept. 8, 1858, María Machaca from Azángaro passed her parental Estancia Hucuni, located in parcialidad Hurinsaya, to her illegitimate son Simón Mango, sired by Colonel Vicente Mango of the kuraka family. She had passed most livestock to her legitimate daughter María Copacondori so that she would not have any claim to Hucuni; REPA, año 1858, Manrique (Sept. 8, 1858). Six years later the daughter nevertheless claimed title to half of the estancia; REPA, año 1864, Patiño, F. 32, No. 14 (May 10, 1864).

52. See the will of María Hancco from Azángaro of Sept. 9, 1911, Expediente Judicial, AJA; she excluded her legitimate son Basilio Inofuente from inheriting "because he rebelled against me and stole from me nine cows, one horse, and earlier one yoke of oxen and three further cows as well as a flock of sixty sheep." Further examples of peasant disinheritance are in the wills of Apolinar Coasaca, REPP, año 1909, Garnica, F. 405, No.

198 (Nov. 12, 1909); and Melchora Luque, REPA, año 1908, Jiménez, F. 1272, No. 503 (Dec. 29, 1908).

53. Hobsbawm, "Peasant Land Occupations," 143; Orlove and Custred, "Alternative Model," 50.

54. Fundo Ccatahuicucho, located in the old parcialidad Sillota of Asillo district, in 1908 still the subject of a sales contract between peasants, in the 1940 census appears as an ayllu with eleven families and forty-one inhabitants; REPA, año 1908, Jiménez, F. 775, No. 310 (Apr. 11, 1908).

55. See the case of the Calsina family in Azángaro district between the 1880s and 1910; various siblings and their offspring owned or leased landholdings in the neighboring parcialidades of Tiramasa, Anac Quia, and Hilata. The eight coheirs of one family estancia, Paccaray Lluncuyo, lived spread over all three of these communities. REPA, año 1899, Paredes, F. 69, No. 32 (May 8, 1899); REPA, año 1901, Jiménez, F. 376, No. 139 (Sept. 30, 1901); REPA, año 1903, Jiménez, F. 257, No. 111 (June 5, 1903); REPA, año 1907, Jiménez, F. 166, No. 62 (Apr. 11, 1907).

56. The Calapuja Pachari family from parcialidad Yanico in Arapa owned Fundo Humanasi Choquechambi in parcialidad Curayllo until 1908 by inheritance from their mother Paula Quispe Pachari; REPA, año 1908, Jiménez, F. 837, No. 330 (May 1, 1908). See Orlove, "Rich Man, Poor Man," 5, for examples from Canchis province.

57. Urquiaga, *Sublevaciones*, 10–21.

58. Alcalde José A. Lizares Quiñones to Subprefect, Azángaro, Aug. 26, 1893; Alcalde José Albino Ruiz to Subprefect, Azángaro, Oct. 2, 1894; both in Municipal Archive of Azángaro.

59. Manrique, *Yawar mayu*, 152. This also appears to be the position of Poole, "Landscapes of Power," 367–98, who, mistakenly in my view, sees an increasing association between gamonales and state power even beyond 1920.

60. Mostajo, "Apuntes," 758–59.

61. REPA, año 1910, Jiménez, F. 550, No. 242 (Mar. 12, 1910).

62. Peru, *Informe que presenta el Doctor Pedro C. Villena*, 35–36; Demelas and Piel, "Jeux et enjeux," 55–64; Mallon, *Defense of Community*, 144–67.

63. *Memoria del Sr. Prefecto [1901]*, 27–28. For the period 1888 to 1890 the contribución personal accounted for 80.5 percent of Puno's total departmental tax revenue of 141,283.63 soles m.n.; see Romero, *Monografía del departamento de Puno*, 524; Manrique, *Yawar Mayu*, 172–78. Manrique mistakenly believes that the juntas departamentales were left without funds after the abolition of the contribución personal; but they continued to receive the proceeds from the contribuciones de predios rústicos y urbanos, de industria, and de patentes, as well as the contribución ecclesiástica; see Calle, *Diccionario* 3:511–14, 4:33–42. On the relation-

ship between serrano elites and central government, see my article "Free Trade," 158–59.

64. T. Platt, *Estado boliviano*, 100; emphasis in the original. See also Langer, "El liberalismo," 59–95.

65. Pedro Villena claimed in 1913 that in Lampa "the tax roll was based on the number of people living in an 'ayllu' or an 'estancia,' but not on the income which each taxpayer derives from his property"; see Peru, *Informe*, 10. But this cannot have been the case in Azángaro, because the peasants' property tax was assessed on the basis of some fifteen different estimates of annual income, ranging from 20 to 500 soles m.n., and in some communities many peasants paid, whereas in others few or none did.

66. For the central sierra, cf. G. Smith, *Livelihood and Resistance*, 83.

67. Cf. Hazen, "Awakening of Puno," ch. 2; Gonzalez, "Neo-Colonialism," 1–26.

68. Roca Sánchez, *Por la clase indígena*, 173–74.

69. Sivirichi, *Derecho indígena*, 122.

70. On Buenavista de Conguyo, see REPA, año 1894, Meza, F. 352, No. 172 (July 23, 1894); on San Antonio de Lacconi, see REPA, año 1862, Patiño, F. 332, No. 159 (Oct. 31, 1862).

71. REPA, año 1869, judge not listed (Feb. 15, 1869).

72. The matrícula de predios rústicos of 1897 lists 724 community peasants with annual income of 20 soles m.n. or more, equivalent to at least 100 OMR in livestock. My estimate allows both for the inclusion of some families in the rolls actually owning less livestock and the exclusion of some families owning at least 100 head of livestock. In Santiago district, for example, peasants were nearly totally absent from the 1897 rolls. Percentage estimate based on an estimate of 38,000–40,000 community peasants in Azángaro in 1897 and an average family size of 5 persons.

73. Cf. the descriptions of communities in the western cordillera: Orlove and Custred, "Alternative Model"; Flores Ochoa, *Pastores de Paratía*.

74. In Arapa, with its lakeshore microclimate allowing more crop raising than most altiplano areas, a larger percentage of peasants spoke Spanish, and peasant families such as the Chambis and the Amanquis were prominent in local politics.

75. See Matos Mar, "La propiedad en la isla Taquile," for land transfers among altiplano peasants. For the Mantaro valley, see Contreras, "Mercado de tierras."

76. Cf. Orlove, "Reciprocidad, desigualdad y dominación," 309–10.

77. Michael Ducey found that rebellions in Mexico's Huasteca region during the late colonial period were usually led by affluent members of the community; see his "'Viven sin ley ni rey.'"

78. This estimate is based on other estimates and census data for community population and livestock held in the communities. It includes the affluent or kulak peasants. Because I have not been able to estimate the number of affluent peasants around 1825–29, it is not clear to me whether their share of total peasant livestock increased during the century after independence, although I doubt that it did.

79. On the Mantaro valley, see G. Smith, *Livelihood and Resistance*, 81–83.

80. In his will Pedro Quispe from Muñani granted three cows and ten sheep to his domestic servant María Laura, an orphan whom he and his wife had raised since early childhood; REPA, año 1872, Patiño, F. 30, No. 17 (June 22, 1872).

81. See the case of one Mamani family residing on the land Vilacucho, part of the Puraca's Buenavista de Conguyo; REPA, año 1869, Patiño, F. 3, No. 3 (Jan. 13, 1869), and REPA, año 1880, Torres Nuñez, F. 66, No. 39 (Aug. 31, 1880). On landless retainers in Bolivian communities, see Langer, *Economic Change*, 73; on the Mantaro valley, see G. Smith, *Livelihood and Resistance*, 82–83; on the Callejón de Huaylas, see W. Stein, *La rebelión de Atusparia*, 43.

82. Orlove and Custred, "Alternative Model," 38–39.

83. Delgado, *Organización*, 39–40.

84. Will of Casimira Mamani, REPA, año 1910, Aparicio, F. 293, No. 336 (Dec. 27, 1910).

85. See, for example, the grant of Fundo Huacamocco-Adobe-Canchapata in parcialidad Llallahua (Santiago) to Mariano Chambi in 1852, REPA, año 1902, Jiménez, F. 781 (Aug. 23, 1902, prot.); and of Estancia Huaichaccasani in parcialidad Jayuraya (Putina) to the Arenas family in the early 1820s, REPA, año 1902, Jiménez, F. 582 (Feb. 21, 1902, prot.).

86. For the appropriation of an estancia belonging to a peasant family who died in an epidemic, see REPA, año 1892, Meza (Dec. 21, 1892, prot.). According to Romero (*Monografía del departamento de Puno*, 524), the state turned over land to Indian peasants in Puno in the aftermath of the War of the Pacific in exchange for renewed payment of the contribución personal.

87. Leases were rare among peasants; see chapter 6.

88. Martínez, "El indígena," 180.

8. GAMONALES, COLONOS, AND CAPITALISTS

1. Between 1920 and 1940 some newly formed haciendas disappeared, and others lost land and shepherds. For the 1829 estimate, see Jacobsen, "Land Tenure," 837, app. 2. The figures for 1876 and 1940 are calculated from national population censuses.

2. See the case of Hacienda Achoc in Achaya; REPP, año 1869, unnamed judge (Feb. 15, 1869).

3. Fischer to Castresana, Picotani, Aug. 29, 1909, AFA-P.

4. REPA, año 1867, Patiño, F. 109, No. 51 (May 19, 1867).

5. "Lista de pagos de los alcances de los empleados y pastores de la Finca Picotani de Setiembre 1908 al mismo de 1909," Picotani, Sept. 30, 1909; "Plan general del recuento general de ganado de la Hacienda Picotani, Toma y Cambría," Picotani, Aug. 31, 1924; both in AFA-P.

6. Mendoza Aragón, "El contrato pecuario de pastoreo," 38–39; Avila, "Exposición," 39; Aramburú López de Romaña, "Organización," 57.

7. Cf. G. Smith, *Livelihood and Resistance*, 82.

8. See legal action in 1869 by ten community peasants from Acora, Chucuito province, whose estancias lay contiguous to Hacienda Sacuyo of José María Barrionuevo and who fought against being forced to render labor services for the estate; REPP, año 1869, unnamed judge (Apr. 3, 1869).

9. G. Smith, *Livelihood and Resistance*, 82.

10. Urquiaga, *Sublevaciones*.

11. Jiménez, *Breves apuntes*, 10–12; Romero, *Monografía del departamento de Puno*, 435–36.

12. REPA, various contracts, 1903–10.

13. Romero, *Monografía del departamento de Puno*, 435–36.

14. Santisteban to Pérez, Arequipa, Mar. 27, 1925, AFA-P.

15. Pedro Balero to Juan Paredes, Toma, Oct. 14, 1874, MPA.

16. Urquiaga, *Sublevaciones*, 28–29; Tauro, *Diccionario enciclopédico del Perú* 3:21.

17. Urquiaga, *Sublevaciones*, 31; "Propuestas que hase [*sic*] el suscrito [Genaro Nuñez] para la administración de la Hacienda Picotani y sus anexos Toma y Cambría," Arequipa, Sept. 20, 1924, AFA-P. On some estates further categories of subaltern positions existed, such as *jatun quipu* and *quipillo*.

18. Romero, *Monografía del departamento de Puno*, 435–36.

19. "Lista de pagos," Picotani, Sept. 30, 1909, AFA-P; for Cuzco haciendas, see Burga and Flores Galindo, *Apogeo*, 28–29.

20. Urquiaga, *Sublevaciones*; Maltby, "Colonos on Hacienda Picotani," 99–112; Kaerger, *Landwirtschaft* 2:329–30; Burga and Flores Galindo, *Apogeo*, 20–33; Bustamante, *Apuntes*, 17–18; Romero, *Monografía del departamento de Puno*, 435–36; Ponce de León, "Situación del colono peruano," 98–121; Mendoza Aragón, "El contrato pecuario de pastoreo"; Pacheco Portugal, "Condición."

21. Urquiaga, *Sublevaciones*, 26–32; Mendoza Aragón, "El contrato pecuario de pastoreo," 26–27; Giraldo and Franch, "Hacienda y gamonalismo," 97–103, 205–7; Aramburú López de Romaña, "Organización," 13–14, 31–32; Maltby, "Colonos on Hacienda Picotani."

22. For exceptional written labor contracts in 1920, see Roca Sánchez, *Por la clase indígena*, 286–88.

23. Martínez Alier, *Los huacchilleros*, 13.

24. Urquiaga, *Sublevaciones*, 32; Maltby, "Colonos on Hacienda Picotani"; Aramburú López de Romaña, "Organización," 33.

25. Burga and Flóres Galindo, *Apogeo*, 39; Aramburú López de Romaña, "Organización," 37; Belón y Barrionuevo, *La industria*, 17–18.

26. Cf. the estates of César Salas Flores, discussed in ch. 6; see also Avila, "Exposición," 34.

27. Formally landless peons who accumulated a modest affluence through their own livestock operations confounded Azángaro's tax commissioners. They assessed some of them for property taxes, whereas others had to pay *contribución industrial*. See "Matrículas," 1897, 1902, 1907, 1912, BMP; Urquiaga, *Sublevaciones*, 32; Avila, "Exposición," 34, 39; Maltby, "Colonos on Hacienda Picotani."

28. Maccagno, *Los auquenidos*, 33–34.

29. In some cases communities formally existed within southern Peruvian estates; cf. Plane, *Le Pérou*, 64–65; Reátegui Chávez, *Explotación agropecuaria*, 13–17.

30. "Arancel de los jornales del Perú, 1687," in Macera, *Mapas coloniales de hacienda cuzqueñas*, 145–46.

31. Markham, *Travels*, 190; *El Nacional* (Lima), May 16, 1867, cited in E. Vásquez, *La rebelión de Juan Bustamante*, 347; Martinet, *La agricultura en el Perú*, 88ñ-88o.

32. It is unclear whether the length of service refers to the time the colono actually had a flock or merely to the time of his or her physical presence on the estate.

33. T. Davies, *Indian Integration in Peru*, 63.

34. "Cuaderno de la Hacienda Quimsachata," MPA.

35. "Lista de pagos," Picotani, Sept. 30, 1909, AFA-P; accounts of the shepherds of Hacienda Santa Fé de Sollocota, Sept 9. 1918, AFA-S.

36. Accounts of the shepherds of Sollocota, Sept 9. 1918, AFA-S.

37. Maltby, "Colonos on Hacienda Picotani"; Aramburú López de Romaña, "Organización," 37.

38. Urquiaga, *Sublevaciones*, 32.

39. Fischer to Castresana, Picotani, Sept. 20 and Oct. 9, 1908; "Planilla de fallas de Setiembre de 1907 al mismo de 1908," Aug. 1909; all in AFA-P.

40. "Planilla de los saldos de lana que adeuda la indiada de la Finca de Picotani al 1 de Octubre de 1909," AFA-P.

41. Fischer to Castresana, Picotani, Aug. 30 and Sept. 20, 1908, AFA-P.

42. Medina to Castresana, Picotani, Aug. 11, 1907, AFA-P.

43. Cf. Bauer, "Rural Workers in Spanish America."

44. On hacienda stores in Cuzco, see Anrup, *El taita*, 128–29; Burga and Flores Galindo, *Apogeo*, 124–28.

45. Maltby, "Colonos on Hacienda Picotani," 103.

46. Urquiaga, *Sublevaciones*, 35.

47. Maltby, "Colonos on Hacienda Picotani," 102; "Planilla de los saldos de lana," AFA-P.

48. Giraldo and Franch, "Hacienda y gamonalismo," 115.

49. Contract betweeen Mullisaca and administrator Julio La Rosa Galván, Picotani, Nov. 30, 1909, AFA-P. The patronym "Mullisaca" appears limited to Muñani district and the ayllus around San Juan de Salinas; perhaps both groups of Mullisacas derived from one clan that had established use rights in different ecological zones. Benito Mullisaca might have maintained rights to entradas de sal or exchanged the salt against livestock products with distant relatives from his ancient clan in Salinas.

50. Fischer to Castresana, Picotani, Apr. 12, 1908, AFA-P.

51. Cf. the classic portrayal of paternalism by Genovese, *Roll, Jordan, Roll*.

52. On Andean notions of reciprocity in late nineteenth-century haciendas of Bolivia's Chuquisaca department, see Langer, *Economic Change*, 60–61; in Peru such notions remained more powerful in some of the large, mixed pastoral-agricultural estates of Cuzco's Quispicanchis province than they did in the altiplano; cf. Burga and Flores Galindo, *Apogeo*, 28–31; Plane, *Le Pérou*, 65; Anrup, *El taita*, esp. ch. 5.

53. Giraldo and Franch, "Hacienda y gamonalismo," 109.

54. Urquiaga, *Sublevaciones*, 25–35; various letters, 1907–11, AFA-P.

55. Gamarra, "La mamacha," 26–30.

56. Ponce de León, "Situación del colono peruano," 105. On violence as constitutive of gamonal power, see Poole, "Landscapes of Power," 367–98.

57. Burga and Flores Galindo, *Apogeo*, 112–13.

58. Quoted in Tamayo Herrera, *Historia social e indigenismo en el altiplano*, 228.

59. Quoted in Burga and Flores Galindo, *Apogeo*, 28

60. Genovese, *Roll, Jordan, Roll*, 96–97.

61. Scott, *Weapons of the Weak*, esp. 279–86.

62. Fischer to Castresana, Picotani, Jan. 10, 1909, AFA-P.

63. Quoted by Burga and Flores Galindo, *Apogeo*, 28.

64. Kaerger, *Landwirtschaft* 2:330; Declerq, "El departamento"; Min. de Fomento, Dir. de Fomento, *La industria lechera*; V. Jiménez, *Breves apuntes*; Barreda, "Carneros," reprinted in Flores Galindo, *Arequipa*, 156–61; Rivero y Ustáriz, *Colección* 2:244–45; Bustamante, *Apuntes*, 17–18.

65. Declerq, "El departamento," 186.
66. León, *Cartilla de ganadería*, 42–43; León, *Lanas, pelas y plumas*, 11–12.
67. According to one description, the cattle were small, with disproportionately large bones, "hardly [had] udders and completely lack[ed] any of the characteristics of good milk cows." During a short period of lactation of four to six months they produced only one to two liters of milk per day. But the quality of the milk was considered high. In the case of cattle, meat was the more important product. Cattle was sold on the hoof to cattle traders for supplying fresh meat in Puno, Juliaca, or as dried meat (*cecinas*), both for consumption on the estate and for sale throughout the altiplano and in the ceja de la selva, in Cuzco, La Paz, and Arequipa. But the animals produced little meat, which was "far from being tender and tasty." Declerq, "El departamento," 193; Min. de Fomento, Dir. de Fomento, *La industria lechera*, 19–20; Jiménez, *Breves apuntes*, 88; Kaerger, *Landwirtschaft* 2:367–68.
68. "Libro de cargo y descargo de ganado lanar de los pastores de la Hda. Santa Fé de Sollocota para los años 1905 y 1906"; "Planes de existencia de ganado ovejuno, vacuno, de llamas y alpacas y de caballos de la Hda. Sollocota . . . , recontados el 1o. de Agosto de 1927 y el 1o. de Setiembre de 1928"; both AFA-S.
69. Aramburú López de Romaña, "Organización," 15–16; I have subtracted lambs from the total number of sheep; I also subtracted 65 quintales from the estate's 1909 wool crop (588.11 quintales), an estimate for wool from colonos' huaccho herds acquired by the estate.
70. Martinet, *La agricultura en el Perú*, 131–32; V. Jiménez, *Breves apuntes*, 82; Declerq, "El departamento," 183.
71. Bringing alfalfa from Arequipa to the altiplano was deemed too expensive; the barley planted by some hacendados was reserved for cattle, mules and horses; Declerq, "El departamento," 185.
72. "Libro de cargo y descargo de ganado lanar . . . , 1906–1907," AFA-S. On the "ruin" of riding horses in Picotani because of drought, see Galván to Castresana, Picotani, Nov. 7, 1909, AFA-P.
73. See, for example, extension of irrigation in Hacienda Potoni by Rufino Macedo, REPA, año 1865, F. 35, No. 19 (May 22, 1865).
74. Romero, *Monografía del departamento de Puno*, 418–26.
75. Esteves to Castresana, Picotani, July 3, 1911, AFA-P.
76. Perú, Min. de Fomento, *El mejoramiento del ganado nacional*, 3.
77. Barreda, "Carneros," rpt. in Flores Galindo, *Arequipa*, 157.
78. Kaerger, *Landwirtschaft* 2:361–62; for more optimistic figures, cf. León, *Cartilla de ganadería*, 34; for even lower estimates, see Belón y Barrionuevo, *La industria*, 21–34.
79. Harris, *Mexican Family Empire*, 181, table 6; Hultz and Hill, *Range Sheep*, 63.

80. Possibly the reproductive capacity of both ewes and rams was low because of malnutrition and disease. Altiplano ranchers calculated 10 rams to serve 100 ewes, whereas in sheep-ranching areas of the United States, Argentina, and Australia 1 to 3 rams per 100 ewes sufficed to procure larger lambing crops. Cf. Hultz and Hill, *Range Sheep*, 57; H. Gibson, *History*, 108.

81. Walle, *Le Pérou économique*, 205–6; Declerq, "El departamento," 189. See V. Jiménez, *Breves apuntes*, 9, for somewhat lower mortality rates.

82. Esteves to Castresana, Picotani, Sept. 8, 1911; C. Luza to Eduardo López de Romaña, Picotani, Oct. 3, 1924, AFA-P; Romero, *Monografía del departamento de Puno*, 418; Urquiaga, *Sublevaciones*, 32.

83. Kaerger, *Landwirtschaft* 2:361; Declerq, "El departamento." Four lambing seasons were still described as the norm in V. Jiménez, *Breves apuntes*, 7–8.

84. Ernst to Eduardo Lopez de Romaña, Picotani, Nov. 21 1924, AFA-P; Lavalle y García, "El mejoramiento," 55.

85. Lavalle y García, "El mejoramiento," 55; Romero, *Monografía del departamento de Puno*, 418–26.

86. Kaerger, *Landwirtschaft* 2:360.

87. REPA, Jiménez, año 1906, F. 1119, No. 352 (May 18, 1906), referring to livestock recount from 1896.

88. V. Jiménez, *Breves apuntes*, 13–14.

89. Cf. Kula, *Teoría de la economía feudal*.

90. This is one of the methodological problems of studies on Latin American businesses before 1900 that rely exclusively on price theory to "explain" their performance as well as entrepreneurial decisions of the owners. Obviously, prices of output, input, labor, transactions, and capital are important for understanding the conjunctures of haciendas, just as they are for obrajes, mines, or commercial enterprises. But how are we to come up with meaningful "market prices" for these factors if different actors have to pay different amounts for the same amount of land, labor, and inputs, depending on the power they can bring to bear and on their particular networks of clients and kin groups? In an economy like that of the Peruvian altiplano, market prices can be calculated as an aggregate mean for large numbers of producers over the median and long term, but such figures render confusing results in analyzing the performance of individual producers from one year to the next. "Externalities" consistently exert a large influence here. For a methodologically consistent application of price theory, see Salvucci, *Textiles and Capitalism in Mexico*. Burga and Flores Galindo (*Apogeo*, 27) point out difficulties with that approach.

91. Walle, *Le Pérou économique*, 206.

92. In 1893 Picotani was sold for 41,000 soles to Colonel José Maria Ugarteche; REPAr, J. M. Tejeda, año 1893, F. 539, No. 361 (Aug. 5, 1893);

an approximate doubling of the estate's value until 1909 takes the incorporation of additional lands into account. According to Aramburú López de Romaña ("Organización," 16), Picotani sold 588.11 quintales of wool in 1909. Again I have subtracted 60 quintales bought from colonos at market prices. The average price for sheep wool placed in Arequipa, 16.70 soles per quintal in 1909, is taken from Burga and Reátegui, *Lanas*, 208, table 6; I have subtracted 1.50 soles per quintal as the cost of transportation from Estación de Pucará to Arequipa.

93. Urquiaga, *Sublevaciones*, 24.

94. Barreda, "Carneros," in Flores Galindo, *Arequipa*, 156–61.

95. Cf. Hunt, "La economía," 7–66; Burga and Flores Galindo, *Apogeo*, 27; Florescano, "Formation."

96. Cf. calculation of production costs and net revenues of average altiplano stock estate in Belón y Barrionuevo, *La industria*, 21–34.

97. Giraldo and Franch, "Hacienda y gamonalismo," 203–4.

98. Stordy, "Breeding," 118–32; Bertram, "Modernización," 8–9.

99. Maccagno, *La producción*, 9–15.

100. Villarán, "Condición legal," 1–8. See also Mariano Cornejo's juxtaposition of property as "simple source of rent" and "as instrument of labor" in his *Discursos políticos*, 235.

101. Giraldo and Franch, "Hacienda y gamonalismo," 196.

102. Kaerger, *Landwirtschaft* 2:330.

103. "Huacahuta Sheep Ranch," *West Coast Leader*, Mar. 16, 1926, cited in Martínez Alier, *Los huacchilleros*, 22 (my own retranslation into English).

104. "Lista de pagos," Sept. 30, 1909; Fischer to Castresana, Picotani, May 3, 1908; Fischer to Castresana, Picotani, Sept. 6, 1908; all AFA-P.

105. Esteves to Castresana, Picotani, Sept. 8, 1911, AFA-P.

106. Cited in Maltby, "Colonos on Hacienda Picotani," 106.

107. Ibid., 106–7; Aramburú López de Romaña, "Organización," 49–51, app. 6, 87–89.

108. Aramburú López de Romaña, "Organización," 54–58, table 14, 71–72.

109. Ibid., 54, 62; Min. de Agricultura, Zona Agraria 12, Puno, "Informe técnico de afectación, Picotani," Sept. 5, 1969; Maltby, "Colonos on Hacienda Picotani," 105.

110. Aramburú López de Romaña, "Organización," 28.

111. Maltby, "Colonos on Hacienda Picotani," 103, 108.

112. Ibid.; "Lista de pago," Sept. 30, 1909, AFA-P.

113. Tamayo Herrera, *Historia social e indigenismo en el Altiplano*, 224–27.

114. Burga and Flores Galindo, *Apogeo*, 124–29; Bertram, "Modernización," 5.

115. Mendoza Aragón, "El contrato pecuario de pastoreo," 26–27; Pacheco Portugal, "Condición," 84–94. By the late 1950s wage levels on

altiplano livestock estates had become widely differentiated, ranging from a minimum of 0.40 soles to a maximum of 3 soles per day. It is not clear that estates paying the highest wages were the most modern, capital-intensive enterprises. See Diaz Bedregal, "Apuntes," 83–84, app. Correspondence between Sindicato Unico de Trabajadores de la Hacienda Posoconi, the management of the Sociedad Ganadera del Sur and the Director of ONRA (Oficina Nacional de Reforma Agraria), Zona Puno, about labor conditions on Hacienda Posoconi, May 12, 1968–May 29, 1968, Expediente de Afectación, Sociedad Ganadera del Sur, vol. 1.

116.   In contrast, wage labor predominated on Argentine sheep ranches as early as the mid-nineteenth century, and no later than the 1880s something approaching a free labor market was in place; see Sabato, *Agrarian Capitalism*, ch. 3.

117.   Bustamante, *Apuntes*, 18; Kaerger, *Landwirtschaft* 2:360; Martinet, *La agricultura en el Perú*, 88ñ–88o; Universidad Mayor de San Marcos, *Discurso académico*, 21–23. Burga and Reátegui (*Lanas*, 90–93) stress the success of stock selection between 1900 and 1930, in my view exaggeratedly.

118.   Avila, "Exposición," 34; Giraldo and Franch, "Hacienda y gamonalismo," 203; Aramburú López de Romaña, "Organización," 14. For greater advances on a few larger estates in the central sierra, see Walle, *Le Pérou économique*, 203–7, and León, *Cartilla de ganadería*, 42–43.

119.   Aramburú López de Romaña, "Organización," 71–72, table 14.

120.   "Explicaciones para la administración de Picotani i anexos," Arequipa, Sept. 12, 1924, AFA-P.

121.   Aramburú López de Romaña, "Organización," 42; Urquiaga, *Sublevaciones*, 27; Declerq, "El departamento," esp. 190–91; Burga and Reátegui, *Lanas*, 90–91. On most estates sheep were sheared with broken bottles; see Romero, *Monografía del departamento de Puno*, 418–26, 435–36.

122.   Maltby, "Colonos on Hacienda Picotani," 105; Appleby, "Exportation and Its Aftermath," 119–21. Cf. Wilson, "Conflict," for the impact of trucks on peasant commercialization in the central sierra.

123.   For the dramatic change in ideal-typical accounting methods during the early twentieth century, compare the first and second handbooks for altiplano livestock haciendas. V. Jiménez's volume of 1902, *Breves apuntes*, represents a summary of the most efficient traditional stock-raising practices, replete with conventional methods of measuring, classifying, and recording. Cazorla, *El administrador* (1930), lectures the rancher with the authority of modern science on new forms of accounts and livestock-raising techniques.

124.   Arturo Arias Echenique, son of the notorious founder of Hacienda San José, was an exception. See his "La ganadería en la provincia de Azángaro."

125.   Gadea, "Informe"; Lavalle y García, "El mejoramiento," 69; Dir. de Fomento, *La industria lechera*; Declerq, "El departamento."

126.   Bertram. "Modernización," 7.

127.   Bertram, "New Thinking"; Hunt, "La economía"; Martínez Alier, *Los huacchilleros*. For a review of historical hacienda studies up to the early 1970s, see Mörner, "Spanish American Hacienda."

128.   Bertram, "New Thinking."

129.   Maltby, "Colonos on Hacienda Picotani," 109.

130.   G. Smith, *Livelihood and Resistance*, 82–90.

131.   Martínez Alier, *Los huacchilleros*, 18–22; Romero (*Monografía del departamento de Puno*, 173–74) judges the situation of community peasants as more favorable than that of colonos. A classical statement of the deteriorating social and economic position of Andean community peasantry through the advance of "feudal latifundism" is Mariátegui, "El problema de la tierra," in his *Siete ensayos*, 50–104. For an orthodox view of colonos as dependent serfs, see M. Vásquez, *Hacienda*, esp. 26–36. An early, original exception to this orthodoxy, written as an apology for altiplano hacendados, is Urquiaga, *Sublevaciones*, which portrays the multifaceted exploitation of community peasants compared to a great degree of autonomy and economic well-being of colonos. For later apologetic pamphlets with low analytical value see, for example, Drapoigne, *La verdad*; for a revisionist interpretation of hacienda social relations, see Bauer, "Rural Workers in Spanish America," 34–63.

132.   Avila, "Exposición," 39. In 1952 Roberto Mendoza observed that "in the small estates the fluctuation of shepherds is constant and this is caused by the fact that pastures scarcely suffice for the livestock of the hacienda and beyond this the shepherd inevitably tends to overstock the pastures; thus in the long run the situation becomes critical and the livestock mortality obliges the shepherd . . . to emigrate [i.e. to leave the estate] in search of better sites"; Mendoza Aragón, "El contrato pecuario de pastoreo," 39.

133.   Lehman, "Dos vías de desarrollo."

134.   This argument follows that made for slaveocrats of the antebellum southern United States by Genovese, *Political Economy*, esp. 17–18, 34–35.

135.   S. Miller, "Mexican Junkers," 263.

136.   M. Jimenez, "Travelling Far."

9. CONCLUSION

1.   Kapsoli, *Los movimientos*, ch. 1; Gonzales, "Neo-Colonialism"; Hazen, "Awakening of Puno," ch. 2.

2.   Ramos Zambrano, *Movimientos*, 15–28; D. Mayer, "La historia."

3. Ramos Zambrano, *Movimientos*, 29–34; Bustamante Otero, "Mito y realidad," 126–30; I would like to thank Scarlett O'Phelan Godoy for sending me a copy of this thesis.

4. Villarán, "Condición legal"; T. Davies, *Indian Integration in Peru*, 50–52; Hazen, "Awakening of Puno," ch. 3.

5. In 1901 President López de Romaña dispatched a commission headed by Dr. Alejandro Maguiña to investigate peasant protests against local authorities in Puno's Chucuito province; see Maguiña's report of March 15, 1902, in Macera, Maguiña, and Rengifo, *Rebelión India*, 19–56. In June 1913 the early populist president Guillermo Billinghurst commissioned lawyer Pedro C. Villena to investigate abuses in Puno department. Villena's report detailed specific cases of fraudulent land usurpations by several prominent citizens in Lampa province; see Peru, *Informe que presenta el Doctor Pedro C. Villena*. I would like to thank Gordon Appleby for providing me with a copy of the report. In what was to become the most fateful of all these commissions, a few months later Billinghurst dispatched Major Teodomiro Gutiérrez Cuevas to investigate the violent clashes in and around Saman; the resulting report disappeared after Bustamante's overthrow in 1914. Two years later, during the administration of José Pardo, Peru's Ministry of Foreign Relations sent Dr. Victor Cárdenas to Puno to investigate the relationship between peasant uprisings and border conflicts with Bolivia; see "Informe que presenta a la Cancillería el doctor Victor R. Cárdenas sobre la influencia boliviana en algunas provincias de Puno, la condición del indio en ese departamento y las medidas que deben adoptarse," Archivo General del Ministerio de Relaciones Exteriores, as cited in Bustamante Otero, "Mito y realidad," 180v n. 1.

6. Hazen, "Awakening of Puno," ch. 2; Ramos Zambrano, *Movimientos*, 20–26.

7. Details of these events vary in different accounts. The most reliable study is Ramos Zambrano, *Movimientos*; see also Bustamante Otero, "Mito y realidad"; Hazen, "Awakening of Puno," 139–50; D. Mayer, "La historia"; Paredes, "El levantamiento"; Urquiaga, *Sublevaciónes*, 53–59; Tamayo Herrera, *Historia social e indigenismo en el Altiplano*, 202–17; Burga and Flores Galindo, *Apogeo*, 115–19; Flores Galindo, *Buscando un Inca*, 241–48.

8. Gutiérrez Cuevas himself was captured in Arequipa in April 1916. In January 1917 he escaped from prison and fled to Bolivia, where he died sometime between the late 1920s and 1937. He kept in contact with indigenistas and revolutionaries in southern Peru and Bolivia and wrote a revolutionary plan of vast proportions that shows influences of anarchism, indigenismo, and Freemasonry, as well as his military background. See Ramos Zambrano, *Movimientos*, 40–41, 47–70; Bustamante Otero, "Mito y realidad," 157–61.

9. Lizares Quiñones, *Los problemas*; Bustamante Otero, "Mito y realidad," 156.

10. Tamayo Herrera, *Historia social e indigenismo en el Altiplano*, 201; Burga and Flores Galindo, *Apogeo*, 118, 127–28; Flores Galindo, *Buscando un Inca*, 248.

11. The reconstruction of community through memory is emphasized in Rivera Cusicanqui, *Oppressed but Not Defeated*, ch. 2; see also Glave, "Conflict and Social Reproduction," 143–58.

12. Tamayo Herrera, *Historia social e indigenismo en el Altiplano*, 209.

13. Florencio Diaz Bedregal, "Los levantamientos indígenas en la provincia de Huancané," *Ideología* (Ayacucho), no. 1 (1972): 37, cited in Kapsoli, *Los movimientos*, 74.

14. During 1915 altiplano peasants may have felt especially frustrated by the paradox of rising wool prices and stagnating or falling purchases by traders because of a shortage of cash, temporarily created by Peru's monetary disturbances at the beginning of the war; see Bustamante Otero, "Mito y realidad," 130–31.

15. This argument has been made for the mid-nineteenth-century peasant communities of the Mantaro valley by Contreras, "Estado republicano."

16. Reátegui Chávez, *Documentos*, 32–36.

17. For a detailed account of this crisis, see Burga and Reátegui, *Lanas*, 43–49.

18. Bertram, "Modernización," 18–19, tables 3.a, 3.b; Burga and Reátegui, *Lanas*, ch. 3.

19. Burga and Reátegui, *Lanas*, 46.

20. Appleby, "Exportation and Its Aftermath," 70–71.

21. Sociedad Ganadera del Departamento de Puno, *Memoria*, 5–6.

22. Min. de Agricultura, Zona Agraria 12 (Puno), Sub-dirección de Reforma Agraria, Expedientes de Afectación: Huasacona, Sociedad Ganadera del Sur.

23. Hacendados were especially angry because they knew that the wool prices offered by Arequipa export houses had fallen much more steeply than international prices had; see Sociedad Ganadera del Departamento de Puno, *Memoria*, 5–6.

24. Hazen, "Awakening of Puno," 109.

25. "Seismic wave" is from Flores Galindo, *Buscando un Inca*, 240.

26. On indigenismo in Puno see Tamayo Herrera, *Historia social e indigenismo en el Altiplano*, part 4; Hazen, "Awakening of Puno," chs. 3, 6. For the movement in Peru generally, see Degregori, Valderrama, Alfajeme, and Francke Ballve, *Indigenismo*; Chevalier, "Official Indigenismo."

27. Hazen, "Awakening of Puno," 190.

28. Ibid. The commission report of 1921 was published by one of its members; see Roca Sánchez, *Por la clase indígena*.

29. Kapsoli, *Ayllus del sol*, 218–38.

30. Hazen, "Awakening of Puno," 156–59; Ramos Zambrano, *La rebelión de Huancané*, 19.

31. Sociedad Ganadera del Departamento de Puno, *Memoria*; Hazen, "Awakening of Puno," 179–82, 190–92.

32. Appleby, "Exportation and Its Aftermath," 89–90. Based on a single case from the department of Cuzco, Burga and Flores Galindo claim that small traders and peasants were on the verge of forging an alliance; see their *Apogeo*, 128.

33. Sociedad Ganadera del Departamento de Puno, *Memoria*, 14–16; Drapoigne, *La verdad*, 24–30.

34. Burga and Flores Galindo, *Apogeo*, 125. This demand was not surprising in the case of Lauramarca, as communities had continued to exist within the vast estate; see Plane, *Le Pérou*, 64–65.

35. Florencio Diaz Bedregal, "Los levantamientos de indígenas en la provincia de Huancané" (thesis, Universidad Nacional de San Antonio Abad del Cusco, 1950), 64–71, as cited in Tamayo Herrera, *Historia social e indigenismo en el Altiplano*, 237.

36. L. Gallegos, "Wancho-Lima"; Tamayo Herrera, *Historia social e indigenismo en el Altiplano*, 229–43; Hazen, "Awakening of Puno," 170–78; Ramos Zambrano, *La rebelión de Huancané*.

37. Burga and Flores Galindo, *Apogeo*, 128.

38. Law No. 605 of October 6, 1922, of Leguía's short-lived Regional Congress for Southern Peru had actually abolished the old communal offices; see Sivirichi, *Derecho indígena*, 123. In Cuzco the law was not heeded, and communities continued to appoint their *varayocs*; see Delgado, *Organización*, 15–16, 57–58. For their abolition in Azángaro, see Macedo, *Apuntes*, 39.

39. Hazen, "Awakening of Puno," ch. 5; Orlove, "Landlords and Officials," 119.

40. Appleby, "Exportation and Its Aftermath," 187–212.

41. For the case of the central sierra during the 1930s, see Wilson, "Conflict," 125–61.

42. Ramos Zambrano, *Movimientos*, 26; Appleby, "Exportation and Its Aftermath," 205; Favre, "Evolución," 244–45.

43. Romero, *Historia económica del Perú*, 284; Zea, "Constatación de clases"; Romero, *Monografía del departamento de Puno*, 235–36; Bertram, "New Thinking," 105–7.

44. Martínez Alier, *Los huacchilleros*, 12; Flores Galindo, *Arequipa*, 129–31; Belón y Barrionuevo, *La industria*, 13.

45. Burga and Reátegui, *Lanas*, 52.

46. "El Comité de Salud Pública" to Cámara de Comercio de Arequipa, Sept. 30, 1923, cited in Bertram, "Modernización," 10; "La granja modelo de Puno."

47. Bertram, "Modernización," 10–13.

48. In 1926 Colonel Stordy suggested to the U.S.-owned Foundation Company, a major contractor for President Leguía's public works program, that it should buy up 500,000 acres of hacienda and community lands between the Estación de Pucará and Hacienda Picotani, in effect forming one vast sheep ranch on a central swath of territory across Azángaro province; although negotiations began, the Foundation Company soon lost interest; ibid., 13.

49. Burga and Reátegui, *Lanas,* 58–59.

50. Belón y Barrionuevo, *La industria,* 53–54; Min. de Agricultura, Zona Agraria 12 (Puno), Subdirección de Reforma Agraria, Expediente de afectación: Sociedad Ganadera del Sur; Burga and Reátegui, *Lanas,* 57–59. See the announcement of Belón's candidacy in the Partido Aprista Peruano's departmental weekly, *El Collao,* Sept. 29, 1931, 5.

51. Beals, *Fire on the Andes,* 232.

52. Fitzgerald, "Review," 209–11.

Glossary

aguardiente	Raw liquor distilled from wine or sugar cane
ahijadero	Plot of pasture with abundant moisture reserved for the dry season and frequently fenced with a stone wall
alcalde	Municipal magistrate; officeholder in indigenous communities
alquila	Tenant laborer who is carrying out transport tasks for his or her patrón
arroba	Spanish weight of 25 pounds (11.5 kilograms)
avíos	Food rations distributed to tenant laborers on altiplano estates
ayllu	Prehispanic Andean social unit based on kinship; Indian peasant community
aynoca	Parcels of agricultural land worked under communal regime of fixed crop rotations with usufruct for individual families
buscadores	Estate employees during the colonial period, charged with recapturing runaway hacienda laborers
cabaña	Sector of pastures of livestock estate assigned to one shepherd family
carga	Regionally variable measure of weight; in Puno it equaled four to five arrobas
caserío	Central building complex of livestock hacienda
ceja de la selva	Eastern escarpment and piedmont of the Andes, bordering on the tropical rain forest
censo	Mortgage imposed on real estate yielding an interest
chalona	Dried and salted carcass of a sheep

429

chuño	Freeze-dried potatoes
collpares	Eroded spots of altiplano pastures with a surface of saline or nitrate minerals
compadrazgo	Ties of fictive kinship between the sponsor of a life-cycle ritual (baptism, wedding, etc.) and the parents of the person or persons sponsored
composición	Compact between the Crown and a private person that adjusted defective land titles during the colonial period in return for payment of a fee
en casco	Livestock estate without livestock capital
encomendero	Colonist entrusted with right to tribute of a group of Indians and with responsibility for their physical and spiritual welfare
fanega	Spanish measure of grain and seed; usually about a hundredweight
forastero	Indian peasant during the colonial and early republican periods with no or limited rights to communal lands and paying lower tribute rate
guataco	Estate employee during the colonial period charged with forcefully recruiting Indian peasants as hacienda laborers
hilacata	Officeholder in traditional altiplano peasant communities
juanillo	One-time, nonrefundable deposit for leasing an altiplano livestock estate
kuraka	Officer in Indian communities during the colonial period, often descended from prehispanic Andean nobility
leva	See *aynoca*
lihua	See *aynoca*
manda	See *aynoca*
masa	Traditional altiplano land measure equal to 760 square meters
merced	Royal grant of land
mita	Prehispanic and colonial system of draft labor
mitani	Indian peasant woman doing domestic service in the household of a local authority or estate owner on a rotational basis
mitayo	Draft laborer
moya	See *ahijadero*
obraje	Textile manufactory
originario	Indian peasant during the colony and early republic with unrestricted communal rights
parcialidad	Moiety; Indian peasant community

pongo	Male Indian peasant doing domestic service in the household of a local authority or estate owner on a rotational basis
quintal	A hundredweight; 4 arrobas, or 46 kilograms
quipu	Foreman on altiplano livestock estates
repartimiento	Forced distribution systems: either of labor or of goods
segunda	Officeholder in altiplano peasant communities
sobrino	See *forastero*
tiana	See *cabaña*
topo	Land measure of prehispanic origin employed for equitable land distributions in communities; variable according to region and quality of land
uros	Members of an ancient altiplano ethnic group; by the republican period, they had often been integrated as the poorest stratum of Aymara or Quechua peasant communities
yanacona	Servile labor tenant on altiplano livestock estates

Bibliography

PRIMARY SOURCES

Archival Sources

Archivo de la Prefectura, Puno:
  Expediente judicial (judicial case file) concerning Estancia Caiconi, 1808;
  Matrícula de contribuyentes industriales, provincia de Azángaro, 1850.
Archivo del Fuero Agrario, Lima (AFA):
  Picotani Correspondence (AFA-P);
  Ricketts Correspondence, selected letterbooks (AFA-R);
  Sollocota Accounts (AFA-S).
Archivo del Juzgado de Primera Instancia de Azángaro (AJA):
  Various expedientes judiciales, 1899–1933.
Archivo General de la Nación, Lima, Sección Ministerio de Hacienda (AGN):
  Padrón de contribución de predios rústicos y de arbitrios de la leal villa de Lampa,
    capital de la benemérita provincia del mismo nombre, según la enumeración
    practicada por los Señores Subprefecto Don José María Recavarren y Apod-
    erado Fiscal Don José Luis del Carpio: rige desde el semestre de navedad de
    1843;
  Padrón de contribuciones prediales e industriales de la provincia de Lampa, 1850.
Archivo Nacional de Bolivia, Sucre, Materias sobre Tierras e Indios (ANB):
  Various expedientes judiciales concerning landholdings, Indians, caciques, and
    corregidores in Azángaro and Paucarcolla provinces, 1759–82.
Biblioteca Municipal, Puno (BMP):
  Censo de población para el año de 1862, provincia de Azángaro;
  Matrículas de contribuyentes de predios rústicos, urbanos, industriales y eccle-
    siásticos, provincia de Azángaro, 1897–1912.
Biblioteca Nacional, Lima, Sala de Investigaciones (BNP):
  Expediente formado a consecuencia de la representación que los Indios de Pupuja
    hacen ante el justicia mayor de Azángaro para no volver a ser alistados para

433

la expedición y dicho justicia mayor lo dirige original a la exma. Junta provincial, Cuzco, October 9, 1813;

Expediente sobre la queja presentada por el pueblo de Azángaro para que el gobierno virreynal ponga término a los desmanes que comete el subdelegado Escobedo, April 2, 1813;

Partido de Lampa de la provincia e intendencia de la ciudad de Puno, estado que manifiesta en primer lugar el numero de pueblos y habitantes clasificados y en segundo lugar los valores de todos los frutos y efectos de agricultura, de industria y minerales que ha producido este partido en todo el año de 18.. [sic], distinguido por el numero, peso o medida de cada clase, May 23, 1808;

Regimiento de dragones del partido de Azángaro, provincia de Puno, October 6, 1806.

Ministerio de Agricultura, Zona Agraria 12, Puno, Subdirección de Reforma Agraria:

Expedientes de Afectación: Huasacona, Picotani, Sociedad Ganadera del Sur.

Private Archive of Mauro Paredes, Azángaro (MPA):

Cuaderno de la Hacienda Quimsachata que corre desde el primero de Agosto de 1841 a cargo del mayordomo Manuel Machaca;

Paredes Correspondence.

Private Archive of Augusto Ramos Zambrano:

Contribución General de Industria, Padrón de Contribuyentes del Pueblo de Vilcapaza, Capital de la Provincia de Azángaro que empieza a regir desde el semestre de San Juan de 1850.

Registro de Escrituras Públicas de Arequipa (REPAr):

Deposited in the Archivo Departamental de Arequipa.

Registro de Escrituras Publicas de Azángaro, 1854–1920 (REPA):

Deposited in the offices of the notaries Francisco Santa Cruz Zegarra and Manuel Aparicio Gómez in Azángaro.

Registro de Escrituras Públicas de Cuzco (REPC):

Deposited in the Archivo Departamental de Cuzco.

Registro de Escrituras Públicas de Puno, 1852–1920 (REPP):

Consulted between 1975 and 1977 in the office of the notary Guillermo Garnica González in Puno; after Don Guillermo's death, these papers passed into the possession of his son, the notary Julio Garnica, Puno.

Registro de la Propiedad Inmueble, Puno (RPIP):

All entries on rural property in Azángaro province, 1897–1920.

Government Documents

Great Britain. Parliament. Commons. Sessional Papers: 1837–38, vol. 47; 1847, vol. 54.

Memoria del año judicial de 1893, leida por el Presidente de la Ilustrísima Corte Superior de Puno, Dr. Daniel Rossel y Salas. N.p.: n.d.

Memoria del Director de la Sociedad de Beneficencia Pública de Puno, Dr. Andrés Miguel Cáceres, correspondiente al año 1910. Puno: Tipografía J. Cano, n.d.

Memoria del Presidente de la H. Junta Departamental de Puno, Sr. J. M. Gerónimo Costas. Arequipa: Tipografía Medina, 1909.

Memoria del Sr. Prefecto del departamento de Puno [Manuel Eleuterio Ponze], año de 1901. Lima: Imprenta de "El Nacional," 1901.

"Memoria del subprefecto de la provincia de Azángaro, Daniel Rossel y Salas." *El Peruano* (Lima), July 22, 1874.

Memoria leida en la ceremonia de apertura del año judicial de 1913 por el Presidente de la Ilustrisima Corte Superior de los departamentos de Puno y Madre de Dios, Dr. J. Teófilo Nuñez. Puno: Imprenta del Seminario, 1913.

Memoria leida por el director de la Beneficencia Pública de Puno, Sr. Dr. Enrique Robles Riquelme, año de 1928. Puno: Tipografía Comercial, 1929.

Memoria leida por el director de la Beneficencia Pública de Puno, Sr. Dr. Washington Cano, año de 1930. Puno: Tipografía Comercial, 1931.

Peru. *Informe que presenta el Doctor Pedro C. Villena, comisionado por el Supremo Gobierno para investigar las quejas de los indígenas de la provincia de Lampa, en el departamento de Puno.* Lima: Imprenta del Estado, 1913.

——. *Juicio de limites entre el Perú y Bolivia, contestación al alegato de Bolivia, prueba peruana presentada al gobierno argentino por Victor M. Maúrtua, abogado y plenipotenciario especial del Perú.* 8 vols. Buenos Aires: Imprenta de G. Kraft, 1907.

——. *Registro electoral de la provincia de Azángaro, departamento de Puno, 1897.* Lima: Imprenta La Industria, 1899.

——. Dirección de Agricultura y Ganadería. *Estadística general agro-pecuaria del Perú del año 1929.* Lima: Gil, 1931.

——. Dirección de Estadística. *Censo nacional de población de 1940.* Vol. 8, *Departamentos Cuzco, Puno.* Lima, 1949.

——. Dirección de Estadística. *Resumen del censo general de habitantes del Perú hecho en 1876.* Lima: Imprenta del Estado, 1878.

——. Dirección General de Aduanas. Sección de Estadística. *Estadística del comercio especial del Perú en el año 1915.* Lima: 1916. [Same for 1919, 1928, and 1929; title of series varies.]

——. Dirección Nacional de Estadística y Censos. *Boletín de Estadística Peruana. Estadística Económica y Financiera,* año 7, fascículo 3 (1964).

——. Dirección Nacional de Estadística y Censos. *Censo de 1961,* vol. 4, *Centros Poblados, Pasco–Piura–Puno–San Martín–Tacna–Tumbes.* Lima, 1966.

——. Ministerio de Fomento. Dirección de Fomento. *La industria lechera en los departamentos de Arequipa, Puno y Cuzco, por L. Hecq, especialista en lechería, profesor de la Escuela Nacional de Agricultura.* Lima: Imprenta Americana, 1911.

——. Ministerio de Fomento. Dirección de Fomento. *El mejoramiento del ganado nacional; conferencia sustentada en la Sociedad Nacional de Agricultura por A. Declerq.* Lima: Imprenta del Estado, 1907.

——. Ministerio de Fomento. Dirección de Obras Públicas y Vías de Comunicación. *Economía y reseña histórica de los ferrocarriles del Perú.* Lima: Imprenta Torres Aguirre, 1932.

——. Ministerio de Hacienda. *Memoria que presenta a la lejislatura ordinaria del Perú del año 1849 el oficial mayor del Ministerio de Hacienda encargado de su despacho José Fabio Melgar.* Lima: Imprenta del Eusebio Aranda, 1849.

——. Ministerio de Hacienda. *Memoria que presenta el Ministro del Hacienda del Perú al congreso de 1847.* Lima: Imprenta de José Masías, n.d.

———. Ministerio de Hacienda y Comercio. *Memoria de hacienda y comercio presentada al congreso constitucional de 1890 por el ministro del ramo [Eulogio Delgado].* Lima: Imprenta de "El Nacional," 1890.

———. Ministerio de Hacienda y Comercio. *Plan regional para el desarrollo del sur del Perú.* 28 vols. Lima: Talleres del Servicio Cooperativo Peruano-Norteamericano de Educación, 1959.

———. Oficina Nacional de Estadística y Censos. *Censos nacionales, VII de población, II de vivienda, 4 de Junio de 1972. Departamento de Puno.* Vol. 2. Lima: ONEC, 1974.

SECONDARY SOURCES

Abascal y Sousa, José F. de. *Memoria de gobierno.* Ed. Vicente Rodriquez Casado and José A. Calderón Quijano. Publicaciones de la Escuela de Estudios Hispáno-americanos de la Universidad de Sevilla, series 3, Memorias, relaciones y viajes, no. 1. 2 vols. Sevilla, 1944.

Actas del Coloquio Internacional 'Túpac Amaru y su tiempo.' Lima: Comisión Nacional del Bicentenario de la Rebelión Emancipadora de Túpac Amaru, 1982.

Albert, Bill, and Paul Henderson. *South America and the First World War: The Impact of the War on Brazil, Argentina, Peru, and Chile.* Cambridge: Cambridge University Press, 1988.

Alcedo, Antonio de. *Diccionario geográfico-histórico de las Indias occidentales ó América.* 5 vols. Madrid: Imprenta de Benito Cano, 1786–99.

Altamirano, Nelson. "La economía campesina de Puno, 1820–1840: Repercusiones de la presencia militar y la producción textil." *Allpanchis* 23, no. 37 (1991): 93–130.

Amat y Junient, Manuel de. *Memoria de gobierno.* Ed. Vicente Rodriquez Casado and Florentino Pérez Embid. Publicaciones de la Escuela de Estudios Hispáno-americanos de Sevilla, no. 21. Sevilla, 1947.

Angelis, Pedro de. *Colección de obras y documentos para la historia antigua y moderna de las provincias del Rio de la Plata.* 2d ed. 5 vols. Buenos Aires: J. Lajouane y Compañía, 1910.

Anrup, Roland. *El taita y el toro, en torno a la configuración patriarcal del régimen hacendario cuzqueño.* Stockholm: Nalkas Boken Förlag, 1990.

Appleby, Gordon. "Exportation and Its Aftermath: The Spacioeconomic Evolution of the Regional Marketing System in Highland Puno, Peru." Ph.D. diss. Stanford University, 1978.

———. "Markets and the Marketing System in the Southern Sierra." Paper presented at the Symposium on Andean Peasant Economics and Pastoralism, Jan. 1980.

Aramburú López de Romaña, Clemencia. "Organización y desarrollo de la hacienda ganadera en el sur: Picotani, 1890–1935." B.A. thesis. Póntifícia Universidad Católica del Perú, 1979.

Arias Echenique, Arturo. "La ganadería en la provincia de Azángaro." Thesis to obtain the degree of Ingeniero Agrónomo. Universidad Agraria, Lima, 1928.

Avila, José V. "Exposición e causas que justifican la necesidad de la reforma agraria en el distrito de Azángaro de la provincia del mismo nombre, Puno." Bachelor's thesis. Universidad Nacional del Cuzco, n.d. [probably 1952].

Bagú, Sergio. *Economía de la sociedad colonial, ensayo de historia comparada de América Latina.* Buenos Aires: El Ateneo, 1949.

Bairoch, Paul. *The Economic Development of the Third World since 1900.* London: Methuen, 1975.

Bakewell, Peter. *Miners of the Red Mountain: Indian Labor in Potosí, 1545–1650.* Albuquerque: University of New Mexico Press, 1984.

Balmori, Diana, and Robert Oppenheimer. "Family Clusters: The Generational Nucleation of Families in Nineteenth Century Argentina and Chile." *Comparative Studies in Society and History* 21, no. 3 (1979): 231–61.

Barriga, Victor M. *Memorias para la historia de Arequipa, 1786–91.* 2 vols. Arequipa: La Colmena, 1941.

Bartra, Roger. *Estructura agraria y clases sociales en México.* Mexico: Ed. Era, 1974.

Basadre, Jorge. *Historia de la república del Perú.* 6th ed. 11 vols. Lima: Editorial Universitaria, 1968.

———. "El régimen de la mita." *Letras* 8 (1937): 325–64.

Basadre y Chocano, Modesto. *Riquezas peruanas. Colección de artículos descriptivos escritos para 'La Tribuna.'* Lima: 1884.

Bauer, Arnold. "The Church and Spanish American Agrarian Structure, 1765–1865." *The Americas* 28, no. 1 (1971): 78–98.

———. "Industry and the Missing Bourgeoisie: Consumption and Development in Chile, 1850–1950." *Hispanic American Historical Review* 70, no. 2 (May 1990): 227–54.

———. "Rural Workers in Spanish America: Problems of Peonage and Oppression." *Hispanic American Historical Review* 59, no. 1 (1979): 34–63.

Beals, Carleton. *Fire on the Andes.* Philadelphia and London: Lippincott, 1934.

Bedoya, Guillermo. *Estadísticas de exportación de la región sur del Perú.* Annual. Mollendo, 1923–39.

Behnsen, H., and W. Genzmer. *Weltwirtschaft der Wolle.* Berlin: J. Springer, 1932.

Belón y Barrionuevo, Carlos F. *La industria ganadera del departamento de Puno y su economía social.* Arequipa: Tipografía Acosta, 1945.

Benavides, Julio M. *Historia de la moneda boliviana.* La Paz: Ediciones "Puerta del Sol," 1972.

Bergad, Laird. *Coffee and the Growth of Agrarian Capitalism in Nineteenth-Century Puerto Rico.* Princeton: Princeton University Press, 1983.

Bertram, Geoff. "Modernización y cambio en la industria lanera en el sur de Perú, 1919–1930: un caso frustrado de desarrollo." *Apuntes, Revista Semestral de Ciencias Sociales* 6 (1977): 3–22.

———. "New Thinking on the Peruvian Highland Peasantry." *Pacific Viewpoint* 15 (1974): 89–110.

Biografía criminal de Don José María Lizares y su hijo Angelino Lizares Quiñones o Arteaga Alarcón con sus respectivos apéndices y el famoso 'mancha que limpia,' comentado. Pisagua: Imprenta del Pueblo, 1903. [Ascribed to Luis Felipe Luna.]

Blackbourn, David, and Geoff Eley. *The Peculiarities of German History.* New York: Oxford University Press, 1984.

Boloña, Carlos A. "Tariff Policies in Peru, 1880–1980." D. Phil. thesis. Oxford University, 1981.

Bonilla, Heraclio. "Aspects de l'histoire économique et sociale du Pérou au XIX siècle, 1822–1879." 2 vols. Thèse du troisième cycle. Ecole Pratique des Hautes Etudes, Paris, 1970.

———. *Guano y burguesía en el Perú.* Lima: Instituto de Estudios Peruanos, 1974.

———. "Islay y la economía del sur peruano en el siglo XIX." *Apuntes, revista semestral de ciencias sociales* 2 (1974): 31–47.

———, comp. *Gran Bretaña y el Perú, 1826–1919: Informes de los consules británicos.* 5 vols. Lima: Instituto de Estudios Peruanos, 1975.

Bonilla, Heraclio, Lía del Río, and Pilar Ortíz de Zevallos. "Comercio libre y crisis de la economía andina, el caso de Cuzco." *Histórica* 2, no. 1 (July 1978): 1–25.

Bonilla, Heraclio, and Karen Spalding. "La independencia en el Perú: las palabras y los hechos." In *La independencia en el Perú,* edited by Heraclio Bonilla and Pierre Chaunu, 15–65. 2d ed. Lima: Instituto de Estudios Peruanos, 1981.

Borde, Jean, and Mario Gongora. *Evolución de la propiedad rural en el valle de Puangue.* 2 vols. Santiago: Universidad de Chile, 1956.

Bosch Spencer, M. H. *Statistique commerciale du Chili, de la Bolivie, du Pérou, de l'Equateur, de la Nouvelle Grenade, de l'Amérique Centrale et du Mexique; Importations et exportations par les ports situés dans l'ocean pacifique; Industrie agricole et minière du Chili, de la Bolivie et du Pérou.* Brussels: Impr. de D. Raes, 1848.

Bourricaud, François. *Cambios en Puno.* Instituto Indigenista Interamericano, Ediciones especiales, no. 48. Mexico, 1967.

Brading, David. "Hacienda Profits and Tenant Farming in the Mexican Bajío, 1700–1860." In *Land and Labour in Latin America,* edited by Kenneth Duncan and Ian Rutledge, 23–58. Cambridge: Cambridge University Press, 1977.

———. *Haciendas and Ranchos in the Mexican Bajío, León, 1700–1860.* Cambridge: Cambridge University Press, 1978.

"Breve reseña histórica del pueblo de Arapa." *Makaya, organo del pueblo de Azángaro,* no. 5 (Mar. 1976).

Bueno, Cosme. *Geografía del Perú virreinal (siglo XVIII).* Edited by Daniel Valcarcel. Lima: n.p., 1951.

Burga, Manuel. *De la encomienda a la hacienda capitalista, el valle de Jequetepeque del siglo XVI al XX.* Lima: Instituto de Estudios Peruanos, 1976.

———. "El Perú central 1770–1860: Disparidades regionales y la primera crisis agrícola republicana." In *América Latina en la época de Simón Bolívar,* edited by Reinhard Liehr, 227–310. Berlin: Colloquium Verlag, 1989.

Burga, Manuel, and Alberto Flores Galindo. *Apogeo y crisis de la república aristocrática.* Lima: Ediciones Rikchay Perú, 1979.

Burga, Manuel, and Wilson Reátegui. *Lanas y capital mercantil en el sur, la Casa Ricketts, 1895–1935.* Lima: Instituto de Estudios Peruanos, 1981.

Bushnell, David, and Neill Macaulay. *The Emergence of Latin America in the Nineteenth Century.* New York: Oxford University Press, 1988.

Bustamante, Juan. *Apuntes y observaciones civiles, políticas y religiosas con las noticias adquiridas en este segundo viaje a Europa.* Paris, 1849.

―――. *Los Indios del Perú.* Lima: J. M. Monterola, 1867.

Bustamante Otero, Luis Humberto. "Mito y realidad: Teodomiro Gutiérrez Cuevas o Rumi Maqui en el marco de la sublevación campesina de Azángaro (1915–16)." Bachelor's thesis. Pontifícia Universidad Católica del Perú, Lima, 1987.

Caballero, José Maria. *Economia agrária de la sierra peruana antes de la reforma agraria de 1969.* Lima: Instituto de Estudios Peruanos, 1981.

Cahill, David. "*Curas* and Social Conflict in the *Doctrinas* of Cuzco, 1780–1814." *Journal of Latin American Studies* 16 (1984): 241–76.

―――. "Towards an Infrastructure of Gamonalismo: The Cuzco Region at Independence." Paper presented at the Forty-sixth International Congress of Americanists, Amsterdam, July 1988.

Calle, Juan José. *Diccionario de la legislación municipal del Perú.* 4 vols. Lima: Impr. Torres Aguirre, 1906–11.

Campbell, Leon. "Recent Research on Andean Peasant Revolts, 1750–1820." *Latin American Research Review* 14, no. 1 (1979): 3–48.

Cardoso, Fernando Henrique, and Enzo Faletto. *Dependencia y desarrollo en América Latina.* Mexico: Siglo XXI, 1973.

Castelnau, Francis Conde de. *Expédition dans les parties centrales de l'Amérique du Sud, de Rio de Janeiro à Lima, et de Lima à Pará executé par ordre du gouvernement français pendant les années 1843 à 1847 sous la direction de Francis Conde de Castelnau.* 6 vols. Paris: 1850–51.

Castro Pozo, Hildebrando. *Del ayllo al cooperativismo socialista.* 2d ed. Lima: Editorial Juan Mejía Baca, 1969.

―――. *Nuestra comunidad indígena.* 2d ed. Lima: Perugraph Editores S.A., 1979.

Cazorla, Juan Manuel. *El administrador de haciendas de ganadería.* Arequipa: Ed. La Colmena, 1930.

Celestino, Olinda. *La economía pastoral de las cofradías y el rol de la nobleza india: El valle del Mantaro en el siglo XVIII.* Universität Bielefeld, Universitätsschwerpunkt Lateinamerikaforschung, Arbeitspapier No. 25. Bielefeld, 1981.

Celestino, Olinda, and Albert Meyers. *Las cofradías en el Perú, región central.* Frankfurt a.M.: Verlag Klaus Dieter Vervuert, 1981.

Cephalio [José Baquijano y Carrillo]. "Disertación histórica y política sobre el comercio del Perú." *Mercurio Peruano* 1, no. 26 (1791).

Céspedes del Castillo, Guillermo. *Lima y Buenos Aires: repercusiones económicas y políticas de la creación del virreinato del Plata.* Publicaciones de la Escuela de Estudios Hispánoamericanos de Sevilla, no. 34. Sevilla, 1947.

Chevalier, François. "Official Indigenismo in Peru in 1920: Origins, Significance, and Socio-Economic Scope." In *Race and Class in Latin America*, edited by Magnus Mörner, 184–96. New York: Columbia University Press, 1970.

———. "Témoignages littéraires et disparité de croissance: L'expansion de la grande propriété dans le Haut-Pérou aux XXe siècle." *Annales, économies, société, civilisations* 21 (July–Aug. 1966): 815–31.

Choquehuanca, José Domingo. *Ensayo de estadística completa de los ramos económico-políticos de la provincia de Azángaro en el departamento de Puno de la República Peruana del quinquenio contado desde 1825 hasta 1829 inclusive, formado por el ciudadano José Domingo Choquehuanca, diputado que fue de la M. H. Junta Departamental de Puno.* Lima: Imprenta de Manuel Corral, 1833.

Cisneros, Carlos B. *Frutos de la paz.* Lima: Oficina Tipográfica "La Opinión Nacional," 1908.

Clay, Christopher. "Marriage, Inheritance, and the Rise of Large Estates in England, 1660–1815." *Economic History Review,* 2d ser., 21 (1968): 503–18.

Coatsworth, John. *Growth Against Development: The Economic Impact of Railroads in Porfirian Mexico.* De Kalb: Northern Illinois University Press, 1981.

———. "Railroads, Landholding, and Agrarian Protest in the Early Porfiriato," *Hispanic American Historical Review* 54 (1974): 48–71.

Cobb, Gwendolyn B. "Supply and Transportation for the Potosí Mines, 1545–1640." *Hispanic American Historical Review* 29, no. 1 (Feb. 1949), 25–45.

Cobo, Bernabé. *Historia del nuevo mundo.* Edited by Marcos Jiménez de la Espada. Sociedad de Bibliófilos Andaluces, Obras Publicadas, primera serie. 4 vols. Sevilla, 1890–95.

Cole, Jeffrey A. *The Potosí Mita, 1573–1700.* Stanford: Stanford University Press, 1985.

Comité Arquidiocesano del Bicentenario Túpac Amaru, ed. *Túpac Amaru y la iglesia, antología.* Lima: Edubanco, 1983.

Contreras, Carlos. "Estado republicano y tributo indígena en la sierra central en la post-independencia." *Histórica* 13, no. 1 (1989): 9–44.

———. "Mercado de tierras y sociedad campesina: El valle del Mantaro en el siglo XIX." Paper presented at the annual meeting of the Latin American Studies Association, San Juan, Puerto Rico, Sept. 1989.

———. "Mineros, arrieros y ferrocarril en Cerro de Pasco, 1870–1904." *HISLA* 4, no. 2 (1984): 3–20.

———. *Mineros y campesinos en los Andes.* Lima: Instituto de Estudios Peruanos, 1988.

Cook, Noble David. "La población de la parroquia de Yanahuara, 1738–1747: Un modelo para el estudio de las parroquias coloniales peruanas." In *Collaguas I,* edited by Franklin Pease G. Y., 13–34. Lima: Pontifícia Universidad Católica del Perú, 1977.

———. "Population Data for Indian Peru: Sixteenth and Seventeenth Centuries." *Hispanic American Historical Review* 62, no. 1 (Feb. 1982): 73–120.

———, ed. *Tasa de la visita general de Francisco de Toledo.* Lima: Universidad Nacional Mayor de San Marcos, 1975.

Cornblit, Oscar. "Society and Mass Rebellion in Eighteenth Century Peru and Bolivia." In *Latin American Affairs,* edited by Raymond Carr, 9–44. Oxford: Oxford University Press, 1970.

Cornejo, Mariano H. *Discursos políticos.* Lima: Imprenta del Estado, 1913.

Cornejo Bouroncle, Jorge. *Pumacahua, la revolución del Cuzco de 1814*. Cuzco: H. G. Rozas, 1956.

Costa y Martínez, Joaquin. *Colectivismo agrario en España [1898]*. Vols. 7 and 8 of *Obras completas*. Edited by George Cheyne and Carlos Serrano. 10 vols. Zaragoza: Editorial Guara, 1983.

Cotler, Julio. *Clases, estado y nación en el Perú*. Lima: Instituto de Estudios Peruanos, 1979.

Crotty, R. D. *Cattle, Economics, and Development*. Slough, U.K.: Commonwealth Agricultural Bureau, 1980.

Dancuart, P. Emilio, and R. M. Rodríguez. *Anales de la hacienda pública del Perú*. 24 vols. Lima: Imprenta de "La Revista" and Imprenta de Guillermo Stolte, 1902–26.

"Datos para un estudio monográfico del distrito de Putina." *Makaya, organo del pueblo de Azángaro*, no. 3 (1971): 2–13.

Davies, Keith. *Landowners in Colonial Peru*. Austin: University of Texas Press, 1984.

Davies, Thomas M. *Indian Integration in Peru: A Half Century of Experience, 1900–1948*. Lincoln: University of Nebraska Press, 1974.

Deane, Phyllis, and W. A. Cole. *British Economic Growth, 1688–1959, Trends and Structure*. Cambridge: Cambridge University Press, 1964.

Dechesne, Laurent. *L'évolution économique et sociale de l'industrie de la laine en Angleterre*. Paris: Librairie de la Société du Recueil général des lois et des arrêts, 1900.

Declerq, A. "El departamento de Puno y sus industrias ganaderas." In *Memorias presentadas al Ministerio de Fomento del Perú sobre diversos viajes emprendidos en varias regiones de la república por los ingenieros agrónomos G. Vanderghem, H. van Hoorde, J. Michel, V. Marie y el médico veterinario A. Declerq, profesores de la Escuela Nacional de Agricultura de Lima, traducidas al castellano por Manuel F. Albertini*, 180–213. Lima: Tipografía Fabbri Hermanos, 1902.

Degregori, Carlos Iván, Mariano Valderrama, Augusta Alfajeme, and Marfil Francke Ballve. *Indigenismo, clases sociales y problema nacional: La discusión sobre el 'problema indígena' en el Perú*. Lima: Editorial CELATS, n.d. [ca. 1981].

de Janvry, Alain. *The Agrarian Question and Reformism in Latin America*. Baltimore: Johns Hopkins University Press, 1981.

Delgado, Julio. *Organización de la propiedad rural en la sierra*. Lima: Facultad de Derecho, Universidad Mayor de San Marcos, 1930.

Demelas, Marie-Danielle, and Jean Piel. "Jeux et enjeux du pouvoir dans les Andes: Les cas des départements du Cuzco et de La Paz (vers 1880 jusque vers 1920)." In *Les frontières du pouvoir en Amérique Latine*, edited by Université de Toulouse–Le Mirail, Centre de Promotion de la Recherche Scientifique, 55–64. Toulouse: Université de Toulouse–Le Mirail, Service de Publications, 1983.

Deustua, José. "El ciclo interno de la producción del oro en el transito de la economía colonial a la republicana." *HISLA*, no.3 (1984): 23–49.

———. *La minería peruana y la iniciación de la república, 1820–1840*. Lima: Instituto de Estudios Peruanos, 1986.

———. "Producción minera y circulación monetaria en una economía andina: El Perú del siglo XIX." *Revista andina* 4, no. 2 (Dec.1986): 319–78.

Diaz Bedregal, Florencio. "Apuntes para una reforma agraria en el departamento de Puno." *Revista universitaria* (Cuzco) 49, no. 118 (1960): 195–297.

Diez Canseco, Ernesto. *La red nacional de carreteras*. Lima: Impr. Torres Aguirre, 1929.

"Documento para la historia de Azángaro." *Makaya, organo del Pueblo de Azángaro*, no. 2 (June 1971): n.p.

Dollfus, Olivier. *Le Pérou, introduction geographique a l'etude du developpement*. Paris: Institut des Hautes Etudes d'Amérique Latine, 1968.

Drapoigne, J. E. *La verdad en la cuestión indígena (apuntes)*. Arequipa: Tipografía S. Quiróz, 1922.

Ducey, Michael. "'Viven sin ley ni rey . . .': Rebellions in the Colonial Huasteca, 1750–1810." Paper presented at the Workshop on Social Movements and Popular Ideology in Latin America, University of Chicago, Feb. 1990.

Duffield, A. J. *Peru in the Guano Age, Being a Short Account of a Recent Visit to the Guano Deposits*. London: Richard Bentley, 1877.

Duncan, Kenneth, and Ian Rutledge, eds. *Land and Labour in Latin America*. Cambridge: Cambridge University Press, 1977.

Dunn, William Edward. *Peru: A Commercial and Industrial Handbook*. U.S. Bureau of Foreign and Domestic Commerce. Department of Commerce. Washington, D.C.: Government Printing Office, 1925.

Echenique, José Rufino. *Memorias para la historia del Perú, 1808–1878*. 2 vols. Lima: Ed. Huascarán, 1952.

Erickson, Clark L. "An Archaeological Investigation of Raised Field Agriculture in the Lake Titicaca Basin of Peru." Ph.D. diss. University of Illinois, Urbana-Champaign, 1988.

Escobar, Gabriel. "El mestizaje en la región andina." In *El Indio y el poder*, edited by Fernando Fuenzalida et al., 153–82. Lima: Instituto de Estudios Peruanos, 1970.

Espinoza R., Gustavo, and Carlos Malpica Silva Santisteban. *El problema de la tierra*. Lima: Biblioteca Amauta, 1970.

Esteves, Luis. *Apuntes para la historia económica del Perú*. 1882. Rpt. Lima: Centro de Estudios de Población y Desarrollo, 1971.

"Extracto de las pruebas de nobleza de don Gregorio Chuquihuanca nombrado Caballero de la Real Orden Española de Carlos III en derecho de 13 de Abril de 1792." *Revista de historia de América* 77–78 (1974): 151–205.

Favre, Henri. "Evolución y situación de las haciendas en la región de Huancavelica, Perú." In *La hacienda en el Perú*, edited by Henri Favre, Claude Collin-Delavaud, and José Matos Mar, 237–57. Lima: Instituto de Estudios Peruanos, 1967.

Figueroa, Adolfo. *Capitalist Development and the Peasant Economy in Peru*. Cambridge: Cambridge University Press, 1984.

Fisher, John R. *Commercial Relations Between Spain and Spanish America in the Era of Free Trade, 1778–1796*. Monograph No. 13. Liverpool: University of Liverpool, Centre for Latin American Studies, 1985.

―――. *Government and Society in Colonial Peru: The Intendant System, 1784–1814.* London: Athlone, 1970.

Fisher, Lillian E. *The Last Inca Revolt, 1780–1783.* Norman: Oklahoma University Press, 1966.

Fitzgerald, E. V. K. Review of Victor Bulmer-Thomas, *Studies in the Economics of Central America* (London, 1988). *Journal of Latin American Studies* 22, no. 1 (1990): 209–11.

Florescano, Enrique. "The Formation and Economic Structure of the Hacienda in New Spain." In *Cambridge History of Latin America*, vol. 2, edited by Leslie Bethell, 153–88. Cambridge: Cambridge University Press, 1984.

Flores Galindo, Alberto. *Arequipa y el sur andino, siglo XVIII a XX.* Lima: Editorial Horizonte, 1977.

―――. "Aristocracia en vilo: Los mercaderes de Lima en el siglo XVIII." In *The Economies of Mexico and Peru During the Late Colonial Period, 1760–1810*, edited by Nils Jacobsen and Hans-Jürgen Puhle, 252–80. Berlin: Colloquium Verlag, 1986.

―――. *Buscando un Inca, identidad y utopia en los Andes.* Lima: Instituto de Apoyo Agrario, 1987.

―――, ed. *Túpac Amaru II—1780, Antología.* Lima: Retablo de Papel Ediciones, 1976.

Flores Ochoa, Jorge A. *Pastores de Paratía, una introducción a su estudio.* Cuzco: Ediciones Inkari, 1968.

Forbes, David. *On the Aymara Indians of Bolivia and Peru.* London: Taylor and Francis, 1870.

Frank, André Gunder. *Capitalism and Underdevelopment in Latin America: Historical Studies of Brazil and Chile.* New York: Monthly Review Press, 1969.

Frisancho, José. *Algunas vistas fiscales concernientes al problema indígena del agente fiscal de Azángaro.* Lima: Tipografía El Progreso Editorial, 1916.

―――. *Del jesuitismo al indianismo.* Cuzco: Talleres Tipográficos Imperial, 1931.

Frisancho Pineda, Samuel, ed. *Album de oro.* 6 vols. N.p. [Puno]: Editorial Los Andes, 1973–76.

Fuenzalida V., Fernando, Enrique Mayer, Gabriel Escobar, François Bourricaud, and José Matos Mar. *El Indio y el poder en el Perú.* Perú Problema, no. 4. Lima: Instituto de Estudios Peruanos, 1970.

Gadea, Alberto, "Informe sobre aclimatación de pastos en el departamento de Puno." *Boletín del Ministerio de Fomento* 1, no. 7 (July 1903): 37–79.

Gallegos, Luis. "San José: Una comunidad cautiva." *Makaya, organo del pueblo de Azángaro*, no. 8 (Aug. 1978): 6–13.

―――. "Wancho-Lima, la tragedia de un pueblo en el altiplano." N.p., n.d. [about 1975].

Gamarra, Abelardo. "La mamacha." In his *Cien años de vida perdularia*, 26–30. Lima: Casa de la Cultura del Perú, 1963.

García Jordán, Pilar. "La iglesia peruana ante la formación del estado moderno (1821–1862)." *Histórica* 10, no. 1 (July 1986): 19–43.

Garland, Alejandro. *La moneda en el Perú, estudio económico sobre los medios circulantes usados en el Perú durante el imperio de los Incas, época de coloniaje, época republicana.* Lima: La Industria, 1908.

Genovese, Eugene D. *The Political Economy of Slavery: Studies in the Economy and Society of the Slave South.* New York: Random House, Vintage Books, 1965.

————. *Roll, Jordan, Roll: The World the Slaves Made.* New York: Pantheon, 1974.

Gibson, Charles. *The Aztecs under Spanish Colonial Rule.* Stanford: Stanford University Press, 1964.

Gibson, Herbert. *The History and Present State of the Sheep Breeding Industry in the Argentine Republic.* Buenos Aires: Ravenscroft and Mills, 1893.

Giraldo, Martha, and Ana Liria Franch. "Hacienda y gamonalismo: Azángaro 1850–1920." M.A. thesis. Pontifícia Universidad Católica del Perú, Lima, 1979.

Glade, William. "Latin America and the International Economy, 1870–1914." In *Cambridge History of Latin America,* vol. 4, edited by Leslie Bethell, 1–56. Cambridge: Cambridge University Press, 1986.

————. *The Latin American Economies: A Study of Their Institutional Evolution.* Washington: American Book, 1969.

Glave, Luis Miguel. "Conflict and Social Reproduction: The Andean Peasant Community." In *Agrarian Society in History: Essays in Honour of Magnus Mörner,* edited by Mats Lundahl and Thommy Svensson, 143–58. London and New York: Routledge, 1990.

————. "Demografía y conflicto social, historia de las comunidades campesinas en los Andes del sur." Paper presented at the FLACSO Conference on the Andean Community During the Nineteenth Century, Quito, 1989.

————. *Trajinantes, caminos indígenas en la sociedad colonial, siglos XVI/XVII.* Lima: Instituto de Apoyo Agrario, 1989.

Glave, Luis Miguel, and María Isabel Remy. *Estructura agraria y vida rural en una región andina: Ollantaytambo entre los siglos XVI y XIX.* Cuzco: CERA Las Casas, 1983.

Golte, Jürgen. *Bauern in Peru.* Indiana Beiheft No. 1. Berlin: Gebr. Mann Verlag, 1973.

————. *La racionalidad de la organización andina.* Lima: Instituto de Estudios Peruanos, 1980.

————. *Repartos y rebeliones, Túpac Amaru y las contradicciones de la economía colonial.* Lima: Instituto de Estudios Peruanos, 1980.

Gonzales, Michael J. "Neo-Colonialism and Indian Unrest in Southern Peru, 1867–1898." *Bulletin of Latin American Research* 6, no. 1 (1987): 1–26.

————. *Plantation Agriculture and Social Control in Northern Peru, 1875–1933.* Austin: University of Texas Press, 1985.

González, Luis. *Pueblo en vilo, microhistoria de San José de Gracia.* Mexico: El Colegio de México, 1968.

González Navarro, Moisés. *Anatomía del poder en México, 1848–1853.* El Colegio de México, Centro de Estudios Históricos, n.s., 23. Mexico, 1977.

Gootenberg, Paul. "Beleaguered Liberals: The Failed First Generation of Free Traders in Peru." In *Guiding the Invisible Hand: Economic Liberalism and the State in Latin American History,* edited by Joseph Love and Nils Jacobsen, 63–97. New York: Praeger, 1988.

———. *Between Silver and Guano: Commercial Policy and the State in Postindependence Peru.* Princeton: Princeton University Press, 1989.

———. "Merchants, Foreigners, and the State: The Origins of Trade Policies in Post-Independence Peru." Ph.D. diss. University of Chicago, 1985.

———. "Population and Ethnicity in Early Republican Peru: Some Revisions." *Latin American Research Review* 26, no. 3 (1991): 109–57.

———. "The Social Origins of Protectionism and Free Trade in Nineteenth Century Peru." *Journal of Latin American Studies* 14 (Nov. 1982): 329–58.

Gosselmann, Carl August. *Informes sobre los estados sudamericanos en 1837 y 1838.* Edited by Magnus Mörner. Stockholm: Instituto de Estudios Iberoamericanos, Escuela de Ciencias Economícas, 1962.

Grandidier, Ernest. *Voyage dans l'Amérique du Sud, Pérou et Bolivie.* Paris: Michel Lévy frères, 1861.

"La granja modelo de Puno (articulo informativo)." *Boletín de la granja modelo de Puno,* no. 1 (July 1931): 2–11.

Grieshaber, Erwin P. "La expansión de la hacienda en el departamento de La Paz, Bolivia, 1850–1920, una versión cuantitativa." *Andes, Antropología e historia,* nos. 2–3 (1990–91): 33–83.

———. "Survival of Indian Communities in Nineteenth Century Bolivia: A Regional Comparison." *Journal of Latin American Studies* 12, no. 2 (Nov. 1980): 223–69.

Griffin, Keith. *Underdevelopment in Spanish America: An Interpretation.* London: George Allen and Unwin, 1969.

Guevara Velasco, Agustín. *Apuntes sobre mi patria, volumen del departamento de Puno.* 3 vols. Cuzco: Editorial H. G. Rozas, 1954.

Guía general del sur del Perú. Cuzco: Imprenta Rozas, 1921.

Haenke, Tadeo. *Descripción del Perú.* Lima: Imprenta de "El Lucero," 1901.

Haigh, Samuel. *Sketches of Buenos Aires, Chile and Peru.* London: J. Carpenter and Son, 1829.

Haitin, Marcel. "Urban Market and Agrarian Hinterland: Lima in the Late Colonial Period." In *The Economies of Mexico and Peru During the Late Colonial Period, 1760–1810,* edited by Nils Jacobsen and Hans-Jürgen Puhle, 281–98. Berlin: Colloquium Verlag, 1986.

Halperín Donghi, Tulio. "Argentina: Liberalism in a Country Born Liberal." In *Guiding the Invisible Hand: Economic Liberalism and the State in Latin American History,* edited by Joseph Love and Nils Jacobsen, 99–116. New York: Praeger, 1988.

———. *Historia contemporánea de América Latina.* 3d ed. Madrid: Alianza Editorial, 1972.

———. *Revolución y guerra: Formación de una élite dirigente en la Argentina criolla.* Buenos Aires: Siglo Veintiuno Editores, 1972.

Hamilton, Thomas R. *A Statistical Survey of Wool Prices.* College Station: Texas Agriculture and Mining Press, 1938.

Hamnett, Brian R. "Church Wealth in Peru: Estates and Loans in the Archdiocese of Lima in the Seventeenth Century." *Jahrbuch für die Geschichte von Staat, Wirtschaft und Gesellschaft Lateinamerikas* 10 (1973): 113–32.

Handelman, Howard. *Struggle in the Andes: Peasant Political Mobilization in Peru.* Austin: University of Texas Press, 1975.

Haring, Clarence. *The Spanish Empire in America.* 2d ed. New York: Harcourt, Brace and World, 1963.

Harnisch, Hartmut. *Die Herrschaft Boitzenburg, Untersuchungen zur Entwicklung der sozialökonomischen Struktur ländlicher Gebiete in der Mark Brandenburg vom 14. bis zum 19. Jahrhundert.* Weimar: Hermann Böhlaus Nachfolger, 1968.

Harris, Charles. *A Mexican Family Empire: The Latifundio of the Sánchez Navarros, 1765–1867.* Austin: University of Texas Press, 1975.

Hazen, Dan C. "The Awakening of Puno: Government Policy and the Indian Problem in Southern Peru, 1900–1955." Ph.D. diss. Yale University, 1974.

Hennessy, Alistair. *The Frontier in Latin American History.* Albuquerque: University of New Mexico Press, 1978.

Herndon, Lewis, and Lardner Gibbon. *Exploration of the Valley of the Amazon Made under the Direction of the Navy Department.* 2 vols. Washington: A. O. P. Nicholson, 1854.

Herr, Richard. *Rural Change and Royal Finance in Spain at the End of the Old Regime.* Berkeley and Los Angeles: University of California Press, 1989.

Herrera Alarcón, Dante. *Rebeliones que intentaron desmembrar el sur del Perú.* Lima: Colegio Militar Leoncio Prado, 1961.

¿He vivido en vano? Mesa redonda sobre 'Todas las sangres,' 23 de Junio de 1965. Lima: Instituto de Estudios Peruanos, 1985.

Hinojosa Cortijo, Iván. "Población y conflictos campesinos en Corporaque (Espinar), 1770–1784." In *Comunidades campesinas, cambios y permanencias,* edited by Alberto Flores Galindo, 229–56. Chiclayo and Lima: Centro de Estudios Sociales Solidaridad, CONCYTEC, 1987.

Hobsbawm, Eric. "Peasant Land Occupations." *Past and Present* 62 (Feb. 1974): 120–52.

Hultz, Fred S., and John A. Hill. *Range Sheep and Wool in the Seventeen Western States.* New York: John Wiley and Sons, 1931.

Hünefeldt, Christine. "Poder y contribuciones: Puno, 1825–1845." *Revista andina* 7, no. 2 (1989): 367–407.

Hunt, Shane J. "La economía de las haciendas y plantaciones en América Latina." *Historia y cultura* 9 (1975): 7–66.

———. "Growth and Guano in Nineteenth-Century Peru." In *The Latin American Economies, Growth and the Export Sector, 1880–1930,* edited by Roberto Cortés Conde and Shane Hunt, 255–318. New York: Holmes and Meier, 1985.

———. *Price and Quantum Estimates of Peruvian Exports, 1830–1962.* Research Program in Economic Development, Discussion Paper no. 33. Princeton: Princeton University, 1973.

Husson, Patrick. *De la guerra a la rebelión (Huanta, siglo XIX).* Lima and Cuzco: CERA Bartolomé de las Casas, Instituto Francés de Estudios Andinos, 1992.

———. "1896—La révolte de sel dans les provinces de Huanta et La Mar (département d'Ayacucho, Pérou)." N.p., n.d. [1979].

Hutner, Francis Cornwall. *The Farr Alpaca Company: A Case Study in Business History*. Smith College Studies in History, vol. 37. Northampton, Mass.: Department of History, Smith College, 1951.

"Informe del médico titular de Azángaro sobre las condiciones higiénicas del indígena [August 10, 1920]" In *Por la clase indígena*. By P. Erasmo Roca Sánchez. Biblioteca de la Revista de Economía y Finanzas, No. 1. Lima: Pedro Barrantes Castro Editor, 1935.

Instituto "Libertador Ramón Castilla." *Archivo Castilla*. 7 vols. Lima: Impr. de la Universidad Nacional Mayor de San Marcos, 1963.

Inter-American Committee for Agricultural Development. *Tenencia de la tierra y desarrollo socio-económico del sector agrícola*. Vol. 6, *Perú*. Washington, D.C.: Union Panamericana, 1966.

Jacobsen, Nils. "Between the 'Espacio Peruano' and the National Market: Trading Regimes in Southern Peru During the Nineteenth Century." Paper presented at the Annual Convention of the American Historical Association, San Francisco, 1989.

———. "Campesinos y tenencia de la tierra en el altiplano peruano en la transición de la colonia a la república." *Allpanchis* 23, no. 37 (1991): 25–92.

———. "Cycles and Booms in Latin American Export Agriculture: The Example of Southern Peru's Livestock Economy, 1855–1920." *Review* 7, no. 3 (Winter 1984): 443–507.

———. "Desarrollo económico y relaciones de clase en el sur andino, 1780–1920: Una réplica a Karen Spalding." *Analisis* 5 (May–Aug. 1979): 67–81.

———. "Free Trade, Regional Elites, and the Internal Market in Southern Peru, 1895–1932." In *Guiding the Invisible Hand: Economic Liberalism and the State in Latin American History*, edited by Joseph L. Love and Nils Jacobsen, 145–76. New York: Praeger, 1988.

———. "Land Tenure and Society in the Peruvian Altiplano: Azángaro Province, 1770–1920." Ph.D. diss. University of California, Berkeley, 1982.

———. "Livestock Complexes in Late Colonial Mexico and Peru: An Attempt at Comparison." In *The Economies of Mexico and Peru During the Late Colonial Period, 1760–1810*, edited by Nils Jacobsen and Hans-Jürgen Puhle, 113–42. Berlin: Colloquium Verlag, 1986.

———. "Taxation in Early Republican Peru, 1821–1851; Policy Making Between Reform and Tradition." In *Las economías de los paises bolivarianas*, edited by Reinhard Liehr, 311–39. Berlin: Colloquium Verlag, 1989.

Jimenez, Michael. "Travelling Far in Grandfather's Car: The Life Cycle of Central Colombian Coffee Estates." *Hispanic American Historical Review* 69, no. 2 (1989): 185–219.

Jiménez, Vicente A. *Breves apuntes sobre la contabilidad de las haciendas de ganadería en el departamento de Puno*. Puno, 1902.

Juan y Santacilia, Jorge, and Antonio de Ulloa. *Noticias secretas de América sobre el estado naval, militar y político de los reynos del Perú y provincias de Quito, costas de Nueva Granada y Chili: Gobierno y regimen particular de los pueblos de Indios: Cruel opresión y extorsiones de sus corregidores y curas: Abusos escandalosos introducidos entre estos habitantes por los misioneros: Causas de su origen y motivos de su continuación por el espacio de tres siglos*. Biblioteca de Ayacucho 31–32. 2 vols. London, 1826.

Kaerger, Karl. *Landwirtschaft und Kolonisation im Spanischen Amerika*. 2 vols. Leipzig: Duncker und Humblot, 1901.

Kapsoli, Wilfredo. *Ayllus del sol, anarquismo y utopia andina*. Lima: Tarea, 1984.

———. *Los movimientos campesinos en el Perú, 1879-1965*. Lima: Delva Editores, 1977.

Knight, Alan. "The Mexican Revolution: Bourgeois? Nationalist? or Just a 'Great Rebellion'?" *Bulletin of Latin American Research* 4, no. 2 (1985): 1–47.

Konetzke, Richard. *Die Indianerkulturen Altamerikas und die spanisch-portugiesische Kolonialherrschaft*. Fischer Weltgeschichte 22. Frankfurt a.M.: Fischer Bücherei, 1965.

Konrad, Herman W. *A Jesuit Hacienda in Colonial Mexico, Santa Lucía, 1576–1767*. Stanford: Stanford University Press, 1980.

Kossok, Manfred. *El virreinato del Río de la Plata, su estructura económica-social*. Buenos Aires: Editorial La Pleyade, 1972.

Kriedte, Peter, Hans Medick, and Jürgen Schlumbohm. *Industrialisierung vor der Industrialisierung, Gewerbliche Warenproduktion auf dem Land in der Formationsperiode des Kapitalismus*. Göttingen: Vandenhoek und Ruprecht, 1978.

Krüggeler, Thomas. "El doble desafío: Los artesanos del Cusco ante la crisis regional y la constitución del régimen republicano (1824–1869)." *Allpanchis* 38 (1991): 13–65.

———. "Lifestyles in the Peruvian Countryside: Changes in Food, Dress and Housing (1820–1920)." Seminar paper. University of Illinois, Urbana-Champaign, 1987.

———. "Sozial– und Wirtschaftsgeschichte des städtischen Handwerks: Cuzco, Peru, 1820–1880." M.A. thesis. Universität Bielefeld, 1987.

Kubler, George. *The Indian Caste of Peru, 1745–1940: A Population Study Based upon Tax Records and Census Reports*. Institute of Social Anthropology, Publication No. 14. Washington, D.C.: Smithsonian Institution, 1952.

———. "The Quechua in the Colonial World." In *Handbook of South American Indians*, vol. 2, *The Andean Civilizations*, edited by Julian Steward, 331–410. Bureau of American Ethnology, Bulletin 143. Washington, D.C.: Smithsonian Institution, 1946.

Kula, Witold. *Teoría económica del sistema feudal*. Mexico, Madrid, and Buenos Aires: Siglo XXI Editores, 1974.

Langer, Erick. *Economic Change and Rural Resistance in Southern Bolivia, 1880–1930*. Stanford: Stanford University Press, 1989.

———. "Espacios coloniales y economías nacionales: Bolivia y el norte Argentino, 1810–1930." *Siglo XIX, revista de historia* 2, no. 4 (1987): 135–60.

———. "El liberalismo y la abolición de la comunidad indígena en el siglo XIX." *Historia y cultura* 14 (1988): 59–95.

Larson, Brooke. *Colonialism and Agrarian Transformation in Bolivia, Cochabamba, 1550–1900*. Princeton: Princeton University Press, 1988.

Lavalle y García, José A. de. "El mejoramiento de los pastos de la sierra del Perú." *Boletín de la Sociedad Geográfia de Lima* 26 (1910): 42–81, 182–235.

Lavrín, Asunción, and Edith Couturier. "Dowries and Wills: A View of Womens' Socioeconomic Role in Colonial Guadalajara and Puebla, 1640–1790." *Hispanic American Historical Review* 59, no. 2 (May 1979): 280–304.

LeGrand, Catherine. *Frontier Expansion and Peasant Protest in Colombia, 1830–1936.* Albuquerque: University of New Mexico Press, 1986.

Lehman, David. "Dos vías de desarrollo capitalista en la agricultura, ó crítica de la razón chayanoviana marxizante." *Revista andina* 3, no. 2 (Dec. 1985): 343–78.

León, Edmundo de. *Cartilla de ganadería.* Lima: Imprenta del Estado, 1907.

———. *Lanas, pelas y plumas.* Publicaciones del Ministerio de Fomento, Monografía No. 44. Lima: Imprenta del Estado, 1908.

LeRoy Ladurie, Emmanuel. "Die Tragödie des Gleichgewichts, Seuchen, Kriege und moderner Staat [1973]." In *Vom Umschreiben der Geschichte, Neue historische Perspektiven,* edited by Ulrich Raulff, 29–44. Berlin: Wagenbachs Taschenbücherei, 1986.

Leubel, Alfredo. *El Perú en 1860 ó sea anuario nacional.* Lima: Impr. de "El Comercio," 1861.

Lewin, Boleslao. *La rebelión de Túpac Amaru y los orígenes de la emancipación americana.* Buenos Aires: Librería Hachette, 1957.

Lewis, Arthur. *The Evolution of the International Economic Order.* Princeton: Princeton University Press, 1978.

Lizares Quiñones, José Angelino. "J. A. Lizares Quiñones se presenta ante la consideración de su pueblo." Flier. N.p.: n.d. [probably early 1932].

———. *Los problemas de la federación del Perú y del mundo.* 2d ed. Lima: "La Opinión Nacional," 1919.

Lora Cam, Jorge V. R. *La semifeudalidad y la política agraria neocolonial en Puno.* Universidad de Ayacucho "Victor Andrés Belaunde," Instituto de Investigaciones Socioeconómicas, Cuaderno No. 5. Ayacucho, 1976.

Luna, Lizandro. *Choquehuanca el amauta.* Lima: Imprenta Gráfica Stylo, 1946.

Maccagno, L. *Los auquénidos peruanos.* Edited by the Ministerio de Fomento. Lima: Estanco del Tabaco, 1932.

———. *La producción de lanas en el Perú.* Edited by the Ministerio de Fomento. Lima: Imprenta Torres Aguirre, 1924.

Macedo, J. Francisco. *Apuntes monográficos del distrito de Asillo.* Puno: Editorial "Los Andes," 1951.

Macera, Pablo. "Feudalismo colonial americano: El caso de las haciendas peruanas." In *Realidad nacional,* edited by Julio Ortega, 1:239-98. 2 vols. Lima: Retablo de Papel, 1974.

———. *Iglesia y economía en el Perú del siglo XVIII.* Separata de la Revista *Letras,* No. 68. Lima: Universidad Nacional Mayor de San Marcos, 1963.

———. *Instrucciones para el manejo de las haciendas jesuitas del Perú, siglos XVII-XVIII.* Nueva Crónica 2. Lima: Universidad Nacional Mayor San Marcos, Facultad de Letras y Ciencias Humanas, Departamento de Historia, 1966.

———. *Mapas coloniales de haciendas cuzqueñas.* Lima: Universidad Nacional Mayor de San Marcos, Seminario de Historia Rural Andina, 1968.

———. *Las plantaciones azucareras en el Perú, 1821–1875.* Lima: Biblioteca Andina, 1974.

———. *Tierra y población en el Perú (siglos XVIII-XIX).* 4 vols. Lima: Seminario de Historia Rural Andina, 1972.

Macera, Pablo, Alejandro Maguiña, and Antonio Rengifo. *Rebelión India.* Lima: Editorial "Rikchay Perú," 1988.

Macera, Pablo, and Felipe Márquez Abanto, eds. "Informes geográficas del Perú colonial." *Revista del Archivo Nacional del Perú* 28, nos. 1–2 (1964): 132–247.

Malaga, Modesto. "El problema social de la raza indígena." Bachelor's thesis. Universidad del Gran Padre San Agustín de Arequipa, 1914.

Mallon, Florencia. *The Defense of Community in Peru's Central Highlands: Peasant Struggle and Capitalist Transition, 1860–1940.* Princeton: Princeton University Press, 1983.

Maltby, Laura. "Colonos on Hacienda Picotani." In *Land and Power in Latin America: Agrarian Economies and Social Processes in the Andes,* edited by Benjamin S. Orlove and Glynn Custred, 99–112. New York: Holmes and Meier, 1980.

Manrique, Nelson. *Mercado interno y región, la sierra central, 1820–1930.* Lima: DESCO, 1987.

———. *Yawar Mayu, sociedades terratenientes serranas, 1879–1910.* Lima: Instituto Francés de Estudios Andinos, DESCO, 1988.

Marcoy, Paul [Laurent Saint-Cricq]. *Travels in South America from the Pacific Ocean to the Atlantic Ocean [1862–67].* 2 vols. New York: Scribner, Armstrong, 1875.

Mariátegui, José Carlos. *Siete ensayos de interpretación de la realidad peruana.* 29th ed. Lima: Editora Amauta, 1974.

Markham, Clements. *A History of Peru.* Chicago: Charles H. Sergeland and Company, 1892.

———. *Travels in Peru and India While Superintending the Collection of Chinchona Plants and Seeds in South America and Their Introduction into India.* London: Murray, 1862.

Martinet, J. B. *La agricultura en el Perú.* Lima: Centro Peruano de Historia Económica, 1977.

Martínez, Hector. "El indígena y el mestizo de Taraco." *Revista del Museo Nacional* 31 (1962): 173–224.

———. *Las migraciones altiplánicas y la colonización del Tambopata.* Lima: Centro de Estudios de Población y Desarrollo, 1969.

Martínez Alier, Juan. *Los huacchilleros del Perú, dos estudios de formaciones sociales agrarias.* Lima and Paris: Instituto de Estudios Peruanos, Ruedo Ibérico, 1973.

Mathew, W. M. "The First Anglo-Peruvian Debt and Its Settlement, 1822–49." *Journal of Latin American Studies* 2 (1969): 562–86.

Matos Mar, José. "La propiedad en la isla Taquile (Lago Titicaca)." *Revista del Museo Nacional* 26 (1957): 210–71.

Mayer, Arno. *The Persistence of the Old Regime: Europe to the Great War.* New York: Pantheon, 1981.

Mayer, Dora. "La historia de las sublevaciones indígenas en Puno." *El Deber Pro-Indígena,* nos. 40, 48, 49 (1916–17). Rpt. in *Documentos para la historia del campesinado peruano, siglo XX,* edited by Wilson Reátegui Chávez, 46–55. Departamento Académico de Ciencias Histórico-Sociales, Ediciones "Kallpa" no. 1. Lima: Universidad Nacional Mayor de San Marcos, 1978.

Mayer, Enrique. "Tenencia y control comunal de la tierra: Caso de Laraos (Yauyos)." *Cuadernos* [del Consejo Nacional de la Universidad Peruana], nos. 24–25 (1977): 59–72.

Memoria que la Junta Nacional de la Industria Lanar presenta por el año 1942. Lima: n.p., 1943.

Mendoza Aragón, Roberto. "El contrato pecuario de pastoreo." Bachelor's thesis. Universidad Nacional San Agustín de Arequipa, 1952.

Miller, Rory. "British Business in Peru." Ph.D. diss. Cambridge, 1979.

————. "The Grace Contract, the Peruvian Corporation and Peruvian History." *Ibero-Amerikanisches Archiv*, n.s., 9 (1983): 324–28.

————. "The Making of the Grace Contract: British Bondholders and the Peruvian Government, 1885–1890." *Journal of Latin American Studies* 8, no. 1 (1976): 73–100.

————. "La oligarquía costeña y la República Aristocrática en el Perú, 1895–1919." *Revista de Indias* 48, nos. 182–83 (1988): 551–66.

————. "Reinterpreting the 1876 Census." Paper presented at the International Congress of Americanists, Amsterdam, 1988.

————. "The Wool Trade of Southern Peru, 1850–1915." *Ibero-Amerikanisches Archiv*, n.s., 8, no. 3 (1982): 297–312.

Miller, Simon. "Mexican Junkers and Capitalist Haciendas, 1810–1910: The Arable Estate and the Transition to Capitalism Between the Insurgency and the Revolution." *Journal of Latin American Studies* 22 (1990): 229–63.

Mishkin, Bernard. "The Contemporary Quechua." In *Handbook of South American Indians*, vol. 2, *The Andean Civilizations*, edited by Julian H. Steward, 411–70. Bureau of American Ethnology, Bulletin No. 142. Washington, D.C.: Smithsonian Institution, 1946.

Mitre, Antonio. *Los patriarcas de la plata: Estructura socio-económica de la minería boliviana en el siglo XIX*. Lima: Instituto de Estudios Peruanos, 1981.

Molino Rivero, Ramiro. "La tradicionalidad como medio de articulación al mercado: una comunidad pastoril en Oruro." In *La participación indígena en los mercados surandinos: Estratégias y reproducción social, siglos XVI a XX*, edited by Olivia Harris, Brooke Larson, and Enrique Tandeter, 603–36. La Paz: CERES, 1987.

Moll, Bruno, and Emilio G. Barreto. "El sistema monetario del Perú." In *Sistemas monetarios latino-americanos*, edited by Universidad Nacional de Cordoba, Escuela de Ciencias Económicas, 1:141–226. 2 vols. Cordoba: Imprenta de la Universidad, 1943.

Montavon, William F. *Wearing Apparel in Peru*. U.S Department of Commerce, Bureau of Foreign and Domestic Commerce. Washington, D.C.: Government Printing Office, 1918.

Mooser, Josef. *Ländliche Klassengesellschaft, 1770–1848.* Göttingen: Vandenhoek und Ruprecht, 1984.

Moreno Cebrián, Alfredo. *El corregidor de Indios y la economía peruana del siglo XVIII (los repartos forzosos de mercancías).* Madrid: Consejo Superior de Investigaciones Científicas, Instituto "G. Fernández Oviedo," 1977.

Mörner, Magnus. *The Andean Past: Land, Societies, and Conflicts.* New York: Columbia University Press, 1985.

————. *Compraventas de tierras en el Cuzco, 1825–1869.* Estudios Históricos Sobre Estructuras Agrarias Andinas no. 1. Stockholm: Instituto de Estudios Latinoamericanos, 1984.

————. *Historia social latinoamericana, nuevos enfoques.* Caracas: Universidad Católica Andrés Bello, 1979.

————. *Notas sobre el comercio y los comerciantes del Cuzco desde fines de la colonia hasta 1930.* Lima: Instituto de Estudios Peruanos, 1979.

————. *Perfíl de la sociedad rural del Cuzco a fines de la colonia.* Lima: Universidad del Pacífico, 1978.

————. "The Spanish American Hacienda: A Survey of Recent Research and Debate." *Hispanic American Historical Review* 53, no. 2 (May 1973): 183–216.

Moscoso, Maximiliano. "Apuntes para la historia textíl en el Cuzco colonial." *Revista universitaria* (Cuzco), nos. 122–25 (1965): 67–94.

Mostajo, Francisco. "Apuntes etnológicos, modalidades léxicas, usos y costumbres andinos." *Inca, revista trimestral de estudios antropológicos* 1, nos. 2–3 (Apr.–June, July–Sept. 1923): 410–20, 751–60.

Mues, Joachim. *Die Organisation des Wollhandels und der Wollmärkte.* Altenburg: Akademisch-Technischer Verlag F. O. Müller, 1930.

Murra, John V. "El contról vertical de un maximo de pisos ecológicos en la economía de las sociedades andinas." In his *Formaciones económicas y políticas del mundo andino,* 59–116. Lima: Instituto de Estudios Peruanos, 1975.

Nalvarte Maldonado, Nicolás F. *Cuyocuyo, síntesis monográfica del distrito.* Puno: Editorial "Los Andes," 1973.

Nickel, Herbert. "Zur Immobilität und Schuldknechtschaft mexikanischer Landarbeiter vor 1915." *Saeculum* 3 (1976): 289–328.

Obermiller, Tim. "Harvest from the Past." *University of Chicago Magazine* 82, no. 3 (Spring 1990): 26–33.

O'Phelan Godoy, Scarlett. "Aduanas, mercado interno y elite comercial en el Cusco antes y después de la gran rebelión de 1780." *Apuntes* 19 (2d semester of 1986): 53–72.

————. *Rebellions and Revolts in Eighteenth Century Peru and Upper Peru.* Köln and Wien: Böhlau Verlag, 1985.

————. "Las reformas fiscales Borbónicas y su impacto en la sociedad colonial del Bajo y Alto Perú." In *The Economies of Mexico and Peru During the Late Colonial Period, 1760–1810,* edited by Nils Jacobsen and Hans-Jürgen Puhle, 340–56. Berlin: Colloquium Verlag, 1986.

Orlove, Benjamin Sebastian. *Alpacas, Sheep, and Men: The Wool Export Economy and Regional Society in Southern Peru.* New York: Academic Press, 1977.

————. "Landlords and Officials: The Sources of Domination in Surimana and Quehue." In *Land and Power in Latin America: Agrarian Economies and Social Processes in the Andes,* edited by Benjamin S. Orlove and Glynn Custred, 113–27. New York: Holmes and Meier, 1980.

————. "Native Andean Pastoralists: Traditional Adaptations and Recent Changes." Paper presented at the Symposium on Planned and Unplanned Change in Contemporary Nomadic and Pastoral Societies, Amsterdam, Apr. 1981.

———. "Reciprocidad, desigualdad y dominación." In *Reciprocidad e intercambio en los Andes peruanos*, edited by Giorgio Alberti and Enrique Mayer, 290–321. Lima: Instituto de Estudios Peruanos, 1974.

———. "Rich Man, Poor Man: Inequality in Peasant Communities." Paper presented at the Forty-first International Congress of Americanists, Mexico, Sept. 2–7, 1974.

———. "Urban and Rural Artisans in Southern Peru." *International Journal of Comparative Sociology* 15 (1974): 193–211.

Orlove, Benjamin Sebastian, and Glynn Custred. "The Alternative Model of Agrarian Society in the Andes: Households, Networks and Corporate Groups." In *Land and Power in Latin America: Agrarian Economies and Social Processes in the Andes*, edited by Benjamin S. Orlove and Glynn Custred, 31–54. New York: Holmes and Meier, 1980.

Pacheco Portugal, César. "Condición jurídica de los indígenas pastores de haciendas en el departamento de Puno." Bachelor's thesis. Universidad Nacional San Agustín de Arequipa, 1960.

Paredes, Mauro. "Apuntes monográficos de la provincia de Azángaro." In *Album de oro, monografía del departamento de Puno*, edited by Samuel Frisancho Pineda, 1:61–74. Puno: Editorial "Los Andes," 1973.

———. "El levantamiento campesino de Rumi Maqui (Azángaro, 1915)." *Campesino*, no. 3 (1970): n.p.

Paz, Melchor de. *Guerra separatista, rebeliones de Indios en Sur América, la sublevación de Túpac Amaru.* 2 vols. Lima, 1952.

Paz-Soldan, Carlos Enrique. *La región Cuzco-Puno, estudio médico-militar.* Lima: Servicio Geográfico del Ejército, 1913.

Paz Soldan, Mateo. *Geografía del Perú.* Edited by Mariano Felipe Paz Soldan. 2 vols. Paris, 1862–63.

Peloso, Vincent. "Succulence and Sustenance: Region, Class, and Diet in Nineteenth Century Peru." In *Food, Politics, and Society in Latin America*, edited by John C. Super and Thomas C. Wright, 46–64. Lincoln: University of Nebraska Press, 1985.

Peñaloza, Luis. *Historia económica de Bolivia.* 2 vols. La Paz: Editorial Fénix, 1954.

———. *La Paz en su IV centenario, 1548–1948.* Vol. 4, *Monografía económica.* Edited by Comité Pro IV Centenario de la Fundación de La Paz. Buenos Aires: Imprenta López, 1948.

Pentland, Robert Barclay. *Informe sobre Bolivia.* Potosí: Editorial Potosí, 1975.

Peralta Ruíz, Víctor. *En pos del tributo en el Cusco rural 1826–1854.* Cuzco: CERA Bartolomé de las Casas, 1991.

Piel, Jean. *Capitalisme agraire au Pérou.* Vol. 1, *Originalité de la société agraire péruvienne aux XIXe siècle.* Travaux de l'Institut Français d'Etudes Andines. Paris: Editions Anthropos, 1975.

———. "Le latifundium traditionnel au Pérou jusqu'en 1914: Marginalisation et résistance." *Etudes rurales: Revue trimestrielle d'histoire, géographie, sociologie et économie des campagnes* 59 (July–Sept. 1975): 35–50.

———. "The Place of the Peasantry in the National Life of Peru in the Nineteenth Century." *Past and Present* 46 (Feb. 1970): 108–33.

[Piérola, Felipe A. de.] *Anales de la iglesia de Puno.* N.p.: n.d. [approximately 1870].

Plane, Auguste. *Le Pérou.* 2d ed. Paris: Librairie Plon, 1903.

Platt, D. C. M. "Dependency in Nineteenth Century Latin America: A Historian Objects." *Latin American Research Review* 15 (1980): 113–31.

Platt, Tristan. *Estado boliviano y ayllo andino, Tierra y tributo en el Norte de Potosí.* Lima: Instituto de Estudios Peruanos, 1982.

Polanyi, Karl. *The Great Transformation: The Political and Economic Origins of Our Time.* Boston: Beacon, 1957.

Ponce de León, Francisco. "Aspectos económicos del problema indígena." *Revista Universitaria* (Cuzco), n.s., 21 (1932): 137–51.

———. "Situación del colono peruano." *Revista universitaria* (Cuzco), n.s., 23 (1934): 98–112.

Poole, Deborah. "Landscapes of Power in a Cattle-Rustling Culture of Southern Peru." *Dialectical Anthropology* 12, no. 4 (1987): 367–98.

———. "Qorilazos abigeos y comunidades campesinas en la provincia de Chumbivilcas (Cusco)." In *Comunidades campesinas, cambios y permanencias,* edited by Alberto Flores Galindo 257–95. Chiclayo and Lima: Centro de Estudios Sociales Solidaridad, CONCYTEC, 1987.

Porras Barrenchea, Raúl, ed. *Dos viajeros franceses en el Perú republicano.* Trans. Emilia Romero. Lima: Editorial Cultura Antárctica, 1947.

Puertas Castro, Nestor. *José Domingo Choquehuanca.* Lima: n.p., 1948.

Pulgar Vidal, Javier. *Geografía del Perú, las ocho regiones naturales del Perú.* 7th ed. Lima: Editorial Universo, n.d.

Quiroga, Manuel A. *La evolución jurídica de la propiedad rural en Puno.* Doctoral thesis. Universidad de Arequipa. Arequipa: Tipografía Quiróz, 1915.

Quiroz, Alfonso W. "Financial Institutions in Peruvian Export Economy and Society, 1884–1930." Ph.D. diss. Columbia University, 1986.

Raimondi, Antonio. *El Perú.* 5 vols. Lima: Imprenta del Estado and Imprenta Gil, 1874–1913.

Ramirez, Susan. *Provincial Patriarchs, Landtenure, and the Economics of Power in Colonial Peru.* Albuquerque: University of New Mexico Press, 1986.

Ramos Zambrano, Augusto. *José Domingo Choquehuanca y el Peruano de Pucará-Azángaro.* Puno: Comité de Defensa de los Derechos Humanos, 1989.

———. *Movimientos campesinos de Azángaro (Puno), Rumi Maqui.* Puno: Universidad Nacional del Altiplano, Instituto de Investigaciones para el Desarrollo Social del Altiplano, 1985.

———. *La rebelión de Huancané (1923–24).* Puno: Editorial Samuel Frisancho Pineda, 1984.

Reátegui Chávez, Wilson. *Explotación agropecuaria y las movilizaciones campesinos en Lauramarca-Cusco.* Lima: Universidad Nacional Mayor de San Marcos, Seminario de Historia Rural Andina, 1977.

———, ed. *Documentos para la historia del campesinado peruano, siglo XX.* Departamento Académico de Ciencias Histórico-sociales, Ediciones "Kallpa" no. 1. Lima: Universidad Nacional Mayor de San Marcos, 1978.

Remy, María Isabel. "La sociedad local al inicio de la república, Cusco, 1824–1850." *Revista andina* 6, no. 2 (Dec. 1988): 451–84.

Rivera Cusicanqui, Silvia. "La expansión del latifundio en el Altiplano boliviano, elementos para una caracterización de una oligarquía regional." *Avances* 2 (1978): 95–143.

————. *Oppressed but Not Defeated: Peasant Struggles among the Aymara and Qechwa in Bolivia, 1900–1980.* Geneva: United Nations Research Institute for Social Development, 1987.

Rivero, Francisco de. *Memorias o sean apuntamientos sobre la industria agrícola del Perú y sobre algunos medios que pudieran adoptarse para remediar su decadencia.* Lima: Imprenta de Comercio, 1845.

Rivero y Ustáriz, Mariano E. de. *Colección de memorias científicas, agrícolas e industriales.* 2 vols. Brussels: Imprenta de H. Goemaere, 1857.

Robles Riquelme, Enrique. "Episcopológia de Puno." In *Album de oro, monografía el departamento de Puno,* edited by Samuel Frisancho Pineda, 4:75–94. Puno: Editorial "Los Andes," 1976.

Roca Sánchez, P. Erasmo. *Por la clase indígena.* Biblioteca de la Revista de Economía y Finanzas, no. 1. Lima: Pedro Barrantes Castro, editor, 1935.

Roel, Virgilio. *Historia social y económica de la colonia.* Lima: Editorial Gráfica Labor, 1970.

Romero, Emilio. *Historia económica del Perú.* 2 vols. Buenos Aires: Ed. Sudamericano, 1949.

————. *Monografía del departamento de Puno.* Lima: Imprenta Torres Aguirre, 1928.

————. *Perú, una nueva geografía.* Lima: Librería Studium, n.d. [ca. 1972].

Roseberry, William. *Coffee and Capitalism in the Venezuelan Andes.* Austin: University of Texas Press, 1983.

————. *Histories and Anthropologies.* Newark: Rutgers University Press, 1990.

Rossello Paredes, J. Alberto. *Murales de Azángaro.* Puno: Editorial Laykakota, 1954.

Sabato, Hilda. *Agrarian Capitalism and the World Market: Buenos Aires in the Pastoral Age.* Albuquerque: University of New Mexico Press, 1990.

————. "Wool Trade and Commercial Networks in Buenos Aires, 1840s to 1880s." *Journal of Latin American Studies* 15, no. 1 (1982): 49–81.

Sahuaraura Tito Atauchi, Raphael José. *Estado del Perú.* Edited by Francisco A. Loayza. Lima: D. Miranda, 1944.

Salas Perea, Gilberto. *Monografía sintética de Azángaro.* Puno: Editorial "Los Andes," 1966.

————. *Razgos biográficos de Nicómedes Salas.* Puno: Editorial "Los Andes," 1957.

Salas de Coloma, Miriam. "Los obrajes huamanguinos y sus interconexiones con otros sectores económicos en el centro-sur peruano a fines del siglo XVIII." In *The Economies of Mexico and Peru During the Late Colonial Period, 1760–1810,* edited by Nils Jacobsen and Hans-Jürgen Puhle, 203–32. Berlin: Colloquium Verlag, 1986.

Sallnow, Michael J. "Manorial Labour and Religious Ideology in the Central Andes, A Working Hypothesis." *Bulletin of Latin American Research* 2, no. 2 (1983): 39–56.

Salvucci, Richard J. *Textiles and Capitalism in Mexico: An Economic History of the Obrajes, 1539–1840.* Princeton: Princeton University Press, 1987.

Sánchez Albornóz, Nicolás. *El Indio en el Alto Perú a fines del siglo XVII.* Lima: Seminario de Historia Rural Andina, 1973.

————. *Indios y tributos en el Alto Perú.* Lima: Instituto de Estudios Peruanos, 1978.

Santamaría, Daniel J. "La estructura agraria del Alto Perú a fines del siglo XVIII, un análisis de tres regiones maiceras del partido de Larecaja en 1795." *Desarrollo económico* 72 (Jan.–Mar. 1979): 579–95.

———. "La propiedad de la tierra y la condición social del Indio en el Alto Perú, 1780–1810." *Desarrollo económico* 66 (July–Sept. 1977): 253–71.

Sartorius von Waltershausen, A. *Die Entstehung der Weltwirtschaft.* Jena: Verlag von Gustav Fischer, 1931.

Saul, Samuel B. *Studies in British Overseas Trade, 1870–1914.* Liverpool: Liverpool University Press, 1960.

Schwartz, Stuart, and James Lockhart. *Early Latin America.* Cambridge: Cambridge University Press, 1983.

Scott, James C. *Weapons of the Weak: Everyday Forms of Peasant Resistance.* New Haven: Yale University Press, 1985.

Seligson, Mitchell A. *Peasants of Costa Rica and the Development of Agrarian Capitalism.* Madison: University of Wisconsin Press, 1980.

Sempat Assadourian, Carlos. *El sistema de la economía colonial: Mercado interno, regiones y espacio económico.* Lima: Instituto de Estudios Peruanos, 1982.

Sereni, Emilio. *Capitalismo y mercado nacional.* 1966. Barcelona: Ed. Crítica, 1980.

Sigsworth, Eric M. *Black Dyke Mills: A History.* Liverpool: Liverpool University Press, 1958.

Sigsworth, Eric M., and J. M. Blackman. "The Woolen and Worsted Industries." In *The Development of British Industry and Foreign Competition, 1875–1914: Studies in Industrial Enterprise,* edited by Derek H. Aldcroft, 128–57. London: George Allen and Unwin, 1968.

Silva Santisteban, Fernando. *Los obrajes en el virreinato del Perú.* Lima: Publicaciones del Museo Nacional de Historia, 1964.

Sivirichi, Atilio. *Derecho indígena peruano, proyecto de codigo indígena.* Lima: Ediciones Kuntur, 1946.

Slatta, Richard. *Gauchos and the Vanishing Frontier.* Lincoln: University of Nebraska Press, 1983.

Smith, Clifford T. "The Central Andes." In *Latin America: Geographical Perspectives,* edited by Harold Blakemore and Clifford T. Smith, 263–334. London: Methuen, 1971.

———. "Patterns of Urban and Regional Development in Peru on the Eve of the Pacific War." In *Region and Class in Modern Peruvian History,* edited by Rory Miller, 77–102. Monograph No. 14. Liverpool: University of Liverpool, Institute of Latin American Studies, 1987.

Smith, Gavin. *Livelihood and Resistance: Peasants and the Politics of Land in Peru.* Berkeley and Los Angeles: University of California Press, 1989.

Sociedad Ganadera del Departamento de Puno. *Memoria presentada al supremo gobierno.* Arequipa: Tipografía Cordova, 1921.

Southey, Thomas. *The Rise, Progress, and Present State of Colonial Sheep and Wools.* London: Effingham Wilson, 1851.

Spalding, Karen. *De Indio a campesino: Cambios en la estructura social del Perú colonial.* Lima: Instituto de Estudios Peruanos, 1974.

———. "Estructura de clases en la sierra peruana, 1750–1920." *Análisis* 1 (Jan.–Mar. 1977): 25–35.

————. *Huarochiri: An Andean Society under Inca and Spanish Rule.* Stanford: Stanford University Press, 1984.

Stavenhagen, Rodolfo. *Social Classes in Agrarian Societies.* Garden City, N.Y.: Doubleday, Anchor Books, 1975.

Stein, Stanley, and Barbara Stein. *The Colonial Heritage of Latin America: Essays on Economic Dependency in Perspective.* New York: Oxford University Press, 1970.

Stein, William. *La rebelión de Atusparia.* Lima: Mosca Azul Editores, 1988.

Stern, Steve. *Peru's Indian Peoples and the Challenge of Spanish Conquest.* Madison: University of Wisconsin Press, 1982.

Stordy, Robert J. "The Breeding of Sheep, Llama, and Alpaca in Peru with a View to Supplying Improved Raw Material to the Textile Trades." *Journal of the Royal Society of Arts* 69, no. 3556 (Jan. 14, 1921): 118–32.

Tamayo Herrera, José. *Historia social del Cuzco republicano.* 2d ed. Lima: Editorial Universo, 1981.

————. *Historia social e indigenismo en el Altiplano.* Lima: Ediciones Treintaitres, 1982.

Tandeter, Enrique. "Crisis in Upper Peru, 1800–1805." *Hispanic American Historical Review* 71, no. 1 (1991): 35–72.

————. "Trabajo forzado y trabajo libre en el Potosí colonial tardío." *Estudios CEDES* 3, no. 6 (1980): 1–40.

Tandeter, Enrique, and Nathan Wachtel. *Precios y producción agraria, Potosí y Charcas en el siglo XVIII.* Buenos Aires: Estudios CEDES, n.d. [1983].

Tauro, Alberto, ed. *Diccionario enciclopédico del Perú.* 3 vols. Lima: Ed. Mejía Baca, 1967.

Taylor, Lewis. "Earning a Living in Hualgayoc, 1870–1900." In *Region and Class in Modern Peruvian History,* edited by Rory Miller, 103–24. Monograph no. 14. Liverpool: University of Liverpool, Institute of Latin American Studies, 1987.

TePaske, John J., and Herbert Klein. *The Royal Treasuries of the Spanish Empire in America.* 3 vols. Durham: Duke University Press, 1982.

Thompson, L. G., E. Mosley-Thompson, J. F. Bolzan, and B. R. Koci. "A 1500-Year Record of Tropical Precipitation in Ice Cores from the Quelccaya Ice Cap, Peru." *Science* 229, no. 4717 (Sept. 6, 1985): 971–73.

Thorp, Rosemary, and Geoffrey Bertram. *Perú 1890–1977: Growth and Policy in an Open Economy.* New York: Columbia University Press, 1978.

Torres Luna, Alfonso. *Puno histórico.* Lima: n.p., 1968.

Trazegnies, Fernando de. *La idea de derecho en el Perú republicano del siglo XIX.* Lima: Pontifícia Universidad Católica del Perú, 1979.

Tschudi, Johann Jakob von. *Peru. Reiseskizzen aus den Jahren 1838–1842.* 2 vols. St. Gallen: Scheitlin und Zollikofer, 1846.

————. *Reisen durch Südamerika.* 5 vols. 1869. Stuttgart: F. A. Brockhaus, 1971.

Tutino, John. *From Insurrection to Revolution in Mexico: Social Bases of Agrarian Violence, 1750–1940.* Princeton: Princeton University Press, 1986.

Tyrer, Robson. "The Demographic and Economic History of the Audiencia of Quito: Indian Population and the Textile Industry, 1600–1800." Ph.D. diss. University of California, Berkeley, 1979.

Universidad Mayor de San Marcos. *Discurso académico de apertura del año universitario de 1902 pronunciado por el Dr. Wenceslao F. Molina, catedrático de zootécnica de la facultad de ciencias.* Lima: Imprenta y Librería de San Pedro, 1902.

Urquiaga, José Sebastian. *Sublevaciones de indígenas en el departamento de Puno.* Arequipa: Tipografía Franklin, 1916.

Urquiaga Vásquez, Alberto. *Huella histórica de Putina.* Sicuani: Prelatura de Sicuani, 1981.

Urrutia de Strebelski, María Cristina, and Guadalupe Nava Oteo. "La minería." In *México en el siglo XIX (1821-1910): Historia económica y de la estructura social,* edited by Ciro Cardoso, 119–45. Mexico: Ed. Nueva Imagen, 1983.

Valdéz de la Torre, Carlos. *Evolución de las comunidades de indígenas.* Ciudad de los Reyes del Perú: Euforion, 1921.

Valdivia, Juan Gualberto. *Memorias sobre las revoluciones de Arequipa desde 1834 hasta 1866.* 2d ed. Arequipa: Ed. El Deber, 1956.

Van Young, Eric. *Hacienda and Market in Eighteenth Century Mexico.* Berkeley and Los Angeles: University of California Press, 1981.

Vásquez, Emilio. *La rebelión de Juan Bustamante.* Lima: Librería-Editorial Juan Mejía Baca, 1976.

Vásquez, Mario C. *Hacienda, peonaje y servidumbre en los Andes peruanos.* Monografías Andinas no. 1. Lima: Editorial Estudios Andinos, 1961.

Vega, Juan José. *José Gabriel Túpac Amaru.* Lima: Editorial Universo, 1969.

Veliz, Claudio. *The Centralist Tradition in Latin America.* Princeton: Princeton University Press, 1980.

Villanueva Urteaga, Horacio, ed. *Cuzco 1689: Informes de los párrocos al obispo Mollinedo: Economía y sociedad en el sur andino.* Cuzco: Centro Bartolomé de las Casas, 1982.

Villarán, Manuel Vicente. "Condición legal de las comunidades indígenas." *Revista universitaria* (San Marcos), 1907, 1–9.

Vollmer, Günter. *Bevölkerungspolitik und Bevölkerungsstruktur im Vizekönigreich Peru zum Ende der Kolonialzeit, 1741-1821.* Bad Homburg v.d.H.: Gehlen, 1967.

Walker, Charles. "Peasants, Caudillos, and the State in Peru: Cusco in the Transition from Colony to Republic, 1780–1840." Ph.D. diss. University of Chicago, 1992.

———. "La violencia y el sistema legal: Los indios y el estado en el Cusco después de la rebelión de Tupac Amaru." In *Poder y violencia en los Andes,* edited by Henrique Urbano and Mirko Lauer, 125–48. Cuzco: CERA Bartolomé de las Casas, 1991.

Walle, Paul. *Le Pérou économique.* 2d ed. Paris: Librairie Orientale et Americaine, 1908.

Wallerstein, Immanuel. *The Modern World System.* 3 vols. New York: Academic Press, 1974–89.

Warman, Arturo. *Y venimos a contradecir, los campesinos de Morelos y el estado nacional.* Ediciones de la Casa Chata, no. 2. Mexico: Instituto Nacional de Antropología y Historia, Centro de Investigaciones Superiores, 1976.

Weber, Eugen. *Peasants into Frenchmen: The Modernization of Rural France, 1879–1914.* Stanford: Stanford University Press, 1976.

Wibel, John F. "The Evolution of a Regional Community Within the Spanish Empire and Peruvian Nation, Arequipa, 1770–1845." Ph.D. diss. Stanford University, 1975.

Wightman, Ann M. *Indigenous Migration and Social Change: The Forasteros of Cuzco, 1570–1720.* Durham: Duke University Press, 1990.

Wilson, Fiona. "The Conflict Between Indigenous and Immigrant Commercial Systems in the Peruvian Central Sierra, 1900–1940." In *Region and Class in Modern Peruvian History,* edited by Rory Miller, 125–61. Monograph no. 14. Liverpool: University of Liverpool, Institute of Latin American Studies, 1987.

————. "Propiedad e ideología: Estudio de una oligarquía en los Andes centrales (siglo XIX)." *Análisis* 8–9 (May–Dec. 1979): 36–54.

Winder, David. "The Impact of the *Comunidad* on Local Development in the Mantaro Valley." In *Peasant Cooperation and Capitalist Expansion in Central Peru,* edited by Norman Long and Bryan Roberts, 209–40. Austin: University of Texas Press, 1978.

Wittman, Tibor. *Estudios históricos sobre Bolivia.* La Paz: Editorial "El Siglo," 1975.

Wool Year Book, 1930. Manchester: Textile Mercury, 1930.

Wright, Mary Robinson. *The Old and the New Peru: A Story of the Ancient Inheritance and the Modern Growth and Enterprise of a Great Nation.* Philadelphia: G. Barrie and Sons, 1908.

Yambert, Karl A. "Thought and Reality: Dialectics of the Andean Community." In *Land and Power in Latin America: Agrarian Economies and Social Processes in the Andes,* edited by Benjamin S. Orlove and Glynn Custred, 55–78. New York: Holmes and Meier, 1980.

Yepez del Castillo, Ernesto. *Perú 1820–1920: Un siglo de desarrollo capitalista.* Lima: Instituto de Estudios Peruanos, 1972.

Zea, Oswaldo. "Constatación de clases sociales en el Altiplano." *El Collao* 1, nos. 13–14 (Dec. 26, 1931, and Jan. 2, 1932).

Index

Printed in the United States
43918LVS00004B/88

9 780520 082915